LAST
of the
DONKEY
PILGRIMS

LAST
of the
DONKEY
PILGRIMS

Kevin O'Hara

[signature]

FORGE®

A TOM DOHERTY ASSOCIATES BOOK

New York

AUTHOR'S NOTE: This memoir was completed twenty-five years after the journey it recounts. I kept a journal during my travels and, for the most part, I have used authentic names of people and places in recollecting my adventures. The dialogue, however, is reconstructed from memory, and I have engaged in some Irish fantasy and storytelling.

LAST OF THE DONKEY PILGRIMS

Book design by Milenda Nan Ok Lee

This book is printed on acid-free paper.

A Forge Book
Published by Tom Doherty Associates, LLC
175 Fifth Avenue
New York, NY 10010

www.tor.com

Forge® is a registered trademark of Tom Doherty Associates, LLC.

Library of Congress Cataloging-in-Publication Data

O'Hara, Kevin, 1949–
    Last of the donkey pilgrims / Kevin O'Hara.—1st ed.
        p. cm.
    "A Tom Doherty Associates book."
    ISBN 0-765-30983-1 (alk. paper)
      1. O'Hara, Kevin, 1949—Travel—Ireland. 2. Americans—Ireland. 3. Irish Americans. 4. Ireland—
    Description and travel. I. Title.

DA978.2.O38 2003
914.504'824—dc22

                                                                        2003049428

First Edition: February 2004

Printed in the United States of America

0 9 8 7 6 5 4 3 2 1

To my mother, Lella.
And her mother, Mary Ann.
And to my children's mother,
Belita

Contents

Missie's March
'Round Ireland, 1979

© 2003, Mark Stein Studios

1. Kilrooskey
2. Roscommon
3. Athleague
4. Ballygar
5. Monivea
6. Cartymore
7. Oranmore
8. Kinvara
8A. Inisheer Island
9. Ballyvaughan
10. Doolin
11. Lahinch
12. Kilkee
13. Kilrush
14. Tarbert
15. Ballybunion
16. Tralee
17. Cloghane
18. Dingle
19. Dunquin
20. Great Blasket Island
21. Killorglin
22. Glenbeigh
23. Cahersiveen
24. Waterville
24A. Sneem
25. Kenmare
25A. Skellig Michael
26. Laragh
27. Eyeries
28. Castletownbere
29. Glengarriff
30. Bantry
31. Mizen Head
32. Schull
33. Skibbereen
34. Rosscarbery
35. Clonkality
36. Kinsale
37. Cork (City)
38. Youghal
39. Dungarvin
40. Tramore

41. Waterford (City)
42. New Ross
43. Ballynabola
44. Wexford (Town)
45. Blackwater
46. Kilmuckridge
47. Ballygarret
48. Arklow
49. Avoca
50. Glendalough
51. Glencree
52. Dublin
53. Swords
54. Balbriggan
55. Drogheda
56. Dunleer
57. Blackrock
58. Dundalk
59. Newry
60. Rostrevor
61. Kilkeel
62. Newcastle
63. Downpatrick
64. Portaferry
65. Millisle
66. Bangor
67. Holywood
68. Belfast
69. Carrickfergus
70. Glynn
71. Ballygalley
72. Carnlough
73. Garron point
74. Glenariff
75. Cushendun
76. Torr
77. Ballycastle
77A. Portrush
78. Downhill
79. Eglinton
80. Derry (City)
81. Malin
82. Buncrana

83. Letterkenny
84. Portsalon
85. Downings
86. Cashel
86A. Dunfanaghy
87. Falcarragh
88. Knockfola
89. Drumnacart
90. Dungloe
91. Ardara
92. Glencolumbkille
93. Killybegs
94. Donegal (Town)
95. Ballyshannon
96. Red Brae
97. Grange
98. Drumcliff
99. Sligo (Town)
100. Ballysadare
101. Beltra
102. Easky
103. Ballina
104. Killala
105. Belderrig
105A. Glenamoy Bridge
106. Belmullet
107. Bangor
108. Ballycroy
109. Mullrany
109A. Achill Island
110. Newport
111. Westport
112. Louisburg
113. Clare Island
114. Leenane
115. Clifden
116. Roundstone
117. Carna
118. Screeb
119. Inveran
120. Spiddal
121. Galway (City)

Acknowledgments

When it takes twenty-five years to complete a book, one can look back and recall a grandstand of people who have assisted in some way. I wish to begin by thanking Ruth Bass, my editor at the *Berkshire Sampler,* who first published stories of my donkey travels. Secondly, Don MacGillis at the *Boston Globe,* and the current editors at the *Berkshire Eagle,* David Scribner, Bill Everhart, and Dan Bellow.

My newspaper columns were only readable due to the instruction I received from my English professors at Berkshire Community College, Pittsfield. These gifted mentors were Emily Jahn, Sheldon Rothberg, Richard Nunley, and Genie Robbins-Zust.

Following my donkey travels, I worked as a bartender at La Cocina's in Pittsfield. My donkey tales fell on many a customer's ear who, in turn, convinced me to scribble them down. These longtime buddies are Marc DelGreco, Sandy McNay, Dick LaBarbera, John Friend, and Debi Orlando. In time, I also began to write about growing up in our large Irish family, therefore my siblings made me the honorary family scribe. Like an oft-whispered litany, they are Michael, Mary, Jimmy, Dermot, Eileen, Anne Marie, and Kieran.

Next, my parents: Lella, a loving mother whose heart never left the hearth of her old home, and my father, Jimmy, who could walk down Pittsfield's North Street and chat with bank presidents and janitors alike, each dropping their pens or buckets to listen to his tales, told in a rich County Longford brogue.

When this book saw the light of possibility, friends rallied around me, jokingly calling themselves Team O'Hara. But they were no joke to me: Randy Wallingford, Chris Doyle, Rick Glasener, Ceil Roosa, Bill Cormier, Spencer Trova, Pam Culver, Charlie Mendes, Sean Jennings, Frank McCarthy, Deborah Burns, Tom McHugh, Sam Samolis,

Christopher Nye, Alan Kennedy, Steve Young, Joe Murphy, and Bill and Missy Lyon. Also Aunt Nancy and E. T. Carroll, Bob Suarez, Natalie Gingras, Tom Daly, Bill Corby, Dan O'Connell, J. Peter Bergman, and Brian Moore of Brian Moore International Tours (BMIT).

Now, new faces have stepped in to make Team O'Hara's goal a reality. Marc Jaffe, a venerable statesman of the publishing world, who took over the reigns to find Missie a home on Fifth Avenue. Claire Eddy at Forge, who has worked diligently to make my story a better one. And, of course, my dear longtime friend, Steve Satullo, who, for the last twenty years, has guided me tirelessly through every chapter of this book.

Nor can I forget my loving family. Belita, for her support, sacrifice, and understanding, both now and long ago. And our sons, Eamonn and Brendan, who never once doubted their dad couldn't finish his donkey task at hand.

And lastly, the people of Ireland, North and South, who were most generous and accepting to this long-haired wayfarer of the roads.

Introduction

On this brisk June evening in the Irish midlands, I am sitting with Belita and our nearly grown sons, quietly celebrating our thirtieth wedding anniversary, watching my Uncle Mickey throw a few sods of turf onto the fire.

We are also celebrating the completion of this book, just in time for the twenty-fifth anniversary of the events related therein.

Outside in the lingering twilight, three magpies alight on a rosebush behind the house.

"I've seen that sight before." I look out with eerie surprise at the flapping blackbirds flecked with white. "It must be Grannie's handiwork."

"It's her way of welcoming you all home," smiles Mickey. He's talking about his mother and my grandmother, Mary Ann Kelly, who passed away ten years ago, after turning one hundred.

"Now, don't mind me," I announce to everyone, taking a seat to the left of the fire. "I'm going to sit here and work on an introduction for my book, just as I've dreamed about for years, right here in front of Grannie's old hearth."

"Thanks be to God!" exclaims Aunt Mamie, blessing herself. "For all the time it took you to write that confounded book, it wouldn't do you to ever go writing another one. How many years since your donkey-go-round with Missie, tell us?"

"Nearly twenty-five." My face reddens at the staggering amount of time elapsed.

"Well, you'd best mention the changes in our country from that time to this," Mamie comments as she spreads white frosting over a sponge cake at the table. "There's great money in Ireland nowadays, and for a decade now we've been the fastest-growing country in the European Union."

"Oh, I will," I assure her. "Ireland has become a different place in less than twenty-five years, erasing centuries of its struggles. Why, it's gone from farmland to techno-land in one quantum leap. All but this kitchen, that is." I point to the crook and crane hanging above the ancient fireplace.

Our two boys, Eamonn and Brendan, are draped over couch and chair, gazing lazily into the flame, exhausted by our five-day whirlwind tour up the western road, from Skellig Michael in St. Finan's Bay, to this ancestral home here at Ballagh, beneath Slieve Bawn.

"I still can't believe you and Missie walked up Conor Pass," says Eamonn, recalling the mountain passage we drove over three days ago on the Dingle Peninsula.

"I don't see how you survived in the traffic," observes Brendan.

"Fortunately, there were many fewer cars on the road when Missie and I set off in 1979. There was also a major oil crisis, a four-month postal strike, and a major flare-up in the Troubles. Tourism took a major hit that year, so Missie and I had the road to ourselves, relatively speaking. And farmers used to bang around in puttering Morris Minors back then, but now it's powerful Land Rovers that own the road.

"In fact, I haven't seen one old man or woman pedaling down the road on a bicycle," I rattle on, "or a single donkey and cart. No more sheep or cattle being led here or there, either. Gone, too, are the tidy stacks of golden hay that once dotted the fields, replaced by rolls of plastic-wrapped silage."

"So what's the biggest single change you see, Dad?" Eamonn asks.

"All those houses sprouting up like mushrooms have certainly changed the land-scape. And every time I see teenagers with mobile phones stuck to their ears, I think back to the one thin phone book that used to encompass all Twenty Six Counties of the Republic."

"We've gone from Bloody Sunday to the Good Friday accords, and that's a great change," adds Mickey. "Ireland has come into the modern world, and the world has come into Ireland."

"Oh, yes," I agree. "Even the face of the island is changing. I met Brazilians in Cork, Romanians in Kerry, and saw a number of young African families living in Ennis, County Clare."

"Come on, Dad, what's the most dramatic change of all?" Brendan insists with teenage exasperation.

"Well, let me see." I tilt my head thoughtfully into the air. "I'd have to say it's the price of a pint of Guinness. Back in 1979 it was forty-eight pence, and now its three euros and change—five times that amount. And, of course, the currency has changed. No more large colorful bills with Irish heroes, and certainly no more coins with farm-yard animals.

"But I'll tell you one thing that's still the same. When I set out on my travels, I imagined myself to be a latter day Bilbo Baggins, and you boys still go for *The Lord of the Rings* in a big way."

"The biggest change I see," Belita comes over to sit beside me, "is that every village—Kilkee, Kilfenora, Kinvara—could be a Tidy Town winner. Years ago when me and Kevin went traveling Ireland in search of a thatcher, most towns needed a good sprucing-up. Now all the towns and villages have shopfronts painted in lovely pastels. And so many restaurants! Remember, Kevin, the white chipper vans serving fish and chips in greasy newspaper? And years ago, shopkeepers would wrap up your groceries with twine and brown paper. Now the chain supermarkets charge you for plastic bags."

"How about the farmer wearing shorts and a baseball cap in Kerry?" Eamonn reminds us.

"That was a first for me." I laugh. "For a moment I thought I was in Cape Cod. He would've been cut to ribbons by the old farmers years ago for dressing like that."

"He'd be greeted with blackthorns at both market and fair," agrees Mickey with a chortle.

"Such a sight," Mamie comments as she cuts the sponge cake into six large portions. "I'll tell you, Kevin O'Hara, you wouldn't be long on the road with your donkey today until ye'd be knocked into the hedges."

"Oh, don't I know! During my travels with Missie, the roads were filled with colorful characters—now they're filled with colorful Audis and Saabs, zooming around sharp bends like a Celtic Grand Prix. No more crossroad dances on the grassy *boreens* of Ireland, that's for sure."

There's a moment of silence while we each consider what has been gained or lost in the passage of years, but then Mickey asks, "Where have you raised your glass in the past few days?"

"We had a good pint in Knightstown the evening before we set sail for Skellig Michael, and a better one with John Mulvihill at The Red Fox in Glenbeigh, County Kerry. But the best stout was at Joe McHugh's Pub in Liscannor, County Clare, where I told Belita and the boys the story of my memorable night there.

"But sadly, Joe McHugh has long since passed away. In fact, every time I visit, I hear of more folks I stayed with who are now gone. Last week alone I learned that John Burke, Joe Vaughan, and Michael Lafferty are no longer with us, people I knew only in passing, but so vivid and helpful, I felt we had been friends forever. And, of course, most of the old men at Rattigan's are gone, including the 'Four Masters,' who were such an important part of my journey."

" 'Tis the way of the world," sighs Mamie.

"Well, Mamie and meself are still going strong, aren't we?" Mickey jabs at my ribs. "And there's no loss on Vincent or Cella, or our children or grandchildren, thank God. But, tell us, how many miles did you travel with Missie that year?"

"Seventeen hundred and twenty, give or take a few."

"And how many farmhouses?"

"One hundred and fifty. And never once was I asked a penny for lodgings."

"You wouldn't find farmers that accommodating these days," Mamie says, wetting the tea. "Crime is spilling out of the cities and into the country, and the rural folk are afraid to open their doors to strangers. Drugs have also made their filthy way into Ireland, and the tireless telly is filling the heads of our youth with sullied notions. I don't know where it will all lead to in the end." She lets out a moan. "I'm afraid we're all riding the tail of the Celtic Tiger, however it may wag."

Mamie serves up her tasty sponge cake in honor of our anniversary, as the glow of midsummer warms the house as much as the fire. The boys eat contentedly, happy to be back on familiar ground, sharing in their parent's enthusiasms.

"You were lucky Belita let you go rambling off that year," Mamie says as she pours out the tea. "I hope you never forget it." She points at me with her teaspoon.

"Believe me, I won't, and I haven't." I feed Belita a piece of the white-frosted cake.

"My mother always warned me the Irish were wanderers." Belita grasps my hand. "But I didn't know I had married the wild colonial boy. Kevin, you know, has a mole on his leg, and in my native Philippines that's a sign of a rambler."

"He's a right rover, mole or no mole," Mickey snorts.

"That separation must have been hard on you both," Eamonn says.

"Somehow I understood your dad's restlessness," Belita explains to our sons. "I truly felt sorry for him, because this travel bug was even beyond himself. It wasn't that he wanted to get away from me, or run off with another woman. It was his love of Ireland. How could I wage a battle against mountains, lakes, and green fields? His urges were even beyond the understanding of his mom and dad, blaming it on his year in Vietnam. But it was deeper than that, and we were all helpless; we had to let him go and pray he'd come back again full circle."

Belita takes me by the arm: "And, thankfully he did. Pretty much in one piece."

"Even now I can hardly explain what drove me," I add, kissing Belita. "After all these years and all these pages of trying."

There is a lull in the conversation, with everyone's eyes being drawn back to the hearth.

"There's another change to put in your book," Mamie advises. "The EU wants to ban the burning of turf in the country. The company, Bord na Mona, that runs our power stations, has been depleting our bogs at a great rate for decades now, and the Union wants to preserve what's left of them. Rightly so, I suppose, but can you imagine an Ireland without the smell of turf?"

"We'll soon need to be going if we're to have a drink at all." Mickey breaks off to reach for his coat. "We could go to Larry O'Gara's at the Royal Hotel, and maybe have a nightcap at Rattigan's."

"But Dad hasn't done his writing yet." Brendan looks over at my empty pad.

"No wonder it took you twenty-five years to finish that book," Mamie scolds, giving my head a good rub with her knuckles. "Don't go gawking at that blank page. Fill it up, can't you?"

"It's not that easy, Mamie. I'd rather climb Glengesh Pass on my hands and knees."

"Just go writing how you and your Missie were blessed to see the curtain fall on Old Ireland, and that you'll never forget the kindness of the people, and hope their generosity, despite all the changes in our country, never leaves them."

"Boy, Mamie, I should've written my blooming book right here by your side," I say as I jot down her words.

"Let's walk down and visit Dom Tiernan," suggests Mickey, no longer able to watch my painful struggle, "and we'll give the scribe here thirty minutes of peace."

Wishing me luck, Belita and the boys follow Mickey and Mamie out the door, as I read my few random phrases, occasionally lifting my head to gaze into the old hearth. I had looked forward so long to this moment that I can't believe I'm coming up empty. I ought to be a Pentecostal with a gift of tongues, a Mozart with a head full of music, a fervent monk with words just spilling from the pen.

"Fill it up, can't you?" Mamie's voice echoes.

I lift my weary head and stare again into the red coals of the hearth, saying a Hail Mary for enlightenment and thinking back on Grannie Kelly mumbling her beads before this ancient fire. In those days, I felt like an acolyte in the presence of a priestess from some bygone age, those three fluttering birds representing the Trinity. After her beads, we'd have the tea and I'd tell her far-flung stories that would make her howl with laughter.

"Are you coming a'tall?" Mamie pokes her head through the door.

"I'm finished, Mamie." I leap up to give her a hug. "It's a blooming wrap!"

She smiles and kisses me: "God help you, Kevin O'Hara."

Ballincurry, Ballagh
16 June 2003

The Donkey Proposal

CHAPTER ONE

The Irish Midlands
MARCH 1979

I t was at Rattigan's Pub in Kilrooskey, County Roscommon, that I first proposed traveling the coast of Ireland with a donkey and cart. The elderly patrons, biting at pipes and smelling of turf smoke, rolled in amusement.

"Ye're thinking of walking an ass about Ireland?" jawed Hugh Mannion from a high stool. "I have two at home that won't cross Derrane Bog!"

"Arragh, Hughie, now, be fair to your man," chimed Willie Cassidy from behind a hand of playing cards. "There'd only be the one ass that could circle the Ring of Ireland, and that'd be Johnny Rabbitt's jackass who swallowed the umbrella!"

I soothed my throat with a generous swallow of the black native Guinness, and sought refuge by the potbellied stove, flashing back to my inaugural pint here when I was seventeen. That long-ago summer, my younger brother Dermot and I were unwillingly sworn into the Celtic race in a drunken stupor. Now, on this cold winter night in 1979, thirteen years later, nothing had changed in this illustrious parish pub but the Harp calendar.

My uncle Vincent, to whom I had sketchily mentioned my plans, had warned that my "donkey proposal" would be greeted with ridicule by these age-old pensioners, who gathered every Friday evening at Rattigan's. But who else knew more about a donkey's strengths and limitations than themselves?

I took another gulp of the milk-warm stout, thinking back on that wondrous incident days earlier. Pedaling home to my grandmother's on the Knockcroghery Road, I was knocked off my bike like Saul from his horse when I saw a farmer smoothly tipping his donkey and cart down the road. "That's it," I gasped at the vision. "That's how I'm going to travel the whole of Ireland."

Now, taking a deep breath and another fortifying sip, I mustered the courage to speak above their merriment.

"But say, for instance, I was truly willing to go through with it. Could a donkey, a good one, travel the coast of Ireland? I'd take it easy, eight to ten miles a day, and I'd give myself eight months to travel the eighteen hundred miles."

Rheumy eyes glinted and glanced. The Yank wasn't having them on: he was dead serious. The house went silent. Playing cards were flattened. Miserable March rattled outside the panes. Pints were called for and collected as the old gentry of the parish circled their stools to gather their wisdom.

"A jackass, cut-jack, or a mare?" asked Mickey Owens, still eyeing me with suspicion.

"Never a jack," voiced Jack Rattigan, lifting the cap off his brow. "A jack would be braying sonnets in June, bugling day and night in August, and downright altogether mad in the snows of December."

"A cut-jack, then?" suggested Joe Hickey.

"A cut-jack is neither useful nor ornamental," mused Jim Tiernan. "A cut-jack has no heart. Nipped. Dry as polished glass. 'Tis a mare the Yank would need, young and well-handled."

"The very thing," agreed the tall and scholarly Headmaster D'Alton. "A young mare sound of wind and limb, and a fine temperament. You wouldn't want her kicking the stars from the sky."

"A good mouth and square feet," added Hugh Mannion, "free of spavins, curbs, and sidebones. And she'd need to be well-shod with pony shoes and frost nails to cover those miles."

I stood among these wizened fellows—my mother's former schoolmates—nodding my head in agreement, but not having a blooming idea what they were on about.

"A double fistful of oats every morning would do her kindly," continued Willie Cassidy. "But don't go giving her a bucket of water after a good feed, or she'll cripple up and die with the gripe."

"Search Roscommon and Westmeath for your mare," offered Paddy Tiernan, "and don't go to any knackers or horse jobbers. With your Yankee accent, they'd sell you a mule without a tooth in its head."

"Better still," added Dan Madden, "if you're sincere in setting out on this caper, go see the horseman, Jimmy McDermott, in Kilteevan. If there's ever a mare that can circle Ireland, Jimmy Mac would be the one to find her."

"And keep a safe distance from the Spanish jacks," jabbed a smart aleck from the corner, "or your mare will be carrying extra baggage on the road home!"

The donkey seminar ended abruptly as the playing cards, itching in the hands of Willie Cassidy, were reshuffled and dealt again: the quarter-final round of "25" for an

Easter turkey was at stake. Jim Tiernan, however, joined me by the stove. My grandmother's neighbor in the village of Ballincurry, he told me how his donkey could travel twenty Irish miles—twenty-five English miles—a day on a pinch of oats.

"An ass would go forever if you gave her her time," said old Jim, rubbing a plug of tobacco in his hands. "Pity is, too many farmers hurried and abused them. The only worry I see in you traipsing the world with a mare is that she could easily become homesick and lose heart. And when a mare loses heart, nothing will set her going again."

"What makes a mare lose heart?" I asked the affable man.

"'Tis easy enough, I'm afraid," he continued, packing his yellowed briar pipe with his thumb. "Mare asses worked a hard long day in Roscommon. But whether they were off to market with a sow, to the creamery with a can or two, to the bog for a cartload of turf, or to the fields to draw in the hay, they always knew they'd be home by nightfall to be fed and watered. Your mare won't have that luxury, for she'll be traveling the roads day after day, over mountain and bog, and at night be tethered in a different field or placed in some stinking byre. Nor will she be able to make any sense of your wanderings.

"I suppose a jack would be right for your journey if they weren't so ornery," he went on, lighting his pipe. "A jack is a common rogue, a rambler, but a mare likes her home. I heard a story years back of how a County Longford man sold his mare heavy in foal to a County Fermanagh man. The deal was settled over a jar of stout and the mare was boxed and carted up through Longford, Leitrim, and beyond the border town of Enniskillen. Fifty miles, if not more. Well, wouldn't you know, three days later this same Longford farmer was walking his fields, only to spot the sold mare feeding her downy foal. The poor creature had made good her escape and traveled fifty miles in two days to give birth on the third. Now, doesn't that give you some idea of their homing instincts?"

Of course, not everyone at Rattigan's was as helpful as Jim Tiernan. There was a scrum of old wags who brayed and whinnied throughout the seminar, asking one another if both my oars were cleaving the sea and other opprobrious remarks better left forgotten. But, all in all, it had been a fine evening. My proposed journey, however whimsical, now seemed at least plausible.

I sat on a wooden bench by the doorway, finishing my drink and tucking my pants into my socks for the bike ride home, when Hugh Mannion addressed the happy crowd, saying I'd be nothing short of a folk hero if I managed to circle Ireland with a donkey and cart.

"He'd be much like those wise men," he exclaimed, raising his bottle of barley wine, "who climbed Faerymount one clear night in June, all in hopes of catching the rising moon in a burlap bag!"

Everyone had a good laugh at that one, and they were still rolling when I left Rattigan's and mounted my bicycle for home.

On my three-mile spin back to Uncle Vincent's, I became so elated by visions of these donkey travels that I hopped off my bike and shouted up into the star-frosted night. But it was too early to go celebrating just yet. I hadn't a donkey yet nor the knowledge of what to do with one once I had it. And there were those donkeymen at Rattigan's, willing to wager their weekly pension check against any one ass completing the Ring of Ireland.

If this was true, would I have to set up relief stations along the coast—the proverbial Donkey Express? And was the distance of 1,800 miles—Boston to Amarillo in my country—fair for one donkey to travel?

Who was I trying to kid, anyway? I'm no Marco Polo. Not even a Cub Scout. I never toted tents on campouts or annual jamborees, never learned how to read a compass or light a fire with dry sticks. Neither Marlboro Man nor L.L. Bean mountaineer, I was not from that breed of men who tamed the American wilderness. Little wonder those cronies at Rattigan's enjoyed their chuckle, figuring I hadn't the strength to tie a double-knot in my sneakers, and then, to propose this preposterous expedition.

I hopped back on my bicycle, my wheels wobbling down the black country road. There were so many stones in my path: Could a donkey and cart handle the hills and water-crossings, navigate the cities, the Northern boundaries, elude the animal protection league, and avoid encounters with Tommies or the IRA? Would I be gunned down by some trigger-happy sectarian? But easy! Easy! No sense in becoming too anxious too soon.

I stopped to gather myself at the old millhouse in Cloonara where the stars gleamed in winter glory and the River Holywell grumbled through the quiet blackness. Was I really mad, as many at Rattigan's had thought? Who would ever know? But this one time in my life I wanted to leave all worldly concerns behind and embark on this journey with the dizzy abandon of an adventurous boy.

Or like the adolescent I'd been when I first came to Ireland with my parents in 1966, their first trip home since emigrating to America. They'd been in England till 1953, where I had been born, along with four siblings, and three more arrived after we moved to Massachusetts. "The Yanks," we called the latecomers.

Dermot and I had been the chosen pair for this long-awaited vacation, and when we arrived to our grandmother's at Ballincurry, our mother led us to the high-hedged fields of her old homestead. There, uncharacteristically, she took us each by the hand and spun us around, stopping to point out things with a trembling finger.

"There's the white stone where Mrs. Tiernan would sit and wait for us to come home from school with slices of rhubarb tart. Why, you've never tasted the like! And below, there, in the meadow of Coolrua, Aunt Bea kept her blue hens. Yes, blue hens! And look, boys, the fires smoldering in the bogs. Many a long, happy day I spent there gathering turf with your great-grandfather. And do you see Lough Ree? Headmaster Foley would tell us stories of how Vikings sailed their longships there on St. John's Eve a thousand years ago."

Dermot and I looked at her in awe. This wasn't the mom we knew back home in Pitts-field: a tired, worn mother of eight, living in a drafty duplex on Wilson Street. How sad to be brought up amongst the greenest fields, dotted with farmhouses of friends and kin, and to wind up hanging her laundry in a bare backyard where our landlord kept his collection of junked automobiles. Little wonder she was often blue, saving her dimes in a Skippy peanut-butter jar all those years for this short respite to Ireland.

"At your age, boys, I could gather two stacks of hay a day in Jamsie's Field," she continued, her face flushed, her voice young and vibrant. "And I'd deafen swarms of bees with a spoon and tin can in those trees beyond. Oh, and the call of the corncrake. How charming their chatter!"

She told us colorful stories that left us imagining what might have been if she had remained in Ireland and raised her family here, rather than leaving for England at age seventeen to commence her nurse's training there. And how different would we be? Would we have been great men with the cattle, Dermot and me? Would we handle horse and plow, and rest atop the headlands, breathing in the ethereal goodness of turned tillage?

As witness to my mother's awakening that summer of long ago, I felt a great unrest begin to stir in me. What homeland treasures lay buried, never to surface? What hidden springs were never tapped? What balm for the soul never unearthed?

Not that I hadn't been drawn to Ireland long before this first visit. When my mother had suffered low periods back in the States, she would often keep me home from grammar school. I'd do chores and watch the little ones, and then I'd play marbles on our braided rug in the front room while Mom sat sadly by the window, rereading letters from home. I'd beg her to share the contents, and in no time I knew all of Grannie Kelly's family and neighbors. After the letters were read, I was given the stamps from their envelopes—colorful stamps depicting a little stone hut named Gallarus, a seat of kings called "the Rock of Cashel," and a brown-cloaked monk penning a Psalter—which I'd carefully paste into my notebook.

When I asked my mother what she missed most about Ireland, she had said the people, because they were as wholesome as fresh linen on the line. I told her I was going to travel all of Ireland one day, and I'd know it as well as my marbles knew the frayed seams in our braided rug, and sometimes she would smile.

A few years later, Grannie Kelly herself came to America, and I was relieved of my duties. She stayed with us for eleven months, filling the house with lively chat, love and laughter. And stories, always stories. With the evening Rosary said and tea in her lap, she'd tell us tales with her lovely accent and mighty howl. "Aye, and poor Gummy Nertney coming off the mountain after a neighbor gave birth to triplets, you know, and Gummy saying, 'Have ye decided which one ye'll be keeping?'—as if talking about kittens, be God."

So here I was now, alone in the dark of an Irish night with a diadem of stars over my head, ready to reclaim my lost kingdom, determined to travel the roads in search of my heritage, to find some missing part of myself, to recapture an Irish childhood lost to emigration. Call me mad, but I had to embark on this crazy quest.

My cousin Noel Kelly was the only one awake at Uncle Vincent's when I walked the bicycle into the yard. Excitedly, I told him about my planned donkey tour, and how I had to see Jimmy McDermott the next evening in Kilteevan.

Noel, reading the paper at the kitchen table, looked up at me with one eye cocked. "How many pints did you have tonight?" he asked.

"Two."

"Two pints of Guinness," he chuckled, carrying himself off to bed. "Two pints of Guinness and you're out of your flipping mind."

Talk of the Parish

CHAPTER TWO

Are ye getting up this afternoon?" roared Aunt Cella from below in the kitchen. I hated to leave a warm bed, so snug for dreaming on this damp island of mist and faery, wracked by sea-storms and Atlantic squalls. There were recent nights when an eastern storm had raged so fiercely out of Siberia that hundreds of lambs had perished, even in sheltered fields. During those nights I slept between two hot-water bottles and had nine woolen blankets layered over me; blankets so heavy with damp in the dead of night that, if I had an itchy toe, I'd have to wait until morning to scratch it.

"Should I call for a doctor?" bellowed Cella Kelly.

I reluctantly left my bunk and put on a second sweater before walking down the cold hallway to the kitchen, where I crowded up to the heat of the turf-fired range.

"Did Noel tell you about my donkey plans?" I asked, wrapping a playful arm around my aunt.

"He did indeed." She nosed up to my face. "You're one cracked boyo, Kevin O'Hara."

"But I'm serious, Cella."

"Serious about walking an ass about Ireland? God help ye!"

Cella Mannion Kelly, married to my mother's brother Vincent, was a short, plump, pleasant woman with dimpled hands; but she could become mildly vexed at times.

"Is it a hen egg or a duck egg ye'll be having?" she snapped, her face reddening. "I haven't the whole day to entertain your nonsense."

"A hen egg, please. You know I can't eat duck eggs."

"Fine tinker you'll make on the road, as choosey as you are," she scolded, dropping the brown egg into a saucepan of water.

"But honestly, Cella, what do you think of it all?"

"I think you're a half-boiled eejit!" she blurted, never one to be mincing words. "Wasn't Uncle Hugh here this morning telling all at the table how you made a proper fool of yourself last night at Rattigan's? This isn't America where you can go to blazes and home again with no one paying notice. There are those in this parish who'll go wagging their tongues if they see a neighbor wearing two hats in the one day. 'Tis a quare long journey ye're proposing, and there'll be plenty who'll wonder if ye're wise in doing it. And haven't you given them the right to be talking?"

" 'The right to be talking'?" I repeated, somewhat abashed.

"There isn't a soul at Rattigan's who doesn't know you came to Ireland on some crackpot quest for your 'heritage'! Bad enough for an able-bodied man to drop out of his proper life for a year, leaving a good nursing job, not to mention your lovely wife, Belita. How she ever agreed to all of this, I'll never know. And now, three months along, in the frost heaves of March, you sit atop a stool and go hankering on about walking an ass from here to Donegal and back again."

"First off, Cella, I was given a leave of absence from the hospital, and Belita, as you know, is happy and safe with her mother and sisters in California. She agreed to a year's separation hoping I'll get Ireland out of my system once and for all. Believe me, Cella, the hardest thing I ever did in my life was help Belita pack up for the West Coast. We both cried our eyes out, but I can't think about that now. And I know I've had some crazy schemes, like two years ago when I wanted to become a thatcher, but now I've figured out what I really have to do. Last week, when I saw a farmer tipping along with his ass and cart, I just knew. Cella, it hit me like a bolt of lightning—my journey becoming as clear as that smudge of flour on your pretty nose."

She wiped a dishtowel brusquely across her face.

"I'm thirty years old next month," I persisted, "and if I don't do this now, I never will. Besides"—I gave her a playful nudge—"is there any better way to see Ireland than with a donkey? Do those cronies at Rattigan's think I'd be better off hopping a tour bus from Blarney to Killarney?"

"Tell all this to your grandmother," Cella replied sternly, not sold by my romantic notions, "and I'd tell her before she hears it from another direction."

"Why, would she be upset?"

"Upset! Upset in having her grandson make a living spectacle of himself by marching an ass from here to eternity? Your dear grandmother, Mary Ann Gibbons Kelly, has lived in the townland of Ballagh, in the parish of Kilgefin, for eighty-seven years, and her family long before that. The parish talk alone would deafen her."

I ate my boiled egg with a lump in my throat. I had never thought Grannie Kelly would disapprove of my travels, but now that it was pointed out, I could see she might not see the romance and adventure of it. After breakfast and a few chores, I mounted the ancient black Raleigh for Grannie Kelly's. I had no intention of telling her about my plans yet, but a good visit would certainly ease my conscience.

On the way to Ballincurry, my grandmother's village in the foothills of Slieve Bawn—the heart of the Irish midlands, where the River Shannon divides the provinces of Connaught and Leinster—I stopped at Rattigan's to buy Grannie a bag of mints. This mint-buying had developed into a full-blown superstition. In my thirteen years of visiting Ireland, I had never once walked into her house without mints in my hand, as a prescription for her continued good health. So far the mints had never failed me.

Leaving the quiet pub, I pedaled down Beechwood and turned right at "the Clump" for Ballagh Chapel, whereupon I met Dominick Tiernan, son of the neighborly donkey-sympathizer, old Jim, on his red tractor.

"Are ye off to Jimmy Mac's this evening?" he shouted above the din of his diesel.

"I am!"

"You should take your uncle Mickey or aunt Mamie along," he suggested. "Jimmy Mac might take you more seriously if you're with someone he knows."

As we were talking, a car approached and as it passed, three young passengers began to hee-haw out the window.

"The word doesn't take long in spreading, does it?" said Dom.

As I gloomily pedaled down Ballagh Road, I began to realize what I was up against. Just twelve hours after I had opened my gob at Rattigan's, the hedgerow telegraph system was clacking through the seven surrounding parishes. You could blame the old pensioners for that, spreading word of my donkey tour as thin as jam to any idle ear that would listen.

"Did you hear about the Yank last night at Rattigan's?" I could imagine them chattering. "You know him, the thin lad as pale as goat's butter and looking the cut of a weasel, nephew of Vincent and Mickey Kelly. Didn't he go raving on about walking an ass all over Ireland! He did, by Jaysus, and the boys just led him on, feeling sorry for him and all. He can't be well at times, sure he can't."

Catching the wind of their tale, they might continue,

"Ye've seen him, plenty of times. The spindly-looking fella who couldn't lift a stone of turnips without herniating himself, riding all over hell on a high-Nellie bicycle and grinning to all in the heavens. A real village eejit! A right *omadaun*. Why, he's even talking of walking the poor ass through Belfast! 'Tis the truth, I tell ya! I suppose old Paisley will greet him outside the gates of Stormont with a weak cup of parson tea. Oh, the crack last night at Rattigan's was mighty. He's a Fair Innocent, surely, one of God's special children. I'm afraid he left a good part of himself behind in Vietnam. May God bless him and all those afflicted like him."

Oh, yes, Vietnam. One could blame most anything on Vietnam. After my tour of duty there, at loose ends, Dermot suggested we spend the summer of '71 in Ireland. We'd visit ancient haunts and walk western strands, but we always came back to Rattigan's, which became my own private USO, my safe haven, my sanctuary, trying to forget the idiocies and agonies of war.

There, the patrons had been most kind: "Didn't you do well to get out of that place," they'd say. "Now, take your ease, son. You're back home in Ireland."

Grannie Kelly was in the haggard collecting an apronful of turf when I arrived at her two-hundred-year-old farmhouse. I thought the world of her and she knew it. She greeted me with her customary salutation: " 'Glory be to God in the heavens, tonight, tomorrow, and today.' If it isn't himself that's arrived!"

I carried her few sods as she stooped for a moment to weed around the winter cabbage and the shamrock growing along the garden's edge. Straightening her back, she studied the weather.

" 'Twill rain this evening," she said, looking north at Slieve Bawn crouched below heavy clouds, and south toward the gray meandering curls of the River Shannon. "When you can't see Lough Ree from our doorstep, 'twill surely rain."

Inside the kitchen of her whitewashed home, Grannie drew the turf-coal to the front of the grate and stacked fresh sods against the back of the blackened hearth wall. Her chair was well-padded with old coats and jumpers. "All buttonless," she once told me, "so as not to be nagging me back during a good conversing." She sat, as always, to the left side of the hearth, which she believed to be the warmer side of the fire.

She might be well along in her ninth decade, but Grannie kept active by doing the light household chores and minding the kitchen garden. Uncle Mickey, whose family shared her little farmhouse, called Grannie "a topping woman," and the whole parish marveled at her memory and keen senses. She rarely went near the gas range at the far end of the kitchen, calling it "a stinking nuisance," and did all her cooking and baking by using the hobs and skillets of the open hearth.

I handed Grannie her bag of mints.

"Mints. Mints. Mints," she sang, opening the bag of Fox's Glacier Mints and handing me one. "There must surely be a meaning to your bag of mints."

We fell into our usual chatter, discussing her family dispersed throughout Wales, England, and America, the threatened postal strike, the lambs crippled by recent rains, the health of her old friends, and, of course, the weather.

"Do you know, we're only a month away from 'the Days of the Old Cow,' " she began, drawing her chair closer to the flames. "The first days of April are known to be the coldest of winter, and if an old cow is to die within the year, this is the time of their failing. I'm not certain if it's true, but I've never seen an old cow die grazing in a June meadow.

"Time was, every turn of the year had a name. The first days of November were known as 'the Harvest of the Geese,' when all the fatted geese would be sent to market. But you never hear tell of these days any longer, for the new calendars only mark the Bank Holidays, and never a word or mention about fairs or markets, let alone the glorious saints and their holy days."

"As bygone as donkeys and carts, I suppose," I added sheepishly, unable to avoid my fixed idea.

"Thirty years ago you'd see nothing on these roads but asses and carts," she said, building up the fire with the tongs, "but they soon disappeared when the tractor arrived."

"Did you ever drive a donkey and cart?"

"And what would have seen me into town years ago . . . a yellow taxi?" she howled, remembering her visit to the States. "Every Saturday morning for years I'd yoke our little ass to the cart and tip her as easy as you please to town for messages and home again. And there was no rush-rush like a motorcar, but plenty of time to speak with your neighbors along the way. 'Twas your father, Jimmy, who had stories about asses and carts. Surely he told you about his boyhood days in Longford taking cartloads of granite from Cairn Hill to the new convent being built in Newtownforbes?"

"Oh, he did. But it was only last night when talking to Jim Tiernan at Rattigan's, that I learned how far a donkey could travel in a day."

"Jim Tiernan had an ass, God bless it, that could travel twenty miles on a pinch of oats. And your Uncle Bennie, God be good to him, would take our brown lad once a week into Longfordtown and be home again that evening. Forty Irish miles, that would be."

"Forty Irish miles," I murmured, gazing dreamily into my grandmother's hearth, time and distance melting away.

Black weather crossed the kitchen panes as we sat in mild, slow reverie with the fire warming our shins. The wind began to rise, sending swirls of smoke down the chimney flue and scattering cold ash onto the flags. Grannie sat contentedly, leaning slightly toward the portal dolmens of red turf-coals, twittering an old reel through cupped hands and tapping her feet, a habit acquired from her father and grandfather, both champion stepdancers.

We might have fallen into a fireside slumber if not for Mickey's wife, Mamie, arriving home from foddering cattle in the mountain fields, breathing so heavily you'd think she was carrying all of Ireland's misfortunes upon her shoulders.

" 'Tis a wonder I have a calf at all to feed," she gasped, picking up a live coal with the tongs and lighting the butt of a Sweet Afton cigarette. "The weather is shocking to the world!"

Mamie gave me a sharp look, and I guessed that she had found out about my donkey plans.

"I'm surprised to find you here," she said, pulling a wet kerchief from her head. "I thought you'd be gallivanting the roads by now."

"What would have me walking the roads?" I tried to shush her by nudging my elbow in Grannie's direction. "You wouldn't put a dog out on a day like this."

"Nor a donkey," she countered, having me on.

I kept up a lively, nonsensical banter until Grannie had prepared her hot-water bottle for her afternoon nap, but as soon as she had stepped down to her bedroom below, Mamie Kelly was down my throat.

"You're the talk of the parish!" she complained.

"I didn't want it that way," I replied defensively. "Those old men at Rattigans should be working for Reuters or UPI."

"Well, you certainly gave them something to report. And why haven't you told your grandmother?"

"I haven't a donkey yet, have I?"

"And when are you going to see Jimmy McDermott?"

"As soon as possible. And Dom Tiernan thought it would be a good idea if you or Mickey came along with me. We could take the Morris Minor now and be back before Grannie wakens from her nap."

"I'll have nothing to do with your carry-on," she snapped, standing stubbornly before the fire.

"C'mon, Mamie, please. I don't even know how to get to Jimmy Mac's house."

"You'll meet any amount of people who'll be delighted to direct you," she smirked, standing firmer still.

"But, Mamie, this is so important to me. I have my heart set on searching for the heart of the land, seeking out the secrets of its old pathways and meeting people at their front gates. You have no idea what it's like to be an emigrant child—a foot in, a foot out—a bona fide Nowhere Man. I'll never know my true self unless I can discover Ireland. I'm a real mess, Mamie. Please, it's the biggest favor you could ever do for me."

A thin smile crossed Mamie's lips, and with a deep sigh of resignation she traded her Wellingtons for a pair of shoes, swapped coats, brushed a comb through her graying hair and knotted a bright scarf below her chin.

"Well, if you're going to go through with this madness, let's get on with it," she said grudgingly. "And don't go asking me why I'm sticking me neck out for you, for I'm not rightly sure meself."

Jimmy Mac, the Horseman

Bridie McDermott, Jimmy's spouse, answered the door when Mamie and I arrived at the farmhouse in Kilteevan. In their haggard was a high barn filled with pony traps, and a champion horse with its head out a byre window. It appeared Bridie was expecting us, but I couldn't be sure.

"Come in, the two of you, and welcome."

We were led through the house to the kitchen, where Jimmy Mac, a tall trim man in his late forties, sat mending a horse collar. He stood, shook my hand, and studied me from top to bottom, much as a horse jobber might eye a colt at a fair, wondering, no doubt, if my thin shanks had the sinew for the rumored trek . . . and why in God's name didn't I do something with my long mane of hair?

"How can I help you, boss?" he asked, sitting back down and eyeing me dubiously.

"I'd like to travel 'round Ireland with a donkey," I blurted, glancing nervously from Jimmy Mac to his bride.

"Why in hell's bells would you want to do that?" smirked the horseman.

"Oh, it's a long story," I said. "Too long and too confusing, going back as far as my childhood. But it's only now that it's taken on form. . . ."

"Go on," he said, "I'd like to hear more."

"Since my arrival to Ireland, I've been living in Galway, but I've felt hemmed in and out of contact with the land I want to explore. But last week, I saw a farmer tipping a donkey and cart along, and I said, 'That's it! That's how I want to travel the country!' So last night at Rattigan's, after I had voiced my proposal, Dan Madden suggested you could help me find a donkey that could travel the Ring of Ireland."

After hearing my overeager presentation, Jimmy Mac went back to stuffing horse-hair into the leather collar, as Bridie stood up to put down a kettle for the tea.

"Don't mind the tea, Bridie," said Mamie, "we'll have to be leaving now ourselves. 'Twas only Kevin who wanted a quick word with Jimmy before his grandmother awakens from her nap."

"Beg pardon," asked Jimmy, "but weren't you the Yankee lad knocking about these parts a year or two back, looking how to thatch roofs? And hadn't you a lovely bride by your side?"

"Oh, yes," I said, my face turning red.

"How did you fare out with that scheme?"

"Not well," I told him, as Mamie shifted uncomfortably in her chair. "My wife Belita and I lived outside Newtownforbes in Longford and searched high and low for a thatcher. But nothing panned out, so we returned to America six months later, dead broke with my tail between my legs."

"Why thatching? It's a dying trade."

"I felt bad that my grandmother's house in Ballincurry had to be slated after Uncle Bennie, our family thatcher, passed away. I got overemotional, that's all," I conceded, squirming in my seat.

"Where is your bride now?" asked Bridie.

"She's out in California with her family, and she gave me a year off on good behavior," I half joked, trying to bring levity to Bridie's scrutinizing gaze. "Actually, she gave me the okay so I could explore Ireland, hoping I'll be cured from a long bout of displaced homesickness. I'm an extremely lucky man to have such a loving and understanding spouse, and I'm going to make it up to her tenfold when this year is through. In fact, she knitted me this Aran sweater I'm wearing," I said, standing up to show Bridie. " 'The Road Coat,' she called it."

"It's beautiful," said Bridie, fingering the blueberry patterns on my gray cardigan.

"Belita learned the Aran stitch from her neighbor when living in Newtownforbes," piped in Mamie proudly. "A clever girl, Belita."

"She's supposed to come over at Christmas to meet me at journey's end," I chimed in. "That leaves me nine months to travel my road and reach my destination, whatever it may turn out to be."

" 'Tis an odd odyssey, all the same," said Bridie, as I sat back down.

"Can I ask you one thing," said Jimmy, interrupting the women. "Are ye in earnest about this journey?"

"I am, sir."

"Do you know anything about asses?"

"Only from Bible stories—and I've heard they're thought to be the wisest of Irish beasts."

"I mean, have you ever worked with asses?"

"No, sir."

"Ponies or horses?"

"Nope."

"You might be wiser to take a bicycle," said Mamie, "or one of those horse-drawn caravans they hire out in Kerry or Cork."

"The caravans are too touristy," I said, "and a bicycle is too fast, too familiar. A donkey and cart is the old way of traveling Ireland, so it's best for my purposes."

"It would be terribly slow," added Bridie. "You wouldn't cover fifteen miles a day."

"Aye, it would be slow," said Jimmy, suddenly looking at me with a newfound interest. "But when you stop to consider what Kevin is after—to get close to the land of his kin—an ass and cart is the very thing. He'd have the long day to look about him, and in the evenings he could start searching for a farmhouse to shelter himself and his ass for the night. By the time he completes his roundabout, he'd have as much knowledge of Ireland as the tinkers themselves."

"The farmers may not be that obliging," said Bridie.

"What farmer would refuse lodgings to a young man going about the country with an ass and cart?"

"The Troubles in the North have changed things," confided Mamie in a whisper.

"What are you two on about?" bellowed Jimmy, surprising us with a fresh burst of enthusiasm. "Men have flown to the moon and back again, but has anyone ever circled the whole of Ireland with a donkey and cart? 'Tis a powerful undertaking! And mark my words, after a few hundred miles of road, the provincial newspapers will have made Kevin here a celebrity. And there'll be farmers, north and south, who'll be opening their gates at his approach, and women more than eager to put him before a hot meal."

"It won't be that simple," fretted Mamie, "and there'll be a fair amount of hardship as well. Imagine, all those nights with never the same plate before you or the same pillow beneath your head."

"There's no adventure without hardship." Jimmy jumped to his feet and began to pace. "And for the few times Kevin meets up with a contrary farmer, can't he pitch tent down a secluded lane, prepare his own meal, and spancel the ass for the night?"

Mamie looked sadly at me but said nothing.

"How many miles do you figure for your circuit?" Jimmy whirled around, in front of a cupboard filled with trophies and ribbons won at various horse shows.

"Between sixteen and eighteen hundred."

"When might you leave?"—walking toward the wall calendar.

"Before the first of May. And I need to finish no later than Christmas Day."

"That's eight full months," he said, flipping through the calendar. "Eighteen hundred miles in eight months is less than ten miles a day. There'd be no loss on an ass to travel that distance, provided she was well-fed and had a good set of feet. Were there many at Rattigan's who thought an ass could do it?"

"I had the feeling most of them thought it couldn't be done, and I was crazy for thinking of doing it."

"Any wagers, bets?" he went on, smacking his lips.

"None that I saw, but there was talk of it."

"Too early for that just yet, but this could turn itself into a right sweepstakes! Did they say anything else?"

"They said a young mare, free of spavins and curbs, would be best suited for the road."

"They're right about the mare. But how do you know about spavins and curbs?"

"I don't."

"Well, don't go saying things that lead me to believe you know what you're on about!" he erupted, flailing his arms over his head. "We only have eight weeks to prepare you for this journey, and there's more to know about an ass than checking the oil and filling a radiator."

"Yes, sir."

"Now, it will cost you. I'll do my best, but a good ass will go for forty quid and cart and tackle another sixty or more. How does that suit your purse?"

"It'll be fine," I gulped.

"Well, then, be back here a week from tonight and I'll have for you a donkey that will travel the Ring of Ireland."

With that, he shook my hand: a tenacious grip that marked the beginnings of my haphazard apprenticeship.

On our drive home, Mamie and I churned over the evening's events.

"Do you have that sort of money, a hundred quid?" she asked.

"I have a total of two hundred and seven pounds," I said. "A hundred for Jimmy and a hundred and seven for the road. Not much, but it's okay for starters. Why do you think Jimmy suddenly took an interest?" I asked, turning down Beechwood.

"Jimmy Mac has a reputation as a champion horseman, none other like him in these parts. There's great pride in horse folk like himself, and he'll find you the ass, believe me, and he'll wager a tidy sum that you complete your shenanigans. Did you see him licking his lips at the very thought? But this is going to turn into a proper circus," moaned Mamie, slumping into her seat, "and God only knows why I had to go sticking my nose into it."

"Will you stop, Mamie," I said, pulling into the yard at Ballincurry. "It's not the Bataan death march I'm going on."

"Well, it won't be a dance with ham and cabbage," she said, stepping out from the car. "That, Kevin O'Hara, I can assure you!"

Missie and the Fleetwood

Nine donkeys were kicking and snorting in Jimmy McDermott's backfield when I returned to Kilteevan the following week. They were of all sizes and shapes, haranguing in their high, unsettling cries. Jimmy Mac leaned against a gate post and placidly looked out at the bucking asses, jawing them over with a burly man he introduced as Martin Maugham.

"I searched all of Westmeath, Longford, and Roscommon to gather these donks," explained Jimmy, "for it's hard to come by a good young ass a farmer is willing to sell. But I kept my promise and there's two in the crowd that'll do ya the Ring of Ireland."

Jimmy swung open the iron gate as we made our way through the muddy fields to where the asses had gathered themselves.

" 'Tis between those two," he said, flailing his ash stick to shoo away the noncontenders and pointing to a black jack and a brown mare staring blankly in return. "The jack is by far the stronger, but they're pure headers in May and have been known to gallop four counties for three moments of courtship. If a man was so afflicted with a jack's lovesickness, he'd either be a very thin man or a very dead one. 'Tis the mare that's right for your adventure, for she's easily handled and looks the part."

Jimmy sidled over to the mare and grasped her long ears. "Whoa, girl, we just want to look at you. Whoa, girleen!"

"This is the pick of the litter," he said proudly, wrestling with her large handsome head. "She's cart-trained, has good haunches, a firm breastplate, fine mouth, square feet, no signs of abuse." And, prying open her mouth, added, "And she's only cutting her five-year-old tusks."

Martin, in turn, dropped his fingertips lightly on the donkey's back making her coat shiver down the length of her spine.

"A right lively ass," commented Martin, a traveler (i.e., a tinker) whose livelihood depended on equine services. "And do you see those stripes running across her shins? That's a sure sign of Spanish blood. A fine breed of an ass altogether, this one."

She was a small pretty thing, the height of ten hands, with ears pricked high and forward, a sign of intelligence, I was told. She had dark brown eyes with a flash of purple for an iris. A white snout, white circles around her eyes, and white in the depths of her jackrabbit ears. Her coat gleamed with luster, a full nut-brown coat with a black cross on her back. While the others were dopey in appearance, she looked the part of an amused heroine. I was smitten.

"She's the one," I announced.

"A right choice," exclaimed Jimmy, slapping me full on the back. "And you know, she's a Roscommon ass as well. I bought her from the Madden brothers in Ballaghaderreen. Now, as I quoted you earlier, I'll ask forty quid for Her Ladyship and sixty for cart and tackle."

I went for my pocket.

"No, time enough just yet. Let me secure your other gear first."

After the painstaking chore of loading the eight other donkeys onto the lorry, I innocently inquired if Jimmy was taking them back to their owners tonight.

"Owners?" he smirked. "I'm taking them to Dundalk where they'll be tins of dog meal in the morning."

"Dog meal—but why?" I gasped, flinching at the thought of their condemnation.

"There's little need for them any longer, the tractor has all but replaced them," he answered, unmoved. "The ass has seen its day in Ireland and, believe me, its day was a long one. Now, the best thing for you to do is spend time with your mare. Let her get to know your smell and don't be afraid to talk to her. After Dundalk, Martin and I will swing west and make a few inquiries about cart and tackle, and if all goes well you'll have your outfit by the weekend."

The two men climbed into the cab, but as soon as the key fired the ignition, my donkey strained her neck through the gate, and began to bray from both ends.

"Jimmy, Jimmy, there's something wrong with my donkey!"

"There's nothing on her," he chuckled, glancing through the rearview mirror. "She just thinks she's missing out on something and wants to come for the ride."

Jimmy and Martin pulled out onto the main Lanesborough Road with their doomed cargo jamming wet snouts through the lorry slats, and I wondered if the animals had any inkling to where they were bound. When they were gone, I found myself alone with my brown mare, still calling to her erstwhile pals.

"Easy, McDermott," I said, hopping the gate and placing a timid arm over her shaggy back. "Easy, McDermott, you don't know what you're missing, my Miss."

And that, more or less, is how she came to be called Missie Mickdermot.

The cart, as promised, arrived at the weekend. It was a pitiful sight: a homely rubber-wheeled Galway mudbox Jimmy believed to be forty years old. No beauty, it was nailed together by a country carpenter who must have lived a life of poverty if he had persisted in such a trade.

"'Twill do," said Jimmy reassuringly, seeing my face drop.

"I was hoping for iron-shod wheels," I said, looking down at the pair of incongruous rubber tires.

"These are the very things ye'll need." He kicked them with his boot. "Iron-shod wheels are easier pulled and look the part, but if the summer is warm, the old wood of a wheel would swell and the iron bands would fly off, leaving you stranded and looking for a blacksmith a hundred miles away. And where would you be then, tell me? Garages have taken the place of the forge, remember that."

Bridie McDermott pitched in to restore my confidence. She told me how she had painted her father's winning carts in the agricultural shows at Mount Bellew Bridge years ago, and she'd paint my cart the traditional colors—red lead and farmer's blue—to turn this sad specimen into a proud rig.

"Not only is it sturdy, 'twill also be light on your ass's back," added Jimmy, standing between the cart's two long shafts and raising them above his waist. "You yourself could pull this cart about Ireland."

It would be light for the donkey, I conceded, and after a good scrubbing and a generous amount of paint, it might show a respectability hard to envision looking down upon this wooden heap dressed in cobwebs.

"Have you named your donkey yet?" asked Bridie.

"Missie Mickdermot," I offered. "If it's okay to use your surname, though I'll spell it differently."

"No, not at all. Missie Mickdermot is a fine name, isn't it, Jimmy?"

"Finest I've ever heard," he replied absentmindedly, yanking a few useless nails from the mudbox.

"And what will you name your cart?" Bridie asked jokingly.

"*Fleetwood*," I joked, "after the Cadillac of the same name."

That night in the McDermotts' kitchen, I thanked Jimmy for his weeklong search and counted out the correct number of bills onto the kitchen table, thinking all along how the Galway poet, Padraic O Conaire, had bought his *asal beag dubh* ("little black ass") off a tinker for one pound, plus sixpence each to his proliferating children, and how Robert Louis Stevenson had traveled the Cévennes in France with his donkey, Modestine, purchased for sixty-five francs and a glass of brandy.

"Thank you," said Jimmy, stacking the brightly colored bills into a modest pile and handing me a fiver in return.

"That there is your luck money, an old tradition," he said. And, spitting into his palm and waiting for me to do likewise, we shook hands. Missie and the *Fleetwood* were mine.

The days of March remained so wet and miserable I spent many hours in the Reference Room of the Galway Library, reading up on others who had made a circuit around Ireland, by shank's mare or otherwise. These writers—notably, John Synge, William Bulfin, Lloyd Praeger, and Padraic O Conaire—fired my enthusiasm for travel and kept me warm by the cold light of the window.

With five ordnance maps spread out before me, I felt like Bilbo Baggins ready to set out for Rivendell, my pen marking routes along the rugged coastline from Clare to Mizen Head and up the Antrim way to Giant's Causeway. I also worked out various logistics; for example, figuring that I could save eighty miles and avoid Limerick City altogether, by taking Missie across the Shannon ferry.

The planning made my journey feel real, and my apprehensions were drowned during those damp evenings in Galway pubs with friends my own age, who warmed to the adventure. Donal Honan in particular was a cheerleader, rousing my spirits wherever doubts would intrude. "You're on to a winner," he'd say.

I returned to the McDermotts' on the second of April after a three-week absence, and found Jimmy Mac glaring into the pit of the fire, with no hint of greeting.

"Now, Kevin," said Bridie, putting down the kettle and explaining her husband's mood, "there's a great deal of preparation these coming weeks, and Jimmy is afraid you spent too much time in Galway."

"But it's only April second, and I'm not leaving until the twenty-ninth. That gives me four full weeks."

"Four weeks isn't time enough," Jimmy growled, shifting his chair from the heat of the flame. "Your ass hasn't worked a day in months, and after a lazy winter she's liable to go lame after fifty miles of road. You just can't take an ass out of her winter stable and expect her to carry a cart ten miles a day every day for eight months. And if you don't begin to exercise, ye'll catch yourself pneumonia, sleeping in barns and byres and God-knows-where-else, and the *Old Moore's Almanac* predicting frost through the better part of May. You're ill-prepared for this undertaking."

"I suppose I did stay too long in Galway," I conceded, "but March was one of the coldest months on record. What could I have done?"

"You haven't spent a full hour with your mare," Jimmy erupted, his two arms flailing. "You could have had your ass shod! You could have had your cart painted! You could have been walking your ass five, ten miles a day!"

Bridie calmed Jimmy with a touch to his knee.

"To be frank"—he drew in his breath sharply—"I don't think you're serious about this journey. And if you are, you have mighty queer ways of showing it."

I sat humbled in the corner chair, unable to make eye contact with the horseman. Yes, he had found a capital mare ass, but now he had to couple her with the jackass that sat across from him. In the eyes of this ace jobber, I was a puny cut-jack to be sent packing, a hapless dull-lugged, long-haired hippie wanna-be.

I may have cut a harmless figure, but I had reserves of inner strength that Jimmy couldn't see, and I even doubted them myself. But this was more than another notion in a life of notions entertained and abandoned. This was my destiny come to call, and I had to answer. One fantasy I had to make real, whatever it took.

"I'm sorry, I didn't know all that was involved," I said in dire earnestness, "but I'm here now and I'll do nothing but work with Missie until the twenty-ninth. I promise."

"Good, that's all I wanted to hear," said Jimmy, pacified by my resolution. "Now, come Saturday, I'll take you and your Missie to Croghan's forge for a set of shoes, after which ye'll be here every afternoon to tackle your mare to the cart and take her on short jaunts. After these spins, ye'll clean the muck from her byre, put down a fresh bed of straw, and secure her for the night. When you've put your tackle away you'll come in for a bite to eat, and Bridie and I will tell you all ye'll need to know about asses and their ways."

Now he took a deeper breath, and stepped toward me with hand extended.

"We'll keep your Missie in the corner byre until the eve of your departure, and feed her the best of oats and hay. And if you're faithful in tipping her every day, she'll be in good form for your departure. Are you on board with us now?"

"I am," I answered with conviction, standing to shake his hand for a fresh start.

The Apprenticeship

Saturday, the seventh of April, Jimmy Mac and I took Missie to Croghan's forge in Roscommon for her first set of shoes. Stephen Croghan, a thin, bespectacled man in his fifties, with the reputation of a storyteller, walked around Missie thrice before laying a hand on her.

"It's been awhile since I've shod one of these devils," he said gloomily, watching Jimmy excuse himself from the forge to attend to other chores. "You twist her ears tightly," he instructed, looking at me doubtfully, "or this heathen will flatten me to the floor."

I took hold of Missie's ears as she bucked in protest.

"Give them a right twisting!" he shouted, reaching for her kicking hind leg.

Getting a better grip on Missie's nine-inch ears, I wrung them like washcloths, and to my amazement her leg stopped kicking and hung limply in the air.

"That's a good girl," whispered Stephen, cautious with his every move. "I've been knocked out before by one of these buggers."

Taking a deep breath, he cradled Missie's leg between his arm and leather apron, and began to file down her long hoof.

When Stephen went to pare her second hoof, I took the courage to speak.

"What's the reason for twisting my donkey's ears?" I asked, as I kept a firm grasp on her antennae.

"Her ears are extremely sensitive."

"But why would that quiet her down?"

"That's because you have a good hold on them and they're paining her. You've heard about the smart fellow who couldn't walk and chew gum at the same time, haven't you?"

"I have."

"Well, an ass can't be thinking of two things at the one time, or forget about one thing to think about another. With you wringing her ears, she can't think about anything but the ache that's in them. She can't even comprehend what's causing the ache or who's doing the causing, let alone my paring her hooves."

I looked at Missie's deadpan expression: "I have a regular wizard here, don't I?"

"Dumbest animal that ever walked the face of the earth," he stated flatly.

The forge itself was a dark, sooty, low-lying shed where bellows stoked a flaming hearth and an anvil sounded with the dull clang of iron. The hissing plume of forge water cooled the hot-tempered shoes that Stephen fitted to Missie's hooves, which smoked in turn and permeated the air with a pungency so severe a stray dog bolted from the door.

The actual shoeing, along with folktales, legends, and fabrications, took the better part of the afternoon. Stephen asked three pounds for his uniquely skilled and hazardous toils, a small sum when you consider he could have been KO'd by a flying hoof at any time.

"I could have made the shoes heavier," he explained, tying Missie to an iron ring outside on the forge wall, "but a light shoe is better at the start. Check them each morning and see if the nails are still intact. She can quickly go lame with a loose shoe, much like you or I going about with our laces untied. When she loses a nail, as she often will, find a horseman or farmer who'll drive one in for you. If you can't find either, do it yourself," taking a pony nail from his pocket and showing me how.

"When you hammer home the nail, make certain the bevel is pointing out toward the hoof-wall, like so. Or else it will go through her hoof and your walk is finished. It should come as no surprise, but the center of your donkey's hoof is more complicated than her brain.

"She'll also need to be pared every six to eight weeks. You'll know when her hooves need to be shortened, for she'll be walking on her heels like a woman heavy with child. And walking the miles you're talking, she's sure to develop sandcracks . . . fissures in her hooves. Best cure for sandcracks is to rub used motor-oil into her hooves with a cloth each morning. That will lubricate them and keep them supple.

"She'll also need a second and perhaps a third set of shoes if you're hoping to circle the country. I had a few friends here yesterday insisting your mare will go lame within three hundred miles. That needn't be the case. Treat her hooves the way a ballerina does her toes, and she'll tip on for you, no matter the amount of miles."

My brain was still reeling with the complications of Missie's four feet, when Jimmy Mac returned to the forge with his horsebox trailer. He lifted Missie's hooves and commented favorably on her new shoes.

"A topping job, Stephen. They'll see her through County Cork."

The three of us then boarded a stubborn Missie into the horsebox, whereupon

Stephen handed me a bag of nails for the road, and pierced another into the collar of my wool sweater.

"Haven't you noticed the pony nail in my lapel?" He pointed it out to me. "'Mary's Brooch,' we blacksmiths call them, so named after a smith fashioned a clasp from a nail to fasten Mary's cloak on her way to Bethlehem. We consider them good luck. Wear yours and your donkey will never go lame."

My apprenticeship began early the next week.

"Tonight you'll be learning how to tackle your ass to the cart," said Jimmy, pulling the *Fleetwood* from the barn and resting it on its heels with shafts skyward. "Go get your ass, you have plenty to learn."

I led Missie out to the yard and tied her clumsily to a wooden post. I fumbled at a slipknot, and Jimmy tried to instruct me, until he abruptly waved me off in frustration and proceeded.

"Here's your tackle," he grunted, laying out five pieces of harness. "You're familiar with the winkers, and these others are the collar, hames, straddle, and breeching. Ye've seen me tackle my horse, so you should have no trouble in dressing your ass."

I had put on Missie's winkers twice in the past but took no pleasure in it. She hated anything that interfered with her sensitive ears, and the head strap raked and flattened the two of them. I couldn't make heads nor tails out of the collar, and fastened it upside-down around Missie's neck until Jimmy cursed out a few instructions. The hames was like a Chinese puzzle, and I'd still be struggling with it if Bridie hadn't motioned that it secured the collar with the prongs up.

The straddle posed no problem, except for the strap to be secured around her belly. When I reached beneath Missie's starboard side to catch hold of the end-strap, her head swooped down and nearly bit the ear from my head.

But the breeching was the most difficult—a strapped device over the donkey's hindquarters, its main purpose is to keep the cart off the donkey's back when traveling downhill. The problem isn't draping the breeching over the buttocks, but freeing the tail from the breeching after it is properly placed: a difficult procedure further compounded when your mare suspects dalliance.

Keeping a firm grip on her winkers, I went to free her tail but was smartly bitten in the fat of the thigh for my pains. On my second attempt she began rotating away, keeping her entrapped tail just shy of my grasp. After the fifth such roundabout, Jimmy and Bridie were rolling in tears. A comical sight, I suppose, if you're not the one involved.

And the donkey's tail is a peculiar bit of God's handiwork. I had always imagined it to be free of musculature, a flaccid appendage. But no, it is a whiplike muscle capable of swatting the most amorous of jacks back to common sense. After $33\frac{1}{3}$ revolutions on this dizzy donkey-go-round, I lunged for her tail and finally yanked it free. A loud cheer rose from the McDermotts as Missie turned to gape in bewilderment.

"You best be quicker than that, or you'll never set foot again in Roscommon once you leave it," giggled Bridie from behind a handkerchief damp with tears.

"Now pay attention," said Jimmy, "and I'll show you the simplest way to yoke your ass to the cart."

He took hold of Missie's winkers and, clucking a few consonants, he led her about in a half-circle, pivoted her between the upright shafts, backed her in a few steps, and dropped the cart lightly on her back.

"When you drop the cart, the top-band fits into the straddle, the draughts are attached to the hames, the links of the breeching are yoked evenly to the shafts, and the belly-band is placed beneath and behind your ass's forelegs. Do you have it?"

"I think so," I gulped.

I made numerous attempts at leading Missie to the cart, but either she pivoted too early, which left her crosswise between the shafts, or too late, which left her facing the cart. And the few times I had positioned her properly, she was too stubborn to back up the necessary steps to align the top-band with the straddle.

"You've had her every which way but inside out," flared Jimmy—never one to be a kindly teacher. "Go on, talk to her, let her know who's boss! And don't be afraid to give her a taste of the stick!"

"C'mon, Missie," I coaxed, talking from the side of my mouth as Jimmy had done. "C'mon, girl, no kidding. Up, up, uppity-up. Chub, chub, chub . . ."

"You're confusing the hell out of her," Jimmy ranted, pulling the reins from my grasp and forcefully ushering Missie between the elusive shafts and smartly dropping the cart. "Don't make a blooming project out of it—just do it!"

Still fuming, he shouted: "Bridie, swing open that gate. And you, get into this cart!"

I climbed into the mudbox as Jimmy sat on the left side of the dashboard, his lanky legs dangling out of the box.

"Giddeeupthere," he commanded, giving Missie a good swat of the stick which sent her galloping through the gate and onto the main Lanesborough Road.

"When you're tipping along," the horseman explained, as I tried to maintain my balance in the open box of the rumbling cart, "the most important thing is to keep a firm grasp on the reins. When she's tipping at a fair clip, as she's doing, let the reins go slack. If you want to turn right, give a sharp tug to the right rein and leave the left slack. If you want to go left, pull the left rein and leave the right slack. And when you want her to stop, pull both reins together, like so." He demonstrated by smartly pulling the reins simultaneously, which reared back Missie's head and stopped her on a dime.

"And don't be afraid to give the reins a good tugging to stop her," he said, setting her going again with a smart slap of the stick. "She has a good mouth and there's no need to worry about the bit hurting her. What you need to worry about is the heavy traffic you'll encounter on the busy roads and in the cities. She'll be fretful at first, with all the noise, especially air brakes, but she'll get used to it. And when you're tipping her along, watch for windblown newspaper that might skirt up between her legs, for she's apt to raise up and bolt on you no matter how hard you pull back on the reins.

"You also need to keep your eyes open for oil slicks on the side of the road. An ass, for some reason, spooks at an oil slick. And when your ass comes to a manhole cover, she'll never step over it, but will go around it into the road. And if a car or lorry happens to be bearing down on you—*smack!*—you've had it. Asses don't think on the road, so you'll have to do her thinking through these reins."

Jimmy made a swooping U-turn a mile up the road, and tipped Missie back home through the haggard gate as smoothly as a limousine.

"Now, you give it a go," he said, jumping off the cart and holding Missie by the winkers. "Tip her as far as Kilteevan Chapel at a steady pace. And whatever you do, keep a good grip on those reins."

I took hold of the reins and mounted the dashboard in the fashion of the jobber. When I was seated comfortably, Jimmy gave Missie a whooping holler which sent her galloping through the gate and once more onto the main Lanesborough Road.

We were off, with Missie's ears twisting like radar and the *Fleetwood* moving swiftly along the road. Jimmy was right: You really did have to keep a good grasp on the reins. In no time Missie was diving into the hedges, and before we were out of my mentor's glaring sight, she had knocked over an empty milk can. Believe me, it is no joke to trot a donkey down a busy thoroughfare with the reins so tangled in the hames it was only by my Irish luck I didn't go left into hurtling traffic when pulling on my right rein for Kilteevan Chapel.

When we returned to McDermott's after our short jaunt, Jimmy Mac was down my throat.

"You're too gentle with that ass!" he roared, kicking up mud with his Wellies. "If you don't start using that ash plant, she'll make a holy show of you on the road."

"But Jimmy, I'm not one to go raising welts on her back."

"Go on, out of that," he seethed, exploding in a froth of spittle. "An ass is an ass. You'll never find her kind performing tricks at Duffy's Circus!"

With that, he turned and stomped dejectedly into the house, leaving me to figure out how to remove the cart from my stupid donkey's back.

I stood out in the yard, trembling. I had hit Missie, but my stick didn't seem to carry the sting of Jimmy's ash plant. But I wasn't about to swing it like a Louisville Slugger. I was a nurse, after all, not some bullyboy wrangler. And I wasn't too adept at animal psychology, either, having had only one pet in my life, a stray cat I'd named Misery. I wondered if this were more beast than I could handle. And I was thinking of Jimmy as much as Missie.

As I hopelessly fumbled to remove the collar, Bridie was out the door, and together we untackled Missie and placed her in the byre.

"You'll soon get the hang of her," Bridie assured me, as I mounted my bicycle for home. "Chin up, and we'll see you tomorrow evening, please God."

Thanking her, I pedaled out through the gate, little caring if I was flattened by car or lorry.

The Kilteevan Report

CHAPTER SIX

A carillon of bells from the highest cathedral could not have announced my first outing with Missie more widely than did a few spying upstarts from Kilteevan. My first cousin Noel Kelly, scouting the goings-on at Rattigan's in my absence (I hadn't set a foot in the pub since the morning after I announced my donkey proposal), told me "The Kilteevan Report" had focused on Missie's nosedive into the hedges, the toppling-over of a milk can, and my reluctance to give her a taste of the stick.

Noel also reported there still was no fat purse being wagered, nor setting of odds against Missie and me completing the circuit. This was disheartening to hear in a parish known to wager a teat off a cow. Noel thought there were two reasons for this lack of bookmaking: First, Kathleen Rattigan, the proprietress, forbade open gambling in the house; an Easter or Christmas turkey, yes, but the stacking of notes upon a table was strictly forbidden. Secondly, the majority at Rattigan's still thought my proposed journey was a cod, a whim, or "a right wobbly." I simply hoped for a tally of the odds, so I could better gauge what my own chances were.

But whatever they were on about, it was high time to enter Rattigan's and confront these skeptics once and for all. It was also time to tell Grannie Kelly, for I couldn't thrill to thoughts of journeying to "the Pass of the Curlews," or "the Glen of the Downs," until I confessed my plans to the grand woman on the hill.

On Wednesday morning, the eighteenth of April, I tackled Missie to the cart while Jimmy looked on in mild aggravation. I had decided to take Missie to Grannie's without forewarning, and though Cella and Mamie had told me it would give Grannie "quite a hop," they assured me she'd quickly recover.

It would be seven miles to Ballincurry and seven back the following morning, my first overnight trip. This may have made Jimmy Mac proud, but he hid it well by barking out orders as Missie and I rumbled through his haggard gate.

"If you don't get that ass of yours to brighten her step, ye'll be arriving home on her offspring!"

My day's itinerary was to arrive at Grannie Kelly's by way of Rattigan's. So, rather than the Lanesborough Road, I took the narrow lane of Catherain, a quiet, pleasant boreen where blackbirds sang in the ash trees and wrens darted like bandits in the hedges. There were no cars, no distractions, only the ring of Missie's shoes on the cold pavement.

Even in this pastoral setting, however, Missie's slow and stubborn gait began to grate. She just pussyfooted along, stopping to gape at every gap in the hedges. And despite a barrage of whacks that resounded off her back like pistol shots, she wouldn't quicken her pace. Nope, she just lumbered on, walking three times slower than a fat bag-toting caddy in the heat of July, stopping to swing back her head as if to say, *Easy on the stick, jackass, or I won't carry your portage out of Roscommon.*

What really irked me was how she obeyed Jimmy Mac when he was up on the cart. Oh, yes, she would speedily trot for him as if warming up for the Little Brown Jug. But nothing would alter her discourse with me. I could not, despite an infinite number of prods and lashings, get her to move swiftly. Of course, Jimmy Mac would go raging that I was as soft as Joe Soap. Joe Soap! I was breaking sticks over her back.

So on this fresh and breezy day I resigned myself to her listless gait by counting the catkins in the hazel. As she continued at her snail's pace, I slid off the cart and found companionable comfort in walking beside her, guiding her head with shortened reins. *Isn't this the better way to enjoy the countryside?* I thought. Rather than worry about oil slicks, manhole covers, and blown rubbish, I could be safely walking alongside Missie and keeping myself fit as well. Why clip down these picturesque byways when my goal was to cover a mere ten miles a day?

I had mentioned to Jimmy Mac the possibility of walking the country alongside Missie, but he rebuked the idea by saying: "Walking alongside an ass and cart is much like hailing a taxi in the city . . . and then go running home behind it!"

But still, walking beside her would give me a chance to stop and chat with the people at their doors. No need to come down off my "high horse." I'd be like the barefooted postboy in bygone days, leaning against gates and stonewalls to speak with those who'd be in no hurry to see me away. Yes, I'd have the long day to do little but take in at groundlevel the goings-on of this Old World slipping into the New Age: this ancient isle of tradition soon to vanish like Atlantis, a shoal of memories in the western sea.

That was it. It may have been the vision of a farmer trotting his donkey that got me started, but now I had my own path to walk and I was determined to do it on foot, as close to the land as I could get, in touch with the earth in some primordial way.

And why contend with a fractious beast? Why not try to see eye-to-eye with her? Walk the roads as partners, Missie and me, rather than as master and slave?

"Don't go abusing Missie with the stick." My dad's oldest brother, Uncle Mickey O'Hara had offered good advice, enjoying a pint one Sunday evening in Ballinalee, County Longford. "No, give her an apple and a fistful of corn, and get to know her as a friend and companion, not a beast of burden. Talk to her, sing to her, and believe you me, she'd walk the Ring of Ireland if her little legs were crumpling beneath her. That's the nature of the donkey, the way they've always been. But so few know it, and isn't that the way of the world?"

Opinions were divided, of course, on "the nature of the donkey." Jimmy Mac and most of the crew at Rattigan's thought *Equus asinus* was a lazy good-for-nothing, no brighter than a 10-watt bulb. On the other hand, Jim Tiernan told me how his donkey, Nedeen, would bray by his gate each evening and wouldn't "hang its song" until Jim came out from the house to give him a few blasts from his pipe. After taking Jim's mouthful of smoke into its snout, old Nedeen would snort deeply and prance back up the field, evidently content with its lungful. In Patrick Kavanagh's autobiography, *The Green Fool*, the poet tells how he and his mother were lost one evening in their native County Monaghan. After traveling several more miles with their donkey and cart, they found themselves at the very crossroads that began their plight. Patrick's mother, fearful they had stumbled into Faeryland, told her son to let the reins fall and allow the donkey to see them home. The donkey, as strange to these roads as the passengers, made its own decisions at forks and crossroads, and had the poet and his mother safely home by nightfall. So, should I treat Missie as an obstinate beast who was too lazy to breathe, or as a blessed creature who enjoyed a companionable evening smoke?

Missie's kind had always received harsh treatment in Ireland, a symbol of "the hard times." But I couldn't see lashing Missie around Ireland, up on the cart like some Fenian charioteer. It made more sense to walk beside her, as I was now doing, to recast the ancient man-beast relationship and take the trouble to learn her traits and mannerisms, her wants and needs. And if Missie was "innately blessed," as Mickey O'Hara had proclaimed, I should at least give that grace the chance to surface.

Leaving the high-hedged confines of Catherain for the road to Rattigan's, I climbed back onto the cart, thinking it best to remain mounted until the Sunday of our departure to avoid ridicule. Arriving at Rattigan's five miles and two hours later, I clumsily tied Missie to the petrol pump and was met at the door by Hugh Mannion, Willie Cassidy, Dan Madden, Headmaster D'Alton, and Kathleen Rattigan.

"We were expecting you," greeted Kathleen, rushing over to stroke Missie's mane. "She's a prize donkey, so she is."

"So this is the ass that's going to see you through Ireland?" asked Hugh, studying the points of my beast with great interest.

" 'Tis a topping affair," commented Dan Madden, checking out the tackling and cart. "This outfit must have thinned your purse some."

"Ninety-five pounds," I answered.

"Tackle and all?"

"Yep."

"That was right good of the jobber," Headmaster D'Alton observed with a smile.

"Look at her shanks, boys," said Willie. "I say she can tip like the wind. Fifteen minutes from Jimmy Mac's to here, or less?"

"Something like that," I dodged, "but I wasn't really timing her."

"Stephen Croghan do these shoes?" Hugh stooped down to have a look at them.

"He did. And Jimmy Mac thinks they'll see her through Cork."

"Cork be damned!" he laughed. "But a dandy job nonetheless. Look at 'em, boys. Cut-down pony racing shoes with studs to keep her from slipping on the icy roads. I haven't seen an ass shod these twenty years."

"Well, let's not be standing out in the cold," Kathleen suggested, wrapping her arms about her. "Come inside, Kevin, and I'll stand you a pint of Guinness. An American with a donkey . . . dear God," she laughed, as she hurried back into the pub.

I entered Rattigan's for the first time in six weeks, as the Four Masters—my nickname for this quartet—tightened around me for the interview.

"Troth, but you're dead serious," praised Willie, my grandmother's aged godchild. "And we thought you were codding us the whole time."

"I have no choice but to go through with it now," I looked out at Missie standing patiently beside the Esso pump. "And if it's okay with you, Kathleen, I'd like to begin and end my journey here at Rattigan's?"

"I'd be honored," she proclaimed, standing the promised pint before me.

"When might you be leaving?" asked Dan Madden.

"A week Sunday," I replied, "the twenty-ninth of April. I heard it was good luck to start a journey on the Sabbath."

"Jonathan Swift said he loved to begin a journey on a Sunday, so as to be accompanied by all the prayers pouring out from the churches," the headmaster enlightened.

"Where will your travels take you?" asked Hugh, raising his glass of barley wine to toast my first swallow.

"I'll go from here to Galway, and then travel along the coast: Clare, Kerry, Cork, Waterford, Wexford, Wicklow, and up the east coast through Dublin, Meath, and into Armagh, Down, Antrim, Derry, Donegal, Leitrim, Sligo, Mayo, Connemara in Galway, and home again."

"Jaysus, you're a right scholar with your geography," he gasped.

"How many miles do you figure on covering in all?" Willie wet the tip of a pencil and went to scribbling on the back of a brown envelope.

"Between sixteen and eighteen hundred. It's hard to measure with all the peninsulas in the north and southwest."

"And when would you be likely to arrive home?"

"Christmas Eve."

"Will your little brown darling be the only ass you'll use during the loopabout?"

"Yes."

"What if she goes lame or strips a shoulder?"

"I'll stop the journey."

"You won't get another ass to go on with?"

"No. And Jimmy Mac says the *Gardai* would never allow me a second chance."

"He's right about that," said the headmaster. "If your donkey shows the slightest sign of ill-treatment . . ."

"Wasn't a donkey put on this earth to work, same as ourselves?" voiced Hugh in annoyance.

"Enough!" shouted Willie, perturbed with the interruptions. "Let only one of us speak at a time—can't we?—so I can get this straight for the record."

"There's no need for any record," snapped Kathleen, clearing his elbows off the bar with a swoop of her wet bar towel.

"Arragh, now, Kathleen," lilted Willie, his face all innocence like a choirboy, "we only need these specifics for our own personal use. There'll be little gambling, I assure you."

"Do you take me for a fool?" She swiped his elbows a second time.

"A two-pound limit only, Kathleen, on our mothers' gravestones," blurted Hugh, coming to Willie's aid. " 'Twill be as harmless as a football pool set up by the Women's Rosary Sodality, we promise."

"A two-pound limit, so," Kathleen said sternly.

"Now, Kevin," Willie stipulated, "you're telling us today, the eighteenth of April, that you'll travel no less than sixteen hundred miles with the one ass—a mare ass—and be back here at Rattigan's Public House no later than Christmas Eve after circling the country, north and south. Is that correct?"

"It is."

"Boys, have I left anything out?"

"Some may want proof of the distance covered," said Hugh.

"I could do that by sending weekly postcards. The postmarks would verify my route and travels."

"This current postal strike may go on forever," reminded the headmaster.

"Or I could also keep names and addresses of all the people I stay with."

"One or the other should do nicely enough," said Willie, satisfied. "Anything else?"

"I still have to tell my grandmother," I confessed, "and I'm afraid I'd have to drop the whole idea if she's set against it."

"I wouldn't worry about Mary Ann," said Dan with assurance. "I'm thinking she'll look fondly on your caper."

"Would your Missie like anything?" Kathleen peered out the window.

"She enjoys an apple."

"An apple," scorned Hugh, "at two shillings apiece! When we were gossoons we'd be lucky to get an apple for Christmas, and then we'd play with it like a ball till it was bruised and blackened. The only thing I ever gave my ass was a swift boot up the behind. One she richly deserved."

"An apple is a small gift to give a donkey who is setting out to circle the country," retorted Kathleen, picking out a fine Granny Smith from a wooden crate.

While Kathleen stepped out to feed Missie, the Four Masters sat contemplatively on their stools. I may have quieted them for a moment, but I imagined they'd be like anchormen on the nightly news this evening, sharing the details of my travels with the parish crowd.

"You know," I said, breaking the silence as well as covering my departure, "Jimmy Mac told me to tip Missie at a good clip as far as here, but then to take her slowly from here to Grannie Kelly's. Why's that, you suppose?"

"He wants you to break her in slowly after a fat winter," explained Dan. "No sense keeping her on a dead gallop the whole time. The five miles from Kilteevan to Kilrooskey is a good distance for any ass to travel on the run, though she didn't appear winded at all."

"Not a drop of sweat," noted Willie, suspiciously.

"Well, then"—I rushed down the last of my pint— "I suppose it's high time I face the music on the hill."

I left the pub, untethered Missie from the petrol pump, and climbed aboard, as Kathleen and the four pensioners watched from the open doorway.

"It appears she likes to take her time," called Hugh, as Missie began her painstaking stroll toward Ballincurry, two miles away.

"This stick could change her tune," I boasted, raising the ash plant above my head.

"I wonder," answered Hugh, removing his soiled cap in farewell. "I just wonder."

A Birthday Visit to Knock

CHAPTER SEVEN

Sitting up behind Missie Long-Ears like a dunce the whole time, I finally reached Ballagh Chapel at the foot of Ballincurry. I slid off the mudbox and took my time in walking her up the winding village road, hoping the neighbors wouldn't be out to spot my ascent to Grannie Kelly's.

I pulled Missie to a halt every forty yards or so, taking deep breaths of the mountain air and reminding myself how a coward tastes death a thousand times. Missie didn't mind these frequent delays. In fact, she was amiably receptive to them, and soon took advantage by stopping at twenty-yard intervals.

We were closing in on Grannie's next-door neighbors, the Tiernans, when Missie began to bray horribly across the fields. There was no shutting her up once her bugling began, especially after she received a hoarse reply from Jim Tiernan's old, pipe-smoking jack, Nedeen. Missie jumped-to frantically, hotfooting us into the Kelly yard, where Grannie stood laughing and blessing herself at the doorway.

"So, you're the tinker who's come to mend me buckets!" she exclaimed, letting out a long howl of laughter before ducking back into the house. Uncle Mickey, Mamie, and their son Michael, charged out of the house, cheering and clapping wildly. I stood flabbergasted.

"Grannie was expecting me," I said in disbelief. "She knew all along."

"Actually, she was expecting you yesterday," chuckled Michael, throwing an arm around me.

"Why didn't you tell me that Grannie knew?" I asked, still dumbfounded. "Which one of you squealed on me, anyway?"

"You did yourself," smiled Mamie. "One wouldn't need to be a sleuth to know you were spending all your free time in an ass's byre with the stink up on you, and coming into our house every night with muck on your runners."

"Now, just don't stand there," said Uncle Mickey. "Go to your grandmother, for she's eager to hear about your wanderings. Go on, off with ye"—giving me a boot in the pants—"and Michael and I will settle your brown girleen in the backfields for the night."

"But what about Jim Tiernan's jackass, singing below?"

"What about him?"

"Well, it wouldn't do if Missie climbed the hedges and spent the night with him. I mean, I don't want her in foal, you know."

"Jim Tiernan's doddering old ass will be no threat to your young mare, for his candle has long been quenched," chortled Mamie. "Now, step inside, for your Grannie's fretting mightily over her stray kitten."

I left Missie in their care and walked into the farmhouse. There was no sign of Grannie in the kitchen so I walked through the brightly decorated middle room and down to her bedroom door. When I knocked and entered, I found her in bed, covered with a heap of coats, a *shirallee* of blankets, and a brown shawl covering much of her face.

"I owe you an apology." I sat beside her on the bed and handed her a roll of Silvermints. "I should have told you weeks ago but I kept putting it off. And now I find you've known about it all along."

"Dear God, but it wasn't as if you were hiding it from me," she smiled, coming out of her hiding to point at the pony nail Stephen Croghan had pinned on me.

"I'm still sorry, either way," I confessed. "I should have asked your permission from the start."

"Not to worry," she answered, fingering the sleeve of my coat. "But I'll tell you, you had me in pure botheration when I first caught wind of your plans."

I looked out her bedroom window toward Ballagh Chapel, as the long, uncertain road began to unfurl before me. Oh, what a grand rogue I thought myself to be, breaking away from the edicts of reason to travel these ancient highways like the sojourners of old.

With my trek now in the open, I went jabbering on incessantly, telling Grannie of all the places my itinerary would take me. Dreamlike destinations she and my mother had recited countless times to me in poems, laments, and song: "There is a green island in lone Gougane Barra . . ." "The lovely fields of Athenry . . ." "On the green hills of Ulster . . ." "I often think of the Shandon Bells . . ." "The light of evening, Lissadell. . . ." "The little waves of Breffney go . . ."

Yes, I would visit such territories and be home again to tell her about what I had seen and heard, the people I had met and, indeed, if the Mountains of Mourne "swept down to the sea."

"So you don't mind if I set off on this journey?" I asked as I held her warm hand, feeling blessed in the company of my living ancestry.

"I do not, *agra*. But I must warn you, as you may know yourself, there'll be those few at Rattigan's, after the drink's been taken, who'd like nothing more than to see you pack it up early. If God gives you the strength, see it through to the end. Mind ye, 'twould come harder on you to travel the fifteen miles back to your starting point than to walk the thousand-odd miles yet before you."

She went quiet, as I glanced at her cluttered bedside stand, like a display in a folk-park museum, with its carrageen moss, a faithful *naggin* of brandy, mints, chamomile, *Old Moore's Almanac,* Mass cards, Sunday prayer book, a tidy stack of letters from her own scattered about the globe. And, with pride of place, novenas from the Franciscan friary in Athlone, rosary beads in a ball, and holy waters from the shrines of Knock, Lourdes, and Fatima.

"There's another thing I ask," she added, adjusting the brown shawl around her shoulders in this damp room: "that you and I celebrate your thirtieth birthday this Friday by visiting Knock Shrine. I'm not going to allow a wayfaring grandson of mine to roam the earth with a donkey without first making a pilgrimage to Knock."

"Yes, Grannie," I said, kissing her.

"I'll now take me nap, and we'll have the long day Friday to be chatting. And it might be wise for you to check on your Missie." She began to chortle. "It wouldn't do for her to be dancing with Jim Tiernan's old jackeen!"

I pranced like a pony down to the kitchen where I swung Mamie around by the hands. "I've got the queen's blessing!" I proclaimed. "I'm on my way!"

"God help you from this day to your last," she said, wrestling free of my little jig, as Mickey and Michael ambled into the kitchen after having settled Missie.

"I feel like Columbus after meeting with Isabella," I announced to the pair.

"You're off your bloody rocker," said young Michael, grappling me to the floor.

On Friday morning, my thirtieth birthday, Grannie and I set out for the Shrine of Knock, forty-two miles west of Kilrooskey. Our black Morris Minor sped through town and country under a vapor of silvery mist. A few houses were being built along the roads, and in the distance you could see the rubble of stone gables standing in the mist-shrouded fields.

"These new bungalows won't stand the test of time," said Grannie, breaking a thoughtful silence as she kept an observing eye on the road. "The homes left to ruin in the backfields have weathered centuries. And many of these new bungalows have no hearth, but only an ornamental grate, counting on oil for heat, and all the turf left yet in the bog."

We drove along the wet, sinuous road, passing fields of cows lowing mournfully, as sodden lambs, buckling with the heavy weight of rain in their coats, stumbled close to their ewes.

"All one can hear is livestock crying through the countryside," she said, opening her window to the rain. "Starved they are, the lot of them, and if spring doesn't soon arrive, they'll be too weak to complain. And well-to-do farmers asking three pounds for a bale of hay—three pounds, mind ye—not to some stranger, but to their fellow countrymen! Oh, Kevin, the changes I've seen, and so few are good ones. Away from the teachings of Jesus, they are, thinking only of money, money, and not true values. Of course your donkey can feed on 'the long acre,' the high grass along the road's edge, just as the poor of our country have used since time immemorial."

Soon, over the flat Mayo bogland, rose the pinnacle of Knock Shrine—magnet for Irish pilgrims and other faithful, commemorating an apparition of the Blessed Virgin Mary, Saint Joseph, and Saint John the Evangelist, witnessed by fifteen villagers in August 1879.

My first duty after parking the car near the Oratory was to fill two bottles with the holy waters of Knock, running from a series of taps near the Basilica. This done, Grannie and I made our way to the old chapel of Saint John the Evangelist, to celebrate Mass with some forty other pilgrims in attendance. Grannie always preferred Knock on weekdays off-season, forgoing visits when tens of thousands of summertime pilgrims filled the Mayo countryside. She liked prayer without fanfare.

After Mass had been celebrated, Grannie walked the outside aisles to say the Stations of the Cross and I followed, saying them a Station or two behind. When finished, she dropped two coins into an Offering Box, lit two candles, and knelt before them to the right of the altar rail. I sat in the front pew, looking at the statues and flickering flames, and presently discovered we were all alone in this most blessed of Irish chapels, in this centennial year of the Apparition.

When Grannie returned to the pew, she knelt and broke into a litany of prayer, soft and sweet and endless. As her supplications subsided, she took from her pocketbook a pen and paper and began to write in her spidery handwriting. After completing four or five lines, she folded the paper neatly and placed it in a blue linen envelope.

Then she returned to the altar rail, dropped two more coins into the Offering Box, lit two more candles, and slipped the envelope into a brass box beneath the statue of Mary, marked PETITIONS. She then whispered more prayers, lifted her head to the rafters, and knelt quietly for some moments. Finally, as though she had received a heavenly answer, she stood, genuflected, and walked back to join me.

"Now, then," she smiled, taking hold of my hand. "Now you and your Missie can travel the Ring of Ireland."

There was a partial clearing in the western sky on our way home, and all the world seemed peaceful.

"Take your time, now," said Grannie, "for there's no cows to be milked by our hands. And when we reach Castlerea, we'll stop into the Three Counties where I'll treat you to a piping dinner for your thirtieth birthday. God knows, you may not have many hot meals on the road."

"Mamie doesn't think I'm going to eat at all," I joked.

"Now, ye've told me you're planning to seek nightly hospitality from farmers along the road, and I pray to God ye'll find it, even in this day and age. When you do so, knock with the light of day, as you have nothing to hide and ye'd still have time to find other shelter if the farmer refuses you. Days are lengthening now, but when they grow short, you'll need to seek your byre early. Before knocking, don't be afraid to say a decade of the Rosary. There's great power in prayer, and the 'Hail Mary' will ease your countenance and give you the look of trust at any door."

"Amen, Grannie."

"And always do your best to attend Mass on Sunday. There's a wealth of grace in the sacrament of the Eucharist. Imagine, you'll partake the Holy Bread in churches all about the country. Do you know, I've heard Mass in sixty-two different churches during my time?"

"Sixty-two!" I was truly astonished. "You've kept track?"

"Why do you find that so strange?" she playfully scolded, with a pinch to my wrist. "Didn't I read in the *Irish Press* how a Dubliner boasted of having a drink in all of Dublin's seven hundred forty-three pubs? Wouldn't he have been better off going to seven hundred forty-three different churches?"

"I suppose so," I conceded, though I knew which feat I was more likely to achieve.

"And when you're traveling along," she concluded, looking out at the passing fields, "think only of the road at your feet and all that surrounds it, for you may well find the road isn't half long enough when you make your turn for home. And don't worry about lovely Belita. Your love for one another will only strengthen after your short year apart. Remember, there's no pot of gold at the rainbow's end. I'm sure you've learned from your parents that the only pot of gold is the rainbow itself."

She went quiet, her crooked fingers working her handkerchief into a ball, while looking out at meadow and field. *Yes, Grannie, the rainbow itself. Not the destination, but the journey matters. And yes, I'll be mindful of every step, each footfall along these drovers' paths where, since a schoolboy, I have longed to tread.*

The Commencement

CHAPTER EIGHT

I wasn't long back in Kilrooskey when I heard that Rattigan's had erupted in a flurry of rumors and speculation, all stemming from the Four Masters on the Wednesday. Noel Kelly suggested I not enter Rattigan's until the day of my departure, as odds were being freely discussed, ranging between 20–1 to 8–1 against. One oddsmaker reasoned: "If it were one of our own lads setting out on this gambol I wouldn't hesitate in stacking up the odds, a hundred–to–one. But this Yank is a mite peculiar and there's no telling what he can or cannot do."

Noel also advised I not enter Rattigan's again until the day of my departure, keeping my adventure fresh and letting the play have its day.

The week before my departure I alternated nights between Mickey and Mamie's in Ballincurry, and Vincent and Cella's in Cloonara, where I bunked in the back room with Noel and Desmond, ages twenty and eleven, who would pelt me with questions before dropping off to sleep.

"It wouldn't do for you to be out in a bog tonight," said Noel, listening to the wind whistle through a draught in the window.

" 'Twill be fierce hard," seconded Desmond, sitting up on his elbows in the far bed. "Do you really think you can make it?"

"If we get by the first two weeks without a major mishap, we'll be on our way," I answered with blind confidence.

"Who is 'we'?"

"Me and Missie."

"My friends in school are calling you 'the Donkeyman,' " laughed Dessie.

"Desmond!" scolded Noel.

"Well, they are. But I wouldn't mind them. Kieran Gavigan thinks you'll make the history books one day."

"The journey will be hard all the same"—contemplated Noel, eerily silhouetted by the firelight from the bedroom grate—"in someone's barn or shed every night, here and there, and some farmers not kind enough to give you the time of day."

"You may not get to take a bath for weeks," added Desmond.

"No great loss there," I answered. "I almost die of pneumonia every time I step out of the tub."

"How much money have you left?" asked Noel.

"Sixty-seven pounds."

"Sixty-seven pounds won't see you through Clare. I'll have a twenty to give you on Sunday."

"Thanks, Noel, but if my plan works, sixty-seven pounds will be plenty."

"How do you reckon?"

"I hope to earn my food and nightly lodging by telling stories at the kitchen table, the way the old storytellers did it years ago."

"There hasn't been a seanachie traveling the roads since the turn of the century."

"Maybe I can start a revival," I joked, with a half-measure of hope. "I read that farmers long ago would reward a good storyteller with the three b's: bath, beer, and bed."

"That isn't the case any longer. The countryside is full of crackpots."

"Then I'll tell crackpot stories."

"But you haven't any good stories to tell," piped up Desmond. "Isn't that why you're going walking the donkey?"

"Yes, but I'll have a few stories after a hundred miles of road. In the meantime, I can tell everyone how I have a young cousin whose mother is going to put his head in a fox-snare if he doesn't soon catch the vixen that goes stealing her prized hens every other night."

Hearing this, Desmond hurled a hot-water bottle across the room that slapped up against the near wall like a dead fish.

"Stop your messin' and be off to sleep!" roared Cella from the adjacent bedroom. "Ye won't be so quick and lively to get up in the morning!"

On the Saturday before my departure, I brought my belongings to Jimmy Mac's to pack inside the mudbox. The cart had been beautifully painted by Bridie, and a neighbor, John Feeley, with the Ace of Hearts painted on the back tailboard: a symbol copied from my father's carts in Longford years ago. Jimmy had hammered a sheet of plywood over the mudbox, making it rainproof, and in this small compartment I packed a canvas bag full of woolen shirts, socks, pants, and long johns.

I also brought along a series of Ordnance Survey Maps, a stargazer's chart, a paraffin lamp, primus stove, billycan, kettle, jackknife, a dozen American Kennedy half-dollars, a blank journal, and a camera. When all was packed and the tailboard clasped, Martin

Maugham arrived with twelve long ash-wattles, a rigging post, and a 15- by 15-foot sheet of canvas: an original Irish traveler's tent. We secured the wattles to the outside of the cart and folded the canvas over the mudbox.

"'Tis a grand affair," said Martin, admiring my fully equipped *Fleetwood*. "A grand affair, surely."

Bridie then called us into the kitchen where she toasted my travels with a gill of whiskey. With the drink taken, Bridie presented me with a new jumper "to keep in the warmth," and this week's edition of the *Roscommon Champion,* open to the bold headline on the front page: JOURNEY THROUGH IRELAND—WITH AN ASS! I had met with the reporter, Donal Keenan, but didn't know the story would make such a splash.

"He's even mentioned the hour you'll be leaving Rattigan's," said Bridie. "There'll be some crowd tomorrow," she beamed, clapping her hands in joy.

When Missie and I departed from the McDermotts' that Saturday afternoon, Bridie's eyes filled with tears as Jimmy shouted out last-minute tips and instructions. Missie twice cast a longing glance, looked back at her adopted stable, before we turned down Catherain for Uncle Vincent's, where we'd briefly stop before setting out for Grannie Kelly's.

At Vincent's, Cella was out the door, carrying two huge currant cakes, ten wire hangers, and two large pillows.

"Thanks for the cakes, Cella," I said, unclasping the tailboard to pack them along with my basic provisions of yogurt and muesli, "but I don't need that other gear."

"Ye'll need to be hanging your clothes to dry," she argued, "and a pillow for the back of your head."

"I'm going to use the hedges to dry my clothes like any respectable traveler. As for a pillow, I'll use Missie's bag of oats that Jimmy Mac gave me."

"Ye're a right tinker, Kevin O'Hara. Go on, be off with ye, for you're better suited for the road than the hearth."

On Sunday morning, the twenty-ninth of April, the day of commencement, I walked home from Mass with Grannie Kelly. There wasn't a word between us up this winding road—both too much and nothing more to say—so I broke our silence by asking about the weather.

"There's a change on"—Grannie looked glumly toward the brow of Slieve Bawn—"but there's no rain in it, thank God."

After serving me a champion breakfast of egg and rasher, Grannie and Mamie kept quietly busy, though their nostrils quivered in anticipation of the inevitable outburst preceding any departure. The clock struck noon to break our wakehouse silence, and I left the chair by the fire, fetched Missie from the backfield, yoked her to the cart, and brought her to the doorway, where Grannie waited to sprinkle Missie and me with the holy waters of Knock.

Mamie then appeared, whimpering on the upper step, and soon the pair began to blubber freely. We hugged, kissed, and lamented, and, climbing up onto the cart, I put an end to sentiment with a stiff upper lip: "Boy, you'd think I was off to join the French Foreign Legion or something."

With those words, I tipped Missie down Ballincurry toward Rattigan's, leaving my dear grandmother sobbing freely at her door, but now wishing I had said something more—that I loved her and would miss her, a wish for her health and thanks for her stories, which had inspired me onto this road now rumbling under the wheels of my cart.

"Here we go, Miss," I danced the reins in my hands. "We're setting out on a long, long journey for home!"

I had never seen so many people at Rattigan's. Donal Keenan of the *Champion* estimated the crowd at 250 as he introduced me to a television crew from RTE (Radio Television Eireann). Meanwhile, a reporter from the *Sunday World,* a national weekly, hoping for an interview, fought through a wall of children who had surrounded Missie.

"Why are you doing this?" he hollered through the bedlam. "Is it a walkathon for charity, a demonstration for peace, a protest against OPEC?"

But before I could explain my purpose, I was pushed into the pub by a wave of well-wishers.

"A pint for the traveler," shouted Uncle Mickey, calling to one of five women busily attending the bar.

"I might be on TV tomorrow night," I marveled, wedging my way between my two uncles.

"Good show, so," said Jimmy Mac, tipping my glass. " 'Tis good to get all the publicity you can."

"Maybe," I shouted. "But I don't want to get hounded like a celebrity."

"No fear of that. It'll just do nicely to help you along. Believe me, ye'll be going long stretches down the lonely coast with only the odd house spotted miles between. That's the time ye'll be thankful for the publicity."

"The odds are twelve–to–one, against," whispered Noel in my ear.

I handed him a fiver, a gift from Dom Tiernan.

"For or against?" Noel needled.

"Is the betting heavy?" I asked Uncle Mickey.

" 'Tis light. Not many takers; for most think ye'll pack it up in Ballygar."

"They're missing a bet," I said with bravado, smacking my stout-covered lips in blind determination.

"I don't want to hurry you, but you'd best drink up and be on your way," advised Uncle Vincent. "This crowd won't budge until your departure, and Kathleen has to close for Holy Hour, at two o'clock. Now, finish your drink, and may the blessings of the Trinity go with you."

Vincent and Mickey spread the word and the crowd spilled out for our grand sendoff. I made my way toward Missie, through a circle of a hundred admirers, and kissed

Bridie and a dozen other women. I also shook hands with the pensioners, including the Four Masters, an unlikely contingent of cheerleaders.

I hopped onto the cart and was escorted down Beechwood by an entourage of thirty children, as an ovation erupted from the crowd. Of course, Missie was no speed demon, and many a canny eye no doubt studied Missie's gait and assessed my chances. But the children's escort shielded my slow tipping from appraising glances, and the few blackguards hoping to come up with that one memorable line to send me off, had to resign themselves to the maddening fanfare around them.

In time, the last of the children huffed and puffed in exhaustion, leaving a scattered trail of waving good-byes in my wake. When I was a good distance from Rattigan's, I slid off the cart and took Missie by the short rein. "Jimmy Mac will have a bird if he drives by," I said to my mate, glancing back up Beechwood.

"But, oh, what a send-off! We're celebrities now, my friend. So let's get on with it, Missie Mickdermot, because if we fail, we'll be in for 'a hape of shite,' as Noel Kelly would say."

A Gift of Hazel

CHAPTER NINE

I shook as many hands the afternoon of our departure as President Kennedy did at Shannon Airport in the summer of 1963. Families by the carload jumped out to wish me "Godspeed" and "safe home," pressing much-needed money into my hands. Between Rattigan's and the town of Roscommon, a mere five miles, I received twenty-three pounds. At that rate of pounds per mile, I was likely to amass eleven thousand pounds by Christmas Day.

I wasn't long away from yet another generous crowd when a blue squad car with four uniformed guards pulled up before us, making me worry if my windfall of cash was to be confiscated. The young and burly policemen tried to maintain an official air, but in truth they were just out enjoying a Sunday drive without their sergeant.

"Where are you headed?" The driver leaned out his window and eyed me up and down.

"All 'round: I'm doing a circuit of the country," I answered with all humility, cautious not to cross their authority.

"Why are you walking beside your ass, and not up on the cart?" chortled an officer in the backseat.

"I've decided to walk beside her," I meekly replied, "and make friends with my donkey."

A burst of laughter resounded from the squad car.

" 'Make friends with my donkey'?" one of them mimicked me. "The bloody novelty of growing chummy with an ass won't be long in wearing off."

"And you left your grandmother's this morning, is that right?" resumed the driver, trying to keep a straight face.

"Yes, sir."

"Where do you intend on finishing these travels?"

"Back at my grandmother's," I admitted.

"You remind me of an old English board game," joked the troublemaker in the backseat. " 'Willy the Right Wally, and His Walk to Visit Grandma.' "

"And keep your hands off Little Red Riding Hood," snorted another, winking in Missie's direction, as they hooted and roared away.

When Missie and I reached the town, the bells of the Angelus were ringing from Sacred Heart Church, and jackdaws on the neighboring rooftops squawked and squabbled over their nest-building duties. A band of traveling children came skipping across the road from their battered caravans parked in a lay-by on the outskirts of town, and asked why I was traveling without a bride by my side.

"Ye should be twice married, with the age up on ye," said one saucy pots-and-pans girl of fourteen. "Ye can't expect your *asaleen* to tramp the roads all day and then keep ye warm at night."

They circled us and chided gleefully, but were soon called back to their encampment by the elders, who wished me the best of "motoring."

Leaving the Old Jail and the crumbling walls of Roscommon Castle behind, we stopped early for the night in a small vacant field known as Stone Park, a mile out on the Athleague Road. After untackling Missie and leaving her to tumble and graze in this enclosed field, I began to set up my wattle tent: an hour-long exercise that left me wishing I had purchased a more conventional rig in the shops of Galway.

When the wattles and rigging post were finally upright and the large square canvas draped over it—thanks in part to a group of children calling themselves "the Stone Park Gang"—who should show up but Vincent and Cella. They insisted I go back into town for a proper feed instead of "living off that goat food," as Cella maligned my muesli.

We went into the Monument Bar on the Square and enjoyed a capital feed while reliving the day's events. On the drive back to Stone Park, Cella supplied me with another currant cake and once again pressed the case for a pillow. Then, after a mixture of tears and well-wishing, the two drove off into the black night, leaving me standing beside a sniffling donkey at the mouth of my portable hovel.

In the strange surroundings of this tinker's den, I managed to light the paraffin lamp without setting the tent ablaze. That done, I crawled into my sleeping bag and looked up at the shadowy, ribbed ceiling, feeling like Jonah in the belly of a whale. Suddenly a fretful noise came from just outside the tent. I imagined anything and everything, but narrowed it down to a rabid rat burrowing its wet snout through the soil to sink its fangs into my flesh. Fortunately, I took hold of my wild flailing fears and grasped that this stir of nature was simply Missie cropping at the grass.

Thankful for the natural world's return to order, I quenched the lamp and succumbed to the day's excitements. I was falling into a deep slumber when, Holy Bejaysus, I was abruptly aroused by the blinding glare of a flashlamp.

"Ye're a right itinerant," I heard a crawling figure say, "a tinker's son, surely." The intruder lifted my head by the hair, adding, "I've wagered a tidy parcel on you and Missie, so God bless, and begone." My head was then unceremoniously dropped onto my bag of oats.

"Uncle Mickey, is that you?" I shouted through the blackness. "Uncle Mickey?"

The quiet, lonely night fell about me again.

I was up at five next morning, hoping to be on the road by five-thirty. My only thought was to cover distance, ten to fifteen miles if able, and escape this ground zero of popularity. I much appreciated the Rattigan send-off, but now I wanted to be on the road alone, lost in the soft canter of Missie's ringing shoes. So, on the thirtieth day of April, just turned thirty myself, I packed and readied the cart and stepped out onto the sleepy Athleague Road. Soon I fell into Missie's cadence, picking up the rhythm of the first of my many marching songs, Bob Dylan's "Girl from the North Country," a longtime favorite of mine.

By early afternoon we were passing through the wide avenues of Ballygar, County Galway, where a publican greeted me from his door.

"Welcome to Galway," he saluted, introducing himself as Bryan Devine. "Tie your lady friend against the signpost," he insisted, "and step inside for a proper County Galway welcome."

Inside the old family pub, Bryan stood proudly behind a settling pint of black stout, as old mirrors hanging off every wall advertised beverages of long ago. After my pint, Bryan wasted no time in pulling a second. I objected but he insisted, reciting the old publican's adage, " 'Show me a bird who can fly with just the one wing.' "

Out again into the broken Irish weather with my head reeling in "black magic," and Bryan promising a bonfire upon our return to Ballygar in December. I walked Missie down the main avenue in a stupor of goodwill, as scores of shopkeepers waved from their entries, making me feel like a Lord Mayor in the St. Patrick's Day parade.

Brief showers began to spatter, but with Missie showing signs of exuberance, we hastened out the Ballygar Road with all the world reasonable. Abruptly, however, Missie's furry ears began to rotate like radar. She began to buck and bite, rearing up on her heels and trying to make a U-turn. I gave her a sharp whack of my ash plant but she countered with a sweeping swoop of her mammoth head which nearly caught my jaw. If it had landed flush I would have been as bollixed as a fish in oil.

Taking a deep breath after this near blow, I retaliated with a blinding crack to her backside, only to whirl and face an horrendous outcry from two black jacks stalking her from behind.

"So that's it," I deduced, watching the pair strut along with blatant intention. Missie seemed intrigued, to my surprise and regret, with her tail up and out like a question mark, as bold as Mother Nature would allow.

I forced her onward but the jacks continued their feverish campaign, closing in on Missie. In response she seemed possessed, writhing her jaw and soaping at the mouth.

Could these be the cardinal signs of Missie being "in-season"? Why hadn't Jimmy advised me of this hormonal storm on the horizon? Maybe I was the butt of a joke being celebrated this minute at Rattigan's, with Willie Cassidy holding up the Harp girlie calendar with April 30 vividly circled in red, and Hugh Mannion spouting off from his stool, "Well, boys, let's drink to the Yank's mare who, as we speak, is sparking up her heels for a dance with old Neddie!" My blood heated with suspicion as Missie's heated with lust.

Suddenly Missie froze solid, mesmerized in the middle of the road. I chanced to drop the reins and hurl stones at these persistent jacks, but they were clever enough to retreat to the point of my arm's limitations. Missie then snapped from her stupor and began to bray convulsively, rallying her jacko admirers to a demented pitch and bringing on a third trouper, a little gray fellow who couldn't mount a head of cabbage. We continued up the road with the threesome edging closer to Missie's backside. I was thankful the cart would serve as a chastity belt, but Missie's mouth was lathered as if she had mistaken a bar of Ivory soap for a throat lozenge.

Missie then mounted her final bid for romance, heaving against the reins and setting off a tug-of-war. I strained like a deep-sea fisherman with a blue marlin on the line, and would have lost her to the depths of debauchery if not for a farmer arriving on the scene who, after taking glee in my predicament, scattered the three musketeers down the road with his tractor.

Missie and I lumbered on sullenly, following our first fight. I felt like a possessive father who wouldn't allow his stubborn daughter to go out with Stud Stetson, but I couldn't unhitch her from the cart and just say, "Okay, Missie, but I want you back at our campsite by nightfall." No way. A cut-jack for a playmate, yes, but these bugling boyos were a menace to our travels.

We stopped for a rest at Ballinamore Bridge where, after many an urging, Missie finally nuzzled a few oats from my rope-chafed hands. For the rest of the day, we marched on in an uneasy truce.

Having covered thirteen miles on our first full day, we turned in at Caltra where I made bold to ask Tom Nolan, caretaker of the Castle ffrench estate, if we could camp out on the demesne for the night.

"No bother a'tall," the mustached gent replied, unharnessing Missie and leading her to a small field behind his laborer's cottage. "Come in, now, for a cup of tea."

Within Tom's dark dwelling there was nobody but cats of various color: ginger, rum, caramel, licorice.

"I haven't the heart to give them a bath, if you know what I mean," laughed Tom, as I scanned dozens of these slithering felines, from mantel to doorway, from chair to motorbike. Others purred at Tom's feet, slinking in and out of his trouser bottoms, and electric-haired weanlings staggered into the brief spark of firelight.

"Do you have names for all these cats?" I asked, cautiously removing a crescent-clawed kitten from the depths of my lap.

"Aye, I do," answered Tom, fingering the tips of his black mustache. "Do ya see the marmalade girleen beyont the stool?"

"I do."

"Well, her name is Enough. And do you see that toffee-colored tom with the torn ear?"

"I do."

"Well, his name is More-Than-Enough!"

After tea and brown loaf, I was taken to the Norman tower where I met Mrs. ffrench, a relation of Pope Pius XI, who offered me a bowl of soup in her lofty kitchen. Marveling at where my travels had already taken me, I looked out the castlelike window onto the ancient trees of a rookery. Pondering chance and design, I asked this pleasant old noblewoman if she had relations in Stockbridge, Massachusetts.

"I most certainly do," she said, startled to hear this visiting bohemian with kettles and buckets festooned to his cart, betray knowledge of her family in Stockbridge. "Have you met my son, John?"

"Oh, yes. I used to deliver milk from High Lawn Farm to his home, the Dolphin House," I burbled with excitement. "Quite an artistic family; they've gained a nation-wide reputation for their silk-screened calendars."

"So I believe they have," she said, removing my empty bowl and placing a generous slice of sponge cake in its stead. "Now, eat up, and you're welcome to stay as long as you like."

Next morning, the first of May, as the villagers along this western seaboard hung sprigs of hawthorn called "Mayboughs" on their doors to keep out trooping faeries, I began to collect morning dew by soaking a handkerchief and wringing it into a small bottle.

"There's great power in dew gathered on Mary's Morning," my grandmother had instructed me, passing along the small collection kit before my departure. "Sprinkle it on yourself and your donkey, to protect you from the wrongdoers of the road."

There is little enchantment to be had, collecting the dew of May Day in the shivering cold of dawn, especially for one whose faith is shallow at the most fervent of times. After thirty minutes of cockeyed endeavor my bottle contained less than a dram, and my mind was wandering back to my eight May Days in grammar school. There, the good nuns at St. Charles would impose no lessons that day, but would have us write letters to Mary in our finest penmanship. Then we would march out to the schoolyard, all uniformed in blue and white, and sing "Ave Maria" around a bonfire in a barrel, as our intentions lifted smokily to the heavens.

Straightening my back and blowing warmth into my hands, I wondered what those very nuns were now saying from their heavenly lofts. *Can you believe it!* they might exclaim. *Certainly one needs to be dead to see the true wonders of the world.*

"Is it a kettle of water you're after?" shouted Tom Nolan, scaring the life out of me.

"No," I came to and called back. "It's holy water," I raised the bottle with its few precious drops.

Tom did not blink at the absurdity, but had a suggestion of his own:

"Ye'll need a stick of hazel along with that holy water. Faith in the Deity is one matter, but faeries and the Otherworld are quite another. 'Twas Maeve herself, Queen of all Connacht, who said she could walk the world armed with only a switch of hazel. And for all the faery haunts you're likely to stumble upon, ye'd be a foolish man to ever let the hazel out of your grasp. Follow me to Hussion's Grove on the summit of Tycooley-O'Kelly," he beckoned with a rallying cry, "and there I'll cut ye a stick of hazel!"

At first I thought Tom might be having me on, but as we climbed the hillside path, with a last view of Slieve Bawn to the east, I realized he truly believed in the power of hazel.

"There are skeptics who believe the charms of the hazel are just a *pishogue,* a Celtic superstition," said Tom, disappearing into a white-flowering thicket with a sharp knife. "But my father, God be good to him, was a man of honor, and many a night he'd come home with his knees poking out of torn trousers and telling my mother, God be good to her, how the confounded wee folk had tied up his bootlaces, and it was only his stick of hazel that saved him from the Otherworld."

Tom soon emerged with a straight brown hazel stick of custom-made height, the most perfect traveling companion! Then he took his jackknife and carved a few notches like ancient ogham into the handle, rounded off the top and flattened out the bottom.

"There," he said proudly, handing me the bewitching beauty. "Toss away your old ash plant, for this protection will allow you to sleep peacefully in rath, cairn, or stone circle."

Old Coach Road to Galway

CHAPTER TEN

Thanking Tom and waving my new stick high in farewell to the tower of Mrs. ffrench, I was presently walking Missie through Kilasolan Bog—a five-mile stretch of road running across a lonesome moor of bracken and yellowing furze—to Mount Bellew Bridge. A cold, unrelenting wind pummeled us with hailstones, and an old man who pedaled by seemed to be climbing uphill into the gusty weather. Skylarks hovered effortfully against the wind, and starlings hurtled across this barren landscape as if peppered out of a shotgun.

So, these are the bogs, I thought, recalling that these remains of long-ago forests covered nearly a sixth of the country. "We better get used to these barren miles," I said to Missie, whose poor defenseless ears were being pelted by hail the size of rosary beads. "Maybe I should buy some golf-club covers for your tall lugs."

The hail turned to snow as we took the Menlough Road, but we carried on until Jim Ruane, a blacksmith standing by his gate, invited us in for the night. We had covered only eight miles for the day, but I was hungry and longed to be in from the cold. I accepted his kindness, while his three children, Patrick, Mary, and Liam, greeted me with a hero's welcome at the door.

In the warmth of their kitchen, Mrs. Ruane sat me before a champion feed as her children entertained me with riddles and games. *Where would I have ended up tonight if not for Mr. Ruane?* I asked myself later, unrolling my sleeping bag before the warm kitchen range as heavy winds whipped across this wild black night. *Can I expect to be so fortunate tomorrow night?*

Worrisome questions those, but I took my ignorance of any answer for bliss, and consoled myself as I dozed off: "God provides."

The next day came bright and early, and after my blacksmith host checked Missie's shoes for loose nails, he accompanied us down the Menlough Road and instructed me to "stay left and keep left" until I came to the small village of Monivea. Once there, I was to take another left at "the top of the Green," which would put me on the Old Coach Road to Galway: a medieval highway, once the main thoroughfare between Dublin and the City of the Tribes.

"A lovely morning, thanks be to God," greeted a bright-aproned woman, out collecting wildflowers, and then another, whitewashing the winter from her walls with buckets of lime. Flocks of jump-happy lambs bleated their contentment over drystone walls, and gray goslings peeked beneath the hissing, outstretched necks of goose and gander. A drift of calves lay dreamily in the warmth of a meadow, and a blackbird perched high on a song-post of ivy serenaded his brown-feathered hen.

We arrived in Monivea, "Meadow of the Honey," a trim seventeenth-century village once known throughout Europe for its clover and heather honey. I untackled Missie and tethered her securely in an old, abandoned Protestant churchyard, and soon met up with Peig Moyles, caretaker of Monivea castle, having been referred by my earlier hostess, Mrs. ffrench.

"Monivea is best known for the curse Saint Patrick called down upon it," Peig related as she led me down a wooded pathway known as "the Green Avenue" on the estate grounds. "It is said that Patrick went on a prayer-fast in this very wood, but after three days he returned to the hamlet to find his goat milked dry. So famished and vexed was Patrick that he reviled the hamlet, saying it would never grow from that day to eternity."

"That doesn't seem very saintly," I said to the venerable historian.

"Oh, don't I know! I've lived all my life in Monivea," continued Peig, "and as sure as a house is built on the left side of the Green, there isn't much time in passing that one doesn't topple over on the right."

That evening, after settling at the Moyleses' household, I walked through the expansive Green to Kelly's Pub where I began to make entries in my daily log. Mrs. Kelly was down to throw a few sods on the fire and, looking up from her task, said, "Strange, now, the way you're writing, being a *ciotóg* . . . left-handed and all. You remind me of the traveling poet named Husband, a Welshman, who would use this room when we were children. He was a *ciotóg* as well, and would sit at the head of that table like yourself with his hand curled above the page in a most awkward fashion. He kept his poetry in a large black book tied with bits of ribbon, but never allowed any of us to read it."

"You wouldn't want to read mine, that's for sure," I closed my navy-blue journal.

"Mr. Husband came once a year, as regular as the seasons, and I heard he died some years back in a County Home in Mayo. He had a long white beard, I recall, and always dressed in black. A right-looking gentleman of the roads."

"I hope I'm as right-looking," I said, running my hand across the oak table where the Welshman had written his verse.

"You're right as rain," she said, leaving me to my scribbling.

Waking to a fine Thursday morning, Missie and I bid farewell to Moyles, and stopped at McGowen's Granary at the top of the Green, where I checked with a farmer passing on his bicycle if this turn would put us on the Old Coach Road to Galway.

"It will and it won't." He looked me up and down. "The Old Road has broken down over the years but some of it still lies in the fields beyont. You can see ruins of the old stables where they changed coach horses. Yet, I suppose, you can consider this to be the Old Road, what's left of it. But, tell me, why are you walking beside your ass and not up on the dash tipping her along?"

"I'm on a charity walk," I fibbed, having prepared myself for this frequent query.

"A walkathon, is it? But still, there's nobody to spy on you in these parts."

"It wouldn't be fair to my sponsors," I said with a shrug.

"I suppose not," he conceded, looking at me admiringly. "You know," he added, petting Missie between the lugs, "the best thing God ever put on this earth was an honest man. God bless, and it's a pleasure to have met you."

I was abashed. So much for clean linen on the line! Why the cock and bull? What was I ashamed of? *Next time some canny oldster asks me why I'm walking the ass, I'm going to look him right in the eye and say, "Because I want to view old Ireland from donkey level." That's it!* "Tell the truth and shame the devil," as my mother would say.

With the sun winking through pine and sycamore and a soft breeze freshening the world, my spirits soared along this King's Highway. This is what I had envisioned all along, to be on the open road, joining the ranks of drover and poet, piper and tramp— a long, colorful train of Irish pilgrim folk.

The hedges were bursting in wildflower and song: primrose, cowslip, and bluebells in the shade. Speckle-bodiced thrushes, known to fall from their boughs in exhaustion, were singing madly for their mates, as wrens and redbreasts flecked the green hedges with the color of tweed.

No, nothing could dampen my spirits on this bygone highway but my "Abyssinian ass," Missie, who began to snip at the fat of my leg and pull for the inside of the road.

"What's on her?" asked an elderly patron outside the Oasis Pub in Cartymore.

"She's been biting me since we passed the ruins of Belleville Castle." I stated the predicament with shrugged shoulders.

He left his post by the doorway and lifted Missie's legs to check her shoes, dropped his fingers on her back to test her temperament, and pulled open her mouth for God-knows-what.

"Were you the lad written up in the *Roscommon Champion?*"

"I am, yes."

" 'Tis a quare enterprise. Do you not be well at times?"

Before I could formulate a reply, four or five others had made their way out from the pub. Old-timers, mostly. And the few who remained inside were craning their necks out the window.

"Just my luck," I muttered quietly, " 'Rattigan's Revisited.' "

"Had she a fat winter?" asked one.

"Please, sir?"

"Was she wintered in?"

"Yes, sir."

"Tip her along a ways and we'll see if she's gone stray in the gait," suggested another. I led Missie across the parking lot and back again as far as the petrol pumps.

"Musha, she's pulling a mite to the right, all right," said the little farmer who stopped me to begin with. "Best be off with the collar."

The cart was lifted off Missie's back, and the hames and collar removed. And there, beneath a knot of sweaty hair, was an abrasion the size of a half-dollar circled to her chest.

They whistled: "A scalded breast!"

"A what?" I gasped.

"A scalded breast. A stripped shoulder."

"Is it serious?"

"If you had walked on another mile, your journey would be through," said a kindly-looking man named John Burke. "You're very lucky she didn't break the inner skin. Best be getting gall-cure from the chemist in Athenry."

"Gall-cure, not on your life!" snapped the little farmer. "Good old springwater and alum, my father swore by."

"Mushroom paste!" hollered another. "Or, better still, surgical spirits!"

"Egg-whites and pickles! Or boiled oak bark," pronounced a fourth commentator.

"Salt and water, and a good roll in the dust!" crowed a fifth, as those from the windows began to chime in with home remedies, poultices and herbal concoctions not heard of since the passing of the Firbolgs.

I stood numbed among them, looking down at poor Missie's wound. Jimmy Mac had warned me time and again to keep a close eye on her collar. I couldn't believe it. What a jackass! My nursing license should be revoked for such blatant negligence. How soon my pride is humbled. . . .

"Look at your man," said one of the patrons. "He's gone as pale as Rafferty's ghost."

"Not to worry," John Burke draped a reassuring arm over me. "Your donkey will be as sound as a bell in a few days, and can't I keep her for the length of that time in my barn. And wouldn't the publican, Michael Lafferty and his wife Eileen, put you up if you'd be willing to help out with the odd bar duties?"

So, if you had happened to walk inside the Oasis in Cartymore during those three evenings in early May 1979, you would have found the Donkeyman pulling pints for the locals, who were treating me like a celebrity even though we had covered only forty-two miles of road. My popularity soared to greater heights on Friday evening when that week's edition of the *Roscommon Champion* came in with another front-page headline: KEVIN AND MISSIE SET OFF ON TOUR.

The house grew quiet as Paddy Treacy, who still tipped his donkey and cart to the pub and creamery, read aloud Donal Keenan's new installment of our travels, ending with the heartening but dated statement that all was "shipshape" as of the writing.

There was great celebration when the story concluded, with such comments as "a mighty man," "a topping fellow," and an "amazing boyo" resounding throughout the pub.

" 'Tis a powerful journey, altogether," said Michael Lafferty behind the bar. "Christy, would you set out to walk an ass around Ireland?"

"That I wouldn't. Nor to King John's Castle in Athenry, for that matter."

"Martin, what would you say?"

"I say it takes no vocation to be an idiot, and that's all there is to say."

I grinned from ear to ear and served the patrons another round.

For those three nights, I slept in a warm bed, out of harm's way and the unsettled weather, visiting my long-eared darling twice daily, her abrasion steadily healing with applications of gall-cure.

On a wet Sunday afternoon, one week since setting out, Missie and I bade farewell to the fine people of Cartymore and set out through a steady sheet of rain, never lifting our heads till we came to a Norman tower which sat gray and forlorn above the splashing waves of Galway Bay. Catching sight of the ocean's fury and hearing its tumultuous banging along the coast, I knew our march to the sea was now complete and that this, the churning watery world of the North Atlantic, would be our traveling companion for the next sixteen hundred miles.

We crept that night, soaked and shivering, into a high barn outside Oranmore, south of Galway City. It wasn't my intention to be a stowaway, but no one was home and the darkening road offered little hope of shelter. I changed every stitch of clothing and shared fruit and sandwiches with Missie, kindly packed by Eileen Lafferty.

The farmyard where I put Missie was strewn with cow skulls, and I wondered if she could sleep in such ghoulish surroundings. For myself, I shifted a few bales of hay to level a spot for my sleeping bag, and tried to take comfort in one of Jimmy Mac's many axioms: "Rats in the straw, mice in the hay."

Before retiring, I pulled out my maps and journal and calculated that we had traveled eleven miles for the day; not bad, but not enough to make up for lost time. My thoughts were interrupted by Missie's hoarse bawl, bellowing through this rainy night like a foghorn.

"Quiet, Missie," I called from my makeshift bunk. "If you keep up that racket you'll have some farmer running us off with a pitchfork!"

But again, there was no letting up once she began, and squinting through the dirty night I spotted my poor beast shaking terribly in this butcher's yard. I crawled deep into my bag, not wanting to hear her frenzied bawl. It reminded me of her stablemates being driven away in Jimmy Mac's lorry to the meat factory. I called out again but my shouts were no use, a hapless donkeyman without a clue how to comfort his mate. I bit my lip and retreated deeper, as she continued to bray horribly, eastward for home.

The Hollow Bright Fog

CHAPTER ELEVEN

Our passage along the southern rim of Galway Bay turned into a prolonged photo opportunity for package-tour pilgrims. Busloads of American tourists, speeding along in silver CruiseLiners as though being rushed to distant battlefields, poured out like paratroopers to shoot snap after snap of "the tinker and his donkey."

Never in my puff could I have imagined such celebrity. Dozens per bus, sometimes three buses within the hour, armed with Kodaks, Canons, and Polaroids, surrounded us, asking Missie's name, and were we off to market to buy a litter of pigs? But I couldn't answer. After all, I didn't want them to know I was one of their own and spoil all those photographs, so I said nothing and played shy by hitting my hazel stick against the inside of my sneaker.

"My travel agent in Chicago told me tinkers were a thing of the past," braved one woman, freely petting Missie's white snout. "But here we are, just outside Conniecamera and heading for the Cliffs of Mohair, and what do we run into, but a tinker and his donkey."

The group pressed their lengthy questionnaire while I persevered with a vacuous smile. One boastful gent, obviously the self-designated leader, suggested I was either "a Gaelic speaker or deaf and dumb." He was dressed so garishly that Missie reared back upon his approach as if he were a rainbow-running oil slick on the road. He wore caramel-colored slacks, a green Boston Celtics warm-up jacket with white shamrocks emblazoned on the sleeves, topped off by a plaid deerstalker that still had the price tag dangling.

"Can you imagine your son on a Friday night asking for the keys to your donkey and cart?" He played to the crowd, counting on my supposed deafness and dumbness. "'Gee, Dad, I'm taking Denise to the drive-in movies tonight. How about the donkey? Huh, Dad?'"

"Or the rush hour in Boston?" chortled another. "'Attention: This is the WSBK helicopter reporting a jam-up at the mouth of the Callahan Tunnel. It appears some jackass is refusing to move up the ramp.'"

"Did any of you ever hear the story about the tinker sitting on the wall?" Mr. Oil Slick dared, standing alongside me to better illustrate the tale.

"No, Jack," a few shouted, cranked up on Irish coffee.

"Well," he began, throwing a heavy arm over me, "there's this American gentleman, much like yours truly, and when he's touring the Lakes of Killarney he spots this young dirty-faced tinker sitting up on a wall . . . I mean, just sitting there. Well, the American goes off, golfing, stops into a pub for a cold beer—if he's lucky enough to find one—comes back to the hotel late that night and sees this same stinker of a tinker still sitting on the wall. 'Hey, tinker, what the hell are you still doing up on that wall?' shouts the American. 'What do you tink I'm doing, mister?' shouts the tinker. 'I'm tinking!'"

A great guffaw rose from the crowd as I pirouetted from this clown's grasp. I couldn't stand up for the dignity of true knights of the road, but I wouldn't be a prop for this comedian. Better a mute tinker than a bloviating Yank.

Luckily, having to keep to a timetable Phileas Fogg would have found formidable, the bus drivers would soon be out to gather their charges for a three-hour journey to a sham medieval banquet, by way of a five-minute "peer and piddle" at the Cliffs of Moher.

Even when the buses departed—French, Dutch, and German, as well as American—there was still no respite. Passing Dungaire Castle and into the seaside village of Kinvara, I was encircled by a convent of schoolgirls who ardently informed me that Missie and I had been featured on the news program *CountryWide* the evening before, with the film clip from Rattigan's. The young students, ranging from ten to sixteen, went about giggling and blushing as if I were Paul McCartney about to sing "Give Ireland Back to the Irish."

This idolization wasn't too bad, mind you, but I was afraid it was simply a prelude to becoming a full-blown public spectacle. Worse still, I was now pigeonholed from both sides: the foreigners who took me for a tinker and the Irish who knew me as a foreigner.

"Show me a man who has never made a mistake, and I'll show you a man who has made nothing," said Mary Ann St. George to my quandary, standing me a pint in her pub on the Square. Our arrival into Kinvara was to have been a landmark occasion, as it was here that Padraic O Conaire, the well-loved Irish author, had purchased his *asal beag dubh* in 1924 and traveled the breadth of the country to Dublin. Kenny's Book Shop in Galway had found me the English translation of his book, *Field and Fair,* on Headmaster D'Alton's recommendation.

But now, with the uneasy realization that the tube had beamed my face into every sitting room from Bastardstown, County Wexford, to the western reaches of the Mullet,

I somberly sipped my pint and ceremonially read the well-worn copy of the poet's delightful story, while Missie stood quietly out front amid a swarm of adoring school-girls, not taking her celebrity amiss.

The following morning, traveling on the main coastal road from Kinvara to Bally-vaughan, every third car that passed would pull up with its passengers asking me a similar battery of questions: "Are you the lad we saw on the telly with the donkey?" "Why aren't you sitting up on the cart?" "Are you collecting for a charity?" "Do you always manage to find shelter for the night?" "Are you going by way of the Dingle Peninsula?" "How will your donkey ever climb Conor Pass?"

Most interviews were well-intentioned, but it took the pip out of me to prepare for my next interchange fifty yards up the road. Time and again. Car after car. I covered no ground, found no peace, and Missie was becoming lazier than inherently inclined. To compound matters, Missie had scratched her opposite shoulder against a concrete wall the night before. Mr. Kavanagh, with whom we had stayed, believed she was infected with ticks, and suggested a treatment of Alugent, Ticksol, or louse powder, the sooner the better.

Fearing my journey was now way too exposed, I fled my fans by ditching down a grassy lane removed from the rest of the world called the "Green Road," just outside Ballyvaughan in northwest Clare. Removing the cart and tackle, I again faced Missie's aggravated condition. Her scalded breast, though scabbed and hardened, became more grotesque when aligned with the fresh wound on her right shoulder. I coated both sores with the jar of gall-cure, but looked on helplessly as she tossed back her head to gnaw at her flanks, biting away at tufts of tick-infested hair.

With the sky looking dead and thundery, I tethered Missie to a three-foot iron spike, bequeathed to me that morning by two itinerants who took an encouraging interest in my journey. While I hurriedly set up my wattle tent, two children came running down the lane, out of breath, saying their father had seen us pass and wished me back for tea. Then, apologetically, the young girl said I had picked a bad spot to pitch my tent since an unlicensed butcher operated nearby, which meant the place was running with rats.

"Just my luck," I muttered, as the mere mention of the dreaded vermin opened the skies above, that forced us to retreat into the belly of my green-skinned whale. Now I had no choice but to settle here for the night, despite less-than-four-star accommodations. The children, however, were delighted. I asked Noreen and Michael Nilan if they knew of any veterinarian in the area, since my donkey was suffering.

"Not really," replied Noreen, "but once the rain eases and you have the tea, I'll take you to see Dr. O'Dea. He's not a veterinarian, but he does keep horses."

That evening, after a meal of beans and toast with Mr. Nilan, a recent widower feeling the loss of a young spouse, Noreen walked me to the sycamore-lined entrance of Dr. John O'Dea, whose sign announced EVENING SURGERY HOURS.

When I pressed the doorbell, Dr. O'Dea, a young man but a much-respected general practitioner in the county, looked startled to see a tramp of a Yank standing beside a flea-bitten donkey. After I had told him of our plight, he examined Missie's coat and promptly confirmed the diagnosis of ticks, exacerbated by wet weather.

Having no patients at the moment, the doctor led Missie to his adjoining stables, where he prepared a solution of Tick-sol in a bucket of water. As I took up my customary position gripping Missie tightly by the ears, the good doctor scrubbed the length of her back, limbs, and underbelly for a good twenty minutes, assisted by his Connecticut-born wife, Kaethe.

Dr. John handed me another bottle of Tick-sol with instructions to repeat the treatment in eight to ten days, preferably on a sunny morning. Then he turned his attention to Missie's stripped shoulder.

"It's healing nicely," he observed, "and this new wound is simply an unsightly graze. But, quite frankly, the combination of wounds and ticks would justify the guards or any officer of the SPCA in hauling you off the road.

"I'm not telling you to end your journey," he conceded, as he walked us to the gate while refusing payment for his services, "but you best hope for fine weather or her condition will worsen."

I slumped back to my boreen of rats: wet, worn, and lonesome to no end. It poured all night, the incessant rain spilling over the canvas, a cold shower washing away the precious healing solution in Missie's coat as well.

In the morning there was no letup. A teeming deluge. Poking my head from the tent, I spotted Missie in the scant shelter of a flowering blackthorn. She looked pitiful. A hooded crow landed on her back and smartly pulled a hank of hair from her coat before flying off. It flew back momentarily for another clump, yet Missie didn't defend herself. Why was she so passive? Is it within the statutes of Nature for a thieving crow to pull the stuffing from a donkey's coat to line its own nest?

Watching the crow alight a third time, I conjured images of vultures in the Arizona desert circling in an ever-descending vortex on a hapless burro. *Has all the fight left her? Has she suffered quite enough? Will her heart be next to go?*

From the very conception of these donkey travels I had forswore negative thoughts, determined to remain impervious to the doubts and dangers of the road. This was to be a fearless journey of growth, I had promised myself from the outset. The hallmark of my thirtieth year. My personal Acid Test. A journey that would make me forever proud. But now things were collapsing around me. The shadow of uncertainty began to cloud my sunny outlook.

There were the wounds, the ticks, the rain, the rats, the long lonely road, the tourists—and, soon, the authorities on my tail. How could Missie's condition go undetected among the throngs of daily well-wishers? How might the newspaper headlines change any day now? Perhaps the old men at Rattigan's were right: " 'Tis too much for any one donkey to travel."

I had little choice but to end this honorably, while I still had the chance. In time, Grannie Kelly would get over the endless prattle of parish talk. She had gotten over more difficult things in her long life. Jimmy Mac and Uncle Mickey would certainly be disappointed, but what could I have done differently, other than keep a closer eye on Missie's collar? Maybe this whole donkey affair was just a whim, anyhow; a springtide of enthusiasm now unraveling.

Rather than wallowing in the muck of indecision, I put on my leaky raincoat, left Missie in her misery, and walked through a tableland of fissured limestone. I was now properly in the Burren, "the Rocky Place," covering four hundred square miles of northwest Clare. It was here that one of Oliver Cromwell's officers had complained to his commander, Lord Protector of England and Scourge of Ireland, of not having a tree to hang a man, enough water to drown him, or enough soil to bury him. I walked three miles to Aillwee Cave, but even this fantastical underground, with its bear beds, lit grottoes, and thousand-foot passage, only dampened my mood further.

Leaving the bear fossils to the comfort of everlasting peace, and stalactites to the slow measurement of time, I was driven by a kind guide to Poulnabrone Portal Dolmen, a many-tonned capstone resting on two wedge stones where, as legend has it, the run-away lovers Diarmuid and Grainne had sheltered from the clutches of King Fionn. In blissful eagerness at the Galway Library, I had flagged my ordnance map in hopes of sleeping beneath this tombstone from four millennia ago. This sodden afternoon, however, Poulnabrone had no more magic than a neolithic exercise in weightlifting—a few menhirs cleverly balanced, but lacking all romance.

The seven-mile walk back was chill and wet, the few cars hurtling by the disconsolate pedestrian without care or notice. I was nothing without the donkey. A shagging tourist in a bleeding downpour.

When I returned to my den of rats, I found that my provisions, left out carelessly despite fair warning, had been ransacked and chewed. I sat down drained and dull-headed. A pall of depression hung above the place. I didn't even have the heart to look out at Missie, who was urgently summoning me with a dry, heaving cry. Every direction I turned told me to pack it in. The black sky. My rat-sacked rations. Missie's blood-stained collar in the corner of my impractical tent.

I threw myself onto my sleeping bag and wept like a child. It was over. The grandiose traveler succumbs to circumstances after ten days and eighty-two miles of road. I had no choice but to hire out a horsebox and carry Missie back to Roscommon.

But then, in the dim light of the tent, I spotted a small note at the head of my sleeping bag. It read:

Kevin,
   Would you like to come for dinner? We usually eat about 6:30 or so . . . and would you like a steamy bath? (Not insinuating that you need one . . .) I just know that's what I'd appreciate most in your predicament—as you please—
   Perhaps we'll see you then.
   Kaethe, your neighbor, O'Dea

I don't know how long I read over that small note card, but in my rain-soaked solitude I began to cling to boyhood dreams. I called at the house that evening and enjoyed
a hot bath before I sat down to a steaming meal of beef, cauliflower, buttered potatoes,
and a dessert of deep-dish fruit pie and cream. Next we had hot punch and listened to
Irish music as the O'Dea's two children, Feargal and Sinéad, bounced on my knees, and
John and Kaethe told me wondrous stories about the Burren countryside.

I left their beautiful estate on Black Head Bay at midnight, into a blowing gale, but with
an apple for Missie and a refurbished collar that Kaethe had lined with socks and hand-
kerchiefs. Back at my site, I called through the blackthorn to my snuffling donkey.

"Maybe we can march on for another day," I commiserated, feeding her the apple. "I
mean, what other choice have we? You'd probably end up in a tin of Chow-Chow and
I'd be the butt of endless 'Missie' jokes for the next four generations. You're healing
nicely enough, and Dr. John gave me a second bottle of Tick-sol, and now your collar
will ride high, as noble as the ruff on an Elizabethan lady.

"C'mon, Miss," I said, throwing a rallying arm around her, "let's play hide-and-seek
from the SPCA and make a mad dash down the coast."

Inside my tent, I blocked the entrance against visiting rodents before crawling into my
sleeping bag. I thought back to my hootch in Vietnam, where the Dude, a little guy from
the Southwest, had claimed to have seen a rat so large he could sling a saddle over it and
gallop away for home. These Irish rodents seemed less fearful than those Asiatic horrors
which I had survived, so, after tossing and turning, I finally nodded off to sleep.

And as I slept, the fog came.

I may never understand the meteorological phenomenon I witnessed on the Burren
in County Clare, that particular combination of mist and sun, but when I poked my
head outside the tent that next morning, I found the world cocooned in a veil of magic
and mystery. I hurriedly tackled Missie who, in turn, high-stepped gingerly through the
haze until I stopped to ask a farmer by the Pinnacle Well, south of Ballyvaughan, about
this curiosity of the elements. He readily gave me its Irish name, *ceo soilear iseal*, but,
struggling with its English translation, sat back down, and after a long silence blurted,
"A hollow bright fog."

It was just that. A shining mist-laden cloak that shielded us from the rest of the
world. For the next two days, from Ballyvaughan on Friday morning to the Cliffs of
Moher on Saturday evening, this hollow bright fog immersed us in translucent solitude
as we slowly traversed mile after mile of deserted coastline. Not one car passed. Not
one bus. The coast road was bottled in and everybody knew it.

Out on a disappearing sea-rock stood a gray heron, and a hidden cuckoo called from
the hazel thickets. Above us, landward, we could make out the round, soft-shouldered
hills of Cappanawalla, Gleninagh, and Slieve Elva herself, where a herd of wild goats
went clambering up the slippery crags, while the North Atlantic shivered in its shoals
below.

Again the cuckoo called, that tireless advocate of surrogate motherhood, moving invisibly in the shrubs. We were nestled in anonymous, cobwebbed comfort, left alone in the weirdest of Irish landscapes. Above, there was a distant orb of bleached light—a flax-white sun—and all around were high gray boulders strewn carelessly across this limestone table.

"What a passage," I said to Missie, squinting through this tunnel of fog to make out an outline of road wending along the outer ring of these stone-clad hills. I checked Missie's collar, sitting high above her healing wounds, more valuable to me now than the Glenisheen Gold Collar, dated 700 B.C., found in one of these limestone *grykes* in 1930 by a young boy hunting rabbits. The terrain was abundant only of rock and wild-flower: blue gentians and mountain avens tucked into rich pockets of soil between stone.

I leaned against a massive boulder, undisturbed for centuries since last rolled before a moving sheet of ice. "We might as well be on one of Jupiter's moons," I exclaimed, opening a lunch prepared by Kaethe that morning: chicken sandwiches on homemade bread—and, yes, brownies, twelve of them, nut and fudge.

"Eat up," I told Missie, giving her a brownie, as I pondered the local phenomena Dr. John had related last night—disappearing lakes called *turloughs,* and holy wells known to cure headaches and toothaches. There was a mystic haunting about the place, ghostlike and phantom-filled, elicited by the fog, yes, but more so by the *killeens,* crossroad gravesites for unbaptized children in this bleak land.

"Perhaps these vapors are the shrouded spirits of newborns returned from the far regions of Limbo," I whispered to Missie. "Forgotten and unprayed-for, like the pagan ancients in the wedge tombs around us."

Early darkness fell and we were lost to ourselves. We had dallied too long on this remote planet, and I didn't want to spend the night in such barren desolation, when mystery would become misery again. Only seven solitary miles in ten hours. The wattles of my tent couldn't penetrate stone. Tonight I wanted the friendliness of a home. A hot mug in cold hands. Four walls rather than four winds.

There wasn't a house to be seen in the pale, fading light. Only sea air and the calling of gulls in the gloaming. One step following another down the center of this godfor-saken road. But then, the eerie lowing of far-off cattle. A distant cry of donkeys. The smell of turfsmoke—a primeval scent of human habitation—followed by the dim outline of a gable and the unmistakable yellow light of a window.

I tied Missie to the gate and mumbled a few prayers before giving a gentle rap to the door. I heard a grunt and a shuffling of chairs before a man answered.

"Good evening," I began. "My name is Kevin O'Hara and my donkey there is Missie, and I wonder if you might put us up in a shed or byre for the night? I don't smoke and I have my own provisions, and we'll be off first thing in the morning no matter the weather. But I'm sorry to add, I have no money to pay you back for any kindness."

The farmer studied me cautiously before turning to his missus.

"Maura, will you come see who has landed at our door? Sure, such a sight! And isn't it a strange world entirely when you see a young man on your telly one night and on your doorstep the next. Come in, out of the cold," he said, clasping my hands, "and by God, you're welcome!"

A Worldly Man, Indeed!

CHAPTER TWELVE

Inside the cozy and warm-lit kitchen of that friendly farmhouse in the Burren, large sides of bacon, salted and cured, hung from hooks in the rafters, a sight I had seen only in antique picture books of the Irish countryside.

"I say, you won't see many flitches of bacon in your travels," said Jack Casey, catching my glance at the exposed meat when we returned indoors after squaring Missie away with a young calf for the night. "For years we'd buy nothing from the shops but sugar and tea," he boasted genially, as his wife Maura sat me before a ham-and-tomato sandwich.

"There's great talk nowadays of self-sufficiency," went on Jack, a robust man in his late sixties. "There are even books on the subject, and educated people leaving good jobs in Holland and Germany and coming to Ireland to try their hands at it. Well, they certainly picked the right country! In my younger days, we had little choice but to survive on our own, for if you depended on the shillings in your pocket, well, I'll tell you, boy, you wouldn't be long for this world."

I was given a seat by the old black turf-fed Stanley range, where I entertained the pair with a number of stories from my own past.

"Isn't it a treat to hear stories from such faraway places as Cam Ranh Bay in Vietnam and the Green Mountains of Vermont," said Mrs. Casey, walking over to the press and returning with a fresh packet of Jacob's Ginger Snaps. "And isn't it lovely to have you in our company. There you were, two nights back, on our telly, and Jack and I wondering how you might fare and what sort of a fellow would step out on such an uncertain road. And here you are, true as life, sitting in our own humble kitchen.

"Now, move into the range and gather a good blast of heat." She helped me shift my chair. "God knows, there'll be plenty of cold nights before you."

As the night progressed, two of the Casey sons, Joseph and John, stopped in and we chatted on any number of topics. I remembered these travels were meant for telling tales as much as hearing them. There was no sense walking this land with a donkey and then sitting like a lump in such generous households, especially when the pantry shelves were only a tale or two away. I needed to be both traveler and storyteller, as I told my cousins, Noel and Dessie, before my departure. Yes, a character among characters of the road. And if I was to be successful in seeking the warmth of a hundred hearths, I needed to spark and dazzle. Be the clown in every circus. The monkey at every fair.

My fledgling craft, I knew, would pale compared to the great storytellers of Munster a century ago: roaming seanachies who knew so many legends they were never known to tell the same tale twice. Or storytellers from Connacht or Leinster who could recite traditional tales to fill a lengthy tome. Or those Ulster storytellers who could breathe life into a fire, and send the cabin children scampering to the safety of their elders' laps.

But with practice I could entertain. My accent and expressions, I found, were as much a novelty to the Irish as theirs to me. Plus, I could tell stories from Mineola to Mindanao in a single breath. Did the seanachies of the last century have such geographical range? If nothing else, I was a shortwave radio of far-flung tales.

Next morning, after Jack Casey showed me the fine collection of ponies and donkeys he kept on this rocky plateau by the sea, Missie and I set out again through the shining nebula of fog. We didn't halt again until we reached the handsome front of O'Donaghue's Pub in Fanore—painted like Wedgwood china: bone-white and robin's-egg–blue— where I met a gentleman from Brisbane, Australia.

Standing in the quiet road, he began to speak about man's intrinsic drive for progress, and how oftentimes such progress goes against the workings of nature.

"Do you realize Ireland is extremely lucky despite its history of misfortune?" he began in his fine Aussie accent. "This country has almost escaped the blundering of the Industrial Revolution to the present day, so it's left with the cleanest rivers in Europe as well as the Continent's few remaining intact bogs. And the air you're now breathing is the cleanest in the world. Weather satellites have shown this. There's a particular lichen sensitive to pollutants that grows hardly anywhere in the world, yet it thrives in abundance where we stand.

"Take a deep breath," he insisted, buttoning his raincoat to face the misty sea. "Take a long, deep breath, for you'll enjoy no cleaner air than that in the Burren of County Clare."

We continued to tip through the fog at a slow pace, passing through the scattered village of Fanore and out again toward the desolation of this gray, stony world. Soon we passed Ballinalackan Castle, barely visible on a wooded promontory. Bearing right at this junction, we followed the coast road for Doolin, leaving the stone-clad wonderland behind.

We were just outside the village of Doolin, or Fisherstreet as it is often called, famous for its traditional music, when a red-haired boy greeted us excitedly, declaring his parents would give me permission to pitch camp in their field for as many nights as we liked. He introduced himself as Donal Glynn and swung open a gate to a beautiful meadow, bordered by three stone walls and the River Aille.

"You'll be wanting to spend a few days here," said Donal, taking great enjoyment in helping me free Missie from her tackling. " 'Tis a lovely spot, Fisherstreet, and tomorrow is promised fine. If you'd like to sail out to Inisheer Island for the day, can't I look after your Missie when you're gone?"

I rummaged through my camera bag and surprised him with a Kennedy half-dollar.

"John Fitzgerald Kennedy, the pride of our two countries," he exclaimed, studying the large coin on both sides. "But I can't accept this, sure I can't?"

"Of course you can. It's luck money."

"Thank you, sir," he replied, cupping the coin as if it were as valuable as the silver pennies of Edward II found in that locality some years ago.

No sooner had Donal left, when a young man with long brown hair came walking through the field from a house directly across the road.

"Well, well," he said, taking interest in my wattles scattered on the ground, "you must be having a grand time of it. Robert Shannon," he added, offering his hand.

After our introduction, he told me there were thirteen families named Shannon in the parish, the name itself of Spanish origin, brought to the island by sailors of the ill-fated Spanish Armada, shipwrecked off the Clare and Kerry coasts in 1588.

"There is something special about Doolin above other places in Ireland." Robert talked more to the deep, rolling fog than myself. "There's a magic here; you'll hear it yourself tonight in the murmurings of the river or in the playing of our local musicians. I'm no scholar, but I'd say Doolin is an old Celtic outpost like Tara in County Meath or Carnac in Brittany. The only other place I've felt this same magic was on the Dingle Peninsula."

"Well, it's certainly been a strange walk through the fog to get here," I told him.

" 'Tis a wonder," he agreed, "but 'twill soon be burning away with the sun. Why don't you take my bicycle parked at the house and pedal to the Cliffs of Moher? You'll catch yourself a mystical sunset."

I hesitated.

"Ah, do," he persisted. " 'Tis only a five-mile ride, and your belongings are safe in the field. And join me later, can't you, at Gus O'Connor's Pub?"

"You sure about the bike?"

"Why wouldn't I be? You'll not go pegging it into the sea on me, will you? Go on, enjoy the evening."

Thanking his generosity, I pushed off down the road on the bike, unencumbered by Missie's lumbering gait, and felt I was flying over this tabletop of rolling meadowland, until the great sweep of the cliffs came into view.

Leaving the bike in a small parking area, I dashed up a sea-cliff path lined with gray standing slabs of Liscannor stone, and beyond the teahouse known as O'Brien's Tower. There I stood gasping on a grassy headland six hundred feet above the crashing North Atlantic, looking down at the sheer, dizzying drop of cliffs which stretched five miles south to the promontory of Hag's Head, and northward toward Doolin Pier.

" 'A mystical sunset' is right," I said, as the setting sun was steadily burning through the fog's thinning gauze in the west, slowly exposing the Arans one at a time, Inisheer, Inishmaan, and Inishmore—stepping-stones for the ocean god, Manannan Mac Lir, known to skip over Galway Bay toward the mountains of Connemara.

It was the grandest of sights, with the fog lifting its veil from the ocean floor. I marveled at the seastacks below, jutting from the roiling waters like city high-rises, with thousands of seabirds filling the sky as if in celebration. Feeling like God's own lunatic, I raced up a numberless climb of stone steps, tempted to dive headlong into the churning swell of sea, and to rise again like some dolphin-nosed gannet and languidly soar above the heights of Hag's Head. With lungs bursting, I finally fell to the ground and, regaining my senses, curled up in the high sedge of a saucered hollow and lay silent and still in the warmth of this wayfarer's nest.

Oh, what fortune to have witnessed such a sight! Was this a "station," one of those splendid vistas that bygone cattle drovers had told my grandmother about when she was a child, whose lore she had imparted to me? . . . a scene to make these cattlemen believe God had momentarily left Heaven's door ajar.

Who was waiting back at the campsite that evening but Michael and Eileen Lafferty from Cartymore!

"We were so worried when you left the Oasis that rainy Sunday afternoon," said Eileen, "that we decided to drive out and find you."

"Thanks so much." I embraced the pair. "But how did you know I was here?"

"There's an old fella in Ballinadereen who watched you pass Wednesday week," Michael informed me. " 'So you're searching for the Welshman with sticks tied to his donkey cart?' he says, sitting up on a windowsill in the middle of the village. 'Well, now, his donkey appears to be in no particular hurry, so I'll say he'll be no further than Doolin this night.' "

"One can't make a move in this country without someone observing it," I noted in dismay.

"Sure, 'tis near impossible to 'rip the button' or 'hide the bob' without being spotted at the job," Michael agreed.

" 'To go to the bathroom,' " blushed Eileen, noting my incomprehension.

The music of fiddles and melodeons greeted us when we entered O'Connor's Pub on this Saturday night. The house was jammed with people, the four walls vibrantly illustrated with musicians, old and new, who had played in this music box of a place. Robert Shannon was over to greet us, and we all sat together at a crowded table.

To my never-ending amazement, it seemed the patrons at O'Connor's had been keeping a collective eye on our travels. Through snatches of conversation, our where-abouts had been pinpointed with the accuracy of an astronomer trailing a comet's pass-ing. For example, it was common knowledge I had chatted with the Australian outside O'Donaghue's, that I had eaten at the O'Deas' in Ballyvaughan, and so on.

The only mistake repeated was that I was a Welshman. But I had, in fact, arrived in Ireland via the ferry from Holyhead, Wales, on Christmas Eve. Could it be that that pas-sage also had been documented in the ongoing annals of Celtic observation? Have the Irish over the centuries become so acutely aware of a foreigner's presence since the invasion of the Danes back in 795 A.D.?

Even today, the Republic with its twenty-six counties and three million people had had a single phone book only an inch thick. *The Irish have no need for telephones,* I thought, *as the news of a death in the barony travels quicker than the coroner arrives.*

At the close of night, Michael and Eileen drove me back to the Glynns' field, wishing the best and inviting us to stop back at the Oasis on our homeward swing. As I watched their car's headlamps disappear through the black pitch, Missie came sniffing for apples.

"Just think," I said, feeding her a tart Granny Smith, "the Laffertys' will be back in Cartymore, forty-nine miles away, in a little over an hour. And it took you and I six days to get from there to here. 'Missie the Missile,' I'll start calling you. But, Miss, I wouldn't have it any other way. This is the perfect pace. As the wise drinker says, 'Why hurry down a pint when you have the long evening before you?' Dear Missaleen, we have that long evening before us, don't we?"

On Sunday, May 13, after attending Mass at a hilltop chapel outside the village, I stopped into McDermott's Pub in Doolin, where a young man eagerly showed me this week's edition of the *Sunday World*, a tabloid better known for its scantily clothed women than for its journalistic sophistication. There, in the middle of an inside page was a large photograph of me and Missie outside Rattigan's on the day of our departure, with its bold caption overhead: WHY KEVIN IS ASSING ABOUT IRELAND.

A toast resounded throughout the pub as another fellow presented me with five copies of this illustrious periodical. I sat down with the newspapers, looking again at the raucous Rattigan's crowd. I could only wonder what it was like at Rattigan's this Sunday, a fortnight after our departure, with the *Sunday World* spread over counter and lap, and the certain crack that would go with it:

"Will ya look at poor Joe Hickey!" I could just hear Hugh Mannion say. "No closer has he ever gotten to a bikini-clad lassie . . . or ever will again!"

"Whew," I sighed, nursing a noonday pint. "Just think, if I had packed it up in Bally-vaughan? There I'd be today, sulking like an idiot before Grannie's fire as the local tele-graphic exchange signaled my failing quicker than a schoolboy could sneak a peek at the buxom beauty on the *Sunday World*'s center page."

The day itself was fine, as promised by Donal Glynn, and after a Sunday feast with Donal's family, I set out for Doolin Pier and boarded *The Happy Hooker* with a dozen other passengers for the rocky isle of Inisheer. Josh O'Donnell, our flamboyant skipper, went singing, *"O, the sea it comes up, and the fog it comes down,"* during our wet and rollicking ride of seven sea-sprayed miles.

We landed on the lovely strand of Inisheer on a day when "the sun was splitting the rocks," baking this limestone island, which is an outcrop of the Burren itself. Many of the boat's passengers visited the whitewashed dwellings of the natives, or the inviting pub, but I made my way through a maze of stonewalled terraces to the prehistoric fortress known as Dun Forma. There, five boys with long, leafy branches for weapons, sat on the old parapet as if spyglassing for signs of lost galleons with wind-tattered sails from that storm-fated Armada.

Greeting me politely in Irish, the boys went on with their game and I was taken with their innocence, growing up as pure as the cowslip among the rocks. I continued through a labyrinth of endless walls, stones stacked to create small patches of field for oats and potatoes.

I moved along these terraced pathways in brilliant sunshine, my face burnt by the gleam off the flags of stone, and soon came upon St. Keeban's churchyard, half buried in the dunes. There, an old woman, wrapped in a traditional black shawl with red petticoat, was kneeling over a gravestone facing the sea. I passed awkwardly nearby, yet her devotion continued as though not a grain of sand had been stirred.

Rambling within this endless matrix of stone borders, I spotted the other passengers down below, gathering at the pier. Quickening my pace, I was greeted by three islandmen my age who obviously had taken the drink. I shortly exhausted my few Irish salutations and stepped along, when the strangest-looking beast came trotting toward us across its tiny field.

"Do you know the sort of that animal?" one of the islanders asked smirkingly, in English.

I eyed the odd specimen, trying to recall what Jimmy Mac had told me: *If the mother is a pony or a cob and the father a jackass, you'll end up with a short-eared stubborn mule. And if the mother is a mare-ass and the father a pony, you'll end up with a jennet with little donkey hooves.*

" 'A mule has a faraway look, while a jennet is full of roguery,' " I quoted Jimmy Mac to the three. "This one seems a bit of a rogue, so a jennet it must be."

I wasn't certain of my claim, but by the way they prattled away in Irish, I could tell they had taken me for one clever equestrian. They accompanied me down to the boat then, the best of friends, inviting me back anytime, calling me "a worldly man, indeed."

I boarded *The Happy Hooker,* with as much bounce in my step as the bow in the waves. A man of the world, indeed! I squinted into the dazzling blue horizon like any canny explorer bent on far-flung adventure.

Joe McHugh's Pub

CHAPTER THIRTEEN

Back at O'Connor's Pub in Doolin, Ted Furey, father of the Furey Brothers, a popular Irish traditional band, was playing his fiddle alongside Willie Shannon and Micho Russell, who had won "All-Ireland" honors for the fiddle and tin whistle in 1973. I took a seat by the window, enjoying the furious fun of the music, and watching young children, dressed in Sunday best, bounce in the thick-cushioned laps of their elders.

Having met Micho Russell the night before, I sat beside him after the set and asked about his music.

"I have no music theory at all," said the stout, shiny-faced bachelor, collecting a 50-pence piece from a child who had taken a group lesson with him on the tin whistle. "The headmaster once asks me how many notes there were in the scale, and, says I, 'Six,' for there are six holes in the tin whistle, you see. Then he angrily repeats the question, and I, stammering on account of his blackthorn, reply, 'Seven,' thinking of the rosewood flute Brother Ambrose brought back to me from Brazil with, mind you, seven holes. 'Goodness gracious,' sighs the headmaster. 'Here's a lad who plays such a sweet whistle the birds of the hedge hush their song. Yet he doesn't know, perhaps shouldn't know, there are eight notes in the musical scale.' "

Micho then tapped his foot against the hardwood floor and began to play a medley of songs: "Blind Mary," "The Foggy Dew," "Were You at the Mass Rock," "The Lady on the Island," and concluded with his favorite, which had won him the All-Ireland title, "The Fair-Haired Child." Then this jolly man, who looked as though he belonged on an old English toffee tin, gathered his pupils, fifteen in number, to perform "Christmas Day in the Morning." They huddled together, embarrassed by the presence of strangers, but nonetheless pealed out,

"She didn't wash her face in an ivory bowl,
She didn't wash her face in an ivory bowl,
Christmas Day in the morning."

These cherubs and musicians sang the evening to a most mellow conclusion, but early the next morning, Robert Shannon poked his head into my tent, looking drained and forlorn.

"Ted Furey died of a heart attack late last night," he choked out.

I pulled out of my zippered bag and joined Robert, and we looked out over the River Aille in contemplation.

"I suppose it's fitting Ted died here in Doolin," he said, breaking a long silence. "There's no better place for a musician to die. 'The Fiddler of Fisherstreet,' he was, and that's how I'll remember him."

"His four sons will keep his music alive." I tried to comfort Robert. "His legacy will reach far beyond Doolin."

The sun snapped the winter's lingering hold on this fine morning, as the swallows arrived from Tangier, scissoring across the vellum-blue skies in acrobatic flight. Feeling rejuvenated, ready to pack up and go rambling, Missie and I passed Donal Glynn and his mates shouting farewell from their schoolyard, with the same from the friendly men of Doolin, cutting and spreading turf on the high road to Lisdoonvarna.

Our first planned stop was the Donkey Stud Farm on Bog Hill where Lady Averyl Swinfen, author of *The Irish Donkey* and *Donkeys Galore,* took note of My Own Ladyship and invited me in for tea. Missie herself was on her best behavior, as Lady Swinfen's jumping jacks serenaded her without shame. I shudder to think if she had been in-season—the scene atop Bog Hill would have rivaled the Calgary Stampede.

After lunch and an instructive talk on donkey care, the charming equestrienne gave me one of her books, which she autographed to Missie and me. We weren't long down a quiet, sloping road when the Miss began to act up, bawling across the fields at a rheumatoid old jack called Bog Cotton by Lady Swinfen. I couldn't believe it! Was Bog Cotton Missie's grandfather or something? Why hadn't she summoned the good-looking jacks in the near fields? Is love so blind for a donkey?

Struggling with this unaccountable beast by my side, I came to the village of Kilfenora, "Townland of the Seven Churches," which takes the Pope for its bishop. We found a place with Peader and Maura McCormack and family, bunking comfortably in their high barn beside their thatched home. A heavy rain kept us at the McCormacks' a second day, so I took this opportunity to write home. The postal strike was still on, but I had met a woman the evening before who was off to England in a few days, and had offered to post my letters from there.

The McCormacks called me in for every meal and welcomed me into the warmth of their cozy sitting room. While I was writing by the hearth, Mrs. McCormack walked in with a cup of tea and a sweet bread filled with raisins.

"This is a Spotadick cake, my children's favorite." She put the still-steaming treat before me. "Have you heard the old expression, 'There's reasons for everything and currants for the cake'?" she asked, as she thickly buttered a generous slice.

"No, I haven't," I answered, my mouth watering.

"Well, there's reasons—or 'raysons,' as the old people say—for everything that occurs. There's raysons now for you writing home, there's raysons for us chatting, and there's certainly raysons for your donkey travels. Last night, Peader, myself, and our neighbors spoke long about you, and we believe God has put you on this road for some rayson. Are you aware of this?"

"Not really." I accepted a wedge of cake big enough to see me through Munster.

"Oh, yes," she said, pouring the tea, "and at night's close we were all in agreement that a great boon will come to our troubled island if you complete your roundabout with your blessed donkey."

"I don't believe it can be as important as all that," I shrugged, wiping butter from my mustache.

"May God give you the strength to complete your journey, whatever the rayson," she concluded, with a fervency I found mildly disconcerting.

That evening, I walked out to visit the medieval Doorty Cross in the old Kilfenora churchyard, finding the tall stone cross etched with well-worn figures: a bishop with crosier, and a faint outline of a pilgrim with staff walking his donkey. I ran my hands over the weathered High Cross as I thought of Maura's words. Me, a pilgrim? But in a way it had been a strange and blessed beginning—the kindness of natives, the mysterious fog, the sunset at the cliffs. *What have I gotten myself into, pray tell?*

Next morning, Missie and I traveled a loop of roads not found on my ordnance map, but somehow arrived back at the Cliffs of Moher. There I met Joe Vaughan, keeper of O'Brien's Tower, who, having seen our photo in the *Sunday World,* invited me into the tower's small gift shop for soup and sandwiches, where he introduced me to Dinny, an old character who for thirty-some years had been selling tin whistles, and telling wild stories to tourists of his younger days in Chicago.

Joe accompanied me along the cliffs with a pair of high-powered binoculars, pointing out puffins on a sea-rock called Goat Island, as well as the choughs, fulmars, shags, and cormorants that made this sheer precipice their sanctuary.

We witnessed a sea-raven's theft of a kittiwake's egg and its race for home. A commotion followed as hundreds of kittiwakes swirled like a white blanket over the fleeing raven and buried him into the sea.

"Does that happen often?" I asked Joe, looking down hundreds of feet at the spectacle.

"Yes, but more times the raven steals off with the egg. You should see the hubbub when the peregrine falcon arrives in June. And, you know, the United Nations hasn't a say in the matter."

Joe made arrangements for Missie and me to spend the night with his neighbor, Christy Curtin, and for us to meet later that night at Joe McHugh's Pub in Liscannor.

"Now, I don't mean to hurry you out of this place," said Joe, walking us quickly out to the road, "but I'm expecting two busloads of American tourists. And if they see you here, you'll be shutterbugged to death by a brigade of blue-rinsed ladies."

We traveled down a sweeping road where I could see across Liscannor Bay, to the pastel-splashed town of Lahinch, with its lovely strand and the undulating grass dunes of its championship golf course, looking like a sleeping humpbacked serpent by the sea.

On this downslope, I stopped briefly at St. Brigid's Well, a place of devotion along the road. Through a small overhang of shrubbery, I stooped into a grotto adorned with religious statues, holy pictures, and rosaries, above a flowing spring where pilgrims would collect holy water. Close by was a tall needlelike monument, which towered over this modest shrine.

"We had a landowner and MP named Cornelius O'Brien some years back, who tried to outdo the Saint," said an old woman picking up litter by the front gate. "So he had that monstrosity built to honor himself and, believe me, he hadn't a stroke of luck after it was built."

"It's still very peaceful here," I said to this pious-looking woman.

" 'Tis today, mind you. But on the pattern, the Feast of St. Brigid, the first of February, you wouldn't get near the Well with the amount of pilgrims from Clare and Galway, and scores of children selling their rush crosses handcrafted in school. When I was a child, we'd also celebrate Lughnasa here, the first of August, with great crowds arriving from the Arans and beyond."

"Would donkeys have carried the sick and lame here years back?"

"Oh, aye, plenty in my youth, the devout pilgrim riding upon a donkey, praying for a cure. And cures there have been, scores of them, the deaf and blind mostly. Brigid, you may know, is our 'Mary of the Gael.' A gentle-hearted woman who is buried alongside Saint Patrick in County Down."

"I plan on visiting their graves in Downpatrick," I informed her.

"Up north to County Down with that donkey?" she asked, startled.

"It's on our itinerary," I smiled.

"May all the graces of God go with you." She cupped my hands in her own. "And would you say a prayer to Saint Brigid for me when you reach her holy gravesite, please God?"

"I will, gladly."

She then motioned me to stay still, and disappeared into the grotto, only to reappear with a cup of holy water which she splashed lavishly on Missie and me.

"May Patrick, Brigid, and Columcille speed you," she said, crossing herself time and again, as we resumed our way.

I've never touched water from a well more holy than Saint Brigid's, and in all my experience, there is no better watering hole than Joe McHugh's Public House in Liscannor. When Joe Vaughan, Christy Curtin and myself walked through the door that evening, we entered a packed, smoke-filled room with walls the color of grass and honey. Seven musicians were jammed into the deepest recess of this little pub, playing concertinas, uilleann pipes, fiddles, flutes, spoons, and tin whistles, as three canaries, hanging in separate wire cages above the bar, twittered sweetly to the air of "Lucy Campbell."

"God save all here," sang out Joe McHugh, welcoming our entry with a nod of his black cap.

Three pints were promptly and ceremoniously put before us.

"Drink up there, now," said the publican from behind the cluttered bar, and offered me his hand. "I know you're the celebrated Donkeyman, the same fella who told the islanders all about their horses."

"There's no 'hiding the bob' in this county, that's for sure," I answered in amazement.

I had to watch my language later, as a number of elderly patrons took pleasure in making my acquaintance, looking at me admiringly with red-rimmed eyes, as if I were Patrick out to convert the druids, or Galahad in quest of the Grail, or, at least, a whimsical Don Quixote chasing dreams and tilting at windmills.

Behind the bar were black-and-white photos of greyhounds, amidst a jumble of tarnished silver cups and trophies. One such greyhound caught in full sprint was captioned: CLARE BRIDGE, WINNER OF THE TIPPERARY CUP, 1959. I asked Christy Curtin, a bachelor in his sixties, about her.

"There was no better greyhound than Clare Bridge," he answered fondly. "She was gifted with the small paws of a cat, and went on to win the coursing championship in 1959."

" 'Coursing'?"

" 'Tis an ancient sport where a hare goes running out from a slip with two greyhounds in pursuit, and points are rewarded to the dog who *turns* the hare, not the one that eventually captures it."

"Do any of the hares survive?"

"Some do, but only to run another day. Coursing is an old blood sport, and recently many people have raised up against it. But those grown into it, can't see the harm. But, I suppose, like bulldogging in England years ago, coursing will soon die out throughout the country."

I sipped my second pint and fell into a dreamy state brought on by good music and better stout. I looked at Joe McHugh behind the bar—a fiftyish bachelor in failing health, dressed in black tie, white shirt, and black captain's cap, periodically squeezing the rubber end of a brass blowhorn and giving out to anyone in a flash: "I don't care if you're a Higgins, Biggens, Wiggens, or Diggins, I want to see the color of your money!"

He tossed fistfuls of coins and crumpled bills into a little wooden drawer, bagged sweets for young children, winked at toothless old biddies, and openly conversed with the three canaries who continued to warble through the thick welkin of smoke.

"It's hard to believe those birds can last a night in this pub; it's worse than a bad London fog," I said to Joe Vaughan.

"The bird in that middle cage is twenty years old," he answered. "And Joe McHugh has a bird in the back room that's twenty-two, with only one leg."

"A one-legged canary?"

"Oh, aye. It was hanging above his head a year back but it kept falling off its perch, so we'd give out to Joe, telling him to prop a matchstick under the poor thing."

"'Twas the only canary in these parts that needed crutches," laughed Christy Curtin.

Presently two American couples stepped noisily through the door, calling out their order with scant show of courtesy. After Joe McHugh had served them, one of the women asked directions to the ladies' room. The publican pointed the way respectfully, but she was back in a moment, raising her voice above the music.

"There's no lock on the ladies'-room door!"

"No lock?" replied Joe in mock surprise, and squeezed his brass horn thrice, which immediately killed the music, silenced the canaries, and brought a dead calm to the place. "Why, ma'am, I'll tell you something, and not a word of it a lie. But there hasn't been a lock on that door for twenty-five years and—may God strike me dead—but there hasn't been a thing stolen out of there yet."

With that, the house burst in laughter. All, that is, but the four intruders, who weren't long packing for their car, undoubtedly grumbling about stumbling into such a den of unruly Celts.

"Can you imagine?" said Joe McHugh, lifting the black cap from his brow. "You'd think she was the bee's-knees, the Queen of Britannia herself, complaining of having no lock on our bathroom door. No lock, mind ye, as if any of us here had the desire to sneak a peek as she leaked!"

With the pub rolling in glee, Joe McHugh signaled the musicians to resume their play as he began to pull pint after pint, looking up at his chirping canaries and singing, *"Lovely, lovely, all the world is lovely."*

The Grass Widow and Bottle Scrubber

CHAPTER FOURTEEN

I was sleeping soundly on the ceiling of a topsy-turvy caravan overturned by a gale in a trailer park outside the town of Lahinch, a shelter Sergeant Kelly of the Gardai had graciously pointed out the evening before, when I heard the furtive call of a woman drawing me out of my sleep into the cold, clear hour of dawn.

"*Pssst*. Have ye any fags?"

"Beg pardon?"

"Fags. Have ye any fags?"

"Oh, cigarettes," I mumbled, clearing my gaze to look at a hoary harridan from the Dark Ages grinning down upon me like a gargoyle.

"Well, have ye any?"

"No, I'm sorry," I answered blankly.

"Are you the Welshman?" she asked, beginning to peel away the floor tiles above her head.

"I am not," I replied, crawling out of my sleeping bag and walking across the ceiling of this derelict domicile for my sneakers, as disoriented as a Cub Scout on his way to Mars. "I was born in England of Irish parents but spent most of my life watching baseball in America."

"And is that your lovely donkey tied up to the spike?"

"It is," I sat back down to untie the knots in my sneakers.

"'Tis a mighty fine spike. Where did ye steal it?"

"A traveler presented it to me," I answered in annoyance.

"'Twas snitched by him so, before he handed it to ye," she snapped. "A tinker will steal anything not bolted down in a farmyard. So," she went on, sitting boldly beside me, "yer the Welshman, sorra, American, pasted all over the papers. Didn't the two of us meet during the war?"

"I don't think so," I replied, ducking under a faucet as I stood up. "I was born in 1949, after the war."

"He was the spit of ye, I tell ye. A fine wee handsome chap with a bit of a 'tache. A Yankee soldier in Ulster, awaiting Dday."

"Sorry." I turned my back to roll up my sleeping bag.

"Romance hasn't come my way since I fell in with me own husband, God help me, with not a tooth left in his head. And he goes to this young galoot of a dentist in Ennis to be fitted with uppers and downers for eighty quid, mind ye, and to this day he's never worn them, not even on a feast day. 'Ye have eighty quid worth of teeth in a mug,' I give out to him, 'and ye walk the roads with yer chin hanging out like a duck's arse.' But he won't listen, God help me, and to this day he's never stuffed them into his gob, to give him the air of gentry."

I kept turning away to gather my things, but she kept hopping around to confront me.

"Now, do ye see me sole survivor?" She shoved her face close and pulled down her lower lip to expose her one remaining bicuspid. "That's me tombstone, for it will live longer in me head than I will. And this same dentist in Ennis wants me permission to yank it from me skull as if it were a milk tooth, by gum, to clear the way for another eighty quid of plastic teeth in a mug."

Having danced me around once or twice, she pressed on importunately.

"There was a fine nurse down the Gort Road who said I could work me tooth better than a soldier could work a Swiss army knife. Why, I can pare an apple with it, or peel the odd spud if I put me mind to it."

I held my peace, realizing that down the Gort Road was Our Lady's Hospital in Ennis, a large psychiatric facility.

"Well, I'm going to carry me last survivor to me grave," the old woman persisted, still holding down her lower lip. "Troth—a fierce, thick, horrid whore of a dentist in Ennis, with certificates and citations covering his four walls, asking to clear me head for a false set. And they go preaching preventive dentistry! Why, I can gnarl me way through a gamey shank of ham, so I can."

I took up all my gear and made for the exit of this upside-down world, as eager as Alice to escape the rabbit-hole.

"Clearing the way, mind ye," she said, exasperated, sticking to my side as I walked toward more rational companionship, "as if it were a huge rock in the road, so he can go replacing it with rows of teeth that'll leave me grinning like a snail."

"A snail?" I nuzzled up to Missie, trying to keep her snout between mine and the harridan's.

"Aye, a snail. Did ye never learn in school that a snail has twenty-six thousand teeth?"

"I did not," I laughed, even though I had no wish to encourage her.

"Hah, ignorant lot! And did ye ever learn about Biddy Early?"

"Biddy Early?"

"What kind of school did ye go to, a'tall!" she roared. "Biddy Early was the wisest woman in Ireland. Even the poet Billy Yeats knew that! She was born here in Clare, in the townland of Feakle, this last century. But many thought her a witch, for she had in her possession a blue bottle, which was her talisman. If she were alive today, I'd seek her out to cast a curse on that Ennis dentist, so his sporty smile would go blacker than sloes each time he'd smile at man, woman, or beast."

By this time I was awake enough to know there was nothing for me to do but hear this grimalkin out.

"Ye see, Biddy Early stood up against those righteous sorts—priests, doctors, and solicitors—for she was free from the seed of greed. But even those she had helped, went agin' her in the end, thinking her bewitched, because she was a three-time widow. Yes, three husbands gone, for her talisman possessed no cure for her own. So, in a fit of sorrow, she pegged her blue bottle into a lake, and it's there that it lies to this day."

I pulled out two bananas from my cart and offered her one, though she was plenty bananas already.

"I've gone too hard for the soft ones," she said, looking away from the fruit in disgust. "For I, like Biddy Early, am a widow of sorts. A 'grass widow,' without land or livestock, traveling the roads morning and night while me dolt of a husband sits like a lump before an empty grate with no rhyme or reason to his day.

"Now," she asked me, with an amorous eye less appealing to me than the banana was to her, "have ye yerself kept company with any widdy-women along the way?"

"No, I haven't," I determinedly laid the straddle over Missie's back and cautiously reached for the belly-band.

"There's plenty of us, ye know."

"I'm sure. In fact"—I dodged her flirtatious gaze like a boxer avoiding a jab—"I've been reading a book by Padraic O Conaire, and he writes of spending a night with three widows under the one roof: mother, daughter, and granddaughter, with the patriarch dead for fifty years."

"Why, by gum, ye've hit upon it, boy!" She stamped her feet with such force that Missie reared back on her heels. "Ye have brought to mind a secret of the road less known than any other on the five ancient highways to Tara. And if ye only part with enough money to buy me a packet of fags, I'll let ye in on this sealed and guarded matter."

"I don't think so," I declined, busily hitching Missie to the cart.

"But it was Pecker Dunne who told me," she ejaculated in a spigot of spittle, sidling up in my face again, with her lone tooth glistening in the morning sun.

"Who's Pecker Dunne?" I had to ask.

"Ye don't know Pecker Dunne?" she said, in mock disbelief. "Why, he's more famous than Bang-Bang, Pat-in-the-Box, or Birdman—nearly one with yerself . . . donkey, cart, and all—and balladeering with a banjo throughout the known world."

"Never heard of him," I replied, while giving Missie her daily feed of oats, "but I'll keep my eye out."

" 'Keep me eye out!' Oh, such a grand mistake to be making, ye who knows nothing about the road, and I a grass widow of a two-cow boreen. Leave me you the price of a packet of fags in me begging hands and I'll whisper to ye Pecker Dunne's precious secret of the ancient highways!"

I gave Missie a light tug of the reins and stepped out on the coast road toward Milltown Malbay.

"For the price of a packet of fags!" she hollered from the mouth of the caravan park.

I stopped Missie and walked back to the old woman. I pulled two pounds from my pocket, meaning to part with one.

"Bless ye, kind sir," she said, snapping the two crisp bills from my grasp. "May the Lord in Heaven shine on you from this day to your last."

"Pecker Dunne's secret?" I asked.

The old woman looked up the road and down the road and across headland and field, and out beyond the fishing boats that bobbed upon Liscannor Bay, playing it up like a top-billed actress with the Druid Theater in Galway City.

Satisfied that not a wren could overhear her, she cleared her raspy throat and whispered, "Within the year ye must sleep in three different households where five daughters reside. If ye accomplish this feat—and it shouldn't be hard with all your tramping—anything ye wish for will be yer own. And that, me boyo, should set ye right in this world and the next."

I thanked the one-toothed grass widow, with the thought that Pecker Dunne might indeed be onto something.

"Ye're a generous, charitable, Christian man," she cried, stepping lively for the town of Lahinch. "One of Biddy's children, surely, for there's not a seed of greed in yer breed. God bless ye!"

As a psychiatric nurse, I'd had plenty of encounters like this, but I had learned to listen to the ranting for the odd wit and surprising wisdom it sometimes contains, as with this reincarnation of Biddy Early herself.

The day was perfect for traveling, and the road so quiet, we sauntered down its very middle. I had met a farmer the night before who had half joked I would soon have the roads to myself, with another oil squeeze pending, as well as the postal strike into its fifteenth week, crippling commerce throughout the country.

I was so content with the way of the day that I broke into a fine marching song, Woody Guthrie's "Oklahoma Hills."

Wailing away, mind you, without a care in the world, when a big block of a man suddenly appeared from a shed beside the road, scaring the bejabbers out of me.

"You're a fine singer," he said, dropping a brush and a soapy milk bottle at his feet to deliver a sudsy handshake. "A mighty singer, surely."

He was dressed in a suit of dairy-white, black beret, a belt of red rope clasped together by a Yale lock, and a pair of wading boots that crept up to midthigh. He introduced himself as Michael John and spoke so close up that if I pursed my lips, I would be kissing him squarely on the mouth.

"Are you enjoying your travels?" he asked, not awaiting a reply. "And how do you like the little country? Ahh, but it's gone to hell altogether since we've joined the Common Market. I'd rather have my cows in a field of garlic than Ireland in the EEC. Mark my words, they'll do more damage to Ireland than England ever dreamed of doing. We'll be told to dig up plutonium in the Donegal Hills and build nuclear generators in County Wexford. You call that Christian industry? Grain and crops and trees are Christian industry! Feed the world first; then, by God, serve beef on the platters of those who believe they deserve it."

I moved around Missie so her flickering ears offered some buffer from the bottle-man's blurtations. But even her ears began to droop under the assault of his long-winded, in-your-face polemic.

"Do you live hereabouts?" I broke into his relentless monologue on macroeconomics.

"No, I live outside Corofin, but I do be traveling to get the odd bit of work. I'm now scrubbing these bottles for the local creamery. 'Tisn't much, mind you, but it keeps me out of the poor house."

I nodded at the truth of that, but carefully calibrated my response, not wishing to set him off on another tirade.

"I've also tried my hand at publishing short stories," he went on, his eyes dancing in his head. "No luck there, either. I even attended the Writers' Week in Listowel where one uppity writer told us a good story was like a good head of hair. First you write the story, start-to-finish: a ball of tousled hair. Then the story needs to be clipped, snipped, and trimmed. And when you feel you have the story complete, you stand before the mirror and carefully comb it out as an altar boy would before Sunday Mass."

"Did you ever sell any?"

"Not a one," he sighed. "This uppity writer told me that all my stories were full of cowlicks."

Well, here was one who seemed to have a method to his madness, if you could stand in the spray of his sputtering. His monologue swung through the poetry of John Donne, and scholastic philosophy from Thomas Aquinas on, while he went on with his bottle-washing.

"After the Great Deluge"—he arose from his work to nose up to me once more— "a number of beasts from Noah's Ark made their way to Ireland. And when God saw fit, he turned them into mortals. Perhaps you have made their acquaintances along the way, as they still carry their fabled names: Codd and Sammon, Snipe and Woodcock, Rabbitt and Lambe, Crowe and Hare, Fox and Swann, Hawke and Wren, Woulffe and Badger, Hogg and Swyne. Now, people might tell you these families changed their surnames to those of animals, for they were on the run from English agents, English landlords, English soldiers, or English women. Not so. They're off Noah's own gangplank, so they are!"

He pulled back to gauge my reaction, with an eye like Long John Silver's, then zoomed back into aggressive close-up.

"And do ya know how to tell a pagan from a Christian in the way they uncap a hard-boiled egg?" he demanded, his moist breath dampening my nostrils.

"No, I don't," I mumbled, as tight-lipped as a ventriloquist.

"A pagan takes a heavy tablespoon and delivers violent blows to his hard-boiled egg, thus mercilessly shattering its thin fontanel. A Christian, however, uses a more aesthetic approach. A butterknife, sharp and gleaming, circles the air, and with one painless stroke decapitates old Humpty where he sits."

Again I could see his point, but to nod I had to draw back my head like a long-necked crane.

"And do you know why a pearl dissolves readily in champagne, and a tooth in cola?"

"Oh, that's quite okay, I've heard enough about teeth today," I said, tugging at Missie's reins to make good our escape. "We must be going now, so God bless, and the best of luck to you."

"The height of luck to you, too," he said, going back to his chore. "And do enjoy our little country. The Ox Mountains, the Caves of Mitchelstown, Muckanaghederdaughaulia!"

"Muckawhat . . . ?

"Muckanaghederdaughaulia in the County Galway," he laughed. "Go sing yourself a song about that place. Or how about Llanfairpwllgwyngyllgogerychwyrndrobwllllandy-siiiogogogoch, in Wales? Or Lake Chargogagogmanchauagogchaubunagungamaug, in your own Massachusetts? Now, amn't I a right wizard, as smart as any Johnny Forty-Cats you're likely to meet on the road?"

Smarter than most, to be sure, Mr. Michael John.

Old Country Cures

W e took shelter that evening in a tumbledown cabin in a field beside the Armada Inn, a short distance from a grand headland known as Spanish Point. From this promontory, Mutton Island was visible in the southwest; to the north, the Arans and the Twelve Bens of Connemara; and at my feet, a sandy stretch of beach, where men and women were busily collecting seaweed, the sun still high in the west.

With Missie secured for the night, I made my way down the strand and asked the natives if I could assist in some capacity.

"You can pile high the ribbon weed," said a friendly man named Mickey Talty, showing me a sample of seaweed resembling a cat-o'-nine tails. "We can use all the hands we can muster after the May Gurra. 'Tis the highest spring tide."

I went about the work of collecting the stinking seaweed. Mickey explained it would be taken to the Irish Marine in Kilrush, and beyond to England where it would be processed into iodine. There was other seaweed along the strand as well: redweed, black-weed, and carrageen moss. As we began to load the ribbon weed into a cart pulled by a tractor, I heard the bawl of Missie above on the headland.

"Is that your motor giving out?" asked a ruddy-faced man named Charles, working alongside Mickey.

"That's my Missie," I answered, pitching the rubbery seaweed into the cart.

"In my youth," said Mickey, "there'd be nothing but the roar of the sea and the bray of the donkey during the May Gurra. And now, only the tractor."

We knocked off work at nine P.M., with the sun still lapping above the waves, and we were soon enjoying pints of stout at Hennessey's Pub in Milltown Malbay.

"Charles knows every living thing in the hedgerows," said Mickey, after I had mentioned how I was awakened every morning by a chorus of little feathered friends.

"We used to catch songbirds in cradle cages as children." Charles took the prompt from Mickey. "Linnets are fine singers and, of course, goldfinches, thrushes and blackbirds. In fact, it's believed thrushes, sing eighty percent of the day. Truly fascinating, you know, that the birds of our hedges are from all over the world. The redwing is from Iceland, the fieldfare from Norway, the willow warbler from South Africa, and the chiffchaff from the Mediterranean. And what would you say is the smallest Irish bird?"

"The wren," I answered with some confidence.

"Almost, but 'tis the goldcrest. It weaves the most beautiful nest of moss, spider-webbing, and feathers."

Charles brought my attention to the publican behind the bar.

"There's a man there, now, who carries the gift of a cure"—nodding toward Paddy Hennessey. "He has the cure for thrush."

"Really! I've seen babies really suffer from that mouth infection as a nursing student back home where we'd use Nystatin Swish. How did he come by the cure?" I asked, looking at the pleasant white-haired man chatting with his patrons.

"His father died when he was still in his mother's womb," said Mickey.

"And that gave him the cure for thrush?"

" 'Tis the only way I know," said Charles.

"Go speak to him," said Mickey, coaxingly, "and he'll give you a firsthand account of his gift."

Walking to the bar, I waited for a lull before I introduced myself to Paddy and asked if he might tell me about his cure. Clearing a few glasses from between us, he knelt on a high stool behind the bar and leaned across the counter to rest comfortably on his elbows before me.

"I was born," he began, "a month after my father's death and was so given the cure for thrush. My father, you see, was shot dead at Canada Cross, just up the town, on the fifteenth of April, 1920, by a British regiment. There was a great bonfire in town that evening, with hundreds celebrating the release that morning of three Irish prisoners from Mountjoy Jail in Dublin. Suddenly the crowd was indiscriminately fired upon, killing my father and two others—O'Leary and O'Loughlin—and wounding several more. I was born twenty-three days later, on the seventh of May, 1920.

"My mother told me, when I reached the age of ten, that I was to pedal into the country the next morning and cure a young child with thrush, and that I'd possessed this cure since the age of nine, on account of my father's death. I was to fast from midnight onward, she instructed, and I would know what to do upon arriving at the child's house.

"The following morning, I cycled four miles to the parish of Freigh, and walked another quarter-mile through the fields before coming to the house itself. Inside, the mother showed me her child, whose tongue was spotted and swollen. The roof of its mouth was sore with lesions. I took up the child and blew three times into its mouth and did the same every morning for nine mornings, and began to see improvement on the fifth morning."

The publican's story intrigued me. Certainly I believed there was more to health than what modern medicine offered. I asked him a string of questions: "How did healing make you feel? Did it seem like a religious calling? Or do you think it might be a gift from the Middle Kingdom?"

"No such thing as all that," he laughed, amused by my far-fetched queries. "I can neither state nor fathom the reason for it, but, you see, modern-day doctors were scarce in the country during the 1920s and '30s, and cures were the thing at the time. And from that first cure on, I was practically on the move every week until the age of eighteen. I believe I helped many, and the only way I ever felt strange is that I'd often go hoarse or suffer a sore throat after a cure."

"It must be wonderful to have such a gift," I said, admiring the peaceful mien of this healing man.

"It would have been more wonderful to have known my father," he stated plainly. "But God has His raysons, hasn't He?"

He interrupted his restful repose to serve a few customers, but was back again to me.

"If you call back again this way, you should meet the bonesetter, Joe Burke, a little man with a high-pitched laugh, as close to a faery-doctor as any you're likely to meet. His father, Thomas, was elected to the Dail in Dublin, not so much for his political know-how, but that he had set so many people walking again.

"There you have it, now," said Mickey Talty, when I returned to our table. "Old country cures and those who still carry them. Certainly a bit of the Old Ireland you're hunting down."

"Thank you," I said, "but Paddy also mentioned Joe Burke, the bonesetter. Would he have received his gift the same way as Paddy?"

"No," said Mickey. "Bone-setting is in the hands at birth, handed down from one generation to the next. Pity Joe Burke hasn't any children of his own. A few years back, he successfully treated Dr. Staunton, the chief surgeon at the County Hospital in Ennis."

"Are bonesetters like quacks or charmers?" I pursued, intrigued by this Old World topic.

"No, they're a different lot entirely," explained Charles. "A quack or charmer is the seventh son of a seventh son. The most famous is Finbar Nolan, who has offices in both Dublin and New York. He is sometimes called a 'faith healer.' The traveling gypsies also have a host of cures; the wool of black sheep for earaches, the jawbones of fish for toothaches, are just a few."

"There's another cure I heard about," I said, "but I think the fellow was pulling my leg. 'Licking the lizard,' he called it."

"Aye, licking the lizard," said Mickey, knowingly. "'Tis the cure for healing burns."

"How can licking a lizard heal a burn?"

"The *earc luachra* is a small lizard found in the watery drains of bogs," Mick explained. "If you come upon one, catch it, and lick its underbelly from head to tail."

"I think I'll pass."

" 'Tis the only way known to obtain that cure," Charles said matter-of-factly.

"But even after licking the lizard, how would you go about curing a burn?"

"By licking the affected skin with your tongue," added Mickey.

"No thanks, again," I repeated, pulling back my chair. "I think I'd rather be a quack or a bonesetter."

"Mr. Stack in Ennistymon holds the cure for burns," piped an eavesdropper sitting beside us. "I was told that his wife badly scalded her hand one night on a kettle, and he simply licked her hand to lift the sting from it."

"I'd have a hard time convincing my medical friends back home of such a cure," I laughed. "They'd think it was the Guinness talking."

"Speaking of which," sang Mickey, "I think they're calling out to us now. Three pints, Paddy, please!"

Crossing the Shannon

CHAPTER SIXTEEN

When we arrived at the fishing village of Quilty next morning, I stopped into a corner shop for peanuts, fig rolls, and a liter of milk, still living off my scant savings I'd set out with from Rattigan's. The pleasant shopkeeper, amused at seeing Missie peering in through the doorway, buried her hands into a wooden crate and pulled out a dozen bruised apples.

"These are for your little brown friend." She packed them into a bag.

"They will make her day," I thanked her.

I received permission that evening to bed down in a vacant shed in Clohanes, not a three-star affair by any means, but a clean spot with a nice field for Missie to tumble and graze.

It was fun to watch Missie rock and roll in the evenings. There she'd be, sniffing the ground for a suitable spot, and upon finding it, she'd fold her legs beneath her, lay on her right side and go rocking back and forth until she toppled over completely with her metal heels clicking in midair. Once this barrel roll was concluded, she would lay on her left side, momentarily stunned. Then, gathering her wits, she'd right herself, snort deeply, shake her coat free of dust, and stare at me blankly.

Jimmy Mac had explained that these daily tumbles were as refreshing to a donkey as a sound sleep to ourselves. Seeing her tumble was also a sign of good health, thus guaranteeing another day on the road.

I sat down to my meager meal of milk and fig rolls—holding on to my few precious shillings—when a mother and her lovely daughter walked through the gate, asking if I was the fellow in the *Sunday World*.

"I am, yes," I said, rising to my feet.

"When you passed our house earlier I thought I recognized your donkey from the paper, but I couldn't be sure of yourself." The mother reddened.

"Isn't she the right countrywoman?" added the daughter.

"I'm sorry, but your donkey is so distinctive with her white markings." The mother apologized, but made me feel like some nameless donkey-beater from the Middle Ages. "Now, come with us across the way for a spot of tea, and I hope I didn't offend you."

"Not at all. I'm growing accustomed to playing second fiddle to a donkey."

I was soon in a warm sitting room with Pat and Kitty Killeen and family, comprising of two sons and three lovely daughters. The grate was blazing and a pile of freshly made ham sandwiches, slathered in mayonnaise, were put before me. Amply fueled, I rambled on with stories till midnight: stories of the grass widow, the bottle scrubber, and the busloads of tourists.

On Ascension Thursday, after Mass and a send-off feast with the Killeens, Missie and I set out for Kilkee, eleven miles down the Clare coast, passing the villages of Doonbeg and Bealaha along the way. In Bealaha, I spotted a dead magpie swinging on a string attached to a tall pole in the center of a garden. A primitive scarecrow, indeed. As I took a closer look at the hanging specimen, I received an animated welcome from across the road.

"I've had me two eyes peeled out for ye for days," called a bristle-faced old man from his door, beckoning me over. He shook my hand with a grip of banded steel. "What took you so blinking long? 'Twas a woman who detained you, heh? Making honey in yer heart? Why, ye're having the life of Reilly! A blooming holiday! Tramping about the racecourse of Ireland! And by Jaysus, lad, if I was a tad younger I'd be tagging along beside ye, visiting the pubs and stepping out with the pretty women. Now, come in, if only for a moment, and tie your girlie-girl to the knocker on me door."

The lively little man wasted no time in dusting off an old bottle of stout which he poured into a glass with great glee. Never was anyone so enthralled to have me in their company—rubbing his two hands vigorously before him, like a housefly anticipating table crumbs. In the eyes of this old codger, I was a mythological hero, equal to the likes of Conchobhar, Oisin, or Brian Boru. Or better yet, a TV star.

"Ye're a wonder," he kept saying as I took my first sip of the flat bitter stout. "A blooming, blinking wonder to the world!"

I unwisely finished the drink, sacrificed my hand to his viselike grip, and resumed my walk with Missie. She kept stopping every hundred yards for another of the shopkeeper's apples, not convinced she had finished them all until I placed the empty bag over her head.

We arrived in Kilkee late that afternoon, a seaside resort since Victorian times, with handsome two-story houses facing a horseshoe strand looking out on Moore Bay. A number of children playing in the shallow pools at low tide left their games and encircled Missie in admiration.

"You're a dear dapper treasure," they chimed, petting her nose and forehead. "What's her name?"

"Missie Mickdermot."

They giggled: "That's a funny name for a donkey."

When the commotion died down, the children led me by the hand to their "black pools."

"Do you see the little cobblers, mister?" They pointed to tiny fish left behind in these rocky depressions.

The children busily baited hooks with periwinkles and hovered above these miniature loughs—feeling grander, I supposed, than Gulliver himself, kings and queens of this lakeland district by the sea.

As I returned to Missie, a prickling surge of nausea rushed over me. I dropped my head on her back, weak and ready to collapse.

"Anything wrong?" I heard a voice call from a car that had stopped.

"I'm afraid I drank a bad bottle of stout," I said, belching up the soured taste of it.

The man jumped from his car and introduced himself as Manuel DiLucia.

"Make your way to my home," he pointed to his house, a handsome bungalow overlooking the town, "and I'll see to you and your donkey once you arrive."

I made it to Manuel's where, after meeting his fetching German wife Delores, I collapsed into the white-sheeted comfort of a four-poster bed located close to the bathroom, a convenience I called upon repeatedly throughout a wretched night.

The next day was perfect for traveling, but I remained so ill I could step out only in the evening to visit Missie and her newfound acquaintance, a cut-jack in the neighboring O'Mearas' field.

"I'm glad you're having a good time," I weakly called after her, as Missie and the clipped prince went prancing about the meadow in a show of fruitless courtship.

The next day, Saturday, was a total loss, as I felt sicker still, and spent the whole day in the land of counterpane. But Sunday morning, I woke to the fine smell of toast and sizzling sausage.

"Rise and shine," called Manuel from the kitchen, who had come to Kilkee from Italy as a six-month babe in his parents' arms. "Rise out of that bed like Lazarus himself and have the breakfast. Then I'm taking you fishing, where the sea air around George's Head will clear your own."

After a delicious meal I was thankful to keep down, I found myself clumsily helping to row a dinghy out to Manuel's launch to gather lobster pots in the bay. I pulled up two lobsters and a summer velvet crab in no time, and as I filled my lungs with sea air, the promised clearing came over me.

From our seaborne vantage, Manuel pointed out natural features like puffing holes and sea tunnels, and human remnants like the deserted village of Corbally, the seashore castle on Doonmore Head, and the location of "the Well of the Creator of the World."

"It's all a wonderland," I said, squinting through the morning haze toward the bluish headlands.

My three-day bout with gastric distress cut out any further exploration, and would have forced me to pass up the western peninsula of South Clare, but on Monday morning, Manuel kindly drove me through the small villages of Carrighholt and Kilbaha to the lighthouse at the very tip of Loop Head.

A profusion of sea pinks and white campion greeted us at this precipice, also known as Cuchulainn's Leap. A sheer-sided seastack, named Diarmuid's and Grainne's Rock, jutted dramatically from the sea, as the constant boom of waves crashed against these high cliffs.

"Feast your eyes on that view," said Manuel, pointing north toward the Cliffs of Moher and the Aran Islands. "It must be thrilling for you to look back upon all you've traveled."

"It is a sight." I cast a long eye northward.

"But, look now, to the south," he smiled, "beyond the mouth of the Shannon there. Do you see Kerry Head and the rugged mountains of the Dingle Peninsula? You have some fair tipping yet, boy!"

That afternoon, Manuel gave me a new raincoat, which I badly needed, and introduced me to Missie's host as I collected her from the field of her playmate.

"The two of them got along like brother and sister," said Mr. O'Meara, "so don't be surprised if your donkey acts queerly for a few days."

"She acts queerly every day," I answered, thanking them all, and leading my well-rested princess down the quiet coast road.

We had just strode into Moyasta, six miles south of Kilkee, when the publican, Joe Taylor, standing outside his two-story establishment, called me off the road for a pint and a sandwich.

"What kept ye?" asked an elderly patron after I had made my entrance into the pub.

"A gracious old man in Bealaha served me a spoiled bottle of stout," I said. "And if I didn't meet up with Manuel DiLucia, I might well be dead."

"An old bottle can give you the collywobbles," said Joe Taylor. "I suppose the poor fella had it in his press for years. So, by God, Manuel DiLucia saves another one!"

I looked at him inquiringly.

"Did Manuel not tell you he has saved nineteen people from the ravaging waters of George's Head? He has as many commendations as our coast-guard fleet. And now he saves the Donkeyman, who almost sank in a bad bottle of stout. Now, peg back *this* Guinness," Joe encouraged, standing me a creamy pint, fresh from the tap.

After settling Missie in a field belonging to Malachy Browne, I returned to Taylor's where a party had sprung up from a crack in the wall.

"Barring any more mishaps, this is your last night in County Clare," said Joe, "since tomorrow you'll be crossing the ferry into North Kerry."

"Tell us, so," asked the same old geezer from earlier, "how many days did it take you to travel from the border of northern Clare to here?"

"I was in Ballyvaughan on the ninth of May . . ." I began.

"Aye, Ballyvaughan on Black Head Bay, is it?" he interrupted. "And tomorrow, Killimer, on the twenty-ninth. How many miles have you recorded in Clare, so?"

"Eighty-three," I calculated, "and another seven to Killimer will make ninety."

"Ninety miles in twenty days," he said gleefully. "Ye don't need to be a dart player to know that ninety into twenty is less than five miles a day. Powerful tipping, that."

"Will you be traveling through Mayo?" asked a young woman named Mary Devine, home on holidays from England with her husband Jim.

"Sometime in November, I hope."

Mary took a scrap of paper from her purse and wrote: *Cleary's Pub, Ballycroy, Co. Mayo.*

"Ballycroy is the loneliest spot on earth," said Mary, handing me the address, "but Mrs. Cleary is the loveliest woman you'll ever meet. We'll be seeing her before returning to England, and we'll make certain you'll be accommodated when you arrive there."

"And a pint will be standing for you as well," added Jim Devine.

"Please tell her not to pull it until I get there," I requested, my stomach rumbling still.

Later, Joe Taylor and I left the bar and sat comfortably before the den's open fire. He told me how the pub was founded in 1820 by his great-granduncle, Frank Taylor, and how Frank's two sons died during the Famine of 1848.

"This house was also a junction for the West Clare Railway between 1887 and 1961," added Joe, stretching out before the flames. "The engineers would pull in here for a few pints of porter before making their trek to Kilrush or Kilkee. I was told the expression 'flying off the rails' originated right where we're sitting."

I checked Missie out of Malachy Browne's at noon, and we headed for the ferry in Killimer, passing the manufacturing town of Kilrush, a small port on the north shore of the Shannon estuary.

Just out of town, a rough-looking townie left his makeshift shelter in a lay-by and began to walk beside us. I could tell by the cut of him he was up to no good, and Missie, spooked by his presence, snipped at him when he had the gall to sit on the cart's shaft.

"If this was my ass I'd break a stick over it," he spat, sliding off the shaft in ill-humor.

Missie and I hurried along in throes of alarm as the unwelcome encroacher, sockless with torn pant-cuffs, kept pace.

"What's your hurry, boss?" he wheezed, working a cigarette from hand to mouth. He would surreptitiously duck his head each time a car passed. There were fewer cars as we stepped further from town, and our meddler tagged along despite Missie's nips at his lurking legs. It was evident he was waiting for his chance to clobber me and make off with any valuables I might have.

"If you have time," I blurted, keeping a good grasp of my hazel, "why don't you walk with us as far as Killimer."

"What the feck for?" he cursed, looking fore and aft in search of a lonely spot to strike.

"Don't you know?" I pretended surprise. "I'm the Yank going around the Ring of Ireland for charity, and all my sponsors are going to be there when we board the ferry for Kerry."

Seeing a dim apprehension cross his low brow, I pressed my advantage, to outwit his malevolent intent.

"Gay Byrne might even be there, from *The Late, Late Show,*" I added, struggling to keep my voice from cracking. "Didn't you see me on television or in the newspapers?"

He did not reply, but, thank God, his step fell away and the threat passed. As quickly as he had entered my life, he was gone, the poor scrapper dragging his sorry heels back toward Kilrush.

"Oh, Missie, my humble protector!" I gasped in relief, kissing her full on the snout. "Do you know how close that one was! He could've cracked my skull and left me senseless and penniless. But there you were, biting away at him! Why, you're my bucktoothed defender! My long-eared guardian of the road!"

Arriving at the line for the ferry outside Killimer, we took our place behind a dozen cars and lorries, and one driver leaned out to offer advice.

"You know, loose animals aren't allowed to cross, they have to be in a horsebox," he said apologetically. "They might make an exception in your case, but they're usually stringent about such things. Sticklers, in fact."

I stood glumly beside Missie on the queue. Where would I find a horsebox? I had to take the ferry; the long, dreary roundabout through Limerick would take two weeks I'd already lost. The ferry arrived and unloaded, and when the Kerry-bound vehicles had boarded, I stepped up to the tollmaster and sought his permission to do likewise.

"I wouldn't think so," he demurred, studying Missie and me and our trappings. "It's a sticky insurance matter, you see. But I'll ask my boss, Mr. Glynn in Tarbert, and I'll be back with an answer in an hour's time."

The hour passed, as another queue gathered to cross. The ferry once again docked against the pier, spilling its few vehicles landward.

"Well, good news, boy," called the tollmaster, as the last car boarded. "Come along, then," he shouted, waving from the head of the platform.

With a hearty sigh of relief I led Missie to the foot of the steel ramp. But as soon as her front hooves hit the metal incline, she threw on the brakes.

"Come on, Miss." I stood before her and tugged at the reins. "You don't want to go whimpering through Limerick, do you?"

"What's the problem?" asked the tollmaster, glancing at his watch, as passengers became spectators.

"She hates anything that makes her shoes ring out," I puffed, pulling with all my might.

"Best be hurrying," said the tollmaster, unmoved.

Desperation seized my heart as I tried to budge my contumacious beast. Nothing.

Thankfully, four passengers hurried down the gangplank, shouldered the cart's tailboard and pushed from behind, and Missie began to slip and slide up the ramp onto the vessel.

So there the two of us stood, like oddball honeymooners on an oceanliner's deck, gawking as the coast of Clare drifted further away. By the time we were halfway across, Missie was gazing out at the ferry's wake like a seasoned sailor, taking in great gulps of sea air.

The tollmaster, who had finished collecting from the others, saved Missie and me for last.

"Well, now," he said, counting our feet and playing to the audience of passengers, "I'm not certain if I should charge you as a two-, six-, or eight-wheeled vehicle, so I'm not going to charge you at all. And do you know why that is?"

"No, sir?"

"Because ye'll be the first and the last ass and cart who will ever cross the Shannon on my ferry!"

With that, he shook my hand.

"Welcome to the Kingdom of Kerry," he smiled, tearing up my boarding stub in his hands.

A Breather in Ballybunion

If Irish children could vote, I might well have announced my candidacy for prime minister upon our arrival in Tarbert. Scores of children, spilling out from newly-built council houses, shouted out to us, but went scattering back across the Green when I called out for a volunteer to carry Missie's oats around the country.

"You won't catch us, so you won't," they screamed in near frenzy, holding on to one another for dear life. "You won't steal us away to carry your oats for your dear Miss Missie!"

The first registered voter I came upon was Martin Kelly from nearby Carhoona, who stood overlooking a beautiful reach of the Shannon estuary.

"Does she make a good sailor," he asked of our river crossing, "or is she a landlubber like myself?"

"She'll never find work with Cunard Lines," I said, petting my little heroine.

"But you have a smart donkey, nonetheless. You can tell a bright ass by the way they move their ears. A dull-headed donkey has laggardly lugs, but an ass like your own does be watching the road with her ears as much as her eyes."

"Do you know why she sniffs the road?" I asked, concerned over Missie's recent behavior.

"It may be to follow another donkey or it may be to nose out if she herself has traveled the road before. And if she's sniffing at the heel of the day, she's probably telling you she's worn-out and needs a good roll in the dust. But, watching her stroll along, I'd say she's asking for a taste of the stick."

"I like to give her her time, at her own pace."

"You're doing that mighty," he smiled, bidding me good-day.

My first night in Ossian's Kingdom was spent in a corrugated turfshed, where an archaic implement for the skulling of cattle dangled precariously over my head. Before I bedded down, however, two fun-loving grown daughters of the house, Kathleen and Mary O'Carroll, took me out to Monty's Coast Road Inn where a ticking multitude of antique clocks decorated the walls. We stayed till midnight whereupon jillions of tiny brass hammers delicately filled the room with chiming carillons.

" 'Tis the music of trooping faeries," whispered Kathleen.

Mrs. O'Carroll was palpably relieved when her daughters returned safely home with this roving rogue of the road. She served tea and sandwiches, and as I readied to exit and collapse in their shed, the mother said, "We can't let you go without saying the Rosary."

So on my knobs I knelt, between the two daughters who recited the five decades for my safe passage. You'd think I was a right Knight Templar bound for the Holy Land, but I only mumbled the "Hails" and "Holys" until I could flop face-first into my cozy, soft sack.

The following afternoon, Missie and I came to a pub overhung with ivy outside the village of Astee with the unlikely name the Jesse James Tavern. Like a gunslinging cowboy of the Old West, I tied Missie to a post, rambled into the saloon, and ordered myself a cold beer. Soon the publican, Mr. Enright, was eagerly offering up the lore of the namesake.

"Jesse's parents came from this very townland, but moved with so many others to America. Jim James, Jesse's father, married a local girl by the name of O'Connor, but she died shortly after they had settled in Missouri. Jesse actually had a Baptist mother, but didn't he love her like any good Irish boy would. He might be known for an outlaw, but we think of him as a clever leader of a brave band of men, fighting the power, and looking out for the poor. He died decorating his Christmas tree, you know, shot dead by a turncoat from his own gang."

I figured to be stepping out of the tavern into the "lone pray-ree," but instead a hurtling Irish rain soon came barreling down the road on splashing feet, drenching us to the bone.

"Come in out of that!" roared a farmer from the blue door of his pink farmhouse under a thatched roof.

I quickly led Missie through the swinging gate and the farmer, Martin Collins, pulled my cart in the barn and Missie into a small byre. He then led me into the kitchen where his wife, Kathleen, and their eight handsome children, ages ten to twenty-two, were in line to greet the Donkeyman.

They each introduced themselves politely, as I fastened on one snickering boy.

"You're no stranger to children," said Kathleen.

"I come from a family of eight as well," I said, "and this little rascal reminds me of our youngest, Kieran," wrestling the giddy lad to the floor.

After a delicious supper, I sat before the warm range with Martin, a healthy, stout farmer in his late fifties.

"This is the third thatched house I've been in during my travels," I observed.

"This house is three hundred years old, with a new thatch of gilcock and riverweed, a fine specimen of the old ways," he replied. "'Tis also a lucky house, thank God, because our eight children have been raised in it without mishap, and myself and six brothers and sisters before that. And the seven of us survived 'the hard times,' when there was nothing to eat the year-round but potatoes and a spot of milk, and maybe the goose on Christmas Day."

"Which 'hard times'?" I asked. "I'm beginning to learn that Ireland has had more than her share."

"The 1930s, sure, for our country was in a deplorable state back then. No work, little food, sons and daughters emigrating in droves, breaking the hearts of the old folk. Yes, the cream of the nation, two hundred thousand strong, sailing to America, a country mired in its own Depression."

"Oh, yes, where they were greeted with more hardship."

"You'll see the harvest of the 'hungry thirties' throughout your travels," he continued somberly, "as it produced a bumper crop of bachelors. A young man at that time was too poor to take in a bride and raise a family. You'll meet any amount of them, broken-down old souls sitting before a cold grate with only a cat or dog for a companion. And, sure, for every bachelor, isn't there a spinster, keeping up her little empty house? They never had a chance for courtship or marriage. Never a child and, moreover, the priests would strike out at the slightest frolic between them, coming upon crossroad dances with blackthorns swinging. Yes, a whole generation suffering without the joys of procreation and the blessings of family.

"Now, Kathleen and I have our dear eight," he continued, taking a charming daughter by the hand, "but how will they fare in a country with few jobs, tell me? I have even less faith in the Common Market than I do in England owning up to its seven centuries of exploitation."

"At least your children are having a great childhood." I looked across at three of them happily playing a board game. "A loving family in a lucky old house in a beautiful spot of the world."

"Yes," he cuddled the one in his arms, "they're lucky children, all right. Lucky children in a lucky house, indeed."

Next morning, after spending the night in a loft of baled hay, as if I were sleeping in a box of shredded wheat, I was called off my high perch by Martin, waving a newspaper in his hand.

"There's a dandy story about you in the *Irish Press*," he shouted, "and a grand photograph as well."

I climbed down the barn's rickety ladder and was handed the national daily, which gave a glowing account of our travels.

"Look at yourselves," he smiled. "You'll be royally treated from here to kingdom come."

Martin Collins was spot-on in his prediction, for no sooner had we left his lucky house than I was hailed by flock after flock of gaily-frocked women standing at their gates and front gardens. "Arragh, do stop and tell us of your travels. Surely you have time for a freshly baked buttered scone?" They each had their special query to press: "How lovely was County Clare?" "Did you find the people of Galway dark and clannish?" "Are you from County Roscommon, the land of sheepstealers?"

"I can't believe this," I gasped, finding a private moment midmorning to water the hedges after my fifth cup of tea.

With dwindling hopes of reaching the seaside resort of Ballybunion by nightfall, we came upon a long line of farmers with donkeys and carts waiting to empty their milkcans at Kilcoleman Creamery. As Missie and I passed by the ranks of our cohorts, each saluted us in turn.

"Are you the Donkeyman?"

"I am."

"Why aren't you up on the cart tipping her along?"

"My license was revoked."

"Drink, was it?"

"Aye."

"Draining the pints, ladeen?"

"Murdering them."

"A right piss-on?"

"Aye."

"Pulverized?"

"Paralytic!"

"And you're right, by Jaysus."

Cats and dogs were falling from the sky when we passed Kilconly Schoolhouse in Asdee.

"Come in, before you go drowning!" called a woman from her front door.

I led Missie up a flower-lined driveway, adjacent to the schoolhouse, and tied her to a wooden fence.

"Bring yourself a change of clothes, for you'll catch a death in those togs," the woman called again, this time from her back door.

Inside, the woman introduced herself as Sheila Pierce, and her daughter, Anne Pierce O'Dowd, as the present schoolteacher at Kilconly. Mrs. Pierce then directed me to the bathroom, handing me a washcloth and towel.

"Shower yourself up," she said. "You'll go no further tonight in this downpour."

Blessing the editors of the *Irish Press,* I stepped out from the shower spic-and-span, and into the kitchen where I met Sheila's husband, Garrett, the retired schoolmaster of Kilconly, and their son, Gerald, a long-haired fellow my own age.

After a steaming bowl of stew on this damp evening, Gerald and his friend, Liam, took me to Mikey Joe's, a popular pub in Ballybunion.

"You should stay with us a week," suggested Gerald, placing a creamy pint before me. " 'Tis in the west you should take your time. Can't I show you the forts atop Kerry Head and Doon Cove? We could also climb Maulin Mountain to see the whole of the Dingle Peninsula."

"I'd love to," I answered, "but I'm not making much headway as it is."

"Take a breather," Liam chimed in. "Can't you make up for lost time on the east coast? You could travel from Wexford to Dublin in a week's time."

"It never seems to work out that way."

"Suit yourself, but you're welcome," Gerald leaned back and slapped the table with both hands. "It's good to meet someone our own age. Half our mates have gone abroad to England and beyond."

"I have noticed a generational gap," I said. "Sometimes I see nothing but elderly men and women. Are young people still emigrating for lack of work?"

"By the boatload. You talk about hard times, the 1970s have been no joke, with nearly a quarter of our people out of work. There's nothing hereabouts unless you have a farm of land, and many our age want nothing to do with farming."

"Why is that?" I asked, thinking of friends at home being drawn back to work the land.

"For one thing, women are no longer attracted to men driving tractors into town on a Saturday night. And now you need a hundred cows on a hundred acres to make a decent living. What young man has the money to purchase a farm that size?"

"But what about those old farmers I saw at Kilcoleman Creamery this morning?"

"They're the last of the dying breed, barely scraping a living," answered Gerald. "Without the dole or pension they'd be in the County Home long ago. And what man our age," he smiled, "begging your pardon, would be seen riding a donkey to the creamery?"

"Do those farmers at Kilcoleman have decent holdings of land?"

"Paltry holdings," informed Liam, "less than ten acres with two or three cows. Three cows at three gallons a cow in the grass-rich month of June is nine gallons a day. That doesn't leave much for the pub on Saturday night, does it? And when these old bachelors die off, the land is gobbled up by large dairy farmers who receive huge grants and subsidies from the Common Market.

"The EEC, you see, wants nothing to do with a country of ten-acre farms," Liam continued. "To them, farm work is no different from factory work. Output and production. Large herds and larger holdings. The old ways are changing before our eyes. You yourself wouldn't be able to walk this country with an ass in ten years' time. Think about it. What other country could you circle and find a farmer with a field at the close of every night?"

"But is it possible to make a living on ten acres?"

"Who would want the hardship?" shrugged Gerald.

"It sounds better to me than living in a congested city, or having to commute to work five days a week on a clogged expressway."

"That's the side you know," said Gerald, "but believe me, the young people in Kerry are mad to leave the farms and move to American cities, seduced by watching American TV. Some believe everything in America is like that program, *Dallas*. Talk about streets lined with gold. Now they're lined with fast cars and faster women."

"The modern world has finally caught up with old Ireland," Liam concluded, "and what is left of our generation is clumsily leaping over the old. Our country's populace over the centuries has been so abused that we're nothing more than a long ladder full of missing rungs."

"What about yourself, Liam?" I asked.

"I have a small farm of twenty-two acres," he said, draining the remainder of his pint, "and, by jinx, I'm going to work it."

The next day I found Missie in the throes of her in-season derangement, staring blankly at the clouds and soaping at the mouth. Digesting this unpropitious sight, I reconsidered Gerald's kind offer of staying on to visit the local sights, and took this opportunity to douse my stuporous queen with her last Tick-sol treatment, and leave her in Pierce's field to bake in the sun.

Those following evenings, after our daily rambles which sent us as far afield as Killarney, Gerald and I would step into the kitchen where Sheila dished up wonderful meals and we shared our adventures.

"Today we met the playwright, John B. Keane, in his pub in Listowel," I said, "and he told me never to sleep in old boneyards during my travels or I'll always be haunted with bad luck. We also tried to stop in on Bryan McMahon—whose story 'The Homecoming' is one of my favorites—but he wasn't well enough to see us. Just think of it," I reflected, "a publican and a schoolteacher, ordinary folk in one small town, to be such exceptional writers."

"Most Irish writers have always been part of the people," said Garrett. "Why, John B. gets most of his material from his patrons."

"And what do you do back home in America?" asked Sheila.

"I'm a registered nurse on a psychiatric unit," I answered.

"A nurse, really?" Sheila replied in surprise. "I'm a nurse as well, though I no longer practice. How were you drawn to the profession?"

"I was on a MED-CAP team in Vietnam," I explained, "and we went out to villages surrounding Cam Ranh Bay where I was stationed. After my discharge I had big plans of joining the Tom Dooley Foundation, who were desperate for nurses. But by the time I had finished my schooling, the Vietnam War had spread into Laos and Cambodia, where Dr. Dooley's clinics were located and, to be honest, I couldn't face that part of the world again."

"That would be quite understandable," Sheila nodded sympathetically.

"My mother, Lella, and her two sisters, were also nurses, trained at St. Andrew's Hospital in Northampton, England. My mother's letter of acceptance came one August morning when she was saving hay. Three days later, at age seventeen, she was off to

Northampton. Imagine, barefoot in an Irish field on a Wednesday, and working a psych ward in England that Sunday."

"And your father?"

"My father is a Longfordman who met my mom one Sunday outside St. Thomas's Cathedral in Northampton. They soon married and had five children in England, including myself. They returned briefly to Ireland, but a farm once promised my mother slipped away, so back to England we went and boarded the *Queen Elizabeth* for America in 1953. We settled in Massachusetts where my parents had three more children."

"What does your father do for work?"

"My dad is retired now, but he was a chauffeur for the Sisters of Providence at St. Luke's Hospital, driving the good nuns from the Mother House to the Gray House in a sleek black seven-passenger Fleetwood Cadillac. He loved his job, telling his captive audience about his Irish childhood from one end of the turnpike to the other. He would also treat them to ice-cream cones and lead them in the Rosary like a monsignor."

"The right man for the job," smiled Sheila.

"It was made for him," I agreed. "He's a little man as well, like his father before him. In fact, my grandfather, Bernie O'Hara, was said to be the smallest man in Longford, but rode upon the largest horse. A white horse. We always teased our dad, for he is also the smallest man in our parish back home but drove the largest car, that black Fleetwood."

"History repeating itself," smiled Garrett, passing the steaming spuds.

"I often wonder what I might have been if I was brought up here," I said as we ate.

"You'd be a blooming three-cow farmer, that's what you'd be," snickered Gerald. "On line with the farmers at Kilcoleman Creamery with their asses and carts."

"Actually, I think we were raised very Irish in America," I whacked Gerald in the arm. "Or maybe it was very Catholic. The saying of the Rosary every evening without fail, daily Mass throughout Lent, devotions to Mary in May, confession every Saturday. . . . missions, Benediction, you name it. And priests over the house for Sunday dinner where, after the feast of roast beef and Yorkshire pudding, my father would pour strong highballs for these clergy and say, 'Boys, run upstairs for your boxing gloves.'"

"Boxing, really?" Gerald's mouth gaped in astonishment.

"Indeed, and, oh, what fun! In no time our front room would be converted into a makeshift boxing ring, as my brothers and I would go at it, hell for leather, to the delight, and sometimes horror, of our visiting dignitaries."

"A real Golden Gloves, huh?" Gerald shook his head.

"Oh, yeah. My dad even had a bell from a hospital bedside stand that would ring out the rounds. We fought like John L. Sullivan, but real featherweights. One afternoon I landed a roundhouse to my older brother Jimmy's jaw that knocked him out cold, the eyes in his head looking like two Ping-Pong balls."

"Well, now," Garrett explained, "that, really, is an old Irish throwback. Our chieftains were known to have their sons go into mock battle for the entertainment of their guests. Why, you must be true Irish royalty . . . more Irish than the Irish themselves!"

Those nights, I camped out on the Pierces' enclosed front porch, where the lighthouse at Loop Head winked through the windows at three-second intervals. Though off the road, I was more committed to it than ever, eager to catch old Hibernia before it passed, where knitting spinsters and three-cow farmers still greet strangers open-armed at their doors.

Dead Cut of a Weasel

CHAPTER EIGHTEEN

After this weeklong respite in Asdee where an amorous Missie became friends with a cut-jack, who I'm afraid must have been more chump than chum to her, we continued through Ballyduff and out to Rattoo, where a round tower in excellent condition stood above an old monastic ruin. Walking around the tower's base, I met a local named Sean O'Connor who said the tower dated back to the tenth century.

"Were bells rung from those towers, like a steeple?"

"They were used as belltowers, watchtowers, and places of refuge. The monks had ladders that would bring them up so far," Sean explained, pointing to a small entry several feet above the ground, "and within the tower were other ladders that would go to the cone. If there was a Viking attack, the monks would pull up their ladders after carrying their sacred books, chalices, and provisions to safety: provisions they prayed would last longer than their impatient raiders. The bells would also signal the local villagers for help."

"Seems pretty secure."

"Other than a flaming arrow shot through the small windows," he went on, "the monks were safer than a cat up a tree."

We were nosing toward Ballyheigue next morning when an old bachelor called me in for "a mouthful of tea." He had an open hearth in his kitchen, where washed socks were drying over the crane and a brass swastika hung glaringly over the mantel.

"That's a symbol you don't see on display very often," I said cautiously, pointing to the swastika.

"Oh, aye," he said, gazing at it matter-of-factly. " 'Tis an appreciation presented to my sister in Germany."

"When?"

"Toward the end of the Second World War. She was a nurse in Munich and cared for the civilians injured there. God bless her soul, but she told horrific stories of the fire-bombings by the Allied planes, and how she was up day and night with the wounded until she'd collapse among them."

"Did she support the Nazis?" I asked, since his calm demeanor removed any fear of offending.

"Devil a bit, no," he exclaimed. "Didn't she try to nurse in England as well, but it was Germany who sent her fare to be trained. To herself, the difference between England and Germany was like apples and pears before the war. There was nothing in this country at that time, and one simply took what was offered."

After my mouthful of tea, Missie and I resumed our tramping. How hungry the 1930s must have been around here, if people leaped for work in Nazi Germany. Though, then again, in this place at that time maybe the Nazis didn't look all that much different from the English. To the colonized, one empire is as good or bad as the next. As a nurse you serve people, not governments.

Suddenly a blue squad car pulled in front of us, and out stepped two guards in uniform, curtly asking me to unyoke Missie from the cart.

"Anything wrong, Officers?" I asked anxiously, that swastika calling up the image of stormtroopers.

"Routine inspection," one said sternly, without a by-your-leave.

I clumsily untackled Missie in a lay-by and held my breath as they checked her from head to toe.

"What's this?" demanded the senior officer, pointing to the remains of Missie's stripped collar.

"A scalded breast," I said, my voice barely above a squeak. "She had a tight collar in the early going, but I swapped it for another with Crowe the Saddler in Ennistymon. She lost some hair from ticks about the same time."

"Did you treat her?"

"I did, sir. Two treatments of Tick-sol, and gall-cure for the scalded breast."

"Are you putting oil on her hooves?" He stooped down to continue the examination.

"No, sir."

"Well, you'd best, they're cracking. If there was a fever up on them, I'd call you off the road," he warned. "A rag of old oil from any garage will do."

"Yes, sir."

"Are you the Yankee lad from Roscommon?"

"I am, sir."

"We're following up on a complaint lodged yesterday."

"Wh-what sort of complaint?" I stammered.

"Your ass looking sluggish and overworked."

"She's chronically sluggish," I laughed, trying to lighten the mood. "The old farmers are always on to me to give her the stick. She's certainly not overworked. We just took a week off in Asdee with the Pierce family."

"She does have a fine sheen to her coat," allowed the junior officer. "And she's plump, as though in foal."

"Oh, she can't be pregnant," I hastened to declare. "She's only spent a few nights afield with jacks . . . all cut-jacks!"

The bossman cracked a smile.

"She's a pet." The junior officer rubbed Missie's snout and she impishly nipped at his sleeve. "You have this donkey spoilt. Look at this, Sergeant! She's as playful as a pup."

The sergeant glanced, unamused by Missie's antics, and jotted down a few phrases in a black logbook.

"Watch her hooves." He closed his ledger with finality. "And remember, it's our job to follow up on any complaints."

"I understand, Officers."

"Good luck, then," they said, stepping back into the car.

I was trembling like a violin string as I put back Missie's harness.

"Boy, Miss," I exhaled, "they sure caught us at a good time. We would have been dead donkeys if we'd met those boyos in Clare. And look at you," I said, wrestling with her head, "playing up to the young one the whole time. 'Missie the Brownie,' I should call you. The only Irish donkey who's forty shades of brown."

Halfway into June, I had to rally myself, stop dallying, and reach Tralee by day's end. But we were no sooner past Ardfert, than I was harshly called off the road by a brute and buxom woman, who put me in mind of a ribald old ballad: by the eighteenth century poet, Bryan Merriman.

> "She's a powerful, hefty block of a lass!
> A well-thighed, big-pawed, mocking heap,
> Deadened with fault-finding, full of cheek!"

"Unyoke that ass of yours and come in here for a proper feed," she commanded, "and don't be walking this country surviving on apples and biscuits."

My growling stomach overruled my wiser instincts, and I took up her gruff invitation.

She sat me at the table and I meekly acquiesced, as she put down a spread of delft and a lashing of cutlery to accommodate a nine-course meal.

" 'Tis a lonely life you have without a bride by your side." Her tone went more gentle, as she stood bottles of ketchup, salad dressing, and Colman's mustard before me. "And, I suppose, at times, being human and all, you long for companionship?"

"I've been known to miss it," I cautiously replied, afraid of her heat-seeking gaze.

"You see," she bent to whisper in my ear, "I have a daughter upstairs, the youngest and prettiest of five, but old enough to be wed with child. Yet she lays about the house in vainglory, not lifting a finger for man or beast. Would you simply meet her, now?"

"I would," I said with palpable relief, though her eyes continued to bore into me.

"Kitty," she sang, while keeping me fixed in her sights, "come down a moment and meet the fine young gentleman walking the ass about Ireland."

"I won't, then," came the sharp reply.

"See how bold she can be?" said the mother apologetically, only to renew her hollering: "Kitty, get down here this instant!"

"How is it, Mama, that every time a man walks by our door you drag him through the muck of your garden to meet me, when I've told you time and again I'm in no mood to marry?"

"Will you stop painting your face in that blasted mirror and get your lazy arse down here!" the mother roared.

"I won't, I say. And besides," called the determined voice from above, "why should I marry one man when I'm pretty enough to enjoy the company of a hundred?"

My ears pricked at the table.

"See, there, now you have it, the trash learnt over beyont in England!" the mother bellowed, as I patiently fiddled with my butter knife. "She's a plucky girl, I tell you, a right Dimple Dallas."

Abruptly the mother changed tactics, calling for her daughter in a sweet and gentle tone. "Kitty, could you please step down and help me wet the tay?"

"Mama, I saw the Donkeyman's picture in the *Irish Press* and he's the dead cut of a weasel. And sure, if I wanted to meet up with his kind, couldn't I go with one of the Sheridan lads camped outside Tralee?"

"Isn't that fine talk, you bold brassy thing, for a visitor from Massachusetts in the United States of America to hear—and circling the country for some good cause, no doubt."

"I read the papers, too, you know. He's circling the country so he can get back to his grandmother's bedside by Christmas Eve," the daughter chided down the stairs. "Aren't all the Yanks mad for their Irish grandmothers?—but this one's a daft silly header, altogether."

I sat at the table like the guest at a Friar's Club roast, still willing to trade humiliation for a full meal.

"I suppose it's no use," I finally said. "I guess she's waiting for a bonnie prince upon a white steed, not an errant pilgrim with a nut-brown donkey."

"Well, then," the mother said smartly, "I suppose there's little sense in fussing over a hot range, is there?"

"I guess not," I said, tossing my napkin aside.

"Here, take these," she offered me a few tea biscuits from a bin.

"Thanks, but there's no need," I declined, frowning down at the thin dry wafers.

"Arragh, take them, go on," she insisted, forcing them into my hand. " 'Tis a long, trying trek to Tralee, and ye'll soon be famished with the hunger. And, God Bless the Mark, 'tisn't your fault you're the dead cut of a weasel."

I stepped into the dusty road and slowly yoked Missie to the cart, glancing up several times at the bedroom window, hoping to catch a glimpse of this Irish maid in the tower. But not a glimmer of herself did she offer, and as I tramped toward Tralee, more heartsick than hungry, I pondered my likeness to a certain small, unloved carnivorous mammal.

On the Dingle

CHAPTER NINETEEN

Passing the old seaport of Tralee, filled with a myriad of blocks, entrys, and cul-de-sacs that would leave a drunken sailor forever landlocked, we happened upon Ned Kelliher, who was offering rides to tourists on his mule and trap, from the Brandon Hotel to the foothills of Slieve Mish on the Dingle Peninsula.

"Stay with us a night or two," said the plump, beaming horseman, gazing with admiration at my "grand drive," as he distractedly boarded a pair of honeymooners into his trap. " 'Tis only meself and me mother, and our house is easily spotted by its scattering of cartwheels in the front garden, two miles beyond Blennerville. Go on, now, and I'll meet ye at O'Dwyer's Pub later this evening."

"Imagine"—he turned to the happy couple, tossing a Foxford blanket over their laps—"that lad is circling the whole of Ireland with his donkey, and I'll be tipping this same wee jaunt till the wheels crumble beneath me."

Missie and I crossed a stone bridge into Blennerville, a run-down village on Tralee Bay, presided over by a derelict old windmill. But before us stood the magnificent Slieve Mish range, "the Mountains of the Phantoms," extending east to west along the spine of the Dingle Peninsula, thirty miles from the Vale of Tralee to the western ocean.

I ran my eyes across this highland terrain, looking for the precipitous corridor known as Conor Pass: said to be the most spectacular high-level crossing in Ireland, that was to be our passage into the town of Dingle.

Nora Hanlon Kelliher, a kind soul of eighty-eight years who enjoyed her pinch of snuff, wasn't the least surprised that her son, Nedeen, had lassoed the donkeyman in for the night. After I settled Missie in a small paddock, she immediately started to fuss over a skillet.

"A shop egg is of no use," she apologized, cracking two of them over a sizzling pan. "The egg itself is smaller, the shell more brittle, and the yolk paler than the eggs of me own hens that go scratching about in the ditches."

Mrs. Kelliher needn't have fretted her fare, as this eager beggar looked around at the photos that graced the kitchen walls. Ned was pictured with such notables as Ronnie Drew of the Dubliners; Eamon Casey, Bishop of Galway; and Gay Byrne, popular TV host and radio personality. There was also a picture of Mrs. Kelliher embracing a past winner of the Rose of Tralee Festival.

"Doesn't Nedeen know half the country, with all his stories and ballads," said Mrs. Kelliher, sitting me before a meal of most satisfactory eggs, along with rasher and brown bread. "And hasn't he met famous people the world over, coming to spend their holidays in Dingle, and returning years later, asking Nedeen for one more spin on his mule and trap."

Having devoured the meal with the manners of a wolf, I thanked Mrs. Kelliher and walked back to Blennerville and into O'Dwyer's Pub. It was early evening and *The Quiet Man* was being aired on television, a tribute to John Wayne, who had died a day earlier. I watched quietly and listened to the respectful commentary of the patrons, with one local saying "the Duke" was best in cowboy westerns, "where he wasn't afraid to pull back the reins of any man."

Soon the iron-shod wheels of Ned's conveyance were heard, and upon entering he introduced me to all and sundry as "the Yankee lad with the brown ass." Enjoying my chat with this true Kerry character, I asked my fellow wrangler about a donkey's amorous cycles, recounting some of Missie's recent behavior.

"She'll just go on chewing at her teeth," he answered, "and there's little ye can do unless she's mated. And though a donkey doesn't come to foal for eleven months, 'tis wise to keep her barren until her travels are through."

"How often will she come into season?" I queried, turning to accept a free pint from the gracious publican, Michael O'Dwyer. There were certain topics I couldn't take up with Lady Swinfen, and couldn't trust the commentary of old cronies met on the road.

"Three or five days in every twenty-eight, or thereabouts, from April to as late as November. I suppose it's slow going when she's gnashing her teeth and standing blind to the world."

" 'Blind to the world' is right! She just falls into this stupor, staring mindlessly at anything white, passing clouds, sheep . . ."

"Sheets blowing on clotheslines," added Ned.

"Yes," I banged the heel of my hand to forehead. "Especially sheets hanging on clotheslines. Why is that?"

"Beats the bejesus out of me!" howled the horseman.

John Savage, Ned's friend and neighbor, joined us, and it wasn't long before we were talking about *pishogues,* old superstitions of the Irish countryside. It may have been a glance at Maureen O'Hara up on the telly that turned the conversation to redheadedness.

"Red has always been a contrary color in the country," said John. "In bygone days, a farmer off to market would turn for home if he met a redheaded woman on the way, believing there'd be no luck for him that day."

"Really? In America, the redhaired lass is the picture of Irishness."

"Well, it's different here. The redhead recalls the Norsemen, or Judas Iscariot himself."

"Or the villainous Queen Bess of England," interjected Ned. "You'll notice in your travels that a large number of redheads are settled in the eastern counties: Wexford, Waterford, and Dublin, originally Viking settlements. To the west, ye'll find more blackheaded people, the true Celts, living in Mayo, Sligo, and Galway."

The talk shifted to my proposed ascent up Conor Pass.

"Why wouldn't you do it?" said Ned, catching the doubt in my voice.

"I've been warned by many not to attempt it," I confided.

He murdered his new pint with the ease of an open drain, seeming neither to taste nor swallow the contents, but letting it run down his gullet without troubling the gag reflex.

" 'Tis a long road into Dingle by way of Castlemaine"—he wiped the stout's cream from his lips—"and it will leave you backtracking the same road out again. The only way to see the glory of this peninsula is up and over the Conor Pass."

"I don't know." John shook his head worriedly. "It's going to be one hard pull for the donkey, and the sharp blind bends at the summit will leave Kevin at great risk from traffic in either direction."

"Plenty of oats during the ascent," said Ned, paying little heed to his neighbor, "and give your ass the day off before your climb, and the day after as well."

Though it was an hour before midnight, a glimmer of light still mirrored across Tralee Bay, just a few days from the longest of the year, as Ned and I left O'Dwyer's and boarded his jaunting cart for a fifteen-minute ride home. Ned's mule, Cecil, tipped along smoothly toward the gray-penciled mountains of Slieve Mish, as the tipsy jobber chatted away.

"There's a mighty fortress of stone at the crown of Caherconcree," he said, pointing a fleshy finger at the imposing hills. " 'Twas the stronghold of Curio MacDaire, the King of all Munster. There is also a holy well tucked away in the vicinity of Glannagalt, known as 'the Well of the Lunatics,' which the insane of this peninsula would visit in hopes of a cure. Beyond that is a prayer-station known as Maumnahaltora, 'the Pass of the Altar,' where pilgrims would come in droves to hear Mass during the Penal Times. A shelf of unwritten history dwells in those hills, ladeen."

Then he broke into a song, *"Hup, hup, Asaleen is hip hip ho,"* as we sailed through the dream-laced night to the ringing chime of dancing hooves. The roguish face of Nedeen Kelliher continued to bawl out his tune beside me, a face as indigenous to this high land as the coombs and tarns of its hills. With our heads full of spirits and the brisk Atlantic breeze at our back, our chariot galloped toward the Mountains of Phantoms, and I felt at one with the madmen and pilgrims whose steps we traced.

As we approached our destination, however, my splendid rush of reverie was shattered by a strident call scattering the phantoms to the four winds. Who else but Missie! And it wasn't me she was heralding, but Ned's four-legged fool of a mule, Cecil, who answered her urgent plea with the most blasphemous song ever bugled on this third planet from the sun.

"Shall we give them a go at it?" laughed Nedeen, as we wheeled through his gate.

"We will not," said I.

The following afternoon a wet wind gave way to bright weather as we prepared to set off from the Kellihers'. Ned gave Missie the once-over, checking her as a good mechanic would a car. He had arranged that I would stay the night with his cousin, James Bailey, in Aughacasla, thirteen miles down the road.

Missie and I set out on the high path for Camp, but weren't long past Derrymore when we came upon two elderly sisters struggling with a mattress at their door, hoping to air it out in the fine weather. Tying Missie to their gate, I assisted the women and further volunteered to beat the daylights out of three rugs hanging over their clothesline with an antique waffle-faced racket. Coughing up a mixture of ash and dust after my zealous pounding, I was awarded a dish of fresh custard in their parlor.

Traveling along this winding road between fuchsia hedges eight feet high, we came upon three young girls collecting wildflowers for a school project.

"Do you have names for all these flowers?" I asked the giggling threesome, admiring their colorful bouquets.

"We've put our own names up on them." One girl stepped back shyly as she spoke.

"You see," said the second, holding up a spray of foxglove, "our teacher calls these 'Digitalis purpurea,' but we call them 'faery fingers.'"

"Or 'faery thimbles,'" said the third, one of those dreaded redheads, removing a pink tubular flower and sliding it over her finger. "Now, watch." She took another and rolled it gently in her hand till it popped like a tiny balloon, startling Missie.

"Oh, I'm sorry," she laughed, petting my frightened beast.

"Guess what we call scarlet fuchsia?" said the shy one, her face reddening.

"I haven't a clue."

"'Nine-legged ballerinas,'" she giggled, and I whooped a laugh in return.

"You see"—the middle child chose a red, drooping flower from the high hedge—"they all have nine legs beneath their bright dresses."

"Now, if you remove seven, like so," said the redhead, "you'll have yourself a two-legged ballerina. There!" She triumphantly held up the miniature dancer before me.

"Open your hands," coaxed the shy one, "the two of them, and put them together, like so, to make us a proper dance floor."

Doing as I was told, the three girls busily plucked a troupe of ballerinas from the hedge, and proceeded to perform Swan Lake along my lifeline, ending their performance with the tiny dancers bowing as gracefully as Dame Margot Fonteyn.

"Bravo!" I shouted at the conclusion of their program. "Wasn't I a lucky man to have met up with such a charming dance company."

They giggled again and went skipping down the road, leaving the ballerinas sleeping peacefully in my hands.

I walked alongside the flowering fuchsia with ballerinas still in hand, thinking of what it would be like to be young again and grow up with that charming trio. Would I be as knowledgeable of the hedges as they are, would my accent be as lilting? What would it be like to sit beside them in their classroom, with me and my mates chasing them down the lanes to tug at their braids after school? And would I grow up to marry one of them—even Miss Red-Locks, the boldest of the three—and settle hereabouts on a sprawling hillside farm?

Not a mile later, I heard a shout from a woman outside her bungalow. She hurried indoors, and was right out with a generous portion of apple tart.

Kerry must be the friendliest county in Ireland, I said to myself, licking my lips. But as I held out my hands to accommodate this flaky treat, the woman sidestepped me and began stuffing the delectable treat between Missie's grass-stained tombstone teeth.

" 'Tis a pity, my little darling," the woman wailed as she crammed the tasty pastry home, "and Conor Pass, another Calvary, yet before you."

I stood, jaw agape as Missie slobbered all over the woman's hands. After the feeding, this ditsy, doting donkey-lover marched back into her bungalow and returned with another thick wedge, this time wrapped in the waxed paper of a bread loaf.

"For the love of God," she pleaded to me in earnest, "feed this to your donkey when she is most in need. It should be yourself harnessed between those shafts!"

"Yes, ma'am." I swallowed hard, accepting the buttery pie.

"You won't dare eat that yourself, would you?" she challenged me, while Missie gave me one of her sarcastic grins.

"I wouldn't think of it," I fibbed.

We stepped back out on the quiet road, but no sooner were we three bends from the bakerwoman's home than I devoured this succulent feast behind the back of my snuffling donkey.

Following a fine supper in Aughacasla with James and Noreen Bailey, I was invited to spend the night in their spare bedroom, but the night was so clear I opted to camp out on Tullahee Strand, looking north across Tralee Bay to the lighthouse of Loop Head winking through the still blackness. Along the near shore, the lights of Ballyheigue shone like Chinese lanterns. The stars above were so bright it seemed I needed only a stepladder to rearrange them.

I positioned my sleeping bag in the safety of the tufted dunes, and spotted seven satellites in thirty minutes. "Damn," I said, falling off to sleep, "we're cluttering the heavens."

Next morning, before my departure, James presented me with a collection of Irish coins depicting farmyard animals—the "old money," quickly fading out of circulation. He spread the silver and copper across the table, and explained: "Of old, not many rural folk could add or subtract, let alone read or write, so the familiar symbols were helpful in monetary exchange."

I ran my nose over the enchanting display.

"The farthing, you see, has the imprint of a snipe." James said, as he picked each coin up in turn. "The halfpenny has the pig; the penny, the hen; the threepence, the hare; the sixpence, the greyhound; there's the bull on the shilling; the salmon on the two-shilling piece; and the horse stands proudly on the half-crown. Each coin has the harp, Ireland's national symbol, on the reverse side."

I turned over each coin in my palm with fascination, finding them as evocative as my precious stamps.

"I remember going into Tralee as a boy and overhearing the shopkeepers asking the old fellas—many without a day of schooling—for two horses, a greyhound, and hare from their purse" continued James. Today you will still see some old-timers sporting a pen in their coat's breast pocket. They may never need the pen, but are simply proud to know how to use it. In their day it set them apart."

I collected the coins with heartfelt thanks, surprised him with a Kennedy half-dollar, and bid the generous Baileys a fond farewell.

Up the Conor Pass

After an uneventful day of up-and-down progress, we arrived that evening at the small village of Cloghane, aptly meaning "stepping-stones" in Irish, the base camp for our ascent up Slievenea.

Settling Missie into a large mountain field of sheep, I made my way through the village, which crouched beneath the black jagged steeps of Mount Brandon, and entered a pub of red sandstone called Peig O'Neill's.

Inside this public house, a few old fellas invited me to play darts on an old pig-bristle board. But Peig, a single woman in her forties, wouldn't hear of it until I had eaten. Hesitantly she asked, "After your meal, would you mind terribly stepping upstairs and visiting my mother? She's been bedridden for years, but has followed your travels in the *Irish Press*."

I was presently sitting beside Anne O'Neill, eighty, propped up comfortably in her bed.

"'Tis a famous traveler you are," she said, her pale hand holding my own. "When I saw you on the telly, setting off, I told Peig you were a grand, trusting man, to have no fear in walking a strange land. You must have great faith in the Lord to set off on such a journey."

"People have been very kind," I answered.

"And they'll continue to be so, praise God."

Exhausted by my hill-and-dale travels, I soon left Peig's and met her neighbor, Tom O'Connor, who offered me a shed for the night. Before retiring, however, I was invited into the house, where Tom's six young children—Niall, Aine, Ciara, Malachy, Macrina, and Dervla—laughed as I told them "funnies."

"Now I'll tell you a funny," said little Malachy, as his mother readied him for bed. "Ye won't be sleeping alone in our shed tonight, for ye'll be sharing it with me new brood of ducklings!"

" 'Make way for ducklings!' " I squealed, chasing the scampering boy up the stairs.

And ducklings there were: six of them, curled up in a small pen beside their mother, chirping throughout the long night. A brabbling flock of daffy bedmates that left me wishing for a shooting-gallery shotgun to ping them off one by one.

Taking Ned Kelliher's suggestion to give Missie the day off prior to our climb, I set out the following morning on a five-mile walk to Brandon Point, where I sat on a bollard and enjoyed the magnificent sweep of cliff, sea, and sky, as hardy fishermen were unloading their day's catch. A sudden downpour forced me, not unwillingly, into Nora Murphy's Pub, where I was joined by the fishermen who took pleasure in warming their hands around hot glasses of whiskey.

I was informed of the going rate for salmon, and one fisherman off Loop Head had caught 227 salmon in a single day, and sold them for some three thousand pounds, a big winner in the lottery of the sea. But overall, the salmon season was going poorly, and stocks might soon be depleted altogether, what with foreign trawlers fishing the ocean waters with monofilament nets fathoms deep and miles across, to capture every sea-living thing.

Returning to O'Neill's on this Wednesday night before my ascent, I felt like I was walking into my own wake, each patron in attendance with his own autopsy on my fate. The place was buzzing over my proposed climb up Conor Pass, with the locals in wide disagreement whether a donkey, hitched to a mudbox cart, could accomplish such a feat.

"Oh, no, another Rattigan's flashback," I whispered, ordering a pint and sitting in a dark corner.

"I can't see for the life of me how an ass and cart can cross Conor," preached one fellow. "There are motorcars in this village that have blown their gaskets before the summit."

The local weather expert, who had earned his meteorological degree by counting his father's sheep as a boy on Stradbally Mountain, stepped outside to study the hills in the fading light, and returned to his stool, opining, "Tomorrow's weather will be no bother to him, for he'll be in and out of a good day."

I sat in my corner munching nervously on a bag of Pete's Peanuts, keeping quiet but trying to follow the weatherman's oracle and the arguments over our chances. Their speculations were surprisingly ominous. Conor Pass rises only 1,354 feet, hardly comparing to the majestic peaks of McKinley or Everest. But to hear these old fellas, you'd think I'd have to set up various base camps and employ Sherpas along the way.

"I passed the Donkeyman outside Kilcummin," remarked a smart aleck, gesturing in my direction, "and the only thing I see in his favor is that his ass is stuck in low gear."

"For the love of God," exclaimed another, "what brought us into Dingle years ago? 'Twas the donkey!"

"Yes, but that was the old road, mind you," piped another. "The old road before traffic. What will keep your man from a collision when crawling around those three blind corkscrew loops at the summit?"

Too anxious to hear any more prognostications, I downed my pint and said goodnight, receiving a surprising score of blessings and handshakes in return. I was soon bundled up in Tom O'Connor's shed, trying to allay my fears for tomorrow's climb, offering grains of comfort to silence my bedfellows, little Malachy's noisy ducklings.

Next morning, after feeding Missie a double fistful of oats, we set off for Conor, traveling three miles of rocky terrain toward the stony slopes of Slievenea. The sun was moving in and out of the clouds as we came to the foot of the pass, where we were greeted by a large yellow sign with black lettering: ROAD UNSAFE FOR HORSE-DRAWN CARAVANS.

"Pity, that," I said to Missie, reaching into my burlap bag for another fistful of oats, "but you happen to be a donkey, and this is no caravan."

The narrow winding pathway was easy enough for the first mile, but offered little relief as we trudged onward and, discouragingly, upward. Black-faced mountain sheep, with red-and-blue–painted rumps, began to follow us like a Sunday gallery at the Irish Open, as we stopped, not to address our golf shots, but to take long breathers.

The world around us was a scattering of black rock dabbed with white lichen, as though a party of madmen from "the Well of the Lunatics" had scurried over this mountainside with brushes and an endless supply of paint. Onward we climbed; at each stop, further above the dotted lakes of the Cloghane Valley, with a lovely view of brume-capped Brandon, and the Magharee Islands, known as "the Seven Hogs," stretching sandy fingers across the sparkling bay toward Kerry Head.

We continued to ascend higher, step by step, cobblestone by cobblestone, and came gasping to a small lay-by beneath a natural amphitheater. After I removed Missie's cart for a well-deserved rest, I sat on a rock and looked disconsolately upward. A motorcar honked and sputtered by, its gearbox whining in low gear.

I had been told at Peig O'Neill's about three severe turns at the summit that would each leave us blind to traffic for thirty seconds. Thirty seconds left out to dry. Thirty seconds to test the presence of our guardian angels. Thirty seconds to watch a carousel of slides flash my life by: breech birth to rear-ended death.

Without the apprehension of foresight, Missie was itching to get on with it. In fact, she seemed to be wired. Her nostrils flared like an enraged bull. Too many oats? A donkey stuck in overdrive? Equine tachycardia? Would the strain blow out her heart? How does one take the pulse of a donkey?

With Missie the Amphetamine Queen back in harness, we went scraping toward the first of these corkscrew bends, on a gradient so severe her head dipped between her forelegs and her nose skinned the road. Taking strength from panic, I heaved to at the tailboard to help propel her along. The dough-faced bakerwoman had been right: Conor *is* Calvary!

I had kept track of passing traffic, and calculated odds, one slow step after another. They were not good—we were seriously overdue to meet with hurtling tons of metal.

We disappeared into the second round of blindman's bluff, panting and pop-eyed, knowing it could well be bye-bye. Vivid visions of collision danced in my head, and I wondered whether the coroner's inquest would hint of suicide or just plain stupidity.

The third and last loop of this turret staircase twirled higher than the tipsy tip of a soft-serve ice-cream cone. In the gathering gloom of impending doom, the only light was the gleam off a scytheman's blade. We grunted and groaned, until I began singing like a lunatic at the Rapture:

> "Up, up, up she rises!
> Up, up, up she rises!
> Up, up, up she rises,
> Early in the morning!"

But then, unexpectedly, we caught sight of the scenic overlook at the summit. I madly shouldered the tailboard, as Missie heaved and bawled, and, with one last surge of exertion, we went gasping headlong into the car park's safety.

Still gasping, we stood above it all—on the very spine of the Slieve Mish range— gazing south at the Garfinny Valley, and beyond that to the fertile, patchwork fields around Dingle. Further out, we could see the splashing waters of St. Finan's Bay and on the horizon, the Skellig Rocks, blue citadels in the sea's distant offing.

"I tell you, Missie Mickdermot," I said, both of us catching our breath, "this must be our next 'drovers' station' after the Cliffs of Moher. Look, Miss"—I embraced her sweaty head and turned it with mine—"three hundred sixty degrees, and not a blemish to the eye. God's magnificence, surely!"

Overjoyed with our accomplishment, I threatened to squeeze the life out of my beguiling beast.

"Oh, Missie," I said, "if only you could learn to walk on your hind legs. Why, I'd buy you a bright, summery dress and take you dancing this very night!"

Then, being slaphappy-stupid, I kissed Missie square on the snout. And, at the exact moment of my *attouchement*, I heard the *beep-beep* of a motorcar speeding like the devil himself for the town of Dingle.

Celtic Starlight

CHAPTER TWENTY-ONE

I was sorely mistaken to think our travails were over when we reached the summit at Conor Pass, for I quickly learned Missie hated descending great heights more than ascending them.

I tightened her breeching to the last link but it made little difference. The poor beast had to pussyfoot down the steep slope with her rump higher than a giraffe's ass, while I strained to hold back the cart, for fear it would topple over her and away we'd go, ass over wagon, in a somersaulting spin.

Our descent was agonizingly slow, but it gave me time to study the grid of ancient farmsteads that etched the Garfinny Valley below. I could see the remains of beehive huts used as booleys by herdsmen who had taken their kine to summer pasturage there for a thousand years. Dingle, in the sweeping distance, looked the proper postcard amidst its pasture-crowned hills and natural harbor, with brightly painted trawlers bobbing in the azure waters.

The lingering solstice twilight was all but extinguished when we reached the outskirts of Dingle, and after receiving permission from a sleepyheaded farmer to camp in his field, I settled Missie and hurriedly made "last call" at O'Flaherty's Pub on the pier.

"So, you made Conor," a young man congratulated me upon my entrance, "but how will you fare with Abhainn an Ghleanna—the River in the Glen—tomorrow?"

"What's that again?" I shouted above the bedlam that always precedes the flicker of lights and the publican's insistent cry: "Time, please! Time!"

"Abhainn an Ghleanna," the young man hollered into my ear. "A stream of rushing water that crosses the road at Slea Head."

"Will that trouble us?"

"Can your donkey swim?" he laughed, and disappeared into the maddening crowd.

Well, I didn't face Abhainn an Ghleanna the next morning because I gave Missie the day off, and walked back into town. There troupes of schoolboys went about the medieval streets, yapping behind painted masks of cardboard, all in celebration of St. John's Eve, a midsummer's festival night.

"There'll be two grand bonfires tonight," shouted boys running through town. "John Street itself has a hundred and twenty tires to burn!"

Dingle was pulsing with festivity, and I stepped right in. Aswirl through the streets, I crossed the threshold of one of the harbor town's scores of pubs, and was soon in the company of many merry boyos. One told me tonight's bonfires could be seen from as far away as the Iveragh Peninsula, and another informed me the fires had less to do with St. John than the coming of summer.

"You'll notice a bit of the pagan in us yet," smiled Michael Long, a horseman from nearby Ventry. "Many of our saint days simply replaced pagan festivals of long ago. The first of February, Oimelg, for example, became the feast day of Saint Brigid. The feast of Brendan, the patron saint of the Dingle Peninsula, was once a pagan holiday honoring Lugh, the Celtic hero who defeated Balor, a one-eyed tyrant who lived on Tory Island off the coast of Donegal."

A few young lads marched into the pub playing tin whistles.

"St. John's Eve was a great thing altogether years back"—he handed the redcropped leader a few coins—"but like many traditions, they seem to be fading out with the old people. In my youth, we'd have fife-and-drum bands, song and dance around the bonfire, and delicious new potatoes. And when we'd arrive home in the wee hours, our faces were so black with soot that our own mothers were hard-pressed to know us."

" 'Summertime, and the living is easy,' as the song goes."

"Ah, yes, summertime," he said, taking a copious gulp of stout, "and from what I hear, you'll still be trooping the country at the winter solstice. Cancer to Capricorn that, me boy. Let me buy you a pint, for you have a long road yet."

Back on the streets, I had full intentions of staying through the midnight festivities, but a desperate rain began in the late afternoon. With no letup in sight, I returned to camp, where Missie was still raring to go from her recent overdose of oats. So I decided to push on and brave the elements in search of shelter for the night. I donned my raincoat and *Sinbad the Sailor* rainproof pants, and set forth over Milltown Bridge with its old waterwheel, headed for the rugged extremity of this westernmost peninsula.

Two miles along, we were called in from the downpour by a young couple, John and Áine Bradshaw, on holiday. Within thirty minutes of entering their thatched cottage in Ballymote, I had changed, showered, and been seated before a meal of lamb chops, peas, and potatoes, while the generous couple regaled me with tales of their recent five-year sojourn in the Outback of western Australia.

"I swear it was the spiders that eventually drove us home," Áine confided with a laugh, as she passed me a dish of applesauce while bouncing their year-old daughter,

Ciara, on her knee. "There was one spider, the deadly redback, that I swear was out to murder me. I'd find it lurking beneath our bed, under the toilet seat, and even in my shoes. A ghastly thing that can kill you outright."

The long evening passed before a midsummer's fire that glowed like marmalade in the grate of this holiday cottage. On my ordnance map John pointed out their hometown of Blackrock, County Louth, and welcomed me to spend another night with them there.

"Blackrock will be your last stop before you cross the border into the North," John informed me.

Next morning, I lay heavily in the bed, cowering at the thought of facing the rushing river in the Glen.

"Get up out of that and leap your next hurdle," said John, hearing me grumble beneath the covers. "How are you going to walk Ulster, tell me, if you're too yellow-bellied to ford a current of water?"

Áine joined her husband, looking down at my prone figure, and urged, "Come on, now, don't be a slugabed, you must face each day like Saint George himself, ready to slay a host of dragons."

Surrendering to the inevitable, I got up and prepared myself to move on. I told the Bradshaws I'd see them in September, with any luck, and Missie and I set out to face our next challenge.

We passed a scattering of houses near Ventry, and onward to Dunbeg, an imposing Iron Age fortress on a nearby promontory, from which Daire Domhain, "the King of the World," long ago came forth to be slain on a nearby strand.

We continued our march to Slea Head on a narrow winding shelf of road some hundred feet above the crashing Atlantic. Abruptly we came upon a swift-flowing stream that cascaded off a mountainside and bubbled across a cobbled section of road, before tumbling through an arch in the stone wall down to the sea below.

"Egads, the River in the Glen!"

Yet upon further inspection this shallow watercourse seemed to pose little more than a minor inconvenience, nothing like the roaring whitecapped rapids I had envisioned with trepidation.

"C'mon, Miss," I encouraged her, as I stepped into the ankle-depth brook.

Missie, however, jibbed and bucked before the flow, and after a good tussle, positioned herself lengthwise across this hairpin turn. Then she fell into a stupor where neither whack of stick nor promise of apple could bring her back to her marginal senses. Nope, she just stood there, cataleptic before the gurgling stream.

"It's nothing, Miss. Look," I pleaded, splashing my feet in the mountain runoff.

Motorcars traveling east and west began to gather in lengthening queues on the narrow coast road, as Missie's sidewise stance obstructed passage on the tight curve. A few drivers were benignly amused, but others leaned on horns or sang out obscenities that threatened a bloody avalanche.

Smelling the aroma of riot, I searched my fund of donkey lore and remembered Jimmy Mac telling me their vision is distorted, such that Missie would see me as twice my natural height. With such colossal stature, all eleven feet six inches, I stood before Missie brimming with potency and raised my hazel stick menacingly above her head, as if to deliver one cataclysmic blow to the center of her snout, the snout I had been kissing so recently.

But despite my threatening posture she remained frozen. Two men stepped from their car and tried to yank her across the stream—fat chance!—while others were demanding she be hurled into the sea below. But then, just as this poor Georgie Boy was ready to have his bacon fried by the dragon's fiery breath, Michael Long, the Ventry horseman, came upon the scene in a fit of merriment.

"I was thinking she'd trouble you here," he laughed, accepting the reins. He asked for four volunteers to push from the tailboard, as he began to wring Missie's ears as any true jobber would. And then, as easy as you please, he led Missie across Abhainn an Ghleanna.

Everyone had a good laugh, there was a great honking of horns, and even the Dutch couple with porcelain faces managed to crack a smile.

"The sound of the bubbling water fretted her as much as the water itself," explained Michael, handing me back the reins. "Remember, you give those ears a good twisting and she'll walk with you through the Gates of Hell."

I pulled my own ears like a dunce over my failure to learn this simple lesson. The application of a little honest pain was more effective than any amount of empty threat. I had to communicate with Missie in a language she could understand.

Just a little way down the hazard-free road, Liam and Mairin Ni Chonaill, proprietors of the Slea Head House, were out to greet us as we passed, along with a number of lodgers. Obviously it had been broadcast loud and clear there had been congestion at the watery hairpin.

"So, it was you who brought on that long procession of motorcars," Mairin smiled. "Well, you'll travel no further this night. You'll be our guest, for only God knows what obstacle awaits you at the next bend."

As Liam led Missie to shelter under the impressive foothills of Mount Eagle, Mairin invited me into their handsome old inn, overlooking the precipitous cliffs of Dunmore Head and the dramatic islands of Blasket. It may have been the most stupendous view of our travels so far.

A delicious salmon sandwich awaited me when I stepped down from my seaview bedroom, and as I caught up on my journal, an elderly German guest joined me in the sitting room and introduced himself as Heinz Helfgin, a frequent visitor to Slea Head House, who offered the tidbit that Charlotte Brontë had honeymooned there.

This engaging and still-athletic German was intrigued by my travels, taking great interest in thumbing through my maps and journal. He said it was a remarkable idea and an even better achievement, if accomplished. This was something to hear from a man who, I later learned, had circled the globe on a bicycle some years before, a thirty-month adventure, and written a book about it.

That evening I borrowed Liam's bicycle and took a rapturous ride along Dunmore Head to Kruger Kavanagh's Pub. On this winding road by the thrashing sea, I met two brothers, Thomas and Patrick Daly, outside their native home, a stone house on the very edge of Heaven.

"We've been looking out at what people call 'scenery' all our lives," said Thomas, the elder, standing in his doorway facing grassy headlands, serrated cliffs, and limitless sea. "I suppose we'd call it scenery ourselves if it wasn't just there the whole time."

Pedaling on through this fine midsummer's evening, I arrived at Kruger's Pub, perhaps the most famous public house in all Munster, owing its popularity to Kruger Kavanagh himself, now deceased but once a great reporter with a gregarious personality. He had befriended many American and British film personalities while working in Hollywood, and they would visit his pub in Dunquin and fall in love with the place. Thus *Ryan's Daughter* and other films came to be made in the vicinity.

Entering Kruger's, I was surrounded by the lyrical charm and cadence of the Irish language, as I was now officially in the Gaeltacht, one of the isolated geographical strongholds that preserves the language, tradition and culture of the Old Country.

Ordering my pint, I repeatedly heard the word *"asal"* escape the lips of chuckling men and tittering women. Presently, three young fishermen tipped my glass with a rush of Irish blessings. There was roguery in them, to be sure, but they introduced me to Sean O Ciobhain of Radio na Gaeltachta. After hearing my adventures in climbing Conor Pass, he asked if I would be willing to be interviewed for Irish-speaking radio.

Readily accepting his offer, I joined him in a quiet room where he set a tape recorder in motion. Fueled by his apparent enthusiasm, as well as another pint, I rattled on about my travels with Missie, and my hopes of being back to Grannie Kelly's for Christmas.

"You'll be heard on our airwaves tomorrow at noon, and I'll give an update on your travels every day thereafter, provided I know your whereabouts," said Sean, seemingly pleased with the interview. "I'll also have you know that you'll be the first English speaker ever aired on Radio na Gaeltachta. There's a strict rule against broadcasting any language but our own, yet your donkey travels get at the heart of the Irish tradition. We won't let a different tongue interfere with airing such a wonderful journey."

Prouder than a preening peacock, I mounted my bicycle and flirted with absolute death as I raced along the winding coast road back to the Slea Head House. The singsongy language of the Irish speakers rang in my head as I leaned into every sharp turn along this outermost road of the western world.

What a friendly homespun crowd, what grand open faces, I toasted them all in my own mind. *How they listen so attentively, irrespective of one's station in life. Where else would you find a doctor having an informative exchange with a poor farmer, or a learned schoolmaster sharing ideas with a toothless old biddy?*

And to think our travels will be aired throughout this Irish-speaking kingdom tomorrow. I stood into the wind as I sped along. *Sweet Mother of Jaysus, a shimmering son of Eireann, I am!*

The following morning, after a breakfast of porridge and cream, I walked down to Dunquin Pier and boarded a boat with seven others, headed for the Great Blasket.

The friendly fisherman, Thomas Aherne, charging only a quid apiece, acted as our tour guide as he directed his boat through the splashing, blue-sparkling waves of Blasket Sound.

"The Great Blasket, known as the next parish to America, has been deserted since 1953," he began, "but a few fishermen still stay here during the lobster season. The island is four miles long and a half-mile wide, and supported an Irish-speaking community for centuries, raising crops of oats and potatoes. Unlike the Aran Islands to our north, the Great Blasket had plenty of turf and adequate grazing for sheep and the odd cow.

"Charles Lindbergh flew his *Spirit of St. Louis* over the island during his famous Atlantic crossing, and the noise from his aeroplane scattered the asses for days. The writers John Synge and Robin Flower both collected stories here, for the oral tradition in Munster was the strongest in Europe, but stronger still on the Great Blasket where, in their isolation, the islanders continued to recite tales and legends that were older than Beowolf himself.

"In fact," he went on, while keeping a keen eye at the helm, "before Columbus set sail for the New World, the Great Blasket was the last outpost of the known world, and the ancient mapmakers would fill the oceans beyond the Blasket with long-necked serpents and spouting whales."

When we landed on the sandy beach known as White Strand, the other passengers trooped toward the deserted village as I hightailed it up the jackknife pass to the Mountain of the Fort, on the humped back of the island. Huffing and puffing, I fell into the tufted grass at the crown's summit, gazing skyward at the larks flitting in song, with magical wands of bog-cotton waving their tiny flags around me.

"This is certainly paradise," I thought, sitting up to look out at the vast panorama: the escarpment of Sybil Head, the sweeping hillslopes of the Three Sisters, the rugged seastacks and pinnacles of Inishtooskert and Beiginis, Mount Brandon in its kerchief of cloud to the west and, across the narrow waterway, the sunlit slope of Mount Eagle where my dear and precious donkey grazed. I vowed to understand her better in the future, and to hurt her only when it would help.

I continued to roll in the soft grass, feeling like the King of the Island, newly crowned, but quickly righted myself when a young couple appeared over the hillcrest, scattering a warren of rabbits before them. Leaving this couple in loving peace, I went north toward the Sorrowful Slope where, in the churning water pools below, sixteen local fishermen had once perished when a sudden storm arose.

Following a sheep-path which led to a deserted village of whitewashed cabins built in long rows, I arrived at the renowned Peig Sayers's cabin, a woman storyteller whose collected prayers, folktales, songs, and riddles fill many a book. A plaque nearby lamented the passing of the people and the vanishing of an age.

Sitting on her former threshold, as content as a sailor-son home from the Seven Seas, I opened Peig's book, *An Old Woman's Reflections,* purchased in Tralee, and began to read. One passage leapt out: "God gave us all we have and ordered us to help the wanderer." No wonder I liked Peig, I thought, flipping through the pages. If she were alive today I'd be sitting in the comfort of this cabin, hearing her pour out the wisdom of a world now gone.

I walked this desolate village, pretending to be a bold island child, and after peering through a few windows, dashed back to Peig's cabin, and rapidly thumped on her door, shouting, "Pegeen, yer *ould asal* is loose in the garden!" Out she'd bolt, I imagined, squinting into the bright sunshine and shouting, "Morning agony on ye, ye little bag of mischief. The bonham's baptism on ye!"

Sitting back down after my village ramble, I turned to the end of her book where she says, "My spell on this little bench is nearly finished. It's sad and low and lonely I am to be parting with it. Long as the day is, night comes, and alas, the night is coming for me, too. I am parting with you, beautiful little place, sun of my life."

She concludes, "I think everything is folly except for loving God."

On my return to the mainland, as I climbed up the stone jetty of Dunquin Pier, I was greeted by Eileen O'Kane, a widow I had met last evening, whose fisherman husband drowned in these waters a year ago.

"I hope you enjoyed your solitude, since you'll have little now," she smiled bravely, holding her young daughter Nel. "The whole of Dingle and Iveragh listened to you on the wireless at noontime."

"How did I sound?" I asked, taking Nel in my arms.

"Like a proper Yank," Eileen laughed.

When I reached Slea Head House I intended to pack up and move along, but Mairin wouldn't hear of it.

"Setting off at seven in the evening, after running the Great Blasket like a hare," she scolded, as she sat me before a plate of chicken, brown bread, and tomatoes. "Eat up, now, for there's a lively *seisiun* at Kruger's tonight."

Kruger's was brimming with accordions, flutes, and fiddles this night, as the dance floor shook with the stamping of hornpipes, jigs, and Kerry sets.

There I met Ger O Ciobhain, a fellow adventurer who with a friend had taken a native *curragh*—a wicker boat of tarred canvas—and circled the country a few years before, rowing two thousand miles of Irish coastline in six weeks and four days.

"Your *curragh* is seven times quicker than my donkey," I toasted him.

"Wait till you hit the topmost corners of Ireland, northeast Antrim and northwest Donegal," Ger replied in pure delight. "The gales are so strong they'll carry you into the next week!"

It was one in the morning with a lip of light on the western rim of the world, when I finally left Kruger's and prudently began to walk Liam's borrowed bicycle home in a blissful backwash of goodwill. In the shadows of a field, beyond a gate, I heard the low crying of a cow to calf or a ewe to lamb—I couldn't tell which—but it sounded like distress.

In a rush of benevolence, thinking to set things aright, I put down the bicycle and hopped the gate, and to my startlement and hers, I almost fell upon an old woman lying face-up on a blanket in the grass. She bolted upright and asked my business in Irish, and in English I told her I was sorry, and that I thought I was coming to the aid of a laboring animal.

This was her field and she assured me her animals were looked after. I apologized again, and was about to jump back over the gate, when she addressed me in English, "Are you the lad with the *asaleen* staying over beyont at the inn? And didn't I hear you speak on Radio na Gaeltachta this noontime?"

"I am, and you did," I answered, relieved at the recognition. "But are you all right?"

"There's nothing wrong with me, *agra*, just an old woman saying her beads on a night when you can touch the stars above."

"It's some night, all right." I bent back and gazed skyward. "I've never seen the Milky Way so thick with stars."

"The White Cow's Road, that is," she said, pointing to the infinite band of silvery stars. "When we were children on bright clear nights such as this, my father would come in from the milking and say, ' 'Tis a beautiful night to spend in the heavens,' and we'd let out this great roar, my sisters and I, and we'd hurry down with the blankets while Mama would butter the scones and fill the billycan with tea. And up this field we'd go, further than these old legs can carry me now, above the mist of the sea to where the stars shone in all their brilliance."

"A right choice for a late-night picnic," I agreed.

"None better. And after the scones and tea, we'd all lie back on the blanket 'like sardines in a tin,' my mother would say, heads to tails, as my father recited the Rosary using the Plough and stars for the beads as I'm doing this night. He coined such grand names for these constellations: 'Mary's Cape,' there now above the horizon; 'The Monk's Vineyard,' glimmering north of Dunmore Head. And each time we'd spot a flying star, Mama would say it was a guardian angel off on the wing to a newborn child in Dingle, Tralee, or Ballybunion.

"One night, in 1910 or '11 it was, a grand spectacle began in the sky. 'Twas Halley's comet, I learned from Meg thereafter, but Father said it was a flight of angels: 'God's army to save this world.' And we watched their flight, night after night, moving ever so slowly across the sky.

" 'If a flight of angels is so badly needed,' whined Brigid, the youngest, 'why are they moving so slowly?'

" 'But they're moving as swift as swallows,' explained Father. 'It is only because they are so distant that they appear not to be moving a'tall.'

"And kissing us all in the high sedge grass, and carrying young Brigid upon his back, he would gather us up and walk our fields for home."

"It sounds like a magical childhood," I declared as I helped the elderly woman up, her natural piety like a sobering elixir to my already intoxicated spirit.

"Magical, yes, but not without hardship. 'Twas faith that kept us going. *Slan abhaile agus oiche mhaith, agra,*" she said, cupping my two hands. " 'Good night and safe journey, my dear.' "

It was a very good night, indeed, and I mounted my bike for a slow and wobbly ride back to Slea Head, with my head raised to the firmament, mumbling a starry Rosary of my own.

A Souper's Kitchen

CHAPTER TWENTY-TWO

A ringing cheer arose from the guests of Slea Head House as Missie and I set off for the northern hinterland of the Dingle Peninsula.

"God made oceans of time," shouted Liam, "so do visit again when your donkey-trekking is through."

We pushed on toward Dunmore Head where Eileen O' Kane and Nel were waiting for us on a grassy embankment.

"We'll be listening for you on the wireless," said Eileen, lifting little Nel, who decorated Missie's bridle with wildflowers. "And we'll be praying you make it home to your grandmother's for Christmas."

Nel presented me a bag of Cadbury bars as Missie and I set off again on the narrow roads. The sea was a trusty companion, but I was touched with the melancholy of brave, sweet Eileen's lot, to be ever by the churning Atlantic that had swept her husband away.

"Wouldn't she enjoy a day to sit among the midland vales," I said to Missie. "I wonder if she relives her husband's drowning each night in the barking of the Inishvickillane seals, or when the setting sun slinks below the waves of Inishtooskert?"

After a rugged climb out of Dunquin, we were rewarded with a sweeping view of Clogher, Sybil, and Ballydavid Heads—the Three Sisters—as well as the lowland village of Ballyferriter, and the dazzling sparkle of Smerwick Harbor in the pale-blue distance.

When we reached Ballyferriter, we were encircled by a swarm of children rattling on excitedly in Irish, staring at me wide-eyed as if I were John the Baptist.

"*Dia dhaoibh,*" I greeted them in Irish. "God be with you."

"*Dia agus Muire Dhuit,*" they answered, "God and Mary be with you," elbowing each other in amusement at my accent. They accompanied us beyond the village, making me feel like the Pied Piper amidst their happy entourage.

Missie and I bid them farewell and moved onward, as storm clouds enveloped the heights of Mount Brandon.

"We're going to be piddled upon, my Missie."

No sooner than spoken, the skies cracked with thunder, followed by rain-sheets that sent us scurrying for the hedges.

A passing motorist stopped: "I live just down the road. Make your way out of this drenching and you're welcome for the night. My name is T.P. O'Connor.

"Dear Lady Luck," I hallelujahed, as we battled through the driving rain.

After an evening of comfort with T.P., a local politician, and his young family, I was taken by him the following morning to Gallarus Oratory, one of Ireland's most beloved Celtic monuments, more than a thousand years old. We entered this small stone chapel shaped like an overturned boat, and found the ceiling intact and the floor dry despite the recent Irish monsoons.

"Anchorites lived on Smerwick Harbor before the scourge of raiding Vikings," explained T.P., standing in the dark chapel lit only by a small round window in the east gable. "These holy men followed the practice of the Desert Fathers, to pray and contemplate in solitude. In fact, many of the islands along our western seaboard have isolated chapels dating back to the fifth century, founded by such Irish monks as Saints Enda, Senan, and Malachy. Indeed, Saint Ciaran is believed to have celebrated Mass on Cape Clear Island in 352 A.D., a century before Patrick.

"Think of the peacefulness back then," this parish publicist went on, stepping out into the brightness to face the fine view of the harbor dotted with small fishing vessels. "Nothing to distract one's Office but the beauty of God's handiwork.

"And, speaking of handiwork, look at this drystone corbeling," he added, running his hand along the smooth sloping walls of the chapel. "No mortar, just an uncanny knack for choosing and fitting the right stones. Stones that would eventually withstand centuries of North Atlantic gales."

Light showers fell as Missie and I made our way for Tom Leahy's in Cuas that afternoon, referred by T.P. Spotting the high mast of Radio na Gaeltachta outside Ballydavid, I first stopped in to pay my friendly interviewer Sean O Ciobhain a visit. The entire staff stepped outdoors to see me off again, and one stuck a radio bumper sticker onto my cart's tailboard: Corca Dhuibhne 362m 828khz.

"You'll be within our range until you're beyond the Iveragh Peninsula," said Sean, "and we're asking our listeners to contact us when you pass their homes. When you get to Donegal and Connemara, two other Gaeltacht areas, you should stop into their radio stations and they'll do the same. It will be great crack for our listeners to keep tabs on your journey."

When we arrived at Tom Leahy's two-story house at the western base of Mount Brandon, out stepped a tall angular man chiseled by the elements. I told him T.P. O'Connor had sent me, in hopes of a night's shelter for man and beast.

"Well, isn't my house becoming a haven to wayfarers traveling the world in queer ways," he grinned. "First, a fellow named Tim Severin wishing to cross the Atlantic in a *curragh,* and now yourself, circling the country with an ass."

"Tim Severin! Yes, I've heard of him and his famous Brendan voyage!"

"Aye. And it was just below at Brandon Creek where he set sail, to prove to the world our patron saint, Saint Brendan the Navigator, could well have reached North America in the sixth century."

Tom's two grown sons, Tom Junior and John, joined their dad at the door, and within minutes I was sitting before a steaming meal of pollack, peas, and potatoes. After the kitchen cleanup, Tom's sons invited me to their local pub, the Breatnac, a two-mile walk from their home.

I presently found myself walking between these two strapping young men who seemed untouched by any culture but their own.

"It must be grand for you to go walking the world," said Tom, the elder. "There won't be a thing you won't know about our country when you complete the circle."

"Oh, there's a lot I won't know. I should be spending a year in each province, not just passing through."

"Do you find the people in the Gaeltacht as friendly as others?" John made the familiar query. "I've heard we are a bit clannish."

"I've never met people more kind or helpful."

"You would enjoy the pattern of Saint Brendan in June," said Thomas, pointing his walking stick toward the high mountain of Brandon. "We take the Saint's Road to both Mastiompan and Brandon, and the views could fill your camera with pictures of Heaven itself. Then, to Nora Murphy's Pub after the pilgrimage, and home again, exhausted."

"Nine-tenths of the world would love to live their lives here beneath these mountains." I carried on over the beauty and serenity of landscape.

"Aye, and not a tenth of those would stick out a winter, what with the seabirds breaking their wings against the gales," laughed John. "Tonight you're seeing our parish dressed in summer glory."

Entering the Breatnac, I was introduced to a crowd of well-wishers, all Irish speakers, as dancers went twirling across the floor like whirligig beetles. The publican, Mr. Walch, served up pints of stout in heavy ornate glasses, of the sort I had only seen as retired bar relics in the midlands, but standard issue here.

"The old Imperial twenty-ounce pint," Mr. Welch took note of my interest. " 'The glass with the chapel windows.' "

"How old are they?" I asked, studying the heavy goblet.

"Fifty years and then some," he answered.

"Aren't you afraid they'll walk off in somebody's pocket?"

"If they do, they might eventually find their way back home," he confided, washing them carefully in a soapy basin.

I made acquaintance with an older man lamenting the recent loss of his son to emigration.

"He's working now in London, a good lad," the man sighed, "but how I miss him, now that he's gone. I'd give the world to see him walk up the road with his suitcase in hand. Well, God bless," he said abruptly, finishing his pint and not wishing to share his sadness any longer, "and may I see you again, in the land of roses and the valley of the moon."

Next day, old Tom took me to Brandon Creek where Tim Severin had set off on his historic voyage for America in a boat covered with ox-hide.

"Saint Brendan was foremost a holy man," explained Tom, "but also a sailor. He founded parishes up and down the coast, and even sailed to Iona to visit Columcille. His manuscript, the *Navigatio,* tells of his voyage to the Americas, but it may be apocryphal. Brendan writes of sea monsters with fiery eyes and mooring his *curragh* on the back of a whale, which scholars find dubious. But he also spoke of floating pillars of crystal which could be icebergs off Greenland, burning rocks that could be Icelandic volcanoes, and an island teeming with sheep, much like the Faroes.

"So, when Tim Severin sailed his replica of the saint's leather craft safely to North America, he showed that Brendan may well have discovered the New World nearly a thousand years before Columbus, and long before the Vikings."

"And it all began here?" I asked, looking down into the watery chasm.

"Right here. There was a great launching, with the Bishop of Galway and a crowd of dignitaries in attendance, and I, rowing alongside *The Brendan* until it was safely out to sea. My little bit of celebrity, I suppose." He looked out at the sea with a shrug. "A drop of history, boy, much like your own."

Back at the house, young Tom was preparing a fine breakfast as old Tom took *The Brendan Voyage* from the small bookshelf and diffidently read aloud:

> " 'It was Tom's curragh that I had first seen at Brandon Creek so many months ago when I originally visited the area, and I remembered that Tom was the last man regularly working a curragh out of Brandon Creek. Somehow I thought it fitting that the last descendant of a tradition that stretched back for a millennium should see us on our way.' "

"Your sons must be very proud of you," I said, as old Tom closed the book.

"We'd be proud of him whether or not he was ever mentioned in a book," young Tom affirmed devotedly, motioning us both to the breakfast.

Missie and I continued our tramping beneath a hazy sky, looping back to Dingle to meet the long easterly road to Castlemaine, where we'd turn south and west for the Iveragh Peninsula.

In Dingle, I called into John Paul McDonnell's prosperous farm, and got permission in passing from his son, John, to spend the night. As he was hurrying out the door, he told me to settle Missie in the fields and meet him shortly at O'Flaherty's Pub.

Securing Missie in a spacious field overlooking the harbor, I went along to O'Flaherty's and met John there, complimenting him on the beauty of the farm's enclosed cobblestone.

"'Tis fine, indeed, but has seen some ugly history. Not long after being built, it served as 'a souper's kitchen' during the Great Famine of the 1840s."

"A souper's kitchen?"

"Yes, where a starving person could earn a bowl of soup by renouncing his faith."

"You mean, there was a Protestant landlord using hunger to convert the Catholic poor?"

"Precisely. And the hunger was mighty persuasive, with over a million dying of it. Another million emigrated, so we lost a quarter of our population. But not too many traded their souls for a bowl of soup."

A little later I met a couple from Ottawa, who agreed to take some letters back to Canada to mail for me, as the Irish postal strike dragged on. So I spent much of the night writing home, to Belita and my parents, to reassure them their Irish rover was well on the road.

When I returned to the McDonnells', John having gone off with friends, there wasn't a sign of life in the house, so I made a makeshift bunk out of a clean feeding trough in the barn, using fresh straw for bedding and my bag of oats for a pillow, making a nice big Shaker cradle for myself.

I awoke next morning to the clack of hooves in the cobbled yard. Looking up from my crib, I saw a long line of Frisian cattle moving toward the hum of a milk parlor, with sheepdogs snarling and snapping to keep them in line.

The dogs seemed more vicious than usual, and put me in mind of soldiers herding starving peasants. I faded back into an all-too-vivid dream of famine times. I saw landlords and agents heckling and harassing sallow-cheeked villagers, trembling and fainting on line, caught between body and soul like the rock and the hard place.

I floated up high above the cobblestone confines of the yard, saw the faithful scratching for snails by the bay, heard the dry heaves of purple-lipped children burning with typhus, saw old people dropping among the gorse and heather of these famished hills. Further up still, I saw the sea, where grain-laden ships headed for England and coffin ships headed for America packed with emigrants. It was a vision I didn't want to have, and I thrashed in my cradle to fend it off.

"Couldn't my son do any better than this?" I heard a friendly voice pulling me out of my restless rest.

I bolted upright to see Mr. McDonnell standing above me. "The house was dark." I flailed at an explanation.

"You set up this trough nicely." He beamed upon my rustic bedding. "Come in, now, for the breakfast, and my apologies for such accommodation."

I stepped out into the dizzying sunshine and watched a farmhand hose away cow dung and urine from the now-empty cobbled yard.

"A fine morning," I greeted the farmhand, gathering my dazed thoughts.

" 'Tis a lovely morning, thank God," he answered, wiping his brow before returning to the task at hand.

A Night with the Travelers

CHAPTER TWENTY-THREE

Throughout this Kingdom of Kerry, Missie and I would often pass the encampments of the travelers, or "tinkers" as they are slightingly called. Dirty-faced children, accompanied by lean and hungry greyhounds, would gather at the outer boundary of their camps and ask for sweets or coppers as we passed.

These campsites, located in rest areas or lay-bys just outside the towns—with a NO OVERNIGHT PARKING sign defiantly strung with clothesline—are scattered with motor-driven vehicles, horse-drawn caravans, and ash-wattle tents covered with heavy plastic or canvas.

The women would eye me with suspicion as I passed, wondering what brand of gypsy I was—or was I a proper traveler at all? The men, meanwhile, lounging around a central fire in the early evenings, made gruff comments in their own Shelta, a secret jargon based on inverted Gaelic. They would break into English, shouting, "Do you want to buy a billy goat to color your morning tea?" and other scurrilous tidbits better forgotten than repeated.

It is believed the travelers were an early Celtic population who mended weapons for lords and warriors. They were uprooted and scattered throughout Ireland during the Plantation, the campaign of Protestant settlements initiated by King James I of England, and began to ramble about the country after the Catholic defeat at the Battle of the Boyne in 1690, and proliferated again during the Potato Famine.

Besides mending of weapons in olden times, the Irish travelers were also reputed adept at making counterfeit coins. Today they deal primarily in country antiques, scrap metal, and, of course, horses, ponies, and carts.

Next to the northern Troubles, the travelers were the most worrisome topic discussed at the various kitchen tables of Clare and Kerry.

In my journey thus far, I had had mixed dealings with these self-proclaimed "knights of the road." One evening, not long out of Galway, I met two travelers pulverized with drink, who insisted on buying Missie and wouldn't take no for an answer. A fight might have ensued, with myself in danger of a good shellacking, if not for a third traveler who intervened on my behalf.

Another time on the Dingle Peninsula, while I was sampling a generous lady's plate of Queen Anne cakes as she proudly exhibited her fine collection of tea cozies—a hungry man will sit through anything—a tinker's van stopped before the house. Through the window I witnessed the driver hastily removing the canvas from the top of my cart. I jumped from the couch and bolted outdoors, shouting out his license plate number, whereupon he dropped my heavy canvas and was gone.

I also heard endless gossip about the way travelers treat their horses and ponies.

"I see you have a lazy ass," said a farmer to me. "You should hand her over to the tinkers. In a day's time they'll put such a fear of the ash plant into her that all you'll need do is raise it above your ear, and off she'll fly."

In Clare, I heard a story that seemed to sum up their station in society, about a bold schoolboy who received a wicked caning from the headmaster. After a dozen swats to both hands, the master said, "You're a lazy good-for-nothing jackass!" The brazen schoolboy replied, "And you, sir, are no better than the tinker who beats 'em."

So the travelers were painted up to be a bad sort, but I had had a number of pleasant encounters with them. First off, there was Martin and Brigid Maugham of Roscommon, the best and most helpful of people, who'd set me up with my wattle tent. Then there was the traveler in Galway who'd stepped out of his van and presented me with the "honey spike" and length of rope, to tie Missie securely when she grazed overnight in an open field.

When I passed the travelers' untidy dwellings, I would glance admiringly at their crackling fires and the camaraderie of their lively chat; their few prized ponies tethered nearby, the children running barefoot about the place, the adolescent boys and girls dallying in the shadows, the aged men and women with faces mapped like the rocky old landscape.

I wished to spend one night within the inner ring around that enduring fire, and hear firsthand the collected wisdom of the road. Who knew more about Irish highways and byways than themselves, roaming these roads for hundreds of years before me?

Of course, when I brought up this romantic notion to farmers, many would gasp in horror. "I'd rather court the devil himself," said one old gent. "One night with the tinkers and, by God, 'twill be your last until Judgment Day."

On the first of July, after completing our circuit around the Dingle Peninsula, we were just outside the town of Killorglin, the gateway to the Iveragh Peninsula and "the Ring of Kerry," when a traveler left his fire and stepped onto the road to greet me.

"You have a fine spark to your heel," he hailed me with a smile. "Well-suited for this journey, you are. Now, stay with us, can't you, until Puck Fair, when a crowned billy-goat oversees the festivities from Gathering Day to Scattering Day in Killorglin itself?"

"When does that happen?" I replied, intrigued by the prospects of tinker revels.

"The middle of August," the old fellow replied.

"Oh, I'm afraid not," I smiled. "It took us a fortnight just to travel the Dingle Peninsula, and I have a long road to roundabout by Christmas."

"Stay a night, so," he persisted graciously, extending his hand. "My name is Patrick O'Brien, king of the clan. I'll set your donkey grazing with our piebalds, and we'd be honored to have your company."

"King" O'Brien had such a noble way about him that he banished my apprehension and I accepted his invitation without hesitation. After Missie was free of the cart, I was introduced to the king's wife, Queenie, a pleasant woman in a red cardigan who emerged from a half-barrel caravan, as well as their son, two daughters, daughter-in-law, two son-in-law, aunt, and a crowd of children who followed me around the campsite as if I were as wondrous as a walking porpoise.

"We're direct descendants of Bryan Dillon, the first traveler in all of County Kerry," said Patrick proudly, shushing away the children as he parked my cart beside his caravan. "I'm pleased to say I have forty-five grandchildren in Kerry alone."

I was coaxed by two of the older girls, Nellie and Vera, to assist in fetching water from the nearby river, as the king's two sons-in-law, thrilled to host "the Yank" for the night, drove off in their van, vowing to return with a dozen bottles of Guinness.

"This river runs from Kate Kearney's Cottage in the Gap of Dunloe, out to the sea," said Nellie, a freckle-faced redhead of thirteen, as we made our way down the grassy embankment to the black, rushing waters. "Do you know Kate Kearney's Cottage?"

"I do not," I answered.

"'Twas an old public house without a license," Nellie smiled. "And Kate Kearney was so pretty that her patrons came from all over Ireland just to see her pour a drink into a glass. Even Queen Victoria visited her little *shebeen* when she visited Ireland."

"Now fill that kettle in your hands," said Vera, laughing at my tentative approach toward the dark riverbank.

When we returned to the campsite, I was given a seat by the fire, where I was served a mug of tea as black as bog water, and three cuts of thickly buttered bread sprinkled with sugar.

"There's nothing high or mighty about yourself," said the queen, watching me devour the sweet loaf. "Ye'll eat anything that comes your way."

"I'm very thankful for whatever I get," I answered, taking another swallow of the strong, smoky tea. "My aunt Cella in Roscommon thought I was the most finicky eater in the world. But just last night I ate ox tongue for the first time, and I even ate a duck egg the morning before that."

"Ox tongue and duck eggs are a Christmas feast," chided the daughter-in-law.

"Oh, I know that now," I admitted, somewhat abashed. "But when I first set off, I was pretty choosey. I was reminded of that a week ago when a farmer slapped my hand with his butterknife when he saw me peel open the sandwich his wife had prepared. 'Boy,' he snapped, ' "never look a gift horse in the mouth." ' Since then, I eat anything. This bread and butter is a proper treat."

My hostess accepted my thanks like the gracious lady she was.

"This fire is a luxury, too; I usually don't bother. I just crawl into my bag and sleep inside a shed or byre. Last night, I slept under a bridge near Red Cliff, feeling like the troll in 'The Three Billy Goats Gruff.' "

"There's a legend to the bridge at Red Cliff," said the king's son, pausing to accept a heavy bag of pint bottles from his brothers-in-law, and uncapping me a Guinness with a rush of blessings. " 'Donkey Bridge,' they call it, for a power of donkeys, dead and alive, comes off these mountains and gathers there on New Year's Eve. The roar of them alone would deafen the world."

"Did you find your donkey strange when you woke up this morning?" asked one of the king's daughters, an earthy woman clad in a bright dress and red kerchief.

"I find her strange every morning."

Just then, as if on cue, Missie let out a bawl from the backfield which sent the two sons-in-law toppling to the ground.

"They're dead! Yer donkey's kilt 'em!" exclaimed the daughter in glee.

"Oh, my . . . How so?"

"Did you never hear tell that a tinker dies every time a donkey brays?" asked the king. "And now you've left me two daughters widowed. That's why travelers never camp within earshot of Donkey Bridge," he chuckled, as the two in-laws resurrected themselves to uncap their pint bottles they called "sergeants."

"Donkeys are the tinkers of the animal world," said the daughter, "and you, a tinker like ourselves."

"Where do you live in the States?" asked the son.

"On the East Coast, looking back at you: Massachusetts."

"Oh, yes . . . Kennedy country. Around Boston or the Cape of Cod?"

"No, the other end of the state, the Berkshire Hills. Not close to the sea, but we do have Pontoosuc Lake, and Onota, and many others."

"Tell us about your winters," interjected a daughter. "I've heard that ice freezes so thickly over loughs that ye can drive a motorcar over them as if Jesus Himself was at the wheel?"

"Oh, that's all too true," I laughed in return.

" 'Tis a wonder," said the king in genuine awe.

More bottles were uncapped and more questions fielded, as I rattled on incessantly, answering their queries with a mixture of truth and fabrication—fueled, mind you, by the warm intoxication of stout and the fireside glow, like an intrepid explorer fallen in with a friendly circle of natives. Meanwhile, the children went skipping in and out of the firelight, and the daughters cajoled me to buy two ganders and a piebald goat so I could set off "traipsing the world with a grand assortment of God's craytures."

The travelers in turn began to divulge their tangling lore, explaining how to braid Missie's tail to foil a persistent jack in a romantic mood, and how to make a lazy ass "right lively" on Fair Day by sticking a lump of ginger under its tail, and how a few old tinkerwomen could steal the cross off an ass's back by reciting a charm while covering the donkey's back with a concoction of herbs and white ashes.

The night drifted by as the children, one by one, became sleepy in the arms of their parents. The adults grew quieter and stared thoughtfully into the flames. In the near distance I could hear the neighing of two piebald ponies and Missie's occasional blare.

"Why do travelers favor piebalds, both ponies and goats?" I asked the king.

"I suppose there's a little circus left in them, much like ourselves."

"What do you prefer to be called," I interrogated: "tinkers, travelers, knackers, or itinerants?—for I've heard you referred to as each."

"And a lot worse, I'm sure," added the son.

"We're travelers," said the king without hesitation. "If the sun is beaming above and a fresh breeze blowing, we're a hard-kept lot to be penned in a house, squinting out a window only to see our neighbors squinting back. But we do have a council house in Castleisland where we stay during the winter, for the old ways are dying out and we realize our children need their schooling."

"This doesn't seem a bad life to me."

" 'Tis the only life we know," answered the king. "Full of hardship, God knows, and bad luck betimes. But aren't you much akin to ourselves?" he brightened. "How do you find traveling the roads?"

"There's nothing like a long walk to set the mind dreaming," I offered. "But I don't think I could do it forever."

"You would if it was all you ever knew. And, believe me, when your dilly-days are through, there'll be many a night you'll be longing for the road, recalling the sight of a tree dancing before the coming rain, or the sweet scent of woodbine after a passing shower."

"Do you need help in setting up your wattles?" asked the son, cutting short the king's sentiment.

"No, thank you." I didn't want to reveal my awkwardness. "It's a warm night so I'll just sleep on top of my bag."

"You're a right traveler, you are."

As the night slipped away, the children were packed off to bed, but one young toddler kept whining and picking at his nose.

"What's on him?" the king's daughter questioned her older son.

"He put a berry up his nose earlier on," he replied, backing away.

"And you left him to it?" she shouted. "The poor child a breath from his death? Go into your grandfather's caravan and get me some snuff. Hurry!"

The boy shot off into the darkness as his mother took butter from a discarded crust of bread and greased the toddler's plugged nostril, hopping him gently on her lap. When the tin of Clarkes White Cap snuff arrived, she wet the tip of her small finger and dipped it into the stinking brown powder, as the child began to writhe and wrestle on her lap. Then, in a flash, the king's daughter slid her gun-powdered pinkie up the boy's clear nostril as he lurched and lunged and, with one violent sneeze, sent the berry ricocheting off the stones and into the fire.

"Now, hop it to bed, the two of you," she snapped, "and don't be getting into that carry-on again!"

"I went to nursing school for four years," I marveled, "and a team of Emergency Room personnel couldn't do better than your butter and snuff."

I retired well after midnight, sleeping under a canopy of smoky stars between the shafts of my heeled-up cart. I stirred during the night, at the weight of two coats being laid over me. I pulled the well-worn garments to my chin, warming to the kindness of the traveling breed.

A Rock Soars from the Sea

We'll be looking to crown your ass at next year's Puck Fair," shouted King O'Brien, when Missie and I cantered away from their encampment that morning.

"May the heavens be your final bed," added the queen. Their grandchildren, led by Nellie and Vera, chased and circled our cart well down the Glenbeigh Road.

"Thanks for all your kindness to this fellow traveler," I shouted back.

Missie and I walked pleasantly out the Iveragh Peninsula, the second finger of five in the southwest of the country, passing the lovely Vale of Glencar, and continued on the coast road which clings like a stone shelf over the sea. Above, black tunnels wove in and out of the steep northern slope of Beenmore Head: reminders of the Great Southern and Western Railway that operated during the first half of the century, taking its passengers on an exhilarating ride from Killarney to Waterville on Ballinskelligs Bay.

We rested beneath Drung Hill, where I looked across Dingle Bay at the soft blue-pillowed hills I had just traversed. I ran my eyes from the dunes of Inch Strand to the western reaches of Slea Head, recalling the kind people and memorable characters we had met during our peregrinations there. A fulfillment surely, but only part of the long road I was on.

Passing the old Glinsk Viaduct, we settled for the night with an accommodating young couple named Eugene and Marion O'Grady. After a delightful supper of spaghetti, Eugene and I led Missie to a field of high grass where I tethered her securely with reins, bridle, and honey spike.

"We'll be cutting this small field for hay in the next day or two," Eugene commented, "but a donkey traveling the globe deserves at least one night in an uncut meadow."

The following day was suffocating with early July heat, and since Missie was still shedding her winter coat, I asked if I might stay on and help with the hay.

"Why wouldn't ye?" said Eugene's father, John, a healthy man of seventy-five. "Here's a fork," handing me a two-pronged implement, "and if ye can't handle that, I'll give you a twelve-toothed rake."

Taking fork in hand, I worked the long day turning swaths of grass in a fragrant field of clover that looked over the waters at the storied hills of Corca Dhuibhne.

Marion stepped out in the late afternoon with sandwiches and flasks of tea. Gratefully accepting my share, I asked Mr. O'Grady about the lore of taking in the hay.

"Saving hay, is it? Well, one could have cut the meadows anytime during the last fortnight, if it be dry," he began, stretching himself out in comfort across the grass. "Myself, I scythe the meadow, for it keeps me young, but many farmers have great contraptions for the job and some are even into silage, which is a stinking mess entirely.

"Once you scythe or mow your fields, you leave it to dry, turn when ripened with a rake or fork, as you're doing, mighty-like," he winked over at his own, "and if the weather remains favorable, we'll make up small pikes and soon gather them into larger pikes called cocks. The eventual size of the cock depends on weather: small if wet; high if dry. In a good summer, some cocks can weigh three to four hundredweight. Cocks are then gathered into ricks, 'a farmer's loaf,' and placed in the corner of field, haggard, or haybarn and used, of course, for foddering livestock during the winter months."

The O'Grady bunch soon dozed off in their intoxicating field of birdsong and ocean breeze, as I felt the pink warmth of summer on my face and arms. Closing my eyes to this pastoral setting, I recalled childhood stories of my mother, how she would run with bottles of tea to her father and grandfather, turning windrows in the fields of Coolrua and Gannoge, musical meadows where generations of her kin had toiled beneath the foothills of Slieve Bawn.

For no apparent reason, I shot up from this reverie and looked across to where I had tied Missie in the high meadow beside the house. Unable to see her, I dashed across the field and found her lying on her side, gasping for air. Plying my hands through the tall grass, I discovered her left hind foot, which she often used to scratch her jaw, had caught itself in the neckband of her bridle. Her awkward position, as well as her helpless struggle to free the leg, was closing off her windpipe.

Not strong enough to free Missie's leg with its tensile resistance, I shouted to Eugene, who came running, and the two of us barely managed to free Missie's shoe from the neckband. She continued to lay on her side, breathing laboriously. Before I could think, Eugene delivered a smart kick to Missie's backside which brought her struggling to her feet.

"She'll breathe better standing up," Eugene explained, as Missie coughed, sputtered, and finally resumed steady breathing.

"Phew," I trembled. "That was a close call."

Mr. O'Grady arrived at the scene and removed Missie's bridle, studied her hind shoe, and asked me to fetch my rope.

"Make yourself a halter in this manner when you need to tie up your donkey to that spike," he stressed, taking the rope and cleverly looping it around Missie's head. "The back of her shoe, cut like it is, can easily catch the bridle's strap again, but there'll be no fear of that if you use this thicker rope as a halter."

"Thank you." I watched closely to learn the knack of making a halter for my highway queen.

"They say a human being never sees a dying donkey," said Eugene, "but we caught ourselves a glimpse, didn't we? Whatever made you jump up like that?"

"I don't know," I answered, still befuddled. "I looked over at her an hour before and there she stood, gawking back at me. I really don't know."

"The tolling of that beast is in your heart," remarked the father. "There's no other explanation for it. Now, let's say we clean up and go for a pint, shall we."

It was ten P.M. when we walked home from Caitin's Pub, with a huge fireball setting over Slea Head across Dingle Bay.

"A rose in red July." Mr. O'Grady squinted at the sunset across waters dabbed with scarlet.

Before retiring, I checked on my lady beast and found her facing the red sun with a fixed stare, and I laughed with relief at the thought of her near-death experience.

"I hope you weren't being drawn into some luminous gateway, Miss," I said, throwing an arm over her. "Or did I pull you back just at your glorious entrance into Donkey Heaven?"

She burrowed her warm muzzle into my chest, her first such gesture of this kind, and I believed she was thanking me.

"Think nothing of it." I playfully rubbed her snout.

She snorted then and shrugged me away. And with a contented swish of her tail she went back to feeding in this high meadow by the sea.

We left the O'Gradys' on the Fourth of July, traveling the winding coast road bounded by hedges of whitethorn and dog rose.

Missie was a pure pet, a born-again princess, perhaps still appreciative for my rescue the day before. By noontime, however, she had returned to her old pranks, stopping every twenty yards for thistles and whin blossoms, which convinced me that a donkey's gratitude doesn't last the length of a day.

Beneath the foot of Been Hill, a touring bus of Yankee Doodle Dandies stopped up the road, and out they poured for a massive photo shoot. Their cameras clicked like crickets in a midsummer meadow, as Missie and I smiled like a bride and groom on our wedding day. The tourists asked about souvenirs, but again I feigned dumbness, with some made-up sign language.

"This tinker is a dummy?" said the queen of the Q-Tips, as a mass of white-bobbed matrons clustered around.

"It's deaf and dumb," corrected her friend. "See, he's using sign language to communicate with us, poor dear."

"Sign! Why, I read sign language." Another white-top moved to the front of the pack and accosted me with a flurry of genuine hand signals.

Caught red-handed, I did what I had to before this horde of compatriot camera-snappers, and that was to clear my throat and renew a barrage of finger twists, thumb rolls, and pinkie twirls, until my ten digits were knotted in a ball.

"That's not sign language." The knowing woman eyed me suspiciously. "He's a fake."

"How can a tinker be a fake?" asked the queen bee. "He's probably communicating to us in Gaelic."

"I doubt it," my nemesis declared, before heeding the call of their impatient bus driver, who gathered his charges and roared off to who-cares-where.

We reached the market town of Cahersiveen in the early evening, walking the long main street where many traditional shopfronts, boasting the names of O'Sullivan and O'Shea, were abandoned and boarded shut.

A young man approached and introduced himself as John Mulvihill, manager of the Rod and Reel Hotel. "I received a phone call from a patron, John Collins, who spotted you in both Liscannor and Ballyheigue, and he gave me strict orders to put you up once you arrive in Cahersiveen."

Dazed by yet another stroke of fortune, I walked with John Mulvihill to a Dutch-owned hotel by the waterfront, while he raved on about my journey.

"You're a champion, boy," he kept saying with an admiring gaze. "But it broke my heart when I first heard of your travels. I asked myself over and over, why hadn't I thought of that years ago, back when I was free and unanchored?"

John corralled Missie into a large pen, and introduced me to his lovely wife, Olive. Soon I was staring hungrily at a steaming meal of steak, chips, and peas in the dining room.

"What are you waiting on? Eat up," smiled Olive. "Don't tell us you're a vegetarian, like your donkey?"

"Oh, no," I said, taking hold of knife and fork. "I just need to look at this for a moment. I get plenty of sandwiches but, hot meals . . ."

After the feast, we entered the hotel's lounge section and listened to a talented young woman play a medley of American tunes on a guitar.

"Isn't today a holiday in your country?" asked Olive.

"Yes, it's Independence Day."

"Do you have big celebrations?"

"Definitely. There's a big parade every year in my hometown, followed by a carnival and fireworks. When I was a young boy, it was my favorite holiday next to Christmas."

"Really?" said Olive. "What was it like?"

"On the morning of the Fourth, me and my brothers would dress up in cowboy out-fits, and walk downtown with a pair of cap guns slung to our hips."

"Cap guns?"

"Play guns loaded with rolls of firing caps, because all we did that morning was shoot people marching in the parade."

"Who would you shoot?" laughed Olive.

"Soldiers, firefighters, carnival queens, Indians, Boy Scouts, baton twirlers, sidewalk vendors, fat sweltering trombone players, inconspicious men collecting horse drop-pings, and little brats tossing out sweets from antique automobiles. Even pretty majorettes with their high-tasseled boots got riddled with a volley of 'gunfire.'"

"Were you and your brothers the only ones at it?" John inquired.

"Oh, no. Kids were lined up on both sides of the parade route for a mile or more, firing their guns and tossing out firecrackers at anything that moved."

"Little wonder you had no trouble in gaining your independence from England," joked John. "You're all a pack of gun-toting bandits."

"We've been saving our shillings to go to America," disclosed Olive. "But I tell you, it won't be the Fourth of July we'll be going."

"You'll stay on with us tomorrow night as well," John offered. "We've made arrange-ments for you to cross to the Skellig Rocks tomorrow morning. Nine sharp, from Reenard Pier. After all, you can't travel Ireland and miss the Great Skellig. George Bernard Shaw said you can't know Ireland 'through and through' till you stand among the monks' beehive dwellings six hundred feet above the sea."

The next morning was glorious for an ocean splash. I hurried to Reenard Pier and boarded a boat called *An Beal Bocht,* "The Poor Mouth." We crossed over to Knightstown Harbor and down Portmagee Channel, where the boatmaster Des Lavelle shouted over the din of his diesel, "There's an old sea lament, 'Any port in a storm, but please, not Portmagee.' There was absolutely nothing here years ago. Now it boasts two friendly pubs."

Among my shipmates, I made acquaintance with Robert and Carmel Mooney of Dublin, who informed me that even in summer, days go by when rough seas make landing impossible on the Great Skellig, and we were fortunate to have such a calm day.

Chugging smoothly through the open waters of St. Finan's Bay, Des, who literally wrote the book on the Skelligs, had sandwiches passed out to his dozen passengers and shared the history of this mystical isle nine miles from the Kerry mainland.

"Daire Domhain, 'the King of the World,' visited the Great Skellig Rock, or Skellig Michael, around 200 A.D.," he began, "but it was a band of monks who dedicated the island to Michael the Archangel, after witnessing an apparition hovering above the Rock's peaks.

"Despite the everyday hardships of ascetic life, the monks lived a peaceful existence until 823 A.D. when Vikings raided the island, dragging Eitgall the Abbot away in their longboat. Other monks were murdered, and those who managed to hide on the small crag eventually died of starvation, because the Norsemen sank their *curraghs* before departing.

"One can easily imagine the surprise and horror that filled the hermitage during that first raid," Des recited, his ruddy face weathered by a life at sea. "No Irish king or chieftain, despite their penchant for quarreling over gold and prized bulls, would invade a monastic settlement.

"On a later raid, just before the millennium, the Viking Olaf Trygvasson, later King of Norway, was so impressed by the monks' devout faith, he himself was baptized on the Skellig. His son, Olaf the Second, was later to become patron saint of Norway.

"We gather, through old manuscripts," Des continued, "that the hermits of Skellig Michael were the most brilliant minds of the Celtic ecclesiastics, keeping alive the knowledge of Greco-Roman culture, and carrying the light of Christ through the Dark Ages.

"In the Middle Ages, Skellig Michael was revered by the pilgrims of Europe. Special indulgences were obtained by performing the Stations of the Cross there. At the last station, the pilgrim would squeeze through a narrow opening in a chimney-shaped rock called the Needle's Eye, ten feet long and two feet wide, sliding himself precariously forward to kiss the cross inscribed at its very tip, a rock that juts out like a diving board far above the sea. Today, with these swirling winds, I suggest no one attempts this righteous but perilous feat."

No fear of that, I thought to myself.

We soon came abeam the Little Skellig, a seastack over four hundred feet high, whitewashed with guano from thousands upon thousands of gannets, nesting and spreading their six-foot wingspans into flight. Their fervid cries were frightful as they circled above our craft in smothering numbers, some plunging for food into the water's depths, like well-thrown darts.

"A quarter of a million birds—kittiwakes, razorbills, puffins, guillemots, fulmars, and, of course, gannets—make their home on the Skelligs," continued our knowledgeable skipper, steering a path that brought us closer to this cacophonous but magnificent bird sanctuary.

"It's hard to believe, looking up today, that the gannet population on Little Skellig was reduced to thirty pair a hundred years ago, so desperate were the mainland folk for food."

The Little Skellig, however spectacular, became a mere curiosity when we came to Skellig Michael. As we approached the holy rock, a fellow pilgrim handed me binoculars and directed my gaze to the beehive dwellings of the seventh-century monastery clinging six hundred feet above the ocean's surface.

We arrived at Blind Man's Cove, the principal moorage on the Rock, amidst the screams of cliff-dwelling birds. I scooted up the path ahead of the others and came to a stone cross hewn into the rock, marking the stairway up. Exhilarated by the environs of rock and sea, I dashed up hundreds of rough stone steps, on which colorful puffins, undisturbed by my rush, smartly preened themselves in the bright sunlight. At a landing, I found myself in a narrow valley called Christ's Saddle, between two great splintery pinnacles.

On my left was West Peak with its chimney rock, Needle's Eye. But it was the ancient staircase on the near pinnacle that stabbed my senses: a steep rise leading to the heavens. Heart racing but steps slowing, I cautiously climbed these dizzying stairs, passing an outcrop of stone that represented the eighth Station of the Cross, the Wailing Woman of Jerusalem. Breathless, I thought of Olaf climbing these very steps to embrace the Cross a millennium ago.

Entering a small stone gateway, I came upon level ground and into a huddled enclosure, consisting of six beehive huts and two boat-shaped oratories dating to the sixth century. Further exploration revealed stone crosses, two freshwater wells, a small garden, and the ruins of a medieval church with its east window looking down the sheer drop upon Little Skellig.

Alone in this age-old settlement, I stooped into the largest of the beehive *clochans,* and emerged from the dark wondering about the type of person who could survive the rigors of this sea-girt rock. I walked into the graveyard and tried to imagine these holy men into life again—a postulant riding the crashing waves to this stony sanctuary; men in their prime sacrificing all for ascetic communion with a God of extremities; an old man grown wise in uninterrupted contemplation of Christ's Mysteries.

I imagined the lively commerce with passing boats and the terror of Viking raids, and the mournful exodus of the brotherhood back to the mainland in the twelfth century.

Not for me, that hard vocation, but I could feel the saintliness that had seeped into these harsh but exulting rocks. I pulled out my beads and dipped them into the waters of a stony pool. Climbing a peak above the hermitage, a natural spire, I recited a decade to Saint Michael, Archangel of High Places.

Above the world I sat then, looking down on the huts of these ancient anchorites. From this high summit, I watched clouds sailing over the sun-bright Hills of Kerry in the east, and, to the north, south, and west, only the sun-sparkled distance of the rolling wash of sea. A peak experience, to be sure. As George Bernard Shaw would have it, I felt I was beginning to know Ireland "through and through."

Faery-Waxed in Ballybrack

A s I tackled Missie for the road next morning, Olive Mulvihill made a great fuss of decorating Missie's bridle with a spray of wildflowers.

" 'Tis only fitting she looks like a queen in leaving Cahersiveen," she said, admiring her handiwork.

With warm farewell, Missie and I traveled up the town where shopkeepers greeted us from their doorways. In front of the bank, however, a nest of ancient blackguards waited our passing with tormenting zest.

"She's a bouquet of beauty," whistled one old wag.

"She'll soon have a bee in her bonnet," laughed another.

"I may as well dress her up"—I dodged their silver-spittled remarks—"she's the only girl I've got."

"And a right girleen she is, laddie," said a toothless fellow. "But I wouldn't go putting too much shine up on her, for ye'll only be tempting the less fortunate of your brethren."

"If I had a woman of such charm and exquisite beauty," added the fourth chorister, "I'd knock the lights out of any man who'd steal but a glance in her direction!"

Onward we pushed, with Missie bright and cheerful from her day's rest and all the flattery, streaming through the high-hedged fuchsia lanes of Iveragh, peering through gaps in the massed foliage at rich meadows dotted with pikes of hay. Robust families, from industrious grandpas to dutiful children, worked the grassy windrows, as older boys and girls climbed the haystacks to wave as we passed.

A mile outside the seaside resort of Waterville, a comely lass of twenty, clothed in a long red dress, walked out the road to meet us.

"I heard you were coming so I thought I'd be your 'Welcome Wagon' into Waterville," she beamed, introducing herself as "Nancy from Iowa." She was a raven-haired vision, as beautiful as the path she trod.

"That's very kind of you," I said, always pleased to play the gallant with a lady other than Missie.

"I'm here for the summer, toiling away for a rich Irish-American," she explained in her clear Midwestern accent, "but this is my day off, and isn't it spectacular?" she said, gazing at the gold-gilded clouds that floated above Ballinskelligs Bay.

I walked along, tongue-tied.

"This whole country is so blissful, so invigorating, and the villagers so accepting. Do you know they call me a 'fierce-friendly child.' Can you believe it? Me! 'Cantankerous Nancy.' But they're the fiercely friendly ones, with praise for the saints and a kind word for everyone."

We walked on a short distance, looking out at Bolus Head.

"Could I ride up on the cart?" she pleaded, pleasingly.

"My donkey is at your service." I stopped the cart and bowed before her.

She jumped up on the mudbox, smoothed out her long red dress and tidied her flow of black hair, as I wondered what tune the morning roosters of Cahersiveen might be crowing if they could see me now.

"Did you know Waterville was the favorite vacation spot of both Charlie Chaplin and Walt Disney?" she asked, enjoying her vantage from the cart.

"Imagine that." I was distracted by my now-brucklesome beast and had to yank her by the reins. "Sorry for the pigheaded ride."

"Oh, this is fine. Everything's fine—for I've changed." She brushed her hair back from her face and gazed up into the blue zenith. "This land, these people, this day, they fill me with content."

I dragged my obstinate animal into the well-kept village of Waterville. Right in the middle, in front of the Butler Arms Hotel, she spread her hind legs, daintily tiptoed on her back shoes and peed a mighty gallon in the road.

"Nice touch, Miss," I muttered, aching to clobber her.

"There goes Waterville's chances of winning this year's Tidy Town competition," laughed Nancy, jumping from the cart and seeking high ground.

"I hate when she does that," I apologized, as a river of piddle ran down the curbside, floating a candy wrapper into the next county. "We've traveled ten miles today and she has to go right here. Class act, Miss."

"Cut me off at the knees and call me Shorty," proclaimed Nancy, "but I think your donkey is jealous of me."

"I don't know. Maybe she mistook the meaning of the signs saying 'Waterville.'"

"No, look at her," Nancy persisted with mounting hilarity. "That face, whether woman or donkey, is the face of jealousy. Believe me, the look is universal!"

I lifted Missie's drooping flower arrangement to have a better look at my long-eared companion. Missie, in a flash, tried to snap my head off.

"I can't believe it," I said, dropping the flowers as I avoided decapitation.

"Am I right?" Nancy twirled before us like a tintinnabulating music-box ballerina.

"You're right. She sees a rival for my affections," I responded sheepishly.

Making plans to meet Nancy Spain—as I'd dubbed her though she hailed from I-O-Way—later that evening at the Bay View, I walked toward Ballybrack, keeping a safe distance from my grudging beast. A mile out the road, we came to four standing stones on the shoulder of a hill, marking an old druidic ring, where I had hopes of spending the night.

Going up a grassy boreen, I knocked at a small cottage and introduced myself to an elderly couple named O'Sullivan, asking if I might sleep among the stones on their land.

"What in heaven's name for?" asked Mrs. O'Sullivan with a start.

"I've slept in a bed for four straight nights," I said, "and it's time to be a little adventurous."

"Sleeping in a faery circle is not a wise notion," she answered sternly.

"Sleep as you will, if your heart is set upon it," contradicted Mr. O'Sullivan, untackling Missie from the cart.

"Do you get many people sleeping there?" I asked, trying to make light of their difference.

"The odd hare, I suppose," said Mr. O'Sullivan, walking Missie to a small field that overlooked Lough Currane.

"Be it hag or hare!" snapped the warning missus.

"Ye'll be all right." Mr. O'Sullivan nudged me with a wink of the eye. "And if it rains in the night or the faeries go hankering at your toes, come in, whatever the time."

Thanking them both, I hurried back to the Bay View in Waterville to meet up with Nancy.

"Did you find accommodation?"

"I did. I'm sleeping in the Eightercua Stone Alignment."

"What's that?"

"Old druidic standing stones dating back to the Bronze Age. A miniature Stonehenge."

"Will you be all right?" I found her concern for where I might lay my head quite touching.

"I'll probably have to dodge faery darts all night," I joked, "or worry about being stolen away."

"Go on!" She gave me a sharp jab to the ribs, along with a little stab to the heart.

Since Ireland has more ears than Iowa has corn, an old twaddler snookered with drink planted himself in a chair close by.

"Did I hear ye say ye'll be sleeping in that mouthful of stone?"

"Yep."

"You better think twice," he replied with a drooling slur. "The circle at Ballybrack is an old altar where magic was practiced . . . and human sacrifice. It's a jugglery of demons. You're not just putting your life in danger by sleeping there, but your soul as well. Ye're flirting with a cult of pagan mysteries, ye are. Divinities of Darkness."

He stood over us, a nuisance with a mustache of caked stout over his lips.

"There are *pookas*," he said, tottering in his shoes, "who won't be long in running ye out of the place. Why, they can shape themselves into anything, a horse or ass maybe, and ride ye the night long on a deadly gallop from Hog's to Bolus Head, only to hurl ye into the sea at the crack of dawn.

"And *dullahans*, by Jaysus," he continued, shivering at the thought. "They're thicker than flies this time of year. Merciless, headless craytures who blind their victims with basins of bat's blood, and throw them into flying carriages to be deposited, after one long horrific flight, on the fiery flagstones of Hell!"

Unable to restrain ourselves any longer, Nancy and I burst out laughing in the codger's face. Swaying over us, he stared in point-blank shock.

"Is it little ye're making of me warnings?" he swung his hands open, spilling half the contents of his glass to the floor.

"No, no," I tried to pacify him. "I'm struck by your deep concern for my safety."

"Blasted! Ye're gibing me, ye are" he hollered, drawing everyone's attention to his ructions. "Out of it, I tell ye, for ye'll be whillaballooing from the bleak side of Eternity by dawn's light. Courting the red boyo, ould Devilskins himself in his own stony bed!"

Two barkeeps finally ushered him to a distant stool, from which vantage his icy glare never left us.

"What do you think?" whispered Nancy.

"I think the poor guy is corked."

"Well, you shouldn't take him too lightly. I'm sure there's a kernel of truth to his stories."

After we finished our drinks, I walked Nancy to her residence.

"Thank you for the donkey ride today," she blushed at the door.

"You're more than welcome," I stood awkwardly before her.

"Good night, then," she said, kissing me, "and I hope the morning finds you safe and sound."

"Good night, Nancy," I said, backing away.

"You won't tell Missie that I kissed you?" she whispered from the doorstep.

"I won't tell anyone that you kissed me," I assured her, and skipped on the run toward Ballybrack, singing Christy Moore's version of "Nancy Spain" through the dark countryside, footloose but not quite fancy-free.

Returning to my forewarned mound of Hades and climbing through snarling, prickling shrubbery, I reached the four gaunt upright slabs of stone and dropped my sleeping bag in the circle's center.

From the comfort of my bag, I looked up and about. "Gee, the drunkard was right. I do feel like I'm sleeping in a snoring giant's mouth."

Lighthearted from my day's adventures, I considered this stone circle nothing more than an old clock, a simple ancient timepiece, and soon fell into a deep slumber.

Kerr-lew. Keer-lew.

I woke with a start to the creepy sound of lake birds in the dead of night. Ink-black clouds, backlit by a waxing moon, traveled the sky like ghost ships. A stiff breeze blew, whistling through the circle. The quaint, harmless menhirs of day now loomed like the ghoulish teeth of a grinning hag.

Why am I doing this? I sat up to fight off the chill of the place. *I'd never dream of sleeping in a cemetery back home. So why this stony bed in a place of the dead?*

I took up both my hazel stick and rosary beads and mumbled a few prayers to my new protector, Saint Michael, warrior against the wicked, half afraid my prayers would come out backward. *Wouldn't I be a sight if found dead in the morning,* I thought cheerlessly, *with my beads tightly wound around my switch of hazel!* I could hear Mrs. O'Sullivan speaking above my lifeless body laid out on this sacrificial altar, as Nancy keened along the lakeshore.

"He was playing both sides from the middle," I could hear Mrs. O'Sullivan say, as the parish priest was having great difficulty disentangling my beads from the hazel. "You're either pagan or Christian, but, you see, he was entertaining the two deities. Running with the hare and hunting with the hounds. I warned him not to pitch camp in this faery dwelling, but, aye, he was as headstrong as a billy goat in the spring of his youth. Aye, between two stools a man falls. And now he's being whisked through the spirit world by a goblin glede, and it's not Tír na nóg his soul is bound for, but the Dark Chasm below."

"You said it, missus," would add the dipsomaniac by her side. "He was nothing but a pop-buttoned boast at the Bay View, trying to impress the giddy Yankee girl. Aye, a ferretlike Yank drawn to the Devil's Lair, and now he's scalding his fingers on the brassy knob of Hell's door."

I adjusted my position on the stony mound, trying to fill my head with fond memories, to forget I was abed in a boneyard, a potter's field, the very Necropolis of Munster.

I tried to think of the amusing faeries my father used to tell us about, little fellas dressed in red and green and no taller than a milking stool, dashing through fox-runs in the hedges, and up Cairn Hill into the holy wells which led to their faery tunnels.

In this grave of wizards, though, where I could hear only the cry of curlews and moorhens, one thing said by the old sot in the pub rang loud and true: "There are evil spirits among those stones, same as ghosts in haunted homes."

"*Cuidigh liom! Cuidigh liom!*" I cried, with a sudden gift of ancient tongues. "Help me! Help me!"

I curled into the warmth of my sleeping bag and subsided into a shadow world between wakefulness and sleep. But at the rustling of a leaf, demon cats commenced to curse like sailors around me. Will-o'-the-wisps winked their lights from black, beckoning bogs. Washerwomen of Shrouds keened upon the lapping waves below. Banshees screeched like monkey eagles. Air demons fell in squadrons among the dropping mist.

I sat up in my bag, taking comfort in the distant whine of a motorcar. But as soon as I dropped my head, faery processions trooped by, waving penny lanterns in my eyes, screaming, *a-wee, a-wee!* Witch hares hopped the ditches. Radiant lads lit the rushes. Horned women scratched and sharpened the stones. Opalescent specters and phantomhosts went wheeling by. Obscene *sheela-na-gigs* danced. Bronze wands of druids waved o'er my head. Ogres ogled. Pigheaded children grunted, rooted, and groaned.

Much later, after several rounds on my brown and worn rosary beads, I watched dawn peek its timid head over the mountain of Coomcallee. Without delay, I shook off a dread bone-chill and knocked numbly at the O'Sullivans'.

Mrs. O'Sullivan answered the door, and shock covered her face.

"What is it?" I asked, still shivering from my bed.

She pointed a trembling finger toward a mirror on the wall.

My blood turning to paste, I rushed over to the mirror, where no succubus-possessed wretch stared back at me, but only my familiar, weaselly self.

"That'll teach you not to be peeking into pagan places," she said, her hands stubbornly on her hips.

"And how did you sleep, tell us?" Mr. O'Sullivan laughed at his wife's antics.

"I didn't sleep from two o'clock on. I had been planning to sleep out again at the tumulus of Newgrange, but I'll never spend another night among those infernal stones."

"A wise choice," Mrs. O'Sullivan relented as she sat me down for breakfast. "There's little sense in tempting the Middle Kingdom from their dusky nooks, now, is there?"

"There is not," I wholeheartedly agreed.

The Memory Stone

CHAPTER TWENTY-SIX

A brief shower cut through the early-morning haze, making a refreshing day to ascend Coomakista Pass, pride of the Ring of Kerry. Akin to Conor Pass, stark and lonesome, but with gradients a trifle kinder, we were able to traverse nine miles in four hours, as blue-rumped sheep clambered upon the gray-lichened rocks.

I wasn't long at the scenic lay-by on top, when a Japanese family arrived with two daughters. The young girls, wearing colorful silk dresses, dashed merrily toward the crowning knolls, as frolicsome as the mountain lambs that scattered before them. They whirled and twirled, spun by the spectacle of mountain, sea, and sky. Brown larks, startled from their rushy beds, rose above the girls' shining black heads in a twitter of summery song.

The father meticulously photographed every point of the compass with a variety of lenses: toward the long lonesome valley that runs to Hog's Head; toward the rich rolling farmland of Valencia Island; around the stately stand of trees along Derrynane Bay; out to the bejeweled islands of Abbey, Deenish, and Scariff; and across Kenmare Bay to the Slieve Miskish Mountains that unfold in brown heaps along Bearhaven Peninsula. A roll of pictures well worth a trip from Osaka, or Ohara, for that matter.

He approached me with grave politeness, asking if I might take a picture of the whole family beside Missie. When I nodded my okay, the wife and girls came over, petting Missie lightly and thanking me with shy delicate bows.

After the picture was taken, they gathered in front of the statue of the Blessed Mary, whose extended arms seem to protect all in the valley below. I thought there might be another family portrait, but instead the parents instructed their girls reverently. Taking no picture of the statue, but bowing before it, the father led his family back to their car, tooted to me and Missie, and drove north toward Killarney.

Making our descent into Caherdaniel, we were hailed by a pleasant elderly woman outside her two-story home on the southern slope of Cahernageeha.

"How was your climb?" she inquired, standing by a rosebush in full bloom.

"The climb was easier than the descent," I answered. "You'll never find my donkey skiing the slaloms of Switzerland."

She introduced herself as Mrs. Bea Hughes, a retired schoolteacher, and invited me into the house to "hear the kettle's whistle."

"Your flower garden can be seen from atop Coomakista Pass," I reported, listening to the hum of bees drifting by her opened windows.

"The busy bee has no time for sorrow, and neither do I, in keeping this garden." She plopped into her chair with a sigh of relief. "People say I should turn my home into a bed-and-breakfast, since tourists flock here in July and August to visit Derrynane House, the old home of Daniel O'Connell, just beyond those woodlands across the way."

"I've heard his name all my life," I said, peering out the window toward the dense woods, "but I'm embarrassed to say I know little about him."

"Daniel was indeed 'the Great Liberator,' as much as your President Lincoln was. He spearheaded the cause of religious freedom in this country. The story is told that Daniel's parents sought shelter from a storm one evening in a chapel badly in need of repair. They later sent money to the parish priest for restoration of the chapel, and in reply the thankful priest foretold that their unborn son would become a champion of Ireland. The story concludes, with a touch of romancing, that the Kerry Hills pealed in thunderous claps of joy when the child, Daniel, came into the world in 1775.

"He was a splendid barrister," she continued, pleased to have a wayfaring student in her kitchen classroom, "with a tall, regal presence that would have made the Tuatha de Danann, the mythical gods of old Ireland proud. And a voice so magnificent it could be heard by thousands upon thousands at his outdoor meetings."

"What was his career like?"

"After becoming a legendary lawyer, he provided the model for peaceful democratic movements in Ireland, and succeeded in pushing for Catholic Emancipation in 1829. It didn't give the vote to all, by any means, but it did allow Daniel to take his seat as a member for Clare in the Westminster Parliament. He tried to work through 'the system,' as you young folks say, throughout the 1830s. But frustrations in improving the lot of his countryman brought him home to be lord mayor of Dublin in 1841, the first Catholic to hold the post in a hundred and fifty years."

"Must have been like JFK becoming president."

"Exactly. And even before the Famine," the schoolmistress went on, "times were hard for the Catholic majority, with so much of the rich harvests going to the tables of the English, so Daniel became leader of the movement to repeal the Act of Union, to give Ireland its own nondenominational parliament and eventual independence. He made every effort to revive Irish national feeling around symbols like the harp, and organized 'monster meetings' in support of native rights, culminating in a vast gathering on the Hill of Tara, seat of the old High Kings. A million or more strong they came, to express the will of the people."

"Wow, more than Woodstock, or, more to the point, than Dr. Martin Luther King's march on Washington."

"Oh, yes, and another huge rally was planned for Clontarf, where Brian Boru had expelled the Vikings in 1014. This time the English forbade the assembly and threatened military intervention. Now, Daniel was a lifelong pacifist, and the prospect of blood-shed led him to call off the rally. But nationalist passions had been unleashed that Daniel could no longer control. He was superceded by partisans of Young Ireland, who would say, 'Ireland was won at Clontarf and now it is to be lost at Clontarf.'

"The Famine came, and like so many Irish heroes—Parnell, Pierce, Connolly— Daniel died with a broken heart, in a kind of exile, in Italy where he had been ordered for his health. But if you want to gauge his impact, just imagine the career of your Martin Luther King if he had lived a normal span of years, hadn't been cut off by assassination."

Thanking Mrs. Hughes for the tea and the history lesson, I gathered Missie and we continued our saunter down the quiet south coast of Kerry. I saluted Daniel O'Con- nell's Derrynane House in passing, and as I was waving to families who toiled with the hay in sunlit fields, an aged scarecrow jumped out of the hedge at me.

"Sorra to give ye a hop," the antique tatterdemalion apologized.

"Th-that's okay," I stammered, slipping back into my skin.

Eyeing Missie, he commented, "I suppose ye're having the saint's ould luck with your blessed donkey. But how, dear God, were you gifted with the eye to go choosing a turf-colored donkey for your pilgrimage?"

"It was between a black jack and a brown mare," I answered. "But does the color of a donkey's coat mean anything?"

"Troth, 'mean anything'!" He looked around as if he wished to share my ludicrous reply with the world. "Ladeen, a snowy-white donkey is softer than the pudding in a cream pie. The gray fellows faint at a mousies passing. The black boyos are robust, to be sure, but devils entirely 'less they be off to the races. And glory, the piebalds and skewbalds are raving frantic without a thimble of reasoning. The only donkey worth a speckled pullet is the turf-colored donkey."

"A speckled pullet, you say?" I said, petting my little damsel. "Well, she's worth all of that, surely."

That evening, approaching Castlecove, we called into the Black Shop where the publi- can, Brendan Gallivan, invited me to stay for the night. After a ceremonious pint, we chatted out in the lingering twilight, where the dark hulk of Eagle Hill loomed at our backs. Across the road, a small monument had been erected for a local character called "Mick the Blind Piper."

"Mick the Piper boasted of being the hereditary piper to Daniel O'Connell's family," Brendan filled me in. "He emigrated to Worcester, Massachusetts, during the Famine, but returned to Ireland after receiving word he had been left a fortune. But the fortune was a hoax, and it seems thereafter he fell into oddities, fearing spirits and such things, and going about blessing himself the whole time.

"He tied for second place at the Feis Ceoil, a major musical festival in 1899, but blamed his poor performance on faery butter that he said was served to him that morning. Later in life he recorded wonderful tunes on an Edison phonograph, but smashed them to smithereens with his cane when they were played back to him, blaming faeries again for the poor sound. In the end, he became a feeble, friendless, penniless, and eccentric old man who died in the poorhouse at Cahersiveen."

In the fading gloom, Brendan and his neighbor Piel Vander Hlove, who, with wife and family, had recently moved here from Holland to try their hand at self-sufficiency, drove me to nearby Staigue Fort, the best preserved stone cashel in Ireland, built around 1,000 B.C., where small rooms are still standing between thirteen-foot-thick walls eighteen feet high.

"Staigue Fort—'the fort in the bleak place'—is a real mystery," said Brendan, as he and Piel stood amidst tons of dry masonry. "Just about every clump of clay in Ireland has volumes of history, but this fortress has no history at all. It just sits here, silent through the ages. If only stone could talk, hey?"

On a sunlit Monday morning, Missie and I set out from the Black Shop through a rugged landscape of mountain and bog, hoping to reach Sneem by day's end. We weren't long going our ten-mile route when called off the road by a young nurse named Mary, home on holiday from Australia. She sat me before a cup of tea while her querulous mother peppered me with questions.

"'Tis a peculiar gadabout," she said, eyeing me as if I was middling daft. "What will come out of it?"

"I can boast of sleeping in the stone circle at Ballybrack," I offered back, "or, spending a night with a band of Kerry travelers?"

"'Boast,' bedad," she said, puffing at the gills. "Wouldn't that be some queer gabbing? Do ye think ye're Cuchulainn, tempting the Reaper's scythe each and every night? Will you walk the gray battlement of Belfast as if it's a comely stroll through the likes of Parknasilla? Recruit yerself to the Foreign Legion if ye're so fond of dangerous schemes."

"Hold your tongue, Mother, please," scolded Mary, her face red. "I think walking a donkey 'round Ireland is a brilliant idea."

"'Tis senseless," the mother insisted, paying no heed to her daughter. "'Tis like building a lighthouse in the bog."

"'Tis a novelty, a rare scheme," said Mary's dad, an elderly man suffering with arthritis, sunning himself in the open doorway. "Isn't it grand to walk the world and chat with the people? Remember the old proverb, ' 'Tis fortune that favors the brave'?"

"Fortune, bedad," scoffed the missus, cutting me three slices of raisin bread despite her rough demeanor. "Are ye going scribbling a book or something?"

"If I can ever sit down long enough, maybe."

"Who'd buy it?"

"You would, for one."

"Me? And what would I want with a book of pure codology?"

"You'd be in it," I said teasingly, which quickly stilled her wagging tongue.

She huffed from the room as Mary apologized for her mother's brusque behavior.

"She means no harm," said Mary. "She just blurts out anything that comes to mind."

"That's okay," I said, thickly buttering a wedge of her raisin bread. "Your mom is mild compared to the ribbing I get along the roads."

When departing, I was tempted to chaff the mother for spying out from the kitchen window. Winking at Mary and her dad, I led Missie out the road, purposely forgetting to hitch her back to the cart.

"Ye've forgot your caboose, you witless eejit!" the mother hollered from the opened window.

Pretending surprise, I walked back for the cart as Mary and her father laughed aloud. But once the old woman discovered our connivance, she unleashed a salvo of tongue-lashings.

"It's stupider than that donkey, you all are! Off yer hinges entirely. And you two can go to blazes," she added, honing in on her own. "Go fandangling after the celebrated Donkeyman. Go on, out of me sight! And I guarantee it won't be long till ye'll be stretching yer poor sorry necks through me door."

Arriving in the early evening at Sneem, a pretty village of quaint shops with a swift, peat-frothed river tumbling through, I stopped in front of Dan Murphy's Pub where a large white sitting-stone outside its door was occupied by a cyclist.

I knew the popular song "The Stone Outside Dan Murphy's Door," by the late Johnny Patterson, and wondered if this was the actual site that had inspired the lyrics. An elderly farmer, leaning against a walking stick, spoke up from the footpath as if reading my mind.

"That stone is just a setup for the tourists, though the publican himself is a fine honest fellow."

Missie and I walked alongside this affable man eager for the chat.

"Large stones, such as Dan Murphy's, were used as meeting places throughout the country in bygone days," he explained. "Did you happen to pass any Mass-rocks in your rambles, where Mass was secretly celebrated during Penal Times?"

"Oh, yes. I visited a Mass-rock in County Roscommon, and as I was saying a prayer before the altar, a white horse came galloping across the fields and nipped me playfully on the sleeve."

"I don't doubt it." He gleefully tapped his walking stick against my own. "There's great power in stone, and animals are more aware of it than ourselves. Didn't I read how seabirds fly great distances over the gray watery world, and whether day or night, sun or storm, they're able to alight upon the smallest sea-chimneys in the vast regions of sea. And salmon, as you know, swim year after year from the Grand Banks of Newfoundland, to spawn on their very own birthing stones in the streams of Macgillicuddy above."

He walked us through the bustling village to a bench in the Upper Square, where the cleft-chinned fellow continued his seminar on stones.

"The most famous stone in Ireland, Lia Fáil, the Stone of Destiny, crowns the Hill of Tara, and is known to cry out when the rightful king of Ireland stands upon it. Pity, now, how it hasn't cried out for a thousand years and more. There's another Coronation Stone at Cashel in Tipperary, where Saint Patrick crowned Aengus, King of Ireland, in the Year of Our Lord 450. And the Flagstone of Homesickness in County Donegal, where Saint Columcille cured a man from woes that have been shared by many in the long centuries of emigration. And your namesake, Saint Kevin of Glendalough slept, as did many early Irish clerics, on a bed of stone.

"Then, of course, there's the Blarney Stone," he chuckled, "though I don't put much stock into it. The only time I visited Blarney Castle, I overheard a tourist complain of losing a pocketful of change while hanging upside down to kiss it. And, believe me, not a semblance of eloquence sprang from his gob."

He rummaged through his coat pocket for pipe and tobacco.

"Do you know anything about the Eightercua Stones in Ballybrack?" I asked this expert in geomancy.

"Only that it's terribly old. As old as the Pyramids themselves, I've heard, and that human sacrifice was performed there."

"I heard that, all right. But why would they have performed human sacrifice in Ireland?"

"For the very reason other cultures practiced human sacrifice," he replied. "Good crops, fertility, and such things. I read how the druids would plunge a knife through their victims' hearts in Eightercua, and the spasms of their limbs foretold events."

"You know a good deal about stones," I noted, feeling a little weak in the knees.

"I suppose so," he answered with a modest smile, putting match to pipe. "As a lad, I'd often help my grandmother, crippled with rheumatics, to a stone akin to Dan Murphy's outside her little cabin. A great age was up on her entirely, yet she'd rather sit up on that cold stone than beside a roaring fire. She called it her 'Memory Stone,' and, perched upon it, she fell into a swoon like cherished saints of old. During her spells, the villagers would gather and gasp—hushed quiet, you know, so as not to disturb—believing she was in the company of angels.

"I knew little about otherworldly raptures, so one evening I boldly interrupted her swoon, asking how she was keeping and why wouldn't she come in from the cold. She awoke calmly from her trance and answered, 'I'm fine, Thomas, *agra*, but when I sit on my Memory Stone, all pain fades and my mind is drawn to peaceful musings. And, sure, I go sifting through the ages, easy as you please, as far back as my mother's womb and the caul about me. By closing my eyes, I see your father Michael, as a wee lad, with his thin shanks flying o'er the fields, running to help Tishy O'Shea pull the rhubarb for her St. Patrick's Day pies. And Eileen, my sister, may Heaven shine upon her, scrubbing the legs of her four rapscallions who had gone mucking about in the bog. And, Thomas, I see the poor mountain girls off to school, fitted with slippers of mouse-skin, and barefoot tinker children running after our old crock of an ass.'

" 'All that?' I said to humor her, but she went on:

" 'But, of all, I see your grandfather, John, my dear husband, his silvery scythe cutting broad swaths of gold through the ripened meadow, and I am intoxicated by the mown fragrance of bluebell and clover, and dizzied by the sight of himself. Oh, how he could fell an acre into tidy windrows, then stand above it all, triumphant as a grand poet-warrior in Oisin's time.'

"She could sit there half the day," Thomas continued, obviously into his own time-traveling trance, "and I never doubted the wondrous visions she spoke of. But now the poor creature is buried beneath the sod, and of her home only the Memory Stone remains. And I think, betimes, I should have it moved to my place as a memorial to the old soul."

"Sounds like a real good idea," I agreed. "As you say, there's a wealth of power in old stones."

"But wouldn't my neighbors think it a queer job to go shifting a boulder a barony away, with all the stones littering my fields? Yet I might consider it someday," he sighed, sparking his pipe back to life.

"Did you ever sit on your grandmother's Memory Stone?" I asked, as he rose from the bench.

"Oh, aye, several times."

"Did you ever experience anything?"

"I did, now," he answered. "I'd experience the one thing and the one thing only."

"And what was that?" I asked, as he shook my hand farewell.

"A cold arse," he laughed, moving across the square. "A mighty cold arse, indeed."

The Road to Kilmakilloge

CHAPTER TWENTY-SEVEN

Having camped beneath a full moon by the River Sneem, I treated myself to a pleasant noonday lunch at the Olde Ceiling, where I wrote a dozen postcards to celebrate the recent end of the postal strike. I reported that Missie and I were fine, that the people were marvelous, and we'd be stepping into Cork, our fourth county, in a few days' time.

Enjoying my soup and sandwich, I imagined the banter at Rattigan's when Kathleen flourished my postcard, showing the village of Eyeries dwarfed by a patchwork of fields and the tumultuous sea, to the Friday-evening pensioners.

"Will ye look at the poor stony land, and the houses stacked upon one another like playing cards," Dan Madden might say, studying the postcard as a paleontologist would a fossil. "Why the sheep in that country must be wearing their bones on the outside of their coats."

After the card was read, young Donal Rattigan would be summoned to fetch the map of Ireland.

"Not the sacrilegious one, mind you, with Ulster painted in a splash of crimson," Hugh Mannion would shout, "but the old mapeen of the thirty-two counties in a delicate spray of hues, and the Four Provinces outlined, like on the Paddy label."

With old map in hand, Headmaster D'Alton would slowly run his finger along my circuitous route, stopping at the village of Sneem and searching out Eyeries across Kenmare River.

"Why is the Yank sending us a picture card of one place and he still in another?" would grumble Willie Cassidy, extinguishing the butt end of his cigarette between thumb and forefinger.

"Perhaps he'd be in Eyelids today," would reckon Hugh Mannion. "But isn't he getting on well! And here I thought me twenty shillings were safe and snug in the toes of my stockings."

"Remember the Sunday he left," Dan Madden might add, "and the guards pouring in like it was a raid, just to report how the Yank had slid off the cart to walk alongside his donkey. And poor Jimmy Mac, at the counter there, dropping his head into his hands."

"But, look here," Willie Cassidy would interject, calling my expedition into question, the map sprawled across his lap like a field marshal's. "The Yank postmarked this card in Sneem in the County Kerry on Tuesday, tenth July. The *Roscommon Champion* reported he had crossed the Shannon into Kerry on the twenty-ninth of May. Am I right? He'll be, let's see, forty-five days to travel the Kingdom of Kerry. At that pace, he'll never be home this Christmas, nor the one behind it."

"In his card to Jimmy Mac, the Donkeyman said he'd traveled four hundred miles," might pipe up young Donal. "That leaves twelve hundred or more, does it not? Jimmy thinks he has dallied too long in the height of the long days."

"He'll be gone three months in a fortnight, which leaves him five and a half months till Christmas Day," the headmaster would add, thumbing through the Harp girlie calendar. "Four hundred away, with twelve hundred to play. He's near two months behind his timetable already."

"But he's a wonder, nonetheless," Hugh would add. "Almost into Cork with a donkey, be God, and I never stepped a foot into Cork, nor Kerry, nor the watery side of Galway, for that matter."

I sipped my Guinness and smiled up at the ceiling of the Olde Ceiling, on which screen this imaginary dialogue at Rattigan's had played out.

The next morning, Missie and I passed the bucolic resort of Parknasilla, where the Gulf Stream would make you think you had stumbled into Boca Raton. Subtropical plants flourished in well-trimmed yards and gardens, as incongruous to the Irish landscape as an armadillo on a furze-covered moor.

This village, a favorite of George Bernard Shaw's, was no favorite of mine. There is nothing enjoyable about walking an ass past the Great Southern Hotel, where a twitch of her donkey brain littered a score of well-formed briquettes before the disdainful gasps of the hotel's brandy-sniffing, yacht-tanned guests.

Better to walk a donkey through windswept bogs with hail pummeling you both, than to walk before stately holiday homes, where champion wolfhounds, nearly the size of your own beast, sniff your passing with a snooty air. Halfway through the luxuriant resort, Missie let out a tremendous roar.

"What's wrong, Miss?" I pleaded, at a loss to calm her.

No answer, of course, just another bawl, more strident than the first, as she stared pie-eyed at the waving palms. I stroked her withers and looked into her eyes, trying to fathom some past-life bad experience at the hands of desert nomads.

"No, no, Miss, this is not Arabia Deserta, but Hibernia," I tugged forcefully on the reins.

Still no movement, so I was left with but one solution, to rouse my humpless camel from her recalcitrant reverie.

Whap!

Leaving the unsettling confines of Parknasilla and approaching Blackwater Bridge, Missie was encircled in a swirl of flies.

"Cut yourself a few leafy branches and stick them in her bridle," instructed a woman who pedaled by. " 'Tis the only way she'll find comfort when the air is this thick with humidity and flies."

I took my jackknife and cut a few sprigs from the hedge and adorned Missie till she looked like a walking bush. As we were crossing the ivy-clad bridge, the postmistress stepped from the stone post office and doubled over in laughter.

"She's a proper commando," the woman howled. "A right woodkerne!"

Spurred by the lash of embarrassment, we logged a dozen miles before I knocked on the door of a two-story farmhouse belonging to Jeremiah O'Grady, who allowed me the use of his barn by the river's edge.

Pulling off Missie's tackle and giving her a splash-bath and brush-down, I dipped my feet into the flowing waters, as happy as Huck Finn on the run from civilization. I was catching up on my journal when I received a welcome call to supper.

"You're a good lad," said Mrs. O'Grady, sitting me with her family for the evening meal. "I've watched you brushing your donkey after the hot day. I would often see men filling themselves in the pub, never thinking of their poor donkeys who stood outside for hours hitched to the cart in either heat or perishing cold."

"I have to pamper her or she may lose heart," I said, passing the leafy cabbage.

"You're doing that mighty-like," said Jeremiah, passing me a lovely slice of lamb in return.

After supper, young Jeremiah walked me to Spillane's Bar, home to three of Ireland's finest Gaelic footballers: Pat, Mick, and Tom Spillane. It was like walking into an American restaurant where the DiMaggio brothers in their prime would be working happily and without airs for their widowed mother.

Kerry is to Gaelic football what the New York Yankees are to baseball. The name Kerry is synonymous with success, and many a Sunday afternoon Hugh Mannion and his nephew, Pat Joe, would listen to the radio and curse the grand Kerry boys, the Spillanes in particular, who seemed to score goals at will.

Pat Spillane, Ireland's most recent "Athlete of the Year," was pumping petrol when we arrived, and Mick, who had recently scored an electrifying last-minute goal to defeat Cork in the Munster finale before 50,000 stunned fans, was pulling pints and joking with the locals.

When I was introduced by Jeremiah, complimentary pints were pulled and Mick shook my hand in disbelief. "The Donkeyman! The prince of Irish travelers!"

Mrs. Spillane and young Tom, currently the toast of Kerry's minor team, were called from the back kitchen.

"The three lads will be playing together one day, please God," said Maura Spillane. Her brother, Jackie Lyon, was a great footballer as had been her late husband, Packie Spillane. "They always had a knack for kicking the ball," the lovely matron went on, "and I suppose it was Kerry's winning tradition that inspired them after their father's death. It's proud I am of the three. And I'd feel the same way if they couldn't kick a ball at all," she concluded with a sigh.

Hugh Mannion would have given his left ear to be with me that night, for, "after-hours," it was myself, Jeremiah, and the three Spillanes around the table.

They asked about my donkey tour and the nights spent beneath the stars, and I asked what it was like to take a free kick from 60 yards out, before 70,000 frantic fans at Dublin's Croke Park as the entire nation held its breath.

"You just go booting it like you're in the fields beyond," laughed Pat. "It wouldn't do you to think too much about it, would it?"

"But don't you tense up with the chanting crowds, with the president and Taoiseach among them?"

"Noise is noise," answered Mick. "And sure, doesn't Mr. Hillary or Mr. Haughey own the one head like ourselves?"

It was close to two when Jeremiah and I arrived home. He invited me to sleep in the house, but I opted for the riverbank where, on this night, my dear donkey slept like a huge wolfhound at my feet.

After a full breakfast, topped off with Mrs. O'Grady's elderberry jam, we headed for Kenmare. But two miles from the town, passing Dromquinna Riding Stables in Templenoe, I was saluted by a young man named John Hand.

"Your donkey's high on the hoof," he called, "and after dinner I'll pare her for you, if you'll keep a grip on her lugs."

A knowledgeable horseman, John unyoked Missie and checked the tackle, treating each piece with a generous rub of saddlesoap.

"The saddlesoap will keep the tackle supple," John said, laying the pieces out in the sun. "It wouldn't do you to break a breeching on the hilly slopes of Beara."

I sat down to dinner with John's mom, grandma, and an elderly farmhand named Jimmy Harrington. Following the meal, we began the arduous task of removing Missie's shoes, paring her hooves, and nailing back the shoes.

Task complete, John suggested we take two horses and gallop up Knocklomena Mountain. I hesitated, telling him my entire experience on horseback was the occasional pony ride at a church fair. So he teamed me with a twenty-two-year old retired show jumper named Greta who, he promised, would be gentle with me. No sooner had I mounted the gray-dappled mare than Missie let out a cataclysmic roar from her open stall.

"It's a possessive girlfriend you have there," laughed John.

"Don't even bring it up," I said. "You should have seen her when I met a pretty woman in Waterville. I wanted to bury a stick of dynamite under her tail."

We trotted off toward the mountain, as I waved to my bugling gal who, it must be said, suffered sadly in comparison to this tall, graceful champion, retired star of equine ballet.

We trekked hills with lovely views of Kenmare River and mountains of Beara, our mission to check on the dozen horses corralled in the valley. Despite the beautiful surroundings, I was distracted by the jouncing between my groin and Greta's back.

" 'May the Saddle Rise to Meet You,' " joked John, noting my discomfort.

Bowlegged and sore, I was easily coaxed into spending the night in a bedroom with Jimmy Harrington who, before snoring off into raucous sleep, invited me to stay at his place on my swing through Castletownbere.

I limped alongside Missie through Kenmare the following morning, a market town at the head of the river with wide, fair streets and splendid yachts in the harbor. In leaving the lovely town, we were properly off the Ring of Kerry, as it swings northward through the Windy Gap into Killarney, and onto the Ring of Beara, the third of the peninsulas reaching southwest like fingers into the sea.

Our initial passage onto the Beara was canopied by graceful miles of glade—birch, larch, and holly. A tranquil stretch, even though Missie was in bad humor. I had an idea what was bugging her, so I opened the mudbox and produced a lovely red apple.

"C'mon, Miss, do you really think I'd swap you for Greta?" I fed her the shining fruit. "And what about your nights prancing about the fields in Kilkee and Ballybunion? Did you see me get jealous?"

She looked at me with pure disdain.

"Okay, granted, they were cut-jacks. But do you think I'm Mr. Happy Pants? When this trip is over, I promise you'll get your share of romance. But, for now, in the words of Van Morrison, let's 'Hardnose the Highway.' "

Feeling better after our chat, we sauntered on in the late afternoon toward Lehid Harbor, where Pat O'Sullivan greeted me outside the Tuosist Post Office.

"My aunt and uncle, Teddy and Joan O'Sullivan, are inviting you to spend the night at the Pier House in Kilmakilloge."

"I'm on my way," I replied happily, always pleased to have an advance reservation. "Am I far from them?"

"Every foot of six miles," Pat answered. "But it's well worth it. The Pier House was an old coast-guard station built in 1805, converted into a splendid pub. I'll ring and tell them to expect you in, say . . . an hour?"

"Three hours," I confessed shamefacedly.

"Jaysus," he replied, "your ass only travels two miles an hour?"

"On a level surface."

Leaving Pat to marvel at the slowpokes who gad about the world, we pushed on through the wooded wonderland. At times, however, we were bedeviled by squadrons of diptera: gnats, pismires, glegs, bluebottles—a veritable "air show" of swooping and whining fliers, stunting between the pylons of Missie's brown-tufted lugs.

Thankfully, a cool zephyr arrived an hour later, blowing the formation of flies hither and yon, leaving us to a serene woodland and lovely views of Iveragh across the waters. We traveled a narrow descending road lined with moss-covered walls and arched-over by a tangle of leafy boughs, a charmed breezeway to our promised destination for the night.

A car pulled ahead and out jumped an animated Teddy O'Sullivan.

"Are ye finding your way to the Pier House in Kilmakilloge?"

"I am, yes," I said, thanking him for his gracious invitation.

"Are you weak with the hunger?"

"I'm famished, to tell you the truth."

"Good, for you'll have a sip and sup, just two miles now. But I'm to warn you there'll be a *ceili* in your honor since it's your last night in County Kerry. Don't delay, and we'll see you in an hour's time, please God."

He left us to the loveliest walk yet encountered in our travels, a quiet stroll among a world of woodbine, bluebells, and foxglove, as the soft Kerry winds embraced us.

"Imagine," I said to Miss, gazing through the blue twilight at a flock of oystercatchers taking flight, "you and I will have walked a total of eighteen miles today. Templenoe to Kilmakilloge. A new record! We really can be home for Christmas! Oh, what celebrations await us!"

But, of course, Missie didn't answer. She just clipped along, as content as any animal in God's Kingdom, having left Greta far behind, just as I had left my attendant aches and pains, somewhere back along the day's long but magic road.

Lord Tim of the Holly

After a night of revels and good cheer, I woke up in the lounge section of The Pier House in Kilmakilloge to the clink of glasses and the voice of Teddy O'Sullivan rousing me from my sleep.

"Are you dead or alive, or what are you a'tall?" he asked, standing over my head.

I gazed blurry-eyed at the bar clock that showed it was past noon.

"Is it that late?" I asked, sitting up from the comfortable sofa.

" 'Tis, and I was thinking of waking you earlier to visit the holy lake of Mackeenlaun," he answered, collecting a tray of bottles, "but your mouth was opened wider than a pie plate. Now, up for a sup if you're still planning in being in Cork this evening."

After Joan's fulfilling lunch, Ted helped me collect Missie from the foreshore of Kilmakilloge, where an old steam tug had been grounded years before.

"This tug will not taste the salty sea again until the melting of the polar ice caps," said Ted. "Now, follow the road out the Derreen demesne, and by evening you'll come to two bridges. The second bridge is *Glasneanain*, 'the Bridge of Ivy.' Cross that and ye'll be in the County of Cork. Godspeed, and may the saints guide you."

Blessedly free of flying insects, we walked through the lush vegetation of Derreen Gardens, filled with rhododendrons and imported species of ferns and shrubs. The previous evening I had learned how the first landlord of Derreen, Sir William Petty, had acquired 250,000 Irish acres following Oliver Cromwell's confiscations.

"He was 'no knight in shining armor'," said a mustached local historian, "caring little for the land and less for his tenants. Three hundred years ago, a squirrel could hop from tree to tree from here to Allihees. But Petty stripped the forests to smelt the iron ore he took from Beara's hills.

"Early Ireland was filled with oak groves and herds of red deer," continued the chronicler, "but landlords like Sir William cleared them for quick profit. In fact, most English ale shipped to the Continent was casked in barrels of Irish oak."

"Rape and pillage," I commented. "Seems typical of Irish history."

"You can say that again," my informant went on. "Petty once proposed a scheme of sending thousands of Irish girls to England for breeding purposes, so that our bloodline might be improved. He found the Irish crude and primitive, and disdained Derreen, but he was knighted, no less, by Charles the Second. They must have been in dire need to fill a chair at that Round Table."

"There seems to be no shortage of villains, when it comes to the English in Ireland," I concluded.

So this day Missie and I continued on through long rows of spruce and larch, a modest effort at reforestation, but less noble in light of the oak forests that once canopied this now-stark peninsula ahead of us.

In Collorus, we came to a breathtaking vista overlooking the Kenmare River—a view that gave the eye free rein of the McGillycuddy Reeks on the Iveragh Peninsula. I sat on a stone wall trying to name the jagged peaks, and thinking again, as I had done when looking back to Dingle from Iveragh, of the grand people I had met there.

"That's a lovely view to carry home with you," said a gentleman walking his dog.

"I never thought Clare could be topped for scenery or people," I answered, "but now I'm taking my last look at Kerry and wondering the same."

"Your luck won't run dry in Cork, either," he said, his accent so different from those in Kerry. He whistled his sheepdog from the shore's edge. "And isn't it the knack of a traveler to bring out the best in people? I daresay you won't be able to decide on the loveliest or friendliest of Ireland's counties when your circuit's complete. No more, perhaps, than a mother could choose her favorite child."

Missie and I ambled on as the evening sun, peeping through low clouds in the west, brush-stroked this rock-strewn landscape with a palette of eye-popping colors. We soon came to *Glasneanian,* a triple-arched stone bridge draped in rich foliage, taking us triumphantly into Cork, our fourth county since leaving Roscommon.

Passing the village of Ardgroom, I stopped to take a picture of a young curly-topped girl looking out her front gate. After I had squeezed the shutter a second time, the girl's parents, Dan and Carol Sheehan, were out to investigate this roving tinker with Nikon in hand.

Introducing myself, I was soon in their kitchen surrounded by nine young Sheehans, two boys and seven girls, as little Julie, the curly-topped doll, hopped up on my lap like an adventurous kitten.

I entertained the giggling clutch by counting out grains of sugar for my tea, and sitting perplexed with butterknife in hand, confused as to what side of the bread I should butter.

"Butter the top side," said Declan in earnest.

"Butter either side," said Mary. "There's little difference to what side you decide upon."

"No difference?" I gasped, acting the goat amidst their giggles. "Why, there's a top and bottom to everything."

"But bread isn't two-sided like a coin," said Declan, a serious redhead of thirteen. "You just butter whatever side you wish and be away with it. You shouldn't give a bull's notion to such silly things."

Little Monica, age seven, took up my butterknife in a heap of sniggers, buttered my bread on one side, and jellied up the other.

"There, now," she said, handing it to me by the outer edges, "can't you be eating your way out of that?"

When the children retired, three to a bed, Mr. Sheehan and I walked a short distance to the Holly Bar, named for the tree that had been growing in the front window for over a century.

Entering the cozy pub, Dan introduced me to the publican, Ollie O'Sullivan, who pointed out Timothy O'Driscoll, an old eccentric dressed in a gladbag of rags, asking questions of the patrons.

"Lord Tim will buy anyone a pint of Murphy's if they answer him correctly," explained Ollie, looking back at the comical bachelor whose tie was so short it exposed his shirt's lower three buttons.

"Little fear of him ever parting with his money," added Dan, "for he'd stump any scholar, Fulbright or Halfbright, with his queer askings."

Lord Tim was currently face-to-face with a farmer who had, for the second time, ever-so-politely told him to bugger off.

"By the hoax of a fly," said Lord Tim, standing his ground beside the impatient farmer, "you're telling me you don't know the Seven Sisters of the Pleiades, and they gleaming o'er your head from time immemorial. Any schoolchild with a trace of learning knows 'em as easy as Dan Sheehan there knows the names of his seven pretty daughters"— glancing at Dan, but eyeing me boldly. "There's Alcyone, Celaeno, Electra, Merope, Sterope, Taygeta, and Maia, the daughters of Atlas," he replied, smacking his lips in grand gestures. "Hold the Murphy's, Ollie of the Holly, for we have yet to find a winner.

"Teddy Harrington, most learned man of the Beara," Lord Tim went on, skipping over to a passive fellow enjoying a quiet pint, "tell me the price of buttercakes in 1910?"

"I haven't a flipping clue," the soft-spoken man muttered.

"Nine pence a dozen," said Tim, triumphantly.

"Give me a crack at it," said a young man named Michael Mulcahy.

"How old was our own Hag of Beara when a priest turned her to stone?"

"One hundred and ten," guessed Michael.

"And you a proud native son," scolded Tim. "The Hag of Beara, celebrated in verse since the tenth century, lived seven times her natural life span—four hundred ninety years, that, outliving her grandchildren's great-grandchildren. Now, name the second-longest-living woman in Ireland."

"Your blooming mother!" crowed a young patron.

"Kathleen, Countess of Desmond," piped Tim, paying no heed to the upstart, "living to be one hundred and forty years old, and would have lived longer if not for falling from a hazel tree while gathering nuts. And if you don't believe me, look it up."

" 'Look it up'?" said Michael. "Where in heaven's name would anyone look up such nonsense? Only *your* head is so cluttered with fact and fable, legend and lore."

"Ask the Donkeyman a question," suggested Ollie O'Sullivan, introducing me to the old gent.

Lord Tim stepped toward me, eyes agleam. "You mean the celebrated American vaunt-courier himself, Oisin Odysseus O'Hara?"

"The very one," said Michael Mulcahy. "Didn't you see him pass with his donkey this evening?"

"Och, that I didn't!"

"What—a man who misses nothing but the odd laying of a heron's egg?"

"I must have been laying me own egg in the jacks beyont," he replied, keeping his gray watery eyes on me. He shook my hand warmly, and offered, "Better the ass that carries you than the horse that throws you, hey?"

"She's tipping along mighty," I said.

" 'Tipping along mighty,' " he repeated, raising his voice to the crowd, "and it taking you a lifetime to travel from Sneem to Smithereens. Moses himself couldn't have held back the Red Sea long enough to see you two safely across. Now, I'll give ye seven questions pertaining to the ways and nature of your donkey, for a Cork-brewed pint of Murphy's stout. Are ye right, there, O'Hara from Tara?"

"Fire away," I replied, amidst a resounding cheer from the patrons.

"The mule would be a horse but for his father being . . . ?"

". . . An ass," I answered, correctly.

"What is the best time to sire your lady donkey?"

"The moon's last quarter."

"When does a healthy donkey lose its winter coat?"

"In the month it was born."

The house cheered, as the stunned Timothy took a step back, as if clobbered in the jaw. Collecting his wits, however, this champion prizefighter pranced into the next go-round.

"Where is the imprint of the Blessed Virgin's thumb on your donkey?"

"On the inner aspect of her front legs, above the knee."

"How can a husband lessen his wife's labor pains?" he quickly challenged.

"By holding a donkey foal in his arms a day before the birth of his own child," I parried.

A thunderous ovation erupted, as patrons began to cluster close. I had Lord Tim on the ropes, pounding him with a flurry of rights, as jokes rang out about how Lord Tim would be reaching into barren pockets to buy me a pint.

"Two more questions," shouted Lord Tim, quieting the crowd and eyeing me appraisingly, "and, by the powers, if your man answers them correctly, he's the smartest fellow to walk the earth since Einstein took his leave. Now, how could you, this very night, cure a child with mumps?"

"Have the child drink water from a holy well while wearing my donkey's winkers," I stated with assurance.

Lord Tim went white as rice, thinking me a son of a druid. He fell back to his corner, took a healthy swallow of stout, returned to center ring, and raised both arms to the rambunctious throng, "Final question, please!" And, fixing me with a piercing gaze: "Where do your donkey's fingers reside?"

"Fingers?"

"Aye, you know 'em, fingers." He waved his in my face. "Five to each hand. Four digits and a thumb. Why, a few men in this parish have even been known to do a day's work with them. Again I ask, where are your donkey's fingers located?"

I stood flummoxed. Of all the tidbits I had gathered, no one had ever mentioned a donkey's fingers before.

"Well?" he said, doing a little jig before me.

My Adam's apple felt heavier than an iron bucket down a well, as the crowd groaned around me. I could have told him about zedonks and zebrasses; donkey cures for whooping cough and gout, how an onager is a wild ass from Central Asia; that the Australian kookaburra is nicknamed "the laughing donkey"; that the jackass penguin is found around the Cape of Good Hope; that the word *ass* in Irish means "waterfall"; that there's a gallery grave in County Laois called the Ass's Manger; that Samson killed a thousand Philistines with a donkey's skull. . . . But "fingers"?

The steamy, smoky house wrapped itself around me like a clenched fist. Noses flared. Eyes welled. Hearts thumped.

"Her front hooves?" I guessed.

"Och! Goodness gracious," Timothy gasped, pedaling back on his heels.

"Well," said Michael Mulcahy, "is the Donkeyman wrong or right?"

"Never in me puff!" Tim gasped, in glowing histrionics, still withholding the final revelation.

"Do I pull him a pint?" shouted Ollie.

"Well, I never!" Lord Tim bowed his knee, not yet divulging whether in respect or prayer, to signal defeat or thankful victory. "Never in me puff, I say, have I come so close to parting with me few hogs and hens. Why, the very phrase, 'A pint of Murphy's for Your Honor here,' has been humbly forming on me own parched lips. But then, for the famous Donkeyman to say, 'Her front hooves?' "

He stood erect and clapped me on the shoulder: "By the hoax of a fly, I'm sorely sorry, Oisin Odysseus O'Hara, but your donkey's fingers are located in her ears."

"Ears?" The cry went up from the disbelieving multitude.

"Aye, ears, lugs, *clues*—call 'em what you will!" exclaimed Tim in smiling defiance.

"And since you hapless lumps don't believe me, follow me to the Donkeyman's she-ass and I'll show you the ten fingers that's in it."

A great outpouring spilled from the bar, as Lord Timothy O'Driscoll led the way by flashlamp, marching us toward Dan Sheehan's paddock. Poor Missie stood like a dazed hare before Tim's oncoming high-beam, as if facing vigilantes come to avenge her misdeeds on the streets of Waterville and Parknasilla.

"Hold this lamp, you," Lord Tim instructed me, as I tried to console my frightened beast, "and by turning her ear inside out, like so, ye'll see the five fingers in it. Do you see 'em?" he asked loudly, to all and sundry, wrestling with my jibbing beast.

I peered into Missie's well-lit ear and, lo and behold, like a clear X ray, I saw five black fingerlike projections running from its base to tip.

"I do," I conceded, amidst the moans of a dozen souls lost outside the periphery of lamplight.

"Fair play, but you were nearly a winner," said Lord Tim, gracious in triumph, as we made our way back to the Holly. "And, by Jaysus, you've become a fair scholar of the road. 'Tis proud I am to meet you," he added, draping a warm arm around me, "and doubly proud to have a pint with you, begging your kindness for the loan of its purchase."

A Wasp's Dying Sting

CHAPTER TWENTY-NINE

A flying sod of turf, playfully pegged by Declan Sheehan, heralded Sunday the fifteenth of July, St. Swithin's Day. Climbing down from my bed of hay, I noticed a sharp prick among the scratchings of grass. Kneeling at ten-thirty Mass, I felt a burning tenderness in my left leg, but paid it no further mind when I joined the villagers in the customary "gathering" after church, followed by a pleasant exodus to the Holly Bar.

After two pints, followed by a farewell dinner at the Sheehans', where nine giggling children studied my every fun-forked bite, I collected Missie for our journey around Allihees, fourteen miles by way of Coulagh Bay.

I wasn't long going before my leg began to jolt painfully at every step. Limping on, I dragged myself through the lovely Pass of Bofficle, and hobbled gloomily into Eyeries, a quiet village where a string of pastel council houses were ringed by fertile fields amid rocky terrain, as pictured on the card I'd sent to the Four Masters at Rattigan's.

My leg continued to throb as I passed O'Neill's, O'Shea's, and Jack Lynch's pubs, all closed for the Holy Hour. At Eyeries Cross, I ditched behind a vacant shed to examine my leg, and fell aghast at the sight: a deep—reddish purple blotch running from calf to inner thigh, hot to the touch with red streaking.

"Cellulitis," I gasped, my nurse's training coming in handy, "and signs of phlebitis."

I pulled out my map and saw that Allihees led me into the boondocks of Beara.

How can I trudge on to Allihees when my leg looks like a red balloon? I panicked. *What chance have I in finding a doctor in that rock-populated backcountry?*

I sat crestfallen beneath the fingerpost. I had no choice but to cut across for Castletownbere, seven miles southeast, sacrificing the peninsula's western loop of road.

There will certainly be a doctor in the main port town of the area, I reassured myself. More importantly, Jimmy Harrington, my snoring roommate at John Hand's in Templenoe, had offered me a place to stay.

I limped on through Eyeries, a blot on the picture postcard, as a bored sheepdog lying in the middle of the road rose to snip at Missie's heels. He must have sensed my ill-humor, for no sooner had I raised my hazel than he retreated with a loud yap through the dust of this forsaken village.

Back on the main road for Castletownbere, I climbed aboard the cart and let Missie carry me into town, grateful for a gentle descent and her calm demeanor.

On Castletown's outskirts, I asked a local if he knew Jimmy Harrington.

"Jimmy the Tinker, ya mean. Jimmy the Horseman—a sturdy little lump of a fellow? You're not five hundred yards from his house, a two-story turret affair at the butt of the hill. But, being Sunday, ye'll find him playing cards at O'Sullivan's pub, named the Sea View, in town."

"Any chance of a doctor?" I followed up. "I'm afraid my leg is infected."

"A fine young physician by the name of Crowley lives a few bungalows back from Jimmy's."

"Would he have calling hours on a Sunday evening?"

"He would for you, then. 'Tis aisy to see the pain in your brow."

Thanking him, I found Jimmy's house, placed Missie in the back garden, and hobbled across to Dr. Crowley's. Without a grumble, the good doctor led me through the house to a small examining room where he rolled up my pant leg and blurted, "A wasp's dying sting."

"That's what it is?"

"Yes, and a nasty one; so-called, for no wasp could survive it," he replied, opening a cabinet filled with medical sundries. "You have full-blown cellulitis and will need to be off the leg for three or four days. But don't worry," he took note of my anxiety, "your leg should heal completely."

Handing me an envelope of antibiotics, Dr. Crowley instructed me to stay in bed and he'd call in at Jimmy Harrington's the following day. Thanking him, I limped down to the Sea View where I spotted Jimmy playing cards. Seeing me struggling at the door, he rushed over and assisted me to a chair where I divulged my condition.

"Ye'll stay with me till Dr. Crowley sees you fit to go," said Jimmy, with heartening concern. "Have ye eaten?"

"Oh, yes," I answered, a polite lie I would soon regret.

"I'll see you home, so," he offered, quickly introducing me to his card mates before throwing an arm about my waist.

Through the town we walked in a three-legged gimp and up the stairs of his home to where, in a semidelirious state, I took one of Dr. Crowley's pills and collapsed half-dead into a damp and lumpy bed.

I spent the next three days in the land of counterpane, but, unlike the DiLucia home in

Kilkee where I'd had the comforts of fresh linen and victuals, I passed my time at Jimmy's counting the mice that dashed along the skirting boards; or, when I hobbled to the kitchen below, watching them peer out from beneath the lids of the cold range—a range, I'm afraid, that never had heard the sizzle of egg or rasher, but only the kettle's lonely boil.

Nonetheless, I was high and dry from the storms that battered off Bantry Bay, knowing I could have been stranded in a lonesome booley with a leg angrily aflame. Yes, I was indeed grateful for my Good Samaritan, Jimmy. Once my snoring bedfellow in Templenoe, he was now my balding nurse, though in severe need of a crash course in nutrition.

After working the roads for the Council, Jimmy would return home in the evenings and fix us black tea with a few crusts of brown bread with butter. By Tuesday, I began to experience pangs of hunger that recalled the old Famine expression, "Hunger breaks through stone walls."

While my belly grumbled louder than the thunder atop nearby Hungry Hill, Jimmy the Horseman couldn't do enough for Missie, who had become great pals with Rocky, his gray Connemara pony. Before my nightly ration of tea and loaf, standard POW fare, I'd watch from the window while Jimmy served the fat and cheeky pair long swaths of fresh meadow grass, lovingly cut in sun-ripened fields, followed by a silvery splash of brimming springwater.

"Just my luck to be housed with a horseman rather than a butcher or baker," I moaned, turning weakly from the torn curtain.

That Tuesday evening, after our customary bread, washed down with harsh gulps of black tea, Jimmy rummaged through his pockets and presented me with a chocolate bar.

"I thought ye might be fond of sweets," he said, handing me the chocolate. "Sure, I'm not one to be firing up the skillet."

"Thank you," I said, trembling at the very sight of Cadbury's milk chocolate in gold foil and purple wrapping. Breaking the treat into its eight tasty squares, I lined them up to savor one at a time.

"There's a great tick out of your wall clock," I said, offering him a block of chocolate I'll be forever grateful he declined.

"Yes, but a strange clock, that," he said, brightening. "Do ye know, it never chimed for three years after a pony of mine died, and just last month it started up again. Just took itself a notion. But, I tell ye, the faeries must be working those hammers, for when it strikes midnight, it's not till one in the morning before they settle down again."

Our talk soon fell to the wisdom of animals.

"Animals would be as wise as ourselves if they had tongues," said Jimmy, as a band of gray mice brazenly gathered crumbs on the counter. "Isn't it true the whale holds a powerful amount of talk, and the porpoise? But I believe ponies, horses, and donkeys are the smartest of all, though I've come across some clever dogs and cats in me time."

"You're not alone in that view. The famous Irish author, Jonathan Swift, has his character Gulliver travel to a land where horses are smarter than people."

"Aye, the equines, they're the really intelligent ones. A Connemara pony, same breed as my Rocky, woke my neighbor some years ago after seeing a chimney spark ignite his thatch. Only by the pony's warning is the neighbor alive today. I also knew a farmer whose donkey came off Hungry Hill, banging its muzzle against his door, and leading the puzzled farmer up a mountainy drain to where her foal had fallen. Signs of wisdom, that."

"I think my brown-eyed girl would do the same," I said, going to the window to look out at my well-rested heroine.

On Thursday morning, Dr. Crowley gave me a clean bill of health.

"You're a healed man," he said, unraveling the last of my antibiotic bandages. "How does it feel?"

"As good as new," I answered, bearing full weight on my affected leg and walking across the room. I reached for my wallet.

"Two pounds will be grand," he remarked.

"Two pounds?" I queried. "For two visits, plus antibiotics?"

"Two pounds," he repeated. "And the best of luck with your roundabout."

I could only marvel again at the generosity I received at every turn of the road.

That evening, testing my underpinnings, I walked into town and bought six pint bottles of Guinness from the Hole in the Wall, and presented them to Jimmy in his bare kitchen.

"There was no need," he scolded. "It was grand just having you."

"It was grand for you to have kept me," I answered, uncapping two bottles and looking for glasses. "Where would I be tonight if you hadn't invited me here when we were in Templenoe? I could have suffered a leg clot around Ardacluggin Point and never been found. Believe me, it's more than a few bottles I owe you."

On Friday, July 20, I hitched Missie to the cart as a somber Jimmy looked on. I felt exactly the same, leaving a twice-met and never-to-be-forgotten friend in need. Waving a warm farewell, Missie and I made our way toward Hungry Hill, looming before us in a low cloud.

Jimmy added a postscript to his hospitality, by giving me the name of Michael Carey, a friend who lived a day's journey away, at the foot of Tim Healy Pass.

When I arrived at the comfortable yellow farmhouse, the welcoming Mrs. Mae Carey laid out a fine repast before me. As I was devouring the feast, her husband Michael, a large, robust farmer of seventy-odd years, burst into the kitchen, and demanded with a smile, "Did ye throw the traveler a bone with something on it?"

"I did, then," beamed Mae. "He's nearly dead with the hunger. Imagine, being holed up near a week with the likes of Jimmy Harrington, and not a morsel in the house, I'm certain."

Pleased as punch, Michael Carey joined me at the table, laughing at everything I had to say, then he took me down to O'Sullivan's Bar in Adrigole with two of his three sons, Frank and young Michael, where I was introduced to the world at large.

"Tell them the story of how the vain lass wouldn't leave her bedroom mirror to meet 'the weasel,'" Michael Carey egged me on; "or your night spent with the Kerry travelers?"

After a round of storytelling, Michael suggested I stay another day and walk the Tim Healy Pass.

"The Healy Pass was an engineering feat," he explained, "for it cut through the black rock of both Knockowen and Hungry Hill, the very heights of the Caha Mountains. But it came at a great cost to the locals," he added gravely. "It began supposedly as 'relief work' during the Famine, a government scheme to give the hungry work, rather than food. But endless hours in brutal weather yielded pennies a day. Starving people had to eat their wages, simply to keep at their backbreaking tasks for another day. 'Tis blood, as much as picks and shovels, that cleared the Tim Healy Pass. Scores died, until public outcry forced suspension. Seventy years later, work was resumed on the Pass, and completed in a decent manner by Tim Healy, governor-general of the Free State in the 1920s."

The following morning I walked the Healy Pass without Missie, winding through black cliffs and over sparkling rivulets to a crucifix at the summit. There I said a few prayers for all who had toiled and died on these slopes, and a prayer of thanks for my healthy leg.

Returning to the Careys' at noon, I dressed Missie and tied her in front of the house, planning a quick getaway, to reach Glengariff by nightfall. When I entered the kitchen, however, I found the Careys bustling with excitement, with national daily newspapers draped over table and chair.

"Our older brother, Patrick, a detective in Cork City, took part in a huge drug raid yesterday," young Michael informed me.

"My dear Patrick," said Mae proudly, carefully underlining with pencil and ruler each place her son's name was mentioned in print.

I picked up the *Independent* and read: *Up to twenty people are expected to be charged following the seizure of more than £60,000 worth of cannabis in raids in Cork . . .*

"You won't go without eating," said Mae, upon seeing Missie's nose poking at the window. "The meal is only waiting for the call of the plate," she added, dropping the papers to attend to the pots on the range.

With celebration in full throttle, we sat before a hearty meal of chicken, potatoes, and peas.

"There'll be no living with Pat now," smiled young Michael, "with his name in bold print."

"And just think of tomorrow's Sunday papers," added Frank. "Imagine, the largest cannabis bust in Cork's history. That makes our Patrick a hero!"

"What exactly is cannabis?" asked Mae, bewildered. "Do you eat it or smoke it, or what?"

"You smoke it like a cigarette, and the user holds it in his lungs and gets 'high,' " said young Michael.

"They use it a good deal in America, do they not?" Frank asked. "We often see it on the telly."

"Oh, yes," I said, as I bit into a delicious breast of chicken. "Since the 1960s, it's quite common to go to a party and see people smoking it. In fact, there's a grassroots move-ment to legalize it."

"Legalize it?" Mae objected. "So half the country can go raving mad?"

"Well, it's not quite like hallucinogens or opiates," I explained. "In fact, they've found medical uses for it, such as for glaucoma, or for nausea after chemotherapy treatments."

"You seem to know a good deal about it," observed Mr. Carey.

"Well, er, yes."

"Have you ever smoked it?"

"Smoked what, sir?" I stalled, choking on a pea.

"Cannabis."

"Well, yes, I did, sir. I mean, long ago, not regular or anything," I muttered, looking up to see four startled faces gaping at the sort their own boy had just put behind bars. "I was in Vietnam for a year," I tried to extenuate, "and we'd sit out, once in a while, mind you, on the French pillboxes along the South China Sea, and there I'd share the odd doobie—er, marijuana cigarette—with my mates."

"What was it like?" asked young Michael eagerly.

"Easygoing, enjoyable, much like a few pints on an empty stomach. It simply made you gaze out over the ocean and contemplate on things. But it also gives you a ravening appetite. I remember writing a long letter home to my mother under the influence, pin-ing for her chocolate brownies."

I was trying for levity, but Mae looked at me reprovingly.

"Oh, I know it was stupid," I said, forcing a laugh, "but that's all behind me now. Nothing is better than being drug-free—but for the odd pint, that is."

"Do you think it ever did you any damage?" Mae questioned sternly.

"Please?" I hedged, looking down at my plate growing cold.

"Did smoking cannabis or marijuana, or whatever ye call it, ever do you any harm?"

"I don't think so," I answered.

"So, you're saying smoking cannabis never had any ill-effect, is that right?" Mr. Carey tried to pin me down, standing from the table and winking at his own.

"Not that I'm aware of," I replied uneasily. "I mean, I doubt I'd be a rocket scientist if I'd never smoked, but . . ."

"Well," he concluded, lifting me by my ear from the table and dragging me to the kitchen window, "if smoking cannabis never did you any harm—tell us, can't you, why you have an ass and cart parked outside our door?"

I looked out at a beaming Missie, as the table rolled in laughter.

"Now, sit back down for your trifle." Mae softened. "And there's no need for you to write me how much you long for my dessert when you're holed up again with another breaking-the-bread-only bachelor on some desolate stretch of road."

A Run to Mizen Head

CHAPTER THIRTY

Missie and I camped out beneath the stars at the foot of Sugar Loaf, a cone-capped mountain often called "the Irish Matterhorn," in a field by a lake owned by John O'Sullivan of Loughfasta. Waking to the pale dawn, I found Missie Long-Ears had escaped my clumsy halter and gone off to make friends with a black mare and her spindly-legged foal nearby. Wild goats, nimbly navigating these hills, watched marble-eyed—wondering, no doubt, how Missie and I ever had come to camp in their hilly domain.

I retrieved my donk and descended into the "rugged glen" of Glengariff, enjoying a downslope after our uphill heave from Adrigole. Natives of this gentile Victorian village congregated before church on this clear Sunday morn, blessing our passing with a sprinkle of holy water from stone fonts at the church door.

As we were passing Newtown, a mile outside Bantry, Edward Godfrey signaled us off the road just as splashes of rain, hard as pennies, heralded the onset of a sound drenching.

Once unharnessed, Missie sought shelter beneath the lush canopy of a horse-chestnut tree, as Edward invited me into the faded warmth of his ivy-covered Georgian farm-house, where he introduced me to his sister, Mary. The interior, without electricity, was replete with the elegance of a nineteenth-century manor home, and I looked out from their high-curtained windows upon a well-kept garden.

Following a tasty evening of food and tale-telling, I took a flashlight into a nearby shed and dropped my sleeping bag onto a few potato sacks, quickly falling into the black abyss of sleep.

Grrrrrrr.

My head tumbled headlong in ribald dreams.

Grrrrrrr.

"Your breath is as sweet as honeysuckle." I pursed my lips.

Grrrrrrr!

My eyes rolled open to see a chainsaw of gnashing teeth; the snarling mouth of a ravening dog frothed above me.

I froze with this angry mongrel inches from my exposed jugular. It rivaled my nastiest awakening ever, one night in Vietnam when a fellow firefighter named Hank had assaulted me in my bunk with a sharp knife jabbing my throat, the smell of Jim Beam on his hot breath, as he slurred repeatedly that he was going to make me "bleed purple peanut butter." The Viet Cong had tossed a barrage of rockets our way that night, and Hank had tossed back one—or six—too many to calm his nerves. It didn't work, but he didn't slash me, either.

Now, with this canine madman, only my eyes could negotiate an appeal. Pleading eyes telling bloodshot eyes that it was all a mistake. I held perfectly still, my only motion the pulsing of the veins in my neck, driven by a jackhammer heartbeat. But, you know what? The cur's growl turned into a sniff and then a snuffle, and finally he snorted in disgust, shuffled across the floor, and lay before the open door, sighing deeply before collapsing into sleep.

A dusty stream of morning light awoke me from a troubled snooze, and I was relieved to find "the Hound of the Baskervilles" had retreated into the depths of the moor. I hurried into the Godfrey kitchen where I reported my nocturnal visitor.

"You mean Skipper?" laughed Ed, passing the brown bread. "Old Skip wouldn't hurt a flea."

"Old Skip wanted to rip my head off."

"And where, pray tell, did you go laying your sleeping bag?" asked Mary, pouring the tea.

"On top of the potato sacks in the far corner of the open shed," I answered, going for the marmalade.

"Wouldn't you have recognized that as being a dog's lair?" asked Ed. "And you, traveling the roads since the beginning of Time?"

"Can you believe it, a stranger sleeping in Skipper's bed?" Mary dipped two brown eggs from a saucepan of water on the Stanley range.

"Faith, Skipper's been sleeping in that bed since the day his mother birthed him as a pup!" Ed slapped his knee. "Poor Skip, about to lie down after a night of rambling, only to find the King of Ramblers in his bunk!"

The next morning we pushed on for Durras, hoping to cover fifteen miles by day's end, alongside Dunmanus Bay on the northern loop of the Mizen Peninsula. Over this hilly terrain, I was beckoned off the road four times for tea, confirming what I'd heard: that West Cork folk were the friendliest in the country. But then, each county had seemed that way in turn.

Despite poverty and privation, a long history of famine and emigration, the people displayed no stinginess. Far from it. As I passed a shabby trailer in a soggy field, a stout boy came running out with a few potatoes in hand, saying they might help fill my dinner plate. He was startled by my accent, so knew nothing of my small celebrity. To him, I was simply a bone-weary traveler bound for God-knows-where.

His kindness stayed with me for the following miles, and I wondered why the poorest are often the most charitable. Is it that they know the value of a little, or that God's bounty of grace rewards them?

Reaching the crossroads at Durras, as I was contemplating a jumble of fingerposts pointing to such places as Schull, Goleen, and Ballydehob, a man on his bicycle informed me I was standing on the driest spot in all Ireland.

"There isn't a pub within ten miles of here," he chortled, leaning comfortably against his bicycle. "Your thirst won't be quenched now, lad, until Dunmanus Village."

"That's okay, I've had a quantity of tea from kind folk by the road today. My kidneys are floating."

"That hospitality is in us yet," he observed. "The West Cork people were known to help every traveler during the Famine, even though they had little or nothing for their own. The old people, mind you, believed that Jesus could show up at your door dressed as tramp or beggar."

As he mounted his bike, he offered a final thought that echoed my own: "It's said that charity is both medicine for the heart and grace for the soul."

Along the quiet road to Dunmanus, looking over the bay and winding through heath and around rocky knolls, I passed a number of ring forts that suggested this lonely peninsula once supported a large population: a time when boars and wolves hunted the oak groves and giant elk bugled atop the crags of Knockaughna and Knocknamaddree.

Evening fell amongst these hills in a tapestry of lavenders, as my little beast of burden tipped along without a worldly care. She suddenly stopped and put her ears in motion, rotating like antennae, until both ears froze together at a specific point on the compass.

When this happened I would assume the role of gunner, positioning myself behind Missie's earscope and sighting through these crosshairs to see what had caught her attention. Through this eye-line, I had learned she hated pigs. Within sight of a mud-caked sow or within earshot of their rooting, she would drop her head and dig in her hooves like a raging bull. This time, however, I spotted what she'd heard before either of us could see: two giggling girls hiding from us at a bend in the road.

This playful pair showed themselves for a moment, then scampered off, keeping a safe distance from our march. We soon lost sight of them but, passing a large house, we again heard their cascade of giggles, this time from the safety of their parents' arms at the doorway.

"Would you spend a night under the same roof with these rascals?" asked the father, holding them in his grasp.

"I would, gladly," I answered, "but I'm afraid I'll have to tickle them for spooking my donkey."

The two older brothers charged out of the house. "Come in, then," they offered, "and we'll hold them down for you, gladly."

I was soon eating spuds and lamb chops in the comfort of Jerry and Bridie Kennedy's home, a converted police barracks, while their five lovely children—Derry, Pat, Mary, and the two rascals, Catherine and Anne—sat in attendance.

After supper, the TV reported that Pope John Paul II was confirmed to visit Ireland for Knock Shrine's centennial in late September: news that thrilled both myself and the family.

"I wasn't allowed to begin my journey until I spent a day at Knock with my grandmother," I related to the family.

"A woman of faith," Bridie Kennedy nodded, "and very proud of yourself, no doubt. And now the Pope is coming to bless us all as well."

Leaving the Kennedys' the next afternoon, we nosed for the cape of the Mizen Peninsula—Ireland's Land's End—looking across at Sheep's Head with its dazzlingly white promontory.

With dusk falling after a nine-mile day, we found ourselves in a marshy bird sanctuary near Barley Cove. Birds of every feather flew overhead, an ornithologist's delight, as noble swans floated in nearby lakelets watching over their cygnets.

"You'll snap your neck gaping at those flying creatures," called a woman from a nearby cottage. "Come in, can't you?"

I landed in the nest of John and Maggie Wilcox with their clutch of four chirping offspring. They had evidently eaten beforehand and, with no food forthcoming, I discovered a valuable lesson for every hungry rambler: the quickest way to a mother's heart, thus her pantry, is through her children.

"I have a riddle that no child in either Clare nor Kerry could answer," I began. "Liam, are you willing to give it a try?"

"I am, then."

There it happened. The simple utterance of the name, "Liam," triggered a congenial response in Maggie Wilcox as she sat idle in her kitchen. She had heard the name of her beloved son spoken warmly by a total stranger, and stirred forward.

"And if you don't answer correctly," I went on, picking up on this hopeful cue, "I'll give Stephen or Ann or Siobhán a go at it. Are you ready?"

"We are," they all squealed, surrounding me.

Yes, I had stumbled upon a formula, a magic spell, a godsend, for each time I mentioned their names, Maggie Wilcox visibly paused as she moved about the kitchen, as if catching the remembered note of a Chopin nocturne.

"Will you give it a go, Stephen?"

"I will."

"I'm a hopper of ditches, a cutter of corn, a brown little cow without any horns. What am I?"

"A hare," he answered triumphantly.

Perhaps a meal was coming anyway, but, believe me, by the time I reached the halfway mark in my nightly repertoire of jokes and riddles, a hard-boiled egg was waiting in its cup, brown bread was thickly sliced on its plate, and hot tea was steaming from its generous mug.

Filled to satisfaction and exhausted by clowning, I retired for the night to a couch in their back kitchen, where a lantern beneath a picture of the Sacred Heart cast the room in eternal glory. That light, however, also silhouetted a noisy parakeet in a cage above my head.

"Is this my punishment for manipulating a meal tonight?" I mused, wide-awake to the bird's endless gibberish. "A bleeping, peeping parakeet in my bedchamber," I moaned, throwing a blanket over my head, "and all the blooming birds flying over this place."

The next day, leaving Missie in the care of the Wilcox children, I set off on the run across the soft sand of Barley Cove for Mizen Head, the extreme southwesterly point of Ireland.

I reached a suspension bridge leading to the Mizen Signal Station at the tip of the headland, looking down on the slippery sheen of brown seals amongst the rocks below. Braving a sign that read, STRICTLY NO ADMITTANCE, hoping my radio celebrity would gain me access, I dared to cross and was warmly greeted by three lightkeepers at the door.

" 'Tis the Donkeyman," said Martin Hassett, shaking my hand. "Manuel DiLucia of Kilkee told me you'd be coming. Any bad bottles of stout since, heh?"

I stood flabbergasted.

"Amn't I from Kilkee as well?" he laughed, introducing me to Dick Driscoll and Bryan O'Regan, the principal keeper.

I was shortly sipping tea seven hundred feet above the gray tumultuous sea, hearing tales from the Outer Hebrides and about every ill-fated shipwreck between.

"We work four weeks on and four off," said Martin, "five years on land, followed by four on rock or island, until we retire after thirty years of service. And the rocks are ungodly places . . . Fastnet and Bull Island. Then we repeat the cycle in any of two dozen manned lighthouses."

"But this is wonderful," I said, looking out at the churning waters as herring gulls and gannets wheeled about us, and dark cormorants skimmed the ocean below.

"Aye," said Bryan, long past any romantic appreciation of the scenery, " 'tis grand to be spending your good years looking out at a big tub of water that spits its angry salt at ye night and day. We can't get enough of this grand view, can we, lads?"

" 'Tis lovely on the twenty-eighth day," joked Martin.

"You can certainly see the weather coming at you from up here," I stared, mesmerized.

"Seals are great forecasters," said Bryan, "and the west wind pushing up against the setting sun is surely a sign of bad weather. When you see that front forming in your travels, find shelter and brace yourself for a proper gale."

" 'Mackerel sky and mare's tails,' " recited Dick, " 'make loftier ships carry low sails.' "

Bryan broke in with a cheerful voice: "Now, Martin, 'tis only proper you escort Kevin to Norma Sheehan's Pub in Goleen. 'Twouldn't be right to send him from the southern tip of this country without sampling Norma's stout, now would it?"

"That it wouldn't, Principal Lightkeeper," smiled Martin, jumping to attention.

"Now, make sure you visit the signal station at Malin Head in Donegal," added Dick. "Then you can boast to your grandchildren how you once walked from Mizen to Malin."

"I will," I said, "and thank you."

"Cheerio, then," they called, as I caught up to Martin, already halfway across the bridge, smacking his lips at the thought of his assignment.

Wood of the Pilgrims

CHAPTER THIRTY-ONE

On Saturday morning, July 28, I boarded a converted fishing boat at Schull Harbor for Cape Clear Island, an Irish-speaking outpost seven miles beyond Roaring Water Bay, my itinerary in hand, drawn up last night by my knowledgeable host, Pat Hayes of nearby Coosheen.

On the pleasant voyage out, we passed Castle and Sherkin Islands, as humpbacked Cape Clear loomed before us with its patchwork of farms, deep glens, and burst of furze and bracken at its crown.

This blessed isle of Saint Kieran was filled with attractions I eagerly anticipated: Dunanore, the Fort of Gold; Lough Errul, a small lake with mystical cleansing properties; Fir Breaga, "false men," a line of standing stones to fool approaching marauders into thinking the isle was well-guarded; Cill Ciarain, a graveyard where it is said anyone buried there goes to heaven, including Cruathuir O'Careavaun, an eight-foot-tall giant buried there; and finally, St. Kieran's Well, where the saint had sanctified an ancient standing stone with the inscription of the cross, the oldest known Christian relic in Ireland.

As we approached Cape Clear's North Harbor, the skipper slowed to navigate cautiously through a narrow passage between high cliffs, but at this low idle, the engine began to sputter and choke. On shore, meanwhile, a crowd of islanders chattered excitedly in Irish, communicating in a universal language that something was amiss.

Finally, after bobbing for some anxious moments at the mouth of the harbor, our pilot grimly announced we had little choice but to return to Schull.

A middle-aged redhead, who hadn't rested her tongue since boarding, blew her stack. "You were down in the hole working on your engine when we first boarded," she roared. "You knew all along something was wrong, but you took us out anyway. Am I right?"

"I'm terribly sorry," he panted, wiping his brow with an oily rag, "but can't I take you out tomorrow, Garland Sunday?"

"I won't be here tomorrow, and I demand me three quid back!" she hollered, inciting a near-riot, as a dozen passengers joined her mutiny.

"Ye'll get your money when we land," he rejoined stiffly, turning the boat for home.

I sat glum at the prow, my pilgrimage off, and my wooden beads missing a blessed dip in the oldest holy well in Ireland. We nosed back for Schull, sheltered by Mount Gabriel, in whose shadow Saint Kieran's mother is laid to rest. By the spew of curses, it would be a miracle if our skipper didn't join her before the day was through.

"Listen to those tongues," said an elderly woman who, on our hopeful passage out, had confided she and her husband hailed from Tipperary. "Can't they offer up this lost outing to the Vietnamese boat people, suffering through long journeys on open boats, thirsting upon the waters, the sun scorching, turned away at every port or holed up in some garbage-strewn refugee camp?"

"But isn't Ireland a refuge, with a hundred Vietnamese planning to settle here next month?" said her husband, trying to ease her discomfort.

"A scant few to the numbers riding the waves," she added sorrowfully.

The boat continued to chug asthmatically back to the mainland, as the woman's remarks set my mind to thinking of the Vietnamese people I once knew: Tuyet, Kim, Phuöng, Duc, Huynh, Willie Joe. I'd thought of them often after the fall of Saigon. I fell into a deep funk wondering if they, too, were boat people, lost baggage on the high seas.

"Are you all right?" asked the Tipperary woman, tapping me lightly on the knee.

"I'm fine, thank you," I said, gathering myself. "I'm just disappointed, that's all."

"We all are," she said, patting my leg with a smile.

When I returned to Pat Hayes's that evening with a creme cake in hand, Mrs. Annie Hayes told me about tomorrow's festival of Lughnasa.

"Garland Sunday took the place of Lughnasa, the beginning of Harvest in the old calendar," she explained. "The practice of young girls making garlands from corn on this day gradually replaced the old Celtic traditions in most of the country. 'Tis also the time when the new potatoes are eaten, putting an end to Hungry July."

"I heard it was a day of great pilgrimage."

"It was, and still is," she went on. "Tomorrow morning at sunrise, thousands of pilgrims will climb to the summit of Croagh Patrick in County Mayo, some barefoot, just as they've been doing for a thousand years, to honor Saint Patrick who fasted there for forty days and nights."

"There's still some pagan festivals at play tomorrow as well," Pat added. "The great fairs of Lammas in Antrim, and Gooseberry in Donegal, are two of them."

"I remember my father on Garland Sunday," said Mrs. Hayes, "how he'd come through our half-door saying, 'The nights are growing long, and the hay is in the barn.'"

All this talk of changing seasons made me sag at the table.

"Anything wrong?" asked Pat.

"Well, yes. I'm here at the bottom of the country and it's almost August. I'm dangerously dallying."

"Do you have a set itinerary?"

"Not really. I just go at it day by day."

"Bring out the maps and we'll section out your journey," Pat said encouragingly. "You need goals and time lines. And names for your mission. No battle has ever been waged, no expedition achieved, no campaign won, without a code name."

With five ordnance maps spread across the table, Pat and I worked like field generals throughout the evening, emerging from the war room with plan in hand at precisely 2100 hours.

"Have you it all figured out?" asked Mrs. Hayes, serving up cake and tea.

"We do," proclaimed Pat. "Go ahead, Kevin."

"In order to be home by Christmas and win my wager with those crusted cronies at Rattigan's," I announced, "I commence tomorrow, Garland Sunday, on 'the Great Northern March,' needing to travel six hundred coastal miles in eighty days, seven-point-five miles a day, and reach Malin Head at the crown of the Inishowen Peninsula in County Donegal by the twentieth of October."

A cheer arose from the table.

"Next," I continued, "'the Great Western Perambulation'" holding up the map that showed the northwest of the country—" needing to travel four hundred seventy miles in forty nine days, a nine-point-six–mile–a–day clip, and reach Clifden in Connemara, County Galway, on the feast day, December eighth.

"And lastly," I concluded, "'the Homeward Swing,' one hundred twenty miles in sixteen days, giving myself plenty of time to reach Rattigan's Pub by Christmas Eve."

"And may God see you home safe," said Mrs. Hayes, cutting me a second wedge of creme cake.

We commenced on "The Great Northern March" next morning, tipping smartly through Ballydehob, Kilcoe, Meen Bridge, Church Cross, covering thirteen miles before camping out in Newbridge, a mile shy of Skibbereen—a Sunday we earned our garlands, surely.

After pitching camp, I was informed by a passerby that Skibbereen was celebrating the day with its annual "Maid of the Isles" festival, a night that would be "great crack, entirely."

As I walked into town, I recalled listening to my mother recite "Dear Old Skibbereen," one of a hundred poems she had memorized under the waving blackthorn of Headmaster Foley at Ballagh School:

Oh, son! I loved my native land with energy and pride,
Till a blight came o'er my crops—my sheep, my cattle died;
My rent and taxes were too high, I could not them redeem,
And that's the cruel reason that I left old Skibbereen.

This night, however, was the feast of Lughnasa, and the drab market square had been magically transformed with banners, bunting, and a dozen lovely maidens from Ireland and the United Kingdom.

Neil Blaney, an outspoken member of the Dáil from Donegal, spoke of Skibbereen's misfortunes at the hands of the English, and reflected on the injustices of Ulster today.

After his rousing speech, brass bands blared as black-gowned beauties paraded onto the stage to start the competition. Working my way closer—to better assess the most worthy of the candidates, of course—I passed throngs of old bachelors who evaluated the attributes of these charming women in a most poetical fashion.

"Will you look at the high lovely cheekbones on Miss London," said one rooster. "And her delicate chin. As soft, I'm sure, as a baby's heel."

"And look at the glint in Miss Galway's dark Spanish eyes," said his mate. " 'Tis as if she stole them from a jeweler's case in Barcelona."

Some remarks, however, were more coarse: "Did you ever see such a healthy pair of briskets as those on Miss Waterford?" Or, "I'd gladly take me last nitroglycerine tablet for one good roll in the hay with Miss Cork."

After Miss London was crowned Maid of the Isles, the crowd, amid the reels of traditional bands, retreated to pubs where more ribald talk and much merriment ensued, sparked by visions of these visiting maidens.

On Monday morning, Miss and I walked through an empty Skibbereen. Lughnasa was over and the Maids had vanished.

"Dear old Skib is weaker than Lazarus today," remarked one council worker sweeping the square, "and Jesus is nowhere to be found."

My first business was to buy new laces for my sneakers, so I stopped into a shoe shop where I was greeted by mounds of loose shoes of all colors and descriptions, as though they, too, had come alive to hold their own festival. Among the heaps of leather, a young clerk nursing a nasty hangover, tried hopelessly to match the shoes into pairs.

"A bloody cyclone came through here Saturday afternoon," he said apologetically. "Dances and functions, you know, and we fell terribly behind."

"So didn't most of Skibbereen," said a bloodshot customer, rummaging through a cairn of shoes and miraculously matching a pair to his size and liking. "There's cows in the fields still crying to be milked, and not a farmer able to rise to tend them."

He tried them on and decided, "I'll buy these and wear them home." The clerk tossed a half-dozen left-footed loafers aside and placed the customer's old clogs into an empty shoebox.

"Twelve pounds will be grand," said the clerk, walking to the counter.

The customer pulled a dirty twenty from his pocket and, waiting for his change, opened the shoebox and hollered, "You moron! You've sold me back me old clogs."

"Beg pardon," replied the clerk, not the least perturbed by the name-calling, "but I believe you're wearing the new pair."

The old masher looked down at his shining new brogues.

"You're right, I'm sorry there, me bucko," the customer apologized, leaving the shop in his midday stupor.

"The whole town goes bloody daft when the Maids arrive." The clerk cradled his head as he rung up my laces on the register.

A soft rain from the southwest was working itself into a frenzy when Michael Minihane, a photographer for the *Cork Examiner,* stopped to take pictures of me and Missie outside the town, while his six-year-old daughter, Claire, made friends with my little road warrior.

We pushed on wetly, still rallied with thoughts of "the Great Northern March," through Leap and Connonagh, and into Rosscarbery, a picturesque village of Victorian homes. As the evening cleared, we crossed a causeway, where seven swans took flight, their white wings swishing overhead.

"Isn't that a grand flyover for a champion of the roads?" remarked an elderly farmer, stepping down a grassy lane from a fine wooden farmhouse surrounded by luxuriant fields of golden barley.

He introduced himself as Jeremiah Hayes—no relation to Pat in Coosheen—and I soon found myself at his kitchen table alongside his wife, Mary, and five of their grown offspring, ranging in age from twenty-five to fifty.

"Mary and I have been blessed with a lucky thirteen of children," said Jeremiah, passing a huge bowl of spuds. "Six in New York, five at the table, and two married living down the road."

"A fine family, and a lovely house!" I exclaimed. "I haven't seen many wooden houses in Ireland. In fact, I'm not certain I've seen another."

"This house was a gift from God," he said, passing the gravy. "A great blast of wind in 1957 knocked down scores of trees from the wood beyond, and our daughter, Mary, who was with Pan American Airlines in New York, worked extra hours so we could hire laborers to plank the trees and build this house. A godsend, surely, for we were living in an old thatch given in to hard weather at the time."

After our meal, Pat, the youngest, walked me to where he had corralled Missie for the night. I was startled, given her severe prejudice against our porcine brethren, to find her sharing a byre with a grinning sow squealing in delight.

"Will you look at your donk's face," chuckled Pat. "Well, I never . . ."

"She hates pigs," I explained, trying to avoid her seething glare. "I'll have the devil to pay for this."

I opened my cart to feed Miss an apple but, coming up with a rotten one, I tossed it unthinkingly to her roommate, who oinked in sheer satisfaction. When I turned and presented my lady with a polished apple of perfection, I realized my mistake. If a donkey's looks could kill, my dusty remains would be buried in Rosscarbery Churchyard. It was clear she didn't know which was the worse swine, and I could feel her anger as she threatened to bite the hand as well as the offered fruit.

That night, Jeremiah walked me into the village to visit his sister, Katty Hayes, a frail octogenarian with a lively sense of history.

"Ross Carbery, *Ros-ailithir,* means 'the Wood of the Pilgrims,'" said the bedridden woman, cupping my hands warmly in hers as if those of a long-lost relation. "Scholars and pilgrims from all over Europe gathered here, and Rosscarbery became so popular that the monks of St. Fachtnan had to set up a second center in Schull, which literally means 'school.' By the ninth century, *Ros-ailithir* was one of the most important ecclesiastical centers in all Europe. I like to think the spirit lingers to this day.

"And, now, aren't you a twentieth-century pilgrim," she said, looking at me admiringly. "Walking a donkey to the Wood of the Pilgrims and, by glory, staying in the house built from those sacred trees?"

"'The Wood of the Pilgrims,'" I repeated. "But I'm afraid I'm more of a vagabond than a pilgrim. I doubt any devotee would have the thoughts that reel about in my head."

"Do you hear this, Jeremiah?" she said in mock surprise, sitting more upright in her bed. "Not a pilgrim? We're all on a pilgrimage, and you most of all. Remember: 'God hath chosen the foolish things of the world to confound the wise. And God hath chosen the weak things of the world to confound the things which are mighty.'

"Look proudly upon your endeavor," she concluded, as she sank back against the pillow, extending her hand for a final blessing. "Though it may not change the course of Irish history, it will certainly change the course of your own."

Having bid farewell, Jeremiah and I retired to the Carbery Arms where we joined two of his friends, and it was after midnight when we stepped onto the causeway and into the black of night. I lagged behind, eavesdropping on their musical chat amidst the calling of gulls and lapping of waves.

"Look at the vast assemblage of stars," said one of the trio, as they paused on the causeway. "There must be great goings-on in the heavens above, and life so simple for the likes of ourselves below. What do you say to all that, me bucko?" he asked me, pulling me into the conversation.

"I think you're the three luckiest men in the world," I said. "Imagine, this is your nightly walk home from a great pub."

"'The three luckiest,' is it?" smiled Jeremiah, throwing an arm over me. "Well, we're certainly not the least luckiest, that's for sure."

Over the River Blackwater

CHAPTER THIRTY-TWO

Next morning, Jeremiah waved a newspaper under my sleeping nose.

"Wake up, me boy. You're a celebrity."

I focused my bleary eyes on the front page of the *Cork Examiner,* where a banner headline read, DONKEY ADVENTURE EXTRAORDINARY, and below it were three photos of Missie and me taken the day before, and a short piece glorifying our travels.

After breakfast, I hurried to the newsagent and he gave me a dozen complimentary copies. I returned to the Hayes's where I prepared to mail these clippings to friends and family back home, as well as Rattigan's Pub, to show all was well after 525 miles of road.

"I'd give anything to see the faces on the Rattigan crowd when they receive their copy," I said to Jeremiah as I addressed the envelope. "Their briar pipes will be roaring like blast furnaces for the next three days."

After my run to the post office, I collected my ill-humored donkey from her byre with Miss Piggy and set out at a comfortable pace, hoping to reach Timoleague by day's end. I soon realized my offenses would not be soon forgotten or forgiven by my companion of the road. Missie Malicious was in a cantankerous mood, pulling against the halter and lunging her head at me. I was keeping guard, but she found an opening and sunk her teeth deep into my thigh, knocking me to the pavement.

I never wanted our relationship to turn violent, I never wanted to turn into an animal-beater, but sometimes a lesson must be driven home.

"That was real dumb, Miss," I said, picking myself up and raising the hazel above my head.

Whap!

We trudged along, silently looking in opposite directions, as would any couple after a good row. I really hated to hit her; and though farmers assured me that such a whap on her leathery backside was a mere slap on a wrist, I was bothered by the hostility itself, the brandishing of the stick, my flushed face and holler, the antithesis of our pastoral venture. And though she showed neither pain or distress after the wallop, I was certain a surge of bad karma had been let loose upon the world.

Fortunately, our glumness was interrupted by several well-wishers who had seen our photos in the *Examiner*. Unlike earlier encounters, I enjoyed this bout of celebrity immensely, posing for photos alongside children and accepting the generosity of a much-needed six pounds, as well as a quart of strawberries. Missie, too, seemed mollified by the attention, happily sharing the fresh fruit.

We passed along through a countryside of ripened barley, wheat, oats, and sugar beet. The true harvest was upon the land, unimaginable that "the Great Hunger" once gripped this bountiful region. It must be true as the lament has it: " 'Twas God who willed the potato blight, but 'twas the Saxon who caused the Famine, for he took nine times more out of the country than was needed to feed those in it."

When we arrived in Timoleague, I settled Missie, and walked through the remnants of the friary, one of the best-preserved of the Franciscan monasteries that had flourished in Ireland before Cromwell's invasion. There I met two young missionaries home from Africa, eager to make conversation, and we were soon touring the church and cloistral buildings together, their brown robes swishing through austere remains of gray stone.

"A hardened fellow by the name of Lord Forbes burnt both the friary and the town in 1642," said Brother Charles, after walking 'round the tower in prayer. "But earlier, Brother Michael O Cleary, chief of the Four Masters, had studied the famous Book of Lismore here."

" 'The Four Masters'?" I said, thinking of my own quartet back at Rattigan's.

"Aye," he said, touching the stones with his rough hands as if each were sanctified. "Four monks who worked tirelessly to collect the history of Ireland from the time of the Deluge. They gathered every old Irish manuscript they could find, fearing the country's history would be wiped out by English invasion. Writing in an old bardic dialect, they completed their task at Donegal Abbey in 1636."

The younger of the two, Brother James, noticed a rash of insect bites on my forearms.

"Horse doctors," he said, inspecting them closely. "You work with horses?"

"Donkeys," I answered. "Or more truthfully, a donkey."

"Well, watch yourself: 'Tis the season of the warble fly—miserable insects that bury their larvae into the hides of cow, horse, or donkey, leaving thick welts and abscesses."

We wound up sitting on the banks of the River Argideen, the extensive ruins of the abbey at our backs, talking about the wonders of the Dark Continent.

"We can see both the Plough, or Big Dipper, as well as the Southern Cross from our mission, as we're just north of the equator," said Brother Charles. "The Irish sky is thick with stars, but in Africa, the sky is milky-white with them."

They talked about their school and infirmary, their deep affection for the African people, and their homesickness for Ireland, this their first time back in three years.

"But we're not that far away," joked Brother James, fanning out his robes to lay on his back. "My parents, who live in Cork, collected a vial of fine sand blown up from the Sahara and settled on the windscreens of motorcars."

"You're stretching it there, aren't you?" I asked wryly.

"I am not," he stated, sitting upright. "A dry southerly wind can carry desert sand for thousands of miles. My father has great fun showing the pink sand to our neighbors, saying, 'We can't be too far away from our son when his sandals go kicking up sand into our eyes.'"

"What you really need for your travels is an African wild ass," joked Brother Charles. "If you could ever hop up on its back, and stay on it, you'd be back in Roscommon by nightfall."

After a mile-eating march the next day, we set out from Knocknahilan for Ballinagaonulia, an eight-mile jaunt that would leave us within striking distance of Cork City on Sunday. The road, however, rose to a punishing grade after Kinsale, so we stopped to rest beneath a green fingerpost that read: O'NEILL'S CAMP, 1601. ONE MILE.

I took the mudbox off Missie's back and hid it in deep foliage, as we walked down this quiet lane leading to the old encampment of Hugh O'Neill, famous for a bloody battle on December 23, 1601, that led to the defeat of the Irish clans and the subsequent Flight of the Earls.

I sat in this clearing and looked about the solemn grounds where thousands of Irish were left dead and mangled after the clash, which had pitted the powerful Ulster chieftains, Hugh O'Neill and Hugh O'Donnell, against Lord Mountjoy, under the orders of the crowned redhead, Queen Bess. Historians say the battle favored the Irish, but somehow O'Donnell lost his way the night before and, when dawn arrived, he found himself vulnerable to English cannon, muskets, and horsemen. And so lost a campaign that, if won, might have given the Irish an independent kingdom.

I pulled myself out from the country's painful history and glanced over at Missie, busily feasting on spear thistles a few yards away. I jumped upright, however, at the sight of three thumb-sized warble flies, hovering lazily above her head, the dreaded bombers mentioned by Brother James.

I grabbed my hazel stick and approached my pet, as she grazed, oblivious to imminent danger. One warble fly alighted on her hindquarters, the second on her back, and the third on her shoulder, where they boldly surveyed her short matted hair, for Missie had recently shed her lustrous coat and now looked more like a clipped poodle than a shaggy dog.

I quickly decided to work hind to fore, and with a flash of my hazel, I tattooed the first fellow to Missie's rump, nailed the second chump to her cross, but the third took to the air, hovering like a hanging curveball. Splat! Over the hedge and gone! Three swings. Three dead warble flies. Adios, amigos.

I was inclined to savor my victory after this heroic vanquishing of the invading pest. But Missie had a different view of my martial exploits, mistaking them for a resumption of our "marital" hostilities, and responded with another nasty bite to my leg.

I raised my stick but halted. No, not again. I was tired of domestic violence. She braced for a retaliatory strike, but instead I smothered her with hugs and kisses. I picked up a dead warble fly and put it before her for her own inspection; she snorted and looked away, but somehow I thought she had understood. At that moment, I pledged never to strike her again.

Now with leg wound and my stick stained in enemies' blood, I turned to imagining myself the last of the great Irish woodkernes, called to defense of clan and land. I flailed my stick wildly, a self-proclaimed "Sultan of Swat," and rushed into battle over these bloodstained fields against the phantom Mountjoy and his ranks of rancid men.

There, on a small rise, I withstood thundering horsemen and booms of cannonade. There, beside a copse of trees, I scattered brigades of cavalry, causing their horses to tumble in a wild tangle of hooves. And there, returning to my faithful brown steed, I sent foot soldiers scurrying back to Merry Olde England.

"Sail away!" I shouted to the retreating redcoats. "Let our own chieftains squabble! Leave the monasteries peaceful during compline! And, by God, let the native tongue ring out above crib and cradle!"

Exhausted after this battle, I tossed my stick into the dog-rose and fell onto a grassy bank, squinting up into a high ash. Rested, I took up my hazel, cut that frosty May morning by Tom Nolan; my thin defender, who had just made mincemeat out of three vicious warble flies.

"Mystical Hazel," I proclaimed, standing it upright to wipe it clean in the grass. "Sacred tree of August. Queen Maeve's walking stick. Wooden wand of kings. Divining rod for holy wells. Staff of faith. No one needs to convince me of your royal and bewitching powers after all these miles of road. I dub you Ty O'Kelly, for the noble hill from whence you came."

We weren't long back on the Heathfield Road when we met an old woman laboring up her pathway with a heavy kettle of water. She bid me good-day and asked if I wanted a sup of water. When I responded gratefully, she ducked into her old farmhouse and out again with an enamel cup, accompanied by a pair of wispy-bearded billy goats. As I took refreshment, she pointed down the straight line of road, and said, " 'Tis 'The Rising Sun,' this road you're on."

Back on the beeline, I asked Missie: "Now, that's odd company for an old woman to keep, is it not? Imagine if people came to visit me years from now, and found you lazing about in the kitchen. What strange notions would fill their heads, tell me?"

Dusk fell at nine o'clock, reminding me the long summer nights were indeed over, as we found accommodation with Mr. and Mrs. Dennis Cullinane of Ballinagaonulia, five miles from Cork City.

Sunday morning I woke to a torrential downpour.

"You won't see the city today," said Denny, during breakfast. "Content yourself with staying on."

After Mass in Bishopstown, my dampened spirits were cheered by Mrs. Cullinane's Sunday roast.

Piling the mashed spuds onto my plate, I began to shape the Knockmealdown, Galtee, and Ballyhoura Mountains, all visible north of Cork City, much like Richard Dreyfuss did in *Close Encounters of the Third Kind*. I next plopped peas into the imaginary Gap of Aherlow, and a dollop of gravy, like Guaguane Barra Lake itself, into the midst of it all.

"Are you going to eat your meal or play with it?" asked Jerry, Denny's younger brother, with a laugh.

"Oh, I'm sorry," I said, catching myself. "My head is so full of the outdoors that this heap of potatoes remind me of the mountains on Tipperary's horizon."

After the filling feast, I dumped myself onto the couch in their musty front parlor. When I woke from my doze, a cowboy movie was blaring on the telly.

"Do the Irish enjoy westerns?" I asked Jerry, sitting in a chair beside me. "They seem to be aired every Sunday afternoon."

"They're great value," he answered with a grin, enjoying his day out of the rain. "Open spaces, horses, sheep and cattle, and plenty of drinking and fighting in the saloons. We old Irish go for that sort of thing."

On Monday, the August Bank Holiday, I harnessed Missie with only one thought in mind: *Cork City or bust!* Cork was our first urban dragon, and we had no choice but to attack it head-on. Yes, lovely Corcaigh, "the Marshy Place," situated at the mouth of the River Lee.

We traveled the main highway until we came to the city's Grand Parade, marveling at white limestone buildings, gleaming cathedral spires, and a busy riverfront of quays and bridges. Bells rang out from the city at this hour of noon, bells from St. Finnbar's Cathedral—and, high on St. Anne's Hill, the sweet sound of Shandon's bells, made famous in lyric and song.

"This is it," I said, screwing up my courage and feeding Missie a handful of oats. "Remember, Miss, be alert and behave yourself. There'll be plenty of lights, manhole covers, flying paper, horns and air brakes. Pay them no mind. Stay close, move along, and, please, I beg you, try not to drop a basket of briquettes in front of the Custom House."

Initially it seemed an easygoing passage, but when we hit the main thoroughfare of Patrick Street, my jaw dropped at the long receding row of traffic lights that stretched from St. Peter and Paul Cathedral to the limits of sight. Worse still, thousands of merry Corkonians were enjoying this summer respite, gathering at every curbside to herald our passing as if we were on parade for Barnum and Bailey's "Greatest Show on Earth."

Waving blankly to hordes either hailing us or falling "ass over teakettles" in laughter,

I experienced all the ambiguities of my little celebrity. I might have been happier slinking through the city incognito, but, no, thanks to the *Cork Examiner,* I was the fandangling Donkeyman, traveling through a hurtling sea of gas-belching vehicles in sublime incongruity.

Oh, how I wished time would skip ahead, as my poky mate became trapped at each pedestrian crossing within a stampede of city folk, circling Her Highness as though they'd never laid eyes upon a donkey—the cause of incessant *beep-beep*ing blockages in Cork's central artery.

I carried on, my head throbbing, when a snickering party of young women accosted me at Merchant's Quay. What could I do but stammer in woeful embarrassment as their summer dresses billowed pleasantly in the updraft of the North Channel. Lovely lasses who pointed at me with such uninhibited laughter you'd think I was the Prince of Clowns, as they begged me for forgiveness before high-heeling away.

Years from now, when I lay weak on my deathbed, the oils of extreme unction greasing my brow, one little grandchild of mine might ask, "Grandpa, is it a terrible thing to die?"

I'll clear my death-rattled throat and dryly reply: "Not as bad, my dear child, as walking an ass through Cork City on an August Bank Holiday."

Onward ho! We hightailed it away from the city's environs and through Midleton where, hot and exhausted, I would have been happy to dive into its local landmark: the world's largest pot-still in the world's oldest distillery. But we pushed on, like bandits on the run, a record twenty-two miles, until Missie rolled in a high meadow and I collapsed face-first into a horse butt—a horse cart—owned by Dan Kelliher of Castlemartyr, feeling like a fallen martyr myself.

Recuperated, we arrived two days later in Youghal, passing the lighthouse and an esplanade of fine mansions. The narrow, one-way streets would have yielded another impasse if not for a kind old soul who took it upon himself to direct traffic, thus allowing us to pass beneath an archway spanning the cobbled street, with four floors piled atop it.

"That's the Clock Tower," he explained, leading us out of the tight spot. " 'Twas a gift from George the Third to the people of Youghal in 1776 to house offenders under the Penal Laws. By 1785 it was so crowded the bloody jailkeeper had to move out."

Bidding our guide farewell, Missie and I came to Youghal Bridge which spans the River Blackwater, connecting the counties of Cork and Waterford. Despite surging traffic, all was well in our crossing until we came to the expansion plate at the center of the bridge. There, Missie Ignoramus threw on the brakes. No way she would walk that steel plank.

It was déjà vu all over again, as Missie assumed the same crosswise posture she had back on the Dingle, but this wasn't the pastoral "River in the Glen," but the main bridge linking two populous counties. Mass commotion threatened to ensue as horns blasted. Just a warm-up, mind you, like the blare of tubas and trombones before all members of an orchestra are seated, a serenade of fury just tuning up.

I considered the stick in my hand, but decided not to brandish it over my poor pan-icked animal, thus upholding my pledge made at O'Neill's Camp. Three German boys on bicycles came pedaling by, and I begged them to push the cart from behind. As citi-zens from both counties watched, I took hold of Missie's ears, wrung them like dish-towels, and, praise be to God, with the assistance of the good lads, didn't my lovely Miss Lily tip-dance over the metal plate to the toots of a thousand motorcars.

"Welcome to Waterford!" the motorists called.

"Glad to be here!" I shouted back, waving a peaceful Ty O'Kelly in the air.

Washerwoman from Tramore

W e weren't long in County Waterford when a kettle-black sky dipped its wet spout, drenching me so thoroughly I had little choice but to seek refuge in a reed-thatched pub in Grange.

When I entered the pub, the owners Tom and Sis Fleming made a great fuss of my arrival, and as quick as I could peel off my oilskins, Missie was housed in a neighbor's byre and myself before a roaring fire fanned by "a firing wheel," a century-old revolving bellows. Noticing the Flemings' soft Waterford accent, as different from Cork's as Cork's was from Kerry's, I marveled at these dialect changes over the span of a bridge.

Next morning, after a sidetrip tour to St. Declan's Cathedral in nearby Ardmore, where an intact twelfth-century round tower rises nearly a hundred feet above the ruins, I gathered Missie and bid farewell to the Flemings. We were walking the wooded area of Gorteen amid the dreamy Drum Hills, when we pulled off the road for a black hearse and its long funeral procession to pass. With head still bowed, I was accosted by an elderly man who literally popped out from the hedges.

"They call Ireland a poor country," he leaned against his walking stick and commented, "but did you ever see such a fine line of motorcars? And isn't it grand for the dead fellow to have such a loyal following in the end?"

"Is he a dignitary of some sort?" I asked, as the lengthy line continued without hint of a letup.

"It wouldn't matter if he was a baron or a two-cow farmer," he remarked. "It's the practice here and, indeed, in most country parishes, that one from every household attend the funeral of a neighbor. Out of respect, of course, but sure, doesn't it guarantee each of us a grand send-off in the end."

"I suppose it does," I agreed.

"The old people prayed for three blessings long ago," he went on: "memory, truth, and respect. And it's this long memory of the rural Irish that binds us together still, for many old country folk today can go back hundreds of years in recalling their ancestry. And if you go back far enough, isn't everyone related?"

"Seems so, in this country."

"With our tattered and war-torn history, we've been little more than a land of funerals." He wound up his memorial reflections as the last car in the procession trickled by. Not about to let go of a willing audience, he quickly queried, "Do you know our little red weasel, the Irish stoat, also holds funeral services?"

"No, I never heard that."

"Oh, yes," he smiled broadly. "The dead stoat is carried away by a pair of his own with seven or eight in attendance. They behave like proper Christians."

Having found another topic, the wayside commentator launched into tales of Irish wildlife, but I was more than content to let this engaging old man have his say.

"In bygone days, we had bog elk with antlers of ten-foot span, and more recently we had grand packs of wolves, and herds of red deer and wild swine. But those, I'm afraid, vanished when England stripped our forests. 'Tis a wonder we Irish didn't become extinct during those times as well.

"Yet we still do have the native species like the lovely otter and the cute fox," he continued. "But then there's the vicious badger, brought in by the Vikings. It was said that the starving during the Great Hunger refused to eat badger because they had been introduced by these invaders."

"I've heard the badger's jaws are strong enough to snap a human bone, and to avoid them at all costs."

"You heard right," he answered, "for they don't let up on their bite until they hear the snap of bone. That's why wise farmers working the lowland areas place burnt cinders inside their boots, to fool the badger into thinking the bone itself has snapped, not the cinder. And who, tell me, can steal from an apple orchard quicker than a mischievous schoolboy?"

"A mischievous schoolgirl?"

"Good answer, that, but 'tis the hedgehog," he divulged gleefully. "Don't they climb the trees to the high boughs, shake the branches loose of its fruit, climb down, roll onto their backs, and pick up five or six apples with their quills, and home again to their happy clutch."

I smiled encouragement, as the old fellow rolled out more animal tales that ought to be true, even if they weren't. At length, he asked, "Have you heard the cuckoo in your travels?"

"I did, just outside Ballyvaughan in County Clare."

"Did you hear it out of your left ear or your right?"

"Well, it would have been my left ear," I calculated, "for my right ear was against the sea."

"Ah, a pity, that. 'Tis the right ear that always brings the luck. But, cheer up: I say you're a lucky man. No doubt a rich fella, with heaps of money in the banks beyont in America. Mr. Moneybags, is it?"

"I'm afraid not."

"Enough of the poor mouth." He shook his head in disbelief.

"I have thirty-eight pounds to my name," I answered honestly.

"You can't fool an old cadger like me! You're as straight as a ship's mast, not bent crooked with the hard work. And look at your hands . . . those of a priest. 'Tis easy to see you're gentry," he laughed. "The only thing you can't buy is poverty."

"But . . ." I interrupted.

"It's no bother to me who you are," he concluded, tapping his walking stick against mine in farewell. "And when it's time for your own funeral which, please God, will be ages 'pon age, I hope your procession is longer than the Wexford Mail, and the saints in Heaven singing your praises when you arrive at Glory's Gates."

With that, the old man limped back from wherever he came.

As we approached the outskirts of Dungarvan, another oldster, on the further side of seventy, was leaning over his gate, intent on the chat. I pulled into his little driveway and he regaled me with the history of Dungarvan, relating how a Mrs. Nagle saved the town from ruin by offering Cromwell and his men cups of milk after they had plundered the Augustine priory nearby.

"Supposedly, the Lord Protector was so grateful to Mrs. Nagle that he spared our town, though I say it was out of exhaustion he allowed it to stand. Just the week before, didn't the black-hearted devil lay waste to the town of Wexford, slaughtering thousands of its citizens."

Another senior citizen came out of a house across the road, headed for town.

"How is the old fella keeping?" he called out to my new friend.

"Up for the pipe and breakfast this morning, thank God. And now down for the nap. And how is your mother?"

"Ornery as a Kilkenny cat. Nothing will please her today, though she slept like a lamb the whole night."

"You're bearing your cross well."

"The cross is no bother," his friend retorted. " 'Tis the splinters in it that do be killing me."

The following evening, as we trekked toward Bunmahon on a tiring, hilly road, we were caught in an angry downpour. It was short-lived, however, as the sun burst through a tatter of western cloud, sending glints of light across the barley, making the countryside shimmer like a gold collar crafted in an era of Celtic glory.

In the freshly wet hedgerows, two girls busily picking black currants stopped to pet Missie.

"We're collecting berries for the jam man," one fluted, her mouth and fingers blue-stained. "He's coming first thing in the morning and gives us a fair penny for our labors."

"What counts as 'a fair penny'?" I asked the industrious pair.

"Two pound a stone," answered the other, dropping the ripe fruit into a yellow Hillman tin.

"A stone is what, fourteen pounds? Well, God Bless the Work," I said, adopting the often-heard colloquial expression, as they giddily fell back to the task, their fingers darting through the brambles like the beaks of hungry songbirds.

Arriving in Bunmahon, I spotted a field that had Missie's name written all over it: a secure meadow with luxuriant tufts of high grass. A four-star accommodation in any donkey guide.

"Is there any chance my donkey could spend a restful night in your field?" I asked of the family by the farmhouse.

"She can stay as long as she likes!" squealed the two children, Killian and Ide, running toward us.

After supper the children's uncle, Jim Cullinan, walked me through the village on the River Mahon.

"Bunmahon was a prosperous copper town during the last century," he explained, "until cheaper copper came from Cuba. After that, half the town emigrated to Butte, Montana, to dig copper and silver there. But at least Bunmahon was well off during the Famine, doing what it could for its neighbors."

Next morning, young Killian came running to the kitchen table.

"You have to see your donkey," he gasped, dashing off as fast as he came.

Recalling that dreadful day in Kerry when Missie nearly choked to death on her bridle, I bolted from the table, leaped a number of gates, and found her lying comfortably on her flank, cradling two kittens in the warmth of her lap.

"Did you ever see such a thing?" Killian asked, watching the kittens play in the white of her belly. "Isn't she a pet to let them have their way?"

Missie was a portrait of maternal tenderness, a comical Madonna, sweet and gentle, the reigning queen of the peaceable kingdom, the lioness protecting her lambs. A vision of coexistence to inspire a strife-torn land. How could I ever have thought of striking her?

We were soon off, leaving the kittens behind but taking along a vision of mother-hood for Missie once our travels were done. Our departure was joined, however, by a wistful entourage of children from the village.

"There's a steep hill out the road," warned the freckled leader, a boy of twelve, "but we'll gladly push the cart to help Missie along, for ye'll be meeting another high hill before reaching Annestown."

"That's very kind," I said, as nine others including Killian and Ide, trooped behind, a jolly exodus cutting Bunmahon's population by a third.

We arrived at the base of Tankardstown Hill, a modest-enough hump, but the road crew put their hearts to the task, shouldering the tailboard of the cart as though ascending Himalayan heights. The children huffed, puffed, and fell into exaggerated exhaustion upon reaching the crown of this green hillock.

As they sprawled out to catch their breath, I introduced them to "Bucktooth Pearl, the Talking Donkey," working Missie's lips like a seasoned ventriloquist.

"Did you hear about the Kerryman who won a gold medal at the Olympics?" Bucktooth Pearl asked the gang.

"No," they squealed in delight, covering their mouths at the sight of Missie's grass-stained buckies.

"Well," my long-eared dummy answered, "didn't he take it home and have it bronzed!"

When their uproarious mirth had subsided and they readied to leave, I offered the foreman a pound note, so each could buy ten pence' worth of sweets in town. But neither he nor his crew would accept this compensation, scattering before my advances as though I were waving a switch of nettles in my hand.

"Cheerio, Mr. Donkeyman," they sang, scuttling down the hillside for their homes.

We passed through Annestown, a tidy village bounded by fields of grain swaying heavily in the summery breeze, and settled that evening outside Tramore with the Rockett family.

After supper, Mr. Rockett, a lively man in his sixties, walked me down to a singing pub owned by his relations, lilting their signature tune on this fine summer evening:

> "I was feeling very thirsty after eating salty grub,
> When Lady Luck directed me to Mrs. Rockett's Pub . . ."

The celebrated Rockett's Pub was rocking on this Saturday night, a musical hotspot where, I was told, the Clancy Brothers got their start. As I sipped a Smithwick's, Mr. Rockett pointed to a woman motioning me out to the dance floor.

One might think such an invitation from the fairer sex would delight this wayfarer of the dusty roads, but it was heart-stopping to see this beefy, inebriated woman shamelessly curling her forefinger in my direction. I dodged her glance, not wanting to offend by refusing, for she was equipped with forearms that could pull turnips from Alaska's frozen tundra, and the most colossal breasts this side of Babylonia.

"Wouldn't it be like her drunken ways to go running her lamps over you, an innocent stranger," commented Mr. Rockett in exasperation.

I peeked over my glass brim at this stupendous bowl of Jell-O, thirty years my senior, swaying before me. She was dressed in a shapeless floral dress the size of a circus tent, and the spattering of cow dung on her stockings did little to add to her total attractiveness.

Mr. Rockett's cronies, noting my hesitancy from afar, were over to roust me from my nest.

"She's waiting to flatten your ears, Mr. Donkeyman," voiced one old spalpeen.

"Is it a snorkel you're waiting on?" crooned a chinless piper.

"Arragh, give her a whirl," choked the third, wiping his teary eyes. "Ye wouldn't let the villagers down, would ye?"

"Dance with her the one time, and be done with it, so," advised Mr. Rockett, sensibly. "She's a decent sort when her gills aren't awash with the drink."

I reluctantly left my sanctuary as she jerked me to the floor, grabbed me close, and trapped my face in cleavage deeper than Kerry's Paps of Dana.

She pulled me from her Valley of Knockmelons only to press her powdered cheeks against mine, and twirled me about the dance floor to a swift-stepping medley of double jigs. Numerous couples, knocked askew or scattered by our bumper-car ride, regrouped to clap and stomp around us, as the band kicked into a series of high-stepping reels.

I felt I was spinning on a mad carousel, hundreds of painted faces blurring grotesquely all around me. She wheeled me about aimlessly, upsetting tables and chairs, her heaving pillows battering me like waves as I gasped for air, afraid to drown between them. My legs went limp and lifeless, sagging across the floor like a drowned man dragged to shore.

But still, fiddles screeched and goat-skinned bodhrans pounded until, finally, the woman cradled my head, gazed at me with a frightful passion, and planted a big fat wet cigarette kiss square on my lips.

"Are you all right?" laughed Mr. Rockett, assisting me to my chair, as the crowd dissolved in mayhem.

I could only wheeze as my unsteady hands groped for a generous gulp of lager.

"You look like a battered boxer!" crowed a blackguard. "But, now, can't you go telling the whole world how you danced with the buxom Washerwoman from Tramore!"

Having played my part, suffered my initiation, I won great favor from the crowd, and basked in the jovial limelight. Rubbing my arms where they'd nearly been pulled from their sockets, I joked, "I heard about a Kerry woman who used to wrestle boars at county fairs, and wore a necklace of tusks to prove it. But I never believed it till tonight, when I witnessed first-hand how strong a Waterford woman could be!"

The Cock and Hen

On Sunday morning, after church and a banger of a breakfast, I said farewell to the Rockett family and passed the aforesaid seaside resort of Tramore, whose Ferris wheel along the strand appeared through the morning haze like the enchanted playground of a child's dream.

We took the main road to Waterford City, and arrived by midafternoon. Within the city, we confronted a high bridge, from which Missie looked down unsteadily upon the swelling River Suir. Fortunately, a glimpse of an apple was all it took to coax her along.

We traveled past the flour mills of Ferrybank, looking back across the dark river at Waterford's mile-long quay of pastel homes, warehouses, and its most famous landmark: Reginald's Tower, the remnant of a fortified wall built by the Danes in 1003.

When we came to open country, I found accommodations with Thomas Doyle, who placed Missie in a stable with his old draught horse.

Next morning, Mr. Doyle checked Missie's shoes.

"They've worn terribly thin and may split on her," he said. "Why not walk her into Power's Forge on Jail Street for new slippers?"

Heeding his advice, I slipped Missie's winkers over her head and sauntered back to Waterford City, two miles away.

"So these are the shoes that carried you from County Roscommon?" said Peter Power, studying Stephen Croghan's handiwork. "They're dainty affairs. How many miles, did you say?"

"Six hundred and fifty," I answered.

"How many more to go?"

"At least a thousand."

"Glory be to God!" he exclaimed.

"We'll make our shoes a bit heavier," suggested his older brother Tom, "and with any luck, they'll see you home."

They removed Missie's old shoes, pared her hooves, and began firing and shaping her new ones.

"How do you find her overall?" I asked the knowledgeable pair working over my means of transport.

"She's a champ, God bless her," Tom appraised. "But, to be frank, I'm worried about the sandcracks in her hooves. There's no fever in them, but they're bound to worsen on the hot pavement."

"You can see the splitting yourself." He rubbed his fingers over the sharp, raised fissures. "Are you not applying oil?"

"I was, in the early going," I admitted guiltily.

"She needs a week, maybe two, off the road for daily treatments. 'Twould be a pity to be halted after coming so far."

Oh, no. I sunk onto an old anvil and dropped my head into my hands. Why hadn't I used my head earlier, and listened to the warning of the guards? It's one thing to trust to Providence, but quite another to be improvident. While my head had been in the clouds, Missie's hooves were splintering on the pavement. *Now what?*

"What's a fortnight, if necessary?" Peter tried to raise my spirits. "You can make it up. Didn't you tell us you've managed more than twenty miles in a day when needed? She's a fine ass, and you said yourself you've been dawdling."

"Leave her in Tommy Doyle's care, why don't you, and cycle the boot of Wexford," suggested Tom, patting me on the back. "There's grand touring at the Hook and Kilmore Quay. Or the Kennedy Memorial Park outside New Ross."

"Or venture up the Barrow," piped up Peter. "Full of history, those places. And wouldn't it suit you to be at your own leisure for a spell?"

"I suppose so, but I'll really have to haul ass up the east coast. Do you really think a week off the road will heal her hooves . . . that she'll be okay?"

"Oh, aye, she'll be right as rain. They're not all that bad, really, but why take the chance?" Peter was as reassuring as he could be.

When their task was complete, Tom tossed Missie's old shoes into a rusting heap of metal.

"Oh, I'll keep those as souvenirs," I said, retrieving her dainty slippers from atop the immense work boots of draught horses. "I was told that donkey shoes are lucky."

"Lucky, indeed," they both laughed.

"Your donkey's new shoes remind me of a story about a widower from Kilkenny," said Peter, untying Missie and handing me the winkers. "At his wife's wake, he slipped a brand-new pair of shoes into her coffin. When neighbors questioned him, didn't he raise his glass and proclaim, 'Won't she be needing them? For it's a long walk, I'm thinking, from Purgatory's Door to Peter's Gates.'

"And, sure, 'tis the same with yourself and your donkey," he concluded with a laugh. "A long walk, I'm thinking, from Waterford to Roscommon."

On our walk back to Doyle's, Missie was skittish at the heft and click of her new footwear, stepping to and fro, as if caught up in a jig, before finally moving on again.

"I suppose a week off won't hurt either of us," I said to her, trying to console myself over this unforeseen delay. "We're not far from Wexford, and Dublin is less than a hundred miles from there."

But Missie offered no opinion, for she had become totally charmed by the chiming canter of her new shoes, lifting her head time and again to prance in regal splendor.

Thankfully, Mr. Doyle had no reluctance to keep my princess with his old draft mare for a week, offering to oil her hooves daily. On Tuesday, I stayed out of the fierce weather—high winds and lashing rain—and on Wednesday, August 15, the Assumption of Our Lady, I attended Mass at Trinity Cathedral, where the priest urged the congregation to pray for the score of sailors who had perished in the Fastnet yacht race the evening before. From the pulpit, he commended the bravery of the rescue teams from Cape Clear, Baltimore, and Courtmacsherry Lifeboats, who had risked their lives in gale-force winds and mountainous seas to save scores of others.

With a full week on my hands, I bid farewell to Missie and Tom, her resident podiatrist, and ventured up the River Barrow and beyond: walking the Plains of Curragh in Kildare, where the kings of Tara had raced their horses over miles of rolling grasslands from the third century on. Despite the splendid inland countryside, I worried whether our journey would resume, and could only pray that Missie's hooves were on the mend.

Upon my anxious return, Tom Doyle proudly displayed Missie's treated hooves above her new shoes, "You needn't worry about the SPCA any longer."

"If hooves were fingernails, she could be a model for a Revlon commercial," I laughed with great relief.

With a warm "Godspeed" from the hospitable Tom Doyle, Missie and I continued inland through a sliver of Kilkenny, where we spent a night in Glenmore, reputed to have been the only village in Ireland without a pub for a hundred years. Fortunately, this tragedy had been remedied in 1963 when the Glen opened its doors to thirsty villagers.

We left County Kilkenny where the bridge hops the Barrow at New Ross, and stepped into our eighth county, Wexford, well-shod and footloose, eager to explore all that awaited us here.

That following afternoon, a hot and humid Saturday, we came upon the village of Ballynabola, where a knot of men had gathered outside their favorite watering hole. These men, another batch of roadside critics, as I had come to know them, were waiting for Missie and me to pass like a grand parade, though they wouldn't let on to such, and, indeed, seemed completely absorbed in rummaging through their pockets for pipe or handkerchief, twirling a matchstick in their ear, or looking in every direction of the compass but our own.

Experience had taught me that we wouldn't be long past these highway arbiters before their afterthoughts would pepper my backside like darts shot from Peruvian blowguns:

"Arragh, Jaysus, the collar is choking her."

"Did you ever see such a sorra sight as the hames?"

"By jinx, he has her a link high on the inside draught!"

"Look at her belly-band, boys. 'Tis tighter than Mickey Sweeney's hernia belt."

I had recently developed the courage to stop before these rustic commentators and humbly ask their advice in the matter of harnessing Missie, leaving them without the breath to whistle their poisoned needles after we passed.

This quartet of marvel at Ballynabola were no different from the multitudes before, and since every farmer on this island has his own way of tackling a donkey, I stood back as they proceeded to adjust Missie's tackle with the speed and efficiency of a pit crew at the Indy 500.

After their adjustments, I asked these gentlemen if they knew a nearby farmhouse that might bed us down for the night, worn down as I was with the heat. They looked at one another, scratching Saturday beards and Sunday bellies, until one happy soul, with eight pints down and twelve to play, wrapped a heavy arm around me.

"Wisha, can't ye be staying with me and the missus," he slobbered. "I'm only a ten-minute walk down the road, and won't the little woman blossom in pride at seeing such a celebrity as yourself at our gate. And, I'll tell you, boy, there'll be a grand feast set down before you. So, go now, be on your way, and might I only trouble you to tell the bride of my whereabouts," he added, "lest she be worrying her little head about me, and that I'll be shortly home after a card game or two?"

I should have just gone my own way in the same potluck manner I did most evenings, since I suspected from this man's demeanor—such an instant jovial chum—that I was to be the stalking-horse for his late arrival home, three sheets to the wind. But, then again, I didn't wish to prejudge, and the promise of a fine meal had my stomach squealing in anticipation.

He gave instructions, while the others listened in glee, coaxing me in for a pint "to slake yer thirst."

"Ten minutes to the bridge, now," he said, waving the others off, "after which ye'll take a right at the boreen and land yourself before a farmhouse with a green gate and a splashing of flowers."

"Truly ten minutes?" I asked.

"Ten minutes."

"At the pace you saw us walking?"

"Ten minutes."

I looked at the others who nodded their agreement.

"I don't mean to be rude," I said cautiously to my potential host for the night, "but I've found it rare in this country for anyone to be accurate about distance. If it's ten minutes to your house, that's fine. If it's sixty minutes, that's fine, too. But I'd rather know now, because those fifty minutes in between can be the longest on earth."

"Ten minutes," he repeated.

I looked again at the others.

"A hare's jump," said one.

" 'Tis closer than an ass's bawl," offered the second.

"Quicker than a sausage can fart in a pan," added the third.

I said good-bye to these four masters of the spade and shovel, who adjourned to the comfort of the pub, as Missie and I ventured down the road with the hopeful prospect of a short walk and a long meal.

We were soon past the ten-minute mark, and then the half-hour, with the road giving no hint of anything that could be construed as a bridge. *Perhaps time and distance is too concrete for the spirited Celtic race,* I conceded, wiping my brow.

We arrived at the bridge in the unforetold hour, turned right, and finally came to a green wrought-iron gate attached to an imposing pair of masonry pillars, behind which the crone of the crony stood out in the farmyard.

"Excuse me, ma'am," I called, raising my voice an octave, innocent as a choir lad, "I met your kind husband in Ballynabola, and he said we might be able to spend the night in your barn."

"Who is 'we'?" she snapped, shuffling toward the gate.

"Me and my donkey," I answered, meek as could be.

She was a small, wiry woman in her seventies, with quick, henlike movements, and a face so shriveled by the elements that—God Bless the Mark—she resembled a browned crab apple on a winter's bough. She looked even crabbier when I reported His Lordship was still at the pub with his merry band of Wexford men.

Missie and I were set to back off and continue our trek through the stifling evening, when the lady of the manor abruptly swung the gate wide and led us across the farmyard to a second gate, which led to an enclosed paddock and the haybarn itself. Directing us into this stockade, she closed its gate and fitted a heavy branch through the latch which, I gathered, symbolized our imprisonment for the night. That done, she scuffled across the farmyard and slammed her kitchen door from behind, leaving us to feel like unfed livestock awaiting the butcher's call.

"I think we goofed," I said to Missie, lifting the cart off her back.

Resigning myself to the situation, I rummaged through the mudbox and pulled out a book on the northern Troubles. But before I found my place, I looked out over the deserted prison yard. There was no sign of the quick-jerk missus nor Mr. Hospitality himself; who, no doubt, would not return until the publican's nightly refrain jolted him off his stool: "Drink up, please. The sergeant's outside! Haven't ye beds to go home to a'tall?"

Last call would be after midnight, then the "ten-minute" walk home. No, there would be no food this night. Only the third time since our travels began. I was foolish not to carry provisions any longer, but I had become so spoilt with the generosity of the west that I saw little need to pack any victuals.

I tossed the book aside, in no mood to read about the ravages of Ulster. In sheer despair, I gazed at the gate in hopes of seeing the drunken fellow appear and signal me to play my role as buffer, which now I would do gladly, for a plate of beans.

But rather than espying His Lordship, my eye caught sight of a cat playing with a mouse in front of the kitchen door. I had never witnessed this natural drama of tooth and claw in real life before, outside of *Tom and Jerry* cartoons, and so I watched the proceedings intently.

The cat would allow the mouse to nose steadily away from her, about five feet or so. But as soon as the little mouse sprinted for freedom, it was always apprehended by the adroit feline, who would box the small gray fellow into submission, before dragging him back by the tail to the starting position. This went on for some time, and I'd say the cat was tiring of it, until a magpie landed on a nearby turfshed.

Now baiting the greater prize—the magpie for the mouse—the cat gave the tiny rodent a seven-foot spread. And with the mouse inching further away, the magpie swooped down from the shed, just missing the mouse, with the cat just missing the magpie, but regaining the mouse, who had about as much chance of surviving this affair as a dumpling in a Sunday stew.

Watching this stark life-and-death tableau from my place of internment, I was drawn into this conflict between predator and prey. Rallying my superior intellect to help the helpless, I picked up two stones, thinking it plausible to free the poor mouse by throwing one stone between it and the cat, and the other at the magpie, now perched back on the turfshed.

I cocked my arm as the weakened rodent was released from its captor's claws. But just as I was about to fire my first missile, out stormed the bantam hen from her kitchen.

"Are ye thinking about killing me cat?" she roared, kicking up dust with her Wellies.

"Oh, no." I denied the intent, holding out the stones in my hands. "I was only trying to distract it from that mouse. And I have a second stone here for that magpie on your turfshed."

"What are you on about?" she snapped, moving to the center of the farmyard. "Wouldn't ye be needing a third stone for your crack-brained campaign?"

"A third stone?" I replied blankly.

"Aye, a third stone! For if you take the time to look above and beyont, you'll see a second magpie—much brighter than yourself, I'm thinking—who'd be quick in carrying off your precious little mouse after your second stone was flung."

I slowly looked around to see the second magpie, grinning down at me from a nearby beech tree: a clever bird who had accounted for my presence in the natural realm of things.

"Is it that you Americans are mouse-lovers," she asked, "or are you empty-headed with the hunger?"

"A bit of both," I confessed, dropping the stones.

"Is it a cup of tea you're wanting, then? For if you're waiting on the old lad, you may as well count those wisps of hay, for he'll stay in that confounded jug-house till the last dog is hung."

"I'd love a cup of tea," I answered limply.

"Well, come in, then, before ye go breaking me windows and killing me cat."

I petted Missie between the lugs and hopped the gate, but hesitated as I caught a glimpse of the cat trotting away with the plump little mouse in its mouth.

"Are ye coming, so?" called the Wexford woman, finally betraying a hint of amusement.

"I am," I shouted, hurrying across the farmyard, a happy but most humbled naturalist.

Inside her clean red kitchen, she put on the kettle as I kept a keen eye on the proceedings. After months of belly-grumbling research, I had learned there was no better barometer to an eventual meal than the lay of the cutlery.

One spoon set upon the table was a sad note: a mug of tea, and only a mug of tea. Two spoons, side by side: a mug of tea and a hen egg. A spoon and knife, the most common, would mean a cup of tea and a few cuts of bread with butter, and maybe the jam.

My thoughts were interrupted when tonight's forecast was laid out before me: a spoon and knife. *No, this won't do. Not tonight.*

Recalling the old proverb "A hungry man knows no rules," I decided to employ all my weasel-like traits to gain access to the finer foodstuffs in this woman's fridge and pantry.

When my "grand feast" arrived—tea and brown bread—I attacked it as though it were a seven-course dinner of Nova Scotia salmon and Vermont pheasant. Buttering the bread and spreading the jam, I looked up graciously at Mrs. Rhode Island Red, and exclaimed, "I certainly picked the right farmhouse tonight!"

"But, surely," she said, stopping in her tracks, " 'tis only the bread and tay I have to offer."

"Bread and tea and butter and black-currant jam," I answered, wiping my buttered mustache after a hefty bite. "There's been nights, and plenty, when not even a glass of water was offered, and I was shut away in dairy barns where I was lullabied to sleep by the dull thud of cow droppings."

I took advantage of her first sympathetic glance, to offer the clipping from the *Cork Examiner* by way of introduction.

"You have an eighty-seven-year-old grandmother in Roscommon?" she said, looking up from her reading. "She must be sick with worry."

"The beads are forever going through her fingers," I soberly replied.

"Oh, I say, you are a worry to her, all right. Out on these roads of robbers and rogues, and meeting farmers not kind enough to give you a sup of tay."

She then looked at me pityingly as I picked the remaining bread crumbs off the saucer with a moist finger. Before I could engage in more theatrics of deprivation, she left the table and reappeared from the scullery with the most profound implement on God's table: the four-pronged fork, and with it, ham and sausage.

I made short, though grateful, work of her feast. Then, fully replenished, I repaid her surprising kindness with tales of the road, and was further rewarded with a buttery slice of apple tart before bedtime.

"Are you sure you won't sleep inside?" she called from the doorway, as I made my way across the farmyard. "We have a spare room, we do."

"Oh, no, the night is grand," I answered.

"And will you be in for the breakfast," she lilted, "and stay for the dinner after Mass?"

"Thank you, yes," I accepted humbly.

Missie seemed to sense my tactics and regarded me disapprovingly as I climbed back over the gate.

"I know, I know," I said, walking past her steady gaze, "but what else could I have done? I was starved, Miss. And didn't I pay her back with a wealth of stories? Remember the old proverb, 'He is like a bagpipe—he never makes a noise till his belly is full.'"

My dun-brown confessor seemed to absolve me, so I crawled into my sack and fell into a deep and satisfying sleep.

"Psst! Psst!"

I looked up blearily in the deepest night, to find my tardy host grinning down at me.

"Are ye right?" he asked gleefully, his eyes dancing, though bloodshot.

"I am," I answered, struggling to sit up on my elbows.

"And how did you find the bride?"

"Grand," I answered.

"And a champion feed, no doubt?"

"A capital feed," I conceded.

He sat on his haunches before me, in no hurry to let me be.

"Shouldn't you go in to your wife, now that you're home?" I suggested. "She was expecting you all night, and there may be the devil to pay."

"'Devil to pay'? And what's another minute, pray tell, when our death is as certain as tomorrow's pale dawn? Now, I'll give you a bit of advice when you come home with a snootful to your own bride at a wee hour. And sure, wasn't this wisdom brought to life tonight when my playing-partner, Liam, went fidgeting in his chair long before the publican bellowed his warning call."

I crawled from my sack and leaned wearily against a few loose bales, as my belated host took up his tale.

"When I asked Liam his hurry, he told me his missus gives out to him horribly when he's late. So I further inquired how he behaves when he gets home, you see. He explained he's as quiet as a mouse, slipping off his boots at the door and tiptoeing up the stairs. Next he crawls beneath the covers, only to be greeted by his wife's ballyragging roar that would shame the devil himself."

I nodded, less in encouragement to the storyteller than back to dreamland.

"So I explained to Liam that he's using the wrong strategy altogether. When I arrive home, it's not the boots I do be taking off—no. I clunk heavily about the kitchen in them. And I let the kettle boil till it shrieks like a runaway train hurtling through the lonesome bog. Then up the stairs I go, giving each a good stomping, and go to filling me chamber pot from a great distance, so it roars into the empty bowl like a mountain cascade. And, jumping into bed, I pull down the covers, and offer out boldly, 'Is there anybody looking for a little romance before the cock crows in the haggard below?' "

Here he backhanded my chest, knocking me back down to my sack.

"And I'll tell you, Mr. Tinker-of-the-Road, my dear little bride never utters a word. Do ye hear me, Mr. Shank's Mare?" he crowed, rubbing my sleepy noggin smartly with his knuckles. "I say, she never utters a word."

With that, he stood up and went whistling through the yard, as proud as any rooster who believes he has mastered his hen.

Going Widdershins

CHAPTER THIRTY-FIVE

I was sitting before a sandwich and stout at the Bavarian Girl in Wexfordtown in late August, when I learned that Lord Mountbatten, Prince Phillip's uncle, had been murdered by the IRA the day before, at Mullaghmore, County Sligo.

I scanned the newspapers draped over counter and stool: Lord Louis Mountbatten, born with the century seventy-nine years ago, Sea Admiral, Viceroy of India, Knight of the Garter, Supreme Allied Commander in Southeast Asia during World War Two, friend of Mahatma Gandhi and Eamon de Valera, was killed when his boat, *Shadow V,* was blown to shambles in Donegal Bay. His fourteen-year-old grandson and a friend had also died in the blast, while four other passengers were fighting for their lives.

Commiseration echoed throughout the world: from Queen Elizabeth weeping for her "Uncle Bertie" at Balmoral; to India calling for seven days of official mourning. And with it, condemnation of the rough men of the IRA.

"This will put a damper on the Pope's visit," said one patron, folding the *Irish Press.*

"He certainly won't go north on his itinerary," voiced another. "We've been thrown back to '72 and Bloody Sunday, but this time it'll be the Unionists with their blood up."

"An old man and his grandson," said another in disgust. "And those British soldiers ambushed and killed in County Down yesterday as well. A black day, entirely."

"Say what you will, but Mountbatten had no more right to be in this country than those British soldiers in Ulster had," said another, his fist clenched upon the wooden counter. "Mullaghmore in Sligo is thousands of acres of fine land and a castle by the sea. And how did he get that land? 'Twas confiscated in 1856 by the English prime minister Henry John Temple. If Mountbatten was such a great man, why didn't he do for Ireland what he did for India in 1947? Or offer back the land to the natives of Mullaghmore? And what about the torturing of Irish prisoners in H-Block by the British, as we speak?"

"Two wrongs never made a right," reproached the other. "He was an old man who brought the Axis forces to their knees, the most decorated man in his time, and, by God, his medals didn't come cheaply. And what will his murder ever prove but we're an uncivilized race of brutes, just as the English love to paint us? And don't go preaching to me about English atrocities. Amn't I reminded, each time I step through the Bull Ring where hundreds of our own were murdered? But what future is there in being stuck in the past, tell me? Now nothing will stop the Ulster Volunteers from stepping up their campaign, and that old crank, Ian Paisley, will have a heyday in the pulpit. Mark my words, there'll never be peace in the North through killing."

I walked away from their cheerless chat, having entered the pub in search of the crack, some jolly boyo to fill me in on the history of the vicinity. But no, not on this evening, for the magic and lore of old Ireland had been blown up by a plastic explosive in Donegal Bay.

I stepped into the eerie fog, the dank town quiet but for a few heedless vacationers who went laughing by, unaware of the island's recent calamity. I walked to an old wooden quay and stopped before the Wren's Nest, a pub boarded up for years, where I knocked in vain hope its door would open to less-troubled times. From there I walked the narrow streets to the Bull Ring on the square where Cromwell did his dirty work way back in 1649, with a death toll in the hundreds and thousands which continues to mount till this very day.

It was midnight when I reached my hovel in Newtown, a shed filled with cabbage. Among its leaves crawled plump caterpillars, and their creeping turned my rest into a sleepless tussle. Giving up on sweet slumber, I leaned against the cold concrete wall, cursing my poorly chosen digs, and shuddering in the stale damp air. In this dark chill, I thought of the cells of H-Block in Belfast's Maze Prison. But also of the cold stone floors of Irish parish churches where mothers knelt in fervent but despairing prayers for peace. My small discomforts were nothing next to the suffering of Ireland on this wretched night.

A languid fog hung over the River Slaney next morning, as Missie and I halted for a passing train at Wexford's new bridge. A few grim passengers looked out over their disheartening newspapers at my odd presence and offered the occasional halfhearted wave. In fact, everyone I met that morning was downcast by Mountbatten's death. Meanwhile, dignitaries from as far afield as Argentina and New Zealand gathered for a noonday service at London's Buckingham Palace.

Burial arrangements were also being made for the eighteen soldiers blown sky-high at Warrenpoint. Eighteen kids whose parents were now trying to pick up the pieces of their own lives. Eighteen kids who would rather have kicked a football than patrol the last of England's old empire. And throughout the world, the English tabloids blackened

Ireland in bold print: THESE EVIL IRISH BASTARDS. And me, I was at the southeast limit of my travels, turning toward the long trek north to Belfast.

With sullen thoughts, I looked out at the sea and saw a spring of teal wheeling in the lowering skies, showing their brown plumage before turning all at once to flash their white underwings over the gray waters. An instant of spontaneous beauty to set against age-old human tragedy.

"God is with us yet, Miss." I nuzzled my brown beast.

A short ways beyond Curraghcloe, we passed a string of thatched houses, and atop the last of these roofs knelt an elderly thatcher at his task.

"God Bless the Work," I greeted him.

He stepped down from his rickety ladder and fell promptly into a lighthearted conversation.

"My name is Jim Malone from Blackwater." He tipped his cap. "Lovely day, isn't it, if you don't go minding the fog or the news."

"I wish I had met you two years ago, when I came to Ireland to learn how to thatch," I told him. "After my uncle Bennie died—the family thatcher—my grandmother had no choice but to replace the old straw with Bangor slate. She says her home has never been the same."

"Nor would it be, to the poor creature," he answered. "What is more handsome than thatch, tell me? A golden roof that keeps you cool in the summer, warm in winter, and the birds nesting comfortably in its eaves. Just as God planned it."

He took off his cap, wiped a handkerchief across his brow, and cast an amused eye over me. "So, you wanted to become a thatcher?"

"Oh, yes, but the only offer to apprentice I got came from a man in County Tyrone who asked for a three-year committment. It was too much, so I packed up for home."

"A wise choice, that," he said, "for I'm just puffing hard to the finish line myself. In all, I've thatched one hundred forty houses in Wexford and Wicklow, including a score you passed today. I use oat, barley, and wheaten straw, and I peg or scollop the thatch with rods of sally. My roofs are good for twelve to fifteen years, but my days are numbered, for there's a fellow named Cunningham in Youghal who claims a fifty-year roof using river weed. And where will that leave me, pray tell? In the poorhouse, eating gelatin and soft peaches."

He pointed out his tools spread out in the yard: "These are my knave, rake, and thrasher. But I'm especially proud of me old thatcher's-needle here"—showing me a long wooden stick with a circular hook at its end—"handed down to me by my grandfather."

I handled the pikelike implement with due reverence, a tool I once longed to take up.

"Have no regrets about not becoming a thatcher," he reiterated. "All that's left Cunningham, I'm afraid, will be folk parks and quaint pubs. But sure, God was good to me, giving me an honest trade, where I could meet the people beneath their own roofs. Same as yourself, lad. You're meeting the people on their own level, in garden and field, at work and play. Enjoy your roundabout, and if you ever come knocking about again, give me a shout and I'll show you the tricks of a dying trade."

With a backward glance at the thatcher back on his rooftop, Missie and I set off again and arrived at Blackwater where we were greeted by a contingent of mallard ducks quacking and waddling before us. Missie dipped her head like a bull and sent them scurrying and swimming back to their own little thatched house across the village pond.

I camped three days outside Blackwater, with Missie in-season and out of commission again, compounded by a seeming reluctance to resume our journey after her respite. On the second evening, I ventured into the Blackwater Arms where I joined a few young men who had just came in from playing Gaelic football. Together we watched TV, for the continuing saga of the Sea Admiral's death, as "the Iron Lady," Mrs. Margaret Thatcher, came on to vow that "the people of Britain will wage the war against terrorism with relentless determination . . ."

"I suppose Belfast is out of the picture now?" said one lad, following the newscast.

"I haven't given it much thought."

"You'd best," he added. "The newspapers are full of promised reprisals, and the Protestant paramilitaries will do anything to mar the Pope's upcoming visit. Not to mention the SAS boys—the elite forces of the British Army—after losing eighteen soldiers of their own."

"I drove a supply lorry on the Drogheda-Larne Road for three years," said another, "but you couldn't pay me enough to cross the border now. Why not go as far as Dundalk, and cut through Monaghan, Cavan, Leitrim, and up into Donegal? The North will be dicey for a while."

"I need to go sixteen hundred miles to make good my wager," I explained weakly, not prepared to make any more symbolic claims about my need to include the North in my travels, "and that's not possible unless I travel the northeast coast of Down and Antrim."

"Who would harm the famous Donkeyman?" asserted a third footballer, sporting a fresh welt beneath his eye.

"Plenty, I'm afraid," argued his mate. "There's any amount of madmen on both sides, and Kevin is well-known wherever he goes."

"You're daft," dismissed the fella with the shiner.

"Didn't the IRA kill two Pakistani teaboys who worked for the British army a month back?" his friend stressed. "And what about the Catholic show-band blown to bits by the UDA a year back? Talk about indiscriminate killings! If nothing else," he said, turning to me, "cool your heels until the Pope departs in early October. Things could settle down after that."

"I have to be home by Christmas."

"You'll be fine," assured my supporter, nudging me with his elbow. "You're a smart fellow not to be intimidated by this whole bloody mess. And couldn't you meet up with a murdering lunatic wherever you go?"

Despite our three-day rest, Missie remained slow on the hoof as we sauntered up the coast toward Kilmuckridge. After passing us, a well-dressed man emerged from his car and proclaimed our approach with a quotation from the Gospel of Matthew:

"'Look, your King comes to you; he is humble, he rides on'—well, actually walks beside—'a donkey.'"

I nodded acknowledgment as the gentleman advanced to shake my hand, saying, "Isn't it wonderful to come upon a walker, in the age of motorcars. I had heard you were hereabouts on your long circle journey. It's a grand undertaking, boy."

Understanding by now how these wayside greeters had enriched my travels, I welcomed the pause. This dapper gent took a long look down the road and a long look back, and then, staring at me, grimaced as if heart-struck.

"Anything wrong?" I asked with some alarm.

"Is this the way you've been traveling the whole time, counterclockwise about the coast?"

"Yes. Is there a problem with that?"

"Actually, there is. I'm afraid you're going widdershins."

"'Widdershins'?"

"Aye, *tuathal,* in the Irish: 'to move left, to go the wrong way.'"

I stood perplexed.

"Did anyone not tell you before setting off that you should be moving *deasil*—clockwise, that is—about the coast?"

"People have told me a lot of things," I answered lightheartedly. "Not setting off on a Friday was one, as Adam and Eve were banished from Eden on that day. But no one has ever mentioned I was going the wrong way."

"Going widdershins has been avoided by Celtic people since early times, as a precursor to bad luck," he affirmed with grave solemnity. "Kings, poets, and pilgrims all went sunwise—*a' soliel*—with their royal left shoulder, their hearts to the sea, east to west . . . *deasil,* like 'the heavenly wheel.'"

I shrugged my shoulders apologetically, but he persisted.

"Muircheartch, son of Niall, circled Eire clockwise to Tara upon his inauguration. Even the famous Battle Book of the O'Donnells, penned by Saint Columcille, was carried thrice sunwise around Red Hugh O'Donnell's army before combat. If the precious relic had been carried widdershins, the army would have scattered, fleeing the dire consequences."

"Figures I'd be going ass-backwards," I joked sheepishly.

He did not crack a smile, but remained humorless as if I were committing a sacrilege.

"Anything I can do at this point?" I asked, as I began to take his concern seriously.

"Carry on with chin high, I suppose," he relented, seeing my spirits sink. "You can't backtrack, can you? And who knows?" he added, after a meaningful pause. "Your going against the sun might be a blessing in disguise, unraveling centuries of woe. For, in truth, with all our sunwise ambulating, what good has ever come out of it?"

But it was too late to buck up my spirits after having shown me the error of my ways, and, consequently, the next mile was the longest I'd traveled in Ireland.

Why hadn't anyone instructed me on this "sunwise" business? Surely Headmaster D'Alton knew about *tuathal* and *a' soliel*. And why hadn't anyone else pointed this out over the miles? Was this the curse of the ciotóg, the left-handedness the nuns had tried to coax out of me? Now that I thought of it, wasn't going "against the sun" why I'd heard the cuckoo's call in my left ear that morning in the Burren, rather than in my "wish-to-be-granted" right? Most significantly, if I had gone clockwise from the outset, I would now be *leaving* Ulster, not approaching it!

Confusion reigned as we plodded up the coast, with storm clouds threatening over the Celtic Sea. As a boy, during Lent I used to giggle at a little man named "Frenchie," who'd hurriedly say the Stations of the Cross before morning Mass, starting at the fourteenth Station rather than the first. But now *I* was "Frenchie," walking contrary to the ghosts of pilgrims past, a dunce among sojourners.

I pondered this left-to-right business for the next long mile. A card dealer always deals the deck left to right, and my camera lenses lock in clockwise. Even a pot of porridge is stirred sunwise. Only a witch would stir her slurgullion right to left, the way I was going.

Adding to my misery was Missie Molasses who, stopping dead, fixed her ears to a certain point, and fell into a deep catatonia. Unable to budge her, I took up my position behind her earscope and spotted a young bullock with its tail caught in the briars of a nearby field.

Like a bovine's Good Samaritan, I hopped a fence and managed to free the frightened bullock with my knife—a nerve-wracking operation, as his mates began to stomp and bellow around me. Returning to the crumbling farmyard where I had stashed Missie, I found her being petted by a ginger-haired woman with two young tots.

"You're a great man with the cattle," she jested, a lovely witness to my awkward efforts. "I'm Aggie . . . Agnes, and these are me daughters, Lily and Una. But there's no need to tell me your name," she winked. "Ye're Saint Francis, walking about Ireland to help all the poor creatures that's in it. Am I right? Now, do ye fancy a good drenching or will ye join us? I can drum up the kettle."

"I'd love a cup of tea," I answered without hesitation.

"A cup, is it!" she laughed, puffing the bangs off her forehead. "Well, it won't be a cup, but a mug without a handle, but never mind."

But even this meeting with Beauty, after adventure with Beast, could hardly erase the crestfallen features from my own mug.

"Why the long face? Aggie inquired. "Did your best friend run off with your change-purse?"

"I was just told I've been walking the wrong way since the start of my donkey-go-round," I said to this princess of the traveling breed. "Call me 'Wrong-Way Corrigan.'"

" 'Wrong-Way Corrigan'?" she repeated, picking up the youngest of the pair of girls.

"An aviator back in the '30s who thought he was flying from New York to California, but in the morning he found himself landing in Ireland."

"Why bother about it?" she said, waving away my frown. "Didn't he become famous all the same? And how can your travels be wrong whichever way you go, as long as you're on the move. Am I right?"

"I suppose so," I said, unconvinced but charmed.

Rain spattered the roadway as she led me to her impoverished caravan in a nettle-rich field. Her cramped quarters were dark and cheerless, and the meek glow of candlelight did little to improve the scene: three scrawny cats rubbing against a makeshift stove, two aged *sugan* chairs unraveling their old rope and a wooden table brittle with wormwood. All, in fact, could be heaved into the sea without loss, but for a mantel clock of red mahogany that gleamed like a jewel upon the decrepit press.

As we sat to tea and buttered loaf, lightning ripped through the blackness, followed by a crack of thunder that sent Aggie's curly-headed daughters scuttling to her lap.

"Ye'd see some commotion if me mother was still alive after a blinding flash like that," she reminisced, soothing Una, the toddler, with a discolored pacifier. "She was deathly afeared of lightning, and rightly so, poor woman. As a *gossel*, she came upon a flock of dead sheep in Sinnott's Field. Charred black, the lot of them, with one spike of lightning. Can you imagine the horror, and no age up on her at all?"

"I can't imagine that at all."

"Spooked silly, she was, and if she were here today, God protect her, she'd clear out the cats. 'Out with ye,' she'd say; for their coats, ye know, attract the lightning. Next she'd sprinkle the caravan's four corners with holy water, circle it with a wisp of Easter palm, light the Holy Candle, draw the curtains, throw the cutlery beneath the table, and send us out with horseshoes to place under the nests of our few laying hens. All that, too, in a flash, mind ye!"

Aggie stepped to the lone wide window, rocking Una in her arms as another boomer rolled over the Wicklow Hills. Outside, the wet green world splattered, and it may well have been a boat we were on, rocking in the wind and waves, with heads of sea-cows bobbing indifferently in the distant flowing fields.

"I was weaned in Enniscorthy, a traveler's daughter," she said, sitting back down, "and as a child I'd spend me summer days selling strawberries at Ferns Cross, and dreaming up animals in the clouds—horses and hares and dragons, ye know—wondering if they paid any mind to the little towns they looked down upon. And, sometimes, there'd be glowing sunbursts, all a-glimmer like the chalice of God, or golden mountainy clouds like buttery heaps of cauliflower."

Aggie interrupted her reverie to cast a sly glance my way.

"Putting the hunger to ye, am I?" she smiled, mussing up my hair with her fingers. "And I no more in store but the babby's milk."

Presently, the mantel clock chimed a lovely prelude to the strike of the hour, though a particular note in the musical phrase was missing.

"Pay that no heed," said Aggie, reddening, as the clock tolled six bells. "Me husband, wherever he be this night, took out one of its tiny hammers so I might be reminded of his absence and promise of return. 'The tolling of me heart,' he called it."

This ragamuffin beauty held my gaze a long moment, then puffed up her bangs and continued. "The last I heard, he's working a foundry in Aberdeen, but God only knows. Reminded of his absence," she repeated with a sigh, "and all I've done this long year is worry sick about him—and his two daughters growing up before me on the floor."

She sat quiet and forlorn, weariness tracing her brow, the heavy harness of her heart revealed. Resignedly, my own heart went out to her in a communion of sadness.

"I'd be over the moon if ye stayed the night," she said abruptly. "I have an old cot, lumpy enough, but 'tis better than a wet byre. And there's little fear of me husband running ye out of the place; but sure, wouldn't we be in a right fix if he appeared at the door and me doing me best to explain ye away . . . Saint Francis and all."

"I'd love to stay," I answered, picking Lily up off the bare floor.

As the rainy night wore on, we exhausted ourselves with stories. She spoke of roaming the province of Leinster in a parade of horse-drawn caravans. I, in turn, told her of the wonders and coincidences of my road, and gradually came to realize I couldn't be going in the wrong direction when I had been meeting good people like herself along the way.

But in time there was no need for stories. It was just lovely to sit across from her, out of the weather and harm's way, as she lullabied Lily and Una to sleep in the warm glow of candlelight—their nodding heads of rich tumbling curls draped over her shoulders like an elegant shawl.

I was soon snug in my cot, the rain drumming off the caravan's flat roof, thanking God for sheltering me from the elements once again. During the night, I would wake to a child's whimper in the near room, followed by Aggie's cooing assurance. The rain fell, the wind howled, and the clock on the hour chimed its incomplete song.

A Green Martyr

On Sunday evening—into September now—Missie and I walked toward Bally-garret with the sky a blaze of gold. Trimmed hedgerows led to well-kempt farmhouses, where children ran to knoll or gate to whistle and wave as we passed. Lucky children in fields filled with livestock, soon to be called to supper and a lively family hearth. I thought sadly of Aggie's pair, growing up on poor, rushy land with neither crayon nor book to call their own.

At one point on our trek, a strange stillness filled the air, as if the world had momentarily stopped its spinning. *The evening Angelus, the blessing of the day.* I mused, thinking of Aggie's clock chiming its rich but incomplete song this very moment.

Not having a watch, I called to two girls who passed on bicycles.

"What time is it, please?"

"Six o'clock," came their animated reply.

I walked through the wondrous gloaming with a bright step, believing God had given me this reassuring nudge forward. Yes, Lord Mountbatten was dead, Ulster was on red alert, and I was walking ass-backwards. But I was also near the halfway mark, a fortnight from Dublin. And why *not* approach the Dragon of the North with a blessed donkey? *Sidestep Ulster, they say? Not a chance! Ulster isn't an island floating out to sea. It is part of Ire-land, and will remain so until melting Arctic ice floes submerge the Central Plain.*

We reached Ballygarret and settled with Andy Doyle, a schoolteacher who placed Missie in his nearby schoolyard and myself atop a stool at the Schooner for good stout. Andy's friends, like the footballers in Blackwater, voiced strong concerns over my trav-eling the North. Yet I paid their warnings no mind, the matter now sealed and deliv-ered. *Ulster or bust!*

On the Gorey Road next morning, we crossed the bridge at Riverchapel, where a mother and grown daughter watched me drag my slow float along.

"Do you have a spavindy ass there?"

"No, she's forever in-season."

"Circling the country, is it?" chided the daughter. " 'Twill be a miracle if you ever reach Dublin."

Rather than let my slatternly beast make a spectacle of me, we left the road at Courtown and slept the night in a foddering hall, followed by another in a milking barn. On the third morning, with Missie's wanton fever subsiding, we ambled through Arklow and veered inland to explore the beauties of Wicklow, Ireland's "Garden County."

We sauntered through Woodenbridge and on to Avoca, a lovely valley dressed in rowan and pine, where I was kindly directed to the Greene farmhouse by a Dr. Johnston. Arriving at their handsome two-story Georgian home, I settled Missie with the help of the daughter, Jean, as Mrs. Greene, an ex-schoolteacher, fixed me a fine meal and shared the history of the Vale, including its most historic figure, Charles Stuart Parnell, "the Uncrowned King of Ireland."

"Before 1890 there was great opportunity for Ireland to gain home rule," said the pleasant woman as we sat in her front parlor. "Parnell, you see, was a gentleman of the Anglo-Irish landlord class, the old Ascendancy, and was raised just up the road at Avondale House. Before he was thirty, he became a powerful member of the British Parliament. More powerful, in fact, than any other Irish MP in the long, bitter struggle between Ireland and England. He was a militant nationalist, but used filibuster and boycott instead of violence. He totally captivated the country he loved so dearly, but unfortunately he became involved with another MP's wife, one Kitty O'Shea."

"Yes, I've heard of the scandal."

"Her divorce and their remarriage in 1891 ruined not just Parnell's political standing, but his health. His party split and the Church turned against him. The broken man died in Kitty's arms within a year, and Ireland's best hope for home rule with him."

Next day, we followed the Avonmore upstream through a woodland glade of beauty, stopping briefly at "the Meeting of the Waters," the Avonmore and Avonbeg, where Thomas Moore's tree still proclaims:

> "There is not in this wide world a valley so sweet
> As that in whose bosom the bright waters meet."

We passed Parnell's birthplace and arrived at Laragh, our springboard for traversing the Sally Gap: a long desolate stretch of blanket bog that meanders through the Wicklow Mountains toward Dublin, a passage I had red-inked on my map with enthusiasm when first reading of it at the Galway Library back in March.

After settling with a hospitable woman, Mrs. Miley, I attended a singsong at the

Laragh Inn, where the patrons regaled me with the history of Wicklow's four glens, from the founding of Glendalough monastery in the sixth century, to the short-lived gold rush of Glenmalure in 1935.

"You must walk the holy grounds of your patron saint, Saint Kevin, and visit the tall round tower there," suggested a patron, Ciaran Moran. "During Ireland's Golden Age, Glendalough was a leading center of learning in Europe. The Pope decreed that seven pilgrimages to Glendalough equaled one to Rome. Seven–to–one, mind you! Weren't they right braggarts, those Italian popes!"

I took the Green Road to Glendalough early next morning and walked to the Upper Lake where Saint Kevin had meditated in a cave of slaty rocks on a precipice above these waters. The lake itself was ink-black; it was easy to believe long-necked serpents once swam here, one of which had destroyed Saint Kevin's earliest church.

Revered for his marvelous deeds, Kevin attracted numerous disciples, who built seven churches in the valley below his cliffside hermitage, and survived many sackings by the Vikings. My patron saint, known for his comeliness, could also fly off the handle. Once, he became so annoyed with a redheaded temptress named Kathleen, he took hold of her hair and heaved her into these cold waters.

But his gentle side was beyond compare. As he knelt one morning with arms out-stretched in prayer, a blackbird suddenly alighted and laid three greenish eggs into his palm. Neither closing nor withdrawing his hand, the dear saint held it out for weeks, so the story goes, until the young fledglings hatched and took flight. Besides the blackbirds, Saint Kevin had a number of animal friends, including a wolf who had devoured that troublesome serpent, and an otter who would retrieve the saint's prayer book each time it slipped from his hands into the lake.

Whatever the legends, it was certainly true that Glendalough was a famous infirmary where Kevin and his disciples collected herbs for cures. Perhaps it was my namesake who had drawn me into nursing, I mused, as I climbed cautiously about St. Kevin's Bed, his rocky ledge perched above the inky tarn.

Returning to gather up Missie before noon, I set out on the Military Road, an eighteen-mile strip of tarmac which weaves north-south across the lonely Sally Gap, originally built by the English in a campaign to flush out Irish rebels in the glens after the Insurrection of 1798, with barracks at both ends.

It was a hard pull out of Laragh, yet by midafternoon we had reached the summit above Glenmacnass, where I secured Missie and the cart, and surveyed the deep green valley from the head of its tumbling falls.

When I returned to her ladyship, a robust gentleman hiker in his seventies had made her company.

"A splendid view, Glenmacnass, is it not?" said the retired Dublin doctor, pointing a handsome walking-stick that testified to his seriousness as a walker, sporting metal badges from the Alps to the Pyrenees. "These glens are attractive in all seasons. The win-ters are beautiful with snow and, in the spring, whole areas are white with flowering blackthorn. The summers, too, are red with rowanberry, and now the first hints of autumn—the heather blooming purple. Did you happen to pass Shillelagh on your way?"

"No, it was too far inland for us," I answered.

"Well, do so, if given another chance. The surviving oak forests at Shillelagh will give you a glimpse of what Ireland was like before it was deforested. In fact, its fine timber was used to roof such buildings as Westminster Hall in London and our own St. Patrick's Cathedral in Dublin."

"Did the cudgel get its name from there?"

"Certainly. A most powerful stick, that. The undisputed champion of Donnybrook. Now, are you planning to pitch camp?—for I'm afraid you'll never see Glencree with your slow taxi tonight."

"The plan is to spend the weekend up here."

"Delightful! There's a stand of pine above on the right you can't miss, the only woods you'll see. Camp there, and you'll be just like your namesake, Saint Kevin, a Green Martyr."

"A 'Green Martyr'?"

"Oh, yes. The early Irish monastics felt shortchanged they never had the opportunity to spill their blood for Christ, 'Red Martyrs,' you see, like Rome's early disciples. So the Irish clerics devised their own form of martyrdom, namely Green Martyrs, the great ascetics who prayed in the lonely caves like Kevin, or the holy men in their beehive huts on the western fringes. Then there were 'White Martyrs,' setting off over the foaming seas to spread the Gospel and establish monastic settlements wherever they went."

"A Green Martyr it is, then," I affirmed, shaking the gentleman's hand before he strolled off toward Laragh with an effortless gait.

I pitched camp beneath this spinney of fir in an otherwise stark landscape, a full moon bathing the pine-needled floor in ghostly radiance. Not since the Burren in Clare had we been so isolated. A limitless plain of blanket bog fell away to distant purple-domed hills, as lark, grouse, and snipe called through the chilling mountain air. Invigorated by this isolation, I collected *kippins*—dry twigs—and was soon feasting on my shop-bought supplies of chicken pie and baked beans before a crackling fire, thinking it best to start my days as a Green Martyr on a full stomach.

The sky remained so clear I decided to unfurl my bag outside the tent and sleep beneath the shadows of the moon. "We'll spend all three nights right here," I called to my donkey, who happily feasted on a bag of Mrs. Miley's hay. "Three nights in prayer and thanksgiving. And we have some praying to do, dear Missaleen, for we'll soon be sleeping beneath Ulster's troubled canopy of stars."

The following days, amid ling and heather, I hopped countless wooden stiles, scattered thousands of sheep and spoke to scores of city-dwelling Dubliners who rent small patches of bog for eight pounds a year. One such fellow, originally from County Mayo, stopped his turf-gathering to tell me how he enjoyed this respite from the smoky city.

"It brings back my youth and appetite," he happily professed, generously sharing his thick-sliced ham sandwiches. "I suppose you've heard the expression, 'You can take the man out of the bog, but you can't take the bog out of the man.' All that's missing is me bawling old ass."

In the evenings, I'd walk the lonely moor to say the Rosary, counting the red berries off a mountain ash and dropping each, in turn, into a swift-flowing stream. Or I'd face the undisputed King of Hills—Great Sugarloaf—looking like a cathedral with its dazzling quartzite cone. Or at night, I'd lay out in the spongy bracken and count off the stars like the old woman on the Dingle. Or I'd revert to my old wooden beads, a Confirmation gift, always in my pocket while in Ireland and refreshed in grace by grotto streams and holy wells during my peregrinations.

Only recently had I found comfort in saying the Rosary, a peaceful mantra to lull me to sleep when long nights brought on fright or loneliness. As a boy, my father would lead us in the Rosary every evening—his thick County Longford brogue saying the "Hail"s as his chorus of eight children recited the "Holy"s, an embarrassing devotion during the summer months when the window screens were open wide—as our friends waited impatiently outside to play, good Americans who had long since left behind such strange tribal practices.

As I said the Rosary my last night under the sway of Saint Kevin, I noticed my fingers moving in a clockwise manner. Imagine, through countless prayer rounds, never once had I noticed this sunwise movement. In my newfound peace, I didn't fret superstitiously, but I pondered how many other small but significant matters go undetected in one's lifetime, and they at our fingertips the whole time.

Dawn arrived, a brilliant shivering morn with the sun wheeling across these highlands like a child's spinning top, as a dusty stream of long-fingered sunbeams set the moor ablaze. In as magical a realm as that of Bilbo Baggins, I bridled my well-rested companion for the road, and confided to her, "Smaug, the dragon, is waiting for us, and I have no magic ring like Bilbo. But I do have my beads and hazel and, of course, you, Missie, my dear blessed beast."

On our descent into the village of Glencree, nestled between rugged Knockree and Bray Head, I called to a few farmers working the fields below.

"Excuse me, do you know a farmhouse where I might settle my donkey for the night?"

"Move your arse, or I'll swiftly move it for you!" shouted the boss, halting his work to eye me menacingly.

I paused, waiting for the punch line. But none was forthcoming, only his warning glare. He had mistaken me for a tinker, in rank prejudice, which got my Irish up.

"And a hundred thousand welcomes to you, too," I shouted back, in my clearest Yankee accent. "You should drop your spade and go working for the Tourist Board!"

"Why, you durty tinker!" he said, thrusting his shovel into the soil. "One more crack and I'll settle your ass for the night, and your own with it!"

Thinking it wise to back off, I pressed on to the village, where I was dismayed to find no public house. To find no pub in an Irish village is like being lost in the Great North Woods without a compass. Disoriented, I stuck my head into a shop, where the elderly keeper offered her field to Missie and suggested I stay at the local youth hostel.

Having had my fill of youth hostels last month when Missie's hooves were healing, I walked toward the imposing old English barracks, now a "Reconciliation Center," offering respite for troubled souls—Catholic and Protestant—from the North. There I was welcomed by a young man named Peader from County Armagh, who set me up in a vacant caravan on the grounds.

As I unpacked, I told him about my earlier meeting with "Farmer Bigot."

"He's a right jacko, that one," said Peader, in his strong northern accent. "I've always taken to heart a poem by James Cousins, called, 'A Curse on a Closed Gate,' where the wandering poet curses the stingy farmer, hoping he'll never know good cheer, 'Above the ground or below it.' "

"But don't take it too personally," he added, "the locals simply feel overrun by vagabonds. There's scores in the hostel alone. Every September, the villagers have run-ins with English hippies who come here to graze on 'magic mushrooms.' I saw one crowd last week absolutely daft with hallucinations, stumbling about the fields like lost lambs searching for their ewes after a spring shearing."

"Well, I can understand how this guy might resent what he sees as an alien invasion, but he's the hardest man I've come across in my travels."

"Did you notice those seven large fields he was working?" Peader asked. " 'Twas all stone and rubble decades back, but cleared over the years by young Irish lads, back when this place was once a borstal school. Many young Irish backs were broken in those fields for the pettiest of crimes. And another nearly broken today," he added with a smile.

Later, Peader and I went to check on Missie in her stonewalled field.

"That shopkeeper has her hands full, poor woman, caring for her dying sister in the room above," he observed, glancing across at the shop. "The grandest pair, I heard they were, selling everything from soap to Gobstoppers. Now one is failing and the other will follow like the tumbling of thatch after the hearth goes cold. Myself, I live by the credo, 'Live today like it's your last, because someday you'll be right.' "

"I'd join you in that belief."

"It's a lesson you learn up North. Everyone knows someone who was just walking past a milkcan or sitting in a pub or answering the front door, and then, suddenly— boom!—gone, blown to bits. 'Tis a quick end in the end, isn't it? Never a chance to say good-bye or make peace for petty wrongs. A survivor just gets on with it like before, doesn't he, though nothing is ever again the same. Losing a mate is like a pothole that can never be filled, just an ugly old jolt every time you pass over it."

Peader's own rough ride showed in his face, but I could only guess at the road that had brought him to the Reconciliation Center.

That night, he came to my caravan and offered sound tips on my traveling the North.

"Be open and friendly, but stay on safe topics," he advised. "If anyone speaks of the Troubles, say you're an American and don't understand all the botheration. You'll have to pass through both Catholic and Loyalist areas. There's no way around that."

"How will I tell which I'm in?"

" 'Tis easy enough, believe me," he scoffed. "The Protestants have the richest farmland, going back to the land grab of the Ulster Plantation in the 1600s. It'll be Catholics you see on small parcels of rocky soil. Believe me, you'll know what farmgate you're calling upon."

"Thanks. I'll keep a good lookout."

"The towns, too, are easy to decipher. Murals of King Billy on gable walls will mark the Loyalist areas—or painted curbstones of Union Jack red, white, and blue, or on walls: the Red Hand of Ulster. In Catholic areas the murals will be of the Heroes of 1916, and the slogans on the walls, BRITS OUT, or FREE DERRY."

"Sounds like I'll be able to tell the difference right away."

"Aye, but what you must do is to accept everyone and to feign ignorance on touchy matters. Don't rise to the bait like this afternoon. Our fellow in Glencree is just a blowhard, but threats by Northern lads are seldom idle."

Peader rose wearily to leave, heavy with the weight of the wisdom he had to impart.

"Just think, two hundred years ago, it was English soldiers sleeping in these barracks and going out to do battle with the Irish, the so-called Heroes of '98. And, here we are, looking for refuge from this same bloody mess. A long bitter history, is it not?"

"Too long." I shook my head in sad agreement.

Brother Malachy of Mount Argus

On a mid-September Friday, we reached within three miles of Dublin's City Center, arriving at Mount Argus Monastery and being met at the gate by Brother Malachy Daly, a plump, jovial, middle-aged Passionist, smoking a pipe.

"So, you're the lad Jimmy Beirne in Tallacht rung me about. Come in, the two of you, and be our weekend guests."

As a layman from Tipperary named Pat walked Missie to the stables on these spacious enclosed grounds, Brother Malachy led me through a block of graystone buildings to the retreatants' quarters, his brown robes swishing through polished corridors.

"Lucky cell seven, this," he said, opening its door to expose an austere room furnished with table, chair, and a large crucifix over a simple bed. "Now, unpack, and I'll prepare you a meal below."

Presently, the two of us sat alone in the large kitchen.

"You're famished," he exclaimed, watching me eagerly behead my first egg and scoop out its filling. "I say, it's been a hungry road for you?"

"It hasn't been too bad," I conceded. "I have yet to beg for anything but I've gotten pretty good at hinting. It's amazing, really. Every time my pockets are empty, someone stops and hands me a few quid. Same with Missie. When she's down to a handful of oats, a farmer stops out of the blue and gives us a bag. So far I haven't paid a penny for lodgings in almost five months. Heck, I'm seeing Ireland on twenty pence a day."

"God has always provided the pilgrim," said Brother Malachy, pouring out the tea. "In Ireland, especially. We have a long tradition of generosity, going back to the ancient kings of the Seven Provinces who set up countless 'Houses of Hospitality,' for pilgrim, tramp, or wayfarer. A blessing, that, for haven't our roads been filled with the destitute over the centuries, with evictions, wars, and famines? You're living proof such benevolence continues today."

"Amen to that," I said, decapitating my second Humpty Dumpty.

"Many Irish, especially old country folk, believe Jesus takes up disguise and walks our roads," the kindly brother went on. "Saint Caesarius of Arles tells us that 'Christ comes as often as a poor man approaches you.' You wouldn't be Our Lord, now, would you?" he smiled, watching me break bread.

"I'm afraid I'd fail miserably as one of His disciples," I demurred, stuffing my mouth.

"Nonsense! You're the last of the donkey pilgrims, humbling yourself before God and Man about our country."

I was reaching for another slice of bread when Brother Malachy intercepted my hand with a clasp of fervor.

"Tell me, have you been touched by His grace? What has changed within you on this roundabout?"

I looked at Brother Malachy, his eyes fixed and watery.

"Well, I have had some hints of grace lately," I replied, taking back my hand, "but I think it has more to do with being outside all the time, or meeting kind people who thank God for everything but the odd hole in their shoe."

"Go on," pressed Brother Malachy, topping off my tea.

"Sometimes I feel the exact moment of the evening Angelus. It's as if there's a pause, a silence, a moment of thanksgiving. And sometimes prayers just pour out of me, out of the blue, like I'm ready to burst or something."

"A wellspring of grace." He nodded in satisfaction. "Any other movements of Spirit?"

"I don't claim to be any Saint Francis, but whenever the road starts to seem particularly long and lonely, a pied wagtail shows up and hops before us, or a swallow goes zipping between Missie's ears. Just idle fancies of a wandering mind, I suppose."

"Rubbish," he admonished. "You do a great injustice to dismiss these blessings from God as random occurrences. You've tapped into a Higher Power that many strive for, but few attain. Blessed birdbrain, don't discard God's boundless love as mere coincidence. Remember, coincidence is simply God's little miracle in disguise. The Presence is everywhere for eyes that see and ears that hear. Keep your journey on the way of the pilgrim."

I nodded in thoughtful agreement, as my hand grabbled for the breadbasket again.

That evening, I met my first cousin John Conroy at Slattery's Pub in Dublin, and we were soon reminiscing about my first visit to Ireland in 1966, where my brother Dermot and I stayed with John's mother, Aunt Maggie, my father's older sister, on her farm in County Longford.

"Some vacation, that," I said. "Cleaning out cow pies from stinking byres. Our theme song that whole summer was Bob Dylan's, 'I ain't going to work on Maggie's farm no more.'"

"Oh, I remember," teased John. "Honest-to-goodness bellyaching Yanks asking for hamburgers with the ketchup, and my poor mother not knowing what you two were on about. I'd say you're not so fussy these days?"

"I'd eat the feet off a pig, betimes," I acknowledged.

Before we left the pub, John pressed four twenty-pound notes on me.

"I can't take those," I said, pushing them away.

"Take them," he insisted. "No first cousin of mine, grandson of Bernie O'Hara, is going to travel the Six Counties without a few quid in his pocket."

"I can't, John. Besides, I'm doing very well living hand-to-mouth."

"Consider it a loan, emergency funds, anything," he persisted. "It's not hospitable Kerry or Cork you'll be walking through. Just last week, the Rose of Tralee Festival was held under the tightest security in its history, with the crown going to Miss Belfast, in hopes, I suspect, of easing the growing tensions between ourselves and the North. And call me, day or night, whether in Belfast or Derry, if you need anything."

"I'll call you when Missie's in-season again," I ribbed, accepting the four crisp blue bills as a loan.

After the pub's closing, John, who lived in nearby Clontarf, drove me through City Centre and showed me the most direct route out of the city on Sunday, as it was impossible for Missie and me to navigate the Big Smoke any other day of the week.

"Best be off early Sunday morning," he advised me, crossing the O'Connell Bridge. "There'll be a hundred thousand people attending the match at Croke Park to watch Dublin and Kerry battle for the All-Ireland Football Finale. And untold thousands cramming into the city's pubs."

When we returned to Mount Argus, Pat was waiting at the gate.

"So, you've brought him back to us, have you?" Pat joked, shaking hands with John.

"Better you than me," my cousin joked. "I never dreamt there'd come a time when I'd be dropping this galoot off at a monastery."

"Brother Malachy calls him 'the last of the donkey pilgrims,'" said Pat with a benevolent mien.

"Donkey pilgrim!" laughed John, throwing an arm over me. "Our grandfather must be dancing a lively jig in heaven above."

On Saturday, I took a double-decker bus to Trinity College and ventured up Grafton Street, John's cash burning a hole in my pocket, to purchase a conventional tent to lighten Missie's load, the wattles and canvas too cumbersome for our northern travels.

Dublin was bustling with shoppers on this sunny September day. A happy, hearty, healthy race they appeared to be, both the natives and those they called "culchies," recent blow-ins from the west and midlands. Coin-seeking buskers filled the noonday air with song.

Many a time I had walked these streets, but none so fondly remembered as when my uncle Bennie took three days off the farm in 1971 to show me around to everything from the Book of Kells to the Guinness factory. My reverie of bygone days was broken when a dirty-faced redhead poked a soiled kerchief beneath my nose, and charmlessly wheedled, "Spare coppers, mister. Spare coppers!"

This runny-nosed waif, a "knacker" in the Dublin vernacular, was of the traveling breed who had of late given up their painted wagons for the grimy ghettos of the city. The child—God Bless the Mark—had freckles that splotched her face as though God had applied them too hurriedly with a blunt brush. And they ran right up to her matching shock of dreaded red hair.

Confronted with such an imp, Dubliners seemed to respond, *Bugger off, you blooming redhead!* I, however, thinking about Aggie's little ones and having shared the fellowship of the road with the traveling tribe, delved into my left-hand pocket and sacrificed my loose change, eight pence, to her ragged cloth.

Not satisfied with my modest donation, the girl continued to backpedal before me, chanting her beggary, her eyes wide under my nose, insistent and entirely too close for comfort.

"I've given you what I have." I shook her off, not counting the four twenty-pound notes deep and secure in my right-hand pocket. "Now, bugger off, you blooming redhead!"

Hearing that magic utterance, she disappeared through the throngs and was gone.

Proud to have the knack of it, I strutted a few steps before an unsettling intimation entered my brain. Fumbling madly into my right pocket, I scoured a cavernous emptiness of lint and fluff to find I had been picked clean! My sudden wealth had suddenly vanished.

Crazed with adrenaline, I blindly bolted after her, upsetting shoppers, dodging prams, and nearly bowling over octogenarians, and took one desperate lunge at this fleeing itinerant, barely catching hold of her hand.

"I want my money," I gasped, securing her by the wrists.

"Ouch, ye're killing me, mister!" she screamed, kicking my shins, as a swelling crowd encircled us. "For the love of God," she wailed, dropping to her knees in theatrical pain, "is there not a dacent man among you to save me from this madman's grasp?"

"I want my money," I persisted, pleading now as much to the thickening congregation as to herself, for they seemed to be forgetting their own centuries-old disdain for this misbegotten clan of wayfaring robbers.

When I released one wrist, the young lass stopped her struggle and wiped her eyes with her fisted hand, leaving a portrait so angelic, so forlorn, so godforsaken, that it would bring a tear to a glass eye. Then, lifting her head as if to bravely face the consequence of her crime, she slowly opened her paw for all to see. And there, glistening in her sweaty little palm, were my eight pence, which she proceeded to drop one by one into my outstretched hand.

The crowd, won over by this canny performance, began to take me as a pinchpenny and flagrant child-abuser.

"He deserves a swift boot up the arse," fumed one.

"I'll blacken his two eyes," threatened another.

"I'll kick him into next week," volunteered a third.

"It was four twenties she stole from me," I argued, but, feeling the sway of the mob, I began to lose my nerve, and the redheaded miscreant winked at me with a victorious hard-candied smile.

I let go my grasp, and turned as if to set off on my sullen way, but I immediately spun about, catching her off-guard, and snatched the kerchief secured beneath her arm. I gave it one violent shake and, lo and behold, three twenty-pound notes fluttered free from a hidden fold in the cloth.

Now, with the crowd returned to my side, I demanded my last twenty.

"I haven't yer bleeding money," the cheeky colleen replied, tightening her left hand into a knuckled ball. But prying her fingers apart, I extracted my last bill, wadded to marble-size and tucked away like some nimble-fingered magician.

"I'm giving you ten seconds before I call the guards," I warned. "One, two . . ."

The brassy little knacker shoved her fingers into my pocket, pulled out her original eight pence, stuck out her tongue, gave me one parting shot to the shin, and was gone. The crowd dispersed with trailing mumbles, as I walked toward Stephen's Green with pounding heart and aching shin, until I came upon two guards cutting handsome figures in their blue uniforms.

"Excuse me, Officers," I said, "but I just had a run-in with a pickpocket . . ."

"Was she a redhead of eight years?" interrupted one, showing little interest.

"W-why yes," I answered, flabbergasted.

"Well, now, don't you worry about a thing," he stated, as he stared over my head at the passing scene. "We're keeping a close eye on her, so we are."

With that, they continued to saunter down Grafton Street, tipping their caps to all the lovely ladies as they passed.

That night, in the quiet kitchen with Brother Malachy, after I had recapped my day's harried adventures, I showed him the new Black's tent.

"A dandy purchase," he acknowledged, working his pipe in delight. " 'Tis wise to lighten your load. Believe me, Ulster will weigh heavy enough upon the pair of you."

"I know all the enmity of the North goes way back," I said, rolling up my orange tent, "but how did it get so bad recently?" I'd never made it very far into my book about the Troubles.

"Things were peaceful enough in the North following the two World Wars, but Catholics were still being treated as second-class citizens," he shared, pouring out the tea. "But in the '60s, the northern Catholics, inspired by Dr. Martin Luther King, began their own civil-rights movement, pressing for equal rights through a nonviolent campaign. This movement wasn't long taking shape until, in the town of Burntollet in 1969, Unionists armed with rocks and bottles injured hundreds of Catholics, while the Royal Ulster Constabulary, mostly Protestant, stood by and did little to intervene."

"Yes, in those days there was violence in the streets all over, even in America."

"After Burntollet, the Catholic leaders begged Parliament to send British soldiers to Ulster to protect them, as thousands of Catholics had been burnt out of their homes. Ironically, when these soldiers arrived, the Catholics greeted them open-armed in the streets—delighted they were, thinking peace would be maintained. But then came Bloody Sunday."

"Oh, yes, Bogside in Derry, January 30, 1972," I sighed, knowing it too well.

"Aye, when thousands of Catholics marched against 'internment without trial,' under which so-called troublemakers could be swept up and held without charge. The Brits blockaded the route of the march and brought in paratroopers to round up rioters when the inevitable chaos ensued. Well, they got their chaos, and in it, the rattled British soldiers suddenly opened fire, killing thirteen Catholics and wounding dozens more. And rather than admit to their tragic error, the British covered their own and even gave out medals."

"Worse than the police riot outside the Democratic National Convention in Chicago, 1968."

"Yes, and that was it, wasn't it?" he said somberly, cleaning out his pipe over an ashtray. "The IRA, whose campaign had been on the ropes for years, began to recruit heavily and soon started their own rampage, holding their own 'Bloody Friday,' when a number of Protestants were killed in Belfast."

"Blood for blood, an old and sorry tale."

"From then on it's been tit-for-tat. But even so, the peace people never gave up, rallying again a few years back following the deaths of three children killed by an IRA getaway car. And just two years ago, the Catholic Mairead Corrigan and the Protestant Betty Williams were awarded the Nobel Peace Prize."

"Oh, yes. That was a hopeful time."

"For a while," sighed Brother Malachy. "And that, my friend, is the story of the North you're about to enter. A sad tale for a Christian country, is it not?"

Following early Mass on Sunday before the high, marbled altar at Mount Argus, Pat and Brother Malachy led Missie and me to the front gate.

"Do say hello to all the fine people in my native Donegal," said Brother Malachy. "And come back anytime, either as a visitor or young retreatant. Now, may the Blessed Trinity shield you both on your pilgrimage," he added, sprinkling us with Knock water.

Approaching the Dragon

CHAPTER THIRTY-EIGHT

Missie and I were soon cutting through the blue congested haze of An Lar: right at Christ Church Cathedral, left at city hall, and out Capel Street toward the Aerphort Road, where hundreds of cars, headed early for the Gaelic football match, wildly waved flags the colors of Dublin or Kerry.

Recalling my agonizing passage through Cork City on the August Bank Holiday, I kept my head down and walked as determinedly as a soldier headed home on furlough.

We traveled eleven exhaust-wheezing miles to Swords and were taken in by Patrick Moran, an old fellow who placed Missie in his apple orchard, yards away from the main runway at Dublin's International Airport.

"Won't a good drunk do her well," Patrick joked, as we watched Missie feast on a nearby cider heap.

"Will she really get drunk?" I asked uneasily, shooing away a few lazy bees.

"She'll stop before her fill, for she's wiser than many of our own. But doesn't she deserve a good binge, poor creature, with all that's yet before her?"

Leaving Missie content with her apples of Eden, I thumbed back into Dublin to watch the All-Ireland finale at Slattery's Pub, where Kerry romped over Dublin, as Pat and Mick Spillane, my newfound friends from Templenoe, dominated the match from beginning to end.

Returning late to Swords, I found Missie bathed in the sulphurous lights of the runway, as planes slowly descended above her rotating ears.

"Did Swords get its name from a battle fought here?" I asked Patrick, when he invited me in for tea.

"No, indeed," he explained. "Swords is from the Irish *sord,* meaning 'holy well,' a well blessed by Saint Columcille, who also founded a monastery here in the sixth century. The bodies of Brian Boru and his son rested at that monastery on their way to a solemn burial at Armagh in 1014."

"But I thought Brian Boru was victorious at Clontarf that year."

"He was. But bittersweet the victory, for venerable King Brian was slain in his tent by a Danish chieftain, after learning the Irish had won the day."

The roar of a descending aircraft rendered us silent.

"I often wonder if those pilots realize they're landing on such holy ground," Patrick added, after the din had subsided. "And holy ground it is."

We stayed the next night with Phillip Bell in Balbriggan, and then set off for the old Viking seaport of Drogheda, the traffic thick on the N1 with heavy lorries rumbling north and threatening to sideswipe us off our narrow margin.

A thick mist had settled over the old town when we crossed the bridge over the River Boyne, the sky so heavy as to blunt church spires and weigh down the spirit, as does the tragic history of this ancient town. In 1649, Cromwell, on the way to earning his spurs as the so-called Lord Protector, led a punitive expedition to Ireland that culminated in a bitter siege of Drogheda and the brutal slaughter of most of its inhabitants. And again in 1690, this was the site of the Battle of the Boyne, which settled England's so-called Glorious Revolution, and sealed a terrible heritage of dispossession.

I settled Missie outside town with Mickey Foyle, an elderly farmer who lived in a beautiful stone farmhouse surrounded by high wooden walls, and walked back to Drogheda and into St. Peter's Church, on whose steps so many innocents were massacred.

I knelt before the embalmed head of the martyr Oliver Plunkett, Catholic Archbishop of Armagh and Primate of Ireland—hanged, drawn, and quartered after a manifestly false show-trial in London in 1681. Rising after a brief spell before this imposing relic, I was greeted by an enthusiastic old woman.

"Did you hear, the Holy Father will be celebrating Mass in Dunleer, just four miles up the road?" she whispered excitedly, her voice carrying through the hushed aisles. "He can't go north to Armagh, which has been the holy capital of Ireland since Saint Patrick founded his church there in the fifth century. But now, at least, he'll be able to make a pastoral visit to a part of the parish."

"You must be excited for the Pope to be coming."

" 'Tis wonderful." She clasped her hands prayerfully. "An outdoors Mass for the multitudes. And now, thank God, can't the northern Catholics come down and share in the Pope's presence?"

"When is he arriving?" I asked this pious woman.

"Saturday, the twenty-ninth. And he'll celebrate Mass in both Dublin and Dunleer that day." She rattled off his full itinerary: "On Sunday, the Holy Father will be at Clonmacnois, Galway, and Knock Shrine, and will depart from Shannon Airport on Monday after morning Mass in Limerick."

After a walk around the somber, gray-cobbled town of Drogheda, I stepped into a pub and met the barman, Oliver, recently named the second-best barman in Eire. After he served up a perfect pint, he introduced me to Bryan, a keen historian of the locality.

"I've often heard of the Battle of the Boyne," I confessed, "but I know little about it."

"Hurry back your drink, and I'll take you to Oldbridge where a major skirmish was fought. We're only five minutes from it."

We were presently walking across an old stone bridge with high wrought-iron fencing, looking down upon the banks of the Boyne.

"Irish history would be different today if James the Second had been victorious here," began Bryan, looking upon the brown waters. "James was a Catholic, you see, and was deposed by his Protestant daughter, Mary, and her husband, William of Orange. James landed in Kinsale with hopes of regaining his throne, promising the Irish people he would oust the Protestant settlers from their lands in return, if they helped in his campaign.

"There wasn't much of a battle below," he continued, tossing a stone from the bridge, "as William owned the day, leading an army of thirty-six thousand well-trained troops, against James and twenty-five thousand poorly armed men: a ragged lot of French and Irish, many seeing battle for the first time. William's army was able to ford the river at Slane, and again here at Oldbridge, and by noon that July day in 1690, William had his father-in-law outflanked and outsmarted. James was a poor leader and actually left the battlefield that evening with the battle undecided, complaining of diarrhea. After retreating to Dublin he set sail for France, and good riddance to him, last of the Stuart kings."

"As weak as he was, he might have been better for the Catholics in Ireland."

"Yes, but the day belonged to William, Prince of Orange, now revered by Loyalists as 'King Billy.' From here, he cut a bloody swath to Aughrim, where the French-led Jacobites were finally annihilated. So now the Orangemen wear their sashes in all their July Twelfth parades, celebrating King Billy and his victory at the Boyne, parades that heat that old pot to boiling all over again. The Troubles are like a game of 'Snakes and Ladders.' You gain some ground, then, with one roll of the dice, you're back to square one."

"What a sad, unending history this island has had."

"But our history's not all dismal. Going back much further, this valley was a cradle of civilization. It's known as *brugh na boinne,* 'the Palace of the Boyne.' Come on," he said, hurrying me toward the car park, "and I'll take you on a whirlwind tour."

So his car became a time machine, whisking me back thousands of years to Newgrange, Dowth, and Knowth, astounding passage graves and ancient astronomic sites.

That night, with low clouds leaking tears, I returned after my tour of antiquities to the enclosed farmyard of Mickey Foyle, stooping through a little wicket gate he had left unclasped, and retiring to the haybarn. As rain drummed off the corrugated roof, I felt the ghosts of history still clinging like mist to every bough in this region, and not even the strongest Atlantic gale could blow them away.

I could imagine the high squeals of Drogheda's children, as they were slaughtered on St. Peter's steps, and along the Boyne, the banging of kettledrums and splashing of hooves across the ford, the ring of steel and boom of blunderbuss. Three centuries later, these old sounds of battle have evolved into the screech of armored vehicles and the shattering of firebombed glass. Only the cries of children remains the same.

After spending a comfortable night with a kind old woman named Brigid Clarke in Castlebellingham, we set out for Blackrock, five miles from the border, calling on John and Áine Bradshaw, the couple I had met on Midsummer's Eve on the Dingle Peninsula.

They stepped out from their handsome bungalow, not believing their eyes.

"You're still at it," said John, shaking my hand. "How many miles have you now?"

"Eight hundred and fifty. Just over halfway."

"And how is Missie keeping?" asked Áine, petting my affectionate brown nut.

"She's champ and chump all rolled into one," I replied.

Next morning, John took me around the Cooley Hills of Carlingford Peninsula, visiting the Norman king John's Castle and another ancient tomb called Proleek Dolmen.

"You can see Warrenpoint in County Down across the way," said John, "where the eighteen soldiers were ambushed the same day as Mountbatten's murder"—pointing toward a picturesque town on the northern side of Carlingford Bay. "During the ambush, British soldiers fired random shots across this side, killing a young man from London and wounding his cousin from Kerry. I can only tell you to be cautious when you're up there. The only thing in your favor is that you're an American. I wouldn't want to think what would happen if you were one of our own."

On our way home, John suggested we stop at a bank to change my money.

"They don't accept Irish pounds up North," he explained, to my surprise. "Say good-bye to your currency of Irish heroes: Meab, Scotus, Swift, and Yeats. It's Queen Liz until you reach Donegal."

Next morning, it was difficult to know when we actually entered the North, crossing the border into County Armagh. There were no custom posts—I was told they are forever being blown to smithereens—no checkpoints, no barbed wire running the length of the dividing line. I did, however, begin to see a change: better roads, telephone booths painted "Imperial red," billboards to hamper our view, and, finally, an army helicopter hovering over the foothills of Mourne.

A mile shy of Newry, I came upon a show-jumping practice field, and received permission to camp there from its owners, the Hughes family. Escorted by their young son, I checked the outlying boundary for gaps, plugging up a few holes to make it donkey-safe. That done, I stashed my gear in an old cabin in the field's corner, and made my way into town.

Newry's border location made it a focal point for violence. I arrived before suppertime, and at first glance all seemed unremarkable—citizens heading home after a day's work, stopping into shops for milk or newspapers. But soon the scars of the Troubles were visible: motorcars gutted by firebombs, British army vehicles hurtling by stalled traffic, graffiti slashed over abandoned walls.

And within this city at the Angelus there were no children on the Green, no mothers proudly wheeling their prams, no snickering schoolgirls, no old men congregating on bank steps to swap stories. Amongst the few passersby, no pleasantries about the weather were exchanged, no gentle nods of the cap. Even the stores open for business—chemist, newsagent, pub—all gave the outward appearance of being closed.

I ventured into the Bit and Bridle, ordered fish and chips, and looked down the counter in hopes of conversation. But not a single patron looked up from their plate. Back on the street, there was no sign of Friday-evening festivity: Women in quiet clumps window-shopped through iron-latticed gates, their scarfs pulled forward like blinders; and children, so few, here and there, on the run.

In a pub with no name over its door, I sat alone with my journal and logged the day's long, tiring trek. I thought about my encounter with the farmer in Dundalk, driving a lorryload of donkeys, who asked the whereabouts of the meat factory. Missie had fretted at seeing her comrades bucking wildly through the lorry's slats, and I recalled that March morning when her stablemates were loaded by Jimmy Mac for the same fate. *It's a tough world for donks as well as men.*

It was pitch-black when I returned to the Hughes's field. I called out to Missie; but, no answer, no self-pitying whinny. I again called, and rattled hard oats in my bucket. Still no answer. I stumbled around the edge of the field, whistling and shouting madly. Had she fled this troubled land? Had she been snatched by knackers? What butchery might she be facing?

I circled again in growing panic, and nearly leapt from my skin when I knocked into her broadside, standing beneath an overhang of shrubbery and sleeping soundly.

"Oh, Missie," I said, hugging my startled and bleary-eyed heroine.

She snorted deeply, puzzled by my nocturnal embrace, but lazily followed me up the field to the crumbled old homestead. There I pitched my new Black's tent inside the roofless cabin and fell, beads in hand, into a troubled sleep.

I woke late to the hum of traffic, and we were soon into the thick of it, staying to the safe margin of the dual carriageway, and avoided Newry by turning back toward Warrenpoint and the coast road. Along Bayview Drive, large handsome homes offered a grand view back at the Cooley Hills across Carlingford Lough, yet the neighborhood seemed eerily vacant.

Just beyond Warrenpoint, a young boy came pedaling by on a bicycle.

"That roundabout you just passed, at Narrow Waters Castle, is where the eighteen soldiers were killed." He straddled his bike and excitedly pointed back down the road. "It was a terrible loud explosion. The IRA hid the bomb in a parked lorry full of straw and set it off by remote control from across the lough there." He swung his pointing finger to the Carlingford side, and then waved his hands in the air. "There was an ambush, and another explosion, and then a swarm of helicopters came in to take out the dead and wounded."

"Did you see any of it?" I asked this eager scout.

"No, but I heard it. All of it! And the road was cordoned-off after that, and my dad didn't get home till midnight because of it. I never saw so many soldiers."

The lad pedaled off, to whatever new adventures awaited him, leaving me to ponder the difference from my earlier encounters with children along the road. I thought back on the innocence of the playful boys I had met on Inisheer Island, and the girls picking wildflowers on the Dingle, and how this battle-torn province must change its children. *Will they come running out after us like those helpful youngsters in Bunmahon, or will they hold back and gape from afar, instinctively wary of strangers?*

What a great pity, I sighed, for kids to be brought up in a land stained with bloodshed, their minds sullied by senseless murder and occupying forces of men and metal. How many simple joys are lost to mistrust? How many dreams never realized? How immeasurable their lifelong loss?

And Missie and me—what were we in for, leaving hospitality for hostility?

The Kingdom of Mourne

W e pushed along this picturesque but near-abandoned coastline, through the resort town of Rostrevor, and out into a comforting vista of grazing sheep and zigzag drystone walls climbing the granite upland slopes of Mourne. There I asked a farmer, built low and strong like his native hills, for permission to spend the night.

"You can stay in Willie's Loft," he said, pointing to an old cabin stuffed with hay. "My name is Gabriel McGivern, and I have a few lads who'll be happy to help with your donkey"—introducing me to four good-looking sons who shot up from nowhere.

As the boys led Missie to a hillslope filled with horned sheep, I climbed the outside ladder to "Willie's Loft," where a band of curious mice watched me unroll my sleeping bag. I was invited into the farmhouse and seated at the table where a picture of the Sacred Heart gazed down from the wall. The boys scrambled for nearby chairs, as three thick slices of beef were put in front of me.

"You're now in the Kingdom of Mourne," said Gabriel, "and if you can spare a day, my boys will take you on a wee tour. You'll find all sorts of antiquities. A pocket of old Ireland, these hills, undisturbed even by the Plantation itself and, thank God, a safe haven still. In fact, the last Irish speaker died in Hilltown only a few years back."

"We could take you to Kilbroney Graveyard where Giant Murphy is buried," piped up Desmond, the youngest. "He was eight foot two inches tall, so his family sold him off to a traveling circus."

"Pity you weren't six feet taller, so Mama could sell you off," teased his older brother, Niall.

"If I was eight foot two inches tall, I'd bop you one!" retorted Desmond, raising a fist the size of a new potato.

"Manners!" Mrs. Veronica McGivern cast a warning eye at her charges.

"I'd love to stay on and visit these sites, but I'll have to take a rain check, as my timetable is nip and tuck right now," I apologized to the boys. "But what's the story of Willie's Loft?" I asked, referring to my bedposts for the night.

"Willie was a traveler like yourself, who would come about these parts when I was a child," said Mrs. McGivern. "There he'd be at our door, same as yourself, but no donkey, just shank's mare. He came every year for the odd bit of work, and I believe he must have tramped the whole of Ireland, for his accent was a puzzle, to be sure."

I had clearly tapped a vein of reminiscence in the woman, and her eyes took on a dreamy look.

"Every evening he would quiz us on our geography, pulling an old folded map from his pocket and pointing out the Silver Mines of Nenagh, the Caves of Mitchelstown, the Glen of Imeal. Such faraway places. And though your heart would go out to him, traveling the world alone with knotted sack, hadn't he riches beyond compare? He was loved by us children, and wouldn't that be the same of all children? And after his few days of honest labor and nights of storytelling, he'd climb that ladder across the way, and would be gone again that morning before we rose from our beds."

Mrs. McGivern paused for a moment, then continued as she rose to gather up her children's empty plates. "But then Willie stopped coming, and we often wondered what happened to him. He wasn't that old, mind you, and no signs of him settling down or taking a bride. Oh, well, it's a mystery, and life has so many. But somehow he always managed to leave our family at peace, saying how fortunate we were to have a little plot of land beneath these brown hills."

That night, climbing into Willie's Loft, I thought of the rambler who had slept here years ago, speculating on his knowledge of the roads, the drover's stations he had witnessed, and the wild characters he had met. Did he ever meet Husband the Welshman, I wondered, or the balladeer Pecker Dunne?

Who were these circuit-goers that traipsed the island long before me? I mused, adjusting my bag of oats under my head. What were they searching for, and were they successful in their quest? Did they ever find peace and contentment at the end of the highway?

"What if I was to walk this land forever!" I said aloud, clapping my hands to frighten away the gathering mice. "In twenty years' time there wouldn't be a child I wouldn't know in the Four Provinces. Imagine my richness, to hold company with thousands of children."

I finally nodded off amidst the scuttle of mice, happy to sleep in this barn-loft where Willie had rested his wayfaring head years ago, and comforted to know that Ulster, despite my own trepidations, might not be half-bad when such enclaves as these peaceful "brown hills" still existed.

———

On Sunday morning, after Mass and a noonday feast, I said farewell to the McGiverns, promising the lads I'd visit again someday, God willing, and tackled Missie to travel a winding road with the lovely Mournes on our left, the spume of the sea on our right, and nary a soul raising dust but ourselves.

That afternoon we entered the harbor town of Kilkeel, and I took note of the red, white, and blue curbstones—Loyalist markings, as I'd been warned by Peader in Glencree.

Walking down this long row of attached council houses, I felt like a blatant interloper. Missie's shoes rang sharply off the pavement, heralding our trespass into this Protestant domain. I progressed apprehensively, expecting a hooligan to step from his door and slag me, or worse. No one appeared, however—all remained a ghost town, but for the nearly imperceptible shift of curtains as we passed.

I wondered what these peeping occupants might think of my intrusion, my grand Republic of Ireland parade. I wouldn't find out, and perhaps it was just as well. We came to a stone bridge, painted up like a Union Jack, where a handmade placard proclaimed: NO SURRENDER! Crossing it, we were gone from the town, and not a native did we see.

Further down the road, I was stopped by a photographer from the *Mourne Observer*.

"I received a call from a woman in Kilkeel who said you'd make a fine photo for our paper," he said, taking our picture and handing me a pound sterling. "She thinks it's marvelous you decided to include Ulster in your roundabout, and so do I."

Dumbfounded, I thanked him. Peader had told me I'd find the North a puzzling paradox, and I was discovering that already.

That evening, I tied Missie to a farmer's gate in Ballymartin, and asked the missus permission to camp. She eyed me suspiciously, but softened when she looked past me at my sweetly snuffling beast.

"You'll need to ask my husband, Joslin Orr, out back," she said, restraining her family, who began to spill out the door.

Behind the farmhouse, I spotted a score of children ranging from short-pantsed urchin to strapping young adult, standing in line with faces full of hope and enterprise, as Joslin Orr studied each in turn. I hesitated to interrupt whatever this muster might be.

"My father is choosing his pickers for the gathering of potatoes," said one of Mr. Orr's young sons, Keith, who had followed me around the back of the house. "He sorely needs the help, for we have fifty-two acres of spuds in the ground. Whoever's chosen tonight will work for my father these next six weeks."

"After school?"

"No, from dawn till dusk, Monday through Saturday. Pickers won't go back to school now till the end of October."

"That's a long time. Don't their teachers mind?"

"No, half the kingdom does it. There's many people living hereabouts who are desperately in need of money," he explained, awfully knowing for one so young, "and my father gives them five pounds for each ton of potatoes picked."

"Wow," I said, staggered more by the weight of potatoes than the earnings. "How much can one pick in a day?"

"Good pickers, if they don't go spending their day throwing clogs of mud at one another, can make seven pound, fifty pence, a day. A ton and a half of pratties, that is."

"Three thousand pounds of spuds," I whistled. "Backbreaking work, I bet?"

" 'Tisn't bad, mind ya," Keith answered nonchalantly. "I do it as well, and can pick with the best of them."

"I bet you can."

We watched the proceedings as the hopeful children puffed up their chests to show their starch and stamina. It brought to mind my old caddy days, when I had stood before an appraising caddymaster who passed me by for several days, before finally pairing me up with a golfer nicknamed Mickey Shank, a true hacker of the game. Still, the country club was no potato field.

After the ranks had been chosen, and the children scattered for home in this impoverished yet lovely kingdom by the sea, Joslin Orr had no qualms about me staying for the night.

"Come in for the meal and meet my family of nine," he said. "A big family for Protestants, is it not?"

"Yes, even bigger than my brood of Catholics back home in America."

"And do you wish to go picking spuds?" he beamed, throwing an accepting arm over me.

And so I walked into my first Protestant household of the North and, to my great relief, found it more familiar than not.

Next morning, as Missie and I went walking through the Loyalist village of Annalong, I was called in to tea by a pleasant elderly woman.

"Be sure to tell everyone in America that Ulster isn't inhabited by savages, when your travels are through," she urged, as she placed a tray of biscuits on the coffee table before me. "The papers of the world have us blackened, so they do. Didn't I just read how an English secondary school canceled a field trip to the Mournes due to the renewed Troubles? You can't imagine how that pains me! As if some bully would blow up a busload of schoolchildren in the Silent Valley! 'Tis only a handful of blackguards from both sides who keep throwing petrol upon the fire."

"That's the way of it, I'm afraid: the bad blacken the good."

"What about you?" she asked with a sigh of weariness. "How have you found us so far?"

"Warm and accepting," I answered diplomatically. "But, to be honest . . ." I stopped short.

"Go on," she said. "You're safe with me."

"Well, it's a little nerve-wracking, walking through these Loyalist villages with murals of King Billy and the Red Hand of Ulster painted on every other gable."

" 'Tis only to show our solidarity." She made light of it. "Ever since our ancestors were planted here, some without choice, mind you, we've lived in considerable fear. Don't forget, the English made as great a shambles out of Scotland as it did Ireland. The great pity is that we're the one race, Irish and Scot, having meandered back and forth across the North Channel long before history was written."

"One people divided, that's the sad Celtic story."

"And those colorful murals are much like alarm systems placed inside one's homes. They keep out the bad sort. But you yourself needn't worry," she patted my knee, "you're walking with a donkey, and whether Catholic or Protestant, we all know of Our Lord's triumphant entrance into Jerusalem with a donkey."

"Oh, yes," I risked the sacrilege, "but look what happened to Our Lord a few days afterward."

That afternoon, we entered Newcastle beneath a gray-black sky, under the gloomy, looming eminence of Slieve Donard—King of the Mournes—hidden in a vaporous crown, and walked the town's handsome promenade beside the restless waters of Dumdrum Bay. Just out the town, the sky finally collapsed, flattening Missie's ears with pelting rain. Scurrying for cover, we met Joe Kane, spreading plastic over the vegetable stand outside his home.

"The American with the donkey, you say? Well, come in, out of this drenching. But I must warn you, I have a son inside who'll be stone-mad to set out with you in the morning."

Joe Kane was absolutely right. No sooner had the Catholic family finished Grace at the dinner table, than a young John, age eleven, begged to join me.

"I need to travel on my own, this time 'round," I gently told the nearly sobbing boy. "But I'll be looking for a good guide to take me to the top of Slieve Donard, when I return in a few years' time."

"I'm just the fellow for that job," he piped up, clearing his eyes and nearly upsetting his milk. "And there's an old cairn up there, and I'll know every stone that's in it, won't I, Da?"

"Every stone that's in it," agreed Joe Kane, consoling his son with a warm hug. "Every stone that's in it."

Ship on the Sea

CHAPTER FORTY

The inclement weather cleared at noon the next day, as we traversed the tranquil shore of this mountainous land, interrupted only by a convoy of army vehicles speeding to God-knows-where, and a photographer from the *Down Record* who promised, after taking our snap, to send a copy to Rattigan's Pub. By midday we had tipped through Downpatrick, and out the Strangeford Road to Quoile, finding lodgings with a Catholic family named McGrath.

"Do you see that hill?" said old Hugh McGrath, pointing toward a sun-drenched mound. "'Tis Saul, where Patrick celebrated his first mass in Ireland, in 432 A.D. You should see the evening colors dance upon it at times. It's as if God favors that spot above all others, for, in truth, is there anyplace like it in Ireland? Downpatrick is truly the Patrick center of the County Down. You'll find his burial site on the grounds of the Protestant cathedral atop the town."

Hugh responded to my raised eyebrow: "Did you ever hear the like? Aye, 'twas the site of an ancient monastery, but, like so many of our sacred sites, it was appropriated by the English. It probably doesn't bother Saint Patrick much, but it sure gets my goat up."

So, after Missie was fed and watered, I walked back into town and up English Street to the quiet grounds of the cathedral. I searched through weathered headstones until I found a stone slab laying flat, with PATRIC hewn upon it. Kneeling beside this simple monolith, I said my prayers to the three saints reputed to be buried below—Patrick, Brigid, and Columcille—adding another for the old woman I had met in County Clare tending Brigid's Well.

Leaving the churchyard, I was greeted by three friendly young men who said they had seen me pass earlier with Missie.

"You expected more, I suppose," apologized one, who introduced himself as Michael. "But Saint Patrick is no longer in our care. Ironic, isn't it, the patron saint of Ireland buried in a Protestant yard?"

"It does come as a surprise," I agreed, but was leery of taking sides with strangers.

"That huge stone over St. Patrick's Grave was quarried in the Mournes," a fellow named Cormac chimed in. "It lies flat because, in the anniversary year of 1932, pilgrims were taking handfuls of the soil away with them. If they had dug any deeper, they would have carried the saint away as well."

"I've been to Yeats's grave in Sligo and I couldn't believe the busloads of people," said Michael, pressing his point. "And here you are, the only one I've seen visit the saint's grave today."

Thomas was the third and, like his namesake, had his doubts, seeming to have heard his companion's rant often enough. "No one knows whose bones they really are, anyway. It's mostly fairy-tale, and a political tug-of-war. A Norman king claimed to have moved Patrick's remains here to secure his stronghold, but it was a power grab, really. And then just more folklore, like the old poem: *'Three saints one grave do fill / Patrick, Brigid, and Columcille.'*"

Having staked out their usual positions, the threesome changed the topic.

"We'd like to treat you to a meal at the Ivy Bar," said Michael. "It's only a kip of a place, but it's good pub grub."

"Thank you," I said, still cautious, "but the people I'm staying with are expecting me."

Their faces dropped: "A quick jar, so?"

I wavered.

"A pint will do no harm," they encouraged me, their faces brightening.

"A pint, so," I replied, so as not to let sectarian apprehensions change the spirit of my journey.

Even enjoying our round, however, I noticed how the three leaned over the table and spoke softly, quite different from the open, expansive pub demeanor I had come to expect, but companionable enough, after all.

"You're a silly dafter to come North," ribbed Cormac.

"It hasn't been that much different from the Republic, as far as people go," I said. "In fact, you're the first blackguards I've met so far."

The ice well-broken, we soon were laughing foursquare, as the barkeep served up bowls of steaming soup and baskets of sandwiches. As we ate, I told them how Missie and me had been photographed for the *Mourne Observer,* and again for the *Down Record.*

"You might be wise to ring them up and tell them not to print your picture for a week or two," suggested Tom. "I doubt you want the publicity, Papist O'Hara that you are—awfully Green for the Orange territory you'll be going through."

"He's right," agreed Michael. "I'd tiptoe through Ulster if I were you. Some rowdy might give you a hard knock if you stand out too much. Don't make yourself a target for reprisal, because Ulster is ripe to explode, with the Pope's visit this weekend."

Michael turned quite serious and whispered, conspiratorially, "There are people in this town too afraid to take the pilgrim buses to Dublin or Dunleer to see the Pope, convinced the buses will be booby-trapped. A bloody shame, isn't it? Old biddies with their hearts set for years on a chance to see a Pope in Ireland. And here you are," he said, backhanding my shoulder affably, "planning to walk through Belfast with an ass!"

"I won't step into that bloody city even to do me a bit of Christmas shopping," Cormac interjected.

"You best plan your route before entering," advised Tom. "There's one stretch, the Antrim Road, known as 'Murderer's Mile.' Do you know Belfast?"

"I have a good city map," I said, "and I'm planning to pass through early Sunday morning."

"Will you be approaching it from Dundonald?"

"No, Bangor. We're planning to take the ferry out to the Ards Peninsula tomorrow."

"You're taking the ferry out to the Hook?" they roared. "A donkey on a ferry?"

"She crossed the Shannon shipshape in May, like a real sailor," I protested, as their hilarity diffused the growing tension. "And by the time we were halfway across, she was playing shuffleboard with the ship's mate."

"You must be having a right wobbly, or maybe a drop too much," laughed Cormac.

"Or maybe too little," Michael smiled, raising his glass in a toast. "'Twould take a Yank to walk an ass through Belfast. And, by God, you'll manage it!"

Missie and I arrived in Strangeford early the following afternoon, just as the last car was boarding for the four-minute passage to Portaferry. A group of ferrymen hailed our arrival.

"We've been on the lookout all day," one said, encouraging us up the rampway.

Missie balked when she hit the metal ramp, but this quintet made short work of coaxing her up the gangplank, breaking her breeching in the process.

"*Strang Fiord,* is Norse for 'violent inlet,' but the rushing tide is not too bad today," said the tollmaster, looking out at the roiling waters. "But very contrary on a winter's morning, I can tell you."

I handed him two English pounds.

"Put that away," he said. "A few friends you met last evening took care of the toll."

Landing in Portaferrry, we went five miles up the Ards Peninsula to Cloghy, passing a series of whalebacked hills called drumlins, and settled for the night with elderly Pat Watson and his sister Glenda.

Next day, I set off from the accommodating Watsons in great form, looking out at the Isle of Man in the distance, savoring tangy sea air filled with the piping of oyster-catchers on the near shore. At noon I stopped to devour Glenda's ham sandwiches in a setting as peaceful as Cork or Kerry, amidst green hills and blue sea.

The spark in my ragged sneakers dimmed, however, when we entered Ballyhalbert, and a massive mural of King Billy on his white steed brought me up short. Put in opposition, designated an alien, if not an enemy, I was instantly apprehensive, looking for a welcoming party of thick skulls at any corner.

But it wouldn't do to get all paranoid, to be forced to take sides. It was incumbent on me to remain open to all comers. And, indeed, my only greeters were a few children, soon called back from petting Missie by cautious mothers who remained in the shadows of half-opened doors.

Two miles from Millisle, I stopped at what I thought was a shop to buy some milk, but found that the shop had been converted to a home. Excusing myself for the error, I was called back by the elderly man who answered the door.

"You can stay with us for the night. We have a small field out back for the wee donk, and you could sleep in our old boathouse there. We read your spread in the papers."

"Ah, do," beseeched his wife, appearing beside him. "And can't I fix you a chop or two?—for we haven't eaten ourselves. We're Mr. and Mrs. William McCoubrey."

"Kevin O'Hara," I answered, gratefully accepting their offer.

Settling Missie, I stepped into the house, where I was confronted by orange sashes, gaudy banners of King Billy, and a cupboard full of English knickknacks, including teacups from the Queen's recent Silver Jubilee. A bona fide Loyalist parlor.

"I belong to the Orange Order," said William, seeing me appraise the scene. "Doesn't make you too uncomfortable, I hope."

"Oh, no, no—it's fine. I really don't understand what all the fuss is about, anyhow," I said, calling up my well-rehearsed response, and tried to add a tiny twist of irony to the standard line: "Some of my best friends are Protestant. In fact, I was born in England myself."

They both laughed at my practiced reply.

Though frail and in pain from a recent automobile accident, the McCoubreys laid a fine spread before me, while recounting how the accident had prompted them to move from the infamous Shankill area of Belfast, where they had lived for twenty-two years. They were survivors of more than one kind of wreck, though they were most generous to me.

"Shankill was terrible." Mrs. McCoubrey's voice quavered as she cleared the dishes. "But now our days are filled with simple joys. How lovely to look out over the ocean, with all its birds and clouds!"

But it was only minutes later that I heard a sob, and turned to see her weeping at the kitchen sink, seemingly overcome by painful memories stirred by our dinner conversation. William struggled from his chair to comfort his wife, while explaining to me, "Just before leaving Aberdeen Street, my wife cradled the head of a neighbor, shot dead in the street. Shot dead, I say, by young men who had kicked the ball with him a day earlier."

"How awful! I'm so sorry." I stood awkwardly at the table.

"We should have gotten out long ago," he said, as he helped his wife to a chair. "You feel you can put up with anything when you're in the thick of it. But afterward, you wonder how you stuck it out a day, all those long years."

" 'Twas all a shame," said Mrs. McCoubrey, wiping her eyes and composing herself with determination.

A polite order restored, we talked about many things as the night progressed, including William's Military stint in Burma, but the chat always fell back to the Troubles.

"I suppose you're for a united Ireland?" William asked outright at one point, more in sorrow than in challenge.

"I don't know what I'm for"—I opened up a little—"but I don't think it's sensible to have two countries sharing a small island, squabbling for hundreds of years. The people of Ulster will keep struggling as long as this strife continues. New industry is what's needed, to employ all those who are otherwise up to no good, and that won't happen till the Troubles end. It's a circular sort of thing, but from all I've gathered, there'll be no peace in Northern Ireland until the British troops go home."

"The peacekeeping force, go home?" William queried incredulously.

"It's a start," I replied, backing away from my stance. "Their presence is a constant provocation, and those convoys tearing through the dead of night awake the ghosts of history."

"Do you know what would happen if the British troops left Northern Ireland?" William fumed. "There'd be a bloodbath, that's what there'd be. The IRA would stop at nothing."

"I can't believe that," I shrugged, uncomfortably out in the open.

"Did you ever hear what happened at Bloody Bridge, outside Newcastle, in 1641?" he demanded, with a rising vehemence that swamped his kindly nature. "After the Plantation of Ulster, the Catholics killed thousands of men, women, and children. That's what brought Cromwell to Drogheda a few years later. To snuff out the Papists once and for all."

"These old grievances need to be left behind," I argued in spite of myself. "Today, many Catholics and Protestants live peacefully side by side. I've seen it myself. Why, just in Newcastle I stayed with a Catholic, Joe Kane, who ran his vegetable stand totally on the honor system, frequented by Catholic and Protestant alike."

"I don't know about vegetables, but that wouldn't hold out for long; the grabbing and killing would soon begin."

For a silent moment, we contemplated the pessimistic divide between us, before William continued in a calmer manner: "Now, I'll tell you why I personally never want to see a united Ireland. First of all, there's the excellent national health program in the North, which my wife and I severely needed, following our accident. Secondly I sure don't want the Catholic Church telling me what I can or cannot do. And lastly, the Free State can barely run its own affairs. What would it ever do with another million and a half people, tell me?"

"I can't answer that," I conceded, having neither the will nor the matter to contest the argument.

The gentleman's politeness as host reasserted itself, but as the long evening wore on, he couldn't help but come back again and again to the sadness of the situation. When he talked about their long rehabilitation at Royal Victoria Hospital in Belfast, he referred to its world reputation for expertise with burns and severed limbs, another sad legacy of the Troubles.

Eventually he wore me down with tales from the long northern nightmare, giving me another painful perspective on sectarian conflict. He talked of those battered, bartered, and betrayed. The broken bodies and the broken hearts. The unimaginable atrocities and persecutions. And throughout his gruesome litany, Mrs. McCoubrey sat before the telly, the volume loud enough to drown out his chat, as she enjoyed *Coronation Street* and *Keeping Up Appearances,* beamed from across the water in England.

When my patience had almost reached its limit, Mrs. McCoubrey turned off the telly and stood to put on the kettle. "William, isn't it something to have a Catholic in our home?"

"It is, I suppose," he shrugged with a half-smile. "I can hardly wait to tell the members at my lodge. And, O'Hara, aren't you worried you'll be exterminated if your Pope gets wind of this visit?"

"It's 'excommunicated,' " I laughed, relieved to see the hectic flush paling from his brow.

Later in the evening, as I jotted notes beneath an oil lamp, Mrs. McCoubrey peered through the curtain and called out excitedly: "Look, now, the *Sealink* is making its way from Belfast to Liverpool. We watch it every night," she said to me, making room for the three of us at the window.

There we stood, looking out at a sparkling ship floating through the moonless night.

"Not a ripple in the water," said William, his countenance peaceful. "Some nights you'd wonder how it ever gets to Liverpool with the bashing of waves. We often think of those on board hoping for a better life in England, away from the violence and pain."

"Godspeed them," whispered Mrs. McCoubrey, "and may they find a semblance of peace wherever they go."

They stayed at the window till the *Sealink* was little more than a speck on the horizon, a firefly in a dark field, winking back ever so occasionally until it slipped from sight and was gone.

Soon, I readied to retire to the boathouse.

"You'll write and tell us how you fared?" asked William, as I stepped out the door.

"I'll be more than glad to."

"But, sure, won't you call in for the breakfast?" said Mrs. McCoubrey.

"Oh, thank you. No fear I'd miss that."

I walked out into the clear cool night, but rather than going directly to the boathouse, I hiked up the black road, taking in great gulps of sea air and gazing up at the stars. I lay back on a grassy knoll and listened to the lapping waves upon the foreshore below. And when I closed my eyes, they ached for want of tears.

Nursery of Blackguards

On the road past Donaghadee next morning, there were any number of sights—a castle on a hill, a lighthouse by the churning sea—but all were lost to me as I struggled with Missie in one of her bouts of asinine behavior.

Along the Groomsport Road toward Bangor—a Protestant enclave—a red car pulled up with four young men aboard, neither harsh in feature nor mannerism, but full of unsettling queries.

"Are you going to chance Belfast?" asked the driver, without preliminaries.

"I am," I allowed. "From here, I don't really have a choice."

"Aren't you scared?" He wagged his shoulders in exaggeration.

"A little, yes."

I couldn't tell at first whether I was supposed to be afraid of them, or the other guys. Nothing on the car or in their appearance announced which side they were on, or which side they took me to be on. Then one of them made explicit the question on both sides.

"Where do you stand on the Troubles?" asked the fellow in the front passenger seat, adjusting the rearview mirror so he could keep an eye out behind.

"I try not to think anything about them."

"Do you carry any sort of weapon?" he asked peremptorily.

"My stick." I gestured with my hazel, forcing a laugh.

"Not to worry," he rasped in a conspiratorial whisper. "We'll keep a close eye on you."

They pulled out into the traffic and were gone.

Missie and I walked on, but with those four went the goodness of the day.

Where do I stand on the Troubles? Support a campaign where Christmas shoppers are blown sky-high, where old men are shot dead before their grandchildren, where wailing mothers are seen draped over four-foot coffins? Gee, let me think about that for a moment. Have we gone from such a noble race, saviors of Western civilization in dark old times—keeping alive the gospel of light and love—to a people who go recruiting kids to violence?

I'd saved a stamp from one of my grandmother's letters years ago, a bright yellow rectangle to commemorate Mahatma Gandhi, who defeated the British Empire by toting a walking staff, not a carbine. Yet, in the very year that the *Irish Post and Telegraph* celebrated Gandhi, sectarian violence had resumed. But that stamp remains a treasure of hope to me still.

Missie bucked and reared, my anxieties transmitted through her reins like a live wire, as we walked the breakdown lane of this busy thoroughfare. So, was that really the IRA? Didn't sound like the Ulster Volunteers. I'd heard there were more splintered sectarian groups in Northern Ireland than parish football teams. *"We'll keep a close eye on you."* Who is *"we?"* Perhaps they were just four punks. Four nobodies trying to be somebodies in a land of misery. Four young men trying to raise the hairs on my neck, looking for respect in fear.

Trying to dismiss this episode as a random meeting with harmless blackguards, I concentrated on keeping Missie calm in traffic, but it wasn't many moments before the Royal Ulster Constabulary pulled up in a blue patrol car. Two officers, a man and a woman, stepped out in trim green uniforms.

"Good afternoon, sir. And how's it going?"

"Fine, Officers," I said, holding Missie's head close.

"So, this is the famous ass," said the male officer, running his hand down Missie's back. "What happened here to her breeching?"

"It snapped when we boarded the ferry at Strangeford," I conceded.

"Best get it mended," he said sternly.

"Yes, sir."

"You know you'll have to stay off our motorways," he added, checking Missie's shoes like a skilled horseman. "Are you planning to go through Belfast?"

"I am."

"Well, we advise you take the A2 out of Bangor. Do you have anything to report?"

"No, sir."

"Anyone stopping with questions, threats, or the like?"

"No, sir," I repeated, swallowing hard.

"You'll be passing a few British barracks from here on in to Belfast," said the short-haired female officer, standing alongside her partner. "No stopping, no photographs, no sudden movements. Nothing. And do you check your cart each morning?"

"No, Officer, I don't."

"Well, we strongly advise you do so. There's an element in Ulster who'd radio-bomb a pram."

Drained by this second interrogation in less than a mile, I left the Groomsport Road and found accommodation in Ballymaconnell with William Knox. There, I checked my cart's contents and undercarriage, and finally sat myself down to make sense of the day. Red car, blue car? Orange, Green? The colors spun and blurred.

With no sign of my being called in to supper, and too wound-up to sit idle in this Protestant barn through the long evening hours, I walked a dirt road that led from the back of Knox's field to Bangor, where I met a cyclist named Lyndon and his friend, whom he introduced as his "Papist buddy," Lawrence.

"This road is certainly an old survivor," I said, pointing to the deep-rutted cart path that led toward the outskirts of this seaside town.

"William Knox has a fine piece of land, has he not?" said Lawrence, kicking up stones with well-worn shoes. "A picture of rural wonderment it is. In the eighth century, Bangor was the site of one of the grandest monasteries in the world, with three huge choirs of monks singing day, evening, and night. 'The Nursery of Saints,' it was called."

"Aye," scoffed Lyndon, walking his bicycle before us. "Now it could be called 'the nursery of blackguards.' "

In the bustling town on this Friday night, the pair invited me to their favorite watering hole—a Protestant pub, Lyndon informed me, but one where I could take my ease. Lawrence, sensing my anxiety, assured me I was safe, and ordered three pints of Double Diamond.

I joined the night's camaraderie by playing a game of darts, and then placed a tenpence piece on the pool table to await my turn. In no time I was racking up the pool balls, and went on to handily defeat my first two opponents, thanks to countless hours playing with patients on the psych ward back home.

When I held the table a third time, a rough, red-haired townie, who had ruled it earlier, jumped his coin over the others to have a go at me, boasting that no outsider was going to dominate his table. He said it smilingly enough, but, as the game fell in my favor, his visage darkened and he got cruder in his attempts to unsettle me.

"You should have brought your donkey here tonight—I'd love to see you grab hold of her ears and mount her from behind."

Accustomed to every bestial comment since Noah floated the Ark, I paid no mind to his remarks and finished him off by sinking the eight ball. But rather than taking his seat, my foe's face became as red as his hair, and he grabbed another player's coin for a second go at me.

"I hear you're from Boston," he said, angrily thrusting the coin into the slot which brought on an avalanche of balls, "and Boston is full of bloody IRA supporters."

"I'm not from Boston," I corrected, chalking the cue stick, as much to steady my hands as to prepare for my shot. "I'm from the Berkshires in western Massachusetts, closer to New York and Vermont. The Berkshires are a distant rumor to Boston."

Unedified by my geography lesson, he snarled, "For a pint," and ran a tight rack over the well-worn diamond.

"Fine," I answered, flinching away from his hard gaze.

But things were far from "fine." The entire pub had taken on an intensity impercep-

tible a moment before. Even Lawrence and Lyndon, my chaperons, had distanced themselves from the table, offering no allegiance. I scanned the crowd for a supportive face,
but found the only side I was on was my own.

I should have stayed at darts, I sighed, after my initial break had dropped two solids.
But no, I had stepped out boldly into this nursery of blackguards. Why this sudden need
for showboating? Compensatory bravado for my tremors this afternoon? My little
celebrity going to my head? Or was the North slowly unraveling my common sense, as
it had done to so many?

Circling the table for my next shot, I thought it best to throw the game. *Let "Big Red"
be the victor before his home assembly.* But that was easier said than done. I had learned at the
hospital that it was tricky to throw a game, a risky way to appease an agitated patient.
Nothing was more insulting to a strutting peacock than a gift from the competition.

But throwing this game was near impossible, as three solids sat like ducks after my
initial break and, disposing of those, I had an easy runner down the rails, not a shot I
could plausibly miss. I had a bank shot next, and purposefully aimed askew, but, by
unlucky bounce, even that found the pocket, the ball exiting noisily down the long
chute, adding a grating exclamation to its dismissal.

The house circled tighter as the game proceeded, for the cone of light on our little
green arena had become the lone focal point. This was no challenge like Lord Tim's at
the Holly, where I could bask in the attention of my mates, but a pub in the suburbs of
Belfast, filled with shipyard workers whose grandfathers gave birth to the ill-fated
Titanic, notorious for their hatred of Catholic interlopers. More and more, the table
took on the aspect of the boxing ring.

Thick accents whispered, as cigarette plumes wavered beneath the lamp to shadow
the brightly colored Kelly balls. I stopped my seven-ball run with a miss, and then Big
Red, posturing and casting sidelong insults in my direction, proceeded to bury four
high-balls in succession. I stood as expressionless as I could, beginning to see the way
out of this. But he lost all chances when he scratched, giving me, by house rules, two
chances to sink only the remaining eight ball.

I cast a glance at Lyndon and Lawrence, looking detached and indifferent in the
crowd. Who was who in this deceiving clime, this land of suspicion and mistrust?
Whatever the divisions of religion, I was on my own—that much was clear—whether
it meant a cue stick to the skull or not.

I circled the table, thrice sunwise, in a blessing for deliverance. A Catholic in a
Protestant lair, on the eve of the Pope's historical arrival, with two shots to make one.

I took careful aim, for there was no looking back. I had painted myself in this corner
and had to accept the consequences. I studied the green felt table, marked with cigarette burns, beer stains, and torn like the province itself. With one last deep breath, I
struck the cue ball smartly, smacking and burying the black ball in a blur.

Big Red stared impassively at the vacancy on the table, guzzled the remainder of his
drink and clutched his glass as if to throw it. But then he turned and headed for the

bar—I doubted he was going to pay off his bet graciously, but any chance of that was canceled as he disappeared into a scrum of taunting cronies.

Standing blankly with cue stick by my side, I was bumped by a player inserting his coin for the next go-round. It was then that Lawrence sidled up to me.

"Best hurry your drink and be gone," he whispered.

Placing my stick upon the table, I left without another swallow, and crisscrossed many a street before wending my way back to Knox's farm. There, I shuddered and picked up my hazel stick for protection, as I replayed the night's close call, pledging from here on out to heed the warning of my Downpatrick friends and keep a low profile.

It was well past two when I finally fell asleep, Ty O'Kelly still in hand.

Knock Sunday in Belfast

B right and early Saturday morning, William Knox came out to the barn with tea and pastries.

"This should set you going," he said, setting the sugary treats before me.

"Thank you," I answered, before taking a mammoth bite of a creme-filled doughnut, much as Missie would gobble an apple.

"Eat up," he laughed, "and take the remainder with you."

Gazing skyward, he observed, "You have a fine day for your Pope to arrive. I just hope some good comes from his visit."

"I hope so, too." We stood side by side looking up to admire the cloudless day.

Setting out, Missie and I circled the Ring of Bangor, and onto the A2 where we nosed for Holywood. Ignoring the highway traffic, I imagined the Pope's itinerary in time with my own little pilgrimage—landing at Swords in the morning, saying Mass in Dublin's Phoenix Park at noon, visiting in some poor communities, then north to Dunleer, outside Drogheda, to make a plea for peace. I thought of Grannie Kelly, up early, no doubt, not to miss a blink of the three-day telecast, looking away only to press Uncle Mickey's suit for his journey to Knock tomorrow.

Not far along the A2, the RUC stopped in their blue patrol car to check my progress. To complete the reprise of yesterday's encounters, soon after, the driver of those four imposing young men in the red sedan, now traveling alone and in a different vehicle, pulled up to greet me.

"How you keeping?"

"Okay," I said tight-lipped, holding Missie close.

"You've only come this far since yesterday?" he asked in good humor. "You're slower than Gandie's Goats."

" 'Gandie's Goats'?" I shrugged, relaxing at his friendly manner as an individual and not part of a gang.

"Aye, 'tis a northern expression. One you'll hear plenty, if you don't get your ass out of first gear."

With lighter step after that send-off, Missie and I covered nine miles, and in Holywood, just six miles from Belfast City, I asked two shy girls if they knew of a nearby farmhouse.

"There's a large farm beside the Ulster Folk Museum," one blushed. "Go up Croft Road and beyond that to Whinney Hill, where you'll come to a farmhouse."

After amusing them with our "Bucktooth Pearl" routine, I ascended a neighborhood of stately homes, and up Whinney Hill, where we came to a two-story farmhouse crowning its summit. In a large fenced-in field, three men were gathering bales of straw.

"Would there be a chance to spend the night?" I asked, squinting through the hazy brightness.

"Spend the night?" replied a grinning fellow beneath his cap, eyeing me with amusement. "If you help with these remaining bales, you can spend the night and earn a feed as well."

I was soon hoisting bales of barley straw onto a flatbed, the strenuous effort releasing the built-up tensions of our northern trek. Laboring in the heat and dust of the long afternoon, looking out from these beautiful hills over Belfast Lough to the city I would face the next day, I was comforted by the thought of the Pope, just seventy miles away, offering his homily for peace.

"You have the hands of a parson," said the boss of the gang, Hugo Perry, taking note of my blistered hands after the last bale had been tossed, and implicitly confirming my host as a Protestant. "Have you never worked the fields until today?"

"The only fields I ever worked were on a golf course," I admitted, and Hugo's hearty laugh assured me of my welcome, regardless of creed.

When evening came, I found myself at the Perry table with Hugo, his twin sister Anne, and their elderly parents. During the blessing, Hugo, though no kid, started acting the goat, making me laugh by wiggling his ears.

"We adopted these two to comfort us in our later age," smiled Mrs. Perry after the prayer. "A kind and loving daughter, but a rogue of a son. Do you see how good deeds can backfire?" she teased.

"You'd be lost without me, dear Mother." Hugo rolled up his eyes in mock piety.

" 'Tis some journey you've undertaken," remarked Mr. Perry, passing the bowl of steaming potatoes. "Aren't you afraid some sorry pup might do you harm tomorrow in Belfast?"

"Who would harm a man walking a donkey?" said Hugo, forking out the spuds before I could secure my own.

"Plenty, I'm afraid," said Anne, "and the whole world watching, with the Pope and all."

"Your skulls are cracked and in desperate need of repair," said Hugo, leaning across the table for a dollop of butter.

"I still wouldn't want to be in his shoes," said Mrs. Perry.

"I'll drive Kevin through the city after we eat and show him the safest route to Carrickfergus," said Hugo, suddenly shifting his spoon for the trifle in the center of the table.

"Manners!" His mother slapped his hand and pulled the dessert from his reach.

After dinner, I found myself clutching the dashboard of Hugo's beat-up motorcar as he raced like hell's bells down the A2, over the Queen Elizabeth Bridge and through the streets of Belfast, bleakly illuminated by "anti-crime" lights.

"Aren't you worried about being caught?" I asked when he ran a series of red lights.

"Caught?" he laughed. "The RUC has more to worry about than a reckless driver. Now, pay attention, and I'll show you tomorrow's route, and for our second go-round, you call out the lefts and rights, right?"

He made an illegal U-turn and tore back through the desolate streets, the few pedestrians moving quickly through the harsh shadows. After another lap on this Belfast Grand Prix, we stopped into the Railway Bar, a mixed establishment, where we ordered pints of Bass and sat with Barney and Mike Horan, whose father had trained Mick the Miller, a famous greyhound who won the Derby in 1929.

"You don't know Mick the Miller?" Hugo hooted incredulously, when I confessed my ignorance.

"How would I know Mick the Miller?" I objected with a smile. "Do you know Mickey Mantle?"

"But you must know Master McGrath?" said Barney, joining the fun. "The Irish greyhound who brought home the coveted Waterloo trophy in 1869?"

"Aye," Mike elbowed me, "defeating the heavily-favored English bitch, White Rose."

"The only thing I know about greyhounds," I happily joined in the raillery, "is that they're the only ones on the road that look hungrier than me."

Presently the house went quiet as its patrons tuned in to the *News at Ten* on Ulster TV. The broadcast showed clips of the Pope's arrival at Dublin that morning, and the Mass for more than a million people at Phoenix Park, a third of the Republic's population.

"You'd think he was the bloody Queen!" hollered one old wag, responding to the sea of humanity.

"His kingdom is not of this world," retorted a fellow beside us, sending the house up in nervous laughter.

The coverage switched to the Pope's helicopter journey to Dunleer, where he made his dramatic exhortation for peace to both the IRA and Protestant paramilitaries:

"On my knees, I beg you to turn away from the paths of violence and return to the ways of peace. You may claim to seek justice. I, too, believe in justice, and seek justice. But violence only delays the day of justice . . . I say to you, with all the love I have for you, with all the trust I have in young people: do not listen to voices which speak the language of hatred, revenge, retaliation."

"He may as well save his breath to cool his porridge," retorted the same old wag.

Such irreverence did not bode well for the reception of the Pope's message; more than a hint of rancor hung in the air, and the general audience broke up into tables of muttering groups.

"Are you right, there?" said Hugo, finishing his drink.

"I am," I agreed, said good-night to the Horans, and followed his quick pace out the door.

Back at the Perry house, Hugo invited me in for the night.

"There's still a little trifle left, and I'm sure my mother has made up a bed for you."

"Thanks, but I really prefer it out here," I answered. "I find I get up earlier when I sleep out in the air."

"Okay, have it your way. But why so glum?"

"I just have a sick feeling about tomorrow. City streets are no fun with a donkey, and this is one risky city."

"You'll be fine," he assured me. "In a few days ye'll be beyond Larne and traveling the Antrim Glens. Beautiful country, that, a refuge from the Troubles for sure."

"I hope so." I shook his hand good-night.

Having checked on Missie in the nearby haggard, I crawled into my sack and lay staring at the clouded sky. The lights went out in Hugo's bedroom and then, submerged in darkness, I went through the occurrences of the long day. My beads proved a disappointing sedative this night, and, after wrestling wearily for a while, I unzipped my bag and walked the periphery of Hugo's fields, looking out over the sulphur-hued city.

My mind was filled with omens and portents. Why was I on the brink of Belfast on the eve of the hundredth anniversary of the Apparition of Mary at Knock? Why would I be walking through this ravished city while the Pope was celebrating his centenary Mass at the very place I had begun my own pilgrimage, in company with Grannie Kelly, nine hundred rambling miles ago? Alone in the middle of the night, sleepless and anxious, half a world away from home, I began to imagine myself as part of a vast Passion Play.

Haunted by the stories of my parochial schooling, I began to read my situation into them. Imitation of Christ, indeed! In my fretful, abandoned state, I began to envision the end of my journey on the coming day, so many little details of my long road now taking new meaning from the coming climax. The voices of the old and wise I had encountered came to me now in succession—investing my pilgrimage with their piety, a spiritual significance I little foresaw for my whimsical donkey travels.

Yes, now it became clear, falling together with all the clarity of a child's puzzle. Belfast was to be my Jerusalem. I would be cut down on its streets tomorrow. A Red Martyr, after all.

A ludicrous presumption, of course, in the light of the day, but alone in the dark of my own private Gethsemane, I fervently prayed that this cup might pass from my lips. Why had I insisted on traveling the North? Why had I put myself in harm's way? I gradually realized I was doing it for my mother and Grannie Kelly, and the old pensioners at

Rattigan's, to assure them that Ulster was still one of Ireland's Four Green Fields, from its mystic shores to its cairn-crowned hills. Yes, I wanted to penetrate the Black North and return to Rattigan's as a beacon of light on Christmas Night.

Ulster can't be altogether lost if this holy fool can walk a donkey through it, I could hear the Four Masters say.

But now I was certain, with a blind, middle-of-the-night certainty, that with the break of day my journey would reach its conclusion, not back at Rattigan's but on the streets of Belfast. With all the quiet dignity of my newfound resolution, I returned to my cart and wrote out my final message, forgiving my killers, whether IRA or UVA, and adding my prayer of peace to the Pope's.

It was a dull arrival for such an historic day, not a squint of sunlight, but only the gull-gray markings of probable rain. Among the bales of straw, I lay drained and listless, neglecting Missie's cry from the haggard gate. The poor beast was calling for her morning oats, unaware what awaited her worn hooves.

Missie harangued a second time, a frightful bawl that would lift a corpse from its grave. Not wanting to disturb the Perry farmhouse at this early hour, I struggled to my feet, tackled Missie to her mudbox, and quietly departed their farm.

Soon we were walking the breakdown lane of the A2, with Missie jibbing and bucking each time a Land Rover on patrol hurtled by, the British soldiers' eyes staring out of faces painted black-and-green in camouflage. On this grim morning I tried to recall those magical evenings in Kerry and Cork, where children came running down high flowering lanes to greet our passing.

We passed the Harland and Wolff Shipyards, of *Titanic* fame, a sweeping industrial complex of Imperial might beneath its two giant cranes, Samson and Goliath. Further on, we passed a British barracks, surrounded in steel mesh and razor wire, with its grand, dubious ensign: ROYAL HIGHLAND FUSILIERS. Glancing upward, I saw the muzzle of a tommy gun following our path from a slit in the high sentry box. No chances taken here. Since the ambush at Warrenpoint, soldiers were on full alert. Innocent-enough blokes, I suppose, like most of us in Vietnam. Homesick teenagers, perhaps, who had grown restless on the unemployment lines of Glasgow, Cardiff, and Birmingham.

As we crossed the Queen Elizabeth Bridge, the skyline greeted us with a vast array of red, white, and blue—Union Jacks everywhere. Daunted, I scanned the rooftops till I espied a lone yellow-and-white papal flag waving from a Catholic spire, a medieval banner that somehow lifted the heart of this donkey pilgrim.

Making my way through the dingy outskirts of the city, I was accosted by three scruffy teenage boys out for a bit of devilment on a sullen morning. They approached boldly, shouting obscenities, and began to kick an empty can between Missie's legs. In no mood for nonsense, I whistled a cautionary swing of my hazel above their heads. Ducking beneath my stick, they backed off across the street, with only rude remarks to hurl, before carrying their sorry selves back, I'm sure, to sorrier hovels.

A dark cloud closed in around me as I kicked away the empty tin of peaches: SUPREME BRAND. PRODUCT OF NEW ZEALAND. All morning I had been able to fend off my fears by mocking notions of martyrdom as absurdly grandiose and delusional. At that instant, however, I was flooded by the feeling my death was truly imminent, that these shoddy boys had heralded the first Station of my very own Passion Play.

And what was it about tin cans? Somehow this everyday item had an iconic significance for me, a signpost of memory that summoned a host of images, recalling vivid scenes that loom large in my mental landscape. My devotion to Ireland began at my mother's knee with her stories of deafening swarms of bees by rattling spoons in tin cans. I thought of striking incidents from this very journey: back in Wexford watching children collect black currants for the "jam man" in Hillman tins; the tin of snuff at the O'Brien encampment; and just last Friday night in Newry, watching a scrum of boys kicking the archetypal can against an angry wall of graffiti.

"Easy there, Miss," I said, calming my jumpy beast, as I fell headlong into reverie walking along Waring Street.

I remembered standing in a blinding Berkshire snowstorm, on the Mass Pike, hitching a ride to a war moratorium on Boston Common, until some Good Samaritan gave me a lift. The driving was slow and hazardous, and as we passed the miles I told him how I had worked on a MED-CAP team in Vietnam, taking herds of orphans to the beach for a swim. It was all so right and perfect on those evenings long ago, I told him, sitting on a crumbling French pillbox that vainly stood before the great expanse of the South China Sea. The children were out running and giggling through the mist of the incoming combers, their brown silhouettes disappearing into the yellow splash of sea. They'd come staggering out again to dry before the spark of firelight, their black heads as slick as otters' skins.

On the last outing with the group, however, following a frugal meal of fish and boiled rice, a crowd of angry boys, all too familiar with wanton violence, began to chase sand crabs, capturing them in tin cans and torturing them with burning sticks, despite the pleas of myself and the accompanying nuns and nurses to stop their horrible game.

I told him this because there was no one else on the turnpike that morning but him and me and the crazy swirl of thickening snow. He was a poet from Cummington, William Jay Smith, and he reached into his briefcase for a book entitled, *The Tin Can and Other Poems,* reciting:

> "I have gone into the tin can,
> head high, resolute,
> ready to confront the horrible,
> black underside of the world."

Those words came back to me, hauntingly, here in Belfast, passing the Albert Clock. "Head high. Resolute. That's it, isn't it, Miss," I blurted, welling up in tears. "Resolute for this pilgrimage, ready to confront martyrdom. And head high, proud to be chosen, to be guided toward this end. Imagine, Miss, that God choreographed each of your diminutive clip-clopping steps, so we'd be here the very moment the Pope begins his homily at Knock."

Making my peace with the wayward inevitable, I kept on soliloquizing my humble beast.

"Shouldn't we have known all along? Each evening a child greeted us at their gate, or every time a wise or eccentric old person looked on us fondly, as if we represented their greatest hope since the days of Patrick? Weren't we blind, Missie Mickdermot, traveling these ancient highways and never knowing our fate?

"But at least my death won't be a sorry filler in the evening news. A random act of violence, some innocent kid brushing up against an explosive milkcan. No, Miss. This death has been designed to illustrate the Pope's plea at Knock, a message no faction could deny. Just think of the banner headlines in the *Belfast Telegraph* tomorrow: DON-KEYMAN SHOT DEAD IN BELFAST: CEASE-FIRE CALLED!

"Tell me, Miss, who wouldn't take a bullet for such a celestial guarantee, knowing each child in Catholic Falls or Protestant Shankill—kids teethed on rubber bullets—will be running to the heights of Cave Hill and looking down upon a city of harmony?"

Head high. Resolute.

We approached St. Anne's Cathedral, seat of the Anglican Church in Ireland, my heart pounding, my eyes tearing, my nose running free, but my head still high. Gradually I made out the sound of scuffling boots, troops on the run. Looking wildly about, I saw the first soldiers appear around a nearby corner, followed by a full marching band with Union Jacks snapping, brass blaring, drums rat-a-tat-tatting and sabers drawn, glinting, at the ready.

Suddenly, from across the street a brawny bystander in a suit and tie came running right at me. "This is it," I said, putting my arms around Missie's neck, closing my eyes, murmuring a "Hail Mary," and bracing myself for the scalding sear of a skull-splintering slug.

"Would you be so kind to shift your donkey, or you'll be trampled underfoot by this Old Soldiers' Parade for Peace," said the gentleman, flashing the badge of an RUC detective.

I numbly moved Missie to the curbside as the parade passed, baffled yet still poised to receive hot lead from a sniper's rifle. But nothing came my way, not even a rubber bullet, as I watched the parade halt and file in up the cathedral steps.

In a hapless noonday stupor, we continued down the long stretch of York Street toward Carrickfergus. If I was meant to be killed it should have happened there, before the cathedral. But it didn't happen. Never was meant to happen. But I had been ready. Truly ready. Would I ever again be prepared to embrace death so fully?

And now what? Eight hundred more miles, to prove what? That an ass can indeed circle the country? I'd make a cat laugh, thinking myself a martyr whose sole sacrifice would wake all sides from a centuries-long nightmare. As if my poor pitiful death would make a difference after generation upon generation of hatred and bloodshed.

An assassin's bullet. How asinine. *Day of the Jackass.*

Head high? Resolute? *Mr. Fluke.*

A squealing screech of brakes snapped me from my doldrums. I looked up to see a car swing in before us, fishtail in reverse, and brake a few inches in front of Missie's retreating nose.

It was Hugo.

"Boy, oh, boy," he exclaimed, jumping from his cockpit to shake my hand, "lucky for you the RUC has been keeping tabs on your travels. God only knows what those jumpy young soldiers guarding the parade would have thought of your ill-timed caravan. And didn't you make short work of scattering those guttersnipes this morning."

I stood dazed: "You've been following me . . . all day?"

"Well, a bit of it, anyway," he acknowledged. "I mean, it wouldn't do if you had strolled into the wrong neighborhood, would it?" He handed me a large bag of food-stuffs. "But, I'll tell you, my mother gave me hell for letting you sleep in the barn last night. Now, promise to send us a postcard when you reach Roscommon at Christmas. You'll do that, won't you?"

"You bet I will," I choked, pumping his hand. "And thanks, Hugo. Thanks a million for everything."

He laughed: "Well, it's not every day a Catholic comes walking through my gate with a wee kip of a donkey."

With that he climbed into his car, shifted gears, gunned the pedal, made a swooping U-turn, tooted, and roared away in a thick plume of petrol smoke, tearing back toward the heart of that distraught city as if the whole blooming world was in flames.

And the only path through the flames, I could see now, is simple human kindness, not overwrought passions and notions of self-sacrifice.

The Glens of Antrim

CHAPTER FORTY-THREE

I wandered through the long afternoon, thankful, yes, but confused by my life's unexpected postscript. Now what? What would fill the void after my reprieve from a certain end, my death-row pardon at the stroke of noon? I recalled the words of a female patient who awoke after a three-day coma following an unsuccessful overdose attempt: "What do you do when you thought you were out of this place, only to wake to a fresh fall of snow?"

Well, there was no snow, but a refreshing drizzle that washed away my imaginary death mask. We approached Carrickfergus, a well-established trade center when Belfast was just a village. Perched on a rocky spur was its imposing castle, an Anglo-Norman stronghold built to dominate the vast sweep of Belfast Lough. It was here in 1690 that William of Orange landed to commence battle against James II for the English throne, a fount of Troubles for certain.

The misty rain lent a softness to the thick walls and high keep of gray stone, but this fortress was a hard reality to a subject people. Little wonder the Irish take comfort in the prophecy that one day this castle shall appear no larger than the head of a nail in the sea.

Leaving urban industry and agony behind, Missie and I moved into a realm of flowered homes beyond Carrickfergus, where I found lodging with Lester and Margaret Simpson in the townland of Eden.

"You're after walking Belfast with this donkey!" Lester welcomed me in sheer dismay. "Are not all your dogs barking?"

"What kind of chat is that for a champion traveler to hear?" admonished Margaret from the doorstep, ringed by her three children. "Never you mind," she said, extending her hand. "Welcome to County Antrim."

After Lester had placed Missie with the children's donkey, a snowy piebald who gazed up admiringly at my heroine, the three Simpson children asked if I'd play hide-and-seek.

"One . . . two . . . three," I immediately shouted, covering my eyes.

"Try to find us, Mr. Donkeyman!" they screamed, scattering amid peals of laughter.

". . . nine, ten," I concluded, catching a glimpse of their retreat. I chased them around the farmyard like a born-again Peter Pan. "Yes, this is why I have lived on," I exclaimed to myself, grabbing little Eileen and tossing her into the loose hay, "to flush out children in bawn and byre, to catch hold, tickle, and make a grand fuss of them."

Leaving Eileen gasping, I caught Jimmy behind the barn to suffer the same fate, a right tickling beneath the ribs. "Nothing can cross my life again," I puffed, as I ran for Audrey, the last Simpson fugitive. "Certainly not after this resurrection."

Twilight faded on the scene, with me scampering amidst a small flock of laughing children. Oh, how quick and profound my revival. How pristine my life became, washed clean of fear, in the presence of these gamboling lambs . . . and later, how lovely Mrs. Simpson's lamb chops, sizzling on the pan.

Next morning, little Eileen appeared above my sleeping eyes in the living room, where I lay zonked out by the twenty miles I had traversed the day before.

"Are you going to lie about all day, and Missie singing out to you?" she inquired earnestly, knocking her little knuckles against my forehead. "Didn't you say you needed to be at your grandma's by Christmas?"

"I did and I do," I said, catching hold of her fleshy hammer.

"Eileen, you bold girl," called Margaret from the door. "Out of that room this instant."

"I only wanted to say good-bye to the donkeyman before school."

"Well, bring in the others, so. After good-byes, Kevin, you can sleep to your heart's content, and I'll do some washing for you. You can set out for the Nine Glens after you've had a hot bath and an early dinner."

That afternoon, Margaret and I watched the telly to see Pope John Paul board the Aer Lingus 747 called St. Patrick, with a proud green shamrock emblazoned on its tail. The Royal Irish Guard saluted and children waved tiny papal flags, as the airship taxied for departure. The Pope was off to Boston, where he'd be celebrating Mass tomorrow at Boston Common, with some of my own family in attendance.

When the aircraft disappeared into the metallic grayness, Ireland let out a communal sigh of relief. The three-day papal visit had gone off without a hitch, with multiple threats unrealized. The Taoiseach, Prime Minister Haughey, commended the thousands of guards involved in "Operation Papa," the largest security undertaking in the country's history. The only disturbances reported were bands of professional pickpockets from England, called "dippers," who had picked clean the crowds to their hearts' content.

"They weren't all English," I confided to Margaret. "One was a little Irish redhead with a splotch of freckles."

That afternoon, the first of October, Missie and I ambled through Whitehead, a staunch Loyalist area. Newly fearless, I felt no more afraid walking this village than a trick-or-treater in his own neighborhood on Halloween night. The province had been peaceful since the Pope's plea, and, judging by the warm greetings I received in passing, an optimistic feeling enveloped the land.

On the Larne Road, I was stopped by Mr. Gray, a photographer of the *East Antrim Times*, who praised my spunk and took our picture.

"I have a friend, John McKee of the Glynn House, six miles up the road," he offered. "I'll ring him now, and he'll treat you royally."

Given my late start and lumbering companion, it was nightfall when we reached the Glynn House, a centuries-old estate outside a village of the same name. John McKee and grandson, young John, two keen horsemen, greeted me in their cobbled yard.

"We thought you were lost," Mr. McKee extended his hand in welcome, a pleasant white-haired old gent. "You're slower than Gandie's Goats"

Young John eagerly helped me unyoke Missie: "Your tackling needs saddlesoap," he said as he pulled the dry leather straddle off Missie's back. "Oops, and here's a snapped breeching. I can fix that."

I was soon ushered into a lovely sitting room with oak paneling, shelves of leather-bound books, and oil paintings cracked with antiquity, and treated with such courtesy that I began to feel like landed gentry of the Protestant Ascendency.

"When Mr. Gray called, I couldn't imagine what kind of chap you were," smiled Mr. McKee. "A donkey through Belfast! Have you lost your buttons?"

"A few might have popped." I conceded.

"Weren't you frightened?" asked young John, sticking a long sewing needle into a lump of fat before proceeding to stitch my breeching.

"Was I ever!" I admitted cheerfully, still giddy with resurrection. "I already had a list of questions to ask God."

"What kind of questions?" he asked.

"I've been haunted for years thinking I may have placed a 1943 copper penny into a gumball machine in my hometown five-and-dime," I confessed. "There were only a handful of copper pennies made that year due to the war, and now they're worth thousands of dollars."

"And you spent it on a ball of gum?"

"I'm afraid so. A week after I had spent it, I received a coin book along with my stamp approvals, listing its astronomical value."

"What else were you going to ask God?"

"If my guitar teacher, Mr. Fisher, had allowed me to play 'Boots of Spanish Leather,' rather than 'The Hungarian Boatman,' would I be a folk singer today? Or where in the world did I ever misplace my shoebox of 1957 baseball cards? Again, worth thousands."

"Your life has been nothing short of tragedy," roared the grandfather, pouring out two tumblers of Bushmill's whiskey from a crystal decanter. "It's a wonder you survived Belfast at all!"

"How are you doing with your timetable?" asked young John, the breeching draped over his lap.

"We need to reach Malin in Donegal by the twentieth of this month, and Clifden in Galway by the eighth of December, to be right for Christmas," I replied, settling deeply into their couch.

Young John put the breeching aside and proceeded to spread my map over the coffee table. " 'Tis roughly one hundred forty-three miles from Glynn to Malin, if you keep to the coast," he figured. "English miles, now, not Irish."

"That's a break," I smiled, knowing an Irish mile is one-sixth longer, but having discovered by hard practice that it could work out to many times its English counterpart.

"You'll have to cover nearly eight miles a day for the next nineteen days," he calculated for me. "But you'll need all of that, as the Coast Road from Glenarm to Ballycastle is slow going, nothing but braes . . . hills, that is."

"Steep ones?" I rasped out after a swallow, wincing simultaneously at the thought and from the burning whiskey.

"Aye, laddie." Mr. McKee backhanded me playfully. "Steep as the Anglo bridge on your nose."

The next morning, after breakfast and a visit to a nearby graveyard, where worn, bleached headstones festooned with lichen offered a window into the history of this ravished and ravishing old land, Missie and I tipped through the seaport town of Larne, where a high white gable covered with the Red Hand of Ulster gave me pause, but again, all was peaceable.

Beyond Larne, we passed through Black Cave Tunnel, a dramatic gateway over the Antrim Coast Road, marking the end of our long trek up the congested eastern seaboard—Waterford to Larne—and heralding our entrance into the magical Nine Glens of Antrim.

We traversed four miles of this coastal wonderland, delighted by the white limestone cliffs, checkered fields and sparkling sea, and arrived in Ballygalley, meeting landowner Robert McCauley and his Scottish wife, Isabel. After a kind invitation to tea, the genteel McCauleys were happy to share their enthusiasms, as were their visiting neighbors.

"The Glens were never cultivated by the English," explained Robert. "Cut into deep cliffs, black basalt over white chalk, each of the Nine Glens faces the sea and was quite inaccessible by land until the Grand Military Road was built in the mid–nineteenth century. Tis an engineering feat even by today's standards, wending forty-nine miles from Larne to Ballycastle.

"Even today the Glens maintain much of their Scots character." Robert nodded toward his wife. "And traditions as well—you really ought to see the Ould Lammas Fair in Ballycastle. In the distant past, Antrim was part of the Scottish Kingdom of Dalriada, and you, lucky fella, are set to walk it with a donkey."

"You'll see ladder-farms climbing from deep-hollowed valleys hundreds of feet up to the cliffs," chimed Isabel in her delicate Scots cadence, pouring a spoon of heather honey into my tea. "Each glen has its own river as well as its ancient name, like Glencloy, 'the Glen of the Rush Lights,' but Glenariff, 'the Rough Glen,' is the queen of them all. North of the Glens is the Giant's Causeway, the eighth natural wonder of the world. A geological marvel you must surely visit."

One neighbor wanted to know how I occupied my mind on my long walk, and surprised me by referring to "your man Thoreau." After praising the act of walking and the rhythm of thought, he inquired, "Do you compose poetry as you saunter along?"

"I'm afraid not," I answered. "I'm either dreaming or keeping my four-legged lady in line."

"You should do so," he urged. "There was a fellow years back named Dusty Rhodes, appropriately enough, who, at age eighty, was still reciting the poetry he composed when walking in his youth. His parents died when he was a lad, so off he sailed, like many hereabouts, rounding the Horn of Africa in a sailing ship at sixteen, and on to England where he joined the Welsh guard, ending up in India before finally returning home to his little village at the mouth of Glenballyeamon.

"From the large world to a little world unto itself," lilted Isabel.

"His pocket watch, they say, was simply a tin lid tied to a bootlace, but people swore he could tell time to the minute, as though it were a gold watch from a gentleman's vest. Off he'd go, to market and fair, spilling his poetry, with drink fueling his fervor. 'The Smith of Tiveragh' and 'The Causeway Fair' are two I recall. You should set your mind on the same, for what's better tonic for poetry than the long walk, the quiet road, and the clopping of your beast to keep you in meter, hey, lad?"

Next morning, we passed McCauley's Head and the quaint village of Glenarm, surrounded by a thick wooded valley, and pushed on to the fishing village of Carnlough at the mouth of Glencloy. Looking up at a burst of white stone gleaming from its high slopes, I was soon walking beneath an arch of similarly-hued limestone into the village. Up the thoroughfare I noticed portraits of Pope John Paul reverently displayed in the windows of shops and homes, and just outside a school we were surrounded by a flock of youngsters with yellow-and-white papal bunting pinned to their jumpers.

"Do you know the way to Jim Legge's?" I asked these papal guards, heeding the suggestion of Mr. John McKee to look up this colorful character.

" 'Know the way to Jim Legge's?' " repeated one, trying to mimic my accent.

"We do, at that," another chimed, and proceeded briskly to escort Missie and me through the charming village streets to his very door.

"Well, if it isn't the famous roving blade," greeted Jim Legge, his two thumbs stretching out his suspenders. "Leave your donkey in the care of these young muleteers, and come in for the meal."

"I don't mean to disturb . . ."

"Out of that," he scolded playfully. "You're as right as rain, and haven't I been keeping track of your poky march since Glynn, and have it arranged for you to spend the night with Captain Dan Black of Garron Point, four miles up the road."

In the kitchen, I was introduced to Jim's sister, Mary, and three elderly brothers.

"Your timing is perfect," said Mary, making room at the table. "Mr. McKee thinks you're nothing short of a Red Knight. You must have impressed him mighty."

"Mr. McKee thought I was losing my buttons."

"Rubbish!" she said, placing a meal of chicken and potatoes before me. "I think it's a courageous journey, so I do."

"We may have lost a few buttons ourselves?" noted Jim, passing the gravy. "Here we are, four brothers and a sister, the youngest fifty years of age, living under the one roof with none of us married off. Would you ever run into such a queer lot as ourselves in the States?"

"Leave him eat," Mary put in. "Can't you see he's starved?"

"Starved," proclaimed Jim, watching me devour the feast. "He's famished, he is," tossing a leg of his own onto my plate. "You remind me of the story of a traveler who, on a dirty night, sought shelter with a couple above Cushendun. Well, the poor traveler is soon at the table, you see, and after one slice of lovely currant bread, he goes for a second, but gets instead a smart slap from the husband's butterknife, with a stiff warning, ' 'Tis one slice and one slice only for ye, traveling gypsy.'

"What could he do, tell me, and his stomach growling like the Hounds of Hell? Now, there happened to be but one bed in the house, and when it came time to retire, the three fell into it: the farmer between the tramp and his missus. Now, this tramp was a handsome rogue, as handsome as yourself, and the husband a dispirited lout who'd rather drain the Guinness than kiss the missus. So it came as little surprise that she lay restless, separated from this prince of the byways by the loathsome bliggard who snored between them like a beached whale.

"Little wonder, too, that the woman's mind went to romancing, thinking of the grand lovers of the world—Diarmuid and Grania, Tristin and Isolde, Oisin and Niamh—when in truth, she lay there as broken as Deirdre of the Sorrows. Are ye listening to me, laddie?"

"I am," I acknowledged through a mouthful of buttery potatoes.

"In pure desperation, the woman concocts a bold scheme and rallies herself to the task. Smartly jabbing her husband in the ribs, she shouts, 'Get up, you witless beast! Can't you hear the skulk of foxes at me hens, you stone-deaf, good-for-nothing, pride-of-the-dunghill bollux! Will you get out of it, I tell ye, and bag the stinking red devils before me little bantams are a strewing of feathers in the morning!'

"Moaning and groaning, the husband pulls up his breeches, steps into his boots, and makes his way to the back garden where the hens are roosting. The wife, in turn, leans toward the traveler. 'Now's your chance,' she says sweetly, spreading her long red tresses across the soft feathery pillow. ' 'Twill be a good ten minutes before me diddering lackie is back at our door.'

" 'Bless you, ma'am,' gushed the traveler, leaping clear from the bed. 'Bless you kindly, for giving me a second chance to taste your lovely bread.' "

Faery Kingdom of Dalriada

CHAPTER FORTY-FOUR

A fter a pleasant fill of chicken and tall tales, Jim Legge escorted us out the village amidst our entourage of young scallywags, who serenaded our departure, singing a song about Carnloch Bay, along which we traipsed through the dwindling light, lost in this enchanted world of red-streaked headlands, catching the occasional glimpse of the dramatic black crag known as Garron Point. As we neared this otherworldly promontory, a sudden storm catapulted across the sea, drenching us through, turning our magical mystery tour into a sodden slog.

A beat-up Land Rover appeared out of the monsoon.

"I'm Captain Dan Black," he called through the downpour. "I'm a mile further on, so don't go to drowning on me."

We reached Captain Black's home, a lone farmhouse at the base of Garron Point, looking seaward over the North Channel to nearby Scotland, and I settled Missie in his stony backfield, then followed him around the side of the house, where he showed me a foaming torrent of water on its short plummet to the sea.

" 'Tis the Foran River," the captain announced proudly. "The shortest river in all Ireland, measuring thirty-five meters from its source to sea. And you from America, with its mighty Mississippi! Old Mark Twain would have a hard time filling a book of adventure on the Foran, aye, boy? Now, come in, out of this, and bring in a change of clothes before you catch your death."

After being introduced to Ethna, the captain's wife, I sat drying my socks before the fire, studying the mantel filled with curios the captain had collected during his many years in Scandinavia with the merchant marine.

"I was at the very top of the spinning ball, me boy: Stockholm, Christiansands, Gothenberg. Aye, laddie, 'the Land of the Midnight Sun.'"

"How did you become a sailor?"

"By being born on the sea's doorstep," he guffawed. "There was no arable land with my name on it, but miles 'pon miles of ocean. You go to God with what's given you, and for me 'twas the sea. And the sea was good, but for my long absences from Ethna and my son, and for those long winter days when the sun hardly peeped out at all."

Ethna handed me a blue Norwegian eggcup filled with whiskey. "Pour that into you, now, it will warm ye."

"You sitting there barefoot reminds me of a story told years back, about a young lass from the hidden village of Galballey," began the captain. "'Twas called 'the hidden village' for it can only be seen a mile out to sea, tucked behind the black crag of Garron Point, at our very backs.

"The lass, it seems, had been gathering periwinkles at the strand of Red Bay, but returning home she stubbed her toe on what she thought was a stone or seashell. Well, it happened that night her toe went black, and the veins up her leg ran scarlet. The old people knew well what ailed her, for it had been seen before in these parts."

The captain drew out his words slowly and sincerely: "'Twas neither stone nor shell the child had stubbed her toe, but a devil's toenail."

"A devil's toenail?"

"Aye, maneen. Aren't they there still, in volcanic rock on the path toward the hidden village. Hideous imprints of the devil's cloven nails pressed into the hot basalt long since hardened."

"At the dawn of day, the girl had disappeared," Ethna picked up the story, her voice as earnest as her husband's, "and the whole village of Galballey were beside themselves. Vanished outright, abducted her family knew. 'Gone westward into the Glens,' as the old people called it.

"Three days missing, she was," continued Ethna. "But on the fourth morning, she stumbled back into the hidden village, her face pale as the moon, and using a wren's feather to draw the devil's own pentagram in the sand. They brought her in and kept up a holy vigil night and day. And there she remained, poor child, another three days unconscious followed by three days mad."

"But when the lass did finally speak," the captain took up the story, "she said wondrous yet terrible things. Things no young lass could make up, with no age up on her at all, well beyond the ken of any child."

The captain looked at Ethna, and the pair fell into an abrupt oracular silence.

"What kind of things did she say?"

"Stories of angels and devils in clamoring battles," said Ethna, painting her revelation in the air with her hands. "She told of being blinded by the sight of shining armor in the frosted breath of a winter's morn, not a likely vision she could have picked up anywhere else, is it? Dreadful battles, with the fate of the world in the balance. The villagers thought she was raving but, in time, they became less sure. She may have well seen the truth of our world."

"And the poor girl remained touched for the rest of her life," said the captain, "praying incessantly for the victory of the angels, and never growing an inch afterwards, a wee one the size of a half-door. Praying for peace till she left this world, and still praying, I'm sure, up in Heaven this day."

"Clamoring battles, mind you," repeated Ethna, "saying such wars will never cease unless the inhabitants below stop their own squabbling. Now, isn't that a tall order, and we can't even keep peace in our own small province."

Silence followed, and I still wasn't certain if they were actually expressing their beliefs, or if I was simply in the company of a pair of champion storytellers.

"Maybe her prayers are being answered, and the Pope's as well," I said, trying to give the unsettling story a happy ending. "It's been four days now . . ."

"I'm afraid not," the captain sadly shook his head. "The evening news reported a Catholic woman of Falls Road was fatally shot at her door by two men who escaped by motorcycle toward Shankill. It's up and started all over again."

"If only we could find peace here in Northern Ireland, it might spread to the four corners of the globe, like Christianity in Columcille's time," Ethna sighed. "We need to heed what the little girl preached after going westward in the glen. Now, drink that up and we'll settle you for the night."

The Blacks kindly invited me to sleep in their spare room, but I opted for the barn, despite a warning that a sow had recently given birth to eleven piglets.

"You won't stick it a minute with those boniffs," said the captain as he handed me a flashlamp.

"Don't be too sure. I've slept with mad dogs, newly hatched ducks, and asthmatic cows."

"Well, be our guest," he shook his head with a grin. "But if you're driven out, ye'll find the door unlocked."

I stepped into the wet night, where the wink of the Maiden Islands lighthouse in the North Channel eerily exposed at intervals the ominous peak of Garron Point.

"This place is beyond weird," I muttered, clutching the beads in my pocket, afraid I'd stub my toe against a devil's nail-clipping.

Inside the barn, I climbed the ladder to the loft and shined the lamp upon the humongous sow and her piglets, all squealing in a fumbling heap below.

I don't know much about pigs, I thought, crawling into my bag, *but why does it seem the sow is always a teat short in the milk department.*

Let me tell you, counting pigs is not like counting sheep. They carried on endlessly, like professional wrestlers grunting and groaning, emitting the occasional yelp of pain, and I began to regret declining the Blacks' invitation.

"Don't you little pork chops ever sleep!" I shouted over the oinking din. If ten were slobbering in contentment, the eleventh would incite a fresh riot, just like a mob, one or two stirring up trouble and rolling it down the line.

Retreating into the deepest recess of my sack, I found my mind as restless as the squirming heap below. I thought about the woman murdered on Falls Road, the Pope's disappointment, and the little girl from Galballey. It did seem as though there was a battle raging over our heads, between good and evil, but not without human capacity to sway the result. As I tossed and turned, I prayed for an end to the conflict, but there seemed as little chance of that as for these little porkers to fall asleep.

The long night went black to gray before I finally dozed off, but at first light I woke to silence but for the soft breathing and gentle sighs of the boniffs, like a warm breeze stirring through a grove of trees.

"There, now," I said, rolling over to dream in absolute comfort, "the whole world momentarily at peace."

Come morning, I woke to the yeoman's call of Captain Black from the barn door.

"Roll out, matey, and I'll take you up Glenariff, 'the Queen of the Glens!'"

Driving up the coast road that hugged the edge of the vast sea, we stopped by a tall formation of limestone that roughly resembled the outline of a woman.

"The White Lady," said Captain Black. "'The only woman your GIs didn't try to date when they were here in Ulster preparing for D-day."

Standing at a roadside lookout, he gestured with a wide sweep of his hand toward the villages of Cushendun and Cushendall further up the winding coast. "In my grandfather's youth, the sea here would have been filled with sailing vessels, setting out for the far reaches of the world. They used to say you could hear in the sea-wind the crying of emigrants as their ships rounded Torr Head for America. Something, too, wasn't it? The Glens weren't badly hit by the Famine, but emigration took its toll."

We traveled up the bowl-bottomed valley of Glenariff, as I strained my neck to take in the height of a cascade known as the Grey Mare's Tail, and my eyes climbed the ladder farms up the slopes of the glen to the gorse and heather above.

"Would you take me up to the hidden village of Galballey?" I hazarded.

"I could but I won't," he answered firmly and genuinely. "There's nothing there now but a lone monk praying."

Back from our driving tour, I gathered Missie and bid farewell to the Blacks couple, setting out toward Waterfoot. Along the way we were hailed by an oldster weighing heavily on two walking canes. I bade him a quick good-day and moved on, anxious to confront the high braes.

"A man must be in a terrible hurry if he hasn't time to speak to another man," he chided.

I quickly brought in the reins and was happy to meet an engaging man named Martin. After just a few words, he asked me outright if I had stumbled into Faeryland during my roundabout.

"No, I haven't. But last night I heard a chilling story about the faeries," I answered, "and if my hosts were pulling my leg, they did a good job."

"Do you doubt their existence?" he asked incredulously.

"I'm not sure. I mean, I've never seen one."

"And how will you ever see one if you don't believe in them? Just you have a look at the beehive-shaped hill of Tiveragh when you head out the village. Beneath its grassy mound lies a maze of tiny tunnels more intricate than London's Underground. And then explain to me, young man, why sheep won't graze in certain fields there, and why calves have gone stark mad. Explain that away, and ye'll own me two ears, for there's no explanation, but themselves being in it."

The gleam in Martin's eye was more amused than maniacal.

"And, when opportunity presents, walk to Tievebulliagh, the axe-mountain near Ossian's Grave, the greatest poet-warrior of all time. Spend an evening up there and ramble through its hollows and thickets. Or, better yet, poke your nose into the old booleys in any of the ten glens. Aye, laddie, *ten* glens, for one is invisible to the disbelieving eye. I tell you, these faeries will still be dancing when you and I are no more than pouches of dust in our graves."

"What is a faery, exactly?" I asked the affable man, doubting I'd find a more forthcoming expert.

"The true faeries are the fallen angels who were neither bad enough for Hell nor good enough for Heaven but, given a second chance, they were scattered into our surrounding vales. Some are the finest of faeries, helping us without our knowing, a lower class of a guardian angel, they are. But others have turned as wicked as Lucifer, snatching children from their cradles, blighting the potatoes, and leaping for joy each time the Troubles are rekindled. Pity, now, how they're grinning again today."

"Have you ever fallen into Faeryland?"

"Aye, I have now, once, and that was plenty more than enough."

He stopped, wiped his nose in an old checkered handkerchief, and took his sweet time now that he had me in his snare, as villagers hurried by, waving animatedly, suggesting I was but his next victim, in for the earful.

"Home I was walking atop two healthy shanks and the moon late on the rise when I was disturbed by a faery wind that whirled its funnel of dust around me," he whispered in a singsongy breath. " 'Out of it,' I shouted, turning me coat inside out, and away they went, and thought I, *Wasn't I a lucky one?* But as I continued home, I heard the whirring spokes of an approaching bicycle. 'Good night,' says I, tipping me cap. And 'Good night,' says he, a grinning toothless old man who, before me boondoggled eyes, turned himself into a cackling old hag who hissed and spat like a rabidy hare.

"I ran madly for the chapel, hoping to douse meself with the font's holy water, yet he was forever at me side, not pedaling at all, but his feet tucked behind his ears—farting, he was—and sporting a smile of tombstones that sprouted from his gummy jaw. The spokes of his wheel caught me cuffs and hurled me to the ground where I was caught on the staircase to Hell, for I lay with swimming head and me four limbs limp as jelly-sticks.

"Aye, I was left with neither chance nor hope in the black of this wintry night. But with God's strength, I stumbled as far as the pudding-stones in Cushendun—do you know the pudding-stones?—where the hissing cackle of the old male-hag reappeared, raising a gleaming axe above its head. But then, as if a fiery musket rang out, he clasped his throat and vanished into the night, leaving warm droplets of mist in his wake."

He abruptly stopped his story and worked the handkerchief over his brow, suggesting his tale was too terrible to continue.

"Then what happened?" I prompted, which sent him off to the races again.

"I woke up in me own bed, thank God, but the dear missus, always a pure pet, was roaring over me, blaming me condition on the drink, that I was suffering from the jigs and deliriums. But, be God, it was the faery-jigs that had me, for not a drop had I taken! Fortunately a neighbor well-acquainted with the faeries, was beckoned to me side, not understanding how I could have escaped the despicable and dreaded male-hag.

"And searching for clues, he rummaged through me pant pockets and asked, 'And whose hankie is this?' ''Tis mine, right enough,' says I. And says he, 'And who did it belong to before it belonged to you?' 'Me grandmother,' says I. And says he, 'Arragh, now, there you have it,' waving me hankie in the air. 'That's what saved you, Martin, me boy, for there's great power in a grandmother's hankie, and I've never known it once to fail against the dreaded male-hag!"

" 'Never known it once to fail'!" I laughed to this spinner of tales. "How many times in the history of the Faeryworld has one been saved by his grandmother's handkerchief?"

"I can only vouch for this one time," he said, showing annoyance, "but that one time was plenty more than enough. And since that dark and desperate night, I've yet to blow me snout in any other hankie."

"And that's the truth?" I asked.

"Every word of it," he said, grasping my hand, "or may God strike the two of us dead."

As Martin raised his two canes in farewell, we passed on through the Red Arch, as if into a wonderland. Looking down upon the golden strand of Red Bay, I had to wonder whether there was a more astonishing panorama on God's good earth. By the time we passed Tiveragh Hill, a checkered mound of resplendent fields, I was more than ready to acknowledge the existence of faeries.

Passing the ruins of Red Bay Castle, a sixteenth-century fortress perched on a high spur above the bay, and the old Curfew Tower jail in Cushendall, we ascended a steep gradient that never let up for seven miles. Atop the plateau we halted in Layd, where James and Cassie McKay settled Missie, and their neighbor, Joe Ferris, settled myself.

"You have three steep braes facing you tomorrow, laddie," said old James, taking delight in caring for Missie. "Crusheen Brae, Dan-Nancy's Brae, and the Green Hill. Crusheen ye might manage, but the other two will leave your donkey wind-galled."

"What should I do?"

"Honeysakes, what you always do." Cassie playfully slapped my wrist. "Do you think God will abandon you now, after coming so far?"

That night, from a vantage point on the high road, Joe Ferris pointed out the unearthly black crag of Garron Point across the bay, even spookier from this further side, its ancient earthen fort lit solely by a full moon.

"Is there an eerier place on the planet?" he asked from our vantage.

"Not that I've seen," I conceded. "If faeries do still exist in Ireland, I can readily imagine that Garron Point would be their last stronghold."

Next morning, James and Cassie accompanied us down the road.

"Keep a sharp eye on her breeching when ye're spilling o'er the hills," advised James, touchingly full of concern, perhaps more for Missie than myself. "Once you're beyond the three braes, and over Torr Head tomorrow, ye won't know yourself with the flat lay of the land."

"We'll keep you in our prayers." Cassie kissed me. "May God keep you safe, as long as grass grows and water rushes to the sea."

We ambled through Cushendun, the "capital" of Glendun, the deepest-cut valley of the Nine Glens, and came to Crusheen Hill, a steep winding haul which left us panting and weary at the summit, only to descend again immediately into a deep hollow. There we stood and looked up awestruck at the knee-shaking eminence of Dan-Nancy's Brae: a twisty ribbon of black licorice leading to vaporous clouds swirling above, making Dingle's Conor Pass look like a carbuncle on a drunkard's nose.

I sank into a roadside stupor until a native of these hills came chugging by on his tractor.

"Are you behind your luck?" he laughed, sizing up our predicament with a twinkling eye.

"We're finished," I replied with a vacant upward stare. "You'd need to be an alpinist to climb this hill."

"Nonsense! Unyoke your donk and we'll pull the cart up with the tractor. Then I'll bring you back to collect the missus."

"Thank you, but I'm not sure I can do that. My vow is to circle all of Ireland with both donkey and cart."

"I don't think anyone will begrudge you a mile of road that leads to the moon."

"You don't know the crowd at Rattigan's, the pub in Roscommon that I'm circling back to, where bets are laid for my successful return."

" 'Tis either my offer, or the rising moorland tract to Carnighionghea which, personally, I wouldn't ask a healthy hound to cross. I'd say your bet could bend a wee bit."

"I guess there's no other way." I gave in, ultimately happy to let a wiser head prevail. I freed Missie from the cart and tied her to a fencepost.

Hugh McNeil and I were soon making our slow chug up Dan-Nancy's Brae, a switchback climb which tested the tractor's lowest gear, with me hanging on to the cart to make sure it didn't come loose and roll away over the edge of oblivion.

Pointing down to a vacant homestead sinking back into a hollow, Hugh shouted above the tractor's din, "That cabin is where Dan and Nancy used to live, a crazy old pair, from the stories I've heard, and somehow their name stuck on this hill."

Nearing the summit, Hugh gestured toward a distant sea-rock shaped like a mushroom.

"That's Paddy's Milestone, exactly one mile from our coast. And beyond that is Scotland's Mull of Kintyre, thirteen miles from our own Torr Head."

"The top of the world," I exclaimed, looking out upon the edge of the Arctic Circle.

" 'Tis near it, right enough," he nodded.

When Hugh returned me to my fretful beast, I offered him a pound for his troubles.

"Go away out of that," he declined. "Amn't I only doing this white deed to erase my black ones? When Judgment Day comes, I'll say to Saint Peter, 'Hold on there a minute! Don't you remember that October day when I assisted the famous Donkeyman up Dan-Nancy's Brae?' Now, won't that get me off the hook!"

"Don't count on it," I replied, clapping his back in appreciation.

"Well, you know the expression: 'Saints have only a past, but we sinners have a future.'" He remounted his tractor with a laugh and rumbled back down the road.

After a sprightly amble up Dan-Nancy's Brae, side by side with an unencumbered Missie, we collected our cart and struggled through the long afternoon on a tiring roller-coaster ride of hills and dales. But in the evening we came to the foot of Green Hill, the undisputed King of Heartbreak, where we gaped into the stratosphere. Blindly rallying against the insurmountable, we put our heads down and attacked this perpendicular pitch, but after a few measly meters, we rolled back into its deep basin.

Appropriately, a chapel had been erected long ago on this very spot. I unyoked Missie and sat like a lump of lard, pondering the pinnacle before us. Birds flitted about in the hedges, a stand of oats rustled in the comely breeze, a faraway sheepdog cheerfully barked. And, distantly, again came the diesel drone of an approaching tractor with two men aboard.

"Stuck, are ye?" asked the driver, grinning from ear to ear, introducing himself as Joe Murphy, and his passenger, Kevin McKindry.

"That I am," I confessed abjectly.

"Give us the cart, so," said Joe, "and we'll leave it above at John and Ann McCormack's, no finer couple in Antrim."

"But . . ."

"Go on, and enjoy this lovely evening," Kevin added, taking hold of the cart's two shafts. I watched as the tractor slowly sputtered away and disappeared into the misty heights of Green Hill, with my poor little cart in tow.

Without a load to haul, my agreeable beast became a charming companion on a hard but exhilarating climb, with long views at every turn. I had to wonder whether Joe Ferris had orchestrated these much-needed assists, or was it the work of some good faery watching over me, or simply Cassie's reassuring faith that God provides?

"Could it be that simple, to trust without doubt?" I asked Missie, who ambled beside me like a faithful dog. "I don't know those two men from Adam, and who's to say they won't toss our cart over Torr Head? And who are the McCormacks, waiting at the end of the day's road? Maybe, just maybe, the secret of life is to trust without provision or forethought. Could trust be the simple truth that would make the world spin in harmony?

"What if Captain Black's boniffs were capable of trusting instead of hogging? What if they could believe there was milk enough for all? Wouldn't their ructions cease? And wouldn't it work for people, too?

"But, let's forget all these broils and brawls, dear Missie! Look—another drovers' station!" I directed her head toward the beautiful Scottish islands of Islay and the Paps of Jura, appearing like mirages between blue sea and pink sky. "How many drovers' stations, now, Miss? I've lost count."

Throwing an arm over my contented beast, I asked her, "Would you like a song, my damsel fair? Come on, just one, for I have the most perfect song for this glorious evening."

She stared off across the wide, sea-rimmed world, not quite as inspired with the spirit of these giddy highlands.

"Ah, just the one?" I implored, as her gaze zeroed in on seabirds wheeling beneath high stacks of cumulus clouds. I looked beyond, to the crashing sea-foam on which White Martyrs had launched cow-skinned coracles for the western shores of Scotia.

So, on this vast tableland—this geologist's dream—approaching the magnificent heights of Fair Head, I began to croon Paul McCartney's "Mull of Kintyre." And, believe me, atop these lava-formed uplands in this old Scottish Kingdom of Dalriada, my rendition didn't sound half-bad.

Gandie's Goats

CHAPTER FORTY-FIVE

The next morning the rising sun cast a golden glow through a verdant valley, as Missie and I bade farewell to the McCormacks, who had indeed proved hospitable, and walked through a honeyed world of sheep-dotted hills on this northeast shoulder of Eireann. Torr Head up ahead, however, meant Torr-ment and Torr-ture to me, and halfway up this merciless climb, we happily halted when a young couple emerged from their farmhouse with cupcakes and apples.

"This is 'the Big Dipper Road,' the last of the high braes," Hugo Duncan consoled me. "If your donkey can't manage it, I'll pull you up with the tractor."

"As long as it's the last, I think we're willing to give it our all," I said determinedly.

After this welcome respite, we continued our tortuous ascent, leaving the enchanting dell for high bog country. As the orange-billed chough called out from sea-girt cliffs, we trudged on, heads down, step by step, until we reached Torr's summit, with the massive tilting cape of Fair Head visible in the distance, our welcome to the Northeast Corner of the North. Aburst with surmounting energy, we persisted through a prolonged series of dips and rises toward Ballycastle.

That evening, approaching the town with weary satisfaction, I was halted by the spectacle of thousands of rooks blackening the sky, captivated by the sight and sound of their vast circling return to deep-nested rookeries atop a stand of sycamore trees. After each cacophonous roundabout, they would settle into the treetops where, seemingly settled for the night, one would take the notion for a last whirl. So off they'd go, each countless squawking member, and I wondered if they weren't cursing the perpetrator of this latest go-round . . . or, indeed, was it the same rook who instigated each encore? Above all, how could the villagers put up with such nightly clamor?

"Are you a bird-watcher of sorts?" An elderly man startled me from behind.

"I've never seen so many rooks," I replied, settling my own feathers. "Don't they bother the residents?"

"They do," he acknowledged. "But it's unlucky to go shooting rooks, for it's said they carry three drops of the devil's blood in their hearts. And who would want that raining down upon you after a blast of gunshot?" He introduced himself as Jack Woodside and I gladly accepted his offer to spend the night.

Next morning I continued my westward course, but I soon found myself picnicking on a black cliff beyond Ballintoy, gazing out over the chalk-white headlands and half-moon beach around White Park Bay. Suddenly a rubber-tipped arrow bounced off Missie's nose. A moment later, a middle-aged chap leapt from the brambles wearing an Indian headdress.

"Ambushed by an Apache in Antrim," he yelped, doing a war dance around us. "Never expected that, did you?"

"You gave us quite a hop," I answered warily, stroking Missie's withers.

"Sir Charles, at your service." He bowed his feathers to the ground. " 'Tis marvelous to meet you, O renowned Donkeyman. Are ye bound for the Giant's Causeway?"

"I'm planning to get there tomorrow," I answered, cautiously watching him notch another arrow.

"Smashing!" he said, the brightly-feathered warbonnet dangling off his head. "It was built by Finn McCool, you know, lonesome for his bonny lass on the Isle of Straffa."

He moved in close to hiss this advice: "When ye visit, don't miss the Wishing Chair!"

"Where will I find it?" I asked, recognizing he meant no harm, and happy to encourage this eccentric.

"Why, right in the midst of the Honeycomb. You can't miss it, among all the thousands of hexagonal pillars which make up this wonder of the world. But be careful what you wish: Don't be like that merry-andrew from the Sperrin Mountains years back who wished never to be without a golden guinea in his pocket."

"A golden guinea?"

"Aye, twenty-one shillings in the old money, a goodly fortune at the time. Well, no sooner had the bloke discovered his wish come true, than he marched straight into a public house, secured himself to a stool, and drank up its worth in one mighty session. The following day, waking in a dead stupor, what does he discover but the same golden guinea in his pocket. So off he marches to the publican and inquires, 'Do I owe ye for the power of drink I consumed last night?' And the publican replies, 'Not a penny, for you were rolling in the coinage, me boy.'

"Dumbfounded, he set off to buy a litter of pigs. But by the time he led them home, didn't he find the same golden guinea burning his pocket? Spooked by his own wish fulfilled, from that moment on he did all he could to rid himself of it—buying everything from Rahery horses to cartloads of yellow toffee. Why, he'd even buy drinks for the speckled-shinned old biddies who loitered at bread-and-jam dances. Pure mad, he became, certain that the coin was an advanced payment from Hell and not the gift of Finn McCool. So, after three months of whiskey wobblies, didn't he heave the golden guinea into the sea beyond Dunluce Castle, where it remains to this day."

Passing vehicles tooted at the odd apparition of tinker and Injun chatting along the Coast Road, but I was moved to offer my new compatriot one of my sandwiches. We sat awhile together, swapping tales and taking in the view, though I never did find out what the Indian getup was all about. When I set off again, Sir Charles, or "Crazy Charlie," as he referred to himself, gave me the address of his relations just down the road.

He could not have led me to kinder hosts. John and Edith McCurdy were pleasant Scripture-quoting Baptists, full of country charm.

"We never drink, smoke, or sully our minds with the chaotic events of the outside world," spoke Edith, graciously serving me tea so much weaker than I was used to, that I imagined what my aunt Cella might say if presented with such a cup: *"Is it a thimble of tea leaves they've sprinkled into that pot!"*

I spent a good part of the next day hiking the Giant's Causeway, clambering over the Honeycomb of massive basalt columns formed by cooling lava eons ago. I had no trouble finding the Wishing Chair, seeing a cluster of parents taking snaps of their children enthroned on the stone seat. Waiting my turn, I finally sat and covered all the bases with one long-winded, carefully phrased wish, not one to dismiss any marvels the Celtic spirit might evoke. Tradition observed, I was free to roam over all the colorful and uncanny rock formations—Aird's Snout, Giant's Eyes, Onion Skins, Giant's Boot, Irish Harp, and the rest.

Further on, I ascended the Shepherd's Path to the heights of Benbane Head and looked down upon the inlet of a Port na Spaniagh, so-named after another Armada shipwreck, the *Girona* which lost all thirteen hundred hands aboard. Following this lofty, exhilarating four-mile walk, I arrived at the gaunt ruins of Dunseverick Castle, where I rested against its crumbling walls and contemplated the ancient history of the site. Even before these Norman remains had been built, Dunseverick was a major fortress in the old Kingdom of Ireland, home of the Red Branch Knights. I thought of the flows of blood following the flows of lava, all that red seeming to stain the sandstone cliffs to this day.

But rather than dwell on Cromwell's eventual destruction of this castle, I cast my mind further back, to its heyday, when Patrick and his disciples walked the Slighe Midluachra, the Northern Road, from Tara. Yes, I could imagine him swinging his crosier—Bachall Jesu, the staff of Jesus—with great confidence, pleased with his recent successes in Meath and Armagh, recalling his years in slavery as a young herder on nearby Slemish Mountain, and reveling in his newfound freedom to spread the Word, for which he had prayed so fervently.

When I returned to the McCurdys', a party of twenty was in session following their evening prayer service. John happily introduced me to everyone, including William and

Edith Gamble, who presented me with a small leather-bound Bible.

"My wife and I wish you every blessing as you read this book," said William as he inscribed its inside cover. Thanking them, I was encouraged to read from it, so I randomly thumbed to Matthew 18: 18–20, which concluded, ". . . for where two or three are gathered together in my name, there am I in the midst of them."

Everyone commented favorably on how I'd happened upon such a significant passage and, duly inspired, each took turns at reading their favorite psalm or verse. As they read, my mind wandered back to my youth in Massachusetts when a heavy sweltering man, with shirt buttons bursting, came to our front porch one hot summer afternoon, selling Bibles.

My mother invited him inside the house for lemonade, fearing he'd collapse from heat stroke, and after he had wet his whistle he began his sales pitch, showing us vivid illustrations from a white leather-bound bible, with an asking price of $75.

"It's beautiful," said my mother, "but we can't afford it."

"But with all these lovely holy pictures that grace your walls," he persisted, "how can you not afford it?"

"I'm sorry," said my mother.

"But every good family needs a Bible," he continued, as beads of sweat sprung from his brow. "The Protestants embarrass us with their knowledge of the Bible. For example," he said, throwing attention to me and my brothers, "do you know the name of Mary's mother?"

"Yes," we squealed in delight, "Saint Anne d'Auray."

"Very good," he said, flabbergasted, "but can you tell me the age of the Virgin Mother when she was Assumed into Heaven?"

"Seventy-four," we chimed in unison, having been well-tutored by the good nuns of St. Joseph, with their strict faces framed in starched white cornets who marched down our classroom's hardwood aisles with a pointer half-hidden in the folds of their swishing black habits.

"His first miracle, then?"

"Cana," we shouted in glee.

He left in a huff, only to return the following day with a smaller Bible.

"It's a King James Bible." He tugged nervously at his choking collar. "You know, a Protestant Bible, but it's only twenty dollars."

"Whether Catholic or Protestant, I'm still sorry," said my mother.

Now, twenty years later, I owned a King James Bible, and after the readings I placed it carefully in my camera bag, intent on keeping it for all time.

Before the night concluded, Edith McCurdy led the house in a final prayer for my safe passage home, and gave me the names of Mr. and Mrs. William McVicker of Portrush, saying there were few farmhouses beyond Bushmill's, and the McVickers would treat me royally.

————

The following morning, I bade farewell to the McCurdy family and headed toward Portrush, enjoying miles of coastal scenery, including the most impressive ruins of Dunluce Castle, perched on a crag at the edge of the earth, abandoned since part of it plummeted into the sea in 1639, taking a dozen kitchen staff with it.

Our luck held at the end of this perfect day, when we were warmly welcomed, as promised, at the impressively situated White Rocks House, the home of the McVicker family. I was shown to a regal guest room with bay windows looking out upon the pastel houses of Portrush, its golden beaches, and the velvety swales of a golf course.

At a meal as sumptuous as the surroundings, I marveled, "As a boy, I used to caddy for a Scotsman, George Galt, who always talked about his two favorite golf courses, Royal St. Andrew's and Royal Portrush. And here I am this evening, overlooking these fabled links."

"Would you care to play a few holes after tea?" Mr. McVicker offered.

"Would I? But you can't just walk out there and start playing, can you?"

"Oh, I imagine so," he smiled at my gaping enthusiasm, "seven of the holes are on my land."

His three sons—Angus, Alan, and Shane—contended for the privilege of carrying the Donkeyman's borrowed bag of clubs as we strolled through a gap in the fence. I entertained them mightily with pranks and contortions in the tee box before straightening up and driving the ball well into the lengthening shadows of the fairway.

"You've played this game before," Mr. McVicker noted with surprise.

"When I was sixteen, I played a hundred and five holes in one day," I admitted. "I'll never see that again."

"You were lucky to see it at all," he laughed, teeing up his own ball.

While we walked these hallowed holes that had hosted the British Open in 1951— the only Northern Ireland course ever to do so—the boys regaled me with tales of Norse kings.

"There was once a great battle fought hereabouts," said Angus, pointing to the high swardy grass that enveloped these links. "Magnus Barefoot, one of the last Norse sea-kings, lost his life at what's known as War Hollow. While the clash was going against them, the Norsemen hid their booty in the skin of a dead cow and buried it either here or in nearby Ballywillan Bog, where it has yet to be found. When you come back, we could set out on an expedition and find it."

"There's been many oddities found in our bogs," added Alan, "including a young red-headed woman. Once her hair was washed it returned to its natural curls, because of the preserving qualities of the bog."

I stood in the tee box, coiled myself up like Popeye, and whale-hooked my ball two-hundred yards to the left, the trio scurrying over the high dunes with clanging clubs.

"If we're able to find that ball," laughed Angus, "we might find old Barefoot's booty as well."

Waking to a frosty moon-bright morning, I had breakfast with the three McVicker lads before they hurried out to school.

"We must have your address," the mother insisted, opening her book. "Oh, look, you'll be the first O in it. Well, this must be Northern Ireland, mustn't it?"

A schoolteacher himself, Mr. McVicker was hurrying out to school as well, but took time to thank me for making a fuss over the boys. "With all the segregation hereabouts, it's rare for them to spend time with a Catholic, and your being so friendly and entertaining is certain to dispel some of their fears and misconceptions."

I walked away from this charming household that morning with lightness of step—proud of my small accomplishment—and facing a level road and the prospect of accommodations fourteen miles further along, arranged by Mr. Lyons, a colleague of Mr. McVickers's I had met the evening before. Leisurely enjoying this rich agricultural landscape, I stopped often to chat with old farmers working scythes in their high meadows.

We traveled along the quay of Portstewart and over the River Bann into Derry, the fifteenth county of our journey. In the busy college town of Coleraine, I passed a firebombed hotel pub—unfortunately, not an uncommon sight on our northern swing, but encountered no other incident or sign of trouble.

Reaching Castlerock, we settled with James and Raymond Moody, and soon Mr. Lyons and friend, Irwin, showed up as well, offering to drive me to Mussendun Temple, an elegant pile built by a late bishop of Derry, clinging precariously to a high cliff offering a splendid vantage of Magilligan Strand, the longest beach in Ireland.

"An eagle's-eye view, hey?" said Mr. Lyons, peering down from the high walls at diminutive railroad cars snaking alongside the strand. "There's the evening train from Coleraine to Londonderry, said to run as smoothly as a learned finger over braille. And over there, those lights in the distance are from the prison at Magilligan Point, always a full house there, these days. And beyond that, can you make out Inishowen Peninsula in the dimming distance over Lough Foyle? Donegal, that. Be prepared for high adventure, for it's lovely, hilly country."

The next morning, I groggily came down the Moodys' stairs to an extended hand from Maurice McAleese, popular radio host of *Good Morning, Ulster*.

"Don't blame me," grinned Ray Moody, seeing my jaw drop. "Blame it on Mr. Lyons."

I shook myself awake sufficiently to please Mr. McAleese with my praise for Ulster and its people, and to impress him with all we had seen in our short visit, so he left well-satisfied with the interview recorded. With grateful farewell Missie and I nosed for Downhill, a comforting name after our recent climbs, our walk bordered by high sand dunes of wildflower and buckthorn. Just beyond, a uniformed gatekeeper at a railway crossing greeted me.

"I've been on the lookout for you for days," he said, introducing himself as John O'Hara. "You're slower than Gandie's Goats."

"I've heard that over and over since I got to Ulster," I laughed, shaking his hand.

"No surprise, that. You've got to be the slowest one-man parade since Gandie's circuits in the '30s."

"There really was a Gandie in living memory?"

"Oh, yes, poking about these very parts in my youth. Fair play to him, but he never gave in to his handicap, not a leg beneath him—God Bless the Mark—both lost in a railway accident in England, a railway man like myself. Aye, Gandie was a jovial fellow with a bright round face, full mustache, and a burly body. He always sported a cowboy hat, and had fan-bellows fitted to his stumps, and took great pride in jumping three feet from a sitting position."

"And the goats?"

"Pets, the two of them, pulling him along in a little wagon," answered John, glancing habitually up and down the track, "with a railway lantern glowing in the black of night. He used to reason, 'Why put me in the county home when me goats are me two legs, and the world as wide as the day I lost them?' And his goats, not unlike your donkey here, would obey his every command."

"Missie here isn't all that obedient," I answered, patting my little brown jughead, who was beginning to sprout her winter coat.

"Go on. She's brought you to this distant northern shore, hasn't she? And will bring you the long road home? Cheerio, then," John O'Hara waved me on, "and as Gandie might say, 'May the strength of three be in your journey.' Do the name proud, you hear."

A Celebrity in Derry

We walked on through a spat of sunshowers, and on the bridge over the River Roe a double rainbow looped above our heads, and it felt like God's own gateway, as though I were passing through Gandie's triumphal arch. Then the sun lit up these rich fields of tillage, over the backs of laborers working the potato ridges, shaking the spuds free from withered stalks. It was a picture to be painted by Millet; little wonder his *Angelus* adorned the walls of so many homes in this countryside.

As pastoral as the scene was, however, I began to think sobering thoughts about the Potato Famine which began in the neighboring county of Fermanagh in 1845, when a fungus had blackened the potato leaves causing the tubers to putrefy. The following year, this fungus went on a rampage and in 1847, dubbed "Black '47," most of the crop failed, causing the deaths of one million of the rural poor, and another million to emigrate on "coffin ships," the single largest migration of people in the nineteenth century. I was told the western counties of Donegal, Mayo, and Galway were hardest hit by the Famine.

"But the Famine wasn't the greatest of Irish tragedies," had remarked a long-memoried Kerryman back in June. "'Twas the Black Death of 1348, which killed a third of our population in three years' time."

In Myroe, I was warmly greeted by Mr. Gilfillan, another advanced booking courtesy of Mr. Lyons. He settled Missie in his apple orchard and walked me through a portion of his sprawling 650-acre farm, pointing out the immense field where the World Ploughing Championships had recently been held. That evening I took a walk through his fields, humming the "Londonderry Air," since this was the very parish where the tune had been picked up from a roving fiddler and eventually given the words of "Danny Boy."

Despite the gathering dark, many families were still at work. Children, running the length of furrows, would collect white potatoes laid atop the ridges by elders and, after filling their pails, would scamper to a central heap where they poured out their cache. They happily repeated this mad dash, running between the narrow trenches, and I wondered if their collective memories stirred at the feel of healthy potatoes in their hands.

The next morning I listened to *Good Morning, Ulster* with the Gilfillans in their kitchen. They cheered my performance, and set Missie and I off for Greysteel. Not far down the road we were ambushed by James Robbins and a camera crew from BBC-1, who had heard me on the radio and wanted to put us on *Scene Around Six*.

While they were busy setting up for the interview, I dug out a hairbrush and tugged it through my tangled mop, thinking I could get pretty good at this game. Ready for my fifteen minutes of fame, I turned to face the camera, but it wasn't even a quarter-hour before Mr. Robbins was stowing away his gear and telling me to secure a seat before the telly that very evening, when the mugs of Missie and me would be beamed throughout the U.K.

I walked the next mile in a daze. "Wow, Miss, just think who might be looking at us tonight across the British Isles. I wonder if Aunt Mary in Wales and Uncle Josie in Oxford will tune in! And I wonder if the Queen watches TV, or Paul McCartney even? Wait a minute, where am I going to watch it?"

With Missie sniffing the road for a tumble after her three-day, thirty-five-mile output, and myself obsessed by securing a seat before a television by six o'clock, I began to make inquiries for lodging, but had trouble in finding a farmer who had both a field for Missie and a telly for myself. Finally, one old chap gave me the name of Mickey McNicholl in Tullyverry.

"Don't get too excited," I said to Missie, who quickened her pace at the utterance of his name. "Mickey McNicholl is my host for the night, not a frisky jackass."

Believing my meeting with Mr. McNicholl would bode well, I leisurely arrived at his door at five fifty-five P.M.

"Can I help you?" The elderly gent stood firm in his doorway.

"I was told back the road you might have a place for me and my donkey for the night. And a television so I can watch myself on the BBC."

"Really!" he brusquely queried. "And who might you be?"

"My name is Kevin O'Hara, but they call me 'the Donkeyman.' I'm going to be on the nightly news in five minutes." I gestured to the watch I wasn't wearing.

"The nightly news?" he ran his fingers over his bristly jaw. "Are you running from the law?"

"Not with a donkey, I'm not. I'm a bit of a celebrity . . ."

"For walking an ass?" he interrupted.

"Yes," I squirmed, the precious seconds ticking away.

"All right, then," he finally conceded, seeing me about to blow a gasket. "Place your friend in the back garden and come inside."

My heart sank when I entered the kitchen to find old Mickey on his knees before an antique relic of a television.

"Not much use, this," he grumbled, fiddling with the large brown knobs.

"Doesn't it work?"

"Half the time." He crawled beneath the TV table to retrieve a piece of aluminum fallen from one of the antenna's rabbit ears.

I wrung my hands anxiously, staring at the screen as vertical waves flickered like a heart monitor in crisis.

"Make yourself useful and see if the plug is properly in the socket," he demanded, with some asperity. "You fidgeting there isn't helping me any."

I followed a frayed length of cord beneath the kitchen table to the outlet.

"It's okay," I called from my knees, banging my head as I stood up.

He continued to fiddle with the knobs and rabbit ears, and now it was horizontal waves rolling through the static, which momentarily hypnotized us. We stared blankly for a minute, but just as all hope was sinking, Missie and I magically materialized upon the snowy picture tube.

"I'll be damned, it is you!" Mickey exclaimed. "Quite the movie star!"

"I'm the dead cut of a weasel," I disagreed, studying my narrow snout on the black-and-white screen.

After the brief clip was aired, the nightly anchorman added his final quip: "If you see Missie give her a biscuit, and perhaps something a little stronger for Mr. O'Hara. He's off to Derry."

Ten minutes after the news, half of Tullyverry came knocking at Mickey McNicholl's door, coaxing me out for photos and handshakes. As cameras snapped, one Gerard O'Hara from nearby Greysteel offered to take me for a pint and put me up for the night.

"Go on, have a Friday evening with your own clan," said Mickey. "Can't I care for your star donkey for the night?"

I was presently in Gerard's automobile heading for a Catholic club, fielding questions from his three friends in the backseat. Shortly, we came upon a roadblock where RUC officers and British soldiers lined both sides of the road.

"Why the roadblock?"

"Perhaps an ambush or explosion somewhere," said Gerard, preparing his papers.

"Or maybe no reason at all," commented one of his buddies. "Just a simple reminder we live under British rule. Up North, you learn to live with inconvenience."

When we came to the checkpoint, flashlamps glared into our eyes as Gerard was asked our destination. Seemingly accustomed to such interviews, he was concise with each reply, and we were shortly let through.

"Have you seen much trouble in your travels?" asked Gerard, once clear of the checkpoint.

"Not personally," I answered. "But many towns we've been through—Ballycastle, Portrush, Coleraine, Portstewart—have pubs or hotels that look like they've been torched or blown up recently."

"That's why we go to a private club," said his friend, "so we needn't worry about some prig spraying us with gunfire. You made a wise choice to travel Ulster now, and not in July during the height of the Orangemen's parades. They hold more than two thousand annually, bonfires and all, just to remind us that King Billy defeated James at the Boyne . . . and that we're still under their thumb today. As if we need reminding?"

We arrived at our destination, a fenced-in compound where two fellows checked us at the gate before allowing us through. In the center of this compound, we parked in front of a low-lying building as cold and unattractive as the Airman's Clubs in Vietnam. But upon entering, this social club was as warm and inviting as any pub along the Ring of Kerry.

Of course, Gerard introduced me as "the lad on the telly," and it wasn't long before I was in a happy stew of well-wishers. One old man, long in the tooth, approached me after the commotion had died down.

"You said on the telly you've walked a thousand miles with your donkey," he began, looking at me admirably, "yet she's the picture of health. That's a badge on you, my boy. A badge you should carry proudly."

After breakfast with the O'Haras and picking Missie up at Mickey McNicholl's, we set out for Eglington, our scheduled launching pad for Derry City on Sunday. Fortunately, we made an early start on this eight-mile hike, since I was stopped by dozens of well-wishers and invited into four different households for meals.

As dusk approached, I called into a large potato farm owned by George and Elizabeth Lynch of Eglington. The pair were initially hesitant, asking many questions, as I began to realize that a Catholic knocking at their door for nightly lodging was probably as rare as spotting a great auk along the shores below.

"You were the lad on the telly?" asked George, biting his lower lip.

"Yes, sir."

"Why my place?"

"Your farm is close to Londonderry, and I need to make an early go of it in the morning. But if you're uneasy, I can move on for the night. I'm not here to bother."

"Can I tell you something?"

"Yes, sir."

"When I saw you on the telly, my first thought was that you were crackers."

"You're not alone," I said, forcing a laugh.

"But why a donkey?" asked his brother, Thomas, coming upon the scene from a large barn.

"She gets me into places where I'd never get into on my own."

"That's the truth spoken there, anyway." George began to show a hint of friendliness. "Stay the one night, and you can thank your donkey once again."

After supper, where we were joined by Thomas and his wife Nadine, I sensed a lingering iciness that made me most uncomfortable. I received the answer to this unpleasantness when George handed me a picture from the mantel: a portrait of a handsome man in full uniform.

"My brother-in-law, a captain in the RUC," George explained, his voice quavering. "He was in the prime of his life, a good family man, when he was shot down . . . murdered by the IRA."

"I'm sorry." I held the picture before me, and gazed into the other side of the story.

"Now do you understand our hesitancy at the door?" He carefully placed the picture back on the mantel.

"I do," I answered simply.

The night continued in awkward fashion, as my best donkey tales fell on troubled ears. George and Thomas, I found, were weary victims of the Troubles, and I was as helpless at lifting their spirits as I was to fly.

I took a second glance at the portrait of the brother-in-law, and wondered about the circumstances of such: What about his children? What would my greeting be from them? Would they ever befriend a Catholic in their lives?

At times, in pubs and parlors, I had offered tentative suggestions for small steps toward reconciliation of the Troubles, desegregation of schools or promotion of cross-border tourism, for example, and had always met a seething or mocking response. This evening I didn't even try to put a happy face on the centuries of conflict.

At night's close, after George had given me directions through Derry next morning, I asked if there were any neighborhoods of which I should be wary.

"You'll be fine," he said, shaking my hand warmly before retiring. "That telly broadcast will see you home safe."

I was off early to Derry that Sunday morning. Derry—known as "the Maiden City," not just for its encircling walls, the only unbroken fortifications in the British Isles, but also for the lengthy siege of 1689, still memorialized by Loyalists, with bonfires and parades every twelfth of August. Derry—notorious for the Bogside and Creggan neighborhoods, focal points for the Troubles. Derry—whose very name is a point of contention, officially saddled with the alien prefix, *London*derry. But also, holy Derry—founded in the sixth century by Saint Columcille, when he built a monastery in a *doire,* an oak grove.

Facing the city second only to Belfast in the lists of the Troubles, I began to regret more than just the way I'd looked on TV the prior evening. I lamented the missed opportunity to say something to that situation, speak some truth that would make a difference. But what, after all, could I say? I had no special revelation to impart. Why would people listen to a poor donkey pilgrim any more than the Pope? Sad that my journey through the North had amounted to no more than this, I was crossing Craigavon

Bridge when I was hailed by a convoy of British soldiers rumbling out the gate of the city's walls in armored vehicles.

"Good luck, mate!" the young men shouted, giving me thumbs-up from their plated portholes. "We saw you on the telly, mate! Good luck!"

I waved my hazel stick in surprise, and carried on up the Carlisle Road, passing St. Columb's Anglican Cathedral, where thirteen apprentice boys braved to close the gates before the attacking Jacobite forces in 1688. Noonday bells were tolling and parishioners were spilling out from their services. A number of them knotted around Missie and me, surprised at finding the Donkeyman from the telly in their midst.

"Please tell your Americans we're not all brutes," one woman requested. "We're painted far blacker than we are. Most of us get along fine. We just want to live in peace. You'll tell them that, won't you?"

Further down the road, I encountered Catholics with the same message. "The majority of us only want to live in harmony, but the papers only report the bloodshed, not the good between us."

Missie and I continued through "the Diamond," and beneath a second walled arch which led us outside the city walls to Shipquay Gate, where we passed the Guild Hall, a red-sandstone building with a huge four-faced clock, built in 1890 by sixteen London guilds who settled here, after receiving, amongst other incentives, huge tracts of land. Thus the name Londonderry.

Keeping up a good pace, we stepped along the Strand Road to the blast of horns from passing traffic.

"You're a champion man!" shouted one driver.

"A courageous undertaking!" hollered another.

"The right fella!" cried a third.

Amidst this unexpected fanfare, Missie tipped along brightly, reined in only to pose for a photographer from the *Derry Journal*. The salutations continued, even at an army checkpoint where a British sergeant informed his men: "That's the Yankee bloke who's walked all of Ulster."

For a few precious moments, I felt as if peace had come to Derry, or rather, welled up from a reservoir of goodwill just beneath the surface.

"Well, Miss, at least we know good is more prevalent than evil, even in this sad province. It's all one people after all, on this island, in the one boat. They'll come together someday. Can you imagine Lord Tim at the Holly meeting Sir Charles, or Ned Kelliher enjoying a whiskey with Mr. McKee, or Hugo Perry dashing about with Patrick Hayes? What about the handsome McVicker boys dancing with the pretty Sheehan girls from Ardgroom?"

We took our place in the line of traffic at the Irish customs post. Waiting motorists leapt from their vehicles to shake my hand and pat Missie's head, but a no-nonsense customs official broke through the ranks of well-wishers and ordered me to follow him to the post. As I led Missie past the long queue, a white bar was lifted and we were led to a white cabin amidst sandbags and coils of barbed wire.

"Tie that donkey of yours to that pole," the Irish official commanded in a carrying voice. But before I could react, he broke into a toothy grin: "Then step inside for a proper cup of tea!"

With that, he shook my hand, as Irish soldiers, customs officials, and border-crossers suddenly swarmed around us, as though I was Mick Spillane who had just scored an electrifying last-moment game-winning goal.

"*Céad Míle Fáilte!*" they exulted. "Welcome to the Republic of Ireland!"

I lost myself in a sea of joyous faces, reaching out and shaking a multitude of hands.

"You're out of the North," someone shouted. "Nothing now but a smooth road home!"

Yes, I had been safely delivered, I nodded, thanks to a very unlikely crew.

The Questions of Children

CHAPTER FORTY-SEVEN

Three days later Missie and I were crossing the ten-arched stone bridge into Malin, County Donegal, the most northerly village of Ireland. We were taking in the Inishowen Peninsula, and never in my puff could I have imagined a scene so exhilarating—villagers cheering on the tidy green, mist burning off Slieve Snacht, and the western road glistening like a strand of gold before us.

A white-haired man called from the doorstep of his butcher shop.

"Did you happen to meet Mrs. Hutchinson at the post office back down the road in Gleneely?"

"I did."

"And what did she tell you?"

"She told me to look up Bertie Boggs, the victualer in Malin."

"Well, ye've found him," he said, stepping forward to shake my hand. "And you're welcome to camp in my field of sheep, though a few might be lamb chops in the morning."

"As long as there are no slipups," I said, wrapping my arms around the neck of my shaggy roadster. "I still have many miles to go, and I couldn't face the road ahead without my bit of horsemeat here."

A young boy named Will helped me settle Missie in the butcher's field, and tagged along on a trip to the village shop, charming me with his eager inquisitions.

"What are ye doing, mister?" he asked, watching me jot a message on a postcard.

"I promised one Pat Hayes in West Cork that I'd write him as soon as I reached Malin. We figured I'd have to be here in Malin by the twentieth of October to have any chance at making it home for Christmas."

"Ye'll make it," he said reassuringly, chomping on a bar of toffee. "Ye're already three days ahead of schedule."

On my return to the Boggses' establishment, Bertie treated me to a spread of roast beef with his family, along with three laborers working on a new slaughterhouse.

"Where did you spend last night?" asked Bertie, peeling away the skin of a potato with an effortless spin of a butterknife.

"With Rita Quigg of Claggin, just outside Moville," I answered, passing the gravy.

"Rita Quigg is a lovely woman, and has a quaint old homestead," said Mrs. Boggs.

"Just like a folk park," I agreed. "Three whitewashed cabins gathered together like an old clachan, all thatched with flax as white as linen. There's an elderly man in one cabin who's afraid his roof of thatch will be the last, as he's too arthritic to get back up on the ladder."

"Thatchers are a rare and dear commodity these days," said one of the men. "Nor does flax come cheaply."

"You should travel to Banba's Crown tomorrow, the top of Ireland," said Mrs. Boggs. "There's any amount of thatched cabins there, though there seem to be less every year. I'd say Donegal is the last stronghold for thatched houses."

"Who else have you met on Inishowen?" asked a laborer, his arms caked in mortar.

"Jim and Betty Hockley," I said, "who live near the border, and a policeman named Ernie Grey, who drove me out to the Shrove Lighthouse in Greencastle yesterday."

"Ernie Grey?" He rolled the name over his tongue. "I don't believe I know the man."

"You do," his mate insisted, reeling off the man's genealogy to the fourth generation until his identity was established, an amazing knowledge all Irish people seem to possess.

When I was out walking the village Green that evening, an elderly couple, Harry and Kathleen Doherty, called me to their door.

"You'll not go pegging any tent in Bertie's field tonight with the weather promised wild," said Kathleen, handing me a key to their holiday trailer parked nearby. "There's little shelter from the wind hereabouts, and you could be blown into Trawbreaga Bay."

At midnight, after a pint at the Malin Hotel, I bunked in Doherty's caravan, and, as forecast, the gale winds rocked it unceasingly, giving me to understand why, as I'd noticed, the region's thatched roofs are securely anchored by rope and stone. The windstorm blew on with untiring fury, whistling eerily through the trailer's vents like a party of banshees. Brother Malachy had warned me that Donegal tempests could blow the horns off a goat, and I wondered how my little señorita's lugs were faring.

So here I was at the northern extremity of my journey, on a rugged peninsula bordered by two great loughs, Foyle and Swilly, churning up waves of white horses, with a gale howling in from over the North Atlantic. It put me in mind of the famous lines inscribed by an unknown monk of eighth-century Iona on the margin of his psalter:

> "Fierce is the wind tonight,
> It ploughs up the white hair of the sea

> I have no fear of the Viking hosts
> Will come over the water to me."

With that comforting thought I was rocked to sleep.

Next morning, a hard rap came on the caravan's metal door.

"Call quickly for the breakfast," called Bertie. "Master Sweeney has arranged a *ceili* at the school in your honor."

There followed a pleasant morning at Malin School, where I listened to a quintet of young musicians play a medley of traditional tunes for me. My friend, little Will, was among the children and, as his contribution to the festivities, stood on his head atop Master Sweeney's desk, to everyone's amusement. After their lively *seisun,* I stood to address the class, tracing my path on a large map of Ireland.

It was not geography, however, which attracted most of the youngsters' interest.

"Do you talk to your donkey on those lonely roads?" asked one little girl.

"And does she understand you?" chimed in another.

"Does she answer back, that's what I want to know?" added one of the class jesters, raising a titter from the attentive audience.

I paced in front of the class, their eyes following my every move. "I do talk to Missie all the time," I replied. "Now, I don't know if she listens, but it can be comforting to have a pair of long ears to speak to, even if no answer comes back. And I do believe she understands me, though sometimes she pretends not to. As for speaking herself, I haven't heard her yet, but I have been told a donkey is given the power of speech on Christmas Night, in remembrance of its humble role in carrying Mary into Bethlehem. So this Christmas at midnight I plan to be alone with my little beast in my grandmother's fields, and I hope she talks to me—having only good things to say about our journey together."

"Why did you take a donkey and not a horse?" challenged one of the boys. "Donkeys are so slow and lazy."

"Lazy!" shouted Will, his lower lip trembling. "How can Missie Mickdermot be lazy when she's walked to the top of the world? She's a topping mare! Go see her yerself in Boggs's field if you don't believe me."

The teacher stepped between his two charges, while the others continued to gawk at me with wide-eyed curiosity. The small-fry press conference rolled on happily, as I responded to urgently raised hands.

"One last question for Mr. O'Hara before he takes his leave?" asked Master Sweeney, to conclude the session.

"Will you bring Missie back to America with you?"

"I don't believe Missie could take an airplane. Believe me, it was hard enough to get her on board the Shannon ferry. But I'll make sure she's in good hands before I leave Ireland, and I'll visit her as often as I can." I backed out the door reluctantly, waving to my diminutive fans, leaving questions and good-byes hanging in the air.

Unencumbered by my poky companion for the afternoon, I took off out of Malin on the run, setting my sights on the very tip of Ireland, and never stopped my gallop until I collapsed in the high sand dunes of Lagg, looking down on a small chapel isolated in their midst. Catching my breath, I raced on to Five-Finger Strand, and in the solitude of that long golden beach, I took in great gulps of sea air in the face of the ocean's billowing roar.

"Donegal in October," I sighed, having climbed to the prospect from another high dune. "Every time I tell myself there could be no more beautiful place on earth, there comes a new topper."

I thumbed a lift as far as Ballyhillin, and walked to the meteorological station at Malin Head. Entering the cluttered post, I introduced myself to Paddy Delaney and told him I had been sent by his southern counterpart, Bryan O'Regan of Mizen Head.

"Good old Bryan," said Paddy, pumping my hand vigorously. "And congratulations to you. There aren't many who can boast of walking from Mizen to Malin."

He pointed to the maps and weather instruments on his table: "There's rain on the way, but before it gets here, let me drive you up to Banba's Crown—named after a pagan queen—the northernmost point in the country."

On that remote spit of land, Paddy showed me the remains of a Lloyds of London tower.

"Lloyds had these towers built along the Irish coast in the last century to watch for Irish vessels reported missing. Seems these ships would show up in other ports with new names and fresh paint. Now, those Martello towers you also see along your route, they were built by England for defense against Napoleon."

Further along, we came across the word EIRE spelled out with large white stones on a grassy bluff.

"That dates from World War Two, to let German bombers know this was the neutral ground of the Republic. Belfast was hit hard by the Luftwaffe, and Dublin got bombed by mistake as well, but we remained out of it."

The rain had arrived by the time we got back to the station, so I hitched a quick lift back to Malin, where I found Will feeding Missie in Boggs's field, despite the increasing downpour.

"Ye'll be away tomorrow," Will said with a frown, "so I thought I'd give Missie a few new potatoes for strength."

I rummaged through my camera bag and came up with a Kennedy half-dollar to give him as a remembrance. "It won't buy you toffee, but I thought you might like it."

"You're joking! I'll treasure it forever," he said, cradling it in his palms as if it were gold bullion. Then, again shaking my hand vigorously and kissing Missie's white wet snout, he went splish-splashing through the fields for home.

The next morning, as I prepared to set off with Missie, my hazel stick was nowhere to be found.

"We can't go without it." I searched through the field. "Not without my hazel, Ty O'Kelly!" Panicking, I ran to Bertie's front door, where—lo and behold—my bewitching beauty leaned against the wall.

"You left it here the evening you arrived," said Bertie, watching me hug my mystic stick as if it were a lost child. "Did you think it was going to walk off without you? Besides," he smiled indulgently, "who would snatch up a stick that might rise to deliver a bloody thrashing to any who crossed its power?"

Bidding farewell to the kindly natives of Malin, we recrossed the ten-arched bridge, stopping to admire Slieve Snacht, "Mountain of Snows," across Trawbreaga Bay: a summit that hosted the great festival of Lughnasa for centuries.

That afternoon, as we strolled through the village of Carndonough, an elderly man called from across the road, "Are ye off to Pontoosuc Lake?"

"Pontoosuc Lake?" I gasped. The very lake of my hometown, where as a tadpole I took swimming lessons in the goose-bumpy hours of dawn.

"Aye," said the old gent, taking delight in my surprise. "I read in the paper you were from Pittsfield and I worked near there for years, on a rich man's estate. Of a Sunday, he'd often say, 'Frankie, fuel up the Buick, and let's drive to Pontoosuc Lake.' Such beautiful mountainous country, the Berkshires! And where are ye headed tonight?"

"We're off to Drumfree."

"Drumfree, is it? Thank the heavens there's no gale blowing. You're faced with eight miles of lonely bog, laddie, and not a tree from here to there to break the wind."

Undaunted, Missie and I ventured onto this isolated track of heath and rock, under the imposing presence of the Mountain of Snows. It wasn't snow-covered yet but seemed to promise bleak weather ahead. The barren road was a hard, tiring go, but we were rewarded at day's end by a kind invitation from Pat and Betty Doherty in Drumfree. After supper, they took me to their local pub, the North Pole, a name that rang somewhat forebodingly to my ear.

No problem with the weather the next day, however, as we made our way back into the orbit of Derry, to Buncrana, a resort town at the western base of the peninsula, on the shore of Lough Swilly. A large greeting party of fifty or more met me in front of the West End Bar, saying they had seen our picture on television and in the paper, and presented me with a large bag brimming with assorted chocolates, and twelve quid to ease my ailing pockets.

One person asked how far we had to go, and when I answered, six hundred miles in sixty-five days, another whistled in reply, "Six hundred miles! And the almanac calls for a strong northwesterly air flow for the next two months."

"Is that good or bad?"

"It isn't bloody well good," the group laughed collectively.

A white-haired priest asked what I did for work in America, and when I told him I was a nurse, a woman spoke up: "You should visit the grave of Agnes Jones in nearby Fahan, one of a few dozen nurses who served with Florence Nightingale in the Crimean Wars."

" 'Tis a most noble profession, nursing," added the priest. "And I'd say Agnes Jones and her colleagues were as brave as any regiment in the field."

On the outskirts of this friendly town, I was called into the Drift Inn.

"You'll have a pint," shouted the publican, Rory Porter.

Two pints and a chicken sandwich later, I drifted out of the Drift, but on the way out of town I was raucously greeted by a band of camped travelers.

"Now, there's a right-looking Roscommon ass!" bawled a trim woman, keeping her young charges from racing into the road. When I gave her the double take, she followed up: "We were at the Ballinasloe Fair a fortnight back, and were told ye'd soon be tipping by. Stop for a mug, you will?"

Seated before a dying fire in the encampment with a mug of black tea in my hand, I foolishly offered to share my Buncrana spoils, and my candy soon stained the faces of child and adult alike.

"Did you meet up with any travelers in the North?" the thin woman asked, rummaging freely through my bag of treats.

"Just briefly," I answered stiffly, witnessing her unwrap my only Kit-Kat bar. "We camped out in a field where they were staying in Newcastle."

"They're a different breed than ourselves," she went on, breaking up my wafered delight. "Come from the Isle of Man, with names like Douglas, Graham, and Stewart. The English cut them to ribbons in the Middle Ages, so they scattered into Ulster. An odd lot, crippled with superstition."

"Aye," an obese woman added, prying open a tin of marshmallow twirls for her hungry clutch of red-ribboned girls. "They won't play cards after sundown, and they burn the jokers out of every deck."

"Terrified of swans too. Odd, that," interjected an old fella, the only male in the camp, sampling a Turkish Delight.

"But they have gobs of money," said my new acquaintance, daintily lifting a Cadbury chocolate bar from my dwindling cache. "Traveling in elegant caravans you wouldn't find the likes of in the holiday parks of Portsalon, and the long ears of tellys up on the lot of them. They hold things in common and burn all the personal possessions of their dead, to prevent any feuds over property.

"They'll keep nothing belonging to their deceased kin but a small souvenir, a comb or a snuff box maybe," she continued, breaking up my lovely chocolate squares, and distributing them in smeary communion. "Then they torch the whole lot, caravan, money, and all. No superstition there . . . money is where all evil stems."

"There'd be no evil stemming if they pitched it in me two hands," said the obese woman, devouring the last of my nutty truffle logs. "Couldn't I find a hape of uses for it other than ashes, with me poor wee ones groping the hedges for a mouthful of berries."

"Look at us," said another ruddy elder, plowing her fingers through the empty papers in my precious box of Rose's chocolates. "Ya think we hadn't seen sweets from one year to the next."

———

We passed through Burnfoot the next day, and then circled within five miles of Derry before turning west for the Fanad Peninsula, the next of the hard knuckles of land that jut out from Donegal's coast.

Wending through thousands of acres of fertile fields owned by a family named McDonnell, I spotted a stone fortress crowning a neighboring hill. This turned out to be the ancient site of Grianan an Aileach. So, settling Missie behind a modern church named St. Aengus, which mimicked the circular stone construction of the fort, I hiked up Greenan Hill and entered a passageway through the fort's thick walls.

Inside I found a schoolteacher trying to round up her unruly pupils, who had just spilled out of a bus and clearly considered this weekend outing a bona fide holiday. "Children, behave!" the teacher pleaded, while her students, boys and girls alike, wrestled one another in the grass like a horde of Vikings.

"There will be a test tomorrow on what I'm about to say!" Somehow the dread word penetrated the din of battle, peace was suddenly declared, and the class gathered 'round the teacher. I, too, took a seat on the terraced wall and listened in on the history of this place.

"Grianan an Aileach is also known as 'the Sun Palace,'" the teacher began. "Its history may go back as far as 1700 B.C., when it is believed to have been built for Dagda, High King of the De Danann, whose druids used it for sun worship."

"You call this a palace?" crowed a smart aleck. "All it needs is a few cow pies and it would look just like our mucky haggard back home in Sligo."

"Bryan, please. There was a fort here by the time of Ptolemy of Alexandria, who mapped the known world in the second century after Christ."

"Who was Tol-tillie-tell-me?" The boy again drew a few snickers from his peers.

"He was an Egyptian astronomer and geographer," the teacher calmly continued. "His pictures of the world and its place in the universe were taken as authority for more than a thousand years. And this place was the furthermost spot on his map."

She paused to let the span of time and space sink in.

"In the fifth century, Saint Patrick came here and baptized Eoghain—Irish for Owen—whose father was Niall of the Nine Hostages, High King of Ireland, and this fort became the royal seat of the O'Neill kings until the twelfth century. As you may know, Niall divided Ireland among his twelve sons, and Eoghain was given this district known as 'the Island of Eoghain,' or Inishowen, as it is known today. Eoghain's brother, Conall, was given the rest of Donegal, 'the Land of Conall,' or Tyrconnell. The descendants of these two brothers would become the princely and powerful northern clans known as O'Neill and O'Donnell.

"You have to imagine how it might have looked in those days. Within these high thick walls would stand fine structures made from red yew trees. Outside, there were three circular earthen ramparts, which you can still make out. Within those outer enclosures would live the kin of the O'Neills, as well as sheep and cattle. You may recall that cattle was the most prized possession of our ancient people, more valuable than gold. In fact, our roads, boreens, were originally cow paths that meandered to every corner of this country.

"Our ancient kings were privileged to wear seven colors of the finest cloth, and a poet or teacher would wear six. Imagine me, children," she smiled, striking a pose, "wrapped in such fancy hues. Do you see how our people appreciated learning?"

"Only because they had no paper to do homework," young Bryan wisecracked, but the teacher went on, undisturbed:

"The fort was destroyed by the King of Munster in 1101, who ordered each of his soldiers to carry away a stone. What you see here now is a reconstruction from 1870, but still an impressive sight. Now, children, if you'll climb these stone steps to the parapet, we can take in all the surrounding counties. No pushing, please!"

I followed as the children clambered to the top of the fort, looking out over the walls of gray schist.

The teacher's black hair was tousled wildly in the breeze as she swung through the points of the compass. "To the west you can see Lough Swilly and the peninsulas of northwest Donegal. To the north is Inishowen and Malin Head. To the east, there's Lough Foyle and the city of Derry. And to the south, the blue hills of County Tyrone. On a clear day, you might even be able to see our home county of Sligo. Now, enjoy the view for a few minutes before we go down for lunch."

The children ran around the ring of the fort's high wall, the boys shooting pretend arrows at invisible attackers, and the girls pointing out sights across the resplendent patchwork of fields.

"Careful there, Bryan." The teacher came up behind her boisterous favorite, sitting precariously on the wall. "You've gone suddenly quiet."

"I've never seen the North of Ireland before." He pointed somberly. "Tis much like our own country, isn't it?"

"Very much," she smiled. "What did you expect it to look like?"

"Different," he shrugged, and I was struck by his tone of melancholy. "Different, that's all."

Close Call at The Beach

CHAPTER FORTY-EIGHT

From the Sun Palace we took the westward road and logged more than ten miles before finding a welcome with Jim and Ellen Carlin of Moneyhaughley. Their four children gladly led Missie to their small stony field, and, after supper, played board games with me, while Jim, laid up with a bad back, told me of hiring days in Letterkenny, which lasted into the twentieth century.

"Every May and November they held what they called 'Rabble Days,' when rich Protestant farmers would hire out Catholic children for half a year," said Jim, adjusting a hot-water bottle behind his back.

"Think of it, sending off your children, some no more than ten years of age, without any contact or recourse for maltreatment. The children would return home after six hard months with barely enough money to see their impoverished families through the high rents and harsh winter. A hard lot, wasn't it?"

"There's many a sorrowful story there," Ellen added, gazing fondly on her own brood. "But, sadly, child slavery is still a problem in many parts of the world. The ways of the rich and poor haven't changed all that much."

At night's end, as I was taking leave for their byre, Ellen stopped me: "We won't have you out in that. You sleep with Jimmy Tom, a little person in a big bed."

"I couldn't do that."

"I don't mind, as long as you don't snore," piped the young lad.

So I bunked down beside the five-year-old, amazed at the trust of parents who could allow a stranger to tuck in alongside their child, even a daffy pilgrim such as myself. I thought of the Carlins working their sparse fields, while the McDonnell farm spread over thousands of acres. Even today it must be hard for Catholics living under the long shadow of the Ulster Plantation, to pass miles upon miles of rolling Protestant farm-land—"swordland," I had heard it called—knowing it once had belonged to their own. I flipped over my pillow and tried to settle my head, as little Jimmy Tom stirred in his sleep.

On Monday morning, the twenty-second of October, Missie and I turned north from Letterkenny for the Knockalla Coast Road, reputed to be one of the most spec-tacular stretches of the Donegal coast, a twenty-eight-mile route up the Fanad Penin-sula to the resort town of Portsalon. On the way we would confront its lofty rise, the Devil's Backbone.

A car pulled up ahead, and out jumped a lively little man walking toward me.

"My name is Paddy Grace, and I'm inviting you to the Beach Hotel in Downings at the crown of the Rosguill Peninsula, the next cape over," he handed me his card. "We'll see you then, please God, and I'll have the three *b*'s of the traveler waiting for you: bed, bath, and beer."

That evening, with rain spattering, I took refuge in a thatched cottage tucked beneath Carn Hill with Mrs. Edwards and her son, Samuel. Following a bowl of steaming lamb stew, I discussed my route up Fanad.

"You're four miles from Rathmelton and twelve from Rathmullan," said Samuel. "But why go as far north as Portsalon? 'Tis a hard pull over Knockalla."

"I need the miles," I said, referring to my map. "But I don't think I'll go much further north than that. It looks rather bleak from there to Fanad Head."

" 'Bleak,' you say?" smiled Mrs. Edwards, feeding turf into her old black Stanley No. 9. "Between Portsalon and Fanad Head lies the village of Arryheenabin, the last outpost of the known world."

The next morning we passed through Rathmelton, a charming, tree-lined town where I was struck by the way the natives watched our passing vigilantly, but offered no salutations, quite a contrast to our welcome in Buncrana, just a few miles across Lough Swilly.

Further along, we came to Rathmullan in the evening, and outside The White Hart Inn I met a ginger-bearded fellow who was eager to fill me in on the local history. "It's just down the road that the famous Flight of the Earls took place in 1608, the most tragic day in Irish history."

"I'm still waiting to hear of a good day," I smiled wanly.

With a lively sense of grievance flashing from his red beard, he made the case: "After the Battle of Kinsale, when his alliance with Catholic Spain against the encroachments of Protestant England came to grief, the great Earl of Tyrone, Hugh O'Neill, retreated to these parts and tried to make peace with the English, but the plots against him and the other earls, most notably McSweeney and O'Donnell, eventually drove them all from the land, clearing the way for the Plantation of Ulster, under which the Protes-tants took over and settled the province.

"Old Ireland was gone forever after the Flight of the Earls. Law and custom, language and religion, changed overnight. The old bards walked about a grief-stricken land in rags, lamenting the Earls' flight: 'All earthly joy has fled Ireland. The seas have increased with our tears.' Hundreds of years later we still suffer for that day."

My sorrowful shake of the head was all the encouragement he needed to continue:

"This very village was confiscated at that time. Rathmelton was planted as well. To this day, you'll find Rathmelton folk dark-browed and clannish. Like many other planted towns, they found themselves on the wrong side of the fence in 1920, when Donegal was restored from Ulster into the Irish Republic."

"I have to say I did notice a difference passing through Rathmelton."

"They needn't feel so threatened surrounded by a Catholic majority. In truth, the country should never have been divided."

"But it seemed like the only compromise at the time."

"Nonsense! It should have been all or nothing. England could never have ruled all thirty-two counties, and would have soon grown weary of carrying a troublesome weight on its back. But it can garrison the Six Counties of the North and hang on, interfering in our affairs. The first step toward peace is the removal of British troops. There's no more to be said."

"I mentioned that back in County Down, and the fellow said a bloodbath would follow."

"More rubbish. Many's the town in Donegal that's almost half-Protestant, yet people get along fine. I can see it happening in Ulster, as well, if the people there were given the chance."

Pondering his opinions, we found lodgings with Garrett and Margaret Carton, whose three charming daughters—Catherine, Elizabeth, and Rachel—placed Missie in their "sweet native grass in Aughavannon," and myself before a fine stew, topped off by apple tart.

Refreshed by a sound sleep, we rose early to continue our trek north. I looked out across Lough Swilly swathed in morning mist and thought of the great earls sailing away and taking some part of Irish greatness with them, the flame that lit the way out of the Dark Ages.

Turning toward the foothills of Knockalla, we came upon a young black-haired woman breaking a loaf and tossing crumbs to her hens across a half-door.

"Would your donkey like some bread?" she offered.

"I've never known her to refuse food," I answered, leading Missie to her door.

Missie had barely begun to pull bites out of the stale loaf in her hands, when I was startled by a three-legged dog jumping over the door. Missie gave a hop, too, dropping a crust from her startled gob.

"There, now," the lovely woman sparkled, "what would your chances be back home in America to see a three-legged dog leap a half-door?"

"One in a trillion!"

" 'Tis the beauty of travel, isn't it," she looked out wistfully upon her poor but scenic domain, "seeing things you'd never see if you just kicked about the old place. And you'll take it all home with you, won't you, these memories, and be all the better for it. Well, be off with your rambling, so, and I'll keep on with my dreaming." She clapped her hands free of bread crumbs.

"It's only a half-door you're standing behind," I told her. "You could easily hop over it."

"Oh, I know," she smiled, "but could I ever hop back in again?"

Being veterans of more challenging peaks, Missie and I didn't have much problem with the Devil's Backbone of Knockalla, especially with our frequent stops to admire the view: the Urris Hills and the Gap of Mamore over on the Inishowen Peninsula, Ballymastocker Bay at our feet, rimmed by a long stretch of beautiful beach. If the waters were twenty to thirty degrees warmer, one could imagine a string of world-class high-rise hotels taking advantage of such an attraction, but as it was, only a few seabirds soared over the spectacular sands.

So, not surprisingly, we had the resort of Portsalon pretty much to ourselves. I was put up by the postman, James Clinton, and we spent a relaxing evening with a few jars at the Ardglass Inn, where James proved to be an advocate for walking, befitting his profession. He praised my ambulation and mocked those who join fitness clubs.

"Such balderdash!" said James. "People in the big smoky cities stepping onto contraptions better suited for hamsters. And, by God, they're spending a pretty penny at it, even in Letterkenny! Has half the world gone mad, tell me? A good brisk walk of a mile or two a day keeps the body in working order."

Having received the advanced reservation from the hotelier, Paddy Grace, three days earlier, we didn't proceed next day to the extremity of Fanad Head, but leisurely looped back toward Milford for another pleasant overnight, and north again toward Downings, just above Rossapenna at the tip of Rosguill Peninsula.

As we approached our destination, the sky suddenly filled with migrating Bewick swans, a triumphant formation on the wing, trumpeting their own arrival. Watching them elegantly alight on a nearby estuary, I stood awestruck by their grace and multitude. Their sheer numbers and volume of noise reminded me of how the northern travelers are supposed to be spooked by swans. And as I walked past their flocks on the Rossapenna golf course, I mused on the legend of the Daughters of Lir, turned into swans by a jealous stepmother, and also on "the Wild Geese," those emigrating Irish warriors who fled after the Battle of the Boyne, and whose followers manned foreign armies right through the American Civil War.

When we reached the Beach Hotel in Downings, proprietor Paddy Grace, a small but ebullient man, brought the entire staff out to welcome us. His children, Deirdre and Desmond, took Missie well in hand, and I was greeted by his wife Maura, who turned out to be a relative of Congressman Tip O'Neill's, the quintessential Boston politician.

To no surprise, I spent my first night in the bar, listening to Paddy's endless jokes and the Clan o' Malone, a young family troupe of traditional musicians—three girls, two boys—who had just returned from a successful tour in Europe.

Paddy, sidling up beside me, told me one of his many jokes.

"There was a fella out the Fanad way named Aloysius O'Hore, not the full shilling, you see, but he finally landed a job on a building site in Letterkenny. Well, fair play to him, he held his own that first long day; wielding a hammer, carrying the hod, and stacking bricks with the best of them. So much so, that the foreman, who was derided for hiring him earlier in the day, was now being congratulated. But just before the five o'clock whistle blew, a sharp slate slid off the roof and cut away Neddie's left ear. The foreman told his poleaxed worker not to panic, that all they needed to do was find the ear, pack it in ice, and have Neddie taken to the hospital where the surgeons could sew it back on to his head.

"A great search ensued through the dust and rubble until, finally, the foreman found Neddie's ear and raised it above his head in celebration. But Neddie snapped it from his grasp, studied it brusquely and threw it back into the rubble, saying, 'That isn't mine, ya simple eejit. Sure, didn't me own ear have a pencil behind it!' "

Next morning, Robert Elliott took me for an excursion along the Atlantic Drive between Sheep Haven and Mulroy Bay. Both musician and barkeep at the Beach Hotel, Robert stopped along the way before the ruins of an old church and pointed to the ancient cross standing crookedly in its overgrown yard.

"If you ever thought about becoming a priest, this might be the parish for you. It was when his donkey refused to go any further that Saint Columcille founded a church here at Meevagh."

We returned from our scenic drive to find the hotel's receptionist, Caroline, rushing out to us in the throes of anxiety.

"Paddy and Maura are after taking Deirdre to the doctor's!" she gasped. "Missie bit her on the head."

"Is she badly hurt?" Robert had the wits to ask, as I stood by in mute horror.

"There was a spurt of blood, but no telling. If Dr. Kelly can't see to her, Paddy and Maura will take her into the hospital in Letterkenny."

Young Desmond came storming out the door and into Caroline's arms, wailing at me.

"We were only feeding your Missie, and she bit Deirdre with all her might!"

"You must have been teasing the donkey, to have her at that?" Robert interrogated, while I stood dumbfounded.

"We were just playing with her, that's all."

"Playing with her?"

"Aye, pulling at her ears."

"Her ears!" I managed to exclaim, collapsing on a bench.

"She didn't need to go biting Deirdre with all the carrots we were after feeding her," the lad sobbed, with renewed fervor.

I slumped on my seat, imagining the worst—Deirdre maimed, Missie led away by an animal officer, my journey over. Tears welled up in my eyes.

Seeing me nearly as overwrought as the child in her arms, Caroline tried to comfort me as well: "Don't go blaming yourself. You heard Desmond. What donkey wouldn't react the same?"

They left me to collect myself, and after sitting for some minutes with my head in my hands, I stood up and went toward Missie's small enclosure, ready to break my pledge at O'Neill's Camp and clock her good. But when I approached her, she turned an angelic countenance my way, betraying no hint of wrongdoing, and I relented. I let her bask in the sun unpunished, while I paced the nearby strand for an agonizing hour. Finally Paddy's car swung into the hotel's parking lot, and I madly dashed to meet them.

"How is she?" I swung open the door to the backseat, where Deirdre sat wrapped in her mother's arms.

"She'll live another day, please God," Maura snickered at my grim appearance. "Take a look at this."

There, on the crown of Deirdre's head was a miniature monkish tonsure, with one blue nylon stitch in its clean-shaven center.

"I'm terribly sorry," I said, grasping the young girl's hand, and exhaling a long deep breath. Deirdre tucked her head back into her mother's chest.

"No need to worry," Paddy interjected. "We've decided not to report your animal's heinous crime to the authorities. My goodness, you look like the one that needs taking care of. And I know just the thing that will lift your spirits. When was the last time you had a real American cheeseburger?"

"A lifetime ago."

"Come in, then, and bring 'Deirdre of the Sorrows' with you. And Deirdre, haven't you anything to say to Kevin?"

She dropped her little wounded head and whispered to her shirtfront, "I'm sorry for pulling Missie's ears?"

"Sorry, is it?" I said, picking her up in my arms. "Well, I'm sorry you were bitten, but I'm very glad Missie didn't snap away your lovely nose," I added, giving her little snout a tweak. "Now, just to show there are no hard feelings all around, how would you like a ride on Missie's back?"

"No, thank you," she said, wriggling free of my grasp.

"How about if we feed her an apple, then?"

She shook her head.

"A carrot?"

"All right," she agreed hesitantly, wiping away her tears. "But only if it's a really, really long one!"

Mary Hanna's Pub

On Sunday evening, approaching the end of October, after two nights of Paddy Grace's hospitality, I found myself down the road in Cashel, where I stepped into Mary Hanna's Pub and found seven old gents saying the Rosary. Not wishing to disturb their prayers, I signaled the elderly proprietress I'd be back, and walked outside to enjoy the fine view of Doe Castle perched on a rocky knoll above Sheep Haven Bay. It was only five o'clock, but dusk draped the hills, with the clocks turned back an hour the night before.

When I went back inside, one of the pensioners shifted his chair to welcome me into their circle.

"Glad we didn't scare you off," he chuckled. "I don't suppose it's every pub where you'll find the patrons saying their beads?"

Mary brought over a tray of drinks as one gent asked where I had found digs for the night.

"With Robert Moore, just back the road."

"No better man," another approved. "A grand family man with six fine children."

"Not like ourselves," said a fellow as long and thin as the briar he was smoking. "Seven ornery old bachelors under the beguiling spell of one enchanting widow—Mary Hanna, the Star of Donegal."

"Will ya quiet your gob," Mary snorted, swishing a dishtowel over his head. "Will I ever have a Sunday night of peace in my life?"

"Have ye ever wound up your day with our like, wifeless old bliggards?" asked one yeoman with his cap tilted back to expose a band of freckles between his well-weathered face and thinning hair.

"Oh, yes, hungry nights, those," I confessed, drawing laughter. "A plain cut of loaf, tea without milk or sugar, and a mattress as damp as a leaky waterbed. I nearly starved to death once in Cork," I added, thinking of dear Jimmy Harrington.

"County Cork!" exclaimed the fellow with fleshy pouches under his eyes. "The far end of the country, and here I am, with so little spark, I'm thinking of taking to my bed."

"Take to the bed, is it?" Mary burst out. "Are ye that close to heaven's door?"

"I've been lifting its golden knocker these six months." He winked in my direction. "What good am I tripping through the world, eating me bit, tell me, when the woman I favor won't steal a glance in my direction from November to May."

"Do you know what this love-talker is on about?" said Mary, looming over me.

"I'd say he's flirting with you."

"Are you no better than themselves!" She gave my head a good rub with her knuckles.

"Every old sock needs an old shoe," braved one saucy bachelor, as the others enjoyed a hearty laugh.

After that bit of ribaldry, their chat settled on the deceased people of the parish, as the pipe-smoker took another deep draw from his Kapp and Petersen, and fell into reverie.

"As young lads, we would often play football in Packie Doherty's backfields, and we'd often wonder why he never replaced the broken pane of his bedroom window, and how he could stand the harsh winter winds that whistled through. At his wake years later, we learned he had fancied a McGivern girl gone off to America, and it was she, fifty years earlier, who had broken the pane on the morning of her departure, tossing a clatter of stone against it, to awaken him and share their last hour before she went out foreign. A desperate keepsake, was it not?"

A wispy blue contrail curled out of his pipe like a living spirit, and seemed to weave a spell over the circle of old men, all perhaps with reminders of near-romance, each more desperate than the last.

Mary stepped into the circle to place more drinks on the table, and noted, "Tomas, you've grown very still."

"Their stories have me drifting back to my youth, where else?"

"A romance, Tomas? You? I don't believe it," one of his cronies ribbed him.

" 'Tisn't much of a story, but sadly 'tis all I have in this matter of courtship." He fidgeted with a loose button on his frayed tweed jacket.

"Go on, off your chest, man," the others urged him on.

"All right, so. It can't hurt to tell what one can't forget," he conceded. "I was a young man working in Dublin at the time, but home I was headed for the Christmas holidays on the Westport train. Across from me in the carriage sat a young woman, no further from me now than yourselves, the fairest maid in the Four Provinces, but encased on either side by impenetrable walls: a priest as hard and black as coal, and a nun as watchful as a badger over its brood."

"Well-protected, so," the others chuckled.

"Aye, and it was only this invincible pair that kept me from chatting her up, for no more enchanting face had I ever seen, and the kindness simply spilt from her. She betrayed not a blemish, I tell you.

" 'And,' thinks I, 'if she gets off at Westport, my destination, I'll be sure to carry off her luggage, and be bold enough to seek her acquaintance during Christmas Week.' But, as you may know, there are several stops between Dublin's Euston Station and Westport: Portarlington, Tullamore, Athlone, Roscommon, Castlerea, Ballyhaunis, and Castlebar, and well I should know them still, for I zealously studied the train's itinerary that night, praying the docket in my hand matched that in her own.

" 'Portarlington!' cried the porter, and not a budge from the three. Pity no rectory or convent awaited the black pair, for if either had forfeited their seat, I would be quick to claim it, and would pay no notice to the remaining papal guard.

"We rolled on toward Tullamore, the two clerics as black and heavy as granite. Bookends, they were, protecting a lovingly-penned manuscript that would illuminate the firmament if unclasped and gently opened."

"Why, Tomas, you're a bit of a poet," the stout fellow interjected, but was shushed by the others.

"So there we sat, an aisle apart and worlds away, amidst the flicker of lights and the train's dreamy sway. Looking out at the darkening countryside, I discovered I could watch her clearly in the window's reflection without staring directly or infringing in any way. And when our eyes did occasionally meet, my heart pulsed with a magnetism that would pale the Northern Lights. Though I know this may sound full of conceit, I truly believed she thought as much of me as I did her, and however that was, I will never know.

" 'Tullamore!' shouts the porter, and the train bucked to a halt. But again no stir of movement, the black sentinels still in place."

Tomas took a healthy gulp of stout, wiped his mouth with a handkerchief, and continued:

"The world again darkened, but for the white frost layered over fields and fleeting glimpses of cottages candle-lit, anticipating the Holy Family. Overhanging boughs swished across our carriage roof, blessing, so it seemed, our western passage.

"How I prayed, with five stops to go, for if she did disembark in Westport, I'd be as cute as any playboy. I'd see her home along Clew Bay, if permitted, and tell her things I hardly knew about myself, for wouldn't she bring out the best in any man? And when she'd speak, I'd listen like a prize pupil, intent on recollecting her every word.

" 'Athlone!' shouts the porter. Athlone, 'Guardian of the Shannon.' Athlone, watched over by the twin spires of St. Peter and St. Paul. Athlone, where neither priest nor nun vacated their seat, but . . . herself alone."

A groan escaped the audience.

"At first I sat paralyzed, but soon sprang to life, clumsily reaching overhead for her bag, but made a proper circus of it, banging into other passengers who also stood to disembark. But at least I was able to put the suitcase in her hand, little as it was, and received a blushing thank-you in return.

"The clerics slid into her space and chatted on, unaware of any loss, as I directed my gaze to the station's platform, now half hoping she would fall into the arms of another man. But when the platform cleared, it was herself who stood beneath the lamppost. And as the train hissed with impatience, she warmly waved my way, and I had hardly lifted my own hand when the train jolted us forward into the black pitch. And, I tell you, I neither felt nor heard not another thing that long night until my face was being skinned by the bitter winds that skirled across Clew Bay."

"Well, aren't we a cheerful lot," said Mary, noisily clearing away the glasses to break the silence that followed Tomas's story. "They'd have the devil himself weeping into a hankie, wouldn't they," she said to me, "and each of them fine handsome men in their prime, but not one of them to take in a bride."

"What had we to do, Mary Hanna, but wrest a living from the land?" said the freckled fellow. "Should we have trebled our misfortune with wife and child, and many of us caring for the old ones till their dying day?"

"But doesn't Mary make up for the lost ones in our hearts," lilted the pipe-smoker, standing up to put an arm around her waist. "And doesn't she cut a fine figure yet?"

"Be off it, you!" She spun free from his grasp. "I'm thinking there's time for all of you yet, the whole lot of ye!"

Pleasantly drunk on stout and sentiment, we all stepped out of Mary Hanna's, to a great light sweeping across the midnight sky.

" 'Tis the lighthouse on Tory Island," the pipe-smoker informed me, his bowl a faint orange glow. Each of the bachelors shook my hand in turn, wishing me the luck of the saints.

The seven trickled off into the night, walking bicycles or on shank's mare, making their way home as they had done every Sunday night in memory.

I ambled back to the Moores', never knowing the world to be so lonely. Now these seven walk home, to what? The dog, the cold range, the loaf, the heavyhearted tick of a wind-up clock. Each, I surmise, reminiscing his own bittersweet romance. Each fated to unbegetting solitude.

At the Moores', there was no sign of life, so I opened a thatched byre and gathered up a few potato sacks to soften the stone. It was comfortable enough, but my mind reeled, the voices of the bachelors echoing in my head. I rose from the byre to piddle in the hedge. Stillness. Only the distant call of shorebirds.

The beacon on Tory flashed its brilliance across the blackness, a long pause, and then again.

All Hallow's Eve

As I tackled Missie next morning, the older Moore children lined up to say farewell before they set off to gather potatoes beneath the spectacular flat-topped mountain of Muckish, meaning "Pig's Back" in the Irish.

When we passed Mary Hanna's, a young man named Manus Breslin was waiting outside her door. "How are you set for oats?"

"I'm in desperate need."

"I have two stone from last year. Hard as nuggets. You're welcome to them."

"Thank you," I said, reaching into my pocket for a few quid.

"Out of that," he commanded. "Just mention my name if you ever go writing a book."

"I'll mention it twice, Manus Breslin."

Missie and I soldiered on, arriving in Creeslough at noon, a high-perched village which offered stupendous views of the Derryveagh Range. After marveling at this vast expanse of jagged peaks and high country, we continued our trek, passing Ballymore, Marble Hill, Portnablagh, and through the town of Dunfanaghy, situated on a dazzling beach near the headland of Horn Head.

Onward ho! Up and down rugged country lit up by the sun's lowering rays, with tiny lakes gleaming like jewels. Along the road, farmers beside an old dilapidated mill called out to me in English.

"How is your donkey wearing?"

"Fine, but will these roads ever flatten?"

" 'Tis what keeps her going," one shouted back. "She'd lay stone dead if not for the humps that's in it."

We spent Monday night in Murroe, and next day waddled into Falcarragh under a heavy cloudburst, getting a welcomed welcome from the publican, Seamus Gallagher, at the Anchor Inn.

"You're into the barony of Cloghaneely," he said, serving me a steaming bowl of chicken soup. "If you keep to the coast you'll pass the Rosses and Qweedore, which, with ourselves, make up the Donegal Gaeltacht. We're the largest Irish-speaking area in the country, stretching from Fanad Head to Slieve League, broken up only by Dunfanaghy, a Protestant town that. Now, with your permission, I'd like to call Radio na Gaeltachta. I say they'd be interested in your travels."

"Of course, thank you," I replied, fondly recalling how the Irish radio had helped us out on the Dingle.

He was back in a flash, pleased as punch.

"The wireless is going to announce your position twice daily until you're beyond range. They'll also be asking the people to assist you in any way." He clapped his hands in delight. "There'll be bags 'pon bags of eyes upon you, boy. But you'll need it, *Avic*, for you're stepping into desperate country, the poorest I daresay, in the whole of Ireland."

A few locals ventured in, curious to eyeball the gypsy who had parked his donkey before the inn. Following a round of drink, I asked the congenial crowd if they knew of a local smith, since Missie had grown high in the hoof.

"Thomas MacCausland is your man," volunteered one happy trooper.

I was surprised to find that every patron followed me out of the pub and joined Missie and me in a grand parade toward MacCausland's forge, picking up a few stragglers along the way. This spontaneous event was known as a *meitheal*, I was later told, "a gathering at the forge."

"Who made these shoes?" asked Thomas MacCausland, raising Missie's back hoof, while a young apprentice anesthetized her ears.

"The Power Brothers in Waterford."

A thick Irish mumbling filled the forge: "A tidy bit of craftsmanship," he commented, going about his task.

"You'll go no further tonight," said one native, looking out on the downpour. "Ask the O Ceallaighs to lodge you"—pointing to a large shop across the town. "They're a generous family who'd be interested in meeting the likes of yourself."

Pádraig and Mairead O Ceallaigh accepted me warmly, and after supper and the Rosary in Irish, Mairead presented me with a small gift.

" 'Tis Gartan clay," she explained, placing a white chalky block in my hand. "It was collected at Godfrey's Isle on Gartan Lake, a favorite dwelling of Saint Columcille. Keep this in your house back in America and you'll never need worry about a fire."

On Wednesday, All Hallow's Eve, we left Falcarragh for the vast parish of Gweedore with the O Ceallaigh children seeing us off before they set out for school.

"You best watch for the *puca* on the black roads," both Pádraig and Sinéad warned me with a laugh. "'Tis a despicable creature who comes out of hiding tonight to spoil the fruit in the hedge by weeing on it."

The wet, cold weather persisted, appropriately enough, since the next day was Samhain, the first day of winter in the old Irish calendar, as well as All Saint's Day.

We trekked through the village of Gortahork, where pots of geraniums sat in deep-silled windows and behind those pots peered the eyes of the occupants themselves. Unlike the northerners, whose glances were furtive and cursory, these Gaeltacht folk gazed out with childlike curiosity, unembarrassed when caught looking, placidly viewing the passing parade.

As we ascended a lofty road, a fresh wind washed away the troubled sky, allowing us a fine view of Ballyness Bay from our high vantage.

"That's a charming eyeful, is it not?"

I turned, startled, to see a tall old fellow filling the doorway of his thatched cottage behind me.

"Across the bay, peeking back at you, are the islands of Inishbofin, Inishdooey, and Inishbeg, and Tory beyond them all. And there, to our north, is Horn Head and Croagh-namaddy. Wonderful cliffs, those, full of rare sea-fowl. And where are ye headed to-night?—for we've been told to ring the wireless when you're spotted."

"The Bloody Foreland."

"No better place." He ducked to step out from his door.

"How did it get its name?" I asked the genial fellow. "Was a great battle fought there?"

"Battle, no! Cromwell wouldn't bother his head to march through these rocky moors. 'Tis called the Bloody Foreland because the rocks there gleam like flames during early summer sunsets. 'Tis world-famous, you know? Artists from every land go rushing over this very road, hopelessly trying to capture what God accomplishes with a wave of His hand."

After we had passed Meanlaragh, a grocery lorry came out of nowhere and pulled up beside us.

"I have some extra bananas," the driver called out. "Do you and your donkey have a taste for 'em?"

"Do we ever!"

"You're welcome to these, so," he said, stepping out of the lory and handing me three big bunches.

"Thank you," I said heartily, placing them on top of my mudbox. I could hardly believe our luck.

On the lonely stretch to the Bloody Foreland, where numberless boulders were strewn about the limitless moor, I learned not everyone, despite twice-daily mention on Irish radio, knew our identity.

A black Morris Minor pulled up, occupied by a large-eared farmer and his sharp-tongued wife. "What are ye asking for the bananas?" the wife asked, rolling down her passenger window.

"Please?"

"How much for the 'nanas? Are ye selling them or carrying them?"

I was quick to cop on she had mistaken me for a traveling boyo, and so felt obliged to carry this masquerade through.

"A pound a bunch will do nicely, or three quid for the lot."

"Little bargain, that," she snapped. "I can do better in the shops."

"You might and you mightn't," I shrugged.

"You probably lifted them off a lorry."

"They miraculously fell off without a bruise."

"Likely story. You'll have to do better."

"Listen, you couldn't get a bunch of bananas for a pound if the shopkeeper peeled away their jackets before weighing them on his butcher's scale."

"Keep them," she hissed, "and I hope they blacken in tonight's faery frost!"

"A Christian good-day to you, too," I replied with a mock tip of my cap. "Always a pleasure doing business with the likes of yourself."

The pair pulled away in a fuss, and I was amused to note the cab's rearview mirror was angled for her eyes, not his, allowing her to glance back at me as they puttered away down the bog road at a poky pace.

When we reached the outskirts of Knockfola, a Tayto crisps bag, which had been blowing alongside us for a mile, lifted itself in a maddening swirl around our heads. Once it settled, I took my hazel stick and approached it cautiously, as though our lives were imperiled.

"Die, you miserable *puca*, die," I shouted, stabbing the possessed bag countless times before burying it into a soft morass. I looked up from my gravedigging to see a hefty woman gaping at me from her door. She shouted to me in Irish, but forsook her native tongue after hearing my wild Gaelic stumblings.

"I say, are you selling those bananas?"

"I am."

"How much are ye asking?"

"I'll give you two bunches for two quid, for I've decided to keep a bunch for ourselves."

" 'Ourselves,' is it?" she said, looking back and forth at Missie and me. "Fine, so." She waved two crisp notes in her hand.

Knockfola was a scattered settlement of whitewashed cottages, many thatched, sitting in small huddles among these stony hills. A few young mummers, their faces blackened, hurried along the village paths knocking on doors and collecting sweets and coins from these little cabins crouched before the continent of sea.

A brute storm was brewing as we reached the Bloody Foreland and turned the northwest corner of Eireann. I stopped with the angry surf banging against the rocky sea-ledge below, and celebrated by feeding Missie a banana, and then the peel, not sure which she enjoyed the most.

As we continued through the spread-out village, eyes followed us at every window, with the frank curiosity I had come to expect from the Gaeltacht folk. And yet no invitations were forthcoming from these turf-fired cabins. When I called on two dwellings, the elderly occupants apologized, speaking Irish only, but indicating they couldn't house an *asal* in their tiny byres with a solitary cow and a few hens. I had to wonder how they scraped out a living in such inhospitable circumstances, and couldn't hold it against them when they turned me away.

With the heavy cloak of evening descending, we anxiously walked the white-cobbled road out from the village toward the mournful moor. I was just beginning to say my beads in Irish when, from the door of one of the last houses visible, we heard the welcome cry:

"I have a byre full of corn for your *asal,* and pancakes for yourself!"

Sadie McFadden, a plump, cheerful woman who reminded me of my Aunt Cella, ushered me in and introduced her husband, Tom, and their children, Sadie Marie, Tony, and Cathal.

"You're welcome to sleep inside on our fold-out couch," said Sadie, after I had made short work of her pancakes. "Now, freshen up, if you like, for we'll soon be taking a bus to Jack McFadden's Pub in Glasagh. There's a benefit tonight for my sister, Nellie Downey, who recently lost her husband in a car accident."

"I'm sorry to hear that, but I'd be glad to join you."

When we entered McFadden's, a festive air filled the pub despite the somber occasion. Pipes and fiddles played, and dancing couples made a great clacking sound on the wooden floors. With Cathal, a lighthearted adolescent, as my guide, I discovered much about the bereaved family for whose benefit this gathering was called. Nellie Downey was forty-six and had twenty children, and her offspring ranged in age from four to twenty-nine. Six of her first seven children were girls. Six of her last seven were boys. There were two sets of twins and four miscarriages. I tried to learn all their names: Garvin, Aengus, Martin, Sadie, Edward, Madeline . . .

When someone asked Sadie about the staggering size of Nellie's brood, she smiled and replied, "I'd ask Nellie the same, and all she'd ever say was that they were easily come by."

Pints of stout were generously set before me all evening, the last by the publican, Jack McFadden.

"Ye've completed your march to the western sea," he said. "Now, you nose southwest for Mayo, do you not?"

"I do," I answered, sipping a last pint I could well have done without.

"God help ye," he shook my hand. " 'Tis a wild march yet."

On my slightly wobbly way out, I had enough wits about me to drop my two pounds of banana money into the benefit tin, wishing I had a thousand more to give.

It was well after midnight when we reboarded the bus. Sadie sat behind the driver, keeping him company while his eyes remained glued to the looping road. Each time a passenger exited into the fathomless pitch, a mighty wind-gust filled the bus, reminding me where we were: a woebegone exposure along a stony margin of sea.

The rocking of the bus stirred my memories. I thought of the rich farmlands of Meath, Down, and Derry that Missie and I had passed through, the fertile checkered fields filled with livestock, or swaying heavily with golden grain. And now these barren salt-sprayed slopes where the descendants of the uprooted Celts huddle, doggedly hanging on to their language, religion, and music. A proud people still, however humble their habitation, with fond hopes for their children. Sadie, one of the proudest, as her daughter, Sadie Marie, was attending Trinity College in Dublin.

"Seventy-five pounds, twenty pence," said Sadie, counting the last coins in the collection tin. "Won't that help Nellie some."

She pushed a fiver toward the driver.

"Leave it be, Sadie, I won't take a shilling. 'Tis the little I can do but drive."

"You'll take it for the petrol alone, and you hadn't a drink yourself."

"I won't, Sadie, and enough about it."

Sadie sat silent, staring out over the driver's shoulder at the ghostly vapors of sea air rushing through the headlamps like a host of hobgoblins. The old fella beside me asked if he could use my shoulder to rest his head. I nodded okay as Sadie looked back and brightened, rattling to the others in Irish, her voice with the lift and lilt of a fiddle, full of inexhaustible spirit.

"Do you find us coastal dwellers strange, do you?" she asked me.

"Not at all," I answered. "I only wish I knew your language so I could better understand all that's around me."

"The old language is but at the butt of your tongue," she smiled, reaching across the aisle to pat my knee. "And if old Mick keeps snoring into your ear till Samhain's dawn, you won't know what kind of wild dialect you'll be jabbering in the morning."

Missie's March to Drumnacart

CHAPTER FIFTY-ONE

I woke to the sizzle of the pan.

"'Tis All Saints' Day," announced Sadie from the kitchen doorway, "but sure, 'twas like All Souls' with you whimpering throughout the night. Is there any sign of life in your bones, or are you pulverized from the drink?"

I sat up in the fold-out couch in their living room, discombobulated, certain it was my dear aunt Cella calling me from her kitchen in Derrane.

"I say," said Sadie, "can ya eat a bit before Mass?"

Taking inventory of my condition, I thought I could. I sat myself down to a steaming fry, but when the first lump of sausage hit my stomach, it began to churn like the soughing seas all around us.

"Are ye ill-bellied?" asked Sadie, and scooted me into the bathroom.

Between heaves, I heard her call through the door, "How many pints had ye last night?"

"Five," I wheezed back between gasps.

"Five!"

"A new record," I moaned, dropping my head back to the porcelain bowl.

After I had emptied my innards, Sadie assisted me back to the couch.

"Ye'll be going nowhere today, so sleep to your heart's content," she said, pulling up the blankets and calling for Cathal to bring in a cool washcloth.

Like a seasick passenger on a turbulent sea, I lay on my side with knees tucked into my ribs, utterly dying. I couldn't believe it. I was sick with a hangover. Other than that bad bottle of stout in Bealaha, I hadn't been disabled by drink since my military days in Texas when barracks buddies took me out prior to my leaving for Vietnam. I had nine rum-and-Cokes that night, and recall one spirited moment when I jumped up on the table and roared, "I'm going to do this every night of my life!"

I've never tasted rum since.

The day went by in a feverish blur, yet I took a measure of comfort in being in from the elements that buffeted the windows with hard-driven rain. I fell in and out of sleep, waking to the burring chatter of Donegal Irish in the near kitchen, hearing the phrase *"cuig phionta"* repeated to peals of laughter.

In the afternoon, Cathal brought me toast and tea and asked how I was doing.

"Much better, thanks," I answered, nibbling cautiously on the crust. "But can I ask you what *'cuig phionta'* means? It's been echoing in my ears this long day."

" *'Cuig phionta'* means 'five pints,'" he burst out. "The villagers can't believe you're snookered on five pints!"

"Five pints is over half a gallon," I appealed, my head splitting. "Five pints, and I'm the butt of all jokes because I'm grog-headed the next day! I have friends in America who'd be on life support if they drank that much."

"There's a fella in the parish who can drink a quarter-keg and do an honest day's work," Cathal stated with pride.

"Good for him," I dropped my heavy head back to the pillow. "He should think of donating his behemoth liver to the Royal Academy when he departs from this world."

Feeling better by evening, I went for a walk with Cathal and Missie through the village. The skies had cleared and the small thatched cabins breathed like living creatures, exhaling their bluish turfsmoke into the crisp air.

"There's nothing as nice as the smell of turf," I commented to Cathal, taking a deep breath of this earthy tang mingled with sea air.

"I've heard it said that if God smoked a pipe, His tobacco would smell like turf. 'Tis sweet enough, I suppose, but there's better heat in the coal," added the practical lad.

The lighthouse on Tory Island winked across the black sea, the castellated headlands dramatically lit by the rising moon.

"The only round tower in Donegal is on Tory," Cathal followed my gaze to its remoteness seven miles from shore.

"How many people live there?"

"Three hundred or thereabouts. Grand people, they are, but Tory wasn't always peaceful. In early times, the Fomorians settled there—African pirates—who raided the coast along these parts. Their king was Balor of the Evil Eye, who was eventually slain by his grandson, Lugh, who used his 'Sword of Light.'

"When Saint Columcille founded a monastery there," the young student continued, "he befriended a man named Dugan, whose ancestors still live on the island. Today, the head of the Dugan family is in charge of dispensing 'Tory clay' to anyone who asks for it in the name of God. Tory clay has the power to ward off rats."

"Is that true?" I asked, thinking of my own Gartan clay.

"I wouldn't know firsthand, but there's no rats on Tory Island."

Cathal brought my attention to Missie who stood peacefully between us, pondering the limitless ocean at her feet.

"I've never seen a donkey like her," he said. "You don't even need a halter, do you? You'll miss her terribly when your journey is through."

"I sure will," I acknowledged.

"She's a pet, nonetheless," he stroked her white snout. "Not like the mad asses that do be bucking and bawling in these parts."

Early Friday morning we bade a grateful farewell to Sadie, "the wee stout woman," as I had heard her called, and set off at a good clip along sea-rimmed roads, despite ferocious winds that flailed over the frothing shores.

"'Tisn't Christianable weather at all," greeted a woolen-capped farmer, leaning against the gable end of his house that abutted the winding road.

"That, it isn't," I replied, unconsciously adopting his idiom.

Before moseying on, I made mention of the endless stone walls that weaved up the hillslopes beyond his home.

"A learned Englishman stopped here a summer back, and he reckoned that if ye pieced all the stone walls in Ireland together, they could reach from here to the moon."

Despite the punishing cold, we pushed on, but today it was Missie who stepped lively after her day off in a byre of corn, while I was still stewing in a fog of alcohol poisoning. We passed Derrybeg, looking out at Gola Island, and over the River Clady into Bunbeg, where we paid a visit to Radio na Gaeltachta.

"So this is the famous *asal,*" said one of the two welcoming broadcasters, stepping out from the station.

"You'll be followed like a comet across the sky till you're beyond Killybegs," the broadcaster's mate assured me, as he affixed the station's bumper sticker—RADIO NA GAELTACHTA TIR CHONAILL 312M 963KHZ—to my tailboard. "There, what do you think?"

"There'll be no mistaking me now," I laughed, having related to them my brief career as a fruit vendor.

The damp, dreary afternoon cleared at its close, the pale wincing sun sinking to its gray watery bed, looking more like a weary crone than our mother star.

On the westward road to Annagary, I began to search for lodging but, as in Knockfola, the holdings in this loose settlement were sparse and cheerless, the fen-filled landscape broken only by the lone sentinel of Errigal, nicknamed "Cock of the North."

We were now properly in the Rosses, a parish of sixty thousand rock-strewn acres and shivering loughs, a poor old pocket of Ireland. Hungry cows were spanceled here and there, and a few geese pecked for grain before ramshackle byres. Behind these thatched dwellings were the crumbling remains of ancestral homesteads, pitiful domiciles of the dispossessed.

These old folk appeared cautious though apologetic at their doors, the cabin-wives asking if I was the lad on the wireless and suggesting I move out beyond Annagary, where I'd stand a better chance of finding shelter.

The "short-measured" winter day was quick to darken, and a reborn tempest swirled across the sea in gusts that promised sustained fury, so I began to scan this desolate waste of broom and bracken for an old booley or shepherd's hut. Soon after the cold rain began to come down in earnest, a car pulled up beside us, the occupants peering out sympathetically at a disconsolate pair of drowned rats.

The driver rolled down his window and offered, "We have an abandoned cabin beside our home that would do you both. 'Tis in Drumnacart, though, three miles afoot."

"Ye'll find it easy enough." His wife leaned across with a pitying smile. "Ours will be the lone light in the bog."

I thanked James and Sheila Duffy profusely, but my heart sank as I watched their tail-lights snake into the gloomy dark. I tried to take solace in the country expression, "The closing of an autumn evening is like the running of a hound across the moor." Pretty, that. But this was a wet and raw winter evening, with a donkey exhausted after a dozen hard miles, with the added danger of being sideswiped by car or lorry on this winding cow-and-a-half–wide road.

I flirted with despair, yet Missie was fired up and raring to go, so there was little to do but follow her lead. She tipped along tidily through the endless bog, hooves scrabbling over the uneven road, while I lagged behind—cold, tired, and longing for home.

Even as the gale flung hail in our faces, Missie unflinchingly high-stepped through the black moor, while I dragged wearily behind. And it was she who first caught sight of a distant light, well beyond where the twists and turns of the road disappeared into the curtain of night. She bugled me awake and redoubled her pace.

The light disappeared when the road dipped, and when we crested another little rise it seemed mysteriously more distant still. But Missie was not daunted. After another bend in the road, the light seemed to have shifted in another direction. Lost and confused, I began to fear this wandering orb was a will-o'-the-wisp, a well-known but seldom-seen creature who leads wayfarers into bottomless holes of trackless bogs, to lie forever with a well-preserved collection of hermits, tinkers, and redheaded Danes. But Missie's raucous cry again urged me onward, into the dark maze.

The wind howled across this treeless plain, rising with such clamor I seemed to hear the keening voices of Icelandic women wailing over the turbulent sea. Giving up on the fickle, still-distant light, I wrapped the reins about the hames and told Missie, "It's up to you to find our way home. Take whatever boreen you like, for I'm lost and weary, I am."

And off she went, her nose outstretched and her ears stitched back, like a standard-bred trotter in the homestretch of the Little Brown Jug, with the clunky cart for a sulky and no jockey at all aboard. Missie was no equine mutt, but a descendant of the great Hambletonian himself.

In minutes I heard her triumphant bray across the bog, and struggled into a trot of my own to catch up to where I found her at the mouth of a winding lane, at the end of which I could clearly make out a brightly-lit farmhouse in the absolute wilds of these Caledonian highlands.

I threw my arms around Missie's damp shaggy neck, "My dear little trailblazer. Is it you who will see us home after all? A pure blessed creature, you are."

It was the bluff and hearty Brigid Duffy, daughter of James and Sheila, who greeted us at the door.

"We thought you were lost or stolen!" she exclaimed, throwing a coat over her head and leading us down a grassy path to a small misshapen cabin seeping back into the bog.

"Let's settle her first," she proceeded, swinging a lamp before us. "You don't want her out in this mess."

I unyoked Missie, and Brigid pried open the creaking door, but Missie refused to cross the threshold.

"I was afraid of this," said Brigid, obviously no stranger to equine behavior. "Donkeys aren't fond of any shelter that's been peopled. You best take her by the ears and I'll coax her in from behind."

After a tiresome tussle, we wedged Missie into the abandoned kitchen of the wee house.

"She'll be fine here," gasped Brigid, winded by our exertions. "And there's a bedstead below where you can lay your bag." She flashed her lamp into a tiny bedroom off the kitchen. "This old house hasn't been lived in for years, nor is it great, God knows, but 'tis clean and dry. Now, come up to the house for a bite to eat."

Inside the Duffy residence, soup and sandwiches were waiting for me on the kitchen table.

"You can do with a bite of food after that wild march," smiled Sheila, pouring out the tea. "God knows, you must be famished."

"Knockfola to Drumnacart is every bit of fifteen miles," James looked up from feeding the fire with turf. "Whatever put such a wild notion into your head as to walk a donkey?"

"So I could meet generous people like yourselves," I said, and meant it, as I set my wet sneakers before the glowing flames.

After a lovely night of chat, I found my way back to the old cabin, where Missie stood snuffling at the door like a worried bride.

"Sorry I'm late, Miss. I was delayed at the office."

After feeding her the last of our bananas, I closed the kitchen door and dropped my sleeping bag onto the old bedstead, more than ready for a good night's sleep in this primitive but secure shelter. As I settled in, however, the wind outside howled like a glede of banshees, and inside Missie whined like a lonesome pup. After she had provided such noble service today, I had to relent and let her in. She made happy whimpering sounds—the likes I had never heard—as she dropped to the foot of the old bed.

"You know, Miss," I said through the blackness, "I was told the souls of the faithful departed return to their homes on All Souls' Night. If that's true, won't the old residents of this place be in for a shocker, thinking there's been queer goings-on since they took their earthly leave."

Glengesh Pass

CHAPTER FIFTY-TWO

M issie was gawking over me when I awoke late next morning.

"So, you're my guardian angel." I wrestled with her large handsome head. "Give us a hug, you silly little clown."

At just that moment Brigid Duffy appeared at the door.

"Oh, I'm sorry," she snickered. "I hope I'm not interrupting anything."

"Not at all." I pulled myself from the bag. "Missie wouldn't stay in the kitchen last night, so I had to let her sleep in here."

"Likely story," she quipped as she ducked out the door before I could clock her one.

After breakfast, Brigid helped me tackle Missie and accompanied us down the muddied lane to the main road, the landscape not half as wild in the light of day.

"How far will you go today?" she asked.

"Burtonport."

" 'Tis twelve miles, that. Now, you'll never forget your night in Drumnacart, will you?"

"Never in my puff." I gave her hand a heartfelt squeeze.

We journeyed another desolate trek on this Saturday: a hummocky-tussocky road, as the clamorous Atlantic rollers kicked up curtains of wet mist. As we tipped through the seaside village of Kincaslough, a few children, undaunted by the raw day, saluted our passing in Irish, their high-pitched voices blending with the incessant chatter of seabirds overhead.

Night was descending when we entered the prosperous village of Burtonport, famous for its salmon catches off Tory Sound, and the near-shore island of Arranmore, a favorite of day-trippers. We stayed the night, then nosed for Lettermacaward via

Dungloe, a thirteen-mile trek through boggy terrain, peopled by the sparse remains of the royal northern clans, now scattered along this western sea.

"Would you like a song, Miss?" I asked, as we trudged further into this far-flung remoteness.

She nodded, of course, so I sang "Mary from Dungloe," a popular nineteenth-century song I'd learned at McFadden's on Halloween Night:

> "Oh, then, fare ye well sweet Donegal, the Rosses and Gweedore
> I'm crossing the main ocean, where the foaming billows roar.
> It breaks my heart from you to part, where I spent happy days
> Farewell to kind relations, for I'm bound for Amerikay."

We ambled on through a region of orange-tinged grass and rush-encircled loughs, as raindrops, hard as pennies tried their best to dent our foreheads. Along Lough Meela, one titanic gust arose, freezing Missie into a state of catalepsy.

Many cars, returning from Sunday Mass in Burtonport, stopped to see if we needed assistance.

"She's just balking against the storm," I answered them uneasily, fearing one might be associated with the local SPCA.

" 'Tis a right juggernaut, this storm?" agreed one motorist. "You'd better watch your donkey for stringhalts—cold kidneys—in this wet weather. You're out of a hard week, but stepping into another. Wipe her down good at the end of the day and keep her in at night whenever able. 'Twill be terribly hard on her from here on out."

We reached Dungloe by early afternoon, where the bleakness of the landscape is said to have bred a contrasting warmth of welcome from the natives. It certainly seemed so to me. Smiling faces popped out from every window along its main street like jack-in-the-boxes, waving and shouting encouragement before the pelting rain drove them back in again. A young barkeep, in white shirt and black tie, came running out of Doherty's Pub.

"Here ye go," he handed me a bag, as he shivered with the instant soaking. " 'Tis only sweets and sandwiches, but it might help shorten the road."

At a crossroads a mile out of the village we came upon an old fella with a bicycle, hunched beneath the dripping fingerpost.

" 'Twasn't till after I passed you that I began to worry you might go wrong here," he explained, offering a wet hand. "If you're headed for Lettermacaward—seven long miles—you need to stay left at this cross, for if ye go right, the way the signpost is pointed, ye'll end up in Maghery, which will lead you on a long loopabout to nowhere."

"It was extremely kind of you to wait and tell me," I replied through the downpour.

"Wouldn't anyone do the same for a donkey pilgrim such as yourself? Now, God bless, and safe home," he mounted his bicycle and wobbled wetly down the remote track toward Maghery.

The parish of the Rosses remained dark and bleak, and the road at our feet spun forever before us like a spool of gray thread. I began to wonder why the man at the cross didn't pedal back to inform me of the errant signpost, but had held his position despite the downpour.

Journeying across the rust-colored bog, we came upon an old weathered creel basket sunk into the murky blackness. Poking it with my hazel, I wondered if its crofter were still alive and began to ponder the meaning of an expression I had recently heard, "A sod of turf never fell from an empty creel."

I nudged Missie along this barrenness marked by the endless measure of telephone poles poking crookedly to the sky, the lines seeming to hum with the imperceptible carry of voices. Missie again balked, this time her gaze setting upon a gnarled hawthorn tree bent eastward from the western gales: a gaunt arthritic hand that held a snapping black rag in its grasp.

Dropping the reins, I hurtled across the trackless bog and found the black rag to be a woman's woolen scarf flecked handsomely with color. I cautiously freed it from its piercing thorns, thinking it might be useful once washed. Packing it away, we resumed our lonely march toward Lettermacaward, wondering how the woman came to lose her scarf, how far had it flown—the Glenties, perhaps, or Glenveagh—and did she mourn its loss?

After a weary mile contemplating the thorn-tangled scarf's endless possibilities, my thoughts returned to the old man at the cross, speculating . . . if he hadn't been there, how deep we would have ventured into the netherlands before I would have checked my map. In fact, on this lonely stretch, I began to recall many people—friends, sweethearts and strangers alike—who had assisted me at various crossroads of my young life.

A voice shattered my deep reverie.

"I say, have ye gone dreaming over the bog?" called an elderly woman from her door. "Come in, and redden your shin spots by the fire!"

We had reached Neenacarn, three miles shy of Lettermacaward, but I was only too glad to be called to the hearth of Margaret Duffy, a widow living with her son and his young family, and they had a shed for Missie as well.

"Imagine walking a donkey from Burtonport on a day like this," the lively woman fussed, cutting up a handsome loaf while I settled by the fire to get warm and dry. "'Tis pure flummery! Why, I'd rather go dancing a reel with stones in me stockings. Do ye hear me . . . with stones in me two stockings!"

As the evening comfortably wore on, Margaret sat knitting an Aran sweater, just as Sheila Duffy had done two nights before.

"We earn thirteen pence an ounce," Margaret explained over the busy click of her long needles, "and each jumper weighs about thirty ounces. So that's almost four pounds in the purse, and it takes me just a week to finish one, if I keep at it."

"It's a lot of work." I watched her create the diamond and blackberry patterns on its front bodice, knowing that fisherman-knit sweaters fetched thirty pounds–plus in the shops.

"Yes, but you can do it anytime, watching telly or listening to the wireless." She drew another length of *bainin* wool from the ball on her lap. "As children, we'd go knitting socks while walking to school or crossing the bog. Not dreaming away like yourself."

A week into November, Missie and I were traversing the bleak rim of Gweebarra Bay, passing the low country of Maas, Clooney, and Kilclooney, which led us into more foreboding landscape toward Ardara, the weaving capital of Donegal.

On this rain-spattered road, I came upon an old farmer leaning on a two-pronged graip fashioned with a handle of hazel, who poked his capped head from a shed filled with hanging onions.

"How's she cutting?" he asked of Missie.

"She's whipped," I moaned. "And if this weather keeps up, we'll be in big trouble."

"Nothing but a blathering of rain, sure," he agreed. "But watch her for the string-halts, laddie. There's nothing worse for a donkey than constant rain. Keep her in at night, as much as possible."

Night was falling like a blue veil when we descended the steep hill into Ardara, and walked up the main thoroughfare to Tadhg O'Breiglean's Pub, where I asked permission to place Missie in the empty byre behind their establishment.

Teddy Breslin, the proprietor, studied me through the pub's smoky darkness.

"How do you know that byre is empty?"

"There's no hoofprints either in or out," I answered meekly.

He addressed his patrons in Irish, inducing great laughter among them, before turning to me to say, "You've become a right tinker. Place her in the empty shed, so, and step back inside for the pint."

The patrons were joking in Irish when I reentered the pub, but their smattering quickly fell back to English.

"We were after saying 'tis only yourself who would dare walk a donkey down the hill into town," Eileen Breslin, the proprietor's wife, laughed as if saving me from the real source of merriment. "Years ago, we wouldn't chance a donkey and cart down its steepness on the way home from the bog."

As I enjoyed a pint and a lorryload of chat, Eileen presented me with a brown-and-gold knitted cap, with a pom-pom the size of a softball fastened to its crown.

"You'll need this from here on out, or your two ears will be cut away from you," she said, tugging it onto my head. "There, now, have a look."

I gawked into the bar mirror, staring at that fuzzy ball of yarn on top of my head.

"What's wrong?" she asked, as my face dropped.

"I love the beanie, I really do," I hemmed and hawed. "And I've learned never to look a gift horse in the mouth and to be thankful for everything. But I wonder, Mrs. Breslin, if you might be terribly offended if I removed this large pom-pom from the top of your otherwise lovely woolen cap?"

The patrons howled.

"'Tis the style, sure," she said, mildly offended. "But if it's yourself who'll go wearing it, with or without the tuft, that'll give me pleasure enough."

Her husband Teddy, with great pomp, snipped the huge pom-pom from the cap's crest and tossed it to a child sitting wide-eyed in a corner. "There, now," he roared, "doesn't it make a grand football as well."

"Now, look at yourself in the mirror again." Eileen covered her smile with a severe tone.

I did look—a most perfect cap to keep my head warm as I headed for home.

As the evening drew to a close, I asked the patrons about the next day's road.

"I know little about the braes ye've climbed so far," said Teddy, "but if you're bound for the western cape to Glencolumbkille, ye'll be faced with the greatest challenge tomorrow in all Donegal, the Glengesh Pass."

I dropped my cap-covered skull to the counter, wondering if I had another arduous ascent in me.

Eileen handed me a postcard from the wire rack, depicting a spiraling staircase into the sky and captioned, *"Glengesh Pass rises to a thousand feet above the Glen of the Swans, one of the steepest and most dramatic alpine passes in Ireland."*

"Your donkey will need hiking boots," chuckled a local, Columba Diver. "Her white tongue will be dragging in the road when she reaches the summit."

Their chatter fell back into the old language, the better to express their amusement, I surmised, as I wondered why the Irish people, good-hearted as they are, seemed to take such delight in my every highway dilemma.

"Is there any other route?" I pleaded, breaking up their Gaelic singsong. "I've had my heart set on going to Glencolumbkille since I learned Saint Columcille lived there for years before sailing off to Iona."

"'Tis the only way," said Columba with a smirk. "When you get there, if you get there, have any native show you the dear saint's bed, for it's there still, the very way he left it."

"Aye," Teddy clapped my shoulder. "'Tis difficult to muss the sheets of a bed of stone. Why, it's all made up and waiting for you. A hard bed, boyo, where you'll wish you had kept your pom-pom for a pillow."

Next morning, Missie and I set out beneath a low, morose sky to confront Glengesh Pass. We made a steady approach through gently sloping hills, mere molehills to the Matterhorn that slowly materialized before us. At the base we craned our necks up the lofty path of Ardara Falls, which tumbled with a mighty frothing roar at our feet.

Stuffing Her Ladyship with oats, I led Missie up this high brae with our teeth gritted and heads down, undaunted by last night's chatter. We ascended a fourth of the way before stopping to look upon the steepening valley below, down which mountain sheep, near and far, bleated with fragility in this rugged world.

A cold wind swirled about us, and the rain, hinted at all morning, fell in baleful disregard. The grade, however, remained manageable until we came to the first of two hairpin turns, where the pitch was so severe I put my shoulder to the cart's tailboard to assist Missie up the stiff incline. This tactic, unfortunately, was counterproductive, for I quickly learned the more I pushed, the less Missie pulled, and the less I pushed, she didn't pull at all, which in due course left us at a standstill, with the winds piercing our eardrums like icy knives.

With this pause, I put on my newly acquired cap, wondering how I had ever fared without it, but still wavering before this upward passage.

"Where is the Good Samaritan and the sputtering choke of his tractor?" I called out to the great surrounding emptiness.

Left with no other option, I began to empty the cart, planning to carry my possessions beyond this first hairpin to where the rise eased, and return to collect Missie. Taking tent and camera-bag in hand, my two heaviest items, I set off up the mountain pass with a determined stride.

Well, guess who snapped from her listless slumber and began to follow me, bawling in a frenzied bray of desertion, but dear Missie Long-Ears, thinking I had suddenly come to my senses and was bailing out from this road of madness, leaving her to fend for herself.

She lumbered up the brae, her nose scratching the road and her back shoes slipping, as I held my position until she reached me. There, giving her a breather and another fistful of corn, I again deserted, possessions in hand. Up she crawled, bawling in her pagan roar. I hated to do it, but what else could I do? She wouldn't budge when I stood or coaxed her along.

Seven times I deserted, and seven times she strove up the incline, my eyes watering as I helplessly watched her little legs buckle beneath the heavy strain of the cart. Up, up, she persisted with heart-bursting determination, her attachment so achingly apparent that I wondered why she remained so faithful to one so unrelenting in his tactics.

Nearing the summit after her stupendous climb, we stopped before a glass-encased grotto of the Virgin and Child.

"Do you know this pair, Miss? Or have you never been told about the heroic exploits of your noble breed? It's only now, after watching you persevere up this pass, that I understand why Joseph never doubted a donkey could safely carry the Holy Family across the star-studded desert to Egypt, evading Herod's soldiers mounted on thundering steeds."

When we arrived at the car park, I lifted the cart from Missie's back, finding her coat knotted in sweat. Brushing her down, I overlooked the stark world from whence we came: a cold region with Ardara deep in the valley-bowl below, and the weak sun peeping through a rent in the gray-clouded curtain, momentarily casting its numbing light across the brown bracken floor.

"You know, Miss, this journey won't be half long enough when it comes to a close," I said, throwing an arm around her. "Here we are, you and me, the slowest float on the road, but don't you think in some strange, incomprehensible way, we're leading a colorful pageant, a dazzling procession, a grand silver-cymbaled parade?"

Glen of the Saint to Aerie of the Bishop

Glengesh was not our final challenge of the day, as we went uphill and down through an expanse of cheerless bog. We had no chance of making it to Glencolumbkille, and as we reached the top of another tiring rise, I could see a single solitary farmhouse miles off, and beyond that an endless ribbon of empty road unfurling into the gray distance.

"We better pray this farmhouse takes us in, Miss, or we'll be faced with a night we'll bitterly remember."

Dusk settling, we crossed a small bridge toward the lone farmstead. But before I could knock, its four occupants poured out the door.

"God pity you." The matron, Mary O'Boyle, grasped my hand.

"Let our two lads settle your *asal* and you come in to warm yourself." Her husband Charles ushered me into their home. "We've been watching your approach this long hour."

Their sons, Patrick and Colm—the one age as myself, but strapping men dressed in rough woolen coats and caps—led Missie toward a cow byre, and I couldn't help but think what a blessing they were to their parents in such isolation.

"Sit here by the range," Mary insisted, as she fueled the old Stanley with more sods. "Any man who has walked from Ardara to Upper Crove with a donkey deserves a seat at the end of the day."

"He deserves a seat at the right hand of the Lord," joked old Charles.

"You have a corker of a cold." Mary took note of my sniffles. "Best mind your health or your *asal* will arrive home without you."

At supper I could only look 'round and marvel once again at my luck in extremity, finding such hospitality at the end of a lonely road. Afterwards, the family turned on the radio for the seven P.M. news on Radio na Gaeltachta.

I sat comfortably among them, listening to the unintelligible Irish of the announcer, and the wind whistling around their solitary home made me feel strange and faraway.

The broadcaster's voice shifted noticeably to lightheartedness.

" 'Tis yourself they're on about!" Paddy said excitedly.

At the conclusion of the report, the O'Boyles up and cheered.

"They gave you a glowing report." Mary rose to put the kettle back on the boil. " 'The Yankee lad on his way to Glencolumbkille, traveling the old byways of Eireann with a blessed *asal*.' Ye'll be world-famous when your journey is through."

"There'll be no more talking to our like, that's for sure," said Colm. "Ye'll be passing this house in a fine motorcar, and you won't even bother to bleep your horn."

"I doubt that," I smiled.

"How many miles have ye left?" Paddy urged me to spread my maps upon the table.

"Thirteen hundred down with four hundred to go."

"You still have your work cut out for you," whistled Charles, running his finger along the coastal route toward Galway City. " 'Tis a cruel journey yet, and Mayo is a tough old go."

When the table was cleared, Mary served tea and creme roll.

"I certainly picked the right farmhouse tonight," I said, as a huge helping fell to my plate.

"We're the only farmhouse in it." Colm debunked my standard nightly line.

At night's close, after a great night of storytelling, Mary put down a fire in the sitting room, and reappeared from the press with fresh sheets and blankets.

"The Donkeyman will be tucked in tonight, so," Charles joked in sport.

"I wouldn't put out anybody in this weather," she scolded him playfully, as she fit a pillow into its case. "Anyone making a pilgrimage with a donkey to Columcille's Bed, deserves a warm bed of his own."

Next morning, after I ate a humongous hen egg laid by a most majestic hen, I was escorted a distance by Paddy and Colm, as their hospitable parents waved warmly from the door.

We crossed a bridge over the River Glen, and pushed out into empty country where moor-gates clanged unheeded on their posts. High stacks of turf, shaped like beehive cells and covered with rough thatch, stood like sentinels over fallow ground. Further to our north, a cold sleet descended the foothills of Slievetooey, as if trying to establish the first foothold of winter.

Upland, we were rewarded by a sweeping view of Glen Head, the heaving green sea and the russet fields that surround Glencolumbkille. Here and there, on roads that looked more like bridle paths, old men bent beneath wicker creels of turf or potatoes, moving toward their whitewashed cottages above the village, hailed our slow parade with the simple nod of cap.

We made a long descent into the village where three children cheered our entrance.

"We've been waiting for ye since school was let out," giggled the black-headed girl dressed in red tartan, her face glowing with the goodness of wind and rain. " 'Tis lovely you came to visit, 'tis—with a dear donkey that's the talk of the land."

"Glad to be here," I bowed, and proceeded to introduce the trio to Bucktooth Pearl.

With daylight on the wane, we managed reservations in John Byrne's hayshed and, after settling my partner in a small meadow, I walked into Brigid McShane's Pub.

"The wireless has you rightly pegged!" exclaimed old Biddy McShane, introducing me to her son, Jimmy. "They said you'd make the Glen tonight."

My reply was interrupted by a coughing fit.

"Ye have a heavy chest. I'll fix ye either a hot Paddy or a caudle of egg and ale."

"A hot Paddy will be grand."

Biddie poured whiskey into a glass and added hot water, cloves, and sugar.

"Take that down, 'tis medicinal," she ordered. "It wouldn't do you to catch pneumonia with the bogs of Mayo—God help us—still before you."

As I sipped the hot whiskey by the fire, a column of old men began to arrive, talking in their ancient tongue and congregating in small herds like Farmer Brown's cows.

"They've come down from their cabins to see the donkey pilgrim," whispered Standish O'Grady, a recent blow-in from Dublin, drawn by the heritage of Saint Columcille. "Oh, yes, look at them eyeball you, though they won't let on. Believe me, they'll be measuring your mettle all evening."

"I'm afraid I'll fail miserably," I answered the red-bearded man, and glanced at the old cronies still shuttling through the door.

"Don't sell yourself short," said Standish. "They think your journey is powerful."

A popular local, bidding all a good-evening, stepped in with a handsome sheepdog of reddish coat.

"The sheepdog comes from the fox, and the fox came to Ireland from the Danes," announced its owner directly to me. "Now, ye've traveled Ireland, and you may have heard that the best sheepdogs come from the Glens of Wicklow or Antrim. Wrong altogether, that! The best breed of collie is bred here . . . in the Holy Glen of Saint Columcille."

The pensioners, gauging me over the lips of tipped glasses, mumbled their agreement.

As the dog sat attentively, its master hung his cap on a coat peg and slipped a five-pound note beneath an ashtray on the counter. Petting his dog, he wagered, "I'll buy the house a drink if me Napper doesn't impress all here."

"Good man, yourself," a few glensmen chimed.

"Napper will first walk the Nine Steps of Mercy, take me cap off the peg, drop it to the floor, and give us a dance and a fine ballad. Are ye right?"

"Right, you are!" the pensioners called.

The sheepdog took nine steps backwards, an ancient practice upon encountering a funeral. Then he jumped and removed his master's cap from the peg, dropped it to the floor and, on hind legs, danced a lively jig around it, singing in a high yip-yapping cry. As we clapped our approval, Napper, with eyes as bright as a Rhodes scholar, hopped up on the barstool, removed the fiver from under the ashtray, and returned it to his master with a polite bow.

"Bravo!" we all shouted. "Bravo!"

Near night's end, I felt a timid tap on my shoulder.

"Would you mind terribly stepping out for a moment?" asked a young man shyly. "There's a harmless old fella outside, a neighbor of mine, who's thinking of buying a donkey, but the seller is asking a terrific price. Would you just take a quick look, now?"

I walked out into the darkness where, by the window's dim light, an old man was holding a handsome black jack by a *sugan* halter.

"Sorra to bother you, now," the old fella apologized, "and it's an honor to meet a man the likes of yourself, for you're powerful, *avic,* a right kingpin of the road. But I wonder if you might run your knowing lamps over this jacko. I need a new beast, for me old mare has fallen into a chronic class of the pains, and I'm greatly distressed without her?"

"Most certainly," I said, pleased to be called upon for judgment.

From inside, curtains were drawn to throw more light on the specimen, but the light was eclipsed by the sea of faces that crowded to the window. No longer intimidated by any such assembly, I examined the beast in a pondering manner, though in truth it was pure charade—mimicking all the farmers who had offered roadside evaluations of Missie. Even so, I found him to be a healthy two-year-old, a real prize, with a spirited lift to his head.

"He's sound as a bell," I pronounced. "As grand a donkey as ever was foaled."

"Aye, I nearly believe that meself. But, sure, the owner is asking a heavy penny."

"A pity, for he's a right champ and would do you well."

"A heavy penny," he again muttered, as a few of the gang inside the window took out hankies to wipe the heavy-breathing moisture from the panes.

"Will it lighten your purse that much?"

"Lighten it! 'Twill blow away like a blossom in a blast of wind."

"Might I ask the price?"

"Not at all. The bloody lout is asking six quid."

"Six quid!" I repeated, my countenance collapsing as I recalled the forty quid I paid for my little brown nut.

"Aye," he agreed with a deep sigh. "Didn't I tell you the bloody rogue was asking a horrible price, God forgive me for saying it."

"Buy it," I blurted, with an unpleasant vision of Jimmy Mac snickering in my face.

"Are ye certain sure?"

"As certain as our dear Pope was born in Kraków."

"It's decided, so," he said with great finality, giving a thumbs-up to the horde of onlookers in Biddy's window. He reached into his tattered coat pocket, pulled out a 50-pence piece, and planted it into my hand.

"I won't have it," I answered. "There's no need."

" 'Tis but a pint only," he said, his strong hand clamping down on my own. "Sure, 'tis luck money."

Then, after fidgeting with a knot in the donkey's mane, he shook my hand strongly before securing the halter about his wrist.

"Hup, Neddie, hup," he clucked, proudly leading his little black jack up the dark winding road to God-knows-where.

Standish O'Grady met me outside the Millstone Pub next morning, with a kind offer.

"I knew you'd be stepping out early to visit Columcille's Bed, and I thought you might appreciate a lift. Unless, of course, you had plans to be a penitent upon your knees. There's scores of other stones I can show you as well."

I gratefully climbed into his battered Ford Escort, and we soon were standing beside a four-foot-high cross-pillar.

"This is the second station of *an Turas,* 'the journey,' " Standish explained. "On June ninth, the saint's feast day, pilgrims circle fifteen Stations on a lantern-lit march commencing at midnight." His arm swung around the glen like the second hand on a watch. Clockwise again, I noted. "Four hours later they return to that Protestant churchyard below, where the first and last Stations are located.

"These stones date from the sixth century or so," he rubbed his hand along the deeply etched cross markings, "but the valley itself was inhabited for thousands of years before that. It's littered with portal tombs, court tombs, and ring forts.

" *'Na saruigther Seangleann aitreb na leic nimhe,'* said Columcille. 'Let not the Old Glen be violated, the site of the stone slabs of heaven.' "

Motoring a mile through the valley to Columcille's Bed, we could see the morning sun melting the frost that clung to the surrounding heights. Standish continued his narration, while parking his car before a farmer's gate, and nimbly hopping a stone stile.

"Columcille, like any mortal, wasn't born a saint. His name means 'Dove of the Church' in Irish—that's why he's known as Saint Columba in Latin—but he wasn't always so peaceful. Some historians blame him for a battle over a book which cost thousands of lives."

"Really? Over a book?" I followed his agile gait through rough pasture which led to the remains of the saint's chapel.

"Oh, yes, the abiding power of the book goes way back in Ireland. Always tangled up in politics, too, from the time poets sat at the right hand of the ancient kings and the wealth of monasteries poured into volumes like the Book of Kells.

"Columcille was born to power, with royal blood on both sides—from Niall of the Nine Hostages on his father's side, and the O'Donnells on his mother's—but sought his advancement in the church. He had a hand in the establishment of the great monasteries of Derry and Durrow, as well as Kells.

"Among his mentors was Finian of Moville, one of whose Psalters he went copying at night without the abbot's permission. When Finian caught wind of this, he demanded the copy, but Columcille refused. The case was brought to the High King Diarmuid, who pronounced the famous phrase: 'To every cow, her calf; to every book, its little book.' Which is said to be the foundation of all copyright law.

"But Columcille disobeyed the king's order to return it, and after one of his kin was murdered by King Diarmuid's men, a battle ensued between the High King's forces and the powerful O'Donnells, outside Drumcliff in County Sligo. Columcille's side won the clash and he retained the Psalter, which became the famous Battle Book of the O'Donnells, carried as a pledge of victory into all that historic clan's great battles."

When we reached the chapel's enclosure, cluttered with stone crosses and cairns, Standish pointed out the two large flat slabs resting upon an ancient tomb-shrine, which Columcille is supposed to have used for his bed, and finished the story:

"Sources differ on what happened next, but it's generally agreed that reparation for that battle led him to his missionary career. One can imagine him praying for forgiveness on these very stones, until his confessor gave him his penance, to go into exile and win as many to Christ as were lost at Drumcliff. So Columcille set sail for Iona in the Hebrides, not looking back on Eireann's shores for thirty years, saving souls and earning sainthood as 'the Apostle of Caledonia.' Now, enough of my blabbering and make your visitation while I walk the fields. There's no rush, 'tis a lovely morning, thank God."

Left to my own ceremony, I walked outside the crumbled walls and circled the chapel three times clockwise, reciting the mandatory Credo, five Pater's and five Ave's. Then I reentered the ruins and lay flat on Columcille's Bed for some time, making my intentions from this westernmost terminus of ancient Ulster; directing my prayers eastward toward the troubles that divide it still.

Returned by Standish to the village, I set out with Missie at midmorning into an all-too-familiar landscape of brae, bog, and tarn. Reaching Carrick in the afternoon, we were accosted by an excitable old man in front of the church, his eyes brimming with intensity.

"You mustn't miss the marine cliffs of Slieve League," he urged. "They're the highest in Europe and 'twill be a grand evening. So settle your donkey and make your way to Bunglass Head. If you miss the cliffs, boy, your roundabout is not complete."

Swayed by his enthusiasm, I settled early in nearby Bogagh, and told my host I hoped to reach the cliffs for sunset. Michael Galligan was an accommodating policeman and drove me back to Carrick, hailing a fellow on a tractor heading toward Bunglass.

"You're a lucky man," confided Mr. Doherty, making room on the seat for me. "This is the first evening in near a fortnight that you'll have a clear view of the cliffs."

We ascended a steep road as he shouted above the diesel's strain.

"I live in Teelin below," he nodded toward a fishing village to our left, "but I'll take you up to where the path leads to the *amharc mor,* 'the grand view.' You'll have just enough time to follow the Pilgrim's Path and visit the old hermitage there."

He left me a thousand feet above sea level, and I passed a crumbling Martello Tower and scampered up a winding path to where a stupendous view burst before me, the grand view indeed. Initially my eyes could not comprehend the sheer height and dizzying drop of these cliffs down to the sea. Touched by the setting sun, the immense face of speckled stone gleamed in a dazzling display of red, purple, and gold.

Collecting my wits, I dashed up the Pilgrim's Path and came to the remnants of a holy well and beehive cell, the towering outpost of the physician Bishop Aed Mac Bricne, who had resided here in the sixth century. Atop this mystical retreat, I stuck my head over the cliffs' grassy edge, to watch seabirds below wheeling above thrashing waves. In the distance the spilling sun dipped languidly into the sea, extinguishing the cliff's vibrant colors as it doused its own.

From my lofty aerie on this titanic seawall, I gazed southwest across Donegal Bay to where a band of gold cloud hovered above the vast blue tableland of Connacht, with its clutter of romantic hills: Ben Bulben, the Ox Mountains, the cone of Croagh Patrick, and beyond that, the Connemara Pins.

"So that's what's left us," I murmured, surveying our last province from this exalting vantage, this drover's station, this door to the Divine.

A Walk to Ballyshannon

CHAPTER FIFTY-FOUR

Later that evening I found myself babysitting the Galligans' three daughters for a short while, a pleasant change from singing for my supper nightly. The eager trio clustered around the strange wayfarer with the funny mustache.

"Give us a song?" begged little Eimear, jumping up on my lap.

"I won't," I refused with crossed arms. "I only serenade my donkey."

"Why is that?" demanded Geraldine.

"Because she's the only singer I'm better than, that's why."

"Give us a riddle or a rhyme, then," pleaded Anne.

"A gentleman back in Antrim told me walking was the perfect way to compose poetry. So I've made up a few silly verses on the long road."

"Let's hear them, so." Eimear threw her arms about me.

Knowing I'd never have a more rapt and attentive audience, I cleared my throat and recited:

> "I won myself a donkey at the Lammas Fair,
> A wee little donkey from God-knows-where,
> She nipped like a goat and looked pure silly,
> And when she brayed, my head fell dizzy."

They clapped and squealed for another.

> "I've seen pookas and leprechauns,
> Will-o'-the-wisps and dallahans,

But the only one I hope to see
Is the gentle angel who calls for me."

"Ah, lovely, that," they sighed, easily won over. "Another, so."

"I found a bear in Ballintubber,
Took it home and fed it supper,
Washed its face and scrubbed its paws
And kept him then, forever braw."

Face-washing and paw-scrubbing led directly to a game of hide-and-seek, a heart-bursting chase up and down the staircase, until Michael and Anna Galligan returned home to settle their little nest of chicks.

The next day Missie and I made our way out of the Gaeltacht and the helpful reach of its radio station, which had shepherded us from Fanad Head to Slieve League. Like a slow-moving roller coaster we went up and down a number of formidable hills, but at the crest of each we were rewarded with thrilling vistas of Donegal Bay.

On the Killybegs Road, a farmer stopped his tractor beside us.

"Your donkey is high-stepping!" he exclaimed, showing concern.

"Please?"

"Your donkey is high-stepping, meaning she could have the string-halts . . . cold kidneys. Is she having trouble watering?"

"Not that I've noticed," I gulped. "She whizzes whenever and wherever she likes."

"String-halts can be serious," he said gravely, bending down to palpate Missie's underbelly. "She doesn't feel bloated, but best keep an eye on her in fear she's holding fluids."

"Anything I can do?" I asked, having noticed a difference in Missie's gait this last week.

"If you see her struggling at the task, try whistling, as it often relaxes them. Also, try putting a pinch of flour into her water bucket each night. Otherwise, best call a vet before her condition worsens. And, whatever you do, keep her sheltered. God knows, there's nothing worse than the cold rain belting off her back."

"Could it just be a muscle pull?" I asked in a muddle over this newborn crisis. "She had a hard pull up Glengesh, and another out from the Glen."

" 'Tis possible, but the only way to rule out the string-halts is to see her piddling mighty."

Miss and I continued through lovely country, but my day of ambitious adventure had been replaced with high anxiety. However I tried, I could not recall the last time Missie had peed. And if Missie did have the string-halts, would her condition worsen or become chronic, jeopardizing not only our journey but her overall health as well?

We trekked through Kilcar, a center for handwoven tweed, and in the face of a scowling sky I decided to push for the far side of Killybegs. A mistake, that, for the rains came while we were passing through the narrow winding streets of the thriving fishing port—a gray town with a bay full of fishing trawlers and low clouds, smelling like sardines. It was a long, damp mile out of town before we came to a farmhouse with suitable outbuildings.

Tying Missie to the gate after her yeoman effort, I shook off what wet I could and knocked on the farmhouse door. Hmm, no answer, though lights were on in the house, and I heard the unmistakable shuffling of feet within. After my second knock was left unanswered, I circled the yard thrice clockwise in a round of prayer, snooping through the kitchen window at each lap. Then as I raised my icy-blue knuckles for a third pounding, the door flew wide open and I was confronted with the business end of a swinging broom.

"I don't care what you're fixing, mending, selling, or buying!" the vexed old harridan behind it screeched. "I want you off my land!"

The door shut with a slam.

I stood out in the dismal rain, stunned and sodden. I looked at Missie Ragged-Ears, drenched to the bone, her chicklets chattering. Knowing the next village was beyond McSwyne's Bay, I had little choice but to give the door another hard rap.

"Be clearing out of this!" the old grappler sputtered from within her sealed enclosure. "Be streeling along, I tell ya, or I'll deliver such a blow to your cradle-cap, ye'll be stuttering for years!"

"But, please," I begged. "My name is Kevin O'Hara. I'm from America and I'm going 'round Ireland with my don—"

"I don't care if you're John the Baptist proclaiming 'the Good News,' you simple gomeral! Now, get, or ye'll be gimping off, I promise."

I floundered through the muck toward Missie, who read our doom in my face and went to roaring.

A slit of light escaped the farmhouse door. "Arragh, the poor wee donkey," lilted the woman, soft as a mother might lullaby her round-faced, smile-dimpled child. "'Tis been many a year since I've heard the song of ould Nellie . . . God be good to her and all craytures like her. Many a day I gave her a candy-sweet to shorten the long road home with a creel-load of turf on her back."

My hopes reviving, I turned my face into the light with the humble appeal of a blinking idiot. Her own face hardened. "Don't be looking up at me like some sad and sorra pup. There's a shedeen a mile up the road that'll do ya for the night."

With that, the door slammed with pronounced finality, and we were forced to return to the road, gritting our teeth to move on toward that "shedeen," however godforsaken it might turn out to be.

But just then a car pulled up and the driver leaned out with a laugh. "Run off, were ye? A lovely woman, God knows, but living alone these long years she's become a bitteen ornery. Now, can't you stay with us, just up the road? Conal Breslin is my name. I'm a weaver over in the village of Glen, and yourself I know to be the donkey pilgrim who lay atop Columcille's Bed."

Well, the good saint must have been watching out for me, as the Breslins had both bed and byre, and so it only seemed natural to accompany them to Mass in Killybegs the following Sunday morning. Yet it wasn't all as pious as one might imagine. It was the Feast of Martinmas, November 11, but the white-haired priest took the occasion to lash out at his flock during the homily.

"I'm tired of hearing the clatter of tenpenny coins in the collection basket every Sunday morning," he fumed from the pulpit, directing his gaze toward an assembly of men at the rear of the church, "when pound notes will fall as plentiful as autumn leaves later in the pubs."

I glanced back at these fishermen and farmers tugging at stiff collars and sporting a nick or two from a hurried morning shave, though none appeared to be too ruffled by the priest's reprimand. During my donkey-go-round, I had often knelt in gray country chapels and wondered about these vestibule dwellers, whose wives and children sat attentive and well-attired in the upper pews, while they loitered at the back, silent and detached. Not an "Alleluia" would escape their lips, though most of these chaps would lustily belt out "The Night Before Larry Was Stretched," at a publican's last call.

I would get to musing that their stance at the rear of the church was a holdover from Penal Times, keeping an eye out for red-coated dragoons who attacked worshipers at Mass Rocks. I had heard another theory that these rustic Celts were holdouts against the Synod of Whitby in 664 A.D. According to the Venerable Bede, it was assembled by King Oswy of Northumbria to decide between the Celtic and Roman dates for Easter. But the historical fact, that a mere century after the glory of Iona the tide turned against the civilization-saving Celtic church, and meant to these countrymen that the Roman Catholic hierarchy had the gall to say that Patrick, Brigid, and Columcille were second-stringers to the likes of Peter, Paul, and Bartholomew.

Or maybe the reason goes back even further, to the pagan ancestors of these latter-day Celts. They might find it more natural to commune with the Creator in meadow or river or night sky, and see the glory of God in the birth of a lamb, the flash of a salmon, or a falling star in a moment of prayer.

Dead silence fell over the congregation as the collection basket made its way toward the rear of the church. There, the vestibule dwellers one by one dropped their traditional offering in the basket, with the unmistakable clink of a single coin.

"You're a hard lot," the priest roughly chastised as he turned to the altar. "May God find it in His heart to forgive you."

The Breslins saw me off with a splendid Sunday dinner, and Missie and I clipped through a solid dozen miles, looking out at the lighthouse at St. John's Point and pattering past Inver Bay, to wind up in Drimconnor, as guests of Gabriel and Brede Murray in their large farmhouse.

After I told Gabriel of my string-halt worries, this pleasant young man with long blond hair led Missie to a dry shed where he put down a fresh bed of straw.

"We'll soon know if she has a problem," he said, watching her gulp down a half-bucket of water. "Now, come in for the tea, and let's hope nature takes its course."

I was presently in the kitchen being introduced as "the lad on the telly up North," to

Brede, their four handsome children, and Brede's mother and uncle, Mrs. Gallagher and Uncle Charlie.

After tea, I stepped outside to check on Missie.

"No luck," I said, upon my return.

Ten minutes later, I excused myself again.

"Still no luck," I groaned, flopping back into a chair by the door.

"You're like a jack-in-the-box," commented Brede. "You're probably making her so nervous she'll never go."

"He's pure anguished," said Mrs. Gallagher to Brede. "I'd hate to see the state of him if she were ever in foal."

"She wouldn't have gone eleven miles if she had the string-halts," consoled Uncle Charlie. "I think you're right about it being a muscle strain."

Later, after the children were tucked into their beds, Gabriel stepped out to check his cattle as well as Missie. He returned to the kitchen whistling.

"Any luck?" I asked hopefully, lifting myself off the chair.

He gave no answer, but went straight for the cupboard and poured out a glass of whiskey.

"What's this?"

" 'Tis whiskey, sure," he laughed, handing it to me, "for your donkey has thoroughly wet her bed. Now, peg that back, can't you, for the road again is beneath your feet."

After a late night of storytelling and a string of arduous days on the road, I fell into a record-breaking fourteen-hour snooze and woke to a brilliant afternoon.

"Stay on a second day, can't you," urged Gabriel. "Missie is out with the cows, and the sunshine will do her good without those old trappings on her back."

After a king's breakfast, I was lifted into Donegaltown where I visited Donegal Castle on the banks of the River Eske, the former stronghold of the O'Donnells. From there I ambled into the town's diamond and stood at the foot of a tall obelisk, a memorial to the Four Masters, thinking of my own quartet at Rattigan's.

"Do you know anything about the four annalists?" asked an old fella sitting on a nearby bench.

"Just a little."

"Well, the Four Masters literally saved the history of Ireland. In the 1630s they collected, copied, and compiled every existing document of Irish history from the Great Deluge to the Flight of the Earls. Brother Michael O Cleary was the leader of four Franciscan brothers supported by the O'Donnells. He traveled throughout Ireland collecting the precious vellum books of Annals, and here at Donegal Abbey the four labored for four years and more, copying and editing them. Their fears that the original parchments might perish proved only too prophetic, as none survived the Plantation and the invasions of Cromwell and William later that century. But the Annals of the Four Masters survive and remain the primary resource of Irish history up to their time. A great undertaking, was it not?"

"Yes, and a powerful accomplishment," I agreed.

I joined my well-informed old guide in gazing reverently up at the monument. "Yes, they survive to this day," he concluded. "And ourselves with it, thanks be to God."

Tuesday came hard with rain, but we had to bid a fond farewell to the Murrays and set out on the high, wet road, back through Donegaltown and on to Flower Hill, where we bunked for the night in a large barn with eleven hacking cows, which I nicknamed the Kine Sanatorium.

The next day we progressed under a variable sky past the Pullans, limestone caves famous for the "wee people" said to have inhabited them. At dusk, with fresh winds cresting ocean waves, we knocked at the door of an old thatched house in Tullyhart, two miles shy of Ballyshannon.

"You're saying you don't mind sleeping with your donkey in my barn?" said a pleasant old lady, smiling broadly at the pair of us. "Bunk your mate, so, before you're both blown asunder."

I settled Missie and entered the cozy kitchen of Martha Carbery, who introduced me to her son John, himself in his fifties. Long logs of ash wood crackled in an open hearth and paraffin lamps flickered their little light upon the exposed rafters of this old country home.

"One day we might sign on for the electricity," John commented, as I peered around the dimly glowing interior. "But doesn't paraffin do the job to our satisfaction?"

Martha, still a lovely woman well into her seventies, fixed up some eggs and toast for supper, while we listened to the strengthening sea-gales struggle to lift the thatch from over our heads.

"God help you," she smiled, watching me slather my toast with butter. "You must be leading a desperate existence entirely."

"It isn't too bad," I replied through a mouth stuffed with egg.

We ate to the rattling of panes and the whistling of wind, and Martha asked John if he was going out on such a wild and savage night.

"There's a *ceili* beyond the hill where I'm expected. How about you? Will you chance your Mothers' Union Meeting?"

"I think I shall," she affirmed, and turned to me. "I'm going to a church meeting in Ballyshannon, and I wonder if you might accompany me. You could have a pint at a pub while waiting. If we're out on the road at half-seven, there's a good chance we'll be lifted into town."

Martha and I soon stood at the edge of the road in the face of a froth of sea-spittle, but with no sign of headlamps coming down the black road, she conceded, "It might be best to move on. They'll know me if they pass. Are you right, then?"

We walked into the dark of this windswept road beside the turbulent sea, with me recounting my recent travels, and her replying with a verse about Slieve League from Ballyshannon's own poet laureate, William Allingham.

We pushed on, heads down, until a great gust stopped us dead in our tracks.

"Are you right for this?" I shouted into the wind.

"What are you saying?" she called back through the roar.

"Can you walk these two miles into Ballyshannon, and maybe have to walk back home again?"

"I hope so." She took my arm and braced herself anew. "Didn't I do it last night!"

The incessant gale battered away until we had to laugh at the sheer absurdity of trying to make headway against the elements.

"This is surely a comedy," she exclaimed, her free hand gripping the knot of her wet kerchief. "Here we are, heading into a forbidding wind, me an old Protestant mother on the way to her Union Meeting, and yourself a Catholic lad, a fine rebel no doubt, arm-and-arm together in the face of the storm.

"When I first set out on my journey, I was for a united Ireland. Now, I'll gladly settle for a peaceful island."

" 'Tis unimaginable to think of the heartbreak religion has caused this country." She turned suddenly serious, bending her shoulders into the wind. "Ireland, North and South, should be a beacon of light upon our troubled world, not another open wound."

The gale gusted so hard off the white-breasted Atlantic, we were forced to take refuge behind a stone wall, with the ravenous winds whistling through chinks of stone.

"There was a Catholic lad who fancied me once," she continued, hunched low behind the wall, rain dripping from her face. "A young handsome lad, Eddie Connolly, but a right chancer, trying to get into our Church of Ireland dances. But not a hope had he, for everyone knew everybody. Still, he tried on several occasions, even disguising himself once, all for a chance to dance with me."

A pensive expression crossed her usually cheerful countenance.

"It was only a dance, mind you, and I would have danced with him gladly—for wouldn't any girl take notice of a lad so insistent, so willing to risk a bully's beating? A pity, wasn't it, to be separated from the merest contact by the churches we attended.

"But let's get on with it, shall we," she rallied, standing up to renew our march. "We look like a pair of drowned rats, so we do."

We made slow but steady progress until Martha pointed to a sign just ahead. "There, now—Ballyshannon 'on the winding banks of the Erne,' or 'Belashanny,' as Mr. Allingham called it:

" 'The kindly spot, the friendly town, where every one is known,
And not a face in all the place but partly seems my own.'

" '*The kindly spot . . . the friendly town,*' " she repeated with a sigh. "Oh, if only that had been true."

Again it was only for a moment that a cloud crossed her bright but sopping-wet face. "But we made it, you and I, didn't we?" She perked up, her radiance returning. And, taking a better grasp of my arm, she led me through this old British garrison town. Her steps as lively as any reel. The wet shining streets our dance floor.

Beneath Maeve's Crown

CHAPTER FIFTY-FIVE

The next day Missie and I strolled through Ballyshannon in kind daylight, despite the continuing wind and contrary sky. In front of a fine clock tower on the town's main street, we had our picture taken for the *Donegal Democrat*. From this vantage on a steep bluff over the River Erne, we could see the castle of Belleek over in the Northern Ireland County of Fermanagh.

Ballyshannon is situated in a narrow corridor of the Republic between Fermanagh and the sea, and it is easy to imagine the anxieties of the town's Protestants when Donegal was split from historic Ulster in the settlement of 1920. But, as with the other planted towns we had passed through, this one was prosperous and showed no ill-effects of the divorce.

Through miles of checkered fields beyond the Erne, we had a distant view of Ben Bulben, jutting above the plain. From this perspective it looked like a giant icebreaker, its weathered prow plowing toward the seaside resort of Bundoran, where we arrived in due course. So popular in the summer, Bundoran was all but deserted as we walked the mile-long strip of shore. Harsh winds banged up against the corrugated metal facades of closed-up fun parks and arcades. No sauntering day-trippers along Tullan Strand on this raw November day, only twisters of sand playing tag upon the high dunes.

Rejoining the main road to Sligo, with Missie shying away from the heavy rumble of lorries, we soon came to a signpost, WELCOME TO LOVELY LEITRIM, and entered the seventeenth county of our trek.

A young burly man hailed me from his farmhouse: "Leitrim has only three miles of coastline, so you'd be cutting us short if you didn't spend one night in it."

Gladly accepting his invitation, I soon sat in comfort with my two hosts, Don and

Joan Daly of Red Brae, enjoying a hefty helping of shepherd's pie, and a serving of Leitrim lore.

"So, it took you thirty days to get through Donegal, and it wouldn't have taken you an hour for Leitrim unless we stopped you," laughed Joan. "That doesn't say much for our dear 'Cinderella county,' does it?"

"Poorest in Ireland," Don confided. "Our people depart and the tourists don't visit."

"We do have the sea-monster of Lough Allen, though." Joan stood to her county's defense.

"But we may be most famous for the murder of the cruel Lord Leitrim, back in 1878," Don went on. "The only clue was a tuft of bloody red hair found in the clutches of the landlord's fist. The British garrison combed the countryside, searching for any redheaded male with a hank of hair missing from his scalp, but they bitterly discovered that every redhead in the vicinity was sporting a recent bald patch. That shows the indomitable spirit of the Leitrim people, does it not?"

Next morning, Missie and I traipsed through the small village of Cliffony, County Sligo, stopping to gaze seaward at Classiebawn Castle, perched like a fairy-tale dwelling atop the green headland of Mullaghmore: the regal high-turreted mansion of the late Lord Mountbatten, who met his death on August 27 in the bay below.

With a "white" southern wind lending an unseasonable mildness to the next day, Missie and I continued along the main road between the sea and the heights of the Darty Range until we were truly "under Ben Bulben." I called in at a little bungalow just outside Grange, and was welcomed by James and Ellen Waters.

"That's quite a sight parked outside your door," I said to the elderly couple, admiring the fabled mountain.

" 'Tis mighty indeed," agreed James, with as much enthusiasm as if he were seeing it for the first time. "As a lad, I'd spend my summer days on those slopes hunting rabbits or searching for boar tusks."

"Boar tusks?"

"Boyhood dreaming, I confess," he admitted with a laugh. "But there's native forest on the southern slope and once upon a time it was overrun with fierce swine. Diarmuid, the great warrior of the Fianna, was mortally wounded by a wild boar there, fulfilling an old prophecy, and died in the arms of his lover, Grania."

"Did you pass any of their beds scattered about the country?" asked Ellen. "The pair were on the run from King Fionn for many years."

"Oh, yes," I was happy to recall. "I visited one in the Burren in County Clare."

"Poulnabrone," she confirmed. "Do you know that a barren woman only needs to spend a night upon Poulnabrone's capstone if she wishes to have a child?"

"Providing a frisky fella shares the same capstone," James added with a wink.

The couple extolled the other sights of Yeats country and invited me to stay another night, but I sadly declined, citing the hundreds of miles I still had to travel. When they settled before the telly for the evening to watch a horse show, I excused myself and walked back to Grange. I came upon a quaint grocery pub called John Lang's, entered, and was soon chatting with Kevin McHugh, a native who recommended another local sight, the island of Inishmurray, with its extensive ruins of a monastery plundered by the Vikings in 807 A.D. Among the remains are baskets of cursing stones.

" 'Cursing stones'?"

"Oh, aye," he answered. "All one need do is choose one, give it a rub, and recite a curse against your enemy. Presto! Very effective, they are."

"Have you ever tried one?"

"Me?" he howled. "What would I be doing with the likes of enemies?"

Late that evening, a rustic elder burst through the door, waving a check in hand and exclaiming in a cracked voice, "Look what came in today's post! A check for ten thousand pounds!"

"Did you enter the sweepstakes?" asked Mr. Lang, as the few patrons swarmed around the old fellow.

"No, it just came out of the blue," said the bedazzled farmer, bracing himself against the counter.

While several thumped his back in congratulations, one officious local scrutinized the check and declared, "I'm sorry, Mick, but I'm afraid this check is nothing more than a cod. Look, it says right here, 'non-negotiable.' That's a fancy way of saying it's worthless."

"I wouldn't mind all of that!" broke in another old-timer, sporting a huge, dark-veined honker. "Look at the rest, can't you! Your name properly spelt in fine black print, and ten thousand pounds stamped boldly in red. Who'd go to such bother if it wasn't the genuine article? I suppose they go printing 'non-negotiable,' so you don't go straining a heartstring after running your eyes over all those zeros."

"Did it come with a letter?" interrupted the wiser head.

Old Mick hemmed and hawed and reluctantly pulled a letter from his coat pocket, which Mr. Purple-Snout quickly snatched from his grasp.

" 'You are one of a select number of people in Ireland eligible for a grand prize of ten thousand pounds,' " he read aloud. "Sure, now, doesn't that say it all? Why, you're as eligible as a bachelor claiming his bride. 'Non-negotiable' just means you don't have to bargain over it. Go to the Bank of Ireland in Sligo tomorrow, and ye'll come home swimming in money. Think of the soiled stubs the auctioneers do be handing out on fair days, and the banks go cashing them without question. This check is much trustier-looking than that."

"A round for all!" announced Old Mick, his hopes reviving.

The lout with the prominent snout elbowed aside the sensible patron for a spot right at the shoulder of the man of good fortune. Sipping the spoils, he inquired, "And what might you do with your newfound wealth?"

"Buy a few head of cattle, what else?" Old Mick answered, propping up the check before him.

"Now that you're so eligible, you should go to next year's Bachelor's Fair in Lisdoonvarna and bring home a bride," suggested another happy patron, the quiet Friday evening spinning into a night of unbridled promise.

"I'd need a new suit for that," said Old Mick, rubbing his chin and smiling at the thought.

"Buy one at Corcoran's, can't you, then you'd be all made-up," added his new best buddy. "Didn't Leo Gately make a fine catch at that fair last September, a pretty whippersnapper who's been winning baking ribbons ever since. And he a man who couldn't look at a woman unless he was moidered in drink. They say there's magic in those Clare uplands, drawing couples together like nails to magnets!"

I didn't know about nails, but someone was getting hammered.

"Nails to magnets," he repeated, jabbing Old Mick playfully, as fresh pints descended upon the oak counter as if from an unquenchable stream.

"I might try it," Mick mused, eyeing his pint gleefully and lifting a toast to the house. "Sure, I'm only seventy, and there's a little spark in me old horn yet."

So there Mick sat, no more a toiler of soil but a man of means, with each gulp of stout confirming his new status, never mind the walloping dent to his weekly pension packet. As Old Mick's rank in the world was rising to limitless heights, a man and woman came through the door in an uproar.

"Such a bloody hoax!" the fella guffawed, waving a check identical to Old Mick's above his head. "I thought I was made-up, planning to buy a new Leyland tractor to replace my old Ferguson, and over to Mary's I dash, and sure, she's holding the same check as me own."

"And there I was sitting," Mary chuckled in embarrassment, "planning a visit to my sisters in Chicago. Why, my heart leapt clear to my throat when I opened the envelope. Then Tom barges in and spoils it all. We read over the river of print and found we had a million-to-one shot to win the grand prize, and then only if we subscribed to a heap of magazines. Weren't we proper eejits to think money could come so easy? Those people should be fined, raising false hopes in half of Sligo."

They continued to make jolly over their own gullibility, until the publican caught their eye with a nod toward Old Mick, staring lifelessly at the junk-mail check enshrined so reverently before him.

"Jaysus, Mick, we're ever so sorry," the pair quickly apologized to the old man, realizing they had been firing grapeshot into Mick's brittle sides.

But it was a long minute before the cadaver showed signs of resuscitation.

"I suppose the money would have been a botheration in the long run," Mick sighed, picking up the check and tearing it in pieces, as Mr. Purple-Snout slithered away to a dark corner. Mick consoled himself with a copious gulp of stout. "Here I was thinking of buying meself a new suit, and scooting down to Lisdoonvarna next September to find meself a bride."

"Whatever about the bride," Mary teased the resurrected Mick, "but purchase a new suit whatever the cost. Your pants are worn to such a well-chaffed sheen, the choirgirls break out into a fit of giggles when you walk to the altar rail on Sundays."

Tom joined in the needling: "If not for the size, one could take it for your First Communion suit."

"I never knew me suit was the topic of the parish." Old Mick stood on his dignity. "But to hear you bloody bliggards tell it, I'm no better dressed than the scarecrows in your stony fields."

"God forgive me," Mary broke down in sobs of laughter, "but your threadbare pants makes your arse look like two goose eggs tied up in a silk hankie!"

It was drizzling next morning, with Ben Bulben slumbering beneath a gray blanket of mist, as we approached Drumcliff and the churchyard where the great modern Irish bard William Butler Yeats is buried. I had visited the poet's grave years earlier, and would have done so again, but for the tour bus that pulled in ahead of me, dispensing a parade of Yankee Doodle Dandies.

Unfortunately, they turned their backs on the poet's advice to "Cast a cold eye/On life, on death," and would not let this donkeyman pass by, gathering around me with cameras clicking, and so I became the quaint tinkerman I was supposed to be.

"Where are you headed?" one of them asked, with her finger poised to snap my shot.

"My grannie's in Roscommon," I answered in a feigned accent no Irish county would claim.

"Roscommon?"

" 'Tis in the midlands." I pointed to the middle of my raised palm.

"How long will it take you to get to your Grannie's?" asked another, from under a new *bainin* cap.

"Christmas, God willing."

"I hope you're not bringing her her next meal," snorted one toothy mare.

" 'Meals on Donkey Wheels,' " braved another, as they scurried back across the highway, nearly being flattened by an oncoming lorry, for they, like myself, instinctively looked left rather than right when taking their first step off the curb.

Eager to be off the main thoroughfare and back to quiet country roads, Missie and I pushed through Sligo, the largest town in the northwest, after a pleasant Saturday night with Ernie Donaghey and family. We stopped only to salute the truncated limestone cone of Knocknarea looming high above the flatlands west of town. Atop its summit is a gigantic cairn of stone, where the legendary Queen Maeve of Connacht is supposed to be buried, though I remember Headmaster D'Alton arguing she was interred at Rathcroghan, "the ancient palace of the kings," not far from Rattigan's—appropriately enough, since Roscommon was the seat of her kingdom.

No matter. Maeve, or "Meabh," means "She Who Intoxicates," and I meant to pay my respects. The ancient annals tell of her fierce struggles against Cuchulainn and the Red Branch Knights of Ulster over the fabled Brown Bull of Cooley, and goddess-worshipers make much of her magical powers. She offered "the friendship of my thighs" to many noble warriors, and claimed, "I never was without one man in the shadow of another." A truly pagan queen, that.

She also boasted she could walk the world armed only with hazel, so it was only proper that I should raise my own hazel in salute to her.

But in doing so, I noticed a severe crack beginning to extend down my stick's length. And it hadn't been cracked upon Missie's back, I swear—for I hadn't struck my dear beast since the warble-fly attack at O'Neill's Camp—but by the stroke of a thousand stones golfed out of our path along the way. What would I ever do if Ty O'Kelly should fail?

Passing through the pretty village of Ballysadare, we turned off the main road and headed west toward Beltra, the Ox Mountains stretching out before us toward the Mayo border, looking like mud-pies flung far across the monotonous moor. If we had felt crowded off the road through parts of Sligo, here we were now alone without a car or lorry in sight.

Out of nowhere in an otherwise clear sky, a single dark cloud passed over us and sopped us silly, but in the wake of the cloudburst came an iridescent sunburst, and a dazzling rainbow sprang from the bog and made a perfect arch over our path, so vibrant and palpable that Missie balked before it, so splendidly prismatic, I felt I was at the gateway to the Otherworld.

Having logged our daily quota of miles and being slow to dry out even when the sun returned, I secured lodgings at a grocery pub owned by Henry and Joan Collery of Beltra, who showed no hesitation in inviting us in for the night, though they hadn't "a bull's notion" of our travels.

"You'll have a bath before a pint," Joan insisted, appalled by the appearance of the drowned weasel at her door. She led me to the bathroom and began to fill the tub, her arm swishing elbow-deep to test the water's temperature. "Here. Soak yourself in that," she directed, pointing out the soap and shampoo.

"Am I that scruffy?"

"You don't want me to tell you the truth, do you?" she exited with a laugh.

I dropped into the clear water, my first bath since the Beach Hotel—almost a month ago.

Forcing myself to take inventory of my frightful nakedness, I looked down upon my translucent blue-veined body, not well-chiseled but well-whittled. I stepped out of the bath and onto the scales: a paltry 128 pounds—a real skinamalink, but down only seven pounds since I set out, not bad for a fella who'd been living by the hand of generosity for half a year.

"How was your bath?" Grandma Carroll asked, when I had stepped into the lounge section; she was Joan's mother and had a birdlike alertness into her nineties.

"I'm a new man," I pronounced. "Only half a stone lighter since I've been on the road."

"Imagine that," Henry Collery said to three patrons at the bar. "This young man is walking around Ireland with a donkey since April and has only lost a pound a month."

"He wouldn't want to go many months further." One of the three appraised me with a sly look.

" 'Tis remarkable, really." Grandma Carroll leapt to my defense. "What a book it would make. But you'd best write it fast if I'm to get a chance to read it. Here, give us your autograph so I'll have it when the book comes out."

I choked on a peanut, but complied with her embarrassing request.

"Oh, yes, I can see it now," remarked the blackguard, "right on the cover in bold print: *The Mare and Her Jackass.*"

"The Little Mare Who Could," chortled the second.

"I've got it," added the third: *"The Jack Who Would, But the Mare Who Wouldn't."*

"Enough," Grandma Carroll piped up, giving my tormentors a withering glance. "Kevin will go grinning to the bank one day, please God, and it won't be an ass that will carry him, but a fine motorcar."

" 'Tis only sport, Kevin knows," said my mocker, shaking my hand warmly and motioning Henry to stand me a pint. "But you walking the ass reminds me of a story.

"There was this priest from a poor parish who had an idea to raise money by running for stakes. He couldn't afford a horse, so had to settle for a donkey. But he was a man of great faith and entered the animal in a nearby race. And, by God, didn't the little creature come in third. The local paper headlined next morning: Local Priest's Ass Shows!

"The following week, the priest entered his donkey in another race and this time it won outright. Next day the headline blared: Priest's Ass Outshines Them All! The bishop caught wind of the rude captions and forbade the priest to enter his donkey in another race. The paper duly reported: Bishop Scratches Priest's Ass!

"At the sight of this banner, the irate bishop ordered the priest to sell the damn donkey altogether. The priest obeyed his superior and delivered his donkey to a nun at a nearby convent. The tiny tabloid proclaimed: Nun Now Has the Best Ass in Town!

"The bishop, in a state of apoplexy, demanded that the nun rid herself of the beast. Obediently, she sold it to a local farmer, and the rag ran the story: Nun Sells Her Ass for Ten Quid!

"Next week the paper of record had a black-bordered headline: Bishop O'Leary to be Buried Today!"

Refreshed by bath and beverage, I rolled through the lonely western extremities of County Sligo over the next few days, ticking off mile after mile. We passed through Easky, renowned for good surfing in the summer, and turned south from Leenadoon Point, along the eastern shore of Killala Bay toward Ballina.

Our only companions on this solitary road were the skylarks hovering above and the heaving sea crashing against sharp rocks below. Yes, all was as it should be in this vast desolation, that is, until my long-eared siren began to sing out that she was ready for romance.

From the isolated hamlets of Carrowpadeen, Rathlee, and Kilglass she summoned every jack within earshot, her wanton bawl awakening the senses of every ass, from adolescent to senile. Oh, how they came pogo-sticking along! Poor homely jacks, their thin flanks mud-caked, with droopy ears and crusted eyes. Sadder than Eeyore but hopped-up all the same. The way these horned-up soldiers roared at Missie's passing, you'd think she was Raquel Welch performing a USO show in the back of Beyond.

Indeed, the coastal region blared with such blasphemous song, I imagined the heads of selkies and merrows bobbing curiously in the folds of sea, turning as if toward the trump of doom, awaiting the call to emerge from the briny depths and inherit the Earth.

Between Shamrock and Harp

It was Wednesday, the twenty-first of November, when we tramped into County Mayo, and beneath a dove-gray sky crossed the River Moy into the market town of Ballina. The tall spire of St. Muireadach's Cathedral welcomed me like a medieval pilgrim after a lonely trek.

In the town, we were approached by Eilis Ward of the *Western Journal*. "You must be mad," smiled the enthusiastic reporter, gleefully jotting down the particulars of our journey. "Did you escape a booby hatch back home?"

"In a manner of speaking," I nodded knowingly, thinking of the ward where I worked.

Missie and I were strolling up Tone Street when a pack of dogs came trooping toward us. My shaggy beast dropped her head defensively, but the canines sauntered by, paying no heed. What a collection of champions they were: every breed of mongrel—cur, mutt, jeff, pooch, whelp, gyp—bonded only by their exclusion from the Westminster Dog Show. Yet they stepped along proudly as any pampered pets prancing over the royal-blue carpet.

"That pack has run together for years," said a passerby, seeing me turn to watch their procession, "and they'll continue to do so, for Ballina won't follow any leash law laid down by Dublin. Aye, they do soil up the place, but isn't it grand to see the animals at liberty?"

Sensing my confusion, he clarified, "During the Famine you wouldn't see a dog at all in most of Mayo. When one in three people perished, there were much longer odds on any dog's survival."

This was obviously a chap with a story to tell, so I was happy to have him accompany me to the end of Tone Street, where we stopped at a statue of a noble woman with upraised sword and a hound at her feet, dedicated by Maude Gonne in 1898 to commemorate "the Year of the French" a century earlier.

"Since you're nosing for Killala, you'll be traveling the Old French Road," my companion of the moment informed me. "In August 1798, a thousand French soldiers landed on Kilcummin Strand, exporting their Revolution they were—'liberty, fraternity, equality,' and all that—raising the hopes of the two thousand hardy Mayomen who joined them on the road from Killala to here. 'The road of straw' it was called, *'bothnar na sop,'* because the local people lit this road with straw that night to guide them into Ballina.

"Our own men were armed with only pikes and pitchforks, but they moved swiftly and bravely, taking Ballina and marching under the leadership of the French general Humbert and his Irish guides through the wilds around Lough Cullin to surprise the garrison at Castlebar. How the redcoats fled that town is still recalled as 'the Races of Castlebar.'"

He looked up again at the imperious Maude's memorial, and continued: "It didn't turn out so well, of course. Rarely does, in our history. The French-Irish forces were decimated a month later, and our hopes of freedom died again, along with the United Irishmen and its leaders."

"Is that when Wolfe Tone was captured?" I had picked up several references to "the Father of Irish Republicanism," and was, after all, on a street named after him.

"No, that was a little later, when he sailed with a further French expedition to revive the Rebellion and was intercepted at sea, off Lough Swilly, by English men-of-war. He was denied a soldier's death by firing squad, and sentenced to be hung as a traitor, but ended his own life with a penknife, forestalling the savage satisfaction of his captors."

"How horrible!"

"And there's where more bitterness lies, me boy. While the French were treated as prisoners of war, the Irish were hanged as traitors. Traitors, pray tell, as if they had ever willingly pledged themselves to the English Crown. In all, thirty thousand United Irishmen were killed in a four-month span."

The scholarly old gent was working himself into a state, and his voice trembled as he bid us adieu: "Now, take this road out the town, and think of the bloody stamp of Irish history at your feet. Know this country's long and bitter history and you'll be better able to understand the people still in it."

On the Old French Road, all was quiet but the ring of Missie's hooves. That and the historian's words echoing in my ears like tolling bells, his intensity making 1798 seem like just a year or two ago.

A few stars glinted on the eastern horizon, and in the west the last burst of sun-glory dissipated over the tireless sea. The ghosts of Mayomen on the march toward Ballina seemed to pass me on the winding road, the twilight eerily lit with spectral wisps of straw—young and old, brawn and thin, their hearts pounding in the summer night, their eyes wild with fervor and fright, ready to battle British dragoons with farm implements, all in the name of freedom.

I heard their battle prayer murmuring as they passed. *"O Mary, who had the victory over all women, give me victory over my enemies, that they may fall to the ground as wheat when it is mown."*

As dusk gathered at the end of a fourteen-mile day, I knocked on a farm door in Knockatinnole. The door creaked open and a cautious middle-aged woman and her young son peeped out from behind it.

"What is it you're after?" she demanded, clearly not one who had heard tell of our travels.

"A night's shelter for my donkey and me," I squeaked in my most obsequious manner.

"Your name?"

"Kevin O'Hara."

"Your middle name?"

"Brendan."

"Your mother's maiden name?"

"Kelly."

Missie began to fidget, having seen such door-to-gate inquisitions come to naught in the past.

"Where is it your mother hails from?" the matron persisted.

"Ballagh in County Roscommon"—the pitch of my voice going higher by the moment.

She stood pondering, but I took hope from the boys' eyes, lovingly transfixed on Missie.

"O'Hara, is it? And your father's family hail from where?"

"Aughaboy, outside Ballinalee in County Longford. He knew Sean MacEoin, the famous blacksmith there?"

"Well, then," a smile finally broke over her face, "I suppose there must be a little Irish in you somewhere. Come in, so, and we'll try to do better than the old hayshed for the night."

Hearing this, the young lad broke from his mother's side and flung his arms wildly around Missie who, I do believe, winked appreciatively in my direction.

Next morning, a van from the *Western People,* was parked outside Liam and Theresa Harrison's door.

"I had no idea you were so famous," Theresa laughed at the fuss.

"You can be sure I'll sing your praises," I told her over my shoulder, as I tried to coax a smile out of Missie for the photographer.

When the newsmen departed, Liam advised me, "Unless you're dying to see abbeys sacked by Sir Richard Bingham, the so-called Flail of Connacht in 1590, you should get back on the main road to Killala. You'll miss nothing else but potholes and ocean spray."

We took his advice and arrived in due course at Killala, which was bounded by a wall of stones the size of skulls, as if in memory of the five hundred villagers put to the English sword after the failure of the Uprising of '98. Nearby was a round tower, from which I got a preview of the lonely northwest road ahead of us, meandering through Mayo's scattered Gaeltacht, an isolated region of blanket bog bordered by high cliffs and the turbulent North Atlantic.

Out upon this forlorn landscape as the day declined, our laboring breath created a thicket of fog about us as we lumbered beneath the low gloom.

We approached a farmhouse at light's demise, but a gray-whiskered donkey appeared and called to Missie, who celebrated the sorority of she-asses by jubilantly bawling back.

With little hope of settling these ladies in one camp, I passed on, but the old gray mare scuttled along the fence braying, intent on having a chat with my brown heroine. Dropping Missie's reins, I let them go at it, their discordant chorus carrying over the treeless expanse like the belling of stags atop a glen.

After an ear-splitting session, their conversation seized with contented snorts, as the gray she-ass trotted away, obviously pleased with whatever transpired. Missie, too, was pleasantly civil after this brief interlude, and though I cannot be certain if the pair had communicated in some treasured old way, I do know my donkey was thoroughly preoccupied for the next mile of road.

Somewhat shy of Ballycastle, we landed in the household of Peter and Christina Munnelly. Their ten-year-old son, Kevin, turned out to be a real character, with plenty of gibes for his namesake.

"Ye'll be up to your knees in muck for days, bog-trotting from here to Westport," braved the little lad at supper. "And sleeping in ditches with a thick hoary frost over you for a blanket!"

"You seem to take great joy in my suffering, Kevin Munnelly," I answered, pretending hurt from his dire prognosis.

He cackled in reply, "And the Willy Wisps leading you with lit rushes into their bottomless homes!"

"Have you ever met a lad so cheeky?" laughed the mother.

"Should I work the wooden spoon on him?" asked the father.

"No," I blurted, jumping from my chair and catching hold of him. "There's only one remedy for such a bold and saucy lad . . . a flurry of fingers to the ribs."

"Be off me, you jack," he roared, trying to free himself from my grasp. "Can't ye go walking the bogs and leave the simple likes of meself alone!"

Next morning, Kevin and his dad helped me dress Missie.

"If you cover a dozen miles like yesterday," said Peter, "you'll be able to reach Belderrig."

"Ah yes, Belderrig in the barony of Erris," piped up Kevin. "One hundred thousand hectares of bog, and you smack in the middle of it."

I chased the tubby lad around the farmyard until he found refuge in his mother's arms.

"We won't say good-bye," said Christina, shielding her upstart, "so cheers for now."

Promising Kevin I'd come back to haunt him on a stealthy moonless night, I led Missie off to the one-street village of Ballycastle, where I stopped in at the post office. When I emerged, five pensioners astride black bicycles had surrounded Missie like a chapter of Hell's Angels around a vintage Harley hog. This jocular scrum immediately struck me as kin to my Rattigan crowd, to whom I had just dispatched the latest update of our travels.

"Will you have a drink?" asked one wizened oldster with eyebrows thick as a hairbrush.

"I'd love to but I can't. We have to make Belderrig by nightfall."

"Belderrig is barely ten miles," said another, the pockets torn from his old topcoat. "If you climbed up on your float and tipped your girlie along, you could attend both wedding and funeral and still be in Belderrig by nightfall."

This quintet of marvel—likely companions since the cradle—were in no hurry to see a fresh victim leave.

"Why don't you go painting your donkey like our ancestors did? Do ye think it was only the American Indian that put on war paint? Our royal chieftains never stormed into battle without painting their mounts. Even our monks, God save and protect them all, were fond of painting their eyelids before vespers."

"I'd go painting her lugs yellow and her tail green," said the cronie in front of Missie, studying her like a certified cosmetologist. "Wouldn't those colors go grand with her gleaming coat of nut-brown?"

"Has she lost any teeth?" chimed in a fellow sporting a smile that exposed his four lower dental survivors.

"Teeth?"

"Aye, the bitteens of ivory in her gob."

"Not that I'm aware of. But I gladly would have knocked her tombstones out a time or two," I added, winning great favor as a man among men, a countryman after all.

"If she does go losing a tooth, carry it always. They have great potency, for spells and protection and all."

"I'll remember that," I promised, taking up the reins to leave.

"Call into Mary Kelly's in Belderrig," one suggested and each seconded. "She's a fine woman who'll attend to you proper."

"Will her place be easy to find?" I called out as I waved farewell.

"Easy to find?" They laughed in concert. " 'Tis the only place that's in it!"

Across the high moor, we made our way along the path worn by ancient cattle-drovers and barely altered in the millennia since Maeve ruled Connacht. At places the road hung on such a thin margin between sea and sky that I felt afoot on the outer edge of nothingness.

To bring me back from the fringe of this raw windswept coastline, I'd repeat my litany of hosts, by which I could recall every family we had stayed with since our journey began. Through repetition I could rattle off each name, 125 in all, like a coach could run down the lineups of his championship teams: "Tom Nolan of Castle french . . . Jim Ruane of Menlough . . . Peig Moyles of Monivea . . . Michael Lafferty of Cartymore . . ."

Having learned on my journey to look back as well as forward, I turned about to see a splendid long view back along the coast, a lovely succession of steep cliffs climaxing with the rounded sea-stack of Doonbristy off Downpatrick Head. I reveled in the vista, watching jets of foamy spray burst skyward from hidden puffing holes on the grassy capes. Spouting from deep caverns below, they gave the terrain the aspect of an immense pod of green whales. In one such cavern, some fourscore Irish took refuge from the rampaging English after the Uprising of 1798, only to perish when the tide came crashing in, their broken bodies swept out to sea.

At twilight we reached Mary Kelly's in Belderrig, as easy to find as promised, the lone, long two-story establishment in the village. I called in and asked the proprietress if we might spend the night.

"Where else would you spend it?" the engaging matron beamed. "Do you think I'd send you packing to Gortleatilla, Glenamoy, or Annie Brady's Bridge? Settle your friend below, and step in, can't you?"

I was soon enjoying a pint in John and Mary Kelly's antique public house, where slabs of bacon lay bare on counters, brass pots and cooking implements hung from rafters, and four young mothers—tending to toddlers parked in prams before the roaring hearth—chatted away, having traveled a mile or more to seek such amiable shelter.

The Kellys had three charming daughters, Mary, Bridget, and Marcella, and they made great fuss over me, laying out a meal of eggs, beans, and sausage.

Later that evening, when aged Mayomen had replaced the young mothers before the roaring fire, Marcella, just turned eighteen, relieved her even younger sister, Mary, at the bar.

"This is a great old house," I marveled to her in appreciation.

"You think so!" she replied, raising her eyebrows in mock disagreement. "It was meant to be a hotel and train station years back, part of a grand railway scheme for Mayo, but the line rolled over and died at Killala. So here this monstrosity sits, and ourselves in it, a hulking oddity in the middle of nowhere. 'All aboard to the Great Bogs of Erris, the loneliest spot in the world!' " she called out, pulling on an imaginary railway whistle.

"I hear they've discovered *ceide* fields near here?" I offered hopefully. "Those Stone Age farms may bring a swarm of tourists yet."

"Oh, yes!" She rebuffed my optimism. "I can hardly wait to meet the crowd of archaeologists who spend their long days combing the bog with toothpicks, and their evenings in here thrilling to the flints and shards they've dug up. My skin ripples with gooseflesh every time I think of it."

"The surrounding hills are nice, anyway." I kept trying to put a bright face on the isolation she called home.

"If they only danced now and again," she murmured, as she went to serve the pensioners who must have seemed, to her youthful eyes, as dry and yellowed with age as the firkins of butter recently found in these ancient bogs.

The next morning, Marcella came out as I was tackling my brown rose, to bid a wistful farewell.

"Off again, are ye?" she asked.

"Yes, but I'm growing weary of it."

"Weary? I'd be weary of it the day I set out. But you may as well chin up," she added, her turn to console me. "Christmas is coming, and the end of your long road."

She saw me off with kindly directions. "Your next hint of civilization is Glenamoy Bridge, seven miles or so. Across from the church you'll find an elderly brother and sister by the name McDonnell. We'll send them word you're coming. They're the salt of the earth, those two, full of the old stories."

As Missie and I walked the remote back-country road, within its rutted margins rimmed by frost, veils of mist cascaded off the surrounding hills of Benmore, Tawnaghmore, and Sranataggle. It was a bustling Saturday somewhere, but it could have been any day of the week or the millennium upon this gorse-covered tableland. My eyes drooped as I trudged a path without promise toward the low but unreachable sky.

At Glenamoy Bridge, however, John McDonnell was out to greet us, a boisterous friendly man in his seventies. He took Missie and instructed me, "I'll put your friend in the byre, and you go pull her hay from that reek in the haggard."

I went to the large wet haystack and pulled from its base, as I had been taught to do, but ended up with a few scant wisps in my hands. John came upon my struggle, and howled, "Don't you think your donkey deserves more than a few scrawneens?" He bent down to pull great sheaves from the sodden reek, a man seven times stronger than myself, while two and a half times as old.

Inside their snuggery, sister Mary welcomed me like long-lost family. The lids of boiling pots clacked on the range and steam filled my nostrils with the unmistakable aroma of potatoes, cabbage, and ham. Soon Mary was spooning four potatoes onto my large plate, "There, now, do ya see the pitaties breaking out from their skins? 'Tis like they're laughing at us out from the pot."

"And into our bellies, hey?" John chortled, as heaps of cabbage and ham followed.

In the course of our feast, I was telling them where my family came from, and John interjected, "Roscommon is Turlough O Carolan's country. Do you know his story?"

"Wasn't he a blind harpist or something?" I replied casually, as I dropped a dollop of butter upon a mountain of leafygreen cabbage.

"That's a shocking remark for a lad whose mother hails from Roscommon," Mary scolded with a tap to my hand, "where his harp resides to this day and an annual festival celebrates his name. You should know O Carolan was the last and greatest of the traditional Irish harpers. He played so beautifully it was called *ceol na naingeal,* 'the music of angels.' He was eighteen when he lost his sight to smallpox—God bless the Mark—but he had a gift that made his career, even after the passing of the Penal Laws. In the years of the Protestant Ascendency, he traveled the west and midlands, playing for patrons both Gael and Planter. The harp had always been an aristocratic tradition, but O Carolan was beloved by rich and poor alike."

"Before the Flight of the Earls," John filled me in, "every royal Gaelic family would commission a harper to their house, ranked second only to the bard. But the royal Queen Elizabeth proclaimed, 'Hang the harpers wherever found, and destroy their instruments.' Despite her decree, harpers continued to find patrons among old Irish families— why, the O'Haras of Sligo were one—who were allowed to keep their land by giving up their titles, as well as Planters who remained fond of the heritage. O Carolan was careful to avoid controversy, but after his death in 1738, the tradition was suppressed and the harp fell into the hands of beggars in the marketplace. Imagine, an unbroken line of royal musicians playing sweet melodies for centuries—to come to this."

"'From the parlors to the ditches,'" Mary continued. "But a century later, the harp was resurrected as an image of cultural pride, and became the favorite symbol of Daniel O'Connell. The poet Thomas Moore wrote of O Carolan's death: *'The harp that once through Tara's halls / The soul of music shed / Now hangs as mute on Tara's walls / As if that soul were fled.'* "

After supper, we sat before the fire, where the hearth was gold-embossed with a harp and shamrock on either side.

"Well, now I know what this means"—I ran my fingers over the harp's impression— "and I'll think of O Carolan whenever I see it."

"And Saint Patrick," smiled Mary, pointing to the shamrock. "Do you know he converted three-fourths of Ireland before his death, using the shamrock to explain the mysteries of the Blessed Trinity. Fair doings for a bearded evangelist, a foreigner at that, traveling Ireland with only a bell, staff, and milching goat."

"All that's missing from our hearth is the cricket, 'the crowing cock in the ashes,'" John added as he stoked the fire.

After staring into the companionable flames for some moments, I inquired, "I was told there are farmhouses in Glencolumbkille that have kept the same fire alight in their hearths for hundreds of years. Could that be true?"

"Most certainly," Mary confirmed. "Cover the glowing embers with white ashes at night and gently stir the fire back to life in the morning. 'Tis ages since a match has last lit our own, though we can't boast a hundred years. And there's a prayer to say when raking the ashes at the close of night: *'O God, save this house as Christ saved all / Mary and Bridget guard each wall / And may the hosts of angels bright / Guard ourselves and our home tonight.'* Saint Brigid's monastery in Kildare is said to have kept a sacred fire burning from the fifth century to the time of the Reformation. A thousand years, that."

Another moment of silence passed as we watched the fire and imagined it burning for a millennium.

John broke the silence with a fond chuckle, "When Mary was a schoolgirl, near a century ago, she could knot twenty-one different crosses of Saint Brigid."

"Will you stop." Mary's face went red. "And, now, God help me, I have a hard time lacing me old brogues."

John turned on the wireless above the mantel when their old clock struck nine. Following the news, more bloodshed in the North, and the weather, moderate gales forecast, *Ceili House* came on, a weekly program devoted to Irish music.

"That's 'The Lonesome Road to Dingle,'" said Mary as she tapped her feet to the pleasant air. "I say you've traveled that road."

"I have, indeed."

"You've been living the lyrics of our old songs, you 'Gypsy Rover,'" John joined in. "Have you been on 'The Rocky Road to Dublin'?"

"Yes, sir."

"'The Tar Road to Sligo'?"

"Yep."

"And now you're into 'The Hills of Sweet Mayo.'" Mary got caught up in the game. "And ye've certainly traveled 'The Old Bog Road.' And ye'll be traveling it for a spell still!"

After the program, and an invitation to sleep indoors for the night, I made some notes in my journal, while heavy winds swirled outside this cozy firelit interior. When was the last time they had entertained an overnight guest? I wondered. Earlier, they had confided they had lost their parents at a young age, and other than distant relations in New York, there was no one but themselves.

Looking up, I discovered that the old siblings had dozed off before the fire: she beside the shamrock; he, the harp. Proud but weary guardians of tradition, keepers of a vanished age. Their Old World wisdom sinking slowly into the watery depths of their nodding heads.

Mary Cleary's Pub

CHAPTER FIFTY-SEVEN

I went to Mass with the McDonnells Sunday morning and they saw me off, well-fortified with an ample breakfast, for another leg of our long swing through the northwest. The only break in the bleak stretch of heather-clad moorland was the endless row of telephone poles, ticking off like seconds into eternity. I would from time to time see a farmer leading a cow from nowhere to nowhere. Otherwise I felt like a solitary migrating bird, wearily flapping toward some long-sought landfall.

Somehow I had committed myself to touching all the corners of the island of Eire, so was obliged to reach the Mullet at the northwest extremity of Mayo. I would go no further than Belmullet at the entrance of the peninsula to fulfill my pledge, but that required an out-and-back detour that would take a full day or more.

We stopped overnight with Lawrence and Nancy Healey at the Barnatra Post Office, and then pushed out the long neck of land until it narrowed to the old seaport of Belmullet. Along the way, I saluted a young father looking out from the picture window of his new bungalow, holding a toddler in his arms. Oh, how I coveted that man's comfort amidst the warmth of family and home, content to look out upon the grim wet day from his homey confines, while I wandered in self-chosen exile.

But as I raised my stick again in farewell, I was dumbstruck by his unmistakable gaze of envy. He must imagine my ramble to be something like Bran's voyage to the comely Land of Women, while I knew it to be more like Mad Sweeney's, the ancient king of Dalriada who was turned into a bird by Saint Ronan and sent alone into the severities of nature.

Take my stick, for I'm knackered out! I wanted to cry out to him. *I'm weary of begging for daily bread and nightly digs. Weary of wearing the same rags, toileting in nettle-filled ditchbacks and scrubbing an insect-infested head of hair with long harper's nails under every passing shower.*

I long for family and familiarity. I long for home, garden, and the woman I left behind. And I long for a child or two, God willing, to hold in my arms, and look out upon a long wet day with contentment in my heart.

Slogging along, we didn't reach Belmullet till evening was coming on, a tired old town enlivened only by three boys running before us rolling wooden hoops with sticks, a scene I had only ever seen in a Victorian tintype. We walked up the town to the canal that connects Blacksod and Broad Haven Bays on this thin isthmus, and back out again to rejoin the main road. Missie balked and snorted at the U-turn, and I had to sympathize with her displeasure.

A mile down the road, we were most grateful to be called in by Charles and Ann Healy of Attycunnane. That evening the four young Healy lads sat about me on the floor, like some King and his Court, while visiting neighbors shared the intricate mysteries of this remote outpost they called home.

"You must come again in summer to hear the corncrake," urged one. "The Mullet is almost the last place in Ireland you can hear the corncrake's song. 'Tis so comforting that it knocks the loneliness out of a long night."

"We'll also take you to St. Dervila's Well," said another. "And to Kilmore Church-yard where everyone is buried standing up."

"And Inishglora," added a third, "where the Children of Lir lived for three hundred years. Turned into swans, they were, by their wicked stepmother, Aoife."

"That's why sportsmen never go shooting swans," piped young Cathal Healy in earnest: "in fear a child is trapped inside."

They continued to expound on local history, detailing the fate of the *Rata*, the largest galleon of the Spanish Armada, which foundered on the sandbars of the Mullet. But unlike the thousand-odd Spanish sailors who perished further north along Stree-gagh Strand in Sligo, the sailors of the *Rata* survived, with many settling in Mayo.

Before retiring to the couch, I stepped into the black night to check on Missie, her lonely cry from the gate echoing my mental state. As lively as the natives were, they put me in mind of another I'd met when I was a boy. I threw my arm around Missie's neck and recalled a long-ago night spent with my brother, Dermot, visiting an only child at his house in the distant countryside of Vermont.

He was quiet and listless until his mother encouraged him to take us bowling upstairs. He had a set up of little wooden pins at the end of a ill-lit hallway, and it was midway into the game, as he was resetting the pins, that he held one up and finally spoke: "It's a bad night for Saint Peter."

"Saint Peter?"

"Yes, this is Saint Peter," he said, showing us a pin.

"How do you know it's Saint Peter?" asked Dermot, all ten pins looking identical.

"See," he pointed to a small chip in the blue ring of the pin's neck.

"Do you have names for all of them?" we asked, astonished.

"Yes," he stood up Peter with the others. "They're named after the twelve apostles, excluding Judas or James the Lesser. See," he brightened, pleased to share his secret, "this here is Andrew, Thomas, and my favorite, Matthew."

Now, in the dark, as my wet beast nuzzled my pockets vainly for an apple, I understood more than ever the lanky boy's need to name those pins. If I lived out here on the lonely Mullet, I, too, would embrace each bird and saint, legend and locale, as the Healy lads had done. Yes, I'd put names on everything, living and inanimate, just to keep me company.

In the morning, the boys' father helped me get Missie ready for the road. "You'll earn every mile to Bangor Erris today. Gales out of the southeast are forecast up to eighty miles an hour."

"Stay on another day, why don't you?" beseeched their mother from the door.

"I'd love to, but we can't—our timetable is nip and tuck as it is." I buttoned my Road Coat to the chin and bid them a thankful farewell.

For hours we made little headway against the gale-lashed rain, alone with those telephone poles standing picket, crazy-crooked in the soft bog: endless yard-markers with no goal line in sight.

Between the districts of Who-Knows-Where and God-Knows-Why, an elderly woman called me into a shop that stood abjectly alone, as solitary as a desert trading post, but here struggling to stay above the surrounding mire. I entered the dark hovel and noted an old set of bone china set up on the counter, its willow pattern faded and cracked with age, while the pleasant old woman fussed over a pair of tarnished teaspoons.

"Warm your heart, son," she smiled, pouring out the tea, her fingers thin and brittle as old Belleek. "I've watched you this long while, and, says I to myself, it takes great faith in God to go journeying day in and day out, casting yourself before the dangers of the world. But a sorra sight to man, you are, for every three steps you take, doesn't the gale take two back."

She opened a fresh roll of biscuits from the shelf and placed three Custard Cremes onto my saucer's edge. "Well, the weather isn't spoiling any grand sights for you. The only interest in this bygone place, Glencashel, is that an ancient gateway to a rock fortress once stood hereabouts, which guarded the old kingdom of Erris. Imagine, this desperate land hosting royalty."

Suddenly Missie butted the shop's door open, and stuck her head inside. She wanted refuge from the storm and would have come all the way in but for the cart on her back. As I rushed to back her out and shut the door against the wind, the sweet old shopkeeper went searching out a carrot for my highway queen. She reached out with the treat and patted Missie's head, "Dear o' dear, will your poor donkey find a haven at day's end? Will she find peace in this troubled, troublesome world?"

I was surprised to find out how much Mrs. McAndrew knew of the wide world, from the lives of her far-flung seventeen children, and after the refreshing respite she offered, Missie and I braced ourselves for the drab road ahead.

"You're six miles from Bangor Erris," she said, seeing us off. "Six long miles and no one to talk to but Our Lord above."

Her farewell reminded me of a prayer Mary McDonnell had written out for me two nights earlier, so I took out "St. Patrick's Breastplate" and started to memorize it, as she recommended I do before coming to the saint's holy mountain, Croagh Patrick, fifty miles away. The long supplication suited my situation admirably:

> "I arise today
> Through God's strength to pilot me:
> God's might to uphold me,
> God's wisdom to guide me,
> God's eye to look before me,
> God's ear to hear me,
> God's word to speak for me,
> God's hand to guard me,
> God's way to lie before me,
> God's shield to protect me,
> God's host to save me . . ."

After some desolate wayfaring to the brink of despair, I'm afraid it was not God's host, but a fancy BMW that pulled up to save me. The driver leaned out and shouted into the wind, "Call into the West End Bar in Bangor, and tell the Henrys Mr. McGuire sent you."

His power window rose up before my eyes, reflecting my weary but grateful gaze upon the glass, and the vehicle purred off, leaving a glistening track on the wet road. With spirits rising, I found myself singing "Wichita Lineman," now visualizing this long string of telephone poles leading us into the friendly glow of a warm pub.

Which is exactly what we finally, at long last, reached.

"So, we have our orders from Mr. McGuire, do we?" smiled my hosts, Seamus and Monica Henry, more than happy to host me for the night.

"*Baingear,* in Irish, means 'guarding place,'" Seamus informed me, after settling Missie in a byre and me at the bar. "But whatever they were guarding is truly a mystery. Bangor must have been on the border between two old dominions, feuding since the Iron Age.

"You've joined the likes of many a wanderer," he went on, "since Bangor was a stopover for drovers leading kine or sheep over these barren mountain passes. Great old characters, they were, though no bard sang of them. *Ní bheidh ár leitheid ams,* as they say: 'Their likes will never be seen again.' Though you'll do for a wild November night," he concluded with a flourish, serving me up a frothy pint.

"In my youth, a wandering poet named Husband the Welshman stopped here twice yearly on his circuits," said Monica, serving me up a plate of liver and onions.

"Husband the Welshman!" I repeated. "When I was in Galway, a Mrs. Kelly of Monivea told me that Husband had also stayed at her pub prior to the outbreak of World War Two. A white-bearded *ciotóg* who wouldn't let anyone read his poetry."

"That's the fella," agreed Monica.

Later in the evening, when I was well-secured from the rigors of the road, Seamus asked, "Where will you be off to tomorrow?"

"Mary Cleary's of Ballycroy."

"Mary Cleary's is ten miles from our door. Do you know her?"

"No, but I was given her name by a woman I met in Clare named Mary Devine."

"Mary Cleary will give you a grand welcome, I assure you," said Monica, stacking glasses on the shelves. "Tomorrow is Wednesday, the last in November, so it will be the final fair day of the year in Ballycroy."

It was with high heart and good cheer we set out the next morning, despite a hint of inclemency in the sky. We lumbered contentedly across this heath alongside the Nephin Beg Range, where white stone pathways zigzagged upland toward the distant lonely hump of Sleive Car.

At one point on the twisting road I saw a young shepherd leading a great flock of sheep across a vast pastoral panorama—it could have been Saint Patrick himself, or any other avatar of the fifteen hundred years since. Not long thereafter, a beat-up motorcar pulling a makeshift cattlebox with doughnut-sized tires stopped alongside us, and the farmer asked, "Are ye off to Mary Cleary's?"

I told him I was and, satisfied, he drove off in short order.

This began a mystifying sequence of inquiring motorists throughout the day, the hedgerow telegraph system obviously in fine working order in these parts. Where the road touched the inland reach of Tullaghan Bay, we strode over Srahnamanragh Bridge and looked out over the mirrored waters, raising a solitary blue heron from nearby rocks, its long reedy legs dangling as wide wings lifted its tear-shaped body.

A postman pulled up in his orange van. "Are you Kevin O'Hara, bound for Mary Cleary's?"

"I am."

"There's been letters pouring in for you this long month. 'Twill take you a day just to read them."

So that's it, I deduced. Months back I wrote friends and family to send mail *"c/o Cleary's, Ballycroy P.O.,"* and now these locals knew of my letters, and perhaps their contents as well. With word well-advanced, cars continued to salute us throughout the long gray afternoon. From some, children poked their heads out windows like eager pups, waving and calling our names.

As the day drew to its early close, we approached Cleary's and found a long pub reminiscent of Kelly's in Belderrig. At one end, a thick circle of heavy-coated men were appraising sheep and fowl, buying and selling to the last minute of the season, though eyeing my slow approach keenly. Suddenly, the front door burst open and children poured out like clowns from a clown car, followed by a lovely woman with arms outstretched, her seventy years wreathed in smiles.

"You're as welcome as the light of day, Kevin O'Hara," said Mary Cleary, embracing me warmly.

Amidst this clamorous entourage, I was escorted into the warmth of her public house. Besides its fourteen rooms, it included two bars, a grocery, and the post office, and every nook and cranny sparkled with tinsel and holly heralding the Advent of Christmas. After days of lonely bog-trotting, my head spun in this carnival atmosphere, as frolicsome youngsters clambered around me as if I were Saint Nicholas himself.

I emptied my pockets of coins onto the counter, offering treats to all, and they responded in a singsong of sweets. "Three fizzle sticks, two pink squirrels, two pig's-teats . . ." "Four peggy-legs, two brown cushions, three Gob-stoppers . . ." "Five jelly tots, two hedgehogs, three blackjacks . . ." went their litany.

Mary Cleary herself was the image of Mrs. Claus, except for her delightful Mayo accent, and as she served me the pint promised by Mary Devine back at Taylor's Pub in May, she asked, "Tell us, exactly, how many miles have you traveled with your donkey to be with us tonight?"

"Just about fifteen hundred."

"Fifteen hundred!" she gasped, blessing herself. "John Patrick, would you go walking one and a half thousand miles with a donkey?"

"Not for the wealth of the world."

"And you, Fintan James?"

"I'd rather replace the hinges on Hell's fiery door!"

A feeble old man spoke up, with some agitation, "What's fifteen hundred miles, tell me? Can any of you put that in a straight line for me?"

" 'Twould be the distance between here to Greenland," someone offered.

"Here to Greenland?" The elder gawked at me in sheer wonderment. "Jaysus, son, but you're a powerful swimmer!"

Amidst the ensuing laughter, Mary shuttled me into her warm kitchen, where seven goodwives were seated around the range. They peppered me with questions about my travels, which I answered happily, as a plate of chicken and buttery potatoes with scallions was prepared and handed to me. I compared this catechism of the seven matrons with my colloquy with the seven bachelors in Northern Donegal. Finally, one with cheeks ablaze, asked me directly, "Has your journey been worth the effort?"

"Worth the effort!" I replied with gusto. "How else would I have fallen into such charming company?"

"Great value, us," another blushed, chewing on a clove. "You've come a long way for very little, I tell you."

"But if you had come our way forty years ago, it might have been a different story," said another, standing up to plant a wet kiss on my forehead.

"Yet I suppose ye've seen the great sights of Ireland," Mary mused. "All that we've only read about in our schoolbooks."

Delving into a mounded reek of buttered potatoes, I confided to this affectionate audience, "This journey will stay with me forever, but sometimes I feel as though I've seen so little, a thimble of rain from a brimming barrel. And when I pass the ruined abbeys and castles, I can only wonder what Ireland might have been if it had the freedom to flourish. But I have no doubt it will rise again, with all the good people in it."

" 'Tis something to ponder, really," put in another. "Despite our history of heartbreak, we can't be too bad, can we, when a young man can step out and do what Kevin here has done, meeting nothing but kindness throughout the country, North and South."

As I was finishing my feast, Mary suddenly jumped from her chair.

"Och, ye'll have me arrested!" she exclaimed, as she led me by the hand from the kitchen to the small cluttered post office at the end of the house.

"Brede!" Mary called from the half-door, "do you have any mail for Kevin O'Hara?"

"Kevin O'Hara, is it?" the postmistress chuckled, as she emerged with my pile of letters. "I did come upon that name some time or other."

Back in the kitchen, I went immediately to the envelope with the unmistakable handwriting of Grannie Kelly. The seven women watched intently as I opened it, expecting me to share the contents.

"My grandmother, eighty-seven years of age, is as healthy as the day I left," I told them, a quaver in my voice at the good news.

"Thanks be to God," they replied in chorus.

"And she wishes to thank you, Mary, for your kindness."

"She's more than welcome, dear soul." Mary shyly accepted the gratitude. "And who wouldn't be kind to a traveler going about the country putting a little cheer into people's hearts?"

"What will you do with yourself when your journey is through?" asked a woman sitting by the range.

"I'm going to settle back in with my bride, if she'll still have me," I said, holding four unopened letters of Belita's in my hands.

"She must be a very understanding woman," said Brede, "and I hope you never forget her kindness. Believe me, there aren't many women who'd let their husbands go gallivanting for a year."

"Oh, don't I know," I wholeheartedly agreed.

"But she'll be proud of your accomplishment," added another, "circling all Ireland with a donkey."

"I hope so, but I can't go blowing my bugle just yet. Missie and I still have two hundred miles to go, and I've been having this premonition that something is going to go wrong on December seventh."

"Well, we'll all say a special prayer that morning that no harm crosses your path," replied Mary.

"Funny thing," I continued, "this journey was supposed to get Ireland out of my system, but now I feel I've swallowed it whole. It will take awhile to digest it all. But these travels will always stay with me. They've helped me find out who I am, and made me who I will be."

"Tell us," asked the woman chewing the clove, "would you live in Ireland?"

"I would, if I could make a living."

"Why is that, tell us?"

"The people, for starters. It seems that every third person I meet could become a life-long friend. But mostly, I feel I'm a better person here, probably because I'm surrounded by so many good people. There's a cultural undertow in America that can drown the best of one's intentions. Believe me, it's not a culture bent on producing saints."

In time, Mary looked around at her bosom buddies, to see their growing curiosity fixed on the pile of unopened letters in my lap.

"We've made you up a bed above where you can finish reading your letters," she said, standing to show me the way. "When you're finished, you best call down to the men below, for I won't hear the end of it till they search your rucksack for stories. And before you get snookered, we'll ring Mary Devine and tell her how the Yank with the donkey has finally arrived to collect his pint."

After reading letters written by loved ones near and far, I cleared my teary eyes and stepped out to walk the quiet road. Though two of Grannie's close friends and neighbors had passed away, Jim and Lena Tiernan, she herself was fine. My mother and brothers and sisters also wrote, bringing me up-to-date with the doings in their lives. But most affecting were the letters from Belita; she planned to be at Rattigan's on Christmas Eve, and said she loved me as much as the day I left. I joyously clapped my hands and sprinted in a mad dash up the road. Yes, the wanderer indeed had a loving wife to return to at the end of his journey.

When I returned to Cleary's, I found myself holding court in the bar section, where pints were pulled and stories told, into the wee hours.

"Tell us again, can't you, about your dance with the washerwoman from Tramore," said one tipsy farmer, his ribald interest getting the better of him. "Was she truly as buxom as you say?"

"I've seen smaller cocks of hay in Munster in July," I reiterated the tale.

"Bejabbers," he mumbled, his head in the clouds. "Cocks of hay, you say."

From Achill to Clare Island

CHAPTER FIFTY-EIGHT

I woke to the chatter of rooks in the garden below.

"You're alive, are you?" pronounced Mary Cleary, as I dragged myself into her kitchen next morning. "I say you had a power of drink last night."

"Not bad, considering," I replied, as I sank into a chair and nursed a heavy head in my hands. "You could have floated the *Queen Mary* in all the drink offered me."

After I'd eaten what breakfast I could and prepared Missaleen for the road, Mary bid me farewell with open arms. "Give us a hug, can't you? And if you're ever on this lonely road again, don't you ever dare pass without stopping."

We traveled the broad, sweeping bogland where neither the conical peaks of Nephin or Croagh Patrick could be seen beneath the low gloom, as ribbons of wet road stretched out to distant recesses. Motorcars passed with headlamps aglare, and the clouds above weighed down like a sack of coal on an old man's back. But today I took to these dreary miles with a step as bright as May, after the comfort of my letters and the friendliness of Mary Cleary and her establishment.

By midday, we began to emerge from the great blanket bog of Erris. The road ran near the deepest recesses of Blacksod Bay to where it almost touched Clew Bay, but for the isthmus where the village of Mullrany lay, our destination for the night. Sheltered from North Atlantic winds, the area called Beenyvenny seemed an oasis of greenery, as bog gave way to shrubbery—giant fuchsia and other rare plants.

Mist veiled wrinkled hills and rivulets cascaded into a bubbling clatter over stones. On the hillsides I could make out the impressions of long-ago "lazy beds" of potatoes, but their gravelike shapes made me think less of ancient cultivation than of the Famine, most devastating right here in Mayo.

With great relief we arrived by dusk at the cheerful village of Mullrany and the shores of Clew Bay. We found lodging at Hilltop Farm, where Kate and Tom Moran feasted me on a stew of oysters, dredged up by their fishermen sons, Bernie and Kevin, off the coast of Achill Island.

I watched the evening news with the Morans, which highlighted the plight of third-world children, reporting that youngsters in São Paulo are so poor their diet consists mainly of rice water.

" 'Tis deplorable." Mrs. Moran spoke back to the television. "The well-to-do have no sense of obligation to their poorer brethren. The world's rich need a sharp reminder there's no pockets in a shroud."

Next morning, Kevin convinced me to take the day off—our first in over a fortnight—and tour Achill, Ireland's largest island, a Gaeltacht area now connected by bridge to the mainland. Driving me around the black hump of Knockmore, along the rush-choked rim of the Corraun Peninsula, Kevin filled me in on the region's history.

"When the O'Donnells ruled Donegal, they used Achill as a penal colony. And it remained a harsh and primitive place right through the Famine up to our present day. At Slievemore you can see the ruins of a village of stone huts abandoned during the Famine and never resettled. But now the area's becoming famous for its rugged cliffs and wild beaches, quite the spot for fishing and water sports. Tourists are starting to come from all over and soon you won't be able to recognize the place."

The transformation was far from complete, however, as we passed cottages whose whitewash was yellowed by sea and smoke, with farmyards of broken-poled haycocks and crumbling piles of turf, and gates improvised from a startling array of materials: old bedposts, cart wheels, bicycle spokes, hoods from abandoned motorcars, battered black shells of curraghs, and old metal pub signs advertising, SWEET AFTONS, 12 A PENNY. I thought of the famous poster The Doors of Dublin, and smiled at the notion of a sequel, The Gates of Achill.

Kevin dropped me at the bridge where we were to meet that evening, and I hitched a further lift to Keel village. As I walked the strand marveling at the magnificence of Cathedral Rocks and Minaun Cliffs, a cloudburst drove me to seek shelter at the Minaun Pub. There, a dozen old denizens, mumbling a mixture of Gaelic and English, sat on either side of a long wooden plank—ship's flotsam, I was told—with five checkerboards painted down its length, and bottlecaps and seashells serving for game pieces.

The rain continued outside, or it may have stopped, for all I knew, but I lingered through the afternoon in the enchantment of this enduring enclave, this removed relic of old Ireland. I admired the three charming sisters who ran the pub as a triad of heroines, along the lines of Ireland's three legendary heroes: Cuchulainn, Oisin, and Patrick—warrior, poet, saint.

Philomena, the oldest, was the noble warrior of the three; tall, handsome, and burdened with the suffering of the land, from Cromwell's atrocities to the ongoing tragedies in the North. She spoke of the Famine—and she had no doubt who was to blame.

Patsy, the middle sister, about my age, was the poetess, with two languages weaving through her head, as intertwined as the plaited braids that fell to her waist. When I spoke of home, her imagination went flying there: "It must be so beautiful in New England, when the snow drops . . . snow petals—no, snowflakes, isn't it? Aye, snowflakes falling upon a world so peaceful."

Mary was the devoted saint of the three, the Brigid of Patrick's heart. She was forever on the go and had a kind word for everyone, serving tea and sandwiches, sweeping the pub's corners, stoking the fire and running out to pump petrol in the face of a stiff Atlantic storm. She'd come in again with a wet brow, glowing like a rubescent rose. And when she pulled a pint, one might think God had placed her on earth for this purpose alone: setting it before you like a priceless vessel of wine and you a regal king from some faraway land.

"Health and long life to you," she'd say, as you brought the glass to your lips.

Before I departed the next morning, the first of December, the Morans gave me three copies of the current *Western People,* featuring "O'Hara's Donkey Tour," with a large photo of the toothsome pair of us.

Mrs. Moran laughed at my embarrassment, as I contemplated my own mug with queasy fascination, though Missie looked every bit the beaming bride. "There, now," she said, "you'll be king of the road through the rest of Mayo."

"Well, giddy-up, my highway queen. We've miles to go before we reach the next seat of our procession," as I tipped my crown to the Morans and led Missie off down the road.

But Her Highness was regally rebellious after her day off, and we struggled into Newport against a cold wind lashing across Clew Bay. In the lower end of town, we passed the very picture of pauperism, a runny-nosed waif standing in front of a shop window, peering in at a Crolly doll much better dressed than herself. My heart went out to her, but my pockets were empty, and, powerless, my brief kingship melted away. Disheartened, I wondered how any well-to-do could pass this scene without intervening in some generous way.

The next day was First Sunday of Advent, heralded by a sun shower sweeping across Clew Bay, raining light on the green-humped islands that frolicked across its blue-splashing waves, one for every day of the year, it is told. Along the winding road, my heart leapt each time we rounded into view of Croagh Patrick's quartzite crown, over the bay.

By midday we reached the prosperous landlord town of Westport, and walked down its tree-lined mall, and over the bridge that divides it into north and south, with the mountain stream of Carrowbeg rushing to the bay below. Church bells were tolling through this Georgian town, the sidewalks were bustling with pedestrians, and, like an unwitting collection plate, I received a number of gifts from people who had read about our travels on the generosity of the land, and put twelve pounds into my empty pockets.

As we passed through the well-to-do diamond, a car pulled up alongside us and the young couple inside told me they lived in the vicinity of Rattigan's Pub, and knew of our destination.

"You're a terribly slow coach," the wife snickered. "Are you sure you'll be home for Christmas?"

"You bet," I said, petting my little brown engine. "Oh, wait!" I rummaged around in my cart for a copy of the *Western People*. "Could you drop this off at Rattigan's on your way home?"

"We will, gladly," they consented, and I whiled away some miles afterward, imaging the delivery of the newspaper, the sharing of the contents, and the commentary of the Four Masters.

At a sharp bend in the road, I was seized by my first full, up-close view of Croagh Patrick, aglow in a deep shade of lavender. My eyes slowly ascended the tract blazed on its northern slope from foothill to crown: the stigmata of centuries of pilgrims. True to promise, I recited "St. Patrick's Breastplate" from this unobstructed vantage, stumbling in parts, but no matter.

"Now, Miss, there's another drovers' station . . . a real stairway to heaven," I said, wrapping my arm around my companion's neck and pointing up to where the peak of the cone penetrated a bank of wine-dark clouds. "Look up, *asaleen!* This is where Patrick dwelt and fasted, where he took on his mission to spread the Word of God and drive out demons. To us Irish, this mountain is the holiest spot, more sublime than St. Peter's in Rome. Commit this sight to the most treasured vault of memory."

I chose to stop in at a farmhouse nestled beneath the Reek, the local name for Croagh Patrick, but as we walked up the boreen, we were confronted by a yapping fox-terrier who lunged daringly at Missie's hooves. Fearing neither man nor beast after witnessing the saint's ethereal splendor, I raised my faithful hazel and put on my most fearsome Lugh-eyed stare, which sent the whiskery cur scrambling away—straight between the Wellingtons of its masters. I slowly lowered my stick and raised my eyes to the faces of two middle-aged men, obviously brothers. Not the best way, I assure you, to seek bedding for a night.

"You're a hard man with the stick," said one, with a faint smile.

"A brave knight of the road," added the other. "Step in, can't you, before you go drubbing our Tiny senseless."

With no hard feelings, then, I was soon sitting in the kitchen of Peter and Frank McGreal, where a stained-glass light came from the Reek and glinted, plum-colored, off spoon and sugar dish.

"You'll have to forgive us," said Peter, setting the table for tea and loaf. "Our mother passed away three months back, and we've been out of sorts since."

I offered my condolences as the beguiling evening light faded from the room. Tiny, however, eyeing me like a jailer the whole time, rumbled a low growl as I slathered my bread with Dundee marmalade.

"Some dog you have here," I said, offering him a crust.

"Tiny is a grand dog." Peter stooped down to scrub its little head. "He's killed over a hundred fox cubs these last three years."

"Don't be so shook," Frank admonished when I quickly withdrew my hand. "Believe me, the Reek behind us is teeming with hundreds more. 'Tis a pity Patrick hadn't a go at them when he was pitching out the serpents into Lugnademon, 'the hollow of the demons.' For every den of kits Tiny destroys, don't the foxes kill a lamb of our own. 'Tis nothing but an ongoing battle between us."

"Are foxes as clever as they're made out to be?" I asked, winning over Tiny's friendship with a second crust of bread.

"They're very cute," Frank informed me. "Great swimmers, you know, and able to climb trees. They're also able to play dead for hours with their tongues laying out, and when a crow comes landing to sample the tasty red meat, the fox snaps back to life and good riddance to Mr. Crow. Believe me, you'll hear nothing but their sharp treble bark from here to Connemara."

Later that evening I went to Mass with the McGreals back in Westport, and afterwards we stopped in at a pub on the diamond, where we were soon surrounded by an amiable knot of locals.

"The Donkeyman, is it?" said one. "You should forget your tramping and settle hereabouts. Couldn't you make big money by dressing your donkey with cleeve-baskets and go selling tea and twopenny biscuits to the pilgrims on Garland Sunday?"

"'Tis a good trade, that," joked another. "You'll see up to sixty thousand pilgrims climb the Reek that last Sunday in July, though there were twice that many before *an Gorta Mor,* 'the Great Hunger.' The procession begins at dawn and rises in an unbroken line all day long, and many take to the rocky slope in bare feet."

"A few of us thought ourselves great athletes in our youth," shared a burly man in his sixties, "so, one winter's day we decided to race up to the top of the Reek. No round of prayer here, just bragging rights. Well, we did it famously, we did, and—gasping on our backs at the summit, kings of the hill—up from the trackless back of the holy mountain stumbles an old penitent woman through the mist. And paying us jackos no heed, she lifted her heavy black skirt to kneel, where we caught a glimpse of her bare, bloodied feet.

"The sight of her devotion remains with me still," he sighed. "And, believe me, it knocked the boast out of us. And if there's truly a heaven above, 'tis people like herself who'll be sitting at the head table."

Making myself a promise to climb Croagh Patrick on a return visit someday, I took advantage of the opportunity arranged by the McGreals to visit Clare Island, where I could view the saint's mountain from one of the loveliest vantages of all. So next morning, after settling Missie with Martin O'Toole and family in Moneen, I found myself chopping through the waters on a mailboat hauling soap and other sundries to this island that rises out from Clew Bay like an emerging submarine.

"Inis Cliara has less than two hundred full-time inhabitants, but before the Famine it would have been home to ten times as many," shouted my skipper over the wind and waves. "Its heyday was in the sixteenth century, during the reign of the pirate queen Grace O'Malley, 'Graunuaile' in the Irish.

"Graunuaile was born on the high seas, and took command of our western shore when her father was wounded by English pirates, and later reigned supreme in these waters. But when Richard Bingham, the ruthless English governor, arrived to wreak havoc in Connaught, he set out to destroy Graunuaile, stealing her cattle, pillaging her castles, and killing her only son, Owen.

"Powerless against Bingham, Graunuaile set sail for London to seek audience with Queen Bess, 'the Virgin Queen,' whom she would ask for protection against the governor. This was a risky endeavor, as Elizabeth had no time for the Irish and, in fact, had appointed Bingham to subdue Ireland's west.

"Oh, yes, I've heard of Bingham, the notorious 'Flail of Connacht.'"

"Aye, but Graunuaile, a queen in her own right, sailed up the Thames, had her chat in Latin with Elizabeth, and promised she would assist the Crown against all foreign foes if the Queen gave back her lands and kept Bingham off her back. Queen Bess was won over by the sea-pirate's spirit, and granted Graunuaile her wishes.

"So, Graunuaile returned to Inis Cliara after 'the Meeting of the Queens,' and found peace for years until she was eventually killed during a clash with pirates. A bold, seafaring woman, her remains are buried in a Cistercian abbey on the island, with the motto, 'Invincible on Land and Sea.'"

As we approached the quay, the skipper pointed out a castle on the headland by the water. "That there is Graunuaile's own castle." Then, cutting the engine and securing ropes about the bollards along the island's pier, he advised me, "Now, mind yourself along the high sea-cliffs, the path breaks down in places. Go on, I'll manage here, and I'll meet you at the pub in two hours' time."

I went scurrying up the headlands, looking across the bay at Croagh Patrick, outlined against the thin pale sky, and back upon the island's main road, where low-lying cottages were protected by windbreaks of stone and brakes of shrubbery. Farmers, straddling donkeys, climbed the terraced mountain paths toward the extensive bog, and sheep grazed in fields that rose upward toward the dark eminence of Croaghmore.

Bursting with piratical adventure, I clambered along the sheer cliff path, scaring up a warren of rabbits who bounded in countless numbers from hole to hole. After giving them a valiant chase, I went hopping toward an old lighthouse. Face into the wind like the prow of a racing corsair—wild and free, strong and brave—I stood on the promontory and surveyed the watery world at my command.

The winds were whipping mighty when I arrived at the pub, the mailboat pitching about against the tire-lined quay below. I was worried about being stranded, but the skipper casually told me I had time to knock down a pint before we set off.

I sat down next to an ancient mariner, and asked him about the changing weather.

"Nothing to fear today, matey, but tomorrow there'll be a great blow altogether. But, sure, if the wind does begin to batter, and the mailboat battens down, can't I take you back to Roonah Quay meself."

I thanked him for his reassuring offer, and noticed his empty glass performing a little jig on the counter in front of me.

"Two pints, please," I called.

"I've been the world over, sailing the high seas from the Caribbean to the Adriatic Sea," he said, his eyes fixed and gleaming on the fresh pint settling before him. "When I was your age, *avic,* I had seen the world seven times over and witnessed sights that would knock the yolks out of Eric the Red—the champion Viking sailor of the seas—though the Phoenicians might have taught 'em a thing or two, but there was never a sea dog quite like an O'Malley from Clare."

"So you're a descendant of Graunuaile?"

"Aye, and sailed I did," he went on, wiping the stout cream from his lips, "on barques, brigantines, and schooners. By the hokey, I've seen icebergs in the Polar Caps higher than the Andes, and a school of mermaids, heavenly beauties, the lot of them, with ribbon-red hair, gliding after shoals of herring, for ye'll never see a classy school o' maids go chasing mackerel. A durty ould fish, that."

The two-legged jukebox played on until I received a call from the door.

"Was that old parrot telling you how he has sailed the Seven Seas?" the skipper asked as we hurried toward the quay.

"Oh, yes. He told me he has saluted every lighthouse from Alexandria to Cape Cod."

"He did, did he? What else?"

"He said there are seals along the Connemara coastline called selkies, and they belong to certain families, and can transform themselves into women by pulling their sealskins over their heads. And for me to mind any woman who has the scent of seaweed in her hair."

"A fair warning, that," he agreed, boarding the boat and freeing the ropes. "Anything else?"

"He said he was a direct descendant of Graunuaile O'Malley."

"Well, that's the only truth he did mutter, however that was," he cackled, bringing the engine to life. "The islanders call him 'the Admiral,' but, in truth, he has never set foot off Inis Cliara his entire life."

"Really?" My jaw dropped in dismay.

"Afraid of water, he is. Why, he wouldn't cross Clew Bay if Jesus took him by the hand. To tell you the truth," laughed the skipper, piloting us out upon the rough rising waves, "you'd be hard-pressed to plop that old fella into a bathtub."

Hazel to Holly

CHAPTER FIFTY-NINE

A midst a raging gale next morning, I was tackling Missie while the O'Toole children implored us to stay on another night. One after the other shouted from the doorway: "Ye'll be blown away, for sure . . ." "Even school has been canceled . . ." "Look at Missie's ears, can't you? . . ."

I did look at Missie's lugs, stitched to her skull in the face of the wind, and then when she turned her head, they flapped open like gull-wings riding the squall.

I hollered back at Gráinne, Seamus, and Martin, "Sorry, we've got no choice. We only have five days to reach Clifden, and Christmas is right around the corner."

The imminence of the holiday seemed to console them, and they waved us off into the tempest.

I soon regretted not heeding their storm warnings. Missie and I leaned low into the headwind, shouldering into the gale, but at every rise of road we were repelled by pellets of rain hurled off the North Atlantic, stinging our faces and blowing us backward. The wind was relentless, howling and wailing against our progress.

We fought on for a mile or two, but eventually found the gusts impenetrable and, for the first time in our travels, were driven off the road by the elements, turning up a narrow lane toward a rundown cabin. An old man braced the door open just wide enough to shout out at us, "Come in, out of this wall o' wind! Come in, I say, before you catch your death!"

In an instant I was wrapped in a woolen blanket before the range of Bill McNamara of Colacoon, my wet clothes smoking upon the rack. The old bachelor turned up the wireless and we listened to the weather report. All ships were warned into harbor along the Irish coast, with gusts reported in excess of a hundred miles an hour, especially between Louisburg and Killary Harbor.

"That's ourselves," Bill nodded. "We're catching the brunt of the storm."

After tea and loaf, he went to the window to survey Nature's fury, though in this barren landscape the storm's ferocity was barely visible, except for odd bits of flying flotsam. You could certainly hear the icy blasts, though, the wind rattling the house and whistling through loose panes. A severe blow altogether.

Bill mused from his place at the window: " 'Tis storms like this that make me think of the poor souls who walked this very road during the Famine. 'Twas 1849, the worst of the Famine over, but Mayo still starving. Four hundred villagers, young and old, set out from Louisburg to the landlord's hunting lodge in Delphi, a dozen miles down the road, on the rumor that corn meal had been delivered."

"Imagine what hope can make the hopeless do," I replied, with a knowledge I'd never had before.

"The rumor was false, of course, just another torment to desperate people. And the long march home another. A violent snowstorm arose, dreadful, and most of the four hundred perished. This was at Doo Lough, the Black Lake, which ye'll be passing by tomorrow. The bodies were found everywhere, in the lake and on the shore, in ditch and drain, straggling on for miles. 'Tis famous as 'the Doo Lough Tragedy.' "

As I continued to thaw out by the fire, a neighbor burst through the door, bringing in a blast of wind that nearly cut me in two.

"The world traveler, I see," chortled Mr. Heenahan, appraising my thin shanks. "You look more like a plucked goose, you do! This is the picture the *Western People* should have had. But since you're in from the weather, I thought you might take a read of this." He produced a book from under his coat: *Here's Ireland* by Harold Speakman. "He's an American writer who traveled Ireland with a donkey in 1924, much as yourself."

Once back in dry clothes, I spent the long afternoon tucked away in my bag in a spare bedroom, listening to the roar of the wind and reading of Speakman's delightful jaunt with his donkey, Grania. He had correctly taken his thousand-mile journey clockwise around the coast, but otherwise it struck me as an uncanny precursor. So much so, I began to wonder if I were he, reincarnated to circle this enchanted isle once again.

On his first day out, Grania developed a stripped shoulder from an ill-fitting collar, and Speakman was warned he'd be "fined stiffly" if any civic guards came upon them. He paid two pounds for his "joker," as the travelers called his donkey, saying they could have purchased thirty for the same price. A bubbling woman in Cork warned he'd be a "traveling one-ring circus," and several "competent people" said his journey could never be made with the one donkey. The *Cork Examiner* also made "pleasant mention" of his journey.

Speakman was embarrassed when caught singing, and would meet "strange little men" who appeared from time to time. He walked alongside Grania, and helped push their cart up steep hills. He had also been warned not to take a donkey through Belfast, "as she would not be appreciated." Therefore, he left her in Antrim when he visited "the City on Stilts," meeting an agreeable chap named O'Hara there.

I laughed out loud at one passage, recalling the four merry men I had met in Ballyn-abola:

"Gullion's Cross, however, was illusive. Every time I inquired, it was only "five-minutes away." One has to be a little careful of those five minute walks in Ireland. The idea back of it is kindly, for it aims to encourage the walker. But after half an hour's grind . . ."

I was just reading that his favorite road was Leenane to Louisburg, the very road we were traversing in the opposite direction—when I nodded off into a long afternoon nap.

Through the white noise of the ongoing fury outside, a barely audible knock awakened me from a tangle of interwoven dreams of Speakman and myself.

"The Heenahans have invited us over for supper. What do you say?" Bill asked.

"It's entirely up to yourself."

" 'Twill be a better meal than I could ever put before us, that I'm certain."

"The best thing God ever put on this earth was an honest man," I said, jumping from my sack, with a belly outbellowing the storm.

The sky was a tatter of cloud next morning, the storm having hurled itself elsewhere about the globe.

Missie and I set off toward Delphi and into the steep-flanked valley of Glencullin where a grandstand of mountain sheep heralded our passage with bleats of indifference. On one side of the road were the flint-brown Sheefrey Hills and on the other, across the black waters of Doo Lough, the high peak of Mweelra rose in somber eminence, as if commemorating the hundreds of souls who had perished beneath its balding crown.

Contemplating this scene of beauty and tragedy, I trod along until at a step my hazel stick splintered and split in two, the crack I first noticed back in County Sligo finally giving way—surely, an ill omen!

Ever since it was cut for me by Tom Nolan on May Day this staff had been my safeguard and companion. Through our long circuit, it had protected me and staved off disaster in many forms—snarling dogs, stinging warble-flies, threatening young ruffians, and perhaps even unseen mischief-makers from the Middle Kingdom. For me it was both pilgrim staff and shillelagh, alpenstock and waving-wand. It was a vital part of me, and now I was bereft of it. I sat, downcast, by the shore of the lake, a shard of wood in each hand.

I soon realized there was but one thing to be done: I must give my beloved hazel a suitable last rite. Securing Missie in a lay-by, I took the two shafts of silver bark and climbed up a stone ledge overlooking the water.

My funeral oration was brief but heartfelt: "Dear hazel, my companion of the roads, my protector and support, nicknamed Ty O'Kelly, for the hills of home you left to travel with me. Now has come the time for you to rest from our travels; this is the viaticum for my viaticum. So now, Ty O'Kelly, I consign you to the Black Lake in hopes you may one day rise again like Excalibur from the waters of Avalon. God willing, we may meet on the further shore, along with the spirit of Missie, and form again our blessed triad, pilgrim-donkey-hazel, to recommence the ramble."

At the end of my eulogy I heaved both ends of the stick into a watery grave and sat long in reverie, watching my hazel float away like a Viking king headed for Valhalla. I lamented losses new and old, small and large, as fog crept down from the hills like a nebulous glacier and thickened over the lonesome valley.

With a deep sigh, I rose again and went to rejoin my remaining companion. "Well, Miss, now it's just you and me, with only my beads to protect us from the hazards of the road." So off we tramped down our melancholy path, with one last look back at my handstaff, one of a long line of wandering companions reaching back to the De Danaan kings, bobbing on the waves in silent farewell.

We passed through a wooded dell in the deep bowl of the glen, which lent a warm tranquility to the road, and eventually came to an isolated farmhouse, where we gained admittance to a house of three middle-aged siblings, two brothers and a sister named Herarty.

Their two-story cottage didn't have electricity, but did have a cozy open fire. Sitting in the warm glow I noticed a *coileach*—a charming old settle-bed—tucked into an alcove by the hearth wall, and had hopes of settling myself into it for the night. But when the quiet evening drew to its close, Martin pulled the *coileach* covers back for himself, and Pat handed me a hurricane lamp and pointed the way outside to a high barn in the back haggard.

I clambered up to the top of a tall, tall mattress of hay, and soon dropped into welcome oblivion. In the middle of the night, however, I woke with frost bristling my nostrils and the treble bark of foxes coming to my ears from up Ben Gorm. I went grasping for my hazel, forgetting its loss and now wishing I had Tiny the Terrible by my side. Sitting upright in my bag, I imagined this slew of redcoats drawing nearer. Would they be bold enough to strike? Could a skulk of them grabble me by the throat and drag me up the mountain as they had the McGreal lambs? Fortunately, their yaps began to fall more distant, hunting deeper into the silent valleys of this mountainous land.

Sleeping with one eye open and waking with one eye closed, I was pleased to see the peep o' day shimmering o'er these brown hills. I tumbled off the high bales and went inside to find the fire stirring and Margaret preparing a sumptuous breakfast for me to share. After devouring a generous portion, I felt a low rumbling in my belly and asked if I might kindly use their bathroom before returning to the road.

"Why wouldn't you?" said Margaret, opening a door onto a relic of a toilet, a throne as welcoming as an executioner's chair. "Go on," she urged, seeing me pause. "No need to be bashful."

I sat down on the cold porcelain stool to perform my daily task, pleased it would be done and away with. To be frank, this toileting business, which Michael Lafferty had so eloquently coined, "hiding the bob," was the most nettlesome necessity of my travels.

Many a discomforting mile I had walked with a dire urgency to go, and many a chancy spot I had squatted in fear of being caught red-bottomed behind turfbanks or dolmens, in patches of prickly gorse or thorny brambles.

Yes, with belly cramped and complaining, I had searched the Four Provinces for private tuckaways. Somehow Missie always seemed aware of my distress, so she would stop, flash me her toothy smile, lift her tail, and drop a bushel of steaming road apples to the pavement. Boy, that's when I wanted to clock her, but good!

Now, having completed my alimentary function, I pulled the long chain of the overhead tank. A mighty waterfall yielded a swirling whirlpool, circling endlessly to the bowl's confluence, where it exited with a finale fainter than an infant's burp. And there, bobbing unhidden, was my Lincoln Log.

From the bathroom window, I watched the thundering cataracts course down Ben Gorm as I waited painstakingly for the overhead tank to fill with a prostatic trickle, and listened to the Herarty brothers in the yard taking delight in tackling Missie. Finally, the tank ready, I gave the brass chain a determined yank, but again, after setting off a deluge that threatened to drain Doo Lough, I remained face-to-face with my terrible torpedo.

"Are ye right?" called Margaret from the door. "You haven't gone drowning on us, have ye?"

"Oh, no, I'm fine." I fended her off. "I'll be just another minute, thank you."

I closed the lid and sat like a dunce atop it, as the tank slowly filled a third time. Imagine, on an island of tumultuous watercourses enough to quench the briny ocean's thirst, I was forced to wait on this sad pathetic dribble.

One last time, I swung on the chain like Quasimodo tolling the bells of Notre Dame, muttering an Aquarian prayer to the twelve Irish river gods to deliver a cascade not witnessed since the sinking of Atlantis. After the watery vortex subsided to its final soft gurgle, I took a deep breath and lifted the lid. And there, dancing on the waves, floated my unsinkable Mr. Brown.

Dropping the lid in disgust, I escaped the jacks and dashed outdoors to find the Herartys at the gate, with Margaret holding Missie by the winkers.

"May God deliver you home safe." She handed me the reins.

"Thank you so much for everything," I replied, searching for some way to tell her of my unsuccessful evacuation. I settled on the gentlest euphemism I could come up with: "I'm sorry, Margaret, but I'm afraid I left you a little souvenir in the bathroom."

"A souvenir, is it!" she exclaimed, her eyes brightening. "Arragh, love, you shouldn't of. Wasn't it grand just having you. Oh, thank you, yes, but there was no need. No need, a'tall."

She planted a wet kiss on my face, and I was incapable of stuttering a single syllable to this lovely trusting woman. I was still clearing my throat as she pranced off lively toward the house. Rather than chase after her to explain my unfinished business, I guiltily hurried Missie through the gate and down the road. I simply couldn't face the mortification of apologizing for the token of appreciation I had left behind.

Scurrying from my embarrassment, I kept up a frantic pace all morning, out of this enchanting valley, spoiled for me by my own rude memento to Margaret. The wild Bundorragha River roared alongside us, its lush green banks dressed in red fern, but I only stopped to catch my breath when we flowed with it to the edge of Killary Harbor. There, across this deep, narrow fjord, the Maumturks and Twelve Pins of Connemara beckoned to us with sunbursts off their granite crowns.

I was anxious to flee the county, from Mayo to Galway, but that involved a long trek along the high road above Killary's northern shore, looking across at Leenane, our destination so close and yet so far. We finally arrived at Aasleagh Falls at the point of the harbor and crossed over a bridge to start back along Killary's southern shore.

Soon we came upon a second bridge where an old gent in tweed was holding court amongst schoolchildren. It struck me as a scene Norman Rockwell might have painted if he had lived in Leenane, instead of Stockbridge, Massachusetts.

"Where's your staff?" Mr. Coyne gestured with his own handsome stick of holly, after the children had gathered around and we'd introduced ourselves.

"It splintered just back the road and I threw the pieces into Doo Lough."

"Broken over her back, was it?"

"No, no, it finally just gave out, and I'm afraid I'm soon to follow."

"Nonsense, you're weathering well, but you do need a support of some sort. 'Tis well known, going back to Jesus telling his apostles, 'Go out now to the world with walking sticks.' "

"I do feel its absence. The road is suddenly lonelier and scarier."

"Ah, yes, 'tis a protector as well as companion," said the congenial old man, putting on a display of martial arts with his holly to the delight of his youngsters. "Don't you know, we Irish were forbidden swords in bygone days, so over the years we've gained prowess with the blackthorn and shillelagh, hey? Those hard staffs could turn deadly in the right hands," he added, looping his stick above the children's heads. "In my youth, I would see young men fencing one another with sticks at the crossroads and, believe me, they had the talents of any swordsman in the garrison yards."

I lingered for some time, enjoying this gleeman's banter and sharing the amusement of his attentive batch. Finally I gathered Missie for the road, with renewed enthusiasm. After all, by stepping back into County Galway, we were in effect completing the circuit of the isle, if not the journey.

"Take this, will ye," the old fellow offered me his staff. "Every rambler of the road needs a sturdy walking stick for a companion, and the holly is known as 'the Green Knight.' "

"Oh, no, I couldn't."

"Why not, when it's being offered?" he said, mildly offended, holding it up to me with both hands. "What better stick than holly, with Christmas three weeks away? And haven't I others put away, and won't these youngsters be my walking stick home?"

Finally I accepted his gracious offer, sizing up the holly, to the exact dimensions of my hazel, and tapping it against my sneaker.

"A perfect fit. I can't thank you enough."

"Well, then, don't thank me at all." His rosy face beamed. "I'll be honored for you to complete your walkabout with it. So, Godspeed! Now, children, have you any Irish in your heads?"

"*Slan Abhaile,* Mr. Donkeyman."

So, with Green Knight in hand, I led Missie across the Glennagevlagh Bridge into County Galway, looking back to see that the children had huddled around Mr. Coyne, as he limped along amidst their clamorous company.

In turn, Missie and I continued toward Leenane in the daylight's wane, believing God had assigned a band of angels to orchestrate our last leg home.

Rounding Roundstone

We found excellent lodgings in Leenane with the Kings of Killary House, where Missie was led to the mountain slopes of the Devil's Mother behind their home. But despite my comfortable bed, I tossed and turned the whole night. For months, I had been having a recurring premonition that something terrible was to happen tomorrow, December 7. Perhaps this foreboding was inspired by the Day of Infamy, or my need to be in Clifden by the eighth, the final turning point in our journey. Or perhaps it was simply a Vietnam holdover: the closer to going home, the more likely a mishap.

For whatever reason, the night was endless, and it was no help to think of Missie grazing out back at the base of a mountain called the Devil's Mother. It was only too easy to imagine the devilment that might befall her—a tumble on the dark mountainside, a badger bite, an escape through a broken-down gap in the stone wall.

Roused by daybreak, I was relieved to find my little brownie calling happily at the gate. We were soon on the road into Connemara, eager to reach our goal of Clifden and to complete "the Great Western Perambulation," right on the schedule worked out back on Garland Sunday with Pat Hayes in Schull, County Cork, more than four months and a thousand miles ago.

Forewarned by the odd flashes of omen I had experienced leading up to this day, I was extra vigilant for the hazards of the road: the careening lorry, the wheel-busting pothole, the highwayman in the thickets. I would also take extra precautions before disappearing around sharp bends and treacherous curves, glancing back to see what might be gaining on us from behind.

Running through the checklist of potential disasters in my mind, I realized I hadn't examined Missie's hooves recently, habitually still delinquent in this daily task. And sure enough, I lifted her right front leg to find her shoe split in two, a jagged edge pinching into her hoof-bed.

Aghast, I led Missie off the road and quickly removed the cart, fearing the worst. So, this was my premonition come to pass, but would I be able to forestall disaster by anticipating it? Missie showed no apparent discomfort, and I wondered if the shoe had just broken last night on the stony slopes. With a shudder it occurred to me it may have split in eerie synchronicity with my hazel. And now, was my heart the next to break?

I was pacing before the waters of Killary, fighting back the panic, when a car pulled up.

"Are you in trouble?" asked a farmer, father to a full load of bright-faced little ones.

I explained my plight, and in a flash the man took tools from the car's boot and removed Missie's broken shoe with the ready skill of a blacksmith.

"You're in luck, her hoof isn't affected," he reassured me as he worked it with a rasp. "You can still walk her on a bit, but not too far, or her hoof will wear thin."

Thanking the handy Samaritan and clowning a bit with his happy young brood, I retackled Missie to the cart and resumed the road. Yet another band of angels singing me on my way.

A few miles along, I passed a garage where a mechanic was outside leaning against the front door.

"Your ass is limping!" he shouted out to me.

"She's broken a shoe," I explained, holding up the two pieces in either hand.

"Call in to the Kylemore House just ahead—the Naughtons will put you up," Jimmy instructed me, after we had met and assessed the situation. "Then come back to me and I'll drive you to the smith in Renvyle to brace that shoe for you."

As suddenly as the problem had presented itself, it was expeditiously resolved through the multiple of kindnesses of the community. In a span of two hours, I had settled Missie with the Naughtons, been lifted to Renvyle by Jimmy, handed the shoe to smith John Welsh who promised delivery next morning, and been dropped back at Letterfrack Cross by Jimmy on his way home. I stuck out my thumb, and one passing car later I was back at Kylemore House, sitting before a tasty grill of egg and sausage.

"Enjoy that, now," said Kathleen Naughton, "and I'll go upstairs and run you a bath. And if you have any dirty clothes, bring them in to be washed."

I took knife and fork in hand, relieved that I had not ruined the karma of Irish hospitality, and reveling in the life of a lord for the night. Kathleen filled me in on the history of her elegant Georgian home, built by Lord Ardelaun in 1785 and later owned by Oliver St. John Gogarty, famous in his day as doctor, poet, and politician, but best known now as the model for James Joyce's "Buck Mulligan."

Browsing in the opulent library later, I opened a volume of Dr. Gogarty's poetry and came upon the apt selection, "The Forge," struck by the concluding couplet, ". . . For song that is lovely is light and aloof / As the sparks that fly up from the well-shod hoof."

Next morning, a call from the footpath beneath my window shook me from my sleep.

"Oh, Donkeyman! 'Tis the Holy Day, and didn't you say you needed to be in Clifden by day's end!"

I jumped to the window and looked out to see John Welsh. "I have your golden slipper, boy," he shouted, holding up a shining brass shoe.

Soon I was grasping Missie's lugs while John slid the slipper onto the princess's dainty foot. After nailing it into place, he tightened the other shoes as well. Rising again, he wiped his brow and announced, "There you go, son. She's well-nailed for your remaining miles."

I handed him three pounds.

"Do you want me to box you one?" he said, repelling the money with a hard fist. "Go on, out of that."

So, on this cold but sunny feast-day, we set off for Clifden with Missie's four shoes ringing as brightly as Shandon's bells. We strode along the lovely lakes past Kylemore Abbey, crossed Tullywee Bridge, and tipped through the quaint Quaker village of Letterfrack without a wrinkle in our day.

In the afternoon, however, the weather took a turn and a hard rain forced us to take shelter at Moyard Cross. With no sign of a letup, we pushed on, but the unrelenting rain drove us to ground in Streamstown, three miles short of our goal. Martin and Teresa O'Toole proved to be affable hosts, however, and I went to Mass with them that evening at St. Joseph in Clifden, allaying my concern for falling short of my destination.

The church was decorated for Advent, rich purple cloth draped over altar and rail, and the wet coats of parishioners steamed like cattle after a summer rain. My mind drifted throughout the service, lost in the scent of incense mingling with candle wax and the sweet sounds of the young choir from the loft above.

I thought gratefully of the many hands and hearts that had helped me reach this place at this time. After communion, I bowed my head and thanked God for delivering us safely thus far, asking for his continued watch on "the Homeward Swing."

As I lifted my eyes once again, the choir began to sing, as if speaking for me directly:

> "Hail, Queen of Heaven, the Ocean Star.
> Guide of the wanderer here below,
> Thrown on life's surge, we claim thy care,
> Save us from peril and from woe.
> Mother of Christ, Star of the Sea, pray for me."

" 'Guide of the Wanderer.' Of course. Just what I need." I bowed my head again as the choir repeated the chorus. I was filled with humility yet lifted by grace, praying to

Mary on the feast of her Immaculate Conception. Myself anything but immaculate, I felt more than ever the hope of her intercession.

"Mother of Christ, Star of the Sea, pray for me."

"Are ye coming or no?" snickered young Frank O'Toole, tugging at my sleeves. I lifted my head to see the congregation filing out of the church.

"A pretty hymn, that," I mumbled, turning beet-red and scooting out of the pew to join the rest of the family waiting in the middle aisle.

As we left Clifden next morning, I continued upon my appointed coastal route, which would lead me around the immense Roundstone Bog—a stretch almost as lonely as northeast Mayo and, similarly, a Gaeltacht area. It was no surprise now to find Irish speakers pushed to the desolate but beautiful extremities of the island.

The wind whipped up as we walked out of town, and a plastic bag caught on a wire fence sputtered like an engine, much like the biplane of John Alcock and Arthur Brown when they made landfall in a nearby bog on the first transatlantic flight in 1919.

The sun peeked through as we trekked through Ballinaboy and Ballyconnelly, shining on the granite uplands of the Twelve Pins behind us, and gleaming off the many miniature lakes in the black moors to our left. On our right, the tiny cabins of fishermen braved the might of wind and wave, stalwart in the face of the heaving sea. Here and there the rusting carcass of an abandoned automobile defied the embalming powers of the bog.

We earned our dozen miles that day, and wound up knocking on several doors without reply, before we found refuge with Thomas McHugh of Emlaughmore. And even there, the only place for Missie was a tiny wooden byre, formerly an outhouse.

"At least she'll be indoors for the night," Tom apologized, as Missie's pitiful snout poked through the door's small aperture.

I had to laugh at my hapless mate, but I reassured her with a kiss on the exposed nose. "Not to worry, Miss. I'll bail you out first thing tomorrow."

True to my word, we were on the road early on the morrow, another long stretch between bog and sea, with rain persisting through the day and the ocean's spindrift lathering my face with foam like a busy barber.

Reaching the seaside village of Roundstone, the road turned north alongside the bay; I'm sure it was a charming resort in the summer, with a view of the lovely Maumturks over the bay, but today the steady downpour dampened my enthusiasm. A fiery red rooster crowed in the middle of the street and a clamor of seagulls wheeled above. I'd been told further north that "a red crowd" inhabited South Connemara, and was reminded of this when a redheaded mother passed by, wheeling two red-topped children in a pram.

An old woman called me to her kitchen door, saying she would pray to Saint Raphael for us, for he had helped the young traveler Tobias. Although thankful, I would have gladly traded her petition—God forgive me—for the sizzling potato cakes that grilled golden in her frying pan, "boxty" they were called. A few doors down I confronted another redhead, a sixtyish bloke about the height of a rain barrel, dough-faced with round fleshy ears like radio knobs, and trousers hiked so high his belt buckle threatened to scratch his chin. Absurd as he looked, he carried himself like any lord-mayor, and, eyeballing me, he shared some remark to his neighbors in Irish, who broke out in hearty laughter.

Oh, to own the Irish tongue, I said to myself, knowing the joke was at my expense. *Wouldn't I do my best to unplug that human wireless, and fast.*

We plodded ten miles through this filthy squall, and completed our loop around the giant bog by reaching Toombeola and finding refuge at the Fishery, the oldest public house in Connemara, formerly known as Mother Clancy's.

I had been told I would find Connemara folk more fierce and independent than the other Gaeltachts, a people indigenous to their stony land, rather than driven there by Plantation and partition in the North.

One old sage informed me, "Cromwell knew what he was doing when he forbade anyone from Connemara and, indeed, Connaught, from crossing the River Shannon, under penalty of death."

Amongst the natives that long enjoyable evening, I was surprised to run into a fellow veteran of Vietnam. "Aye, I did my time in-country for the Green Card," he confided. "After my discharge from the army, I lived in Chicago for a while, but soon got tired of the rat race."

"I've known people who fled the States to avoid that fight, but you're the first I've met who went in the other direction."

"Well, I suppose it's an Irish tradition of sorts. Have you heard of 'the Wild Geese'?"

"Oh, yes. Fighting on the Continent, after the Flight of the Earls."

"It didn't end there, though. Many Irish were happy to fight the English in your Revolution. In fact, during your War of Independence, one of five colonials who died at Bunker Hill were Irish, and there were Irish brigades on both sides of the Civil War, and in the thick of it, too. I've heard that some Aran islanders returned home from that war and continued to wear their blue or gray uniforms till their dying day. And they remained civil to one another, if you can believe it, swapping war stories in the pubs of Kilronan. Can you imagine their wild chat on a winter's night?"

"Sadly, they had a lot to talk about," I added. "Winchester, Chicamauga, and Antietam, still cursing Burnside for sending his troops across the stone bridge to certain death."

"Before the Famine, nearly half of the soldiers in the British army were Irish-born," piped up an elder from his stool, "being sent all over the globe but to Ireland, of course, in fear they'd turn against the Crown and lead an 'Irish Revolution.'"

"Ireland's greatest exports have been soldiers and priests," summed up the friendly proprietor, Joe Nee, setting up pints in front of us. "Next to the Guinness, of course."

After a sociable and comfortable night at the Fishery, I gathered Missie for another forlorn footslog through a barony of stone and sea spume. High winds pounded our starboard but we held course along the bayside and into the nearly-not-there village of Glinsk. Crossing over another empty peninsula, we reached the scattered settlement of Carna and fought on another mile through the gray mizzle to find digs with John and Katherine Jennings, an enthusiastic pair of middle-aged teachers.

The heart of their home was a sitting room where the light from the fire flickered on shelves of books climbed to the ceiling, while countless volumes were laid open upon table, stool, and chair like a flock of gulls on the wing.

After a delicious bowl of mutton soup and treacle tart, I mentioned to Katherine that their house made me think of how Brother Michael O Cleary's cell must have looked while he was compiling *The History of Ireland*.

"Oh, yes," she replied. "Books are our treasure houses, the salvation of our nation. And we do follow Brother Michael in our own way. But imagine further back, when the substance of all those stories," she gestured toward a bookcase, "was carried in the heads of the esteemed seanachies of Connemara."

Both Katherine and John regaled me with stories and quotations, many they could speak out like oracles, but frequently they'd grab a book to read from, until the open volumes collected around their chairs like heaps of shucked oyster shells. And for whatever I told them of my travels, they had an apt citation.

Starting with my predecessor Padraic O Conaire, writing of "My Little Black Ass":

"I have the little black ass still, and I shall have him until he dies. Many a long mile we have traveled lonely roads in all kinds of weather. He has mended his way in some respects. His master, alas, has not; and I believe the little black rogue knows as well as anybody in the world that he has not."

We continued through the evening reading or reciting favorite poems which included those of Desmond O'Grady, Padraic Colum, Seamus Heaney, John Hewitt, and many more.

As the fire faded on our warm, book-filled evening, Katherine offered some lines from Helen Jane Waddell: " '*Would you think Heaven could be so small a thing / As a lit window on the hills at night?*' "

"Your house was that very thing tonight," I answered her wholeheartedly.

Joe, a neighbor, came blowing in through the door. After he had greeted the house in Irish, he addressed me in English with a shake of hands. "I saw you struggling out from Cashel this morning, fifteen long miles ago, and, says I to meself, 'There's better men in our parish gone east.' "

"That's fine chat for a world-class traveler to hear," scolded Katherine. "Do you know what Joe is on about, Kevin . . . 'gone east'? 'Tis a local expression about poor unfortunate folks who are sent to St. Brigid's Psychiatric Hospital in Ballinasloe. He thinks your journey is a feckless endeavor—a fool's errand—but pay him no heed. He's jealous, he is."

"Oh, aye, jealous, that's it, Katherine," Joe roared, carefully picking his steps through stacks of books. "You have me rightly pegged, you do."

Next morning the northwesterly gales persisted but the rain let up by noon, as the sun punched holes through the clouds. With the wind at our backs, we trooped through the village of Kilkieran where I espied two hookers with rust-red sails rocking by the quay. These handsome three-masted boats, now rare and treasured, used to ply these waters regularly, taking turf and other supplies to the Aran Islands—a ship so significant it adorns Galway City's coat of arms.

We persevered through the long day, with nothing to break our monotony but speculation on the tendrils of gray smoke that curled up from the recesses of the bog. Could they be the campfires of travelers, or stills of poteen-makers? Or daytime manifestations of will-o'-the-wisps? For company we had only the distant hand-waving of elders standing in front of their boxes of government housing near Flannery Bridge.

We persisted to Derryrush, completing another peninsular loop and finding shelter with an extended family of O'Malleys. Grandpa Tom kindly placed Missie in the byre, but took fresh bath towels to wipe her down, which pleased the missus but little.

"Do you want soap and shampoo while ye're at it?" she chided, snapping the wet towels from his grasp.

The elder Mrs. Mary O'Malley certainly proved to be the character of the family, as she sat at supper with her son Eamonn and daughter-in-law Barbara, all chatting away in Irish. The old matron launched a few salvos to great laughter among her kin, but at one point caught herself in midsentence and turned to ask me if I knew much Irish.

"Just a few salutations," I answered, before pouring a battalion of peas down my throat.

Mrs. O'Malley rattled off another volley of the ancient tongue to her clan, and turned again to ask if I had a hint of what she had said.

"Why, yes," I responded with surprising confidence. "You told everyone you'll have to be more careful with what you say, just in case I'm not as stupid as I look."

The family nearly toppled the table in raucous laughter, as Mrs. O'Malley turned redder than her hair was white.

"Bravo, Kevin," Barbara squealed. "You hit the nail right on the head!"

At night's end, old Tom left his chair by the fire.

"Where ye going?" asked the missus

"I'm going out to give the lad's ass a bitteen more hay," he said with a grunt. "Sure, won't it stand to her in the end."

Lamplight to Streetlights

Missie and I set off next morning into a bright but blustery mid-December day, quite refreshing for a trek through mountainous terrain, and were enjoying a gladsome stroll when we came upon a horseman walking two gray-dappled Connemara ponies toward us.

"Me boyos seem to have a yen for your mate," the jobber chuckled, quieting his handsome pair as they whinnied at our approach.

"They're beautiful animals," I observed, as I reined in my own flirtatious brown-eyed girl.

"Remarkable ponies they are, with a legendary lineage," he continued, quick to praise his pets. "They're considered Ireland's only native breed, coming with the Celts some twenty-five hundred years ago, supposedly mixing in the blood of Spanish Arabians who swam ashore when the Armada sunk. Whatever the bloodline, they adapted to a wild life in the harsh Connemara landscape—mountain, bog, and beach—and have become surefooted workers and great show-jumpers as well."

"They're so strong and sturdy-looking," I patted the pair.

"In the old days it was desperately poor farmers who would catch and train the ponies, to help eke a living out of the land, clearing rocks, carrying seaweed, maneuvering over stone and through the muck. But now the breed is famous, and breeders come from around the world to the annual pony fair in Clifden to start lines in other countries. 'Tis only donkeys now, like your own, that carry the heavy creels of turf."

Missie, however, showed no sign of class-consciousness, and would have been happy to gallivant with the dashing ponies, but the horseman and I had to pull our charges in opposite directions. We traipsed along through Screeb and turned south on a solitary road through Lar Connaght toward Costelloe, our night's destination, admiring the high, fluffy stacks of cumulus that towered over the low moor.

"With the world belching out smog from L.A. to Bombay, look at this, Miss," I said, directing her gaze heavenward. "A majestical sight, is it not? The simple beauty of white cloud and blue sky."

The clouds, all adazzle at noon, turned golden as the sun descended, finally bursting into crimson as the day came to its early close, the bleak landscape turning into a fiery wonderland. The colors of the sky were mirrored in the myriad of tiny lakes that dotted the bog, and the horizon just faded away. A distant farmhouse stood out as if at arm's length, and the faraway voices of children at play carried clear in the frosty air.

I unhitched Missie from the cart and sat on a large stone, enjoying a sandwich of Barbara O'Malley's, as I pondered the approach of the hibernal solstice. Missie stepped across the quiet road, looking back at me like a child, not certain how far to go but wishing to show some independence.

She was something to behold, truly first-class: the lithe turn of head, the quick, attentive ears, the graceful gait, the rich, full coat of nut brown. An authentic princess in the unsung world of donkeys, as I was reminded by the oft-repeated refrain, "You're going to miss that donkey terribly."

Finishing my meal, I claimed my little charmer, thinking I should stop more often for such respites, to linger with my pet on our remaining days. I took hold of her reins and backed her in effortlessly between the shafts, before dropping the cart gently on the straddle.

That done, we strolled through this wondrous world of conical peaks toward Costelloe, stopping time and again to gaze up at a ceiling of stars that pierced the thin wintry sky.

After a good night with Mairtin O'Coughaile and family, we made a good start next morning by stopping in at Radio na Gaeltachta in Cashla. I delighted and amazed the friendly staffers by telling them I had now visited all three Irish-speaking stations in the country—*Corca Dhuibhne, Tir Chonaill,* and *Conamara*—and they, in turn, promised to broadcast our passage through this last Gaeltacht toward home.

Our night's destination was Spiddal, and the road showed only hardship as we set out beneath the sky's sulky gloom. As we slogged through this inhospitable terrain, a postman came whirring down the wet road on his bicycle, bag slung over shoulder. He squealed his brakes and dismounted for the chat, leaning against his bike at a perfectly pitched angle of repose.

"We're much alike, you and I," he said, after appraising my rig with a canny eye. "In a few years there'll be no more postmen riding bicycles down country lanes, and certainly no more donkeys and carts. As the saying goes, 'Our likes will never meet again.'"

Pointing to the pony nail pinned to my sweater by blacksmith Stephen Croghan back in March, the postman observed, "When the motorcar made its toehold in Ireland after World War Two, it was those things that kept it at bay for a while, blowing out the tires of the invaders, but their day has passed. The garage has replaced the forge, and the infernal combustion engine has taken over for horsepower, as well as legpower.

"Oh, don't I now know."

" 'Tis the likes of ourselves and every living thing that's being banished from the road. You'd weep at the songbirds I find along my route, knocked dead while darting among the hedges. And the human fatalities, too, old folk in black coats, struck down when walking or pedaling home at night. Why, one in three Irish road fatalities are pedestrians."

At that moment a heavy Volvo lorry came rumbling by, blowing up mist, as we were forced in hurried retreat off the roadside.

"As I was saying," the postman grimaced, straightening his blue cap. "Now that we're safe from traffic for a minute, let me tell you a little postal story that occurred in this barony a few years back. 'Tis a true story," he chuckled, "or as true as any you're likely to hear in Ireland."

The postman resumed his restful slant against the bicycle and launched into his tale.

"Years back, there was an old widdy-woman by the name of Aggie Hackett, living out the Barna way, raising seven lovely lasses. Shortly before the Yuletide holidays, she was boarding the bus for Galway to do her bit of Christmas shopping, but when she reached into her purse for bus fare, didn't a blast of wind come rising up, carrying away her savings of a long year—thirty pounds—flitting off irretrievably across the black bog."

"Oh," I sighed in sympathy to Aggie and in encouragement to the taleteller.

"Aggie stumbled home to sit at her kitchen table and weep into a checkered dishtowel, which is how her nosy neighbor Nora Flaherty found her later that morning. Hearing the tale of woe, the fiery redhead immediately suggested that Aggie write a letter to Saint Patrick, who was known to answer deserving petitioners. Though a woman of considerable faith, Aggie hesitated to make so selfish a plea, but Nora would not relent. So Aggie took pen and paper in hand and laboriously composed a heartfelt letter that would bring tears to a glass eye, thinking only of her poor daughters.

"When it came to the post office, with an undeliverable address and no return on the envelope, the postmaster had little choice but to open it. Well, the letter was so trusting and devoted in its humble way, that he showed it to one and then another of the postmen. In no time, we had all read it, and decided to deliver our own little Christmas miracle to Aggie. We managed to scrape together twenty-odd pounds, and put it in a tidy box with a green ribbon, with 'Saint Patrick,' written in fine Celtic script, as the sender.

"No sooner had the postman pedaled away from Aggie's door next morning, than Nora was over, demanding she open the parcel without delay. Aggie held it tremblingly in her hands, fumbling with the ribbon, but Nora snatched it from her and tore open the package. When the pound notes fell out, Aggie dropped to her knees in prayer, while Nora gathered the bills and began to count.

" ' . . . five, six, seven . . . ' sang Nora wildly.

" 'Praise dear Saint Patrick in his holy grave!' exclaimed Aggie.

" ' . . . twelve, thirteen, fourteen . . . ' on went Nora, stopping only to wet her fingertips.

" 'Praise the Infant Child, on this, His feast day,' rejoiced Aggie.

" ' . . . twenty, twenty-one, twenty-two . . . ' continued Nora gleefully.

" 'May I live to be one hundred to offer my humble prayers to the zenith's glory,' lauded Aggie Hackett.

" ' . . . twenty-three, twenty-four, twenty-five . . . ' Nora stopped abruptly. 'Why, there's only 25 pounds in it!'

" ' . . . Twenty-five pounds!' gasped Aggie, lifting herself up from the floor in pure exaltation.

" 'Aye, twenty-five pounds,' raved the redhead in a froth of spittle. 'And isn't it just like those thieving devils at the post office, to have snitched your other fiver!'

"And thus began Nora's feud against us postal workers, which ended only on that old hag's dying day. Just goes to show you—no good deed goes unpunished, and your poor postman never gets credit for the good he brings."

I was more than happy to give my postman friend credit for his amusing banter, and after sharing more laughs, we shook hands to depart, whereupon he took off his blue cap and removed its silver oval-shaped badge, with a shamrock to either side of his number, 19.

"Take this, you," he insisted, handing me the medal. "A reminder of when progress was nipping us at the heels."

Moved by his kind offering, I took the pony nail from my sweater. "Here, and this is for you. It's as good as Mary's Brooch—it's brought me nothing but blessings since it was pinned on me."

He affixed it to the lapel of his blue uniform while I fastened his badge to my sweater. We shook hands once more before going our separate ways, into the past and future.

Cold winds whipped our faces as Missie and I struggled along on the road beside Galway Bay.

"Where are the halcyon days?" I shouted through the wind gusts. "Where is the great kingfisher who calms the seas a week before the winter solstice?"

The gale ground us to a halt repeatedly, and I stared crestfallen at a signpost outside Inveran—AN SPIDDAL, 6 MILES—knowing the day's brutal hardship was far from over.

"Six long miles beside this churning ocean bed," I said to Missie; feeding her small amounts of oats to warm my hands, the cold feet in my wet squelching sneakers no longer belonging to me. "But it's our final stretch of ocean road" . . . consoling myself as much as her, as we continued through the biting tempest.

We were a fine pair of drowned rats by the time we staggered into Spiddal at nightfall. I could only pray the radio had prepared a welcome for us, moving some listener to pity, leaving a light on to guide the wanderer to shelter. Looking up the deserted main street, where dim Christmas trees hung over shop doorways, I thought of how Spiddal, "hospital" in Irish, had come by its name during the Famine—taking in the destitute who stumbled in from the distant recesses of Connemara. I could only hope my long weary walk found a more comforting end.

As that hope was diminishing with each slow and heavy step, a voice sang out from a closing butcher shop.

"You're quite the hardy trooper!" shouted the victualer, shaking his head in disbelief. John Enda by name, he had my accommodations all figured out. "Step down to Hughes's Bar, and he'll see to you and the *asal* for the night. Then be off to the Buluisce Restaurant where John Glanville has a steak sizzling in your honor. Go on, now, out of this mess."

Spiddal of the Welcomes!

A little later, at Hughes's Bar, I bumped into Angle, a charming young woman I had met that morning at the radio station. Soon I fell into company with her friends, and they invited me to Teach Forbo, a function hall outside town where local children presented the Christmas Pageant in Irish. It was a charming performance, but as the children shuffled off stage, they chattered excitedly amongst themselves in English, which clearly bothered one of Angle's friends.

"For centuries, we feared English decrees would snuff out our language," she objected, "but we kept our mother tongue alive to this very day. And now—now it's that hypnotic television, tirelessly spouting English day after day, that threatens to cut us off. Not English cruelty, but English programming, will wrest the tongue from our heads."

" '*Is lu i an Ghaeilge na an t-uisce sa ngloine sin.*' " One of Angle's friends quoted a saying: " 'The Irish is less than water in that glass.' "

The weather and the road had taken their toll, so I retired early, but I awoke so ill next morning I would gladly have written my name on a toe-tag and awaited the undertaker's arrival. Thick with phlegm and flu, I dragged myself to the window and looked out at sea squalls battering the gray town. I wobbled down to the lounge and asked Mr. Hughes if I could stay on another day.

"Jaysus, by all means." He assessed my condition in a glance. "Take your rest, and what harm? 'Tis a dismal old day, and you'd find little comfort on the road with Saturday shoppers going into Galway to do their bit of Christmas shopping. Go on, upstairs, and I'll bring you some aspirin and a bit of breakfast."

I fell in and out of sleep that long day, waking to the knocks of my keepers delivering steaming lemon drink and hot-water bottles. Icy pellets clicked on the panes like the impatient drumming of a banshee's fingernails, waiting for my last death throe. Homesickness accompanied my fever and chills, as I lapsed back to a childhood when illness meant a loving mother only a cough away.

Bedridden with measles or chicken pox, I'd play with my few toys, my knees making hills and valleys, so like the Berkshires of home, for my little lumber truck to putter through, or trenches for my plastic soldiers. Best of all, I enjoyed my stamp collection, pasting those miniature emblems of the world into my album, dreaming over the prized Irish issues, which had adorned letters from my grandmother.

A gentle rap came to the door.

"Hot whiskey with sugar and cloves," announced Mrs. Hughes, propping up my pillows before handing me the hot glass. "Pour that into you," she cooed, "and I guarantee ye'll be right for morning. And don't fret over your Missie. The lads are having a grand time caring for her."

The long night drifted between bone-chills and the warm smattering of Irish below. Kind as the Hughes family had been to me, I took my main comfort in the idea that tomorrow night, God willing, I'd be staying with friends by Galway City, away for good from the assault of the tireless sea.

I sprang from bed next morning, light-headed but ready to roll. I went to mass at St. Eanna's Church and then collected Missie for our approach to Galway along the bay. Wheezing and snuffling, I slogged a dogged dozen miles. The one respite was tea and cake with a retired American couple living in Salt Hill, who said I reminded them of the old comic strip character Barney Google, with his donkey Spark Plug.

The afternoon was drawing to a close when we reached Galway City, but there was no song to be sung this day of the harbor's glorious sunsets, just low gray turbulence. Nonetheless, I was flooded with the feeling of returning to home turf; it was as though the journey was all but over. I stood on the bridge under which Lough Corrib drains into Galway Bay, looking at the Spanish Arch to one side, and, to the other, what remained of the old fisherfolk quarter of Claddagh, Depression-era concrete houses now, instead of the former huddle of thatched cottages, the glorious fleet of pucans and gleoiteogs now just a memory.

I was to meet my good friends Donal and Helen Honan in town, who had befriended me when I moved to Galway back in January. Recently married, Donal was a schoolteacher who hailed from Clare, and Helen a nurse from London whose father was bred in Mayo.

It was Donal who had filled me in on the history of this excitingly reviving town, from its medieval heyday as an English-speaking city-state lorded over by the families of its aristocratic merchant "tribes," to its sufferings in rebellion against Cromwell and against William. Also, its decimation by the Famine, when the town seemed to have reached the end of its tether, only to stir to life again with the establishment of the Irish state, a comeback putting it on the way to becoming the capital of the west, to balance Dublin in the east. It soon became my favorite city in the world.

I had arranged to meet the Honans in Eyre Square, alongside the statue of the beloved native writer Padraic O Conaire.

"Why, you're nearly one with himself!" Donal exclaimed as he came upon us. "They'll have to erect a statue of you, too. Your little brown ass here will be as famous as his *asal beag dubh*."

Helen embraced me, and then held me at arm's length to marvel, "I can't believe you ever stuck it out."

They guided us out to where they lived, in a new development called Castlelawn Heights, and had arranged for Missie to stay at the only farm left in the neighborhood, a lone thatched cottage amidst the encroaching sprawl of "estate homes." We were welcomed by Walter and Tom Hosty, an aged but lively pair of bachelor brothers, into a close, earth-colored room lit only by a roaring fire. The warm light flickered off portraits of saints looking down with piteous aspect from smoke-stained walls, and danced off the glaze of old earthernware jugs and platters arrayed on a large dresser.

The Hostys were in no hurry to see us away, nor were we in any hurry to leave. They broke out the Paddy and poured us generous glasses, which soon fired our tongues for storytelling. After I shared some far-fetched tale of the road, Tom gasped out, "Blood an' ages, you're a topping explorer. As bold a man as Christopher Columbus."

The Honans burst out laughing, and I demurely declined the comparison. "Thanks, but I'm merely a rover, not an explorer."

"Don't diminish the deed," he said in earnest, putting whiskey to parched lips. "'Tis a powerful journey, and 'twould take some searching to find another lad such as yourself to make it."

"That's for sure," chuckled Donal, giving me a playful jab.

"Did you know Columbus landed at Galway to hear Mass before sailing off to discover America? A fact, that." Tom motioned to Donal, who nodded in confirmation. "Aye, his three ships anchored down by Claddagh. Wasn't that some adventure, sailing over the brink of the known world, where none had dared go before? Except for our own Irish saints, of course," he concluded with a thoughtful smack of his lips.

"Did you murder a postman along the way?" Walter interjected, pointing to the AN POST badge on my sweater.

"No, but we almost died together, under the wheels of a runaway lorry. Actually, he gave it to me to seal our bond as relics of the road, saying progress was nipping us at the heels."

"Nipping, is it?" Walter replied, wiping his nose with a hankie. "'Tis swallowing us up whole! Look out that window there at the rows of new houses," he insisted, standing to draw the curtain aside. "Here we sat the livelong night with no light but the moon itself. Now look out, will ya, it's the blooming Siege of Limerick! All that's missing is the bloody battering ram. I can't tell you the number of offers we've got, just to surrender and move out of the way. I get annoyed in hearing that Galway is Ireland's fastest-growing city, as if it's only ourselves left in the way."

"Not that we mind having fine neighbors like Donal and Helen here, you understand. But it's cruel, too, isn't it," Tom said as he added more peat to the flames, "being offered buckets of money at the heel of one's living days, and nary a drop when we really could have used it. Aye, saving our few shillings in that old jug above, for a pint and card game on a Saturday night."

"We barely managed to keep out the hunger," added Walter, "praying for the hens to keep laying, and for the weather not to wipe us out entirely. Now we're a pen-scratch away from becoming millionaires for our biteen of land."

Tom shuffled toward the old press, bent and bowed, as their sheepdog darted about his legs.

"Another dram of Paddy?" he asked, uncapping the bottle before we could reply. "But, ye know, if me teeth weren't so long in me head, I might truly sell this old plot and go loose and silly about the world."

"Where would you set off to?" I asked, holding out my glass to receive a generous dollop.

"The Wild West, of course! I'd become a cowboy and gallop away on my pinto pony, wearing a ten-gallon hat and rattlesnake boots, and into the saloons I'd go every night to wash away me dusty thirst."

"You would not, then," contradicted Walter with a knowing nod. "If John Wayne himself, may he rest in peace, appeared at our door this very night, you'd find some sorry excuse to stay at home."

"No telling what I might do," replied Tom with a mischievous grin. "Bags o' money does be doin' strange things to people. Why, I might even latch on to some gal in one of those saloons, and wake up in the morning to the flutter of petticoats and the smell of flapjacks on the griddle. Isn't that right, Kevin? Flapjacks?"

"Do you hear the nonsense I've put up with these long years," said Walter, turning a deaf ear toward his brother's rambling, but unable to keep a sly smile from creeping over his face.

The talk returned to the march of progress through Ireland, and Donal observed that it would soon have the youngest population in Europe.

"Well, God bless and protect them all," Tom responded. "May the new Ireland prosper and leave the hard knocks to old times."

"Old or new, 'tis the family that will hold the country together, and the children that make us strong," Walter concluded. "And it's prayer that will keep the family together. Aye, that's the mortar that will properly build our land with bricks of faith."

We left the Hostys' at midnight, walking a short distance to the Honans' tidy new home with all its modern conveniences.

"Have you met many characters like that pair on your roundabout?" Donal asked me, as the lights of the sprawling city shone brightly before us.

"Oh, a few," I smiled, thinking of so many.

"It's amazing when you think of the changes they've seen in their lifetime," Helen mused. "The old Ireland they knew, disappearing from their very doorstep."

"Two good men who knew nothing but hardship, giving way to a hopeful, prosperous future," stressed Donal. "Our generation must never forget how our elders and forebears worked and cherished the land."

"We won't," said Helen with confidence, taking him by the arm.

A Bonfire in Ballygar

CHAPTER SIXTY-TWO

C artymore today, is it?" asked Walter Hosty, helping me dress Missie next morning.

"Yep, just ten miles. And I'll be spending two nights at the Oasis Pub there. Do you know the Oasis?"

"The Oasis!" he scoffed with a smile, as he dropped the cart over the straddle. "How would I ever know a pub in that far-off part of the country?"

"I spent three nights there at the start of my journey, while Missie was getting a gall-cure treatment. I more or less earned my keep by pulling pints and amusing the patrons. The Laffertys were very kind to me, and helped me stay on the road."

"Aye, good people, so. Now, safe home, and may a gallery of saints protect you."

Missie and I cautiously maneuvered through the rotaries outside Galway City, arriving at noon to Carnmore Cross, where I stopped to present a gleaming apple to my road queen.

"Do you know the reason for this treat?" I asked, giving Missie a mighty hug around her neck, as a flock of curious black-headed sheep congregated around us. "This is where our ring comes full circle, where our journey is clasped! This is my toast to you, Missie Long-Ears, for persevering through our roundabout."

Missie gnashed through the apple's core, juices flying, and chomped away contentedly, quite unimpressed by our accomplishment.

"Do you remember that rainy Sunday in May when we walked this road, you with your stripped shoulder on the mend? But we persisted, didn't we? And now look at us, one thousand six hundred thirty-seven miles later! Just think of all we never would have known if we hadn't braved that hollow-bright fog in Clare."

Missie was more interested in the next apple than in the past thousand miles.

"Yes, my princess, we're back on the Old Coach Road!" I proclaimed with a shout, scattering the sheep with a thunderclap of hands.

Of our welcome at the Oasis, I can only say that Ferdinand and Isabella could have done no better for Columbus than Michael and Eileen Lafferty did for me. It was royal court indeed. The roadside pub was bursting with the old gents we had met back in May, along with scores of dignitaries from outlying parishes—wraggle-taggle farmers to Norfolk-coated gentry—all to hear the American spout of his tales. But this wasn't the Yank after a mere forty miles of road, but forty times that amount.

For two nights I fielded questions from all and sundry. I extolled the beauty and bounty of the island I had explored, the spirit and cheek of the natives I had met, the commerce and customs, the history and poetry of the land.

" 'Tis shocking, the tinkers being dacent people," reflected one farmer, after I related my night with the O'Briens in Kerry. "Would anyone here chance a night in a tinker's encampment?"

"That, I wouldn't," my old supporter Paddy Treacy replied to the rapt assemblage. "But hearing this lad's story, I might be inclined to tip my cap, at least."

Another pondered my safe passage through the troubles in the North. "What did you say your man's name was who saw you safe through Belfast? Perry, was it? Well, there's no Irish in that. I wouldn't believe such kindness, but for you there telling me."

"Well, now," said Michael Lafferty, putting an arm over me. "Doesn't that say a wealth for our dear old country!"

Amidst cheers, I sat prouder than the *Santa Maria* billowing in full mast, having dismissed old prejudices with the simple wag of my tongue, leaving the biggest skeptics to reevaluate their age-old mistrusts and positions.

"The O'Haras have been nothing but great travelers throughout the ages," said one local, raising his glass in my honor. "Wasn't the Galway native Robert O'Hara Burke, the first to travel the great Outback of Australia to Cooper's Creek? And Rudyard Kipling's 'Kim' was an O'Hara, wasn't he? Why, Kim's father must be a relation of yours," he joked, "joining the British regiment and off to India, where he could make mischief a continent away."

Cartymore's dear John Burke, who had so diligently nursed Missie back to health last spring, volunteered to put her up again, and when I checked the byre that first evening I found him currying Missie as if she were a champion thoroughbred from the Plains of Kildare.

"She's grand." The sixtyish bachelor stepped back to admire Missie, who was sniffing approvingly at the fresh straw beneath her feet. "When you left us that rainy Sunday, I shook me head and said, 'God will sorely need to intercede in this lad's journey, otherwise he'll fail, and fail surely.' Michael and Eileen came back a week later with news of you safely camped in Doolin, and once you survived that long wet week I believed God would see you through to the end."

"That was the toughest week of all," I heartily agreed.

"And, by the powers, your donkey is living proof of it. Look at her," he said, resuming the long brush strokes which brought out the lustrous sheen of her winter coat. "She's as proud as any donkey who ever graced the Ballinasloe Green. Not even a trace of her scalded breast. She's blue-ribbon," he brushed her down with an emphatic sweep, "and a living token of God's favor and grace."

I had built a margin of safety into my schedule, and now I was able to take advantage of it. So even after two celebratory nights at the Oasis, I had only seven miles a day to cover to reach Rattigan's in Roscommon on Christmas Eve. We weren't long back on the road when we met, standing up ahead, grinning in equine long-toothed splendor, the capital horseman himself, Jimmy McDermott of Kilteevan.

"By God, ye've nearly done it," he threw his powerful arms around me. "And walking your little beast the whole time!"

After giving me a jubilant knockabout, Jimmy gave Missie a thorough twenty-one-point check.

"She's a show donkey." He flashed me the thumbs-up. "You're no joke, Kevin O'Hara. Ye've become a right jobber."

I told Jimmy how Missie's gait had become noticeably brighter since Carnmore Cross, and he confirmed, "She knows she's on the homestretch. I might have told you donkeys are ignorant, but they always know what they want to know. And Missie knows she's nosing home."

I was glad to get fresh news of home myself, delighted to hear that Grannie Kelly, my aunts and uncles, and the Four Masters, were all in good form. Jimmy updated me on the hilarity and general goings-on at Rattigan's, but I had a bone or two to pick with the horseman, for his failure to provide me with a full warranty and a complete drover's manual.

"Jimmy, why didn't you fill me in on the female mysteries of Missie's cycles, when she would go into wanton spells to shame the Sirens in Homer's *Odyssey*?"

"I wasn't sure you were mature enough to understand." He slapped my back with a roguish laugh. "Besides, what could you have done if I did tell you in advance? Mount a machine gun atop your mudbox to keep all the jackos at bay?"

"Still, it would have been nice to know. And speaking of knowing, I wish I had known what a donkey was supposed to cost. I saw a prize black jack in Glencolumbkille going for six quid, and the buyer said that was highway robbery. Six quid! And here I paid you forty for Missie. She's my little heroine, of course, and I wouldn't trade her for anything, but bloody hell, Jimmy, I should have gotten a six-mule team or something, for all that money!"

Jimmy let out a great guffaw: "You asked me to find an ass that could travel the Ring of Ireland, am I right?" he challenged, pinning me up playfully against the door of his lorry. "Do you think that six-quid jack had the heart of your mare? Do you think he could climb Glengesh Pass, like you wrote about Missie in the *Champion*, do you?"

"Not a chance," I conceded, wriggling free of his grasp, thinking back on her more recent march from Screeb to Spiddal.

"Now, rather than you going through Monivea, there's a two-mile boreen atop the village that leads to Abbeyknockmoy," he advised, climbing into the cab. "I just left

Frank Mannion's bar, and he has it arranged that you stay with a sound fellow named Paddy Mulroy. I'll delay no further, but I'll be seeing you soon. When will ye be arriving at Rattigan's?"

"Christmas Eve."

He spat hotly out the window into the hedge: "That's Monday week! Why not this Saturday or Sunday?"

"I want to be like Phileas Fogg in *Around the World in Eighty Days*," I chuckled. "The clock ticking on the wall, edging toward the last minute, while those old cronies wring their pound notes, counting on me to fail. But just as darkness falls, I'll come *knock, knock, knock*ing on Rattigan's door."

"Don't be too cute," Jimmy warned, firing his motor to life. "You might be on the pig's back, but 'tis a slippery back. Your days are numbered and much can go wrong in forty miles. 'Twould be a great blundering if something went awry in the end. And costly to me, I might add."

"I'll be there," I grinned, with foolhardy confidence.

No ill befell us on enjoyable nights in Abbeyknockmoy and then in Moylough, so it was the winter solstice when Missie and I arrived in Ballygar, finding the town abloom with Christmas festivities. At Hanley's Family Grocery, I not only found immediate lodging but an invitation to their holiday party. Promptly escorted up the stairs above the shop into a large sitting room, I was introduced to the hostess, Mrs. Elizabeth Hanley, as the venerable shopkeeper entertained a multitude of friends and patrons.

Food was spread over long tables laid with linen, a bounty akin to the halls of Tara. I grabbed my fill and went to sit in a corner, watching the pageant unfold. The point of the gala seemed to be for people to take turns approaching the comfortable armchair of Mrs. Hanley for a brief private audience.

"A generous queen, Elizabeth Hanley," piped up a man sitting beside me. "But a fading old matriarch, as family markets fall in the face of the supermarket chains. See that heap of bundles over there, they're boxes of Christmas treats the Hanley family prepares each year for their faithful customers. They always include a favorite food of each particular family. Not something a chain store would be likely to do."

I watched Mrs. Hanley present a hefty parcel to a young couple.

"'Tis too good to us ye are, Mrs. Hanley," the young woman answered with a kiss of gratitude.

I had spent so many evenings with seaside folk, who live at great distances, drowned out by the booming ocean, that I was struck by the way the chat of these inland dwellers seemed less demonstrative. Even allowing for the fact it was a house party instead of a pub, the people's demeanor seemed shy and polite, as if they were being watched over by a higher power—or a nosy neighbor.

All around the room were scenes representing Walter Hosty's invocation of the family—little portraits of devotion: mothers feeding their broods or beaming love upon their holiday joy; fathers sipping tea or whiskey-punch with their arms draped affectionately over son or daughter; a grandmother calling to a playful little lad, "Come here to me, my jolly little manikin."

Their language, however, was just as fresh and vivid as any along the coast. From the periphery I would tune in to snatches of conversation that would make me smile.

"Since first plough, I've heard a terrible grunt out of me arm," complained one.

"Winding an alarm clock never guaranteed morning . . ." "She's a fiery hag of mischief who leaves me as vexed as a turkey cock . . ." "Have you seen Joseph?" "Aye, but he was gone and leaving before he arrived a'tall." The voices drifted by in a dream of colorful talk.

Gradually I worked my way closer to Mrs. Hanleys improvised throne, to hear her ask a young girl about her grandpa, "How is the old fella keeping?"

The little colleen blushed in reply, "He's off his bike more than he's on it, fair fallen away since October. In and out of the faeries the long day."

As I edged my way into the inner circle around the dowager, the Hanley party began to lament how Jesus was being left out of His birthday. A white-haired gentleman remarked, "If you haven't Jesus in your heart, what have you at the end of the day?" But then he turned suddenly to me and asked, "How is it with you and Jesus? Have you been blessed with His company along the roads?"

Put on the spot, I reddened every bit as much as the colleen. "I believe Jesus has walked many miles at my side, though maybe it was Missie He was walking with."

"Nonsense," said one woman, not content with my tongue-in-cheek response. "Certainly you must have more to share with us, a beam of light upon this longest night of the year."

"Nothing very profound I'm afraid, no visions or such things," I apologized with a shrug. "But I did feel Jesus was at my shoulder when I'd knock on doors at night, and the welcome I received was due to Him. Since setting out, I've spent one hundred fifty nights in different farmhouses, with hardly a dozen refusals, and never once was I asked a penny for lodgings, even if they were B-and-B's."

"That's remarkable," Mrs. Hanley nodded in affirmation. "Surely Jesus lit your passage and opened doors for you. 'Twas He who put warmth in the hearts of your hosts. Look at yourself, now," leaning forward in her chair, "sitting in a roomful of strangers, but you're as comfortable with us as we are with you, and that's the bountiful grace of Our Lord."

Now that I gave it more thought, I had to add, "I suppose there must have been a band of angels watching over us the whole time. Missie and I have disappeared around a thousand blind bends at a speed of eight miles—a day that is, not an hour—with no collisions or near-accidents. But to tell the truth, I have felt closer to Jesus lately, especially at Communion, where I feel as though I've slipped into His own private snug."

A soft murmuring of assent followed my remarks, the guests seemingly appreciative of the little I had to offer: a few grains of gold panned from a bounteous stream. After a lull, a lady resumed, "I suppose once you're back in America, your travels will be like a dream."

"Yes, in a few months I'll be back at the hospital where I work as a psychiatric nurse. And I'll go telling everyone about my donkey-go-round, and they'll think I'm the biggest cuckoo in the cuckoo's nest. Even to myself it will seem like a fantasy."

Through the early evening, I found myself pouring out my heart's unwritten history to this group of willing listeners. But what matter. The road was nearly at its end, and what I didn't say this night might not be thought of again. Unlike the triumphant adventurer returning to The Oasis at Cartymore, tonight I was the humble castaway washed to shore, where I thanked God for my safe deliverance.

"Here I am, twenty miles from Rattigan's, and despite all that might await me there, there's a part of me that wants this journey to linger on. Once I step foot into that pub, I'm afraid my house of cards will topple and I'll be left to face my own familiar self again. For eight months I've been blessed by this journey God has provided me. But now I face the unenviable task of returning home, where I might forget the valuable lessons I've learned on these roads."

"The Irish poet George Moore once said, 'A man travels the world over in search of what he needs and returns home to find it,' " interrupted the white-haired patron. "May it be so for yourself."

Mrs. Hanley reached over to pat my hand and reassure me, "Your greater journey will go on, but the grace you've obtained from this pilgrimage will go with you."

A young lad came storming up the stairs, out of breath, stammering out an apology for his intrusion, and blurting, "You're wanted up the town, Mr. Donkeyman. Bryan Devine sent me to fetch you!"

"Bryan Devine," I repeated, recalling the innkeeper who had beckoned me off the road when I first passed through Ballygar back in April.

"Best be off, so." Mrs. Hanley released me. " 'Tisn't wise to keep a publican waiting."

Saying hurried good-byes, I followed the young skipper up the long street, past a blur of Christmas lights and a group of scampish teens still dressed in school uniform, the girls running kneesocks to ankles and the boys flailing one another with boughs of fresh holly.

As we approached Devine's Pub, a welcoming fire lit up the sky ahead.

"Look, will ye!" the young lad squealed, with fire in his eyes. "Look what they've laid out for ye!"

There, in front of the pub, Bryan Devine and friends were busily tending to a small bonfire.

"Welcome!" The publican dropped his timber to shake my hand. " 'Tis been many a day since you left my door, and your mare roaring away out the town! Come in for a pint, you will. And a second, sure! After all," he grinned, leading me into a gathering of well-wishers, "show me a bird who can fly with just the one wing!"

A Proper Pair of Pilgrims

CHAPTER SIXTY-THREE

The homecomings continued the next day, when we returned to Athleague, the village where Missie was actually born. We stayed in a lovely two-story house with Patrick Moore and his daughter, Mary, and dawdled pleasantly for a second day to delay our arrival at Rattigan's on Christmas Eve. That long Sunday, I attended Mass at Sacred Heart Church in Roscommon and cleaned out my cart and retired by midnight, but without a single call to pub, eager to be fresh for an early start in the morning.

The foreordained morning, however, I woke with a jolt, as Patrick peeked in early to warn me. "The roads are thick with an overnight frost," he said, drawing open the curtains of my bedroom. "I'm afraid you should have set off yesterday when your goal was at hand."

I stumbled to the window and looked out upon the picture of my folly: a shimmering world of icy roads and gleaming hedges, as the sun, casting its numbing light across the wintry countryside, looked more like a pale moon than our shining day-star.

As I sat downcast at breakfast with the Moores, Mary tried to revive my spirits. "Stay to the soft margin of the road and coax Missie along. 'Tis fairly level from here to Kilrooskey, and ye'll make it yet if the sun warms itself."

"Pity, though, the road crews are already on holiday." Patrick glanced through the kitchen window with a frown. "There'll be no sand spread on the day before Christmas."

After a rushing of blessings at the Moores' door, Missie and I stepped out cautiously upon the Roscommon Road. But despite Missie's frost-nails and my holding the rein short and taut at her head, Missie's forelegs kept slipping beneath her until, inevitably, she smacked her jaw smartly against the pavement.

I righted her and held her head in my hands, murmuring gently as I checked to see if she was hurt. My little trooper was okay, but there was no choice but to pull off the road and pray for a change in conditions.

We took refuge in a lay-by and I looked out upon the solid sheen of ice as my heart splintered into shards, my spirit like a broken wheel. I dropped my head to the cart, on the verge of sobbing when I thought back on Jimmy Mac's stern warning only days earlier. Missie, though, began to buck and fuss, straining to move on in spite of the elements.

She went slip-sliding back on the road, head down, donkey-determined, and dug in strongly with her back hooves, the frost-nails etching deeply into the glazed surface. I skated to catch up to her, marveling as her labored breath steamed from her nostrils like living wraiths, the very picture of her indomitable spirit. Where would I have been without her?

I stopped to feed Missie a grateful fistful of oats, then stroked her head, saying, "You're a credit to your noble breed, you are. This day two thousand years ago, one of your kind was on the long Judean road from Nazareth to Bethlehem, as reliable to its precious cargo as you are to me." I ran my hand over the dark markings on her back and said, "You wear your cross well, dear *asaleen*."

We had the hazardous road completely to ourselves in the cold light of a long morning, as we made our slow, unsteady progress. By midday the sun was thawing out the frozen world, and we gingerly approached the gray medieval town of Ros Coman, St. Coman's Wood, where a noontime carillon sent jackdaws squawking over black-slated roofs and abbey ruins.

We entered the ancient capital of Connaught, and made our way down Convent Road and up Church Street, where well-wishers offered us apples and raisin cake from their doors, and children came scooting down the lanes, singing out, "Missie Mickdermot and the Donkeyman!"

At one doorway, a young boy curled shyly around his mother and held out a small donkey figurine. "Please, sir, would you place my donkey in our manger?"

Honored by his request, I left Her Ladyship with a nest of young admirers and was led to a Nativity that sat in a deep windowsill. I shifted the shepherd and a few lambs as the young lad watched my every move as if it were I, and I alone, who knew where the blessed donkey had stood that Holy Night.

"There," I said, placing the donkey just behind the crib of the Christ Child. "Now, won't her sweet meadow-breath help warm the Infant Jesus?"

"I was hoping you'd place her there." He heaved a sigh of satisfaction. "Isn't it right for the one who has traveled the furthest be the nearest at the end?"

Soon we were on the Lanesborough Road, with just a few miles remaining to fall into the meditative canter of Missie's ringing shoes—to think thoughts that would never surface but for the rhythm of silence.

By the time we made the final turn onto Beechwood, headed for Rattigan's, the late, low solstice sun bathed the tree-lined lane in honey-gold. As we passed a woodland glade, a cock pheasant rose up, rocketing heavenward with a vibrant clap of wings, leaving a flutter of ringed tailfeathers in its wake. I collected a pair, praying I would never again turn a deaf ear to God's constant whisperings.

"A crown of glory for you, Missie Mickdermot," I pronounced, as I placed the long-stemmed feathers into her bridle. A line of motorcars bound for Rattigan's tooted as they passed; I must have looked like a pastoral swain adorning his maiden fair.

"But what of it, Miss, tell me," I confided to my *anam cara,* my soul friend, cutting a sprig of holly from the hedge to accent her bridal bouquet. "Wouldn't they, too, be lovestruck if they had witnessed the wonders of this ancient and numinous road. Can we ever forget the butter roads of Beare, Miss, or the moorland paths of the Erris Plains? Or the Antrim Glens with their sheep-dotted hills? And how about the wilds of Donegal, that night when you spotted the only light in the bleak black bog? Dear o' dear, Miss, but the road that fell forever at our feet is at a close. It's as if God Himself had gently unraveled a great ball of yarn, and is now rolling us home."

A parade of motorcars continued to hoot up Beechwood, and parked three-deep before Rattigan's. A woman cycling past with her child, saluted as they passed. "There's a grand *ceili* in your honor this Holy Night, for you're a proper pair of pilgrims!"

I saluted back with my holly stick and walked on with Missie, now only forty yards from our starting point that long-ago day in April. I stopped twice to adjust her headdress, trying hopelessly to suspend these waning moments in memory. But patrons, young and old, came pouring out of Rattigan's, clapping, cheering, and calling us in from the cold.

A Christmas Ceili

CHAPTER SIXTY-FOUR

ÉAD MÍLE FÁILTE, KEVIN AND MISSIE! proclaimed the yellow banners above Rattigan's door, where happy throngs engulfed us. Out of the sea of familiar faces came my brother Dermot, along with our best American friend, Jack Schermerhorn, and then the woman I had looked around the world for, Belita Suarez O'Hara, wrapping her arms around me.

I held my beaming bride in a long, warm embrace, to the woos and wows of the milling crowd.

"I'll never understand how you could have left such a beauty behind in America to go traipsing the bogs with an ass!" shouted Willie Cassidy.

"My mother warned me that the Irish were wanderers," Belita came up for air. "But I knew our hearts were together, no matter the distance between us."

With an exultant ovation, we were ushered into the cozy precincts of Rattigan's, to the accompanying strains of flute and accordion playing "Paddy's Return" from the corner of the room.

"How is Grannie keeping?" I shouted to Noel Kelly, at first opportunity.

"Topping!" Noel managed to hand me a pint over the crowd. "Topping, she is!"

Hearing that confirmation, and with Belita in my arms, I raised my glass and exclaimed, "Happy Christmas to all!"

Suddenly an avalanche of cheers erupted behind us, and swinging my head around, what did I see but Paul Brennan leading Missie through the pub's front door? To my amazement, she sauntered through the crowd like a seasoned barfly, paying no heed to the young boys who draped themselves across her back like saddlebags.

"Why, I never . . ." Hugh Mannion was awestruck by Missie's peaceful demeanor.

"Bejabbers, she's nearly one with ourselves!" Willie Cassidy scratched his head. "Do you think he had her baptized along the way?"

"I say, she could stand up her hind legs and do a little jig," Dan Madden added in dismay.

Through this churning sea of humanity, however, Missie's wide-eyed glare was fixed on only one object: Belita.

"Uh-oh, Bea." I shielded her in my arms. "There's something I haven't told you. Missie is insanely jealous."

Yet, remarkably, when I cautiously introduced the pair, Missie remained cordial, sniffing placidly at Belita's hands. "Our match must be made in heaven," I said to Belita in disbelief. "You're the first woman who has met Missie's approval."

"Well, good for her, then," Belita nuzzled up to her peaceful rival.

Two strong hands ensnared me from behind: "You gave us quite a fright this morning, you blooming bliggard!" Jimmy Mac put me in a stranglehold. "I looked out on the frosty morning and, says I, 'They're finished. They'll never see home on these slippy roads.' You were terribly lucky the day warmed itself."

Jimmy's wife Bridie planted a smooch on my face: "Did you know your uncles were putting together a road crew just in case?"

"Oh, aye," piped my uncle Vincent, a foreman on the county council. "We were loading sand and shovels just in case. Believe me, we wouldn't have let you fall short of your goal."

Headmaster D'Alton gaveled the heel of his glass to the oak counter, which promptly hushed the spirited crowd—his authority still indelible in the minds of his many former students. He positioned Missie and me by the potbellied stove and raised his lanky arms to the crowd.

"Before we toast Kevin tonight at the close of his remarkable journey, first we must toast his heroine, Missie Mickdermot. No one celebrated her kind better than G. K. Chesterton in his poem 'The Donkey,' so if you will, I'll recite a few lines: the headmaster concluded,

> There was a shout about my ears,
> And palms before my feet.' "

The headmaster's reverent recitation was punctuated by the bray of Willie Cassidy: "How about a bucket of stout before Missie's feet?"

"Oh, could I, Mama?" squealed young Donal Rattigan to his mother, Kathleen, who busily worked the bar with four other women.

"A splash in a bucket, yes, if it's all right with Kevin?"

I shouted back my approval, "She deserves her pint as much as I do. Thank you, Kathleen."

A circle of patrons pressed around my road queen, as a sloshing half-bucket of Guinness was set before her. She snuffled the contents cautiously, but then quickly dove her head into the black liquid and came up with a lathered snout and gleaming eyes.

"By Jaysus, she has a taste for the Guinness!" rollicked Martin Trimble.

The headmaster, with a simple lift of hand, hushed the house once more and with great deliberation delivered a speech in Irish and then repeated it in English:

"This young lad, standing before us all, does honor to two ancient family names. Yes, Kelly and O'Hara, his mother Lella born beneath our own Slieve Bawn, and his father James, beneath Cairn Hill in neighboring County Longford. Across the Atlantic, they raised a son who imbibed their love of the land, and he took it into his head to walk in the paths of the venerable Irish bards, traversing the four ancestral kingdoms of Munster, Leinster, Ulster, and Connaught, his only companion the humble donkey you see here by his side. This Christmas Eve, let us welcome him back into our midst. Céad Míle Fáilte, Kevin Kelly O'Hara!"

Amidst the hurrahs and hoorays following the speech, there came the scrape of a barstool and through the crowd shambled Hugh Mannion, tugging at his frayed collar and clearing his throat for unaccustomed eloquence.

"You'll need this," said my brother Dermot, pressing his way over to thrust a fresh pint into my hand.

"Ye left us that Sunday in April amid great hullabaloo, the likes we had never seen," Hugh began, his blue eyes darting between ceiling and floor. "When ye departed, I said to all here, 'That lad will be back before I finish me bottle of barley wine here.' Well, many a bottle I've drained since, and many a night after your departure I'd look up at the old mapeen and wonder where you might be and how you were faring. And when I'd pedal home at night, I'd catch meself saying a prayer that you might find shelter with kind and charitable people . . ."

Hugh stopped short, his voice catching. He composed himself with a bracing slug of Smithwick's and concluded with a warm smile, "You're a hard nugget, Kevin O'Hara."

Applause followed Hugh back to his spot at the bar and Dan Madden stepped out from his tweed-capped cronies, swaying back and forth on his cane of blackthorn.

"There's an old tale about a poor young lad who traipsed the country during the Famine, going from house to house begging for a scrag of meat to keep out the hunger, but every farmer at their doors asked him the one question: 'Lad, have you a story to tell?'

"But the lad had no story, you see, and back onto the hungry road he was sent. One filthy night, with the Grim Reaper at his heels, he came upon an understanding farmer who bade him welcome without a story. The farmer fed the lad milk and potatoes and put him to sleep by the fire. But then the farmer rounded up his neighbors and dressed them in sheets, to set off a *fothram,* a great commotion. They chased the boy upstairs and down, inside and out, around and around the yard till he fell into a faint."

"When he woke next morning, the lad breathlessly told the farmer about his mad pursuit by screeching ghosts, gamboling goblins, and fearsome phantoms. And the kindly farmer replied with a smile, 'Weren't you the lucky lad to survive such an ordeal, and more lucky still, for from this day to your last, ye'll always have a story to tell.'"

Dan raised his glass toward me. "'Tis the same now with yourself, Kevin O'Hara," he concluded, walking over to shake my hand. "For all your living days and, indeed, in the mansions of the saints above, you'll always have a grand and splendid story to tell."

After another round of applause, it was the turn of the last of my Four Masters, Willie Cassidy, who took the floor with a smile wider than Bantry Bay, and launched into his own tale:

"'Twas a sunny summer Sunday a dozen or more years ago when the Kelly boys, Vincent, Mickey, and Bennie—God rest his soul—brought two nephews into Rattigan's. Young sniffling Yanks, they were, this Kevin here, and Dermot, that ginger-bearded lad in the corner beyont. Well, they took to the stools and asked Kathleen for Coca-Cola with plenty of ice. But it wasn't the Coke they received, but the hard-knocked hello of two pints of Guinness!"

Laughter resounded through the house, and glasses were lifted from every corner. Willie paced before the gleeful crowd, waving his hands like a lawyer orating for a jury.

"Oh, how the pair bellyached, turning their noses this way and that, and coming up with the sorry excuse of some Confirmation Pledge against the drink. Their own uncle Mickey slid the pints toward them and scoffed, 'A pledge, is it? Believe me, your bishop in America will never hear tell a word of this.'"

Another great hurrah echoed through the house, as Mickey took a deep bow.

"With as many wee sips as there were peanuts in a bag, the boys slowly drained their first pints of Guinness, then sat back to wipe their mouths proudly, thinking, no doubt, their initiation into the Celtic race was complete. But before they had time to tear open another bag of nuts, two more pints clunked down heavy beneath their chins.

"Let me tell you," Willie shouted above the din of the delighted crowd, "it didn't take more than a sip from that second jar to send these two galoots reeling. Snookered, they were! Pulverized, I say! Then they went tweaking at their pants, as if fixing to leak at the spout.

"Old Jack Rattigan called out: 'Is it a clothespeg ya need, or is it the jacks ye're after? 'Tis out that way!' He pointed to the back door. The two stupefied lads wobbled off their stools and staggered out that door there, only to find themselves squinting in the sunshine amongst a herd of stomping bullocks. And sure, as they grappled with their zippers, Hughie Mannion calls out, 'And laddies, don't forget to pull the chain!'"

When the raucous laughter subsided, my uncles Vincent and Mickey walked into the light, standing to either side of Missie and me.

Vincent spoke up first: "One day a few months ago while I was working the roads, a townsman stopped to say he had passed my nephew a week earlier in the northwest, a raw day with a wild wind cutting to the bone. From a distance he said he had never seen a lonelier sight to man, but when passing close by he saw Kevin chatting away to Missie without a care in the world, and concluded he had never seen man and beast so comfortable in each other's company.

"That evening, I went to my mother's—Grannie Kelly's—to tell her the news, and no message was ever more happily received. And there will be no warmer homecoming than the one that awaits Kevin in Ballincurry this Holy Night."

Uncle Mickey took the stage, smacking his lips and eyeing me playfully, eager to have his go at me.

"'Tis amazing to think that a proper boyo like me own nephew, a right hooligan, could venture around this island with a donkey and return home without a devil of a loss. 'Tis also heartwarming that our people, despite the divisions that mar our country, would all take kindly to such a roguish imp as himself. So, on this Christmas Eve, I'll toast my long-haired nephew, his lovely wife Belita, and Missie, his long-eared mistress here—but also salute the whole of the country, North and South, for, sure, there's no better place on earth than dear old Ireland!"

As the whole crew drank to that, Mickey pulled me smartly by the ear, which brought on Missie's inaugural in-house bawl, scattering children to the laps of their elders. Headmaster D'Alton ushered Belita to my side, under the dim Christmas bulbs that passed for a spotlight, and we stood before our avid audience as an unlikely Yuletide trio, lovely señorita, bedraggled pilgrim, and shaggy-coated beast. The children scurried back to sit at our feet, and in the eyes of these adoring fans we loomed like Princess Leia, Luke Skywalker, and Chewbacca from the movie, Star Wars.

A yellow Hillman's tea tin had been slowly circling the pub, the patrons dipping into purse and pocket for coins and pound notes, and finally Willie Cassidy popped up before us, cradling the teeming cannister of cash in his hands like a leprechaun gone mad.

"This is truly an odd midwinter's coronation." He jigged in front of us. "Aye, 'tis a mighty quare ceili at Rattigan's this Christmas Eve."

Willie held the tea tin aloft and declared to me, "There's ten quid of me own in this winning cup, but you've earned it, amuck, all three of you really, every penny that's in it, not just your paid-off wagers, but gifts and luck money from the generous people of the seven parishes of Kilgefin, gathered here to partake in this memorable night. I'm proud to present it to you, with all our best wishes."

When Willie handed me the tin, I hoisted it above my head to a thunderous ovation, while the chant, "Speech! Speech!" resounded from every corner of the room.

"On the road people would often ask me why I was so driven to reach Rattigan's Pub by Christmas Eve," I shouted above their carnival din. "Well, if any of them were lucky enough to be here tonight, they'd certainly know the answer!

"How fortunate I've been to begin and end my journey by crossing a threshold so dear to my heart. As you have heard, it was here that my brother Dermot and I were baptized into the Irish race and we've returned regularly to worship in this house of the sacred pint. But it's not because of the drink that Rattigan's will always be a holy place for Dermot and me. Isn't that right, Derm? Not for that jarring initiation, but for the warm acceptance we've found over the years, making us native sons whenever we walked through the door.

"Tonight I am truly blessed because my grandmother, Mary Ann Kelly, waits for me on the foothills of Slieve Bawn, the very center of my circle about Ireland. And before I leave here, I'll call my own mom and dad, and let them hear for themselves the mad bedlam around me.

"There's so many people here I want to thank tonight. The Four Masters and my uncles, of course, for not roasting me too badly. Jimmy Mac and Bridie for matching me up with dear Missiecakes here. My aunts and cousins for putting me up and putting up with me, for making me always feel at home. My brother Dermot and our great friend, Jack Schermerhorn, for coming over the ocean to bear witness to my madness. And this one," I said, embracing Missie. "Years from now, when all is said and done, I will think most fondly of her. True to her breed, she was stubborn at times, but looking back over our miles on the road together, I can honestly say she never let me down.

"And then, especially for Belita, besides lifelong thanks for allowing me to pursue my dream, I want to express special gratitude for the sweater I'm wearing tonight, 'The Road Coat,' which she had knit for me a month prior to my leaving for Ireland. A gray cardigan which kept me warm on the long road back to her."

I wrapped the sleeves of my Road Coat around Belita, held her close and kissed her again, to the thundering approval of the assembly.

"I also wish to thank everyone here tonight, for leaving your homes on Christmas Eve to welcome the Yank and his donkey home. And, of course, to our great generous hostess, Kathleen Rattigan, and young Donal here. Oh, and one last thing before Patsy Hanley and Bertie Mannion play on. I've been in a hundred pubs since leaving here in April, North and South, and I could never so much as reach into my pockets for a handkerchief without being stopped, in fear I'd pull out a few pounds to pay for a round of drink. But tonight," I announced, reaching across the bar to hand Kathleen the Hillman tin, "tonight, let there be drinks on the Yank!"

A great cheer arose, nearly splitting the crossbeams above. The taps flowed as ceaselessly as Galway's Aasleagh Falls, pints passing through the night in fluid communion, and the festive evening drifted away in a whirling wheel of music and merrymaking. When I served Belita a Bailey's Irish Cream, Missie let out a dry cough, and another splash was put in the bucket before her dainty feet. The cronies belted out, "For He's a Jolly Good Fellow!" and finally Belita and I were called out to the floor for a last dance, waltzing to the sweet air of "The Black Velvet Band," while Missie peeped out at us from her entourage of village children, for all the world like a contented bridesmaid.

"Now do you think you'll be able to settle down?" Belita kissed me and asked in earnest.

"I'm sure of it," I answered with confidence.

Fingerpost to Ballagh

CHAPTER SIXTY-FIVE

Giddily drunk, Dermot, Jack Horner, and I eventually stumbled out of Ratti-gan's, dragging Missie along, who showed no desire to depart the festivities. We still needed to walk the final mile to Grannie Kelly's, and as I fumbled with her tackle, I kept up a steady chatter, to which Missie responded with an odd assortment of snorts, whinnies, and playful nips at my sleeve.

"Does Missie talk to you when no one else is around?" asked Dermot in amazement, as we set off down the black road.

"No, but I'm hoping she might tonight. Donkeys are supposed to have the gift of speech on Christmas Eve and when the midnight bells toll at Ballagh, believe me, I'll be alone with her in the fields, praying she'll have a word for me, a final comment on our journey together."

"You've lost it, Shirts," said Jack, calling me by my old caddy nickname. "I've seen you bad before, but never this bad."

We went braying in laughter down Beechwood, and Uncle Mickey's battered Morris Minor went puttering by, beeping wildly, Belita reaching out the passenger window in a passing embrace.

"I know you promised Belita to settle down and try to be respectable," Dermot chuck-led. "But what have you promised this girl here, for all her help and companionship?"

"I'm launching a worldwide campaign to stamp out the hostile and belittling game of 'Pin the Tail on the Donkey,'" I answered, nuzzling up to my partner. "It's a shocking abuse of Missie's noble breed."

"You're cracked, you know it?" My brother slung his arm around me. "Your body may have returned from this journey, but your brain is still out there in the bog."

"You might be right," I confessed.

We arrived at the Clump, where the old metal black-and-white fingerpost read: BAL-LAGH, 1 MILE.

"My first and last fingerpost in all of Ireland," I said, kneeling before the marker as if it were a saint's grotto. "Think of all the fingerposts pointing this way and that into the night, to the wildest corners of the island: Coppeen, Garranstackle, Kilgobbin, Ballyfinboy. But this signpost tells the whole story: Ballagh, *an bealach*, 'the road'—it's the sweetest destination of all."

I rose to my feet and ran my fingers braille-like over the raised black metal letters. " 'The longest road out is the shortest road home!' " I exclaimed. "It's an Irish proverb I've heard again and again, but I never understood it till this very minute, never had a flipping clue."

The wind stirred high in the trees, setting them to rustle and sway around us.

"Look at them dance, boys!" I shouted into the dark. "They're alive, those trees, as alive as ourselves."

"You're raving again, Shirts."

We carried on into the black pitch of the night, lit only by the headlamps of the occasional car zipping by and honking, casting a crazy shadow of three capped heads and two long ears, and then again, the profound darkness.

"The nights here are blacker than ink," said Jack in disbelief. "You can't even see your hand in front of your face."

"Oh, don't I know," I agreed with a sigh. "I'm so glad to be leaving the dark, all those black nights, now drawing close to the light, the warm glow of Grannie's hearth."

Suddenly a bolt of lightning forked through my clouded brain.

"Derm, take Miss." I fumbled her reins into his hands. "Go ahead, walk on toward Ballagh Chapel. I'll catch up to you guys before you make the turn up Ballincurry."

"What's up, Kev? Don't tell me you need another drink."

I rushed off without answering, thankful for the beam of light that had pierced my memory.

"What's wrong?" Dermot called again, as I continued my mad gallop toward Rattigan's.

"Mints! Mints! Mints!" I sang out into the blessed night. "I almost forgot Grannie's bag of mints!"

Epilogue

Minutes before midnight, I hopped the wall in front of Grannie Kelly's farm-house and gingerly made my way through the dark field toward Missie, find-ing her rubbing snouts with Jim Tiernan's old smoking jack, Nedeen. On the high-hedged lane of Ballincurry, I could hear the joyful voices of neighboring children hurrying down to Mass, the second bell already rung.

The night remained cloudy. Pity. Jupiter and Mars were merging these nights in the eastern sky, which some astronomers believe was the alignment that led the Wise Men to the Infant's manger. I had caught a glimpse of the spectacle last night at the Moores', and wondered if the old woman on the Dingle hadn't also been out in her field, saying an old Irish prayer to this "Star of Bethlehem."

Nedeen shuffled away at my approach and I placed both my arms around Missie, waiting for the midnight bells to herald in the birthday of Jesus. I had heard so often donkeys had the gift of speech on Christmas Night, that despite the gathering at Grannie's thinking I had lost my marbles altogether, nothing would keep me away from Missie at this mystic moment.

When the bells shortly rang out over the countryside, Missie uttered nary a word. She did, however, burrow her warm muzzle into my chest for several moments. The only other time she had offered this gesture was in Kerry, after I had helped save her from choking to death on her bridle.

I waited there for some minutes in silence, finally asking, "Well, Missie Mickdermot, do you have anything to say, now that our journey is over?"

She looked at me and I looked at her, expectantly, but no words were forthcoming. I decided to leave the field, not to stay at this foolish game forever, but beforehand, I fed

Missie an apple and gave a warm kiss to her white snout. Nedeen, seeing the smooch, let out a cacophonous bawl, which of course brought on Missie's own horrific harangue. When the pair had finally quieted down, I heard another uproarious roar escape Grannie's house—no doubt at my expense—and I wondered if after my travels I were now better-suited for field than home.

After the mirth within the farmhouse had subsided, I sat up on Tiernan's wall, while the long-lugged pair mingled at midfield. From my vantage I could see the square steeple of Ballagh Chapel, which prompted me to a prayer of thanksgiving, grateful for our deliverance, for Grannie's health, and for the safe passage of Belita, Dermot, and Jack to meet me upon my return.

Missie's head-to-heart gesture had somehow given me a sense of absolution, since my nut-brown confessor had been privy to the worst of this wayward pilgrim, as well as sharing the best with him.

I looked out at the two donkeys standing face-to-face with their necks crossed, and on this most magical of nights, I had to imagine a conversation for them:

"You're the most famous donkey in the world!" I seemed to hear old Nedeen exclaim. "More than the Golden Ass of Apuleius, or Juan Jimenez's Platero."

"Will ya stop," Missie would blush, scratching her dainty hooves before her. "I'm more like Sancho Panza's ass that rode alongside Rocinante."

"Nonsense!" he would disagree. "Imagine, climbing Ireland's highest braes and traveling its ancient cities. Splendid, you are! And I hear you have the gift of clairvoyance. A second sight?"

" 'Tis true," Missie might say humbly, twitching her long lugs. "A gift unknowingly bestowed upon me by Kevin when he sprinkled me with the holy waters of countless grottoes."

"Why didn't you tell him all this at midnight when you had your chance to speak?" Nedeen might ask.

"And have him lose it altogether?" Missie would answer with a knowing snort. "Believe me, he's hanging on to reality by a thread as it is!"

"And how is his grandmother keeping?"

"Devil a loss! This holy evening when we arrived at her door, she greeted him with open arms, saying, 'May all the stars in the Heaven shine upon you in glory this blessed night.' A storybook ending, surely. 'Tis only a pity I can't tell him she'll live to be a healthy hundred years of age, one of his many road prayers answered."

"What will happen to you now, Missie Mickdermot?"

"I'm to be auctioned off for charity on *The Late, Late Show with Gay Byrne.*"

"Gay Byrne! The popular TV host? Doesn't Kevin keep you?"

"How could he keep me when he returns home with Belita to make a proper life for themselves in America? So, he has the thought to auction me off for charity, to guarantee me a good home. He stipulates I can keep any foals I may have, and that he can visit me at any time.

"Oh, what a night, that! Kevin and I on the set at Dublin's RTE studios with half the nation watching. I fetch four hundred ten pounds for the Cherry House in Roscommon. Kevin thinks I'm worth more than a thousand, but the bidding starts late. But I go to a lovely couple, the O'Connells in County Cork. With no land of their own, they put me up with a neighboring farmer, where I soon become yardboss to two other donkeys and an old retired English racehorse named Reginald. 'Tis a good life, I tell you—pared, combed, wintered-in, and fattened with fruit and corn."

"Will you have any foals of your own?" Nedeen flashes his boxy grin.

"Not a one, sorry to say. The O'Connells try to mate me with a racing jack from Buttevant—The Minstrel Lad—a big to-do, you know, 'the road princess and the champion jack.' Nothing comes of it. No matter—God has His raysons."

"Do you ever see Kevin again after he goes off to America?"

"For five years I see him nearly as often as Grannie Kelly. He visits me in Cork with his pockets teeming with apples. But soon Kevin and Belita have their family in Massachusetts, and during that stretch I fall on hard times."

"Hard times? What Irish story doesn't include some?"

"Oh, aye. You see, the O'Connells move to Europe, and the farmer caring for me falls to drinking and sells me off, without permission, to a rogue of the road. For three long years this prince of the ditches works the rod on me, a heavy blackthorn that raises many a welt on my back, as I haul wood in the dire backcountry.

" 'I can't believe you're the ass that traveled Ireland!' he'd give out to me. 'I have me mind set on selling you to the zoo, feed you to the lions, they will.'

"Then, one black November evening in 1986, I see my dear traveling pal approach, a glad sight for a sorry sight. You see me now, the toast of the town, but when Kevin comes to fetch me, he sees a spavined old mare in a field of muck and nettles, scrawny and beaten, with a threadbare, tick-infested coat and forgotten hooves turned up like elfin shoes.

"He's come to spend a year in County Clare with his wife and two young boys, and with the O'Connells' help, has tracked me down. He comes toward me with apple held in trembling hand, not sure he could recognize me in my fallen state. I know his scent immediately, but it takes him a minute to be sure.

"When certain recognition dawns, he cries and whispers to me, 'Missie, I've come to take you home.'

"After a tough negotiation with the donkey-beater, Kevin leads me off for fifty-five quid, though he tells me later he was prepared to go as high as five hundred—a third of his family's savings—just to save me. So, up into the horsebox I go, without fuss or bother and, believe me, there is no happier pair in Ireland that night than Kevin and I speeding out of that tussocky field for the limestone headlands of County Clare.

"Nor was there anything as grand as my year there, grazing in a sheltered field by the sea, where I was pampered by Kevin and Belita and their two young sons, Eamonn and Brendan."

"Do you two ever go traveling again?"

"Just short jaunts up the lane with the wee lads on my back. Usually Kevin just sits with me, looking out across Liscannor Bay and dreaming of things. He's troubled then, trying to write the story of our travels, and not making headway, feeling he's let everybody down, and Ireland itself above all.

" 'If I don't finish this, Miss, I'll die a disappointed man,' he tells me. 'It's what I believe God has put me on Earth to do, after giving me the chance to see an ancient, holy world on the brink of change. I have to tell what I have seen, offer my testimony of grace, but I never feel up to the task. But what a journey we had, hadn't we Miss?' He drapes his arm over my neck and brightens at the memories."

"What happens to you after your year in Clare?" Nedeen sniffs at the faint scent of incense from the chapel below, fondly remembering his dear pipe-smoking master, Jim Tiernan.

"Kevin carts me back to Roscommon, to Vincent and Cella's, where I am royally treated till my dying day. And, yes, Kevin visits me regularly after that, and we stroll sometimes to Grannie Kelly's, stopping in at Rattigan's for old times' sake."

"Can you see your own end?"

"Yes, it comes during Christmas week of 1992. Not quite the proverbial donkey's age, I live almost twenty years, most of them happy, and I go to my rest in a lovely patch of Hugh Mannion's land."

"And what happens to Kevin?"

"Well, it takes him nearly a quarter-century of on-and-off effort, but he does finish the book of our travels, and it's published in time for the twenty-fifth anniversary of our setting out. I can't see any further than that. But I do know he's happy and grateful to have seen the old Ireland before it passed into the prosperous and potentially peaceful young nation it will become in the new millennium."

"Glory be! So you don't see when Kevin dies?"

"No, but I know he asks his sons to scatter his ashes at the spot where he threw his broken hazel stick into the black depths of Doo Lough."

"Fitting, that, for journey's end," Nedeen might snort. "You and Kevin took one step out of the ordinary, trusting to grace and goodwill, and everything followed from that simple sacrament of spontaneity, so Irish at its heart."

"Yes, it was all worth it," I can hear Missie saying, beneath the hidden stars of a long-ago Christmas.

Uncle Mickey broke through my reverie, shouting out, "Have ye gone camping, or are ye coming in a'tall?" Startled, I turned to see a dear congregation standing outside Grannie's front door, a circle of beloved friends waving me inside.

"I'm on my way," I called back, hopping off the wall and running back toward the house for all that awaited me.

References

Irish Names of Places by P. W. Joyce. M. H. Gill and Son, Dublin, 1901.

The Islands of Ireland by Thomas H. Mason. The Mercier Press, Cork, 1937.

The Celtic Book of Days by Caitlin Matthews. Destiny Books, Rochester, Vermont, 1995.

Irish Folk Ways by E. Estyn Evans. Routledge & Kegan Paul, London and Boston, 1957.

The Year in Ireland by Kevin Danaher. The Mercier Press, Cork, 1972.

Rambles in Eirinn by William Bulfin. Sphere Books Limited, London.

The Mountains of Ireland by D.D.C. Pochin Mould. Gill and MacMillan, Dublin, 1976.

The Irish Saints by Daphne D. C. Pochin Mould. Clonmore and Reynolds Ltd. 1964.

The Way That I Went by Robert Lloyd Praeger. Allen Figgis, Dublin, 1980.

An Old Woman's Reflections by Peig Sayers. Oxford University Press, 1978.

The Western Island by Robin Flower. Oxford University Press, 1978.

Sweeney Astray by Seamus Heaney. Faber and Faber, London, 1983.

Geology and Scenery in Ireland by J. B. Whittow. Penguin Books, 1978.

The Aran Islands by J. M. Synge. Oxford University Press, 1979.

The Shell Guide to Ireland by Lord Killanin and Michael V. Duignan. Ebury Press, London, 1967.

Illustrated Guide to Ireland The Reader's Digest. London, 1992.

Ireland Dorling Kindersley Travel Guides. Dorling Kindersley, Inc., London, 1997.

The Encyclopedia of Ireland, edited by Brian Lalor. Gill and Macmillan Ltd. Dublin, 2003.

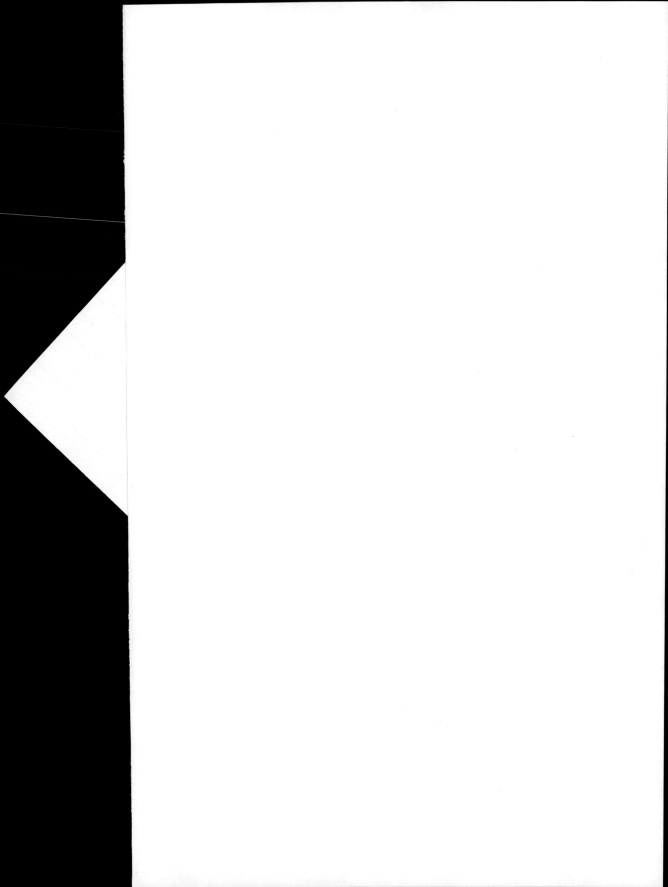